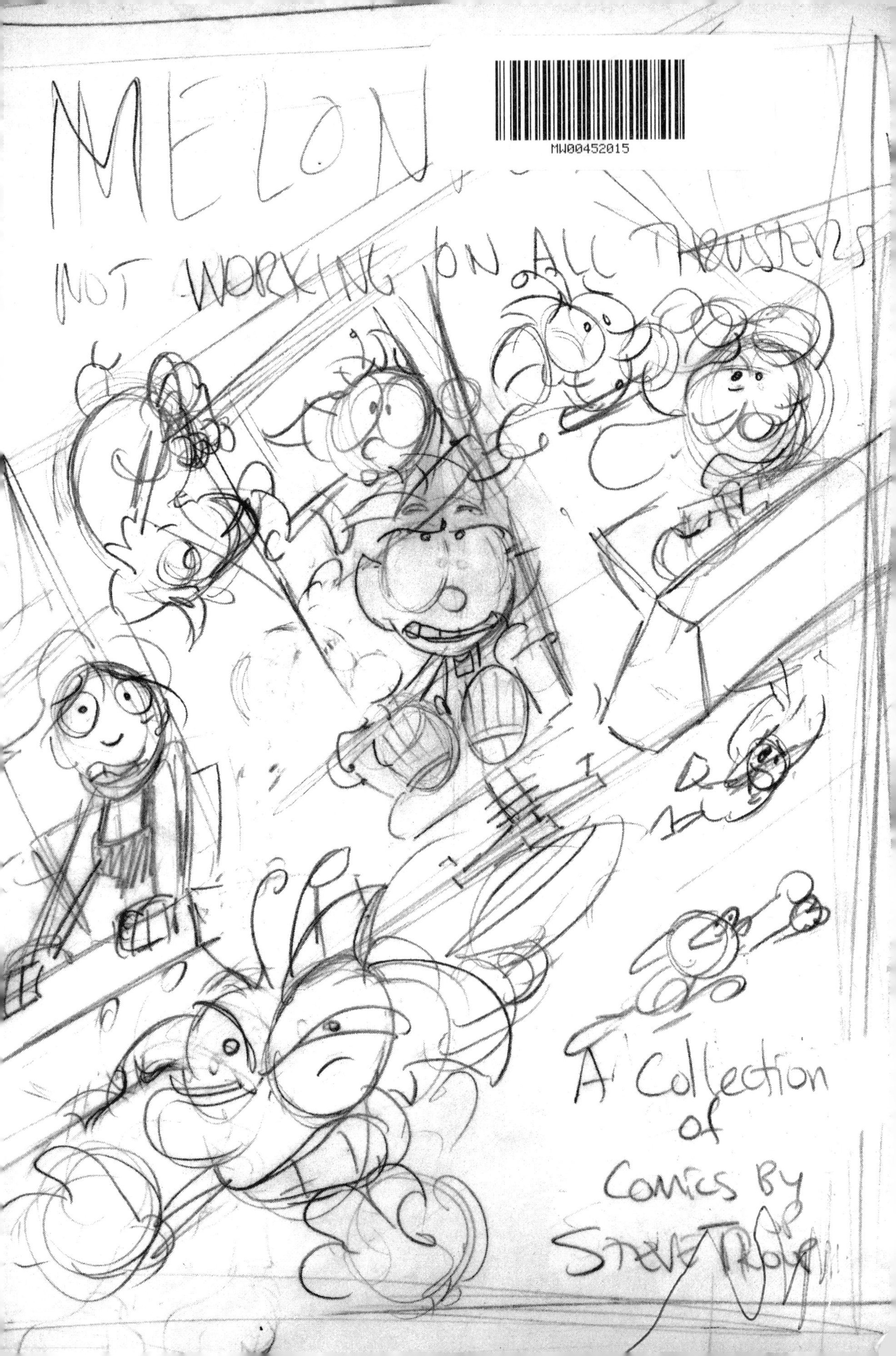
MELON
NOT WORKING ON ALL THRUSTERS
A Collection of Comics By Steve Troop

For my granny, Josephine Troop,
who taught me to sew, so I could build puppets.

ISBN 978-1481037136
First Printing, November 2012

10 9 8 7 6 5 4 3 2 1

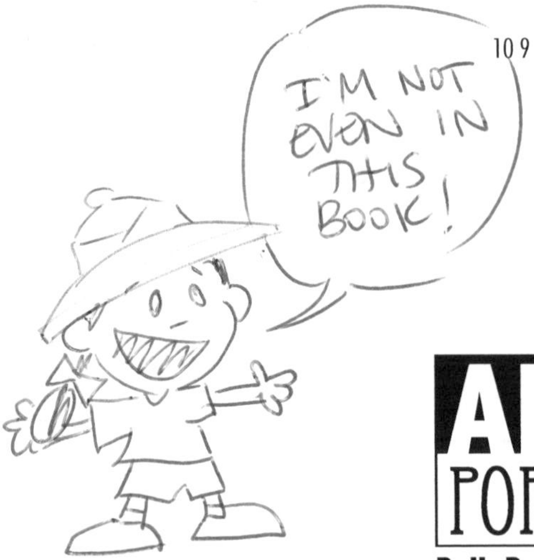
I'M NOT EVEN IN THIS BOOK!

ALIEN PORKCHOP PUBLISHING

ENJOY THIS BOOK! STEVE TROOP '12

OVERDUE

Written by Erik Przytulski

Oh, I've procrastinated far too long
The love that I'd been saving's overdrawn
So I've consolidated all the passion I could find
But I lost interest and the rates were just too high

My heart's indebted
Maxed out my credit
But when love let me go with nothing to show
You gave me a loan
I'm overdue...

I'm overdue for your love
I'm overdue for your love
My hope depleted and I need it renewed
It's your love pure and true that I'll owe it to
I wanna over do it with you

Oh I've invested in some bad affairs
The love that I'd been saving wasn't spared
So I contested and I requested something that would explain
Why this had to happen, and then the final notice came

My heart's suspended
Over-extended
But in time I accrued a love brand new
And the payment was you
I'm overdue...
I'm overdue for your love

I'm overdue for your love
My hope depleted and I need it renewed
It's your love pure and true that I'll owe it to
I wanna over do it with you

So charge me, defer me
Don't pardon the late fee
I'm your chapter 11 woman and you're my repo man
Exempt me, then bill me
When I'm empty, you fill
I've got passion to burn, you've earned my respect
And now it's time for you to collect—oh, whoa, whoa... WOW!

I'm overdue for your love
I'm overdue for your love
My hope depleted and I need it renewed
It's your love pure and true that I'll owe it to
I wanna over do it with you

I'll over do it, I'll over do it, I'll over do it... do it...

TABLE OF CONTENTS

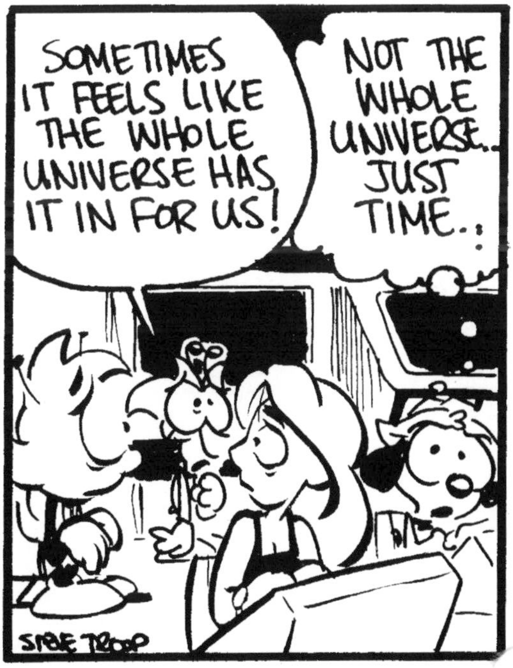
SOMETIMES IT FEELS LIKE THE WHOLE UNIVERSE HAS IT IN FOR US!
NOT THE WHOLE UNIVERSE... JUST TIME...
STEVE TROOP

ACKNOWLEDGEMENTS

As with any book, a lot of people had a hand in making it a reality. This book is no exception which is finally a reality after languishing on my hard drive for the last seven years.

First of all, thanks to my wife **Sarah Troop**, who often believes in my dreams more than I do. Her sons **Koren** and **Chase** always ask me when my next book is going to get done. Finally, I have an answer: NOW!

Thanks to friend, former neighbor and regular writing buddy **Ed Sharrow**, who copy-edited all 216 pages of this book at the last possible moment. Any mistakes that remain are by no means his fault—you'd think after 7+ years, I'd give him more than a couple of days to read the thing, huh?

Of course, I have to thank my parents, **Bill** and **Peggy Troop** and my brother **Dave** who have always encouraged me to pursue my dreams, as well as Dave's wife **Stacey** and daughter **Audrey**, who continue to be exposed to his brother's crazy projects.

In the years since wrapping up the webcomic, I've focused more and more on puppetry. Thanks to **Erik Przytulski**, **Roger Przytulski**, **Chris Gleason** and **Julie Eisenhower** for sticking with the puppetry for going on 20 years now. They, along with **BJ Guyer**, **Jon Stout** and my wife **Sarah** are a driving part of my new dream—a feature-length puppet film based on *Melonpool*. I can't wait to share that with all of you!

Finally, I'd like to take a moment to mention the people that I've lost in the last few years, who have also played a big part in my life. Grandparents **Jo** and **Mel Troop**, **Peggy** and **Frank Mintun**, puppeteer/writer extraordinaire **Earl Kress** and even my dog **Twiggy** will forever be missed and remembered.

After all these years in production, I'm sure I've missed a few people. Next time I take this long of a hiatus, I'll be sure to write the Acknowledgements page first, rather than waiting until the last minute! On second thought, no more hiatuses. I have too much work to do!

—Steve Troop
November, 2012

CAST BIOS

Mayberry Melonpool

Inept captain of the *Steel Duck*. Mayberry's duties include being an all-around scapegoat, janitor and the main source of communication between the pilot that can't use the radio and engineering. Obsessed with *Star Trek*, he happily does whatever it takes to remain captain.

Ralph Zinobop

Somewhat evil, coffee-addicted heir to the Zinoboppian throne. Ralph built the *Steel Duck* while in exile, with the hope of revolutionizing the Planet Zinobop's fossil fuel dependence and reclaiming his rightful place as King. Instead, he got stranded on Earth following the experimental ship's maiden voyage.

Sam T. Dogg

Former test pilot and the only member of the crew who possesses common sense. Sam is forever hindered by the fact that he resembles a common domesticated dog. A telepathic, hat-wearing, hyper-intelligent dog—but a dog, nevertheless.

Sammy The Hammy

One of Ralph's experiments gone horribly awry. Sammy basically eats and sleeps when he's not called into service as the *Steel Duck's* engine—which consists of running on a 12-foot hamster wheel to power the ship.

Roberta Smeffinfeffer

Stranded on Earth by the mysterious GRAISE, Roberta quickly assumed the role of ship's doctor shortly after the *Steel Duck* crashed on Earth. Seemingly the only member of the crew capable of remaining gainfully employed, Roberta puts up with a crew full of male chauvinist pigs because she sees them as her only ticket home.

 **Cast Bios**

Ralphie Zinobop

Ralphie Zinobop is a clone of Ralph—another product of one of his failed experiments. While Ralph is basically evil (or at least, in a bad mood all the time), Ralphie is kind, caring, sympathetic. Ralphie and Roberta have gotten quite close over the years—even producing an offspring as the result of a time paradox.

Jalea Bates

A former pop-singing Protocol droid, Jalea is the closest thing to a human aboard the *Steel Duck*. A bizarre accident transformed her into a living, breathing human being a few years ago. Since then, Jalea has tried to discover her own humanity—at least as well as she can aboard a ship full of aliens....

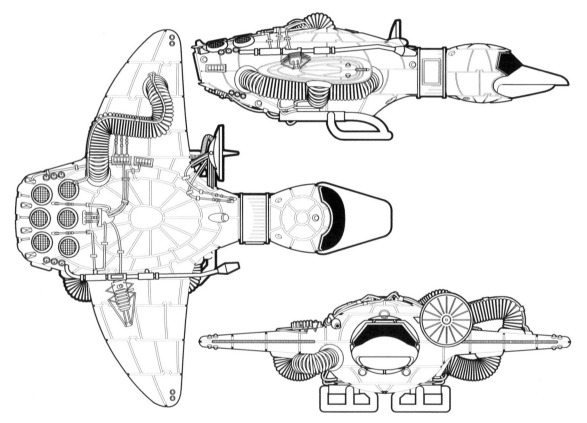

The Steel Duck

A small rusted-out spaceship, lost in space for the last 14 years. The small ship was built by Ralph as a means to test his revolutionary new power source—the hamster-powered engine! Built to resemble a 108-foot mallard duck, the ship has seen her share of adventures.

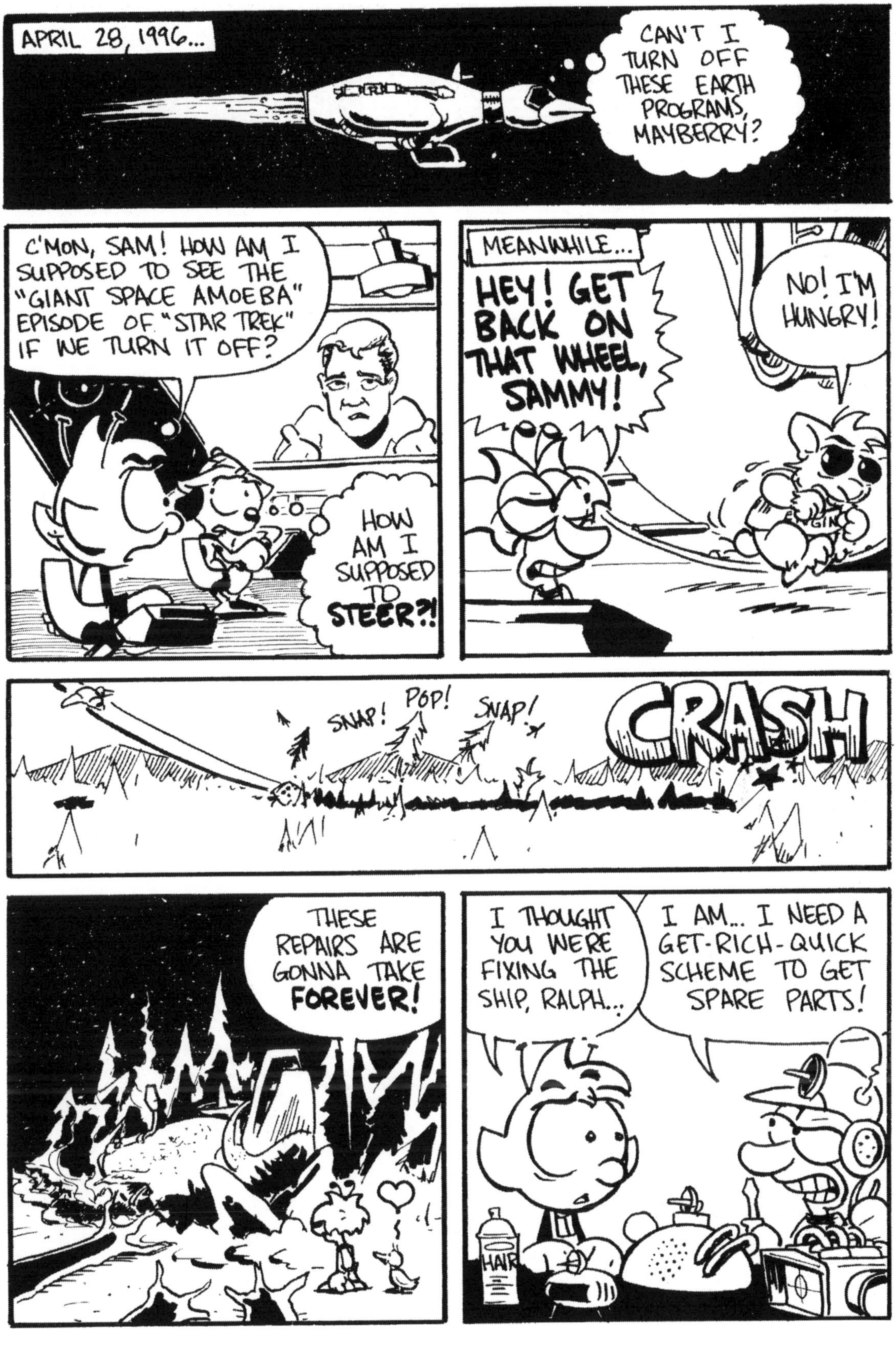

APRIL 28, 1996...
CAN'T I TURN OFF THESE EARTH PROGRAMS, MAYBERRY?
C'MON, SAM! HOW AM I SUPPOSED TO SEE THE "GIANT SPACE AMOEBA" EPISODE OF "STAR TREK" IF WE TURN IT OFF?
HOW AM I SUPPOSED TO **STEER?!**
MEANWHILE...
HEY! GET BACK ON THAT WHEEL, SAMMY!
NO! I'M HUNGRY!
SNAP! POP! SNAP!
CRASH
THESE REPAIRS ARE GONNA TAKE **FOREVER!**
I THOUGHT YOU WERE FIXING THE SHIP, RALPH...
I AM... I NEED A GET-RICH-QUICK SCHEME TO GET SPARE PARTS!
HAIR

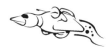

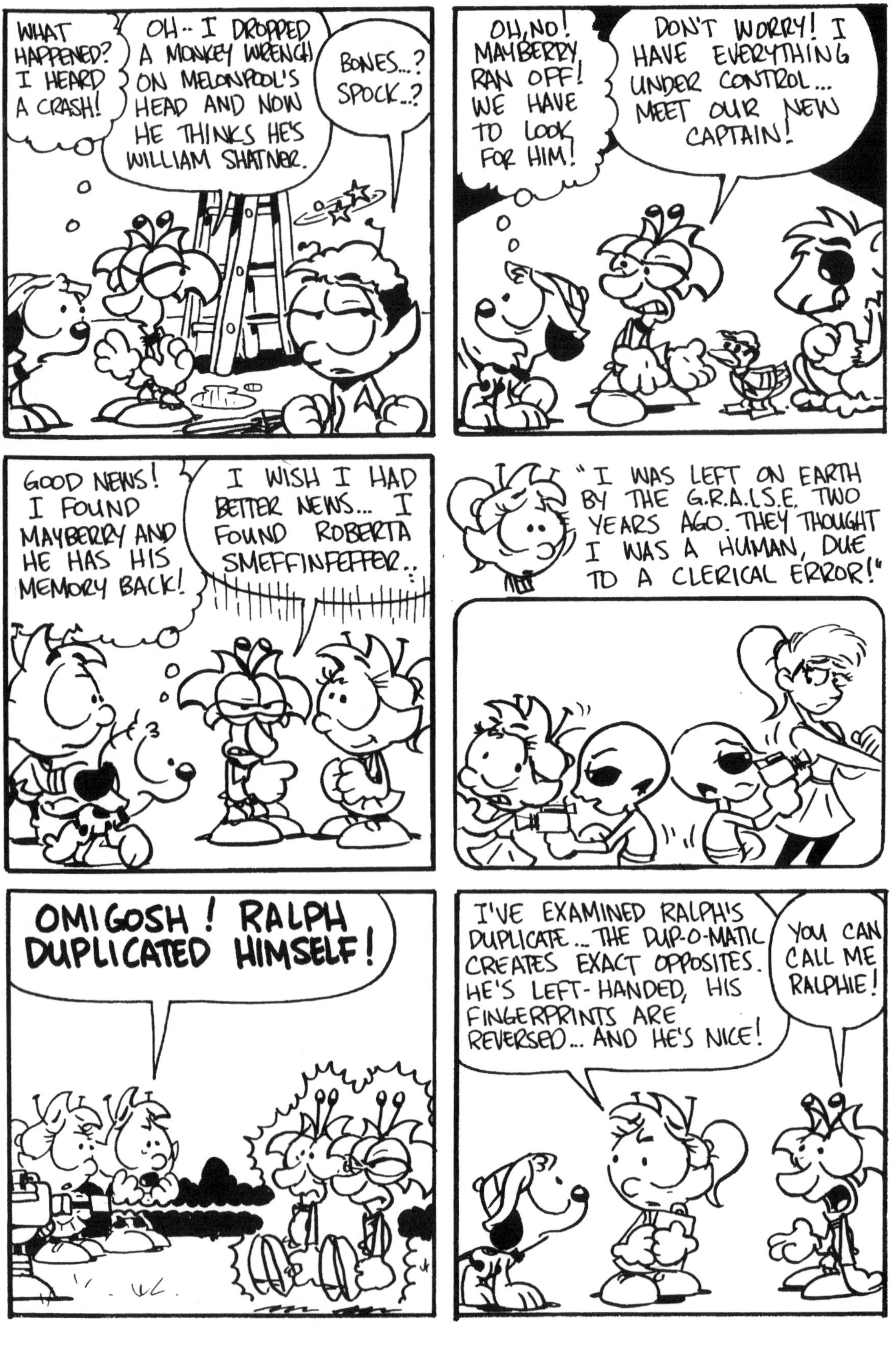
WHAT HAPPENED? I HEARD A CRASH!
OH.. I DROPPED A MONKEY WRENCH ON MELONPOOL'S HEAD AND NOW HE THINKS HE'S WILLIAM SHATNER.
BONES...? SPOCK..?
OH, NO! MAYBERRY RAN OFF! WE HAVE TO LOOK FOR HIM!
DON'T WORRY! I HAVE EVERYTHING UNDER CONTROL... MEET OUR NEW CAPTAIN!
GOOD NEWS! I FOUND MAYBERRY AND HE HAS HIS MEMORY BACK!
I WISH I HAD BETTER NEWS... I FOUND ROBERTA SMEFFINPEFFER..
"I WAS LEFT ON EARTH BY THE G.R.A.I.S.E. TWO YEARS AGO. THEY THOUGHT I WAS A HUMAN, DUE TO A CLERICAL ERROR!"
OMIGOSH! RALPH DUPLICATED HIMSELF!
I'VE EXAMINED RALPH'S DUPLICATE... THE DUP-O-MATIC CREATES EXACT OPPOSITES. HE'S LEFT-HANDED, HIS FINGERPRINTS ARE REVERSED... AND HE'S NICE!
YOU CAN CALL ME RALPHIE!

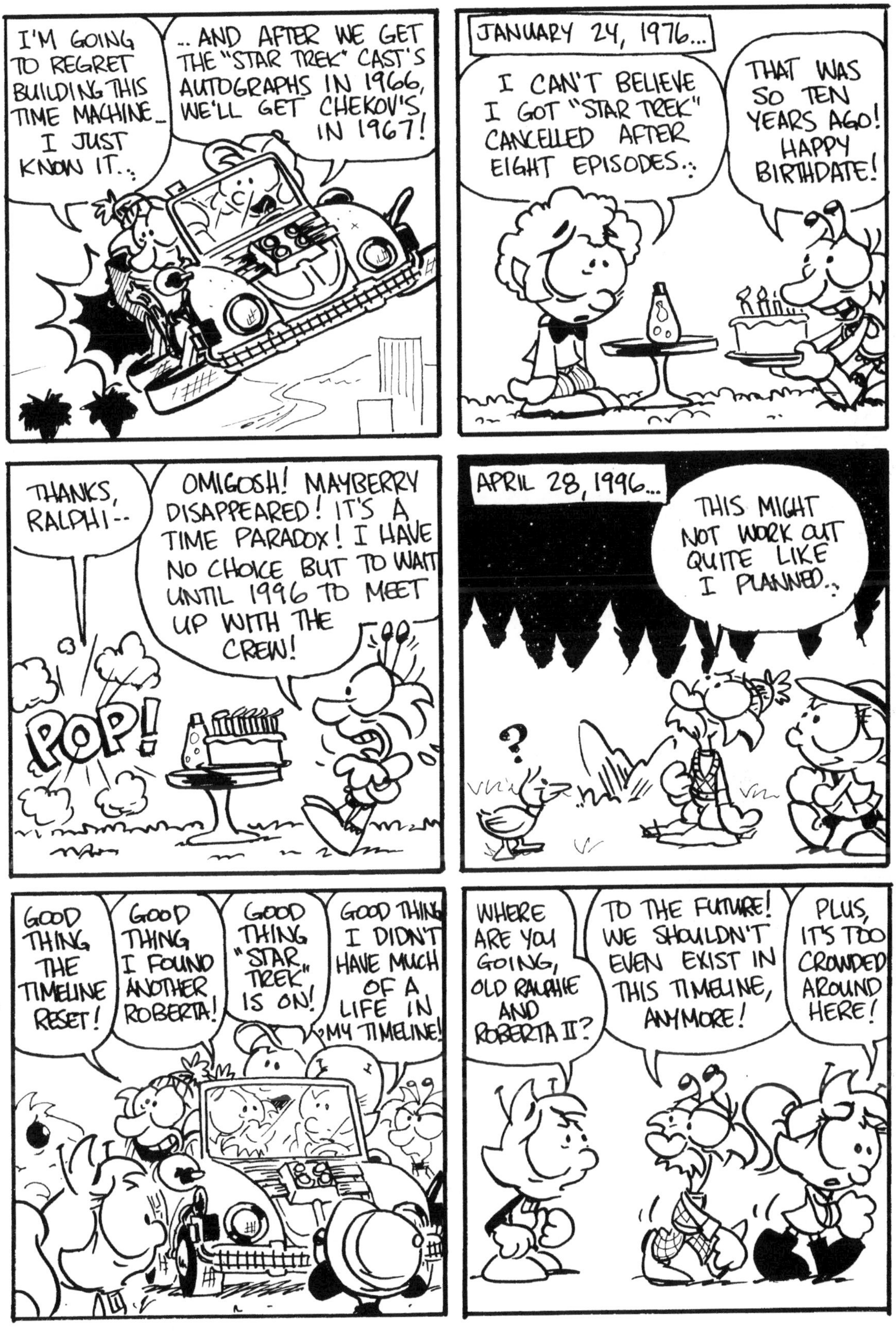
I'M GOING TO REGRET BUILDING THIS TIME MACHINE... I JUST KNOW IT...
...AND AFTER WE GET THE "STAR TREK" CAST'S AUTOGRAPHS IN 1966, WE'LL GET CHEKOV'S IN 1967!
JANUARY 24, 1976...
I CAN'T BELIEVE I GOT "STAR TREK" CANCELLED AFTER EIGHT EPISODES...
THAT WAS SO TEN YEARS AGO! HAPPY BIRTHDATE!
THANKS, RALPHI--
OMIGOSH! MAYBERRY DISAPPEARED! IT'S A TIME PARADOX! I HAVE NO CHOICE BUT TO WAIT UNTIL 1996 TO MEET UP WITH THE CREW!
POP!
APRIL 28, 1996...
THIS MIGHT NOT WORK OUT QUITE LIKE I PLANNED...
?
GOOD THING THE TIMELINE RESET!
GOOD THING I FOUND ANOTHER ROBERTA!
GOOD THING "STAR TREK" IS ON!
GOOD THING I DIDN'T HAVE MUCH OF A LIFE IN MY TIMELINE!
WHERE ARE YOU GOING, OLD RALPHIE AND ROBERTA II?
TO THE FUTURE! WE SHOULDN'T EVEN EXIST IN THIS TIMELINE, ANYMORE!
PLUS, IT'S TOO CROWDED AROUND HERE!

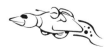

OMIGOSH! WHAT HAPPENED HERE?!
I GOT DUPLICATED AND REALIZED THAT IF I SHOT THE DUP-O-MATIC INTO A MIRROR, IT'D CREATE A "FUSE-O-MATIC!"
YEAH... WHO KNEW MY OPPOSITE WOULD BE SMART?!
ERGH... IT FEELS COLD AND DARK IN HERE...
ARGHH! VOICES IN MY HEAD.. GOOD VOICES!
SO... TELL ME A LITTLE ABOUT HOW THE "STEEL DUCK" CREW MET EACH OTHER.
I'M A TELEPATHIC DOG FROM PLANET K-9, SAMMY'S A MUTANT HAMSTER, MAYBERRY'S AN EX-VIDEO CLERK ... AND RALPH'S AN EXILED PRINCE!
HOW DO YOU FEEL AFTER TAKING THAT "THER-O-QUIL--" OMIGOSH!
WELL... LOOK WHO'S BACK..
SO TO SPEAK!
MEANWHILE, MAYBERRY BEGINS TO LEARN THE WAYS OF THE FORCE...
UM.. MASTER NO-DA... AM I LEARNING THE LIGHT SIDE OR THE DARK SIDE?
THINK OF IT AS THE "GREY SIDE.."
BEER
JEDI KIT
I CAN'T BELIEVE IT! AFTER TWO LONG YEARS, THE SHIP IS READY TO BLAST OFF!
I CAN'T BELIEVE THAT RALPH DIDN'T TRY TO LEAVE WITHOUT US!

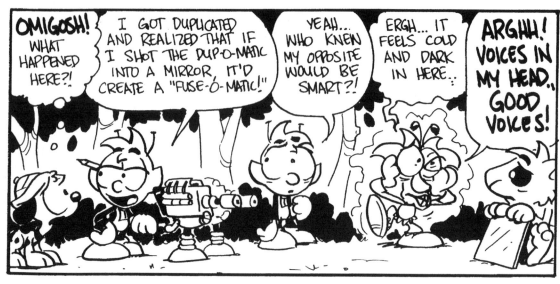

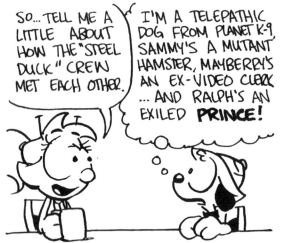

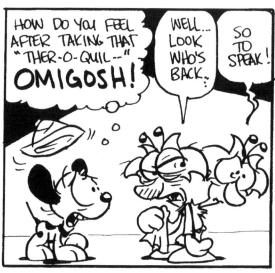

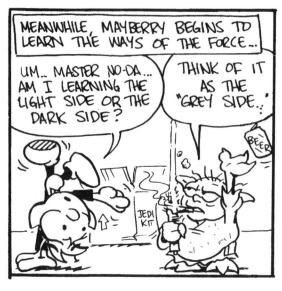

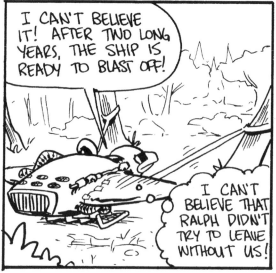

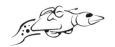

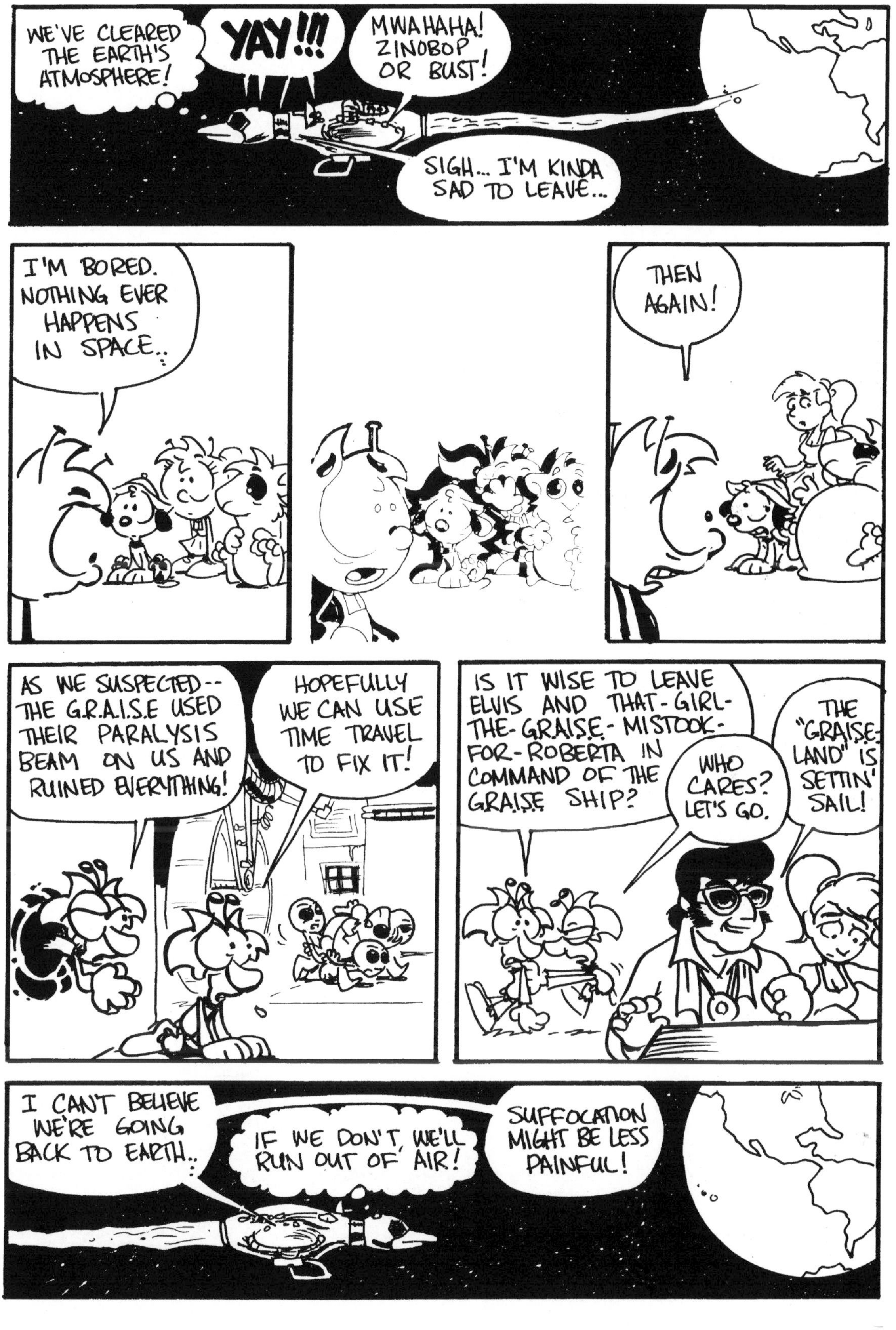
WE'VE CLEARED THE EARTH'S ATMOSPHERE!
YAY!!!
MWAHAHA! ZINOBOP OR BUST!
SIGH... I'M KINDA SAD TO LEAVE...
I'M BORED. NOTHING EVER HAPPENS IN SPACE...
THEN AGAIN!
AS WE SUSPECTED-- THE G.R.A.I.S.E USED THEIR PARALYSIS BEAM ON US AND RUINED EVERYTHING!
HOPEFULLY WE CAN USE TIME TRAVEL TO FIX IT!
IS IT WISE TO LEAVE ELVIS AND THAT-GIRL-THE-GRAISE-MISTOOK-FOR-ROBERTA IN COMMAND OF THE GRAISE SHIP?
WHO CARES? LET'S GO.
THE "GRAISE-LAND" IS SETTIN' SAIL!
I CAN'T BELIEVE WE'RE GOING BACK TO EARTH...
IF WE DON'T, WE'LL RUN OUT OF AIR!
SUFFOCATION MIGHT BE LESS PAINFUL!

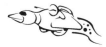

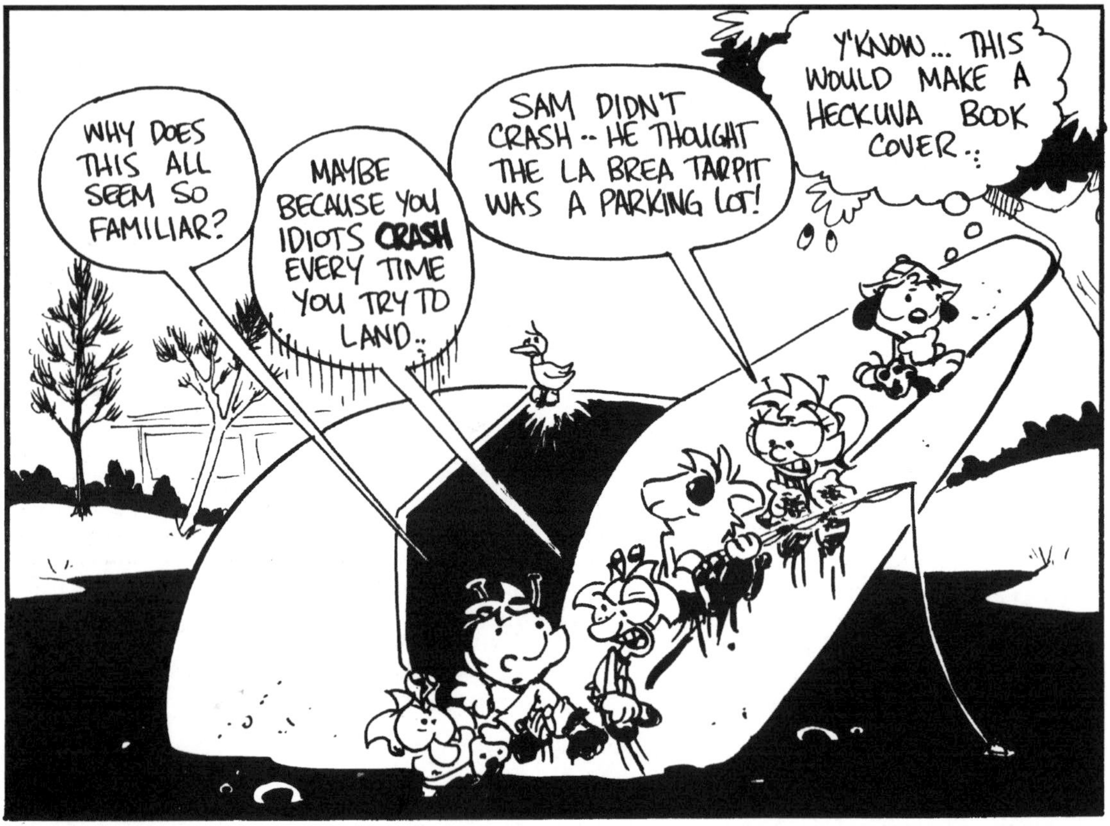
WHY DOES THIS ALL SEEM SO FAMILIAR?
MAYBE BECAUSE YOU IDIOTS CRASH EVERY TIME YOU TRY TO LAND..
SAM DIDN'T CRASH -- HE THOUGHT THE LA BREA TARPIT WAS A PARKING LOT!
Y'KNOW... THIS WOULD MAKE A HECKUVA BOOK COVER..:

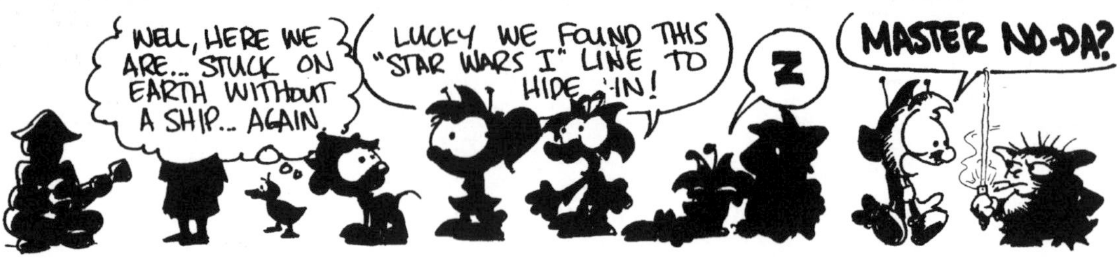
WELL, HERE WE ARE... STUCK ON EARTH WITHOUT A SHIP... AGAIN.
LUCKY WE FOUND THIS "STAR WARS I" LINE TO HIDE IN!
Z
MASTER NO-DA?

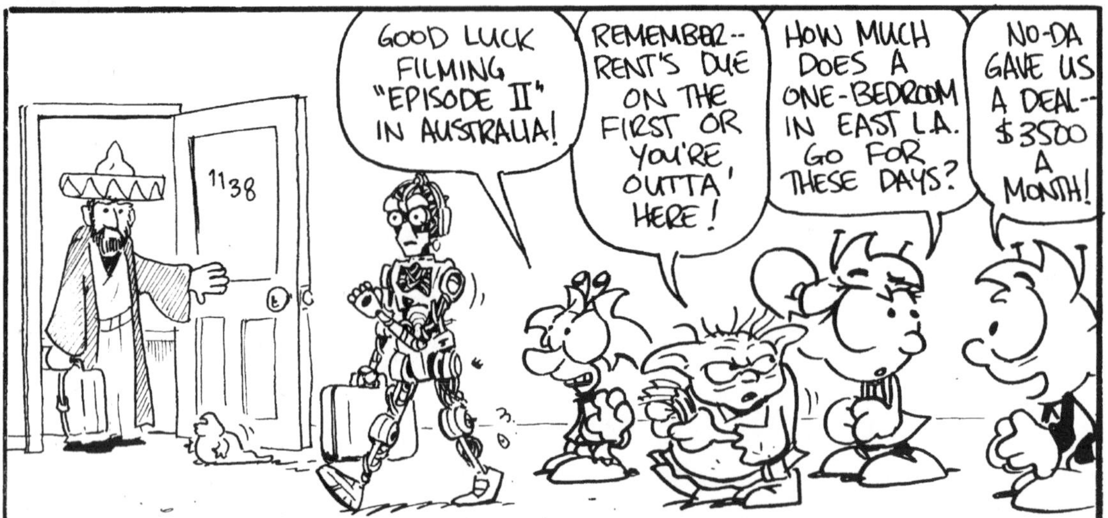
1138
GOOD LUCK FILMING "EPISODE II" IN AUSTRALIA!
REMEMBER-- RENT'S DUE ON THE FIRST OR YOU'RE OUTTA HERE!
HOW MUCH DOES A ONE-BEDROOM IN EAST L.A. GO FOR THESE DAYS?
NO-DA GAVE US A DEAL-- $3500 A MONTH!

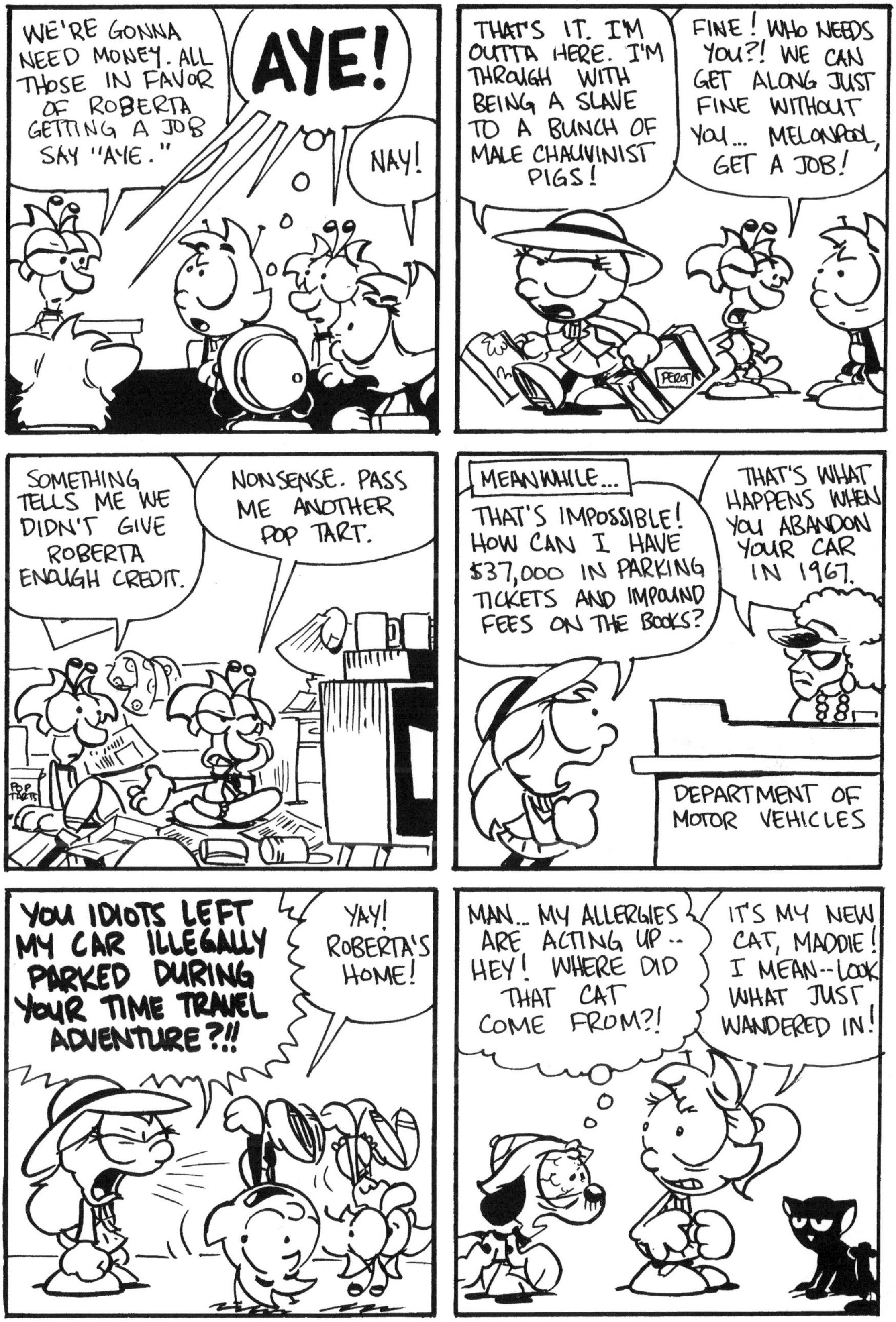
WE'RE GONNA NEED MONEY. ALL THOSE IN FAVOR OF ROBERTA GETTING A JOB SAY "AYE."
AYE!
NAY!
THAT'S IT. I'M OUTTA HERE. I'M THROUGH WITH BEING A SLAVE TO A BUNCH OF MALE CHAUVINIST PIGS!
FINE! WHO NEEDS YOU?! WE CAN GET ALONG JUST FINE WITHOUT YOU... MELONPOOL, GET A JOB!
PEROT
SOMETHING TELLS ME WE DIDN'T GIVE ROBERTA ENOUGH CREDIT.
NONSENSE. PASS ME ANOTHER POP TART.
POP TARTS
MEANWHILE...
THAT'S IMPOSSIBLE! HOW CAN I HAVE $37,000 IN PARKING TICKETS AND IMPOUND FEES ON THE BOOKS?
THAT'S WHAT HAPPENS WHEN YOU ABANDON YOUR CAR IN 1967.
DEPARTMENT OF MOTOR VEHICLES
YOU IDIOTS LEFT MY CAR ILLEGALLY PARKED DURING YOUR TIME TRAVEL ADVENTURE?!!
YAY! ROBERTA'S HOME!
MAN... MY ALLERGIES ARE ACTING UP -- HEY! WHERE DID THAT CAT COME FROM?!
IT'S MY NEW CAT, MADDIE! I MEAN--LOOK WHAT JUST WANDERED IN!

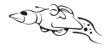

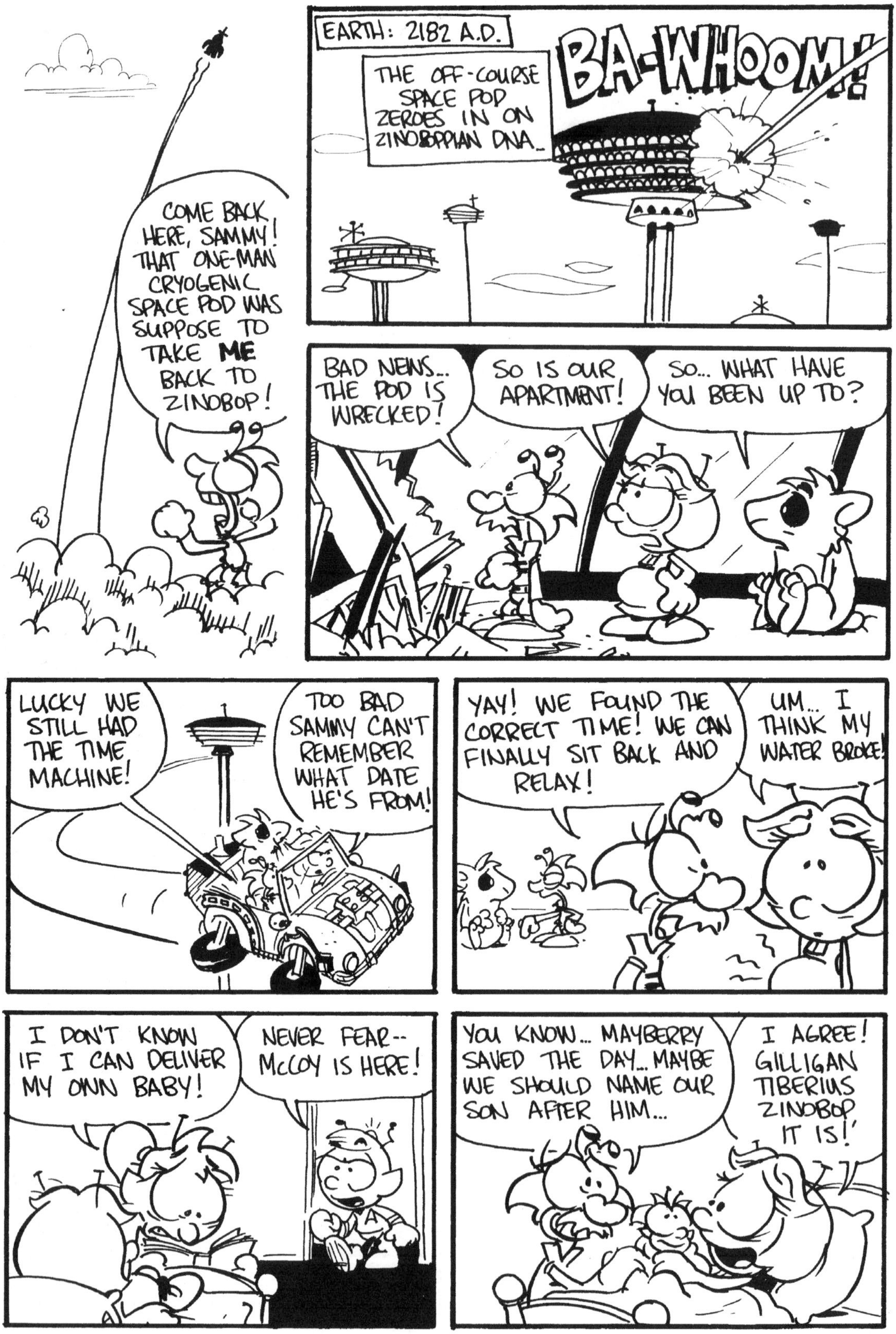
COME BACK HERE, SAMMY! THAT ONE-MAN CRYOGENIC SPACE POD WAS SUPPOSE TO TAKE **ME** BACK TO ZINOBOP!
EARTH: 2182 A.D.
THE OFF-COURSE SPACE POD ZEROES IN ON ZINOBOPPIAN DNA...
BA-WHOOM!!
BAD NEWS... THE POD IS WRECKED!
SO IS OUR APARTMENT!
SO... WHAT HAVE YOU BEEN UP TO?
LUCKY WE STILL HAD THE TIME MACHINE!
TOO BAD SAMMY CAN'T REMEMBER WHAT DATE HE'S FROM!
YAY! WE FOUND THE CORRECT TIME! WE CAN FINALLY SIT BACK AND RELAX!
UM... I THINK MY WATER BROKE!
I DON'T KNOW IF I CAN DELIVER MY OWN BABY!
NEVER FEAR-- McCOY IS HERE!
YOU KNOW... MAYBERRY SAVED THE DAY... MAYBE WE SHOULD NAME OUR SON AFTER HIM...
I AGREE! GILLIGAN TIBERIUS ZINOBOP IT IS!

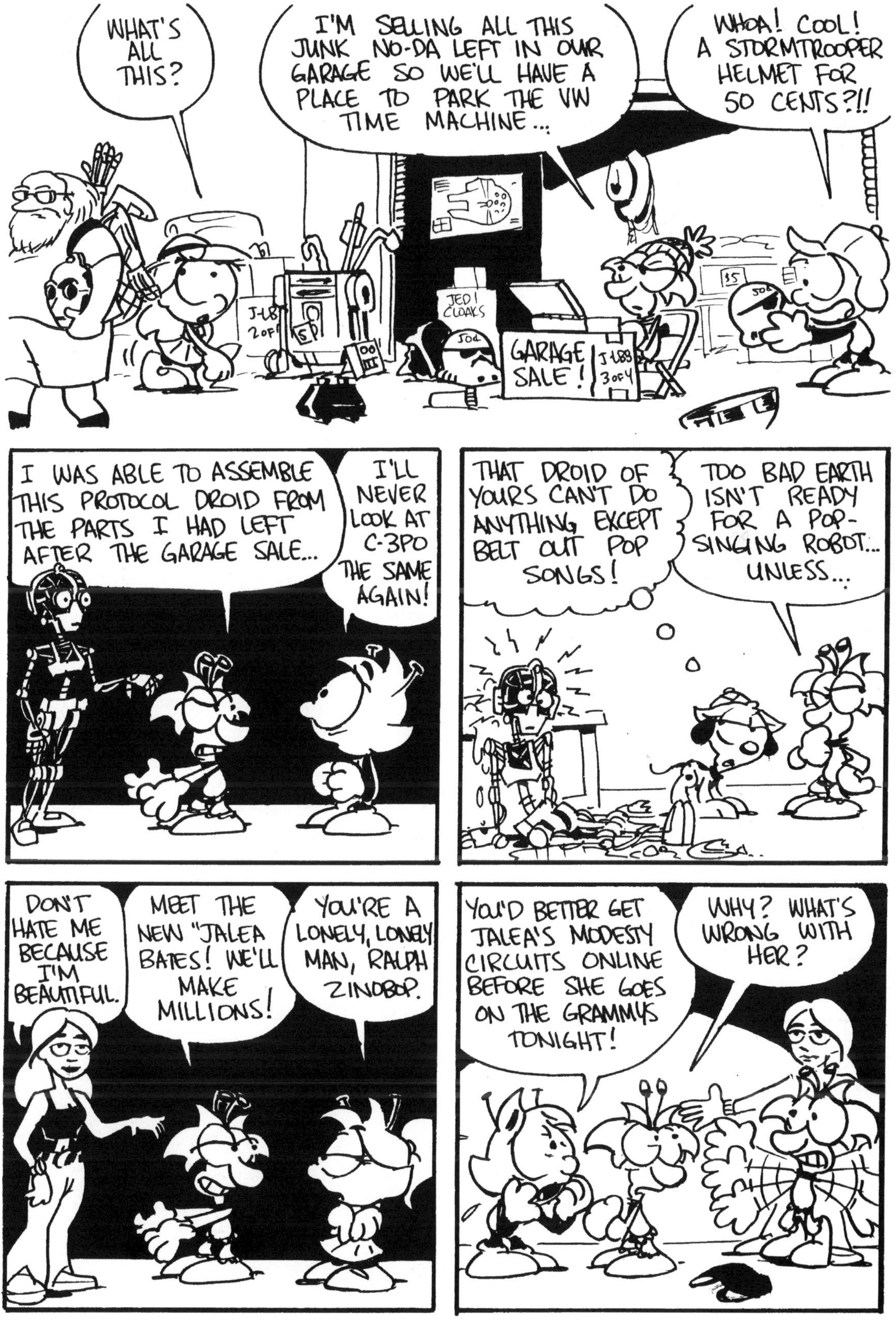
WHAT'S ALL THIS?
I'M SELLING ALL THIS JUNK NO-DA LEFT IN OUR GARAGE SO WE'LL HAVE A PLACE TO PARK THE VW TIME MACHINE...
WHOA! COOL! A STORMTROOPER HELMET FOR 50 CENTS?!!
JEDI CLOAKS
GARAGE SALE!
I WAS ABLE TO ASSEMBLE THIS PROTOCOL DROID FROM THE PARTS I HAD LEFT AFTER THE GARAGE SALE...
I'LL NEVER LOOK AT C-3PO THE SAME AGAIN!
THAT DROID OF YOURS CAN'T DO ANYTHING EXCEPT BELT OUT POP SONGS!
TOO BAD EARTH ISN'T READY FOR A POP-SINGING ROBOT... UNLESS...
DON'T HATE ME BECAUSE I'M BEAUTIFUL.
MEET THE NEW "JALEA BATES! WE'LL MAKE MILLIONS!
YOU'RE A LONELY, LONELY MAN, RALPH ZINOBOP.
YOU'D BETTER GET JALEA'S MODESTY CIRCUITS ONLINE BEFORE SHE GOES ON THE GRAMMYS TONIGHT!
WHY? WHAT'S WRONG WITH HER?

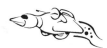

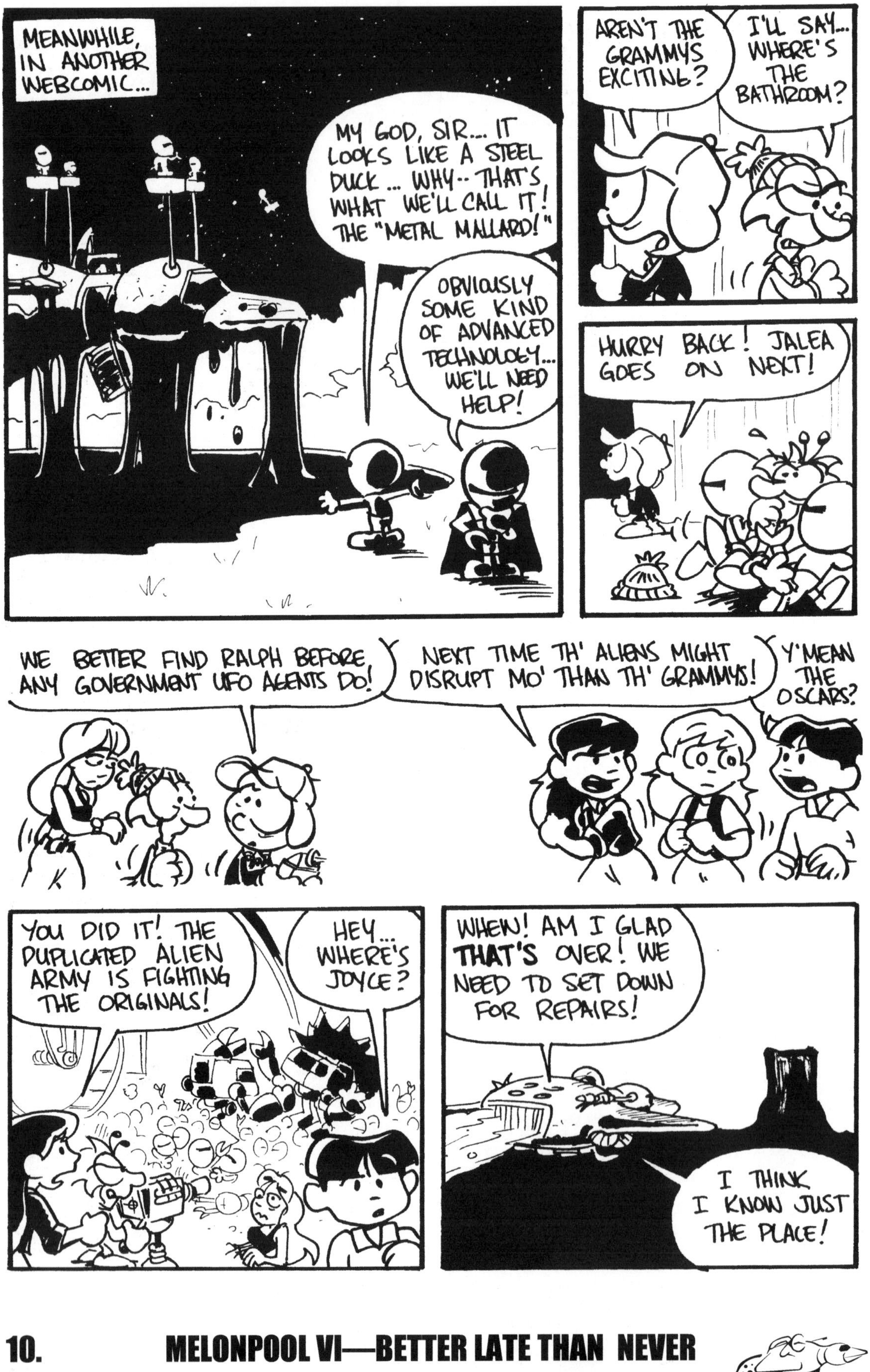
MEANWHILE, IN ANOTHER WEBCOMIC...
MY GOD, SIR... IT LOOKS LIKE A STEEL DUCK... WHY-- THAT'S WHAT WE'LL CALL IT! THE "METAL MALLARD!"
OBVIOUSLY SOME KIND OF ADVANCED TECHNOLOGY... WE'LL NEED HELP!
AREN'T THE GRAMMYS EXCITING?
I'LL SAY... WHERE'S THE BATHROOM?
HURRY BACK! JALEA GOES ON NEXT!
WE BETTER FIND RALPH BEFORE ANY GOVERNMENT UFO AGENTS DO!
NEXT TIME TH' ALIENS MIGHT DISRUPT MO' THAN TH' GRAMMYS!
Y'MEAN THE OSCARS?
YOU DID IT! THE DUPLICATED ALIEN ARMY IS FIGHTING THE ORIGINALS!
HEY... WHERE'S JOYCE?
WHEW! AM I GLAD THAT'S OVER! WE NEED TO SET DOWN FOR REPAIRS!
I THINK I KNOW JUST THE PLACE!

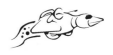

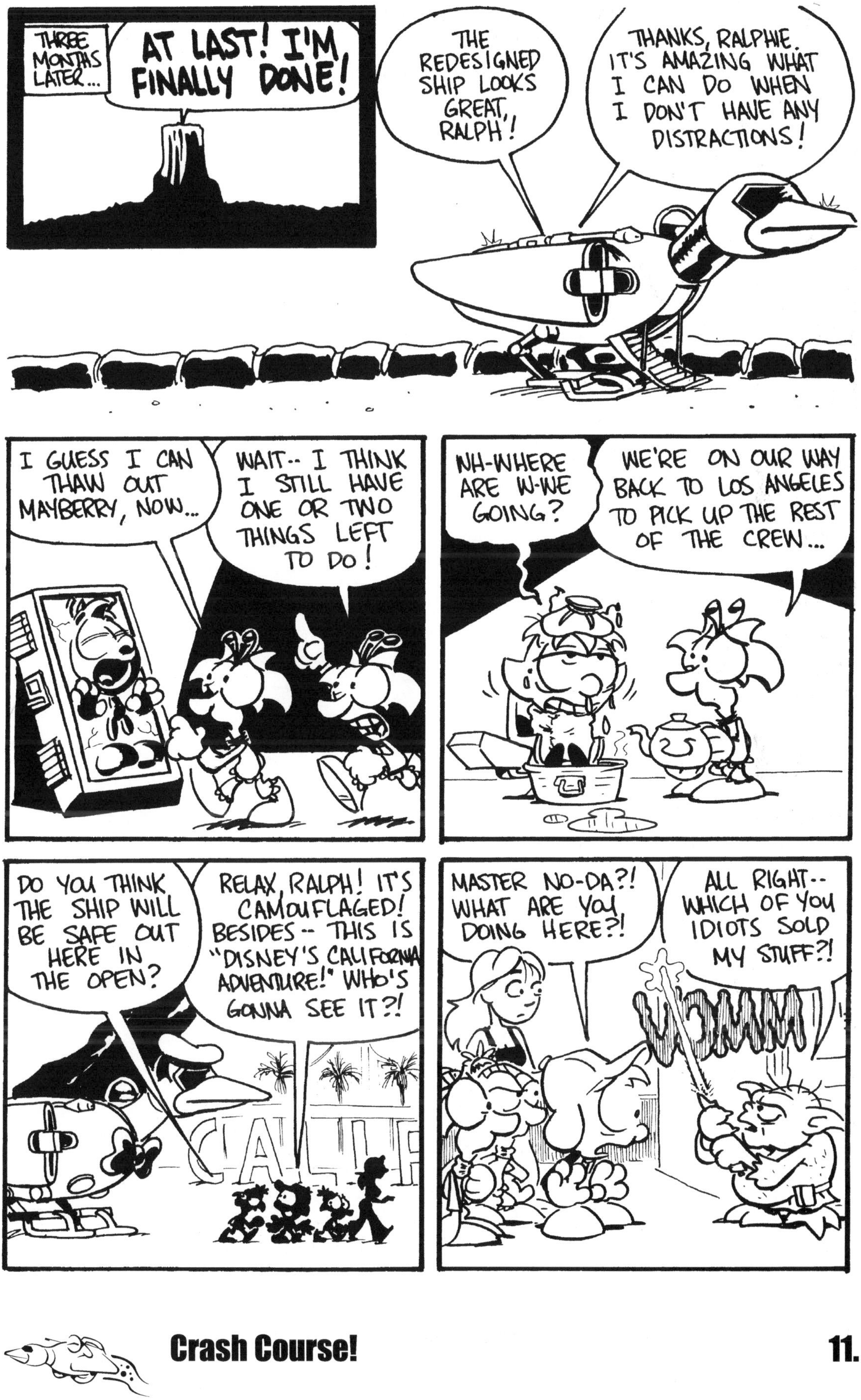
THREE MONTHS LATER...
AT LAST! I'M FINALLY DONE!
THE REDESIGNED SHIP LOOKS GREAT, RALPH!
THANKS, RALPHIE. IT'S AMAZING WHAT I CAN DO WHEN I DON'T HAVE ANY DISTRACTIONS!
I GUESS I CAN THAW OUT MAYBERRY, NOW...
WAIT-- I THINK I STILL HAVE ONE OR TWO THINGS LEFT TO DO!
WH-WHERE ARE W-WE GOING?
WE'RE ON OUR WAY BACK TO LOS ANGELES TO PICK UP THE REST OF THE CREW...
DO YOU THINK THE SHIP WILL BE SAFE OUT HERE IN THE OPEN?
RELAX, RALPH! IT'S CAMOUFLAGED! BESIDES -- THIS IS "DISNEY'S CALIFORNIA ADVENTURE!" WHO'S GONNA SEE IT?!
CALIF
MASTER NO-DA?! WHAT ARE YOU DOING HERE?!
ALL RIGHT-- WHICH OF YOU IDIOTS SOLD MY STUFF?!
VVMMM

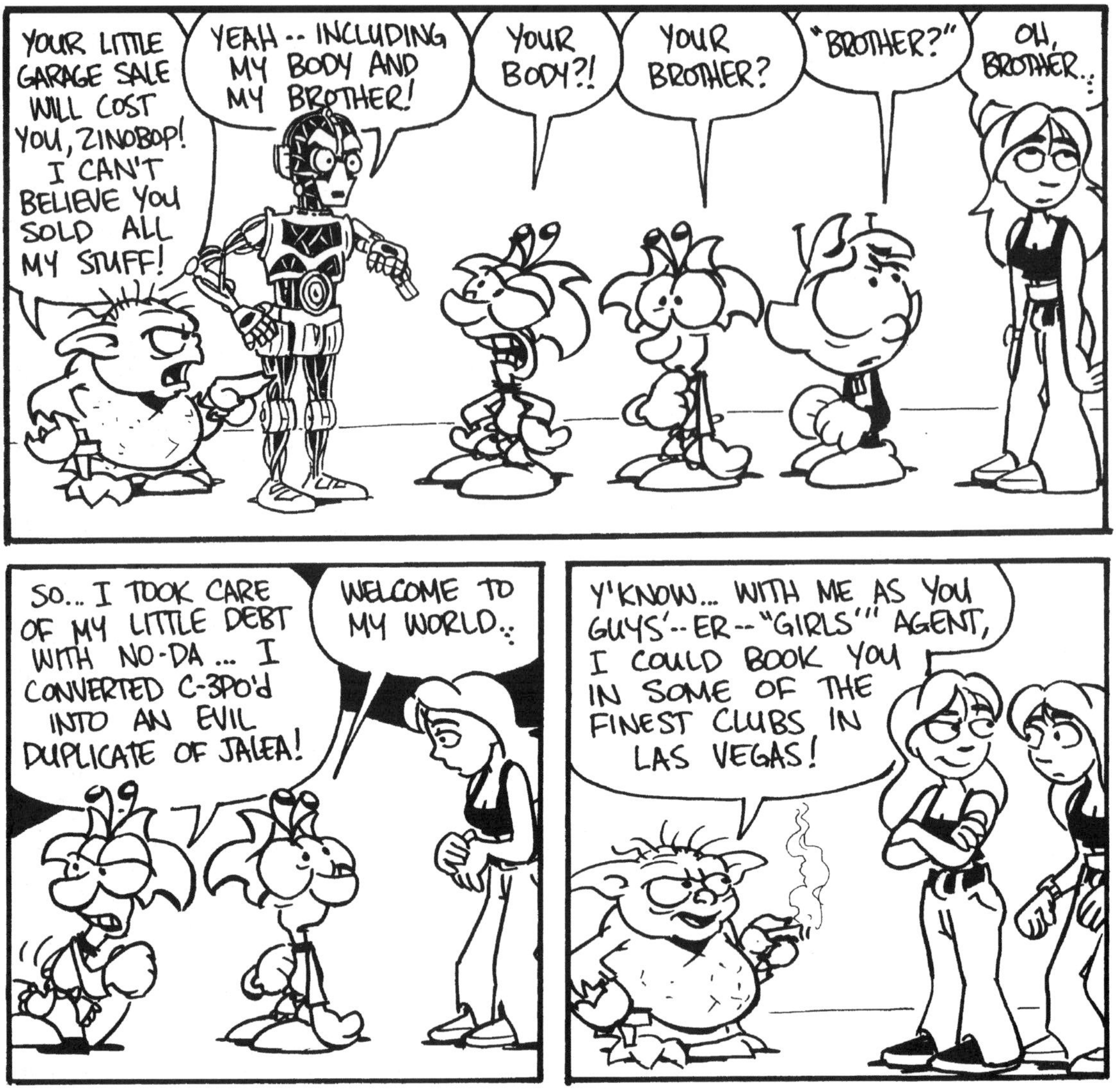
YOUR LITTLE GARAGE SALE WILL COST YOU, ZINOBOP! I CAN'T BELIEVE YOU SOLD ALL MY STUFF!
YEAH -- INCLUDING MY BODY AND MY BROTHER!
YOUR BODY?!
YOUR BROTHER?
"BROTHER?"
OH, BROTHER...
SO... I TOOK CARE OF MY LITTLE DEBT WITH NO-DA ... I CONVERTED C-3PO'd INTO AN EVIL DUPLICATE OF JALEA!
WELCOME TO MY WORLD...
Y'KNOW... WITH ME AS YOU GUYS'--ER--"GIRLS'" AGENT, I COULD BOOK YOU IN SOME OF THE FINEST CLUBS IN LAS VEGAS!
I CAN'T BELIEVE JALEA JUST TOOK OFF WITH NO-DA AND C-3PO'd!
YOU KNOW WHAT I CAN'T BELIEVE--?
THE SHIP IS GONE!

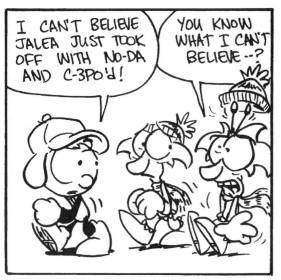

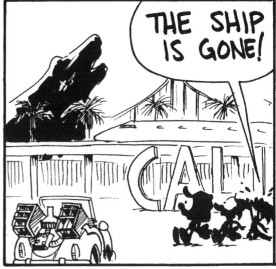

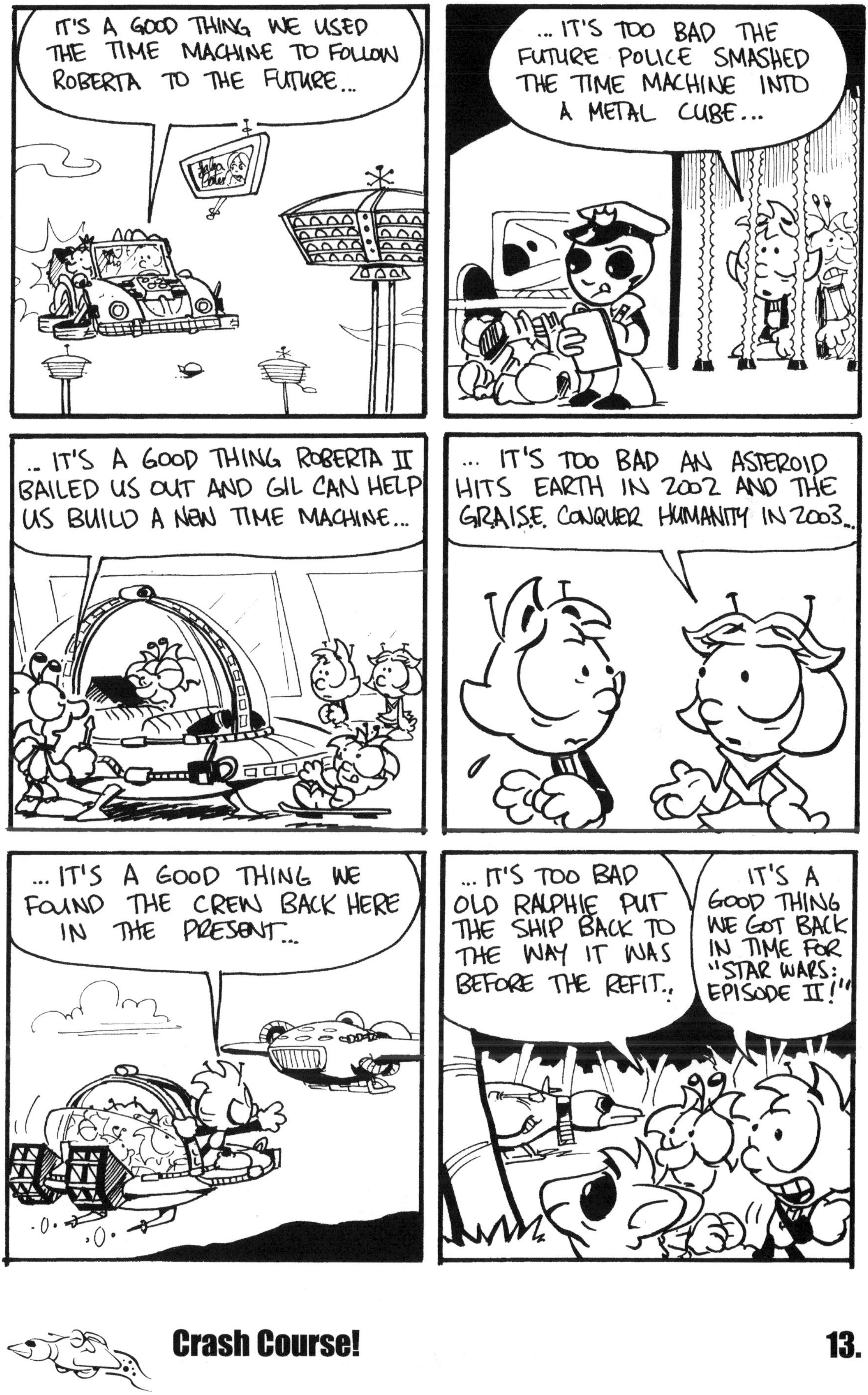
IT'S A GOOD THING WE USED THE TIME MACHINE TO FOLLOW ROBERTA TO THE FUTURE...
... IT'S TOO BAD THE FUTURE POLICE SMASHED THE TIME MACHINE INTO A METAL CUBE...
... IT'S A GOOD THING ROBERTA II BAILED US OUT AND GIL CAN HELP US BUILD A NEW TIME MACHINE...
... IT'S TOO BAD AN ASTEROID HITS EARTH IN 2002 AND THE G.R.A.I.S.E. CONQUER HUMANITY IN 2003...
... IT'S A GOOD THING WE FOUND THE CREW BACK HERE IN THE PRESENT...
... IT'S TOO BAD OLD RALPHIE PUT THE SHIP BACK TO THE WAY IT WAS BEFORE THE REFIT...
IT'S A GOOD THING WE GOT BACK IN TIME FOR "STAR WARS: EPISODE II!"

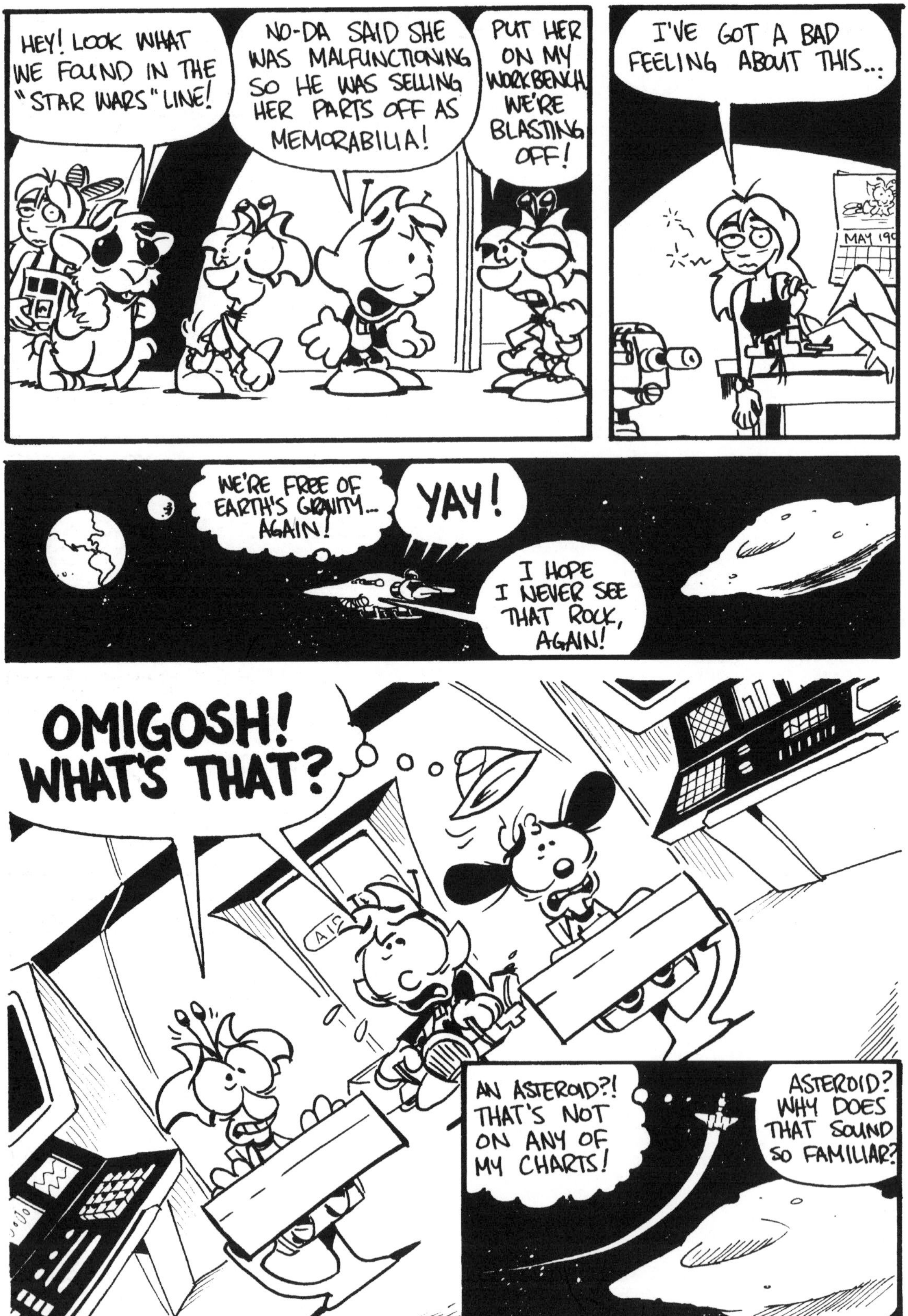
HEY! LOOK WHAT WE FOUND IN THE "STAR WARS" LINE!
NO-DA SAID SHE WAS MALFUNCTIONING SO HE WAS SELLING HER PARTS OFF AS MEMORABILIA!
PUT HER ON MY WORKBENCH. WE'RE BLASTING OFF!
I'VE GOT A BAD FEELING ABOUT THIS...
WE'RE FREE OF EARTH'S GRAVITY... AGAIN!
YAY!
I HOPE I NEVER SEE THAT ROCK, AGAIN!
OMIGOSH! WHAT'S THAT?
AN ASTEROID?! THAT'S NOT ON ANY OF MY CHARTS!
ASTEROID? WHY DOES THAT SOUND SO FAMILIAR?

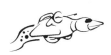

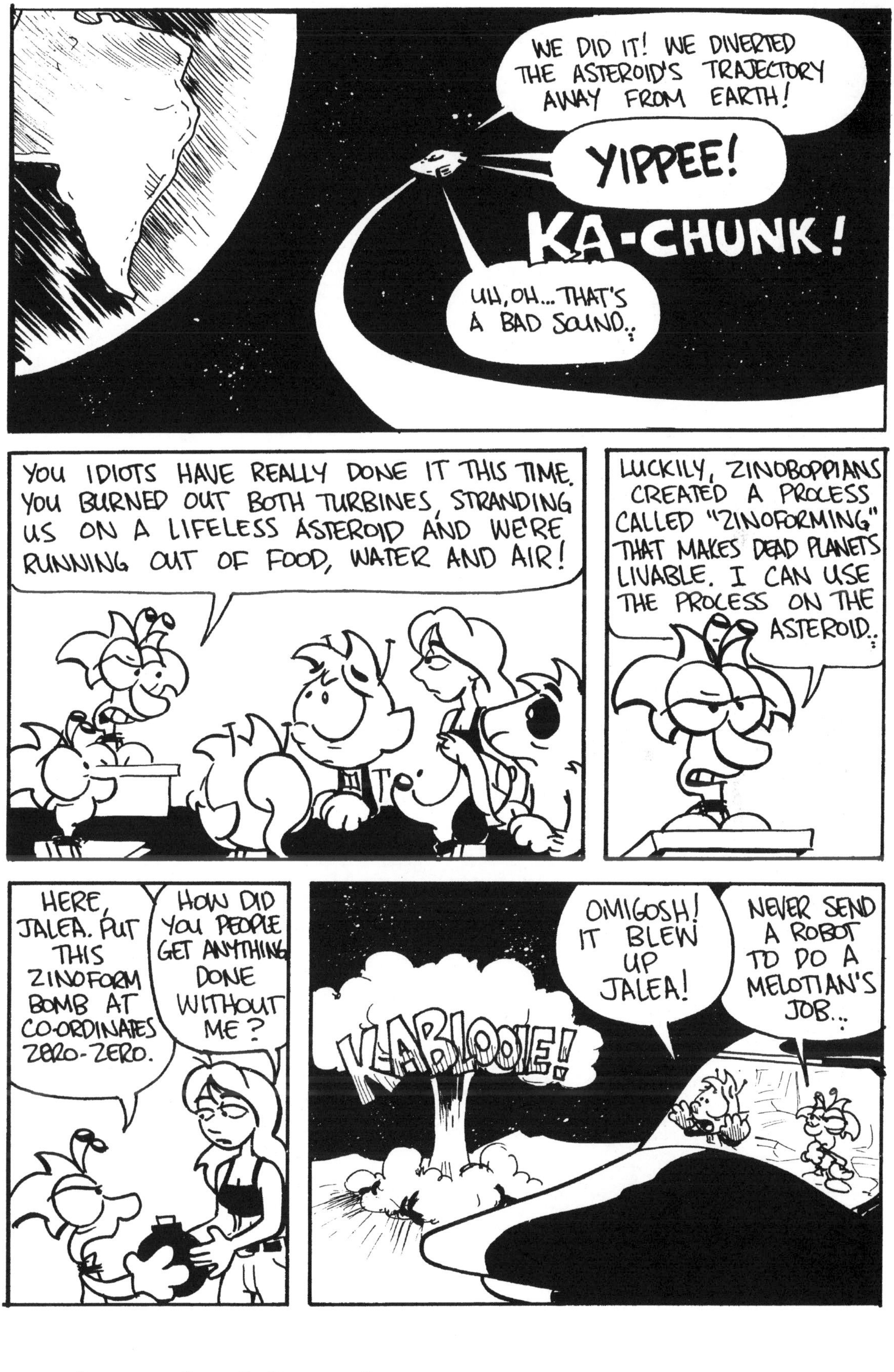
WE DID IT! WE DIVERTED THE ASTEROID'S TRAJECTORY AWAY FROM EARTH!
YIPPEE!
KA-CHUNK!
UH, OH... THAT'S A BAD SOUND...
YOU IDIOTS HAVE REALLY DONE IT THIS TIME. YOU BURNED OUT BOTH TURBINES, STRANDING US ON A LIFELESS ASTEROID AND WE'RE RUNNING OUT OF FOOD, WATER AND AIR!
LUCKILY, ZINOBOPPIANS CREATED A PROCESS CALLED "ZINOFORMING" THAT MAKES DEAD PLANETS LIVABLE. I CAN USE THE PROCESS ON THE ASTEROID...
HERE, JALEA. PUT THIS ZINOFORM BOMB AT CO-ORDINATES ZERO-ZERO.
HOW DID YOU PEOPLE GET ANYTHING DONE WITHOUT ME?
KABLOOIE!
OMIGOSH! IT BLEW UP JALEA!
NEVER SEND A ROBOT TO DO A MELOTIAN'S JOB...

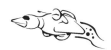

... OF ALL THE SOULS I'VE ENCOUNTERED... HERS WAS THE MOST... HUMAN..
MAN, SAMMY! THAT'S AMAZINGLY GRATING!
WHY DOES MAYBERRY'S EULOGY SOUND SO FAMILIAR?
"STAR TREK II"
OMIGOSH! IT'S JALEA! SHE'S ALIVE!
WAIT.. SHE'S OUTSIDE THE FORCEFIELD-- IF WE OPEN IT WE'LL ALL BE KILLED!
JALEA UPLOADED HER MIND INTO THE SHIP'S COMPUTER BEFORE SHE DISINTEGRATED... MEET HER NEW BODY!
J-LB
THE ASTEROID WAS SUPPOSED TO ZINOFORM INTO A LIFE-SUSTAINING PARADISE... SO, WHY'D IT TURN OUT LIKE "GILLIGAN'S ISLAND?!"
JUST SIT RIGHT BACK AND HEAR A TALE...

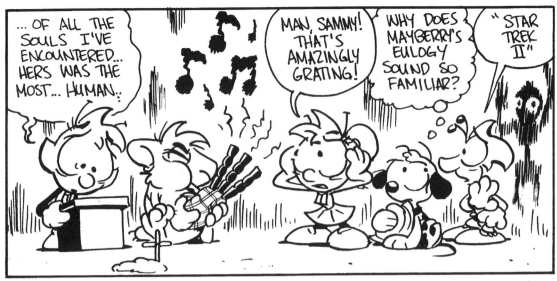

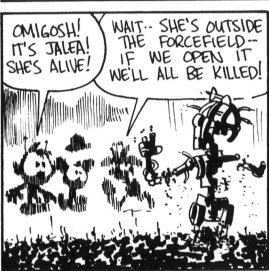

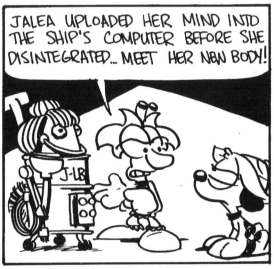

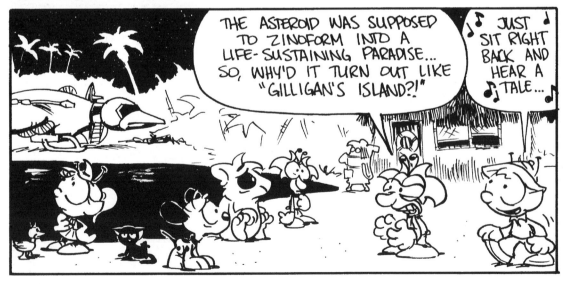

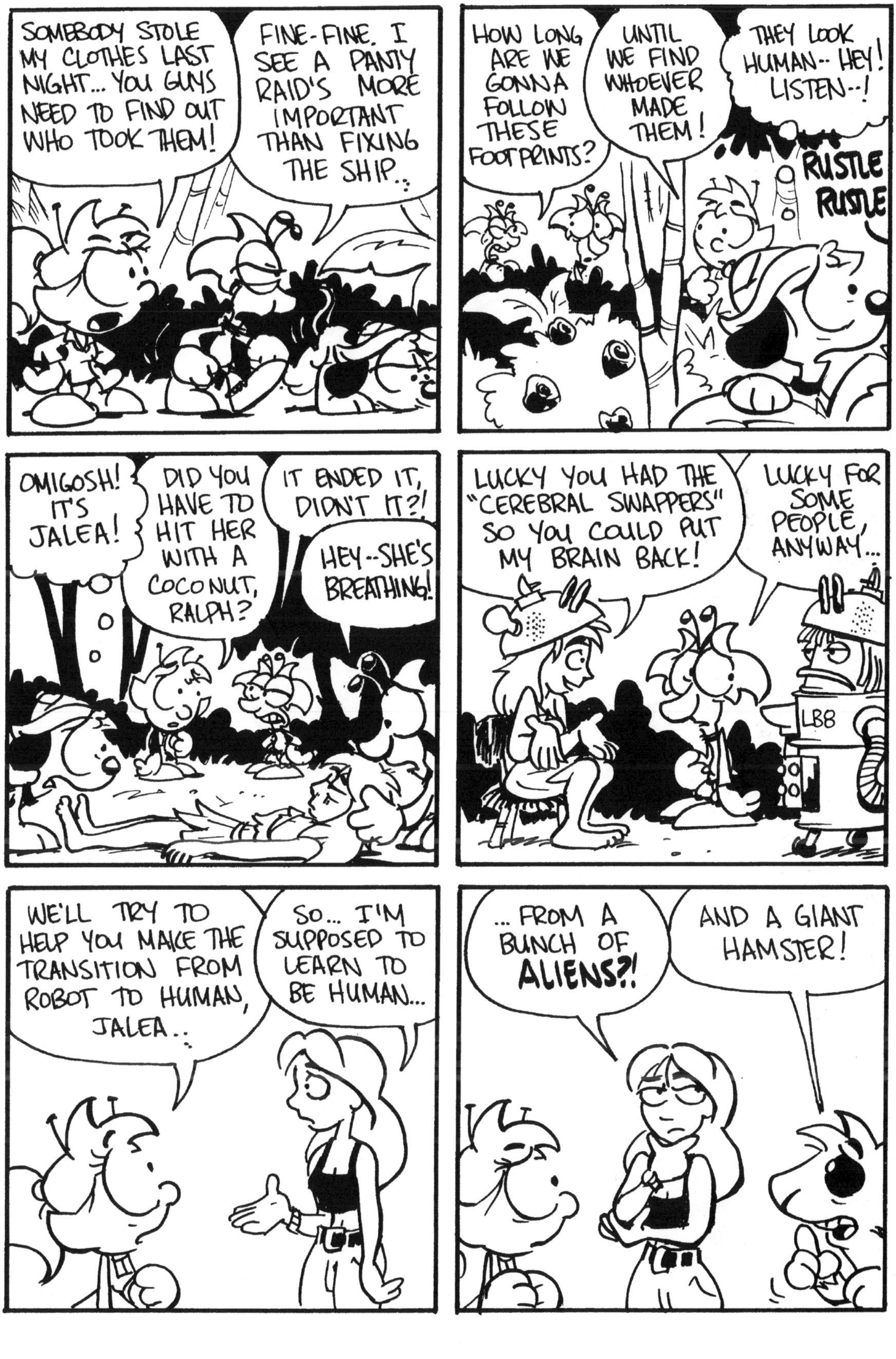
SOMEBODY STOLE MY CLOTHES LAST NIGHT... YOU GUYS NEED TO FIND OUT WHO TOOK THEM!
FINE-FINE. I SEE A PANTY RAID'S MORE IMPORTANT THAN FIXING THE SHIP...
HOW LONG ARE WE GONNA FOLLOW THESE FOOTPRINTS?
UNTIL WE FIND WHOEVER MADE THEM!
THEY LOOK HUMAN-- HEY! LISTEN--!
RUSTLE RUSTLE
OMIGOSH! IT'S JALEA!
DID YOU HAVE TO HIT HER WITH A COCONUT, RALPH?
IT ENDED IT, DIDN'T IT?!
HEY--SHE'S BREATHING!
LUCKY YOU HAD THE "CEREBRAL SWAPPERS" SO YOU COULD PUT MY BRAIN BACK!
LUCKY FOR SOME PEOPLE, ANYWAY...
LB8
WE'LL TRY TO HELP YOU MAKE THE TRANSITION FROM ROBOT TO HUMAN, JALEA...
SO... I'M SUPPOSED TO LEARN TO BE HUMAN...
... FROM A BUNCH OF **ALIENS?!**
AND A GIANT HAMSTER!

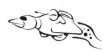

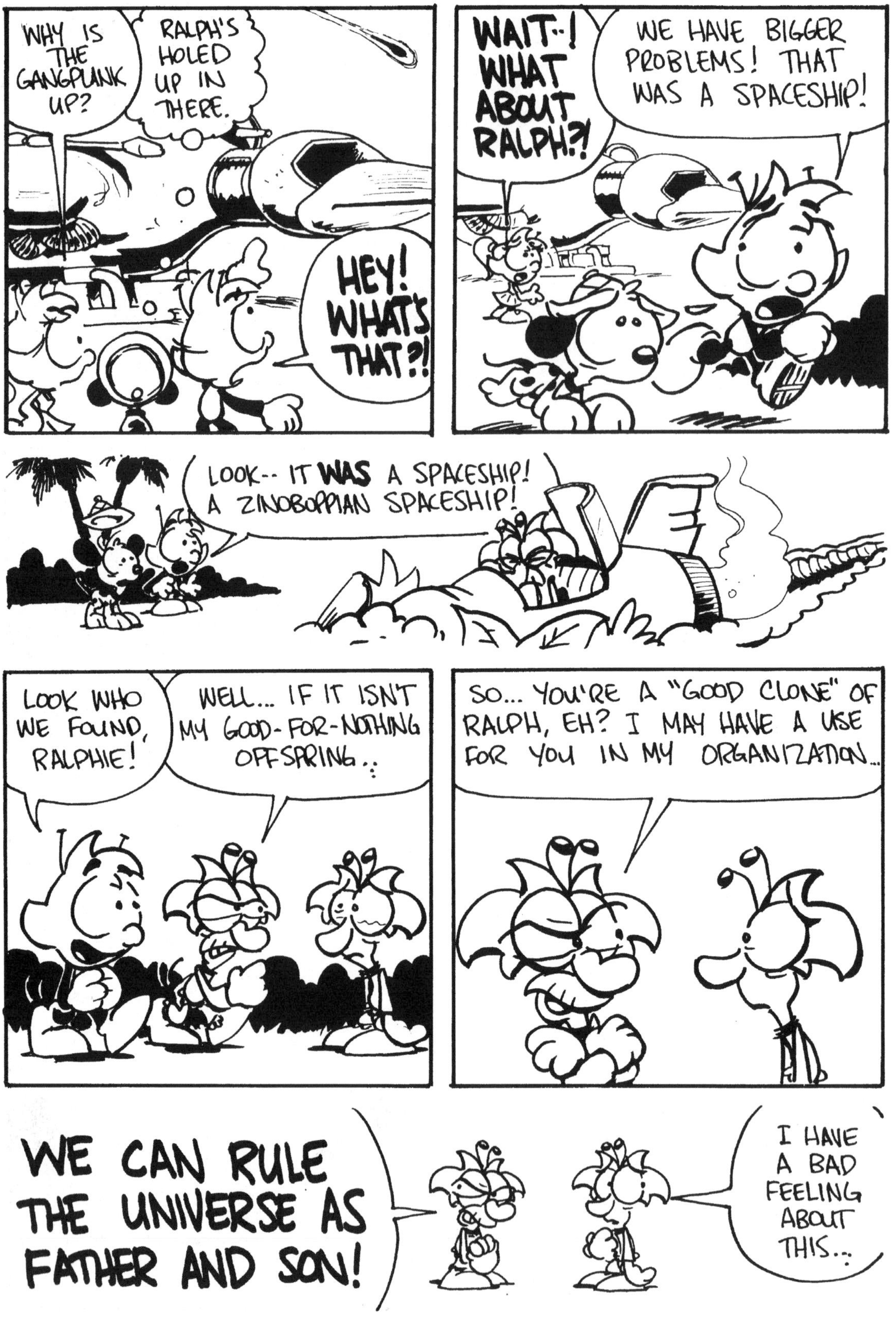

WHY IS THE GANGPLANK UP?
RALPH'S HOLED UP IN THERE.
HEY! WHAT'S THAT?!
WAIT..! WHAT ABOUT RALPH?!
WE HAVE BIGGER PROBLEMS! THAT WAS A SPACESHIP!
LOOK-- IT WAS A SPACESHIP! A ZINOBOPPIAN SPACESHIP!
LOOK WHO WE FOUND, RALPHIE!
WELL... IF IT ISN'T MY GOOD-FOR-NOTHING OFFSPRING...
SO... YOU'RE A "GOOD CLONE" OF RALPH, EH? I MAY HAVE A USE FOR YOU IN MY ORGANIZATION...
WE CAN RULE THE UNIVERSE AS FATHER AND SON!
I HAVE A BAD FEELING ABOUT THIS...

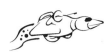

MEANWHILE, INSIDE THE "STEEL DUCK.."
THERE! I'VE FINALLY FINISHED CONVERTING ONE OF THE TURBINES INTO AN ESCAPE POD!
ALL I NEED NOW IS TO COLLECT SAMMY AND IT'S GOOD-BYE ASTEROID-- HELLO ZINOBOPPIAN THRONE! I'LL SNEAK OUT NOW WHILE EVERYONE'S ASLEEP!
RALPHIE..?!
OH, RALPH-- IT'S DAD-- HE'S HERE! HE WANTS ME TO BE HIS PUPPET RULER ON ZINOBOP! I DON'T WANT THAT!
HMM... PUPPET, EH? WE'LL JUST SEE ABOUT THAT... GIMME YOUR CLOTHES...
MY CLOTHES?
OMIGOSH! WHAT'S THAT "EGG-THING" TAKING OFF?! IS IT AN ESCAPE POD?
IT'S OKAY! RALPH SAID HE'D COME BACK FOR US!
I'M REALLY GOING TO BE KING OF ZINOBOP?
"FIGURE HEAD." AND SHUT UP BEFORE I REGRET CLONING MYSELF WITH RALPH'S DUP-O-MATIC...

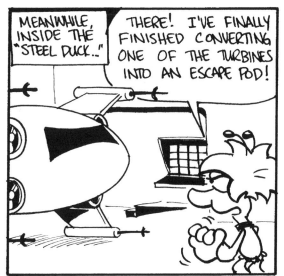

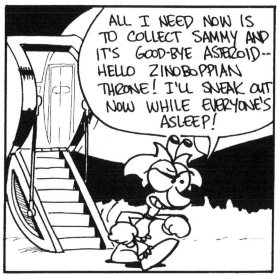

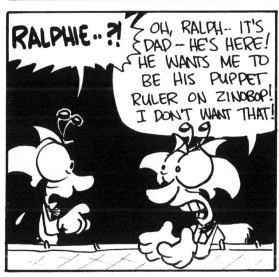

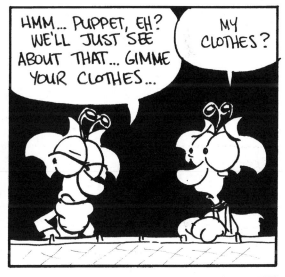

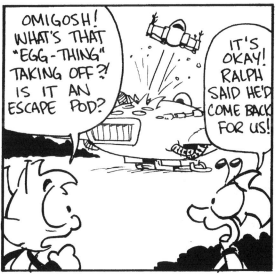

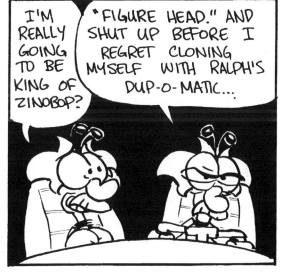

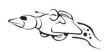

RALPH'S REALLY DOWN... IF ONLY YOUR DAD DIDN'T TAKE OFF WITH ONE OF OUR TURBINES...;

OF COURSE! WE CAN USE THE TIME PORTAL FROM THE G.R.A.I.S.E SAGA!

HERE GOES NOTHING!

WAIT--! I HAVEN'T SET THE TIME CO-ORDINATES, YET!

SOMETHING TELLS ME THAT SAMMY WASN'T THE BEST CHOICE TO HAVE HOLD THE END OF THE GRAPPLING HOOK WHEN I ATTEMPTED TO RESCUE YOU.;

SOMETHING TELLS ME WE'LL BE IN THIS VORTEX FOR AWHILE.;

WHEW! HOOKING ON TO THE TIME MACHINE GOT US OUT OF THAT VORTEX!

BUT... WHAT TIME PERIOD IS THIS?!

WE DID IT--! WE STOLE THE TIME MACHINE FROM THIS ALTERNATE FUTURE!

I HOPE WE CAN FIND OUR OWN REALITY WITH ALL OF THESE PARADOXES!

I WISH I UNDERSTOOD TIME TRAVEL AND PARADOXES BETTER...;

HERE... LET ME EXPLAIN IT TO YOU...

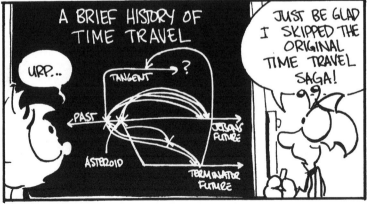

A BRIEF HISTORY OF TIME TRAVEL

URP...

TANGENT

?

PAST

ASTEROID

JETSONS FUTURE

TERMINATOR FUTURE

JUST BE GLAD I SKIPPED THE ORIGINAL TIME TRAVEL SAGA!

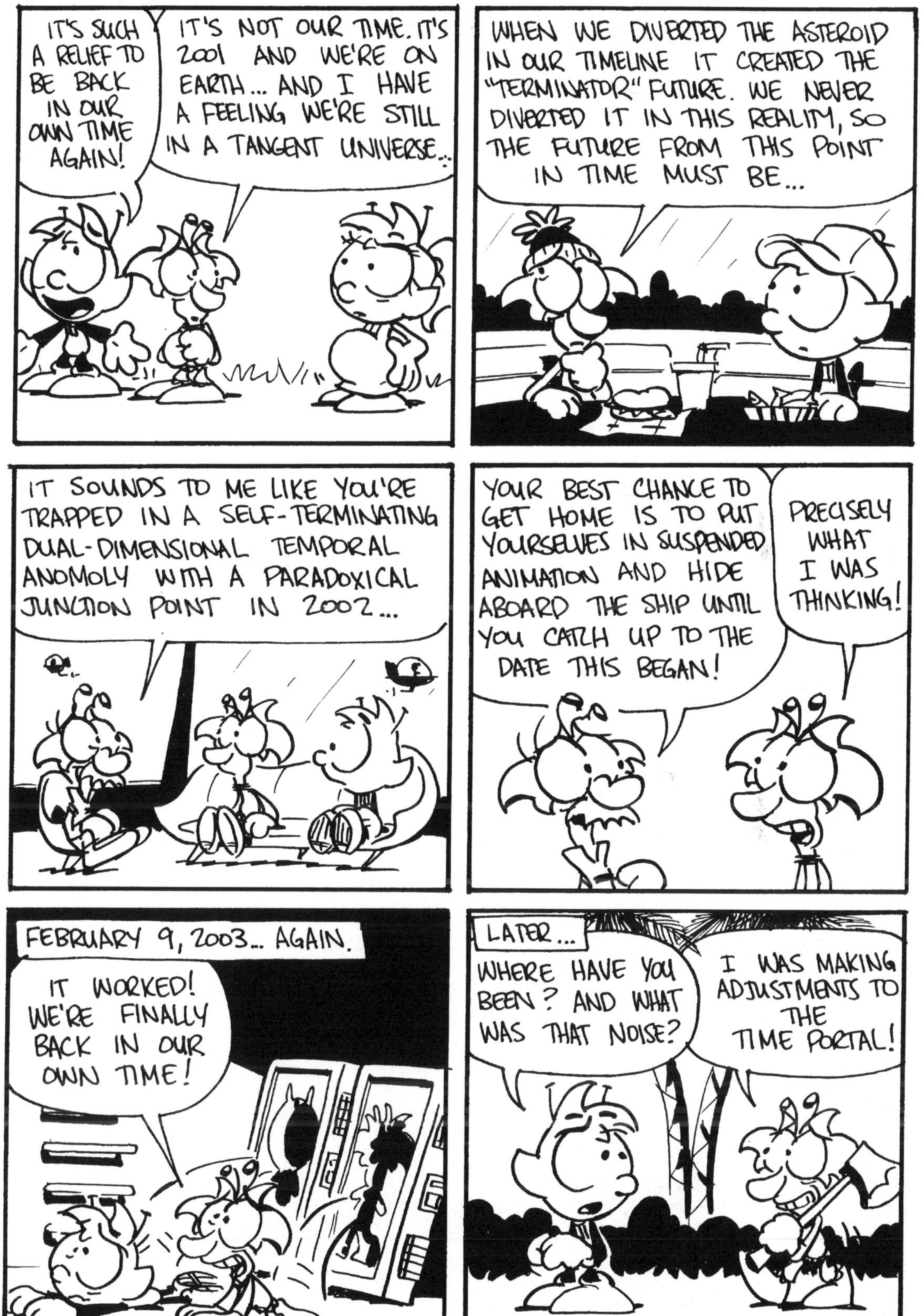
IT'S SUCH A RELIEF TO BE BACK IN OUR OWN TIME AGAIN!
IT'S NOT OUR TIME. IT'S 2001 AND WE'RE ON EARTH... AND I HAVE A FEELING WE'RE STILL IN A TANGENT UNIVERSE...
WHEN WE DIVERTED THE ASTEROID IN OUR TIMELINE IT CREATED THE "TERMINATOR" FUTURE. WE NEVER DIVERTED IT IN THIS REALITY, SO THE FUTURE FROM THIS POINT IN TIME MUST BE...
IT SOUNDS TO ME LIKE YOU'RE TRAPPED IN A SELF-TERMINATING DUAL-DIMENSIONAL TEMPORAL ANOMOLY WITH A PARADOXICAL JUNCTION POINT IN 2002...
YOUR BEST CHANCE TO GET HOME IS TO PUT YOURSELVES IN SUSPENDED ANIMATION AND HIDE ABOARD THE SHIP UNTIL YOU CATCH UP TO THE DATE THIS BEGAN!
PRECISELY WHAT I WAS THINKING!
FEBRUARY 9, 2003... AGAIN.
IT WORKED! WE'RE FINALLY BACK IN OUR OWN TIME!
LATER...
WHERE HAVE YOU BEEN? AND WHAT WAS THAT NOISE?
I WAS MAKING ADJUSTMENTS TO THE TIME PORTAL!

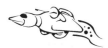

THE ERRATIC ORBIT OF THE ASTEROID PUTS US CLOSE ENOUGH TO ZINOBOP TO TELEPORT ME BACK HOME.
THAT'S GREAT! YOU CAN SEND BACK A RESCUE SHIP!
UH, SURE. YOU'RE IN CHARGE.
OKAY! JUST CALL IF YOU NEED ANYTHING!
HMMMMMM
BEEP BEEP
BEAM ME BACK! BEAM ME BACK!
HMMMMM
ARE YOU ALL RIGHT? WHAT HAPPENED?
IT SMELLED LIKE... DEMOCRACY...
BY THE WAY, I REPAIRED THE REMAINING TURBINE WHILE YOU WERE GONE...

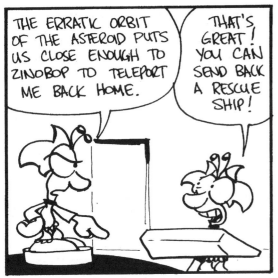

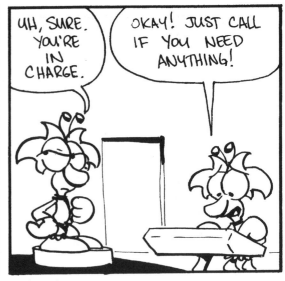

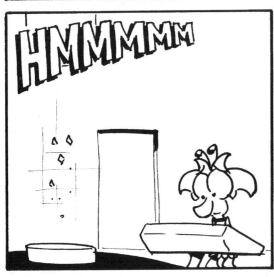

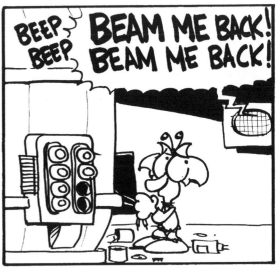

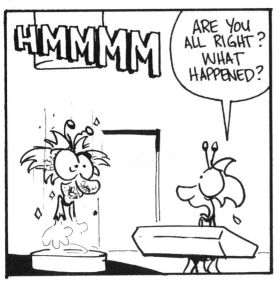

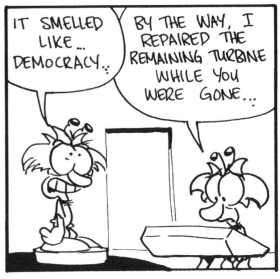

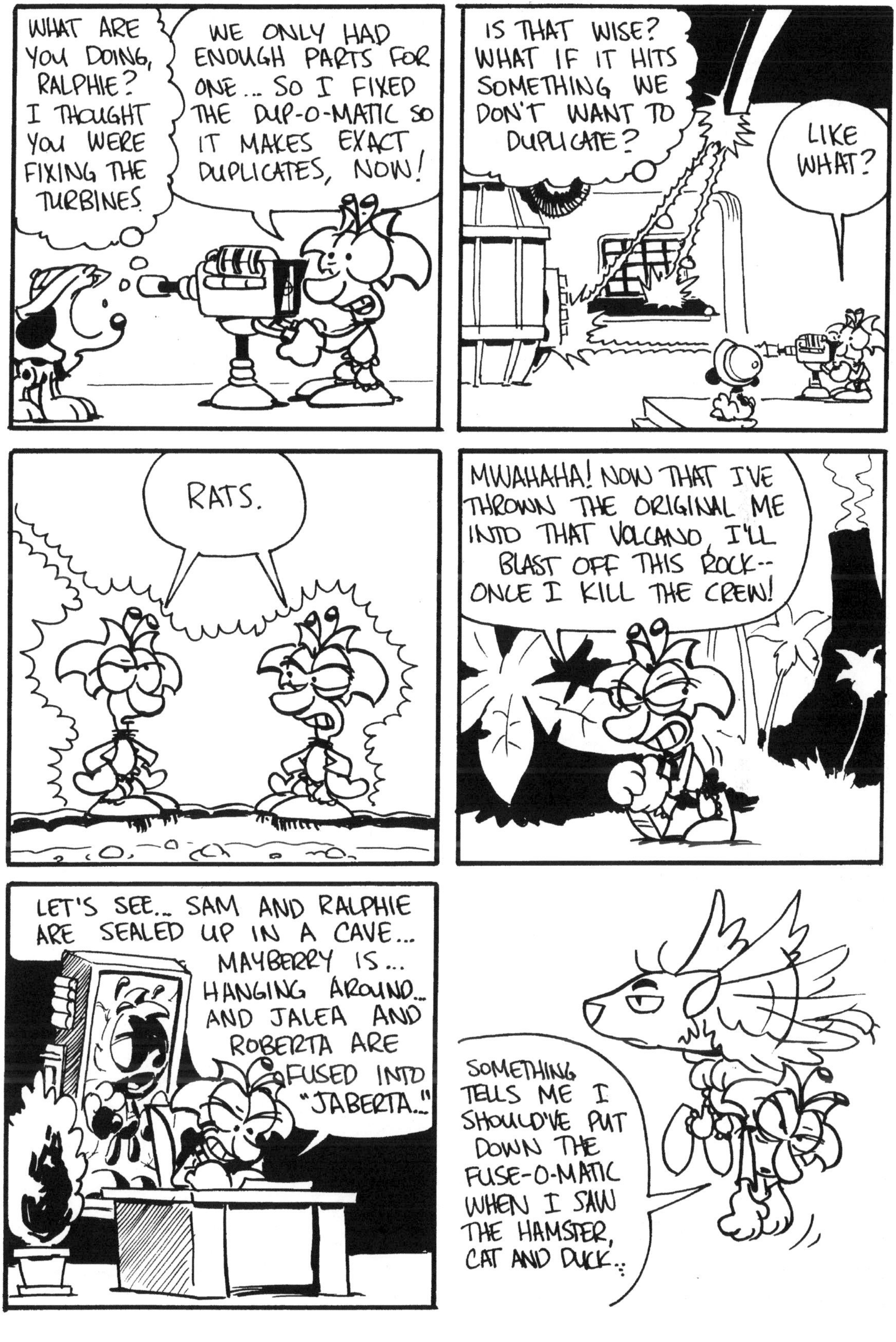
WHAT ARE YOU DOING, RALPHIE? I THOUGHT YOU WERE FIXING THE TURBINES
WE ONLY HAD ENOUGH PARTS FOR ONE... SO I FIXED THE DUP-O-MATIC SO IT MAKES EXACT DUPLICATES, NOW!
IS THAT WISE? WHAT IF IT HITS SOMETHING WE DON'T WANT TO DUPLICATE?
LIKE WHAT?
RATS.
MWAHAHA! NOW THAT I'VE THROWN THE ORIGINAL ME INTO THAT VOLCANO, I'LL BLAST OFF THIS ROCK-- ONCE I KILL THE CREW!
LET'S SEE... SAM AND RALPHIE ARE SEALED UP IN A CAVE... MAYBERRY IS... HANGING AROUND... AND JALEA AND ROBERTA ARE FUSED INTO "JABERTA..."
SOMETHING TELLS ME I SHOULD'VE PUT DOWN THE FUSE-O-MATIC WHEN I SAW THE HAMSTER, CAT AND DUCK...

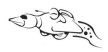

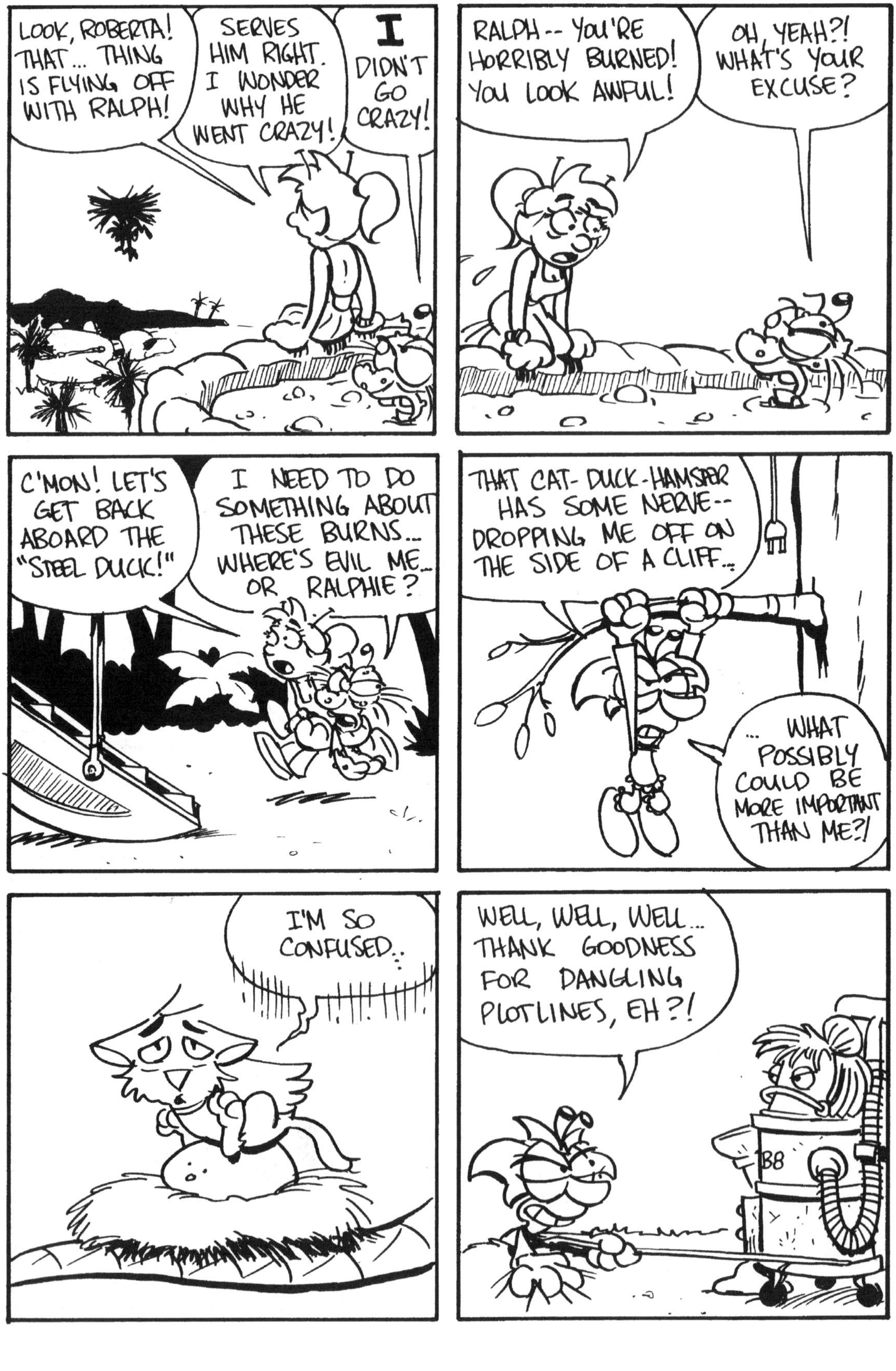
LOOK, ROBERTA! THAT... THING IS FLYING OFF WITH RALPH!
SERVES HIM RIGHT. I WONDER WHY HE WENT CRAZY!
I DIDN'T GO CRAZY!
RALPH -- YOU'RE HORRIBLY BURNED! YOU LOOK AWFUL!
OH, YEAH?! WHAT'S YOUR EXCUSE?
C'MON! LET'S GET BACK ABOARD THE "STEEL DUCK!"
I NEED TO DO SOMETHING ABOUT THESE BURNS... WHERE'S EVIL ME... OR RALPHIE?
THAT CAT-DUCK-HAMSTER HAS SOME NERVE-- DROPPING ME OFF ON THE SIDE OF A CLIFF...
... WHAT POSSIBLY COULD BE MORE IMPORTANT THAN ME?!
I'M SO CONFUSED...
WELL, WELL, WELL... THANK GOODNESS FOR DANGLING PLOTLINES, EH?!
B8

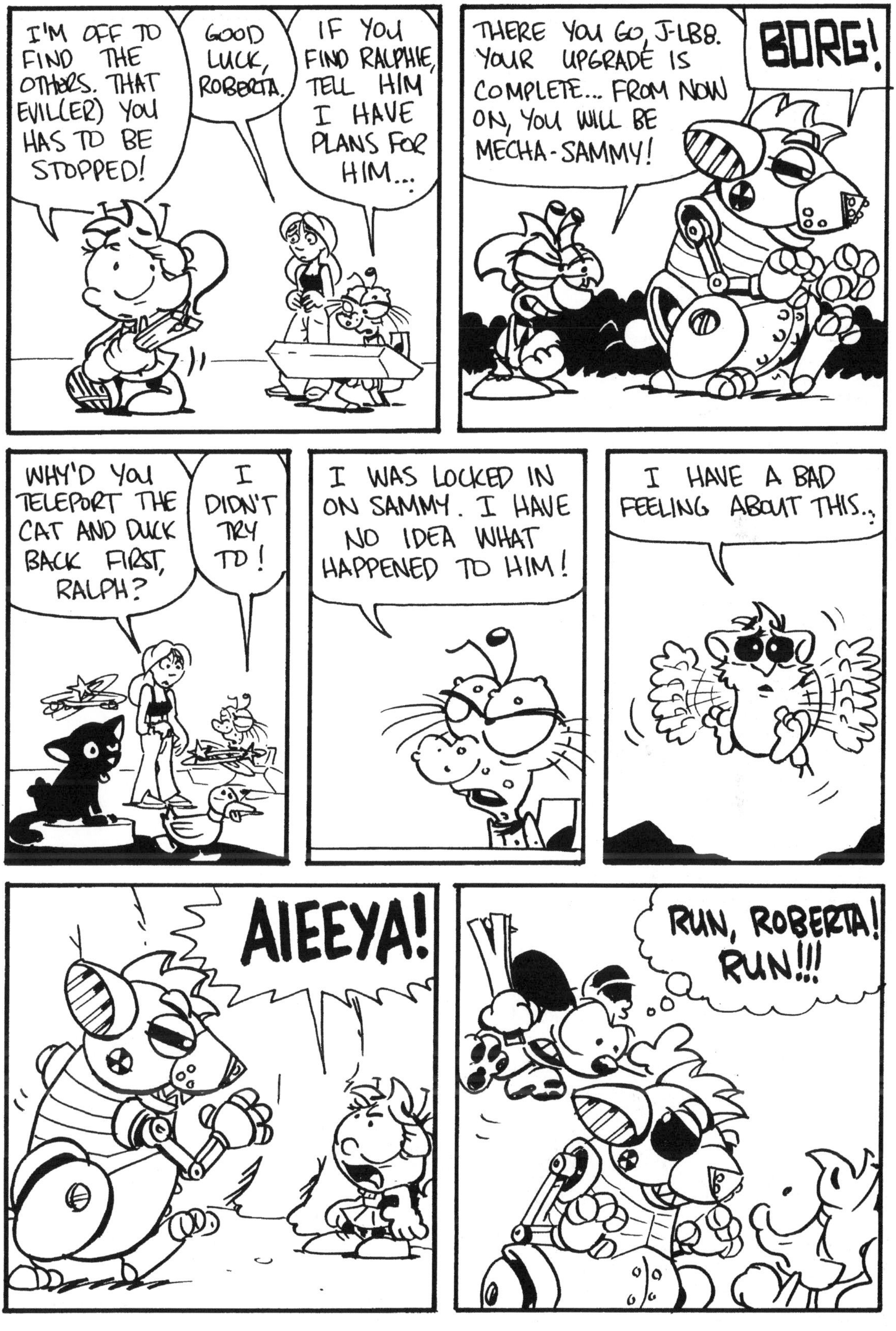
I'M OFF TO FIND THE OTHERS. THAT EVIL(ER) YOU HAS TO BE STOPPED!
GOOD LUCK, ROBERTA.
IF YOU FIND RALPHIE, TELL HIM I HAVE PLANS FOR HIM...
THERE YOU GO, J-LB8. YOUR UPGRADE IS COMPLETE... FROM NOW ON, YOU WILL BE MECHA-SAMMY!
BORG!
WHY'D YOU TELEPORT THE CAT AND DUCK BACK FIRST, RALPH?
I DIDN'T TRY TO!
I WAS LOCKED IN ON SAMMY. I HAVE NO IDEA WHAT HAPPENED TO HIM!
I HAVE A BAD FEELING ABOUT THIS...
AIEEYA!
RUN, ROBERTA! RUN!!!

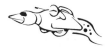

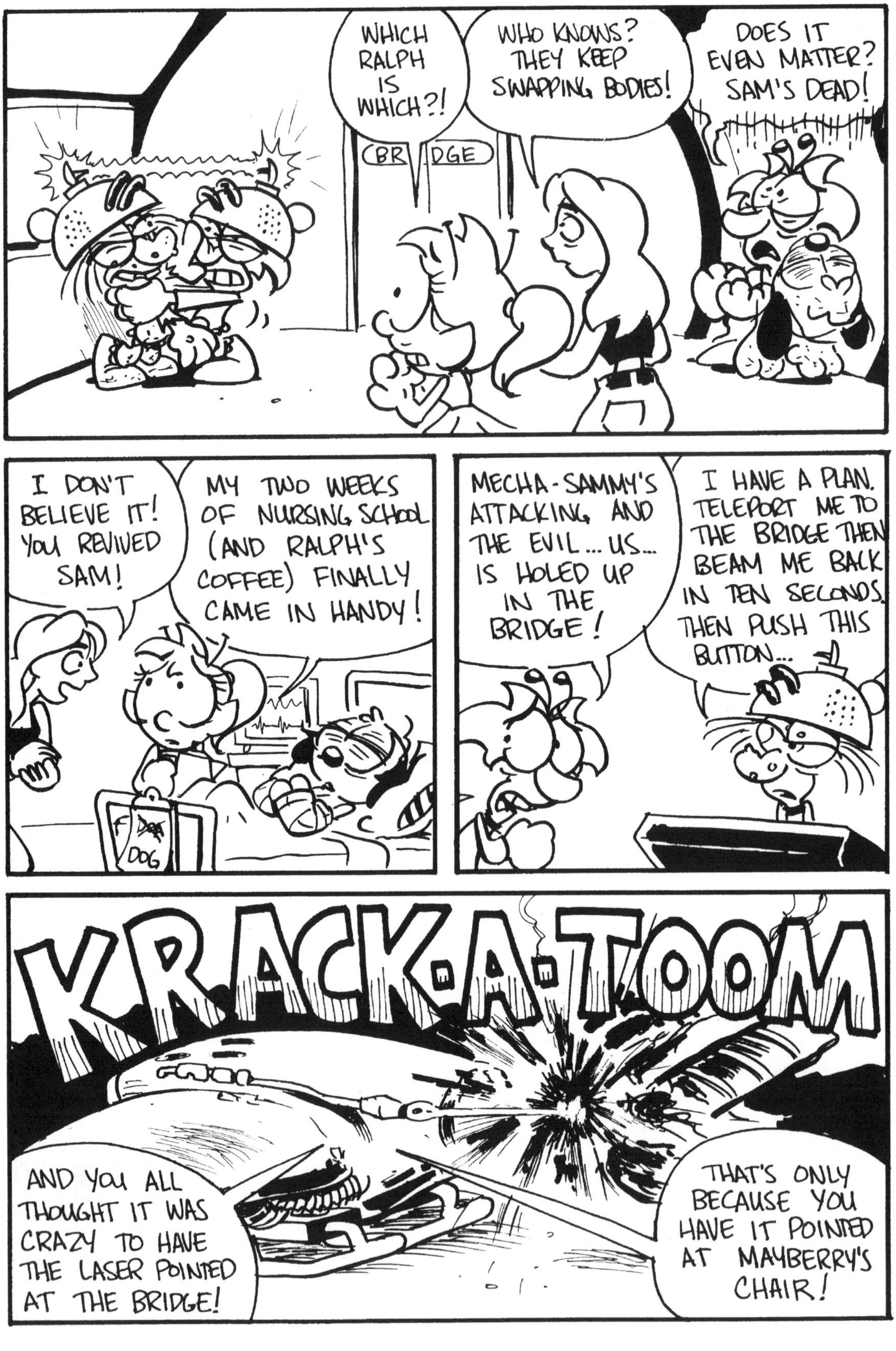
WHICH RALPH IS WHICH?!
WHO KNOWS? THEY KEEP SWAPPING BODIES!
DOES IT EVEN MATTER? SAM'S DEAD!
BR DGE
I DON'T BELIEVE IT! YOU REVIVED SAM!
MY TWO WEEKS OF NURSING SCHOOL (AND RALPH'S COFFEE) FINALLY CAME IN HANDY!
DOG
MECHA-SAMMY'S ATTACKING, AND THE EVIL... US... IS HOLED UP IN THE BRIDGE!
I HAVE A PLAN. TELEPORT ME TO THE BRIDGE THEN BEAM ME BACK IN TEN SECONDS. THEN PUSH THIS BUTTON...
KRACK-A-TOOM
AND YOU ALL THOUGHT IT WAS CRAZY TO HAVE THE LASER POINTED AT THE BRIDGE!
THAT'S ONLY BECAUSE YOU HAVE IT POINTED AT MAYBERRY'S CHAIR!

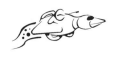

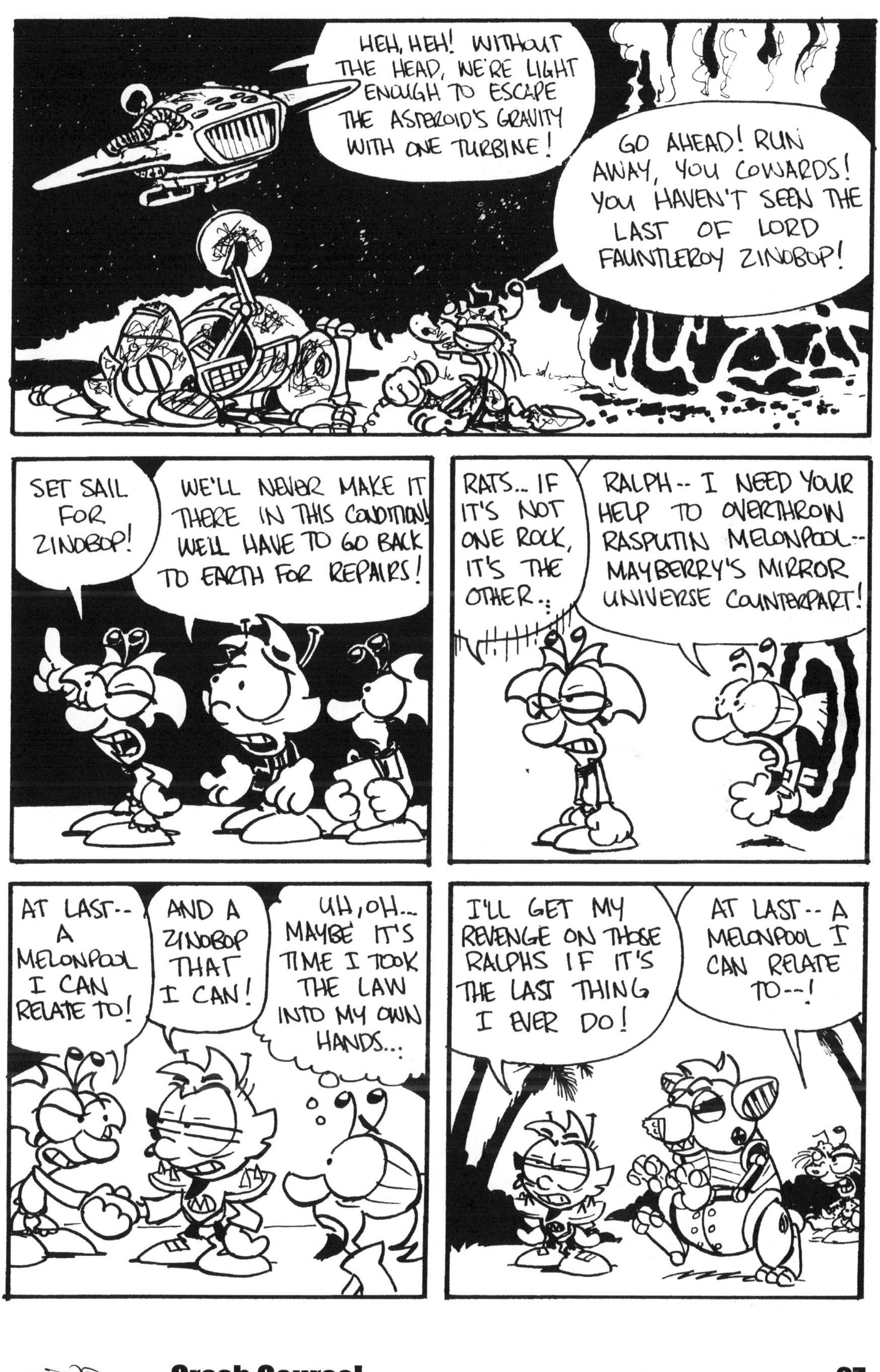
HEH, HEH! WITHOUT THE HEAD, WE'RE LIGHT ENOUGH TO ESCAPE THE ASTEROID'S GRAVITY WITH ONE TURBINE!
GO AHEAD! RUN AWAY, YOU COWARDS! YOU HAVEN'T SEEN THE LAST OF LORD FAUNTLEROY ZINOBOP!
SET SAIL FOR ZINOBOP!
WE'LL NEVER MAKE IT THERE IN THIS CONDITION! WE'LL HAVE TO GO BACK TO EARTH FOR REPAIRS!
RATS... IF IT'S NOT ONE ROCK, IT'S THE OTHER...
RALPH -- I NEED YOUR HELP TO OVERTHROW RASPUTIN MELONPOOL -- MAYBERRY'S MIRROR UNIVERSE COUNTERPART!
AT LAST -- A MELONPOOL I CAN RELATE TO!
AND A ZINOBOP THAT I CAN!
UH, OH... MAYBE IT'S TIME I TOOK THE LAW INTO MY OWN HANDS...
I'LL GET MY REVENGE ON THOSE RALPHS IF IT'S THE LAST THING I EVER DO!
AT LAST -- A MELONPOOL I CAN RELATE TO --!

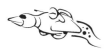

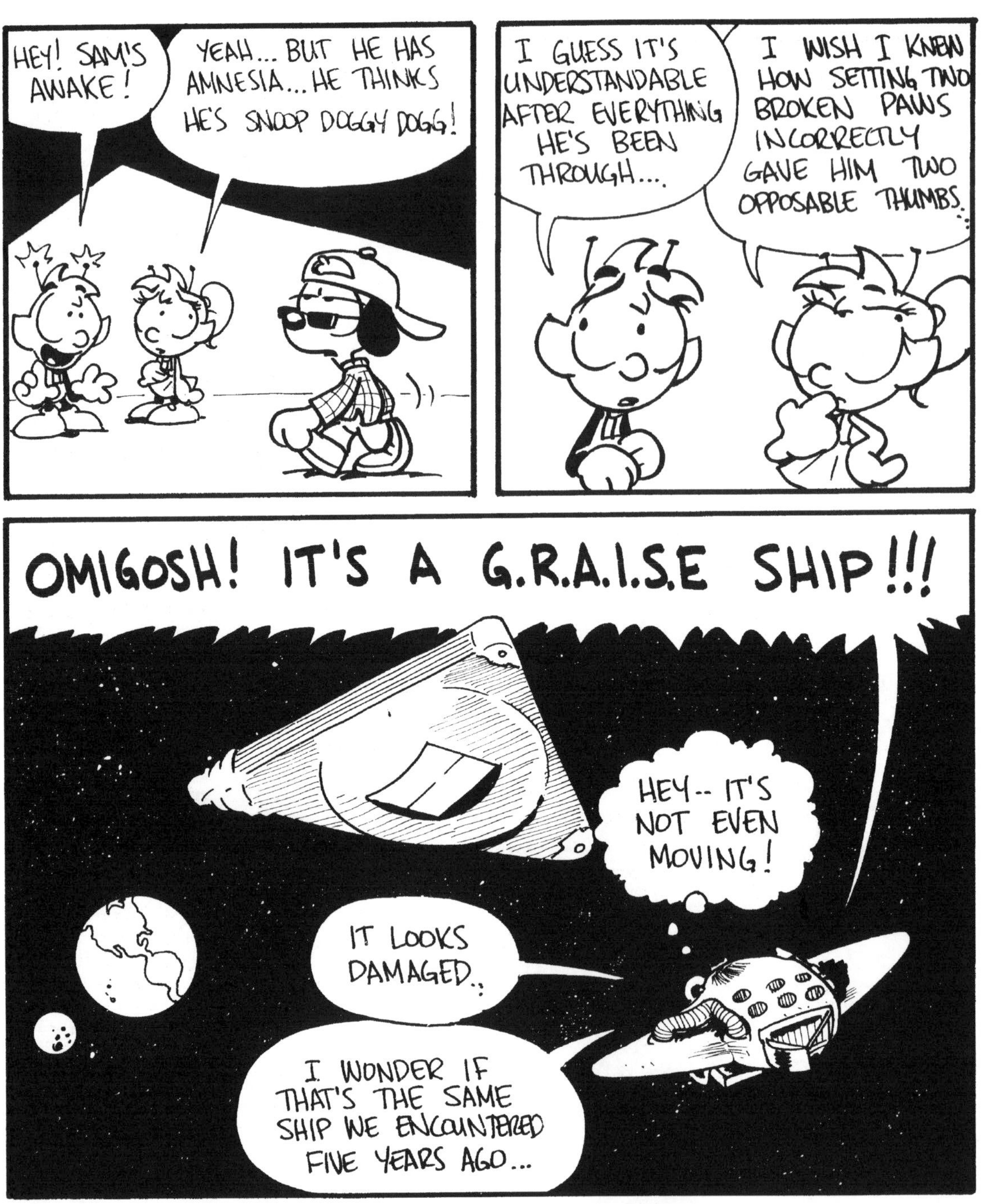
HEY! SAM'S AWAKE!
YEAH... BUT HE HAS AMNESIA... HE THINKS HE'S SNOOP DOGGY DOGG!
I GUESS IT'S UNDERSTANDABLE AFTER EVERYTHING HE'S BEEN THROUGH....
I WISH I KNEW HOW SETTING TWO BROKEN PAWS INCORRECTLY GAVE HIM TWO OPPOSABLE THUMBS.
OMIGOSH! IT'S A G.R.A.I.S.E SHIP!!!
HEY-- IT'S NOT EVEN MOVING!
IT LOOKS DAMAGED.
I WONDER IF THAT'S THE SAME SHIP WE ENCOUNTERED FIVE YEARS AGO...
I'D SAY THAT WAS A DISTINCT POSSIBILITY.

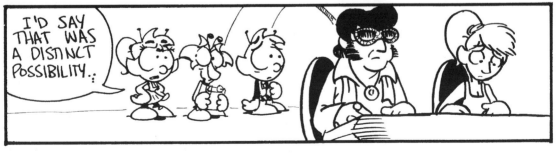

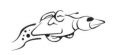

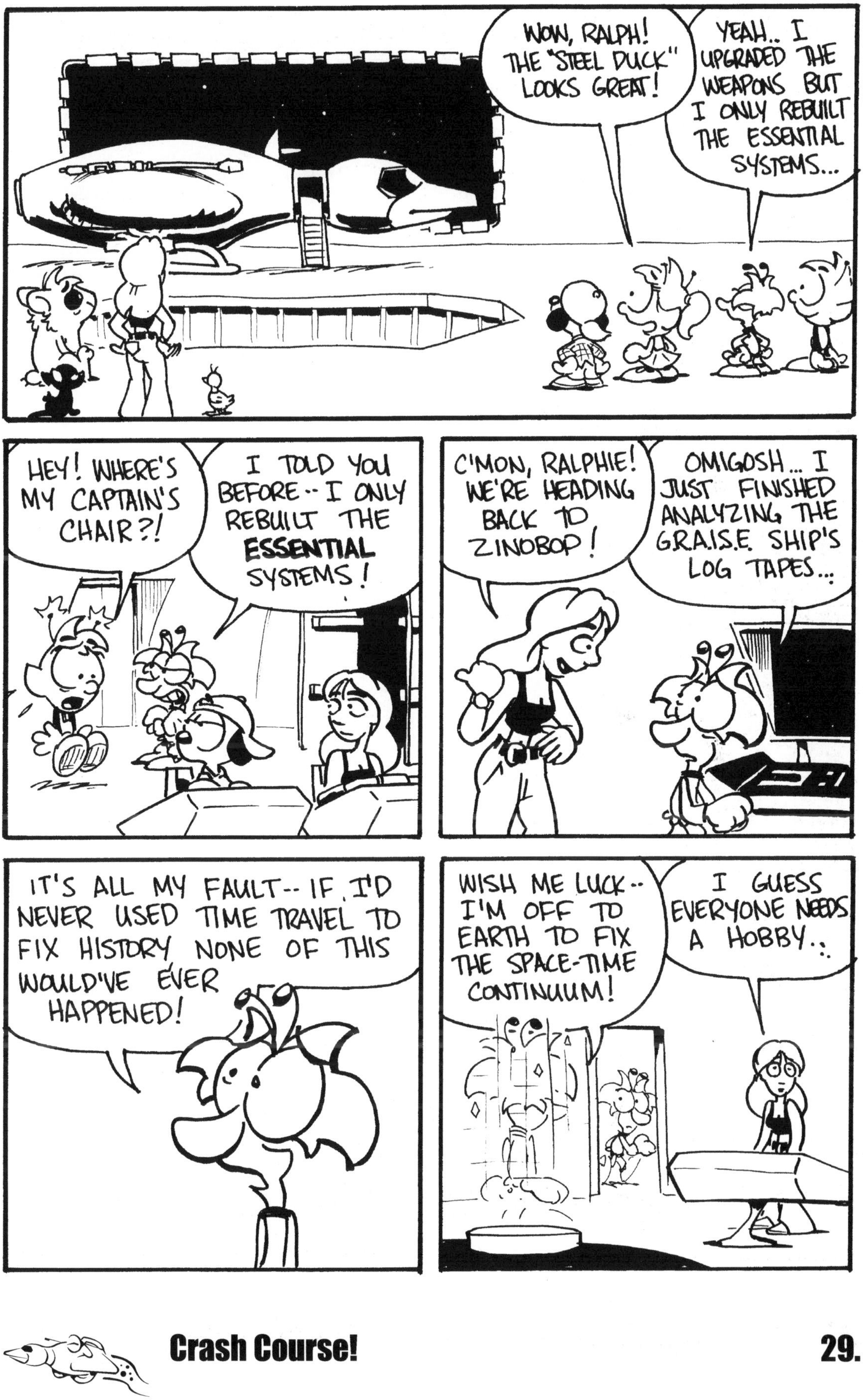

WOW, RALPH! THE "STEEL DUCK" LOOKS GREAT!
YEAH.. I UPGRADED THE WEAPONS BUT I ONLY REBUILT THE ESSENTIAL SYSTEMS...
HEY! WHERE'S MY CAPTAIN'S CHAIR?!
I TOLD YOU BEFORE -- I ONLY REBUILT THE ESSENTIAL SYSTEMS!
C'MON, RALPHIE! WE'RE HEADING BACK TO ZINOBOP!
OMIGOSH... I JUST FINISHED ANALYZING THE G.R.A.I.S.E. SHIP'S LOG TAPES...
IT'S ALL MY FAULT -- IF I'D NEVER USED TIME TRAVEL TO FIX HISTORY NONE OF THIS WOULD'VE EVER HAPPENED!
WISH ME LUCK -- I'M OFF TO EARTH TO FIX THE SPACE-TIME CONTINUUM!
I GUESS EVERYONE NEEDS A HOBBY...

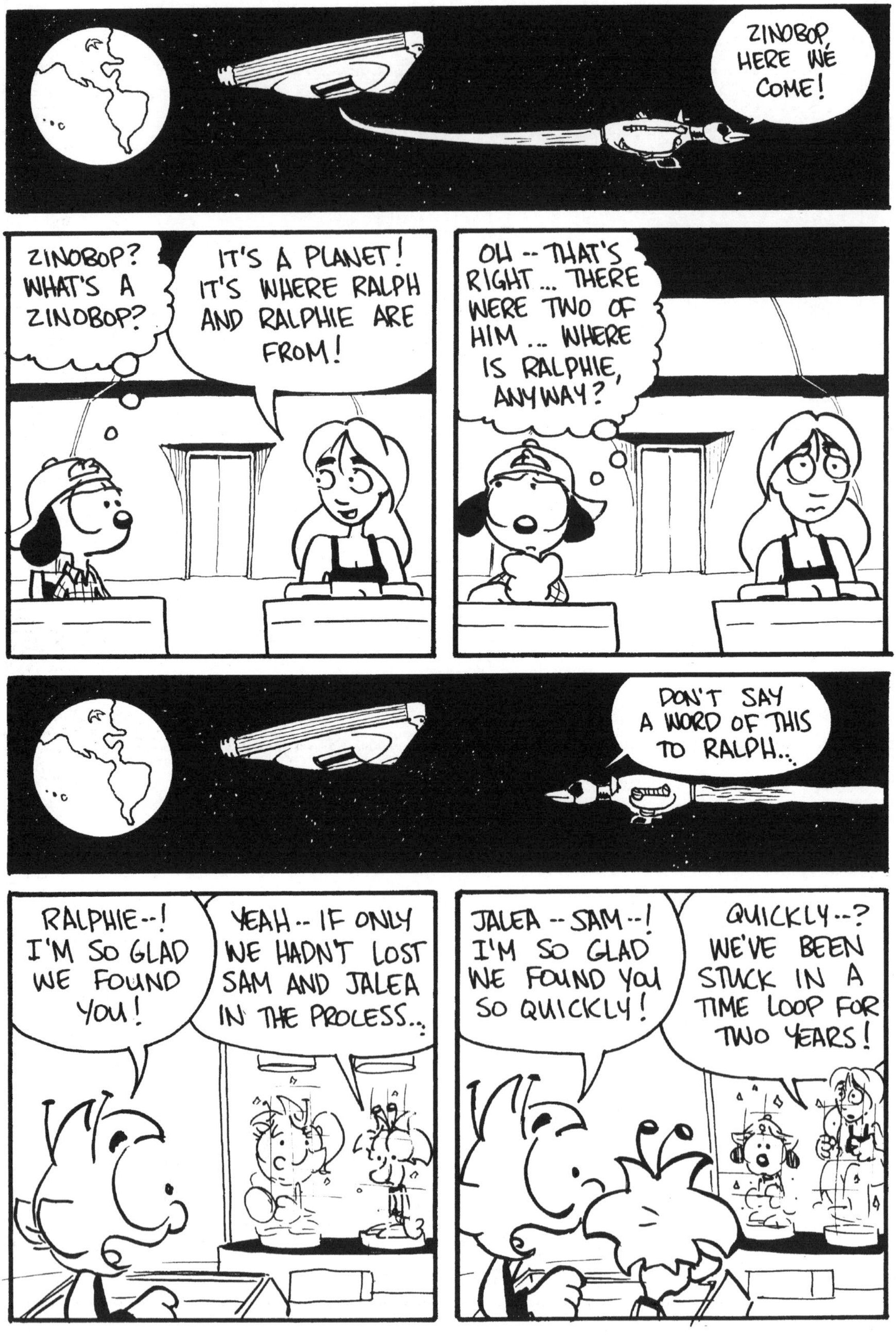
ZINOBOP, HERE WE COME!
ZINOBOP? WHAT'S A ZINOBOP?
IT'S A PLANET! IT'S WHERE RALPH AND RALPHIE ARE FROM!
OH -- THAT'S RIGHT ... THERE WERE TWO OF HIM ... WHERE IS RALPHIE, ANYWAY?
DON'T SAY A WORD OF THIS TO RALPH...
RALPHIE--! I'M SO GLAD WE FOUND YOU!
YEAH -- IF ONLY WE HADN'T LOST SAM AND JALEA IN THE PROCESS...
JALEA -- SAM --! I'M SO GLAD WE FOUND YOU SO QUICKLY!
QUICKLY--? WE'VE BEEN STUCK IN A TIME LOOP FOR TWO YEARS!

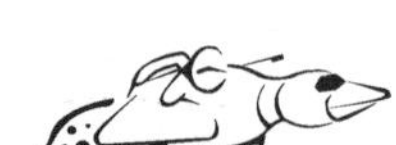

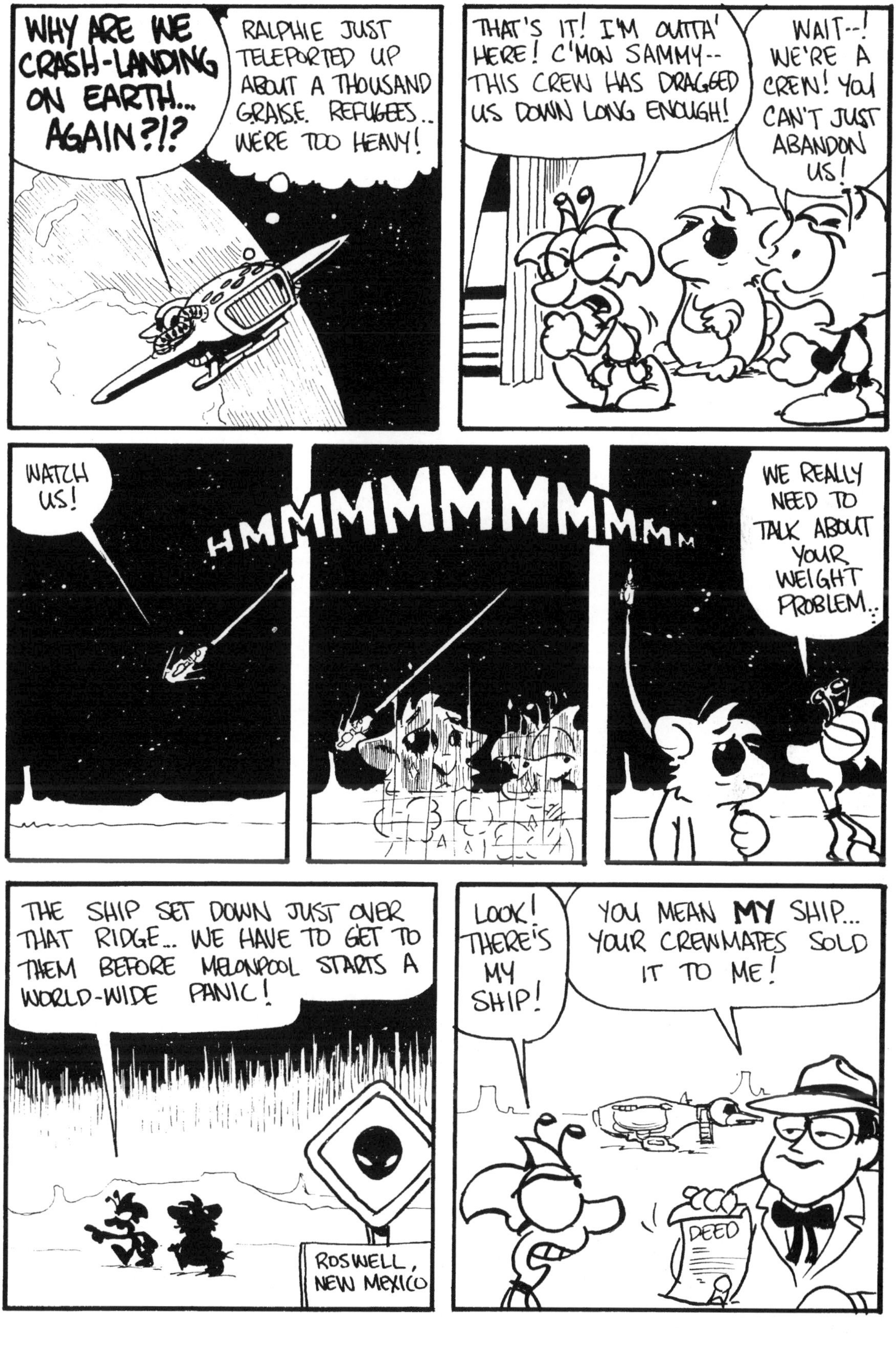
WHY ARE WE CRASH-LANDING ON EARTH... AGAIN?!?
RALPHIE JUST TELEPORTED UP ABOUT A THOUSAND GRAISE. REFUGEES.. WE'RE TOO HEAVY!
THAT'S IT! I'M OUTTA' HERE! C'MON SAMMY-- THIS CREW HAS DRAGGED US DOWN LONG ENOUGH!
WAIT--! WE'RE A CREW! YOU CAN'T JUST ABANDON US!
WATCH US!
HMMMMMMMMMMMM
WE REALLY NEED TO TALK ABOUT YOUR WEIGHT PROBLEM..
THE SHIP SET DOWN JUST OVER THAT RIDGE... WE HAVE TO GET TO THEM BEFORE MELONPOOL STARTS A WORLD-WIDE PANIC!
ROSWELL, NEW MEXICO
LOOK! THERE'S MY SHIP!
YOU MEAN **MY** SHIP... YOUR CREWMATES SOLD IT TO ME!
DEED

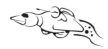

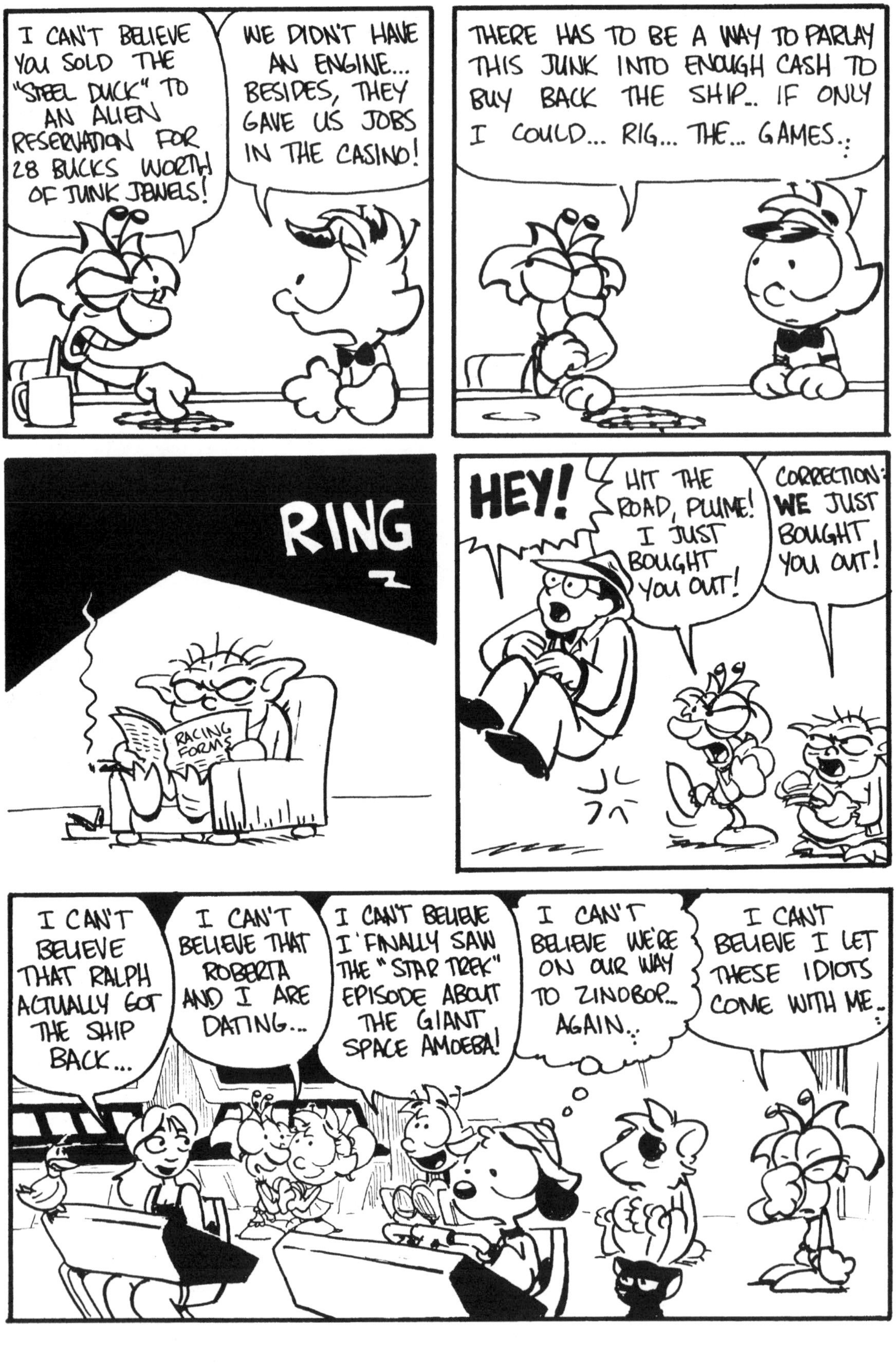
I CAN'T BELIEVE YOU SOLD THE "STEEL DUCK" TO AN ALIEN RESERVATION FOR 28 BUCKS WORTH OF JUNK JEWELS!
WE DIDN'T HAVE AN ENGINE... BESIDES, THEY GAVE US JOBS IN THE CASINO!
THERE HAS TO BE A WAY TO PARLAY THIS JUNK INTO ENOUGH CASH TO BUY BACK THE SHIP.. IF ONLY I COULD... RIG... THE... GAMES..
RING
RACING FORMS
HEY!
HIT THE ROAD, PLUME! I JUST BOUGHT YOU OUT!
CORRECTION: WE JUST BOUGHT YOU OUT!
I CAN'T BELIEVE THAT RALPH ACTUALLY GOT THE SHIP BACK...
I CAN'T BELIEVE THAT ROBERTA AND I ARE DATING...
I CAN'T BELIEVE I FINALLY SAW THE "STAR TREK" EPISODE ABOUT THE GIANT SPACE AMOEBA!
I CAN'T BELIEVE WE'RE ON OUR WAY TO ZINOBOP... AGAIN...
I CAN'T BELIEVE I LET THESE IDIOTS COME WITH ME..

THE INTERNET PART VI

2004–2005

In 2004, after eight years and five books, I ended my webcomic Melonpool. The night the final strip went live, I woke up from a dead sleep and wrote down 13 fully-formed ideas for storylines which picked up right where my "ending" had left off. Eight months later, the strip was back, better than ever, using this fever dream of a list as the blueprint.

After not missing an update for over a year, my grandmother was suddenly diagnosed with stomach cancer, which painfully took her life in less than a year. Around this same time, I was also laid off from my day job after five years with the company. And, to add insult to injury, my girlfriend of three years left me in part due to my devotion to the comic.

In the aftermath, I didn't feel particularly funny anymore. The comic limped along to an unsatisfactory ending and the sixth book, which I was working on at the time, sat untouched on my hard drive for the next seven years.

But, it's not all doom and gloom. I refocused my energies on puppetry— mainly in memory of my grandmother, who had taught me to sew puppets years before she died. As a result, I met my wife, Sarah, while puppeteering at an event and eventually carved out something of a career designing puppets for commercials. In an ironic twist, I actually draw more now designing puppets than when I was trying to make a living as an artist!

But... I always wanted to finish this book. If not for me, then for the fans who have always stood by Melonpool—in whatever form I happen to distribute it in.

I'm really happy with the body of work within this volume. Reading it now, after all these years, I even wonder what might have happened if I hadn't stopped drawing the daily strip all those years ago...

But not very often.

STEVE
TROOP

If this volume is your first experience reading the *Melonpool* Collections, you'll notice that I often refer to "***TUM***s" in the liner notes accompanying some of the strips. This is not a reference to the antacid medication—but an abbreviation adopted by longtime *Melonpool* readers for "The Ultimate Melonpool" books.

TUM I refers to **The Ultimate Melonpool**; **TUM II** is **Melonpool II—The Voyage Home**; **TUM III** is **Melonpool III—A New Hope**; **TUM IV** is **Melonpool IV—Castaway**; and ***TUM V*** is ***Melonpool V: This Island Earth***. All of these strips are also on the Internet at www.melonpool.com... but you'll have to find those for yourself!

When we last left our heroes, Roberta and Ralphie had started dating. At the time, since I felt I was never going to draw this strip again, I figured I should go out with some major plot points that I'd never have to resolve. That's what I figured, anyway.

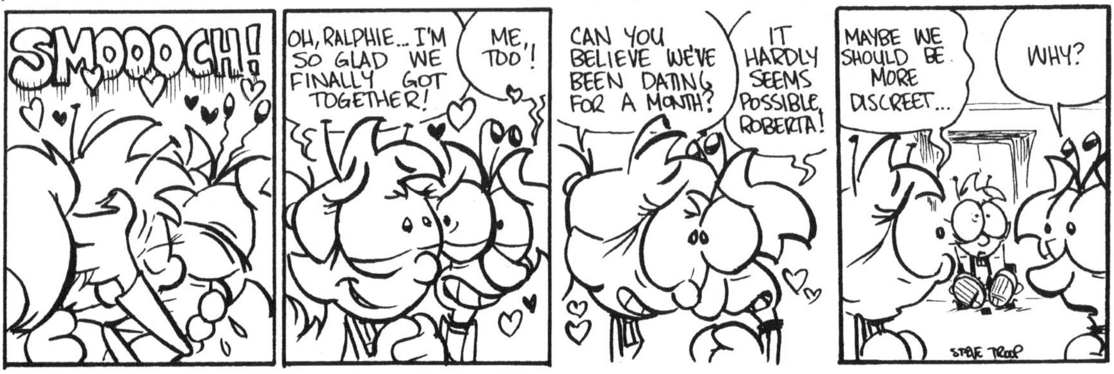
SMOOOCH!
OH, RALPHIE... I'M SO GLAD WE FINALLY GOT TOGETHER!
ME, TOO!
CAN YOU BELIEVE WE'VE BEEN DATING FOR A MONTH?
IT HARDLY SEEMS POSSIBLE, ROBERTA!
MAYBE WE SHOULD BE MORE DISCREET...
WHY?
STEVE TROOP

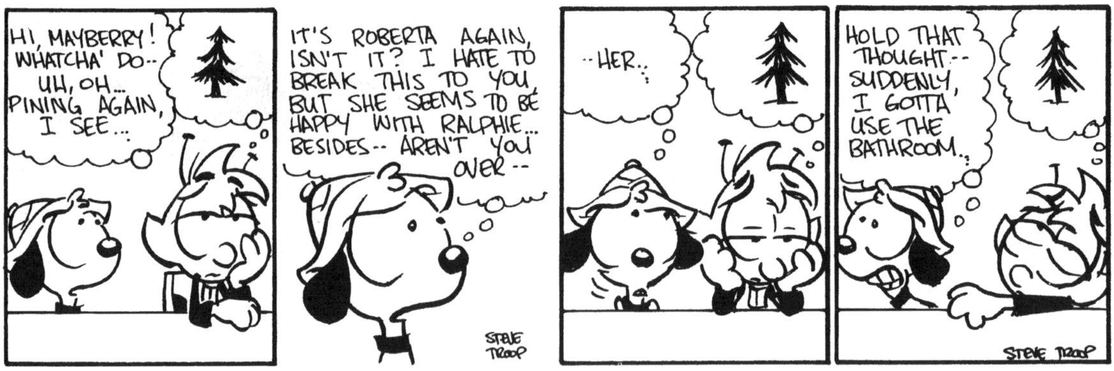
HI, MAYBERRY! WHATCHA' DO-- UH, OH... PINING AGAIN, I SEE...
IT'S ROBERTA AGAIN, ISN'T IT? I HATE TO BREAK THIS TO YOU, BUT SHE SEEMS TO BE HAPPY WITH RALPHIE... BESIDES-- AREN'T YOU OVER--
STEVE TROOP
--HER...
HOLD THAT THOUGHT-- SUDDENLY, I GOTTA USE THE BATHROOM...
STEVE TROOP

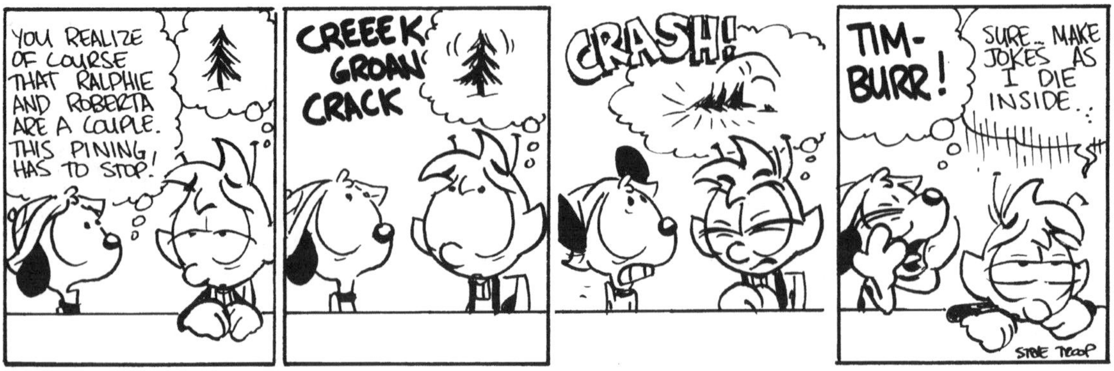
YOU REALIZE OF COURSE THAT RALPHIE AND ROBERTA ARE A COUPLE. THIS PINING HAS TO STOP!
CREEEK GROAN CRACK
CRASH!
TIM-BURR!
SURE... MAKE JOKES AS I DIE INSIDE...
STEVE TROOP

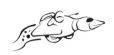

Mayberry finally saw the "Giant Space Amoeba" episode of *Star Trek* near the end of the original run (see TUM V, page 129) after missing it several times (see TUM I, pages 76–77, 116; TUM II, pages 90, 119–120).

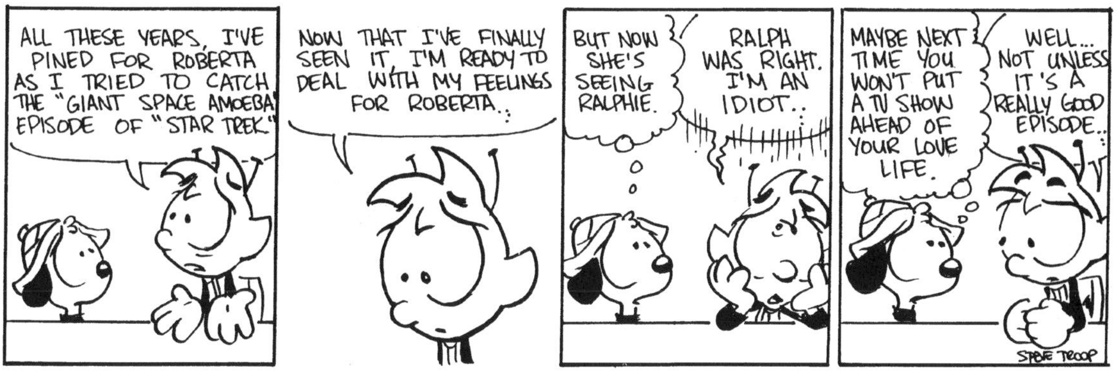

ALL THESE YEARS, I'VE PINED FOR ROBERTA AS I TRIED TO CATCH THE "GIANT SPACE AMOEBA" EPISODE OF "STAR TREK"
NOW THAT I'VE FINALLY SEEN IT, I'M READY TO DEAL WITH MY FEELINGS FOR ROBERTA...
BUT NOW SHE'S SEEING RALPHIE.
RALPH WAS RIGHT. I'M AN IDIOT...
MAYBE NEXT TIME YOU WON'T PUT A TV SHOW AHEAD OF YOUR LOVE LIFE.
WELL... NOT UNLESS IT'S A REALLY GOOD EPISODE...
STEVE TROOP

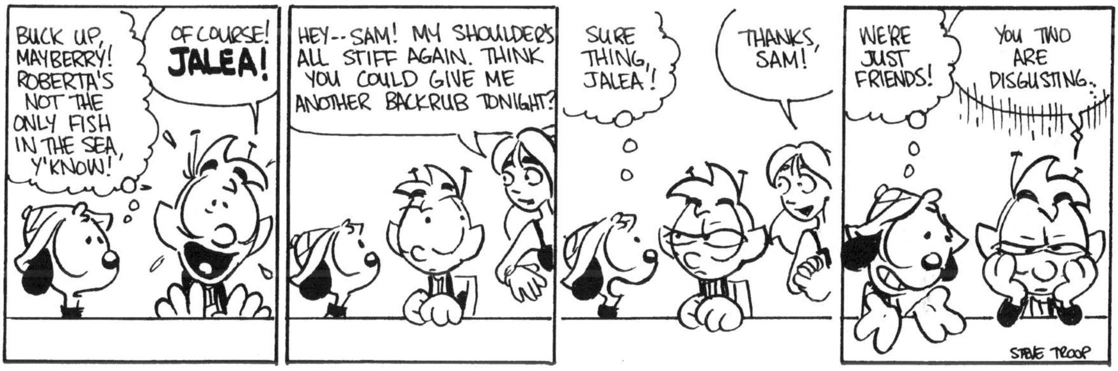

BUCK UP, MAYBERRY! ROBERTA'S NOT THE ONLY FISH IN THE SEA, Y'KNOW!
OF COURSE! JALEA!
HEY--SAM! MY SHOULDER'S ALL STIFF AGAIN. THINK YOU COULD GIVE ME ANOTHER BACKRUB TONIGHT?
SURE THING, JALEA!
THANKS, SAM!
WE'RE JUST FRIENDS!
YOU TWO ARE DISGUSTING...
STEVE TROOP

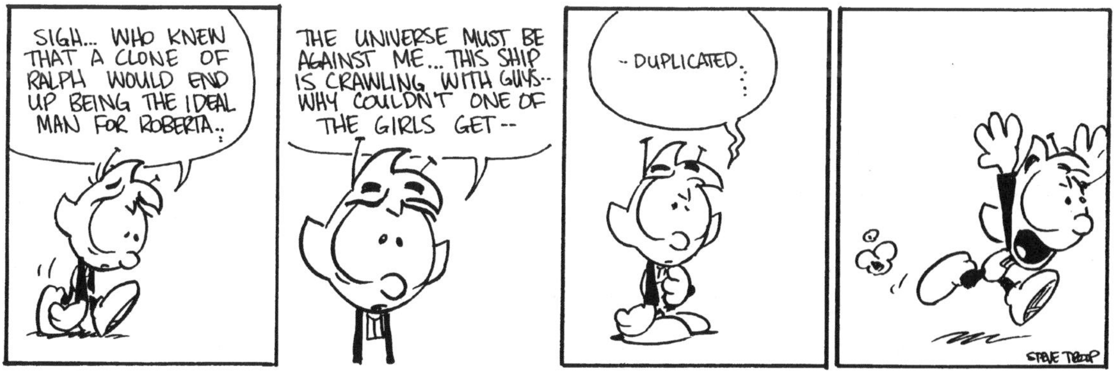

SIGH... WHO KNEW THAT A CLONE OF RALPH WOULD END UP BEING THE IDEAL MAN FOR ROBERTA...
THE UNIVERSE MUST BE AGAINST ME... THIS SHIP IS CRAWLING WITH GUYS... WHY COULDN'T ONE OF THE GIRLS GET--
--DUPLICATED...
STEVE TROOP

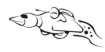

The "Dup-o-matic" was responsible for creating Ralphie (TUM I, pages 142–144), Anti-Joyce (TUM III, pages 92–108), and Fauntleroy Zinobop (TUM V, pages 14–42).

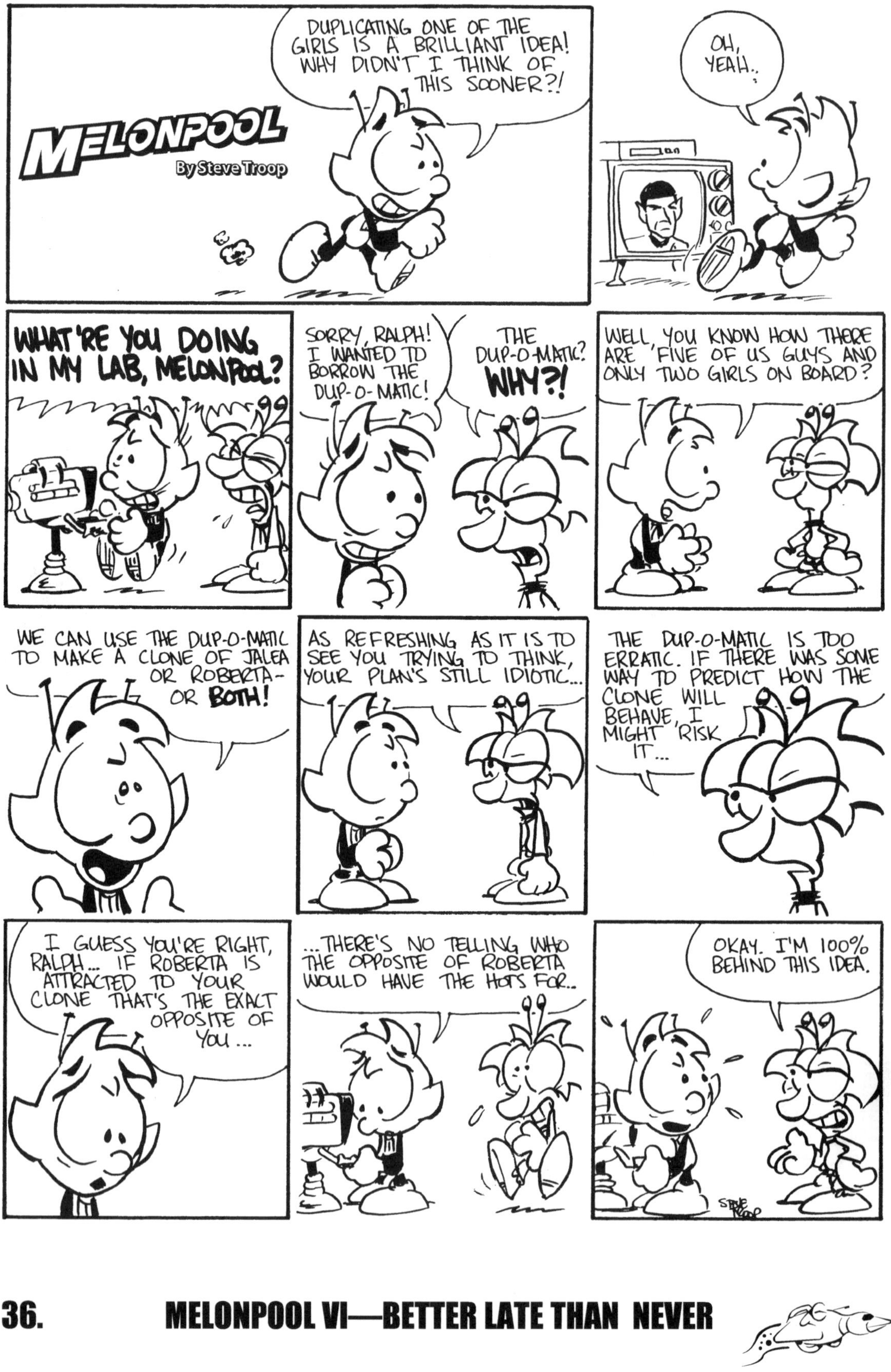

MELONPOOL
By Steve Troop
DUPLICATING ONE OF THE GIRLS IS A BRILLIANT IDEA! WHY DIDN'T I THINK OF THIS SOONER?!
OH, YEAH..
WHAT'RE YOU DOING IN MY LAB, MELONPOOL?
SORRY, RALPH! I WANTED TO BORROW THE DUP-O-MATIC!
THE DUP-O-MATIC? WHY?!
WELL, YOU KNOW HOW THERE ARE FIVE OF US GUYS AND ONLY TWO GIRLS ON BOARD?
WE CAN USE THE DUP-O-MATIC TO MAKE A CLONE OF JALEA OR ROBERTA- OR BOTH!
AS REFRESHING AS IT IS TO SEE YOU TRYING TO THINK, YOUR PLAN'S STILL IDIOTIC...
THE DUP-O-MATIC IS TOO ERRATIC. IF THERE WAS SOME WAY TO PREDICT HOW THE CLONE WILL BEHAVE, I MIGHT RISK IT...
I GUESS YOU'RE RIGHT, RALPH... IF ROBERTA IS ATTRACTED TO YOUR CLONE THAT'S THE EXACT OPPOSITE OF YOU...
...THERE'S NO TELLING WHO THE OPPOSITE OF ROBERTA WOULD HAVE THE HOTS FOR..
OKAY. I'M 100% BEHIND THIS IDEA.
STEVE TROOP

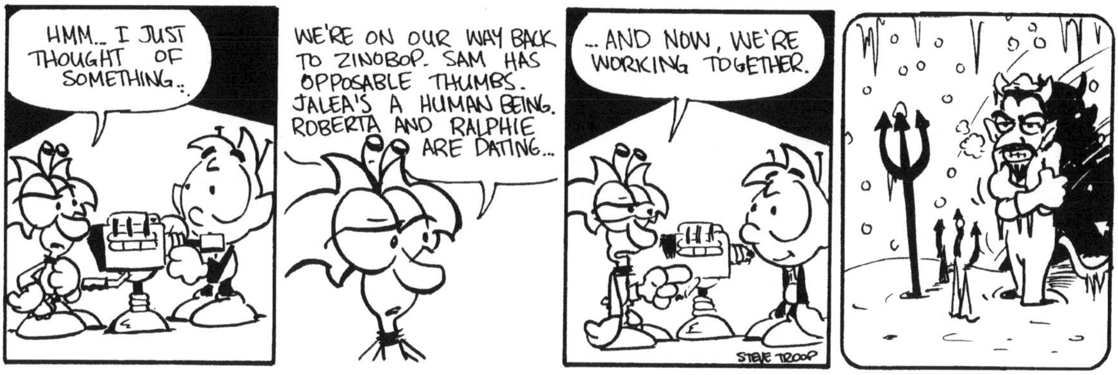
HMM... I JUST THOUGHT OF SOMETHING...
WE'RE ON OUR WAY BACK TO ZINOBOP. SAM HAS OPPOSABLE THUMBS. JALEA'S A HUMAN BEING. ROBERTA AND RALPHIE ARE DATING...
...AND NOW, WE'RE WORKING TOGETHER.
STEVE TROOP

The clone of himself that Mayberry mentions was briefly seen during the **Ralphie Resolution** storyline (TUM I, 172–182).

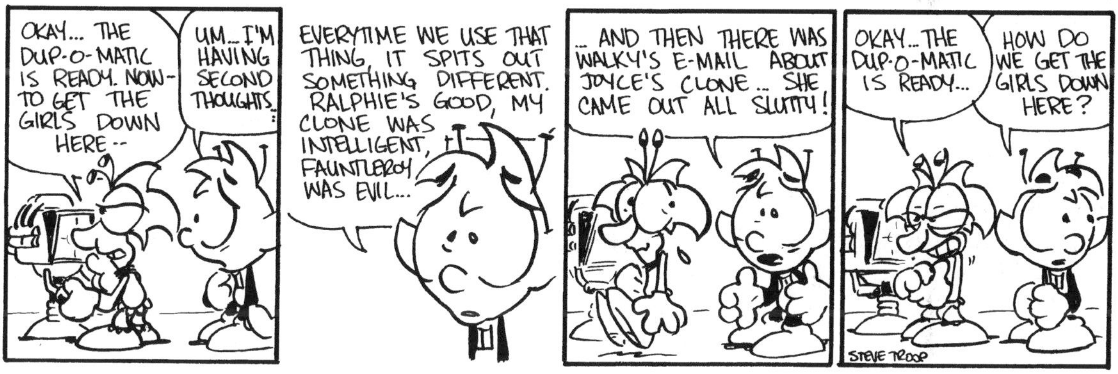
OKAY... THE DUP-O-MATIC IS READY. NOW-- TO GET THE GIRLS DOWN HERE--
UM...I'M HAVING SECOND THOUGHTS...
EVERYTIME WE USE THAT THING, IT SPITS OUT SOMETHING DIFFERENT. RALPHIE'S GOOD, MY CLONE WAS INTELLIGENT, FAUNTLEROY WAS EVIL...
...AND THEN THERE WAS WALKY'S E-MAIL ABOUT JOYCE'S CLONE... SHE CAME OUT ALL SLUTTY!
OKAY...THE DUP-O-MATIC IS READY...
HOW DO WE GET THE GIRLS DOWN HERE?
STEVE TROOP

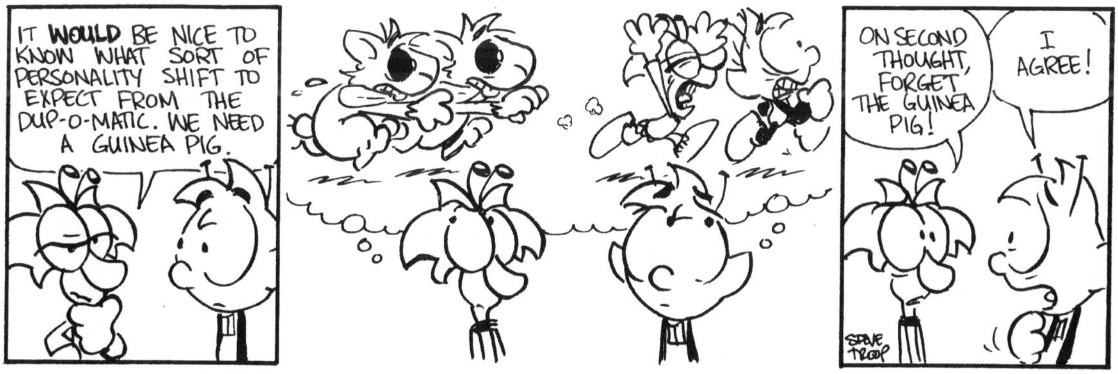
IT **WOULD** BE NICE TO KNOW WHAT SORT OF PERSONALITY SHIFT TO EXPECT FROM THE DUP-O-MATIC. WE NEED A GUINEA PIG.
ON SECOND THOUGHT, FORGET THE GUINEA PIG!
I AGREE!
STEVE TROOP

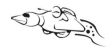

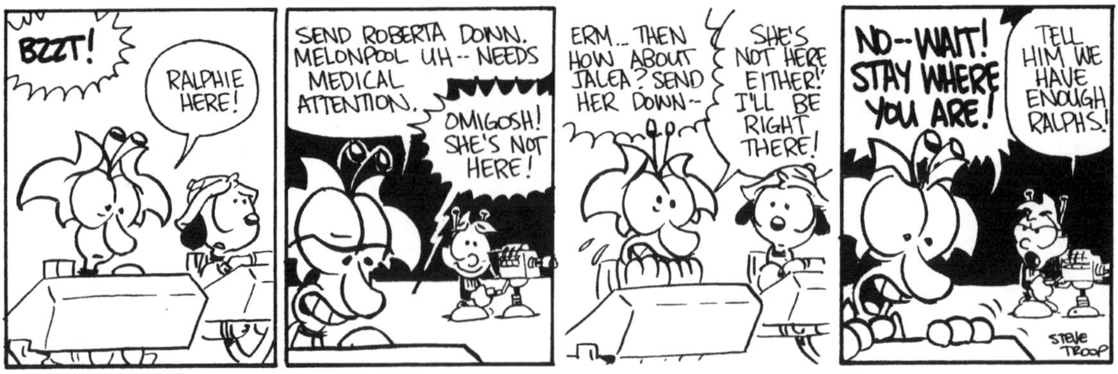
BZZT!
RALPHIE HERE!
SEND ROBERTA DOWN. MELONPOOL UH-- NEEDS MEDICAL ATTENTION.
OMIGOSH! SHE'S NOT HERE!
ERM... THEN HOW ABOUT JALEA? SEND HER DOWN--
SHE'S NOT HERE EITHER! I'LL BE RIGHT THERE!
NO--WAIT! STAY WHERE YOU ARE!
TELL HIM WE HAVE ENOUGH RALPHS!
STEVE TROOP

Ralph and Mayberry again mention the events in **Ralphie Resolution** (TUM I, 172–182).

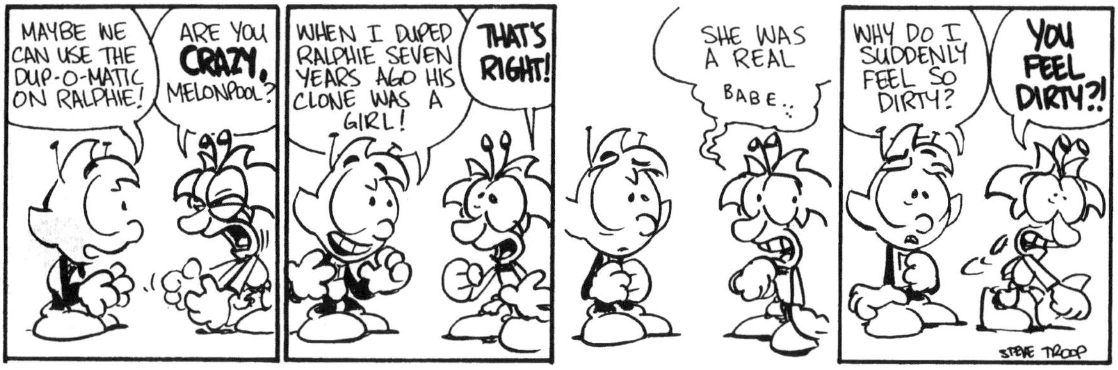
MAYBE WE CAN USE THE DUP-O-MATIC ON RALPHIE!
ARE YOU CRAZY, MELONPOOL?
WHEN I DUPED RALPHIE SEVEN YEARS AGO HIS CLONE WAS A GIRL!
THAT'S RIGHT!
SHE WAS A REAL BABE...
WHY DO I SUDDENLY FEEL SO DIRTY?
YOU FEEL DIRTY?!
STEVE TROOP

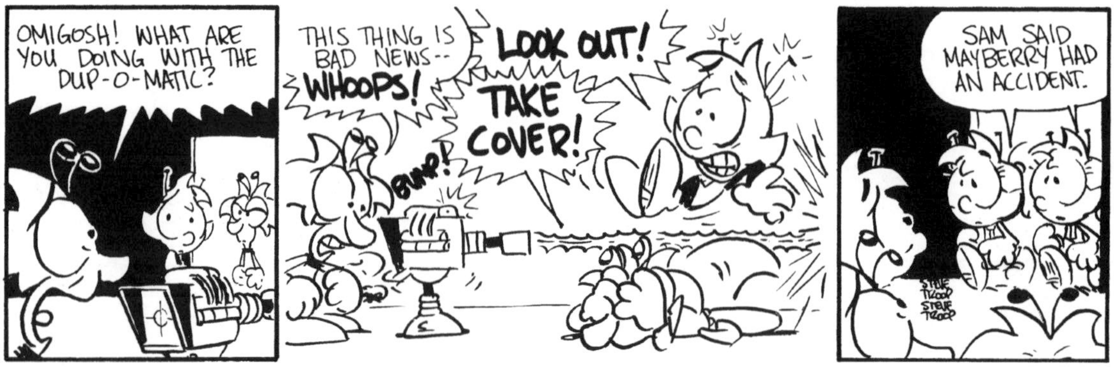
OMIGOSH! WHAT ARE YOU DOING WITH THE DUP-O-MATIC?
THIS THING IS BAD NEWS--
WHOOPS!
BUMP!
LOOK OUT!
TAKE COVER!
SAM SAID MAYBERRY HAD AN ACCIDENT.
STEVE TROOP
STEVE TROOP

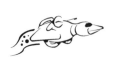

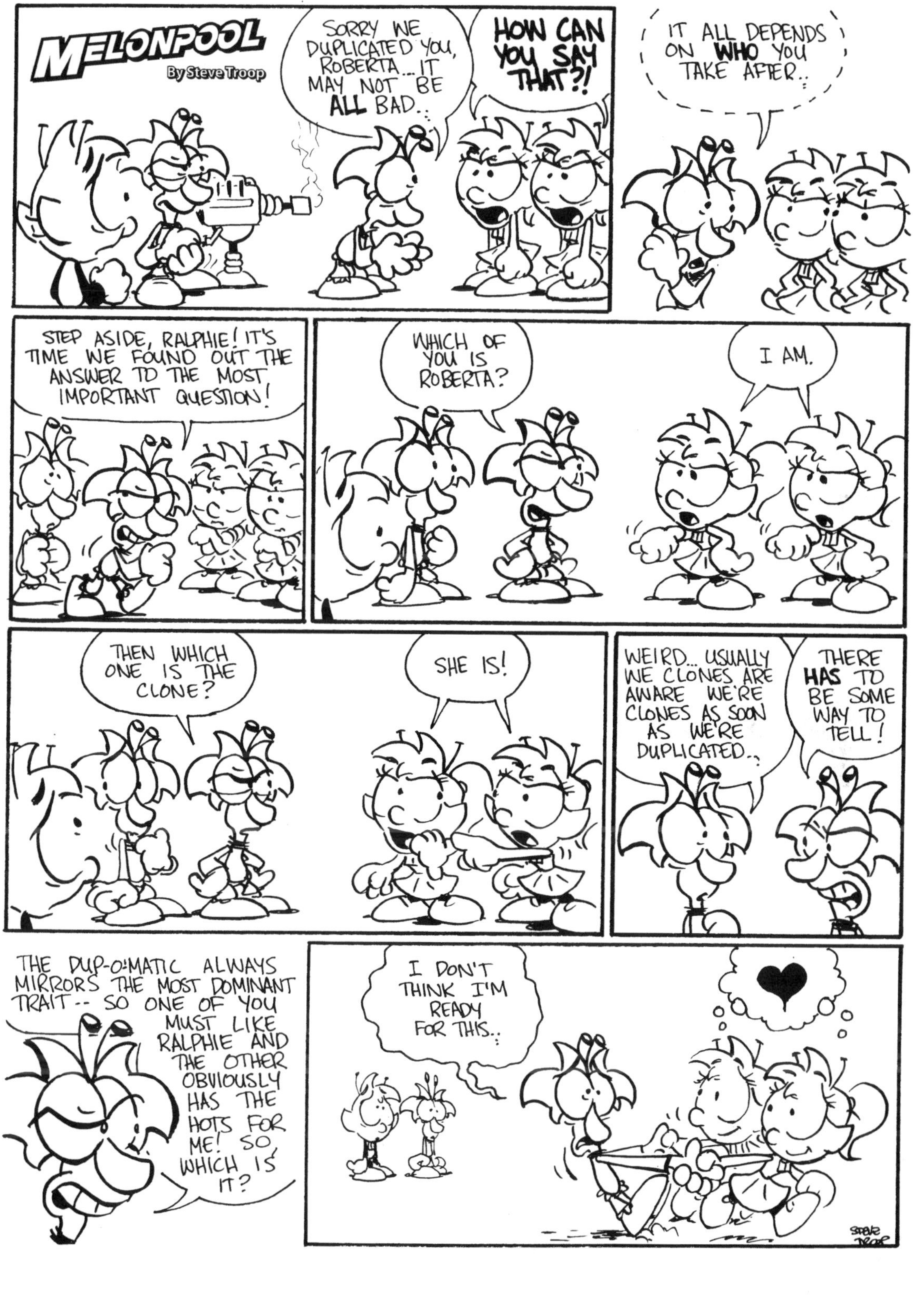
MELONPOOL
By Steve Troop
SORRY WE DUPLICATED YOU, ROBERTA... IT MAY NOT BE ALL BAD...
HOW CAN YOU SAY THAT?!
IT ALL DEPENDS ON WHO YOU TAKE AFTER...
STEP ASIDE, RALPHIE! IT'S TIME WE FOUND OUT THE ANSWER TO THE MOST IMPORTANT QUESTION!
WHICH OF YOU IS ROBERTA?
I AM.
THEN WHICH ONE IS THE CLONE?
SHE IS!
WEIRD... USUALLY WE CLONES ARE AWARE WE'RE CLONES AS SOON AS WE'RE DUPLICATED...
THERE HAS TO BE SOME WAY TO TELL!
THE DUP-O-MATIC ALWAYS MIRRORS THE MOST DOMINANT TRAIT -- SO ONE OF YOU MUST LIKE RALPHIE AND THE OTHER OBVIOUSLY HAS THE HOTS FOR ME! SO, WHICH IS IT?
I DON'T THINK I'M READY FOR THIS...
STEVE TROOP

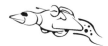

This strip struck a chord with many of Melonpool's fans. I wonder why?

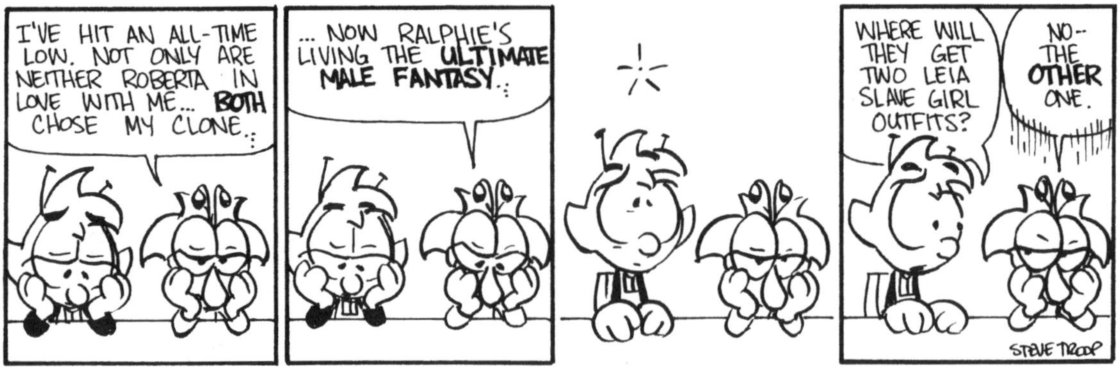
I'VE HIT AN ALL-TIME LOW. NOT ONLY ARE NEITHER ROBERTA IN LOVE WITH ME... BOTH CHOSE MY CLONE...
... NOW RALPHIE'S LIVING THE ULTIMATE MALE FANTASY...
WHERE WILL THEY GET TWO LEIA SLAVE GIRL OUTFITS?
NO-- THE OTHER ONE.
STEVE TROOP

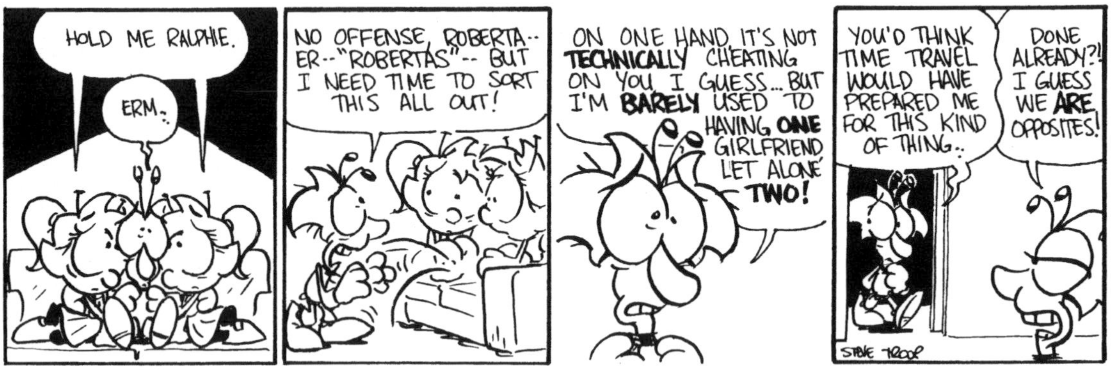
HOLD ME RALPHIE.
ERM...
NO OFFENSE, ROBERTA-- ER--"ROBERTAS"-- BUT I NEED TIME TO SORT THIS ALL OUT!
ON ONE HAND, IT'S NOT TECHNICALLY CHEATING ON YOU, I GUESS... BUT I'M BARELY USED TO HAVING ONE GIRLFRIEND LET ALONE TWO!
YOU'D THINK TIME TRAVEL WOULD HAVE PREPARED ME FOR THIS KIND OF THING...
DONE ALREADY?! I GUESS WE ARE OPPOSITES!
STEVE TROOP

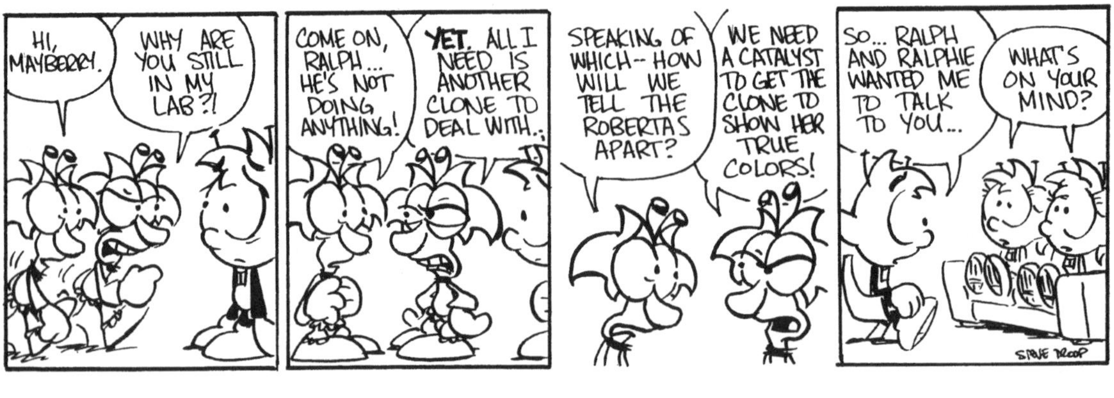
HI, MAYBERRY.
WHY ARE YOU STILL IN MY LAB?!
COME ON, RALPH... HE'S NOT DOING ANYTHING!
YET. ALL I NEED IS ANOTHER CLONE TO DEAL WITH...
SPEAKING OF WHICH-- HOW WILL WE TELL THE ROBERTAS APART?
WE NEED A CATALYST TO GET THE CLONE TO SHOW HER TRUE COLORS!
SO... RALPH AND RALPHIE WANTED ME TO TALK TO YOU...
WHAT'S ON YOUR MIND?
STEVE TROOP

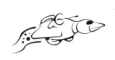

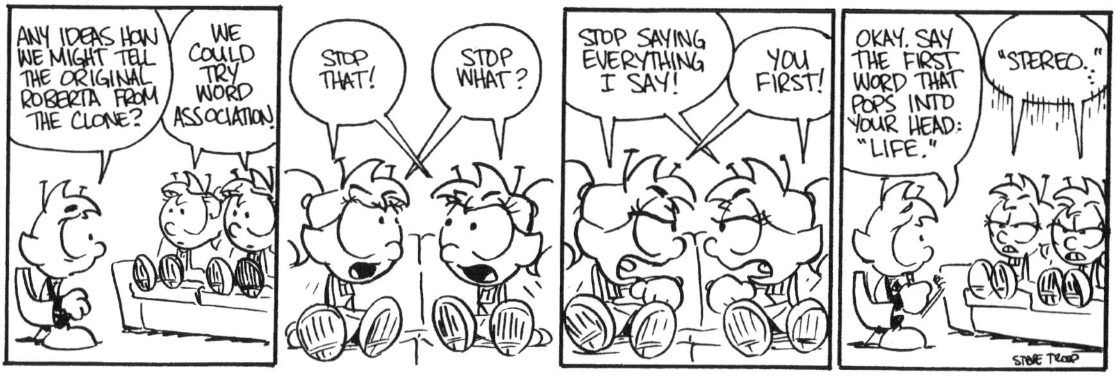

ANY IDEAS HOW WE MIGHT TELL THE ORIGINAL ROBERTA FROM THE CLONE?
WE COULD TRY WORD ASSOCIATION.
STOP THAT!
STOP WHAT?
STOP SAYING EVERYTHING I SAY!
YOU FIRST!
OKAY. SAY THE FIRST WORD THAT POPS INTO YOUR HEAD: "LIFE."
"STEREO."
STEVE TROOP

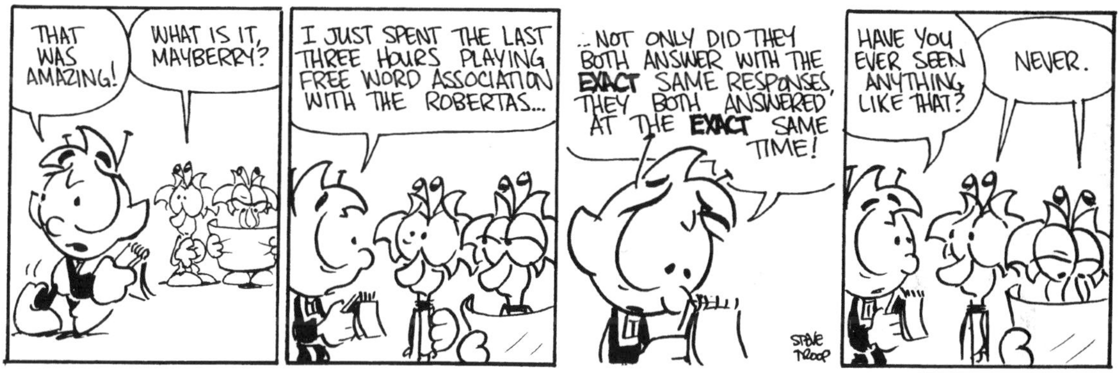

THAT WAS AMAZING!
WHAT IS IT, MAYBERRY?
I JUST SPENT THE LAST THREE HOURS PLAYING FREE WORD ASSOCIATION WITH THE ROBERTAS...
...NOT ONLY DID THEY BOTH ANSWER WITH THE EXACT SAME RESPONSES, THEY BOTH ANSWERED AT THE EXACT SAME TIME!
STEVE TROOP
HAVE YOU EVER SEEN ANYTHING LIKE THAT?
NEVER.

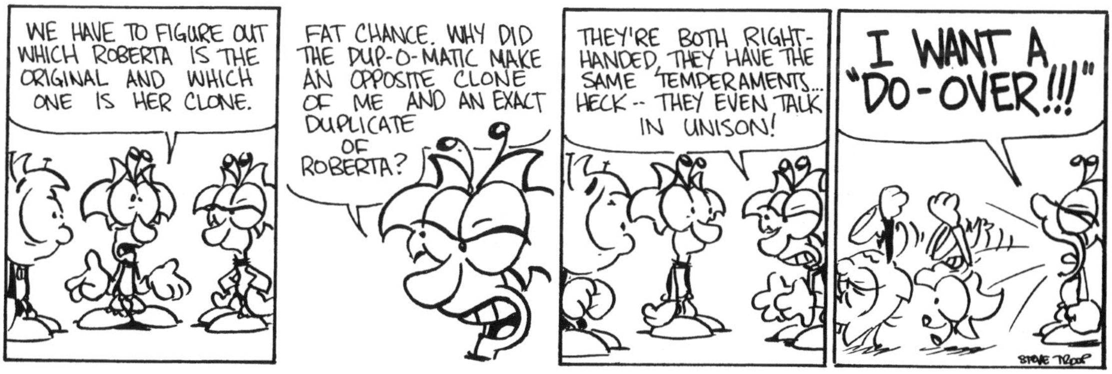

WE HAVE TO FIGURE OUT WHICH ROBERTA IS THE ORIGINAL AND WHICH ONE IS HER CLONE.
FAT CHANCE. WHY DID THE DUP-O-MATIC MAKE AN OPPOSITE CLONE OF ME AND AN EXACT DUPLICATE OF ROBERTA?
THEY'RE BOTH RIGHT-HANDED, THEY HAVE THE SAME TEMPERAMENTS... HECK -- THEY EVEN TALK IN UNISON!
I WANT A "DO-OVER!!!"
STEVE TROOP

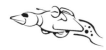

I thought this was a fairly original concept—having the two Robertas saying the same thing at the same time—until one of my readers pointed out that *Farscape* had done the exact same gag a number of years earlier. Oh well, back to the drawing board....

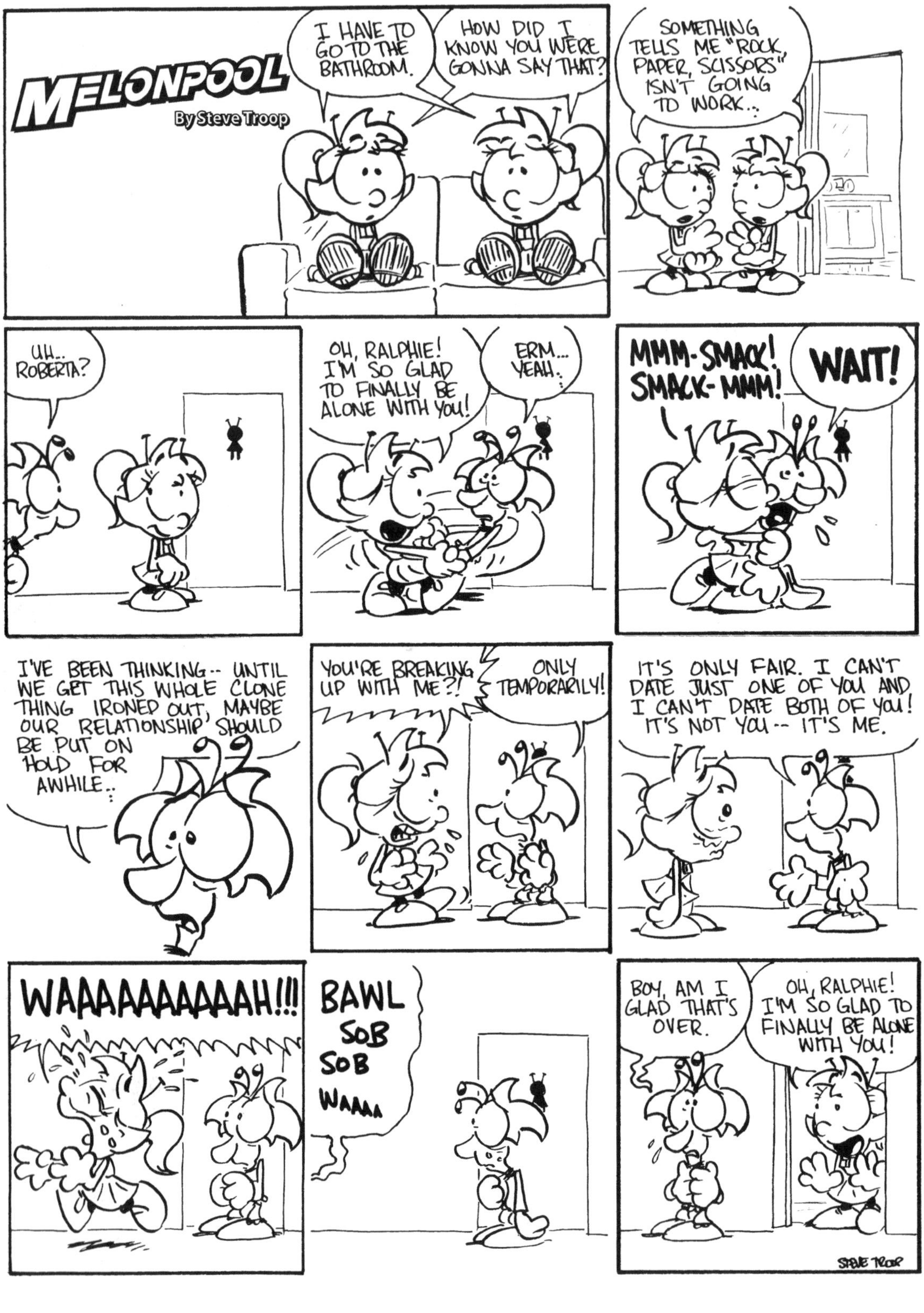
MELONPOOL
By Steve Troop
I HAVE TO GO TO THE BATHROOM.
HOW DID I KNOW YOU WERE GONNA SAY THAT?
SOMETHING TELLS ME "ROCK, PAPER, SCISSORS" ISN'T GOING TO WORK...
UH.. ROBERTA?
OH, RALPHIE! I'M SO GLAD TO FINALLY BE ALONE WITH YOU!
ERM... YEAH..
MMM-SMACK! SMACK-MMM!
WAIT!
I'VE BEEN THINKING.. UNTIL WE GET THIS WHOLE CLONE THING IRONED OUT, MAYBE OUR RELATIONSHIP SHOULD BE PUT ON HOLD FOR AWHILE..
YOU'RE BREAKING UP WITH ME?!
ONLY TEMPORARILY!
IT'S ONLY FAIR. I CAN'T DATE JUST ONE OF YOU AND I CAN'T DATE BOTH OF YOU! IT'S NOT YOU -- IT'S ME.
WAAAAAAAAAAH!!!
BAWL SOB SOB WAAAA
BOY, AM I GLAD THAT'S OVER.
OH, RALPHIE! I'M SO GLAD TO FINALLY BE ALONE WITH YOU!
STEVE TROOP

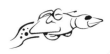

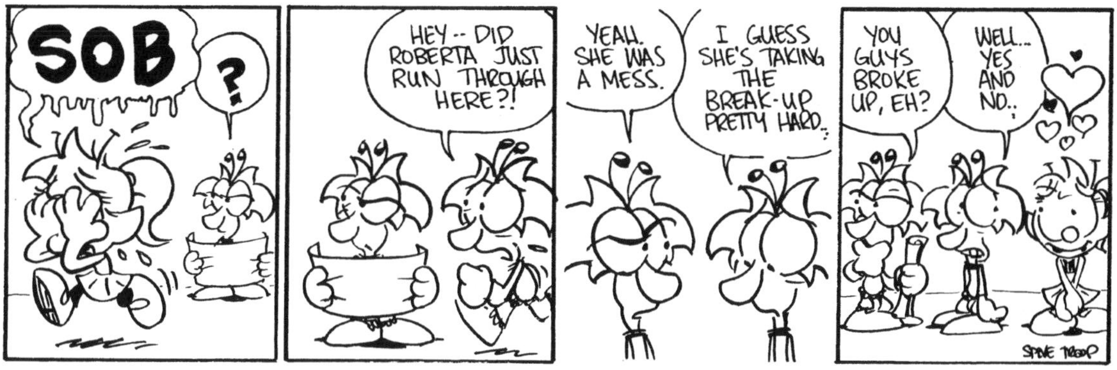
SOB
?
HEY -- DID ROBERTA JUST RUN THROUGH HERE?!
YEAH. SHE WAS A MESS.
I GUESS SHE'S TAKING THE BREAK-UP PRETTY HARD...
YOU GUYS BROKE UP, EH?
WELL... YES AND NO...
STEVE TROOP

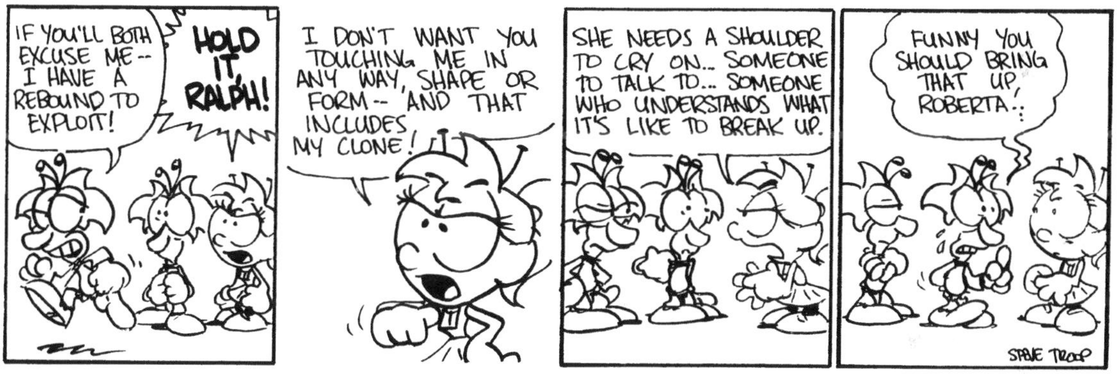
IF YOU'LL BOTH EXCUSE ME-- I HAVE A REBOUND TO EXPLOIT!
HOLD IT, RALPH!
I DON'T WANT YOU TOUCHING ME IN ANY WAY, SHAPE OR FORM-- AND THAT INCLUDES MY CLONE!
SHE NEEDS A SHOULDER TO CRY ON... SOMEONE TO TALK TO... SOMEONE WHO UNDERSTANDS WHAT IT'S LIKE TO BREAK UP.
FUNNY YOU SHOULD BRING THAT UP, ROBERTA...
STEVE TROOP

Actually, Mayberry isn't the culprit this time... Ralphie reversed the polarity during the **Double Trouble** storyline (TUM V, pages 14–43).

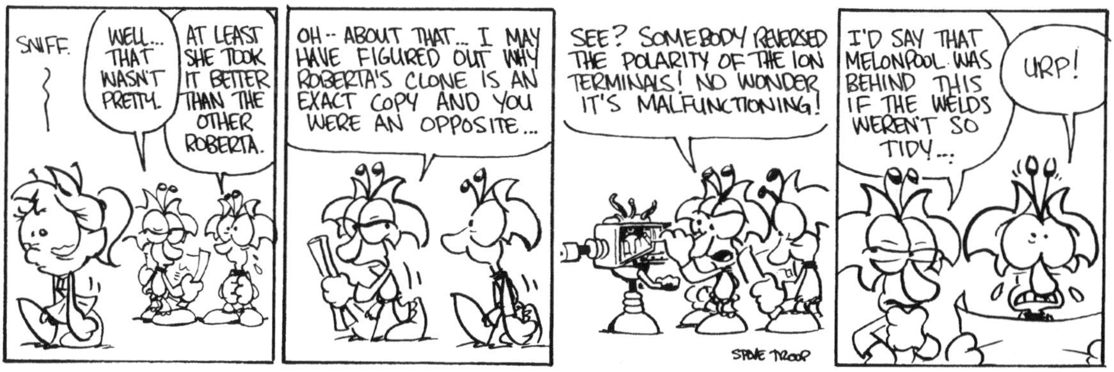
SNIFF.
WELL... THAT WASN'T PRETTY.
AT LEAST SHE TOOK IT BETTER THAN THE OTHER ROBERTA.
OH -- ABOUT THAT... I MAY HAVE FIGURED OUT WHY ROBERTA'S CLONE IS AN EXACT COPY AND YOU WERE AN OPPOSITE...
SEE? SOMEBODY REVERSED THE POLARITY OF THE ION TERMINALS! NO WONDER IT'S MALFUNCTIONING!
I'D SAY THAT MELONPOOL WAS BEHIND THIS IF THE WELDS WEREN'T SO TIDY...
URP!
STEVE TROOP

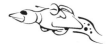

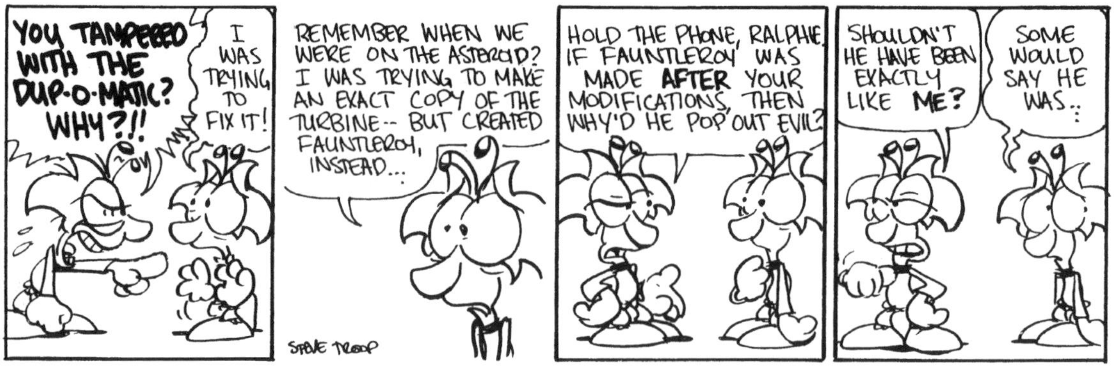
YOU TAMPERED WITH THE DUP-O-MATIC? WHY?!!
I WAS TRYING TO FIX IT!
REMEMBER WHEN WE WERE ON THE ASTEROID? I WAS TRYING TO MAKE AN EXACT COPY OF THE TURBINE-- BUT CREATED FAUNTLEROY, INSTEAD...
STEVE TROOP
HOLD THE PHONE, RALPHIE. IF FAUNTLEROY WAS MADE AFTER YOUR MODIFICATIONS, THEN WHY'D HE POP OUT EVIL?
SHOULDN'T HE HAVE BEEN EXACTLY LIKE ME?
SOME WOULD SAY HE WAS...

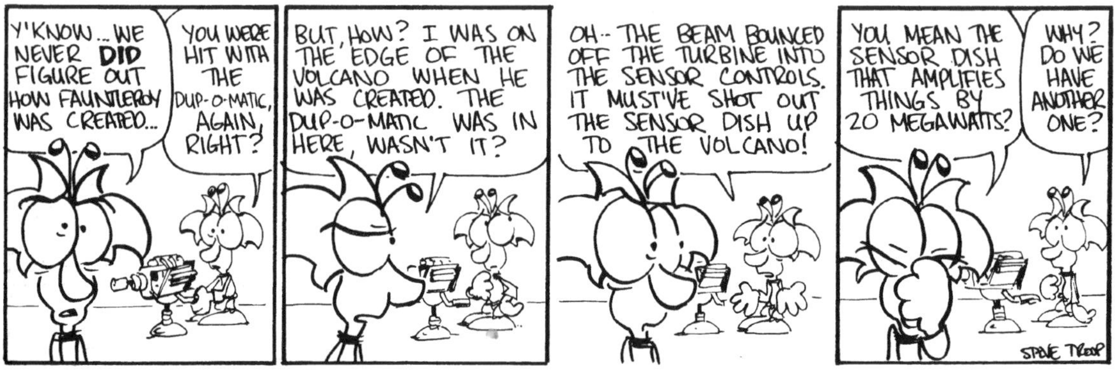
Y'KNOW... WE NEVER DID FIGURE OUT HOW FAUNTLEROY WAS CREATED...
YOU WERE HIT WITH THE DUP-O-MATIC, AGAIN, RIGHT?
BUT, HOW? I WAS ON THE EDGE OF THE VOLCANO WHEN HE WAS CREATED. THE DUP-O-MATIC WAS IN HERE, WASN'T IT?
OH-- THE BEAM BOUNCED OFF THE TURBINE INTO THE SENSOR CONTROLS. IT MUST'VE SHOT OUT THE SENSOR DISH UP TO THE VOLCANO!
YOU MEAN THE SENSOR DISH THAT AMPLIFIES THINGS BY 20 MEGAWATTS?
WHY? DO WE HAVE ANOTHER ONE?
STEVE TROOP

The monitor in the first panel is a reference to longtime Melonpool forumite John Forster, AKA "LCARS"—which I found out later was a reverence to the computer system on *Star Trek: The Next Generation* (AKA the "Library Computer Access and Retrieval" System). See? These *Star Trek* references aren't all my fault!

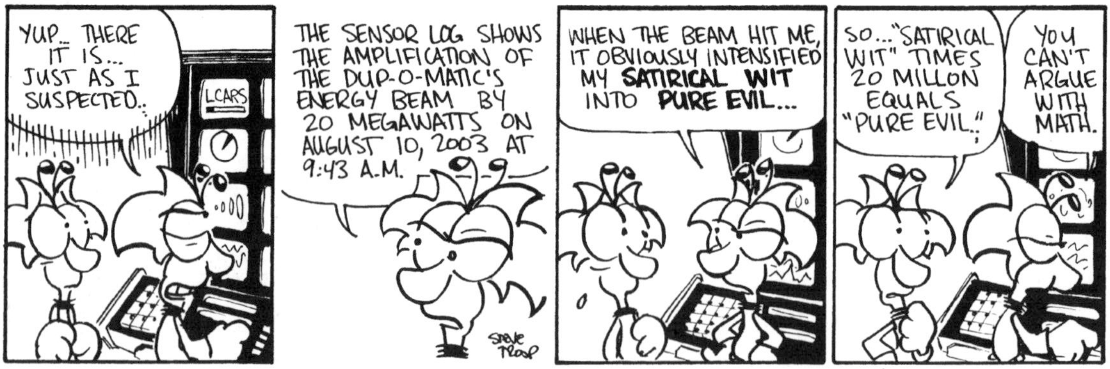
YUP... THERE IT IS... JUST AS I SUSPECTED...
LCARS
THE SENSOR LOG SHOWS THE AMPLIFICATION OF THE DUP-O-MATIC'S ENERGY BEAM BY 20 MEGAWATTS ON AUGUST 10, 2003 AT 9:43 A.M.
STEVE TROOP
WHEN THE BEAM HIT ME, IT OBVIOUSLY INTENSIFIED MY SATIRICAL WIT INTO PURE EVIL...
SO... "SATIRICAL WIT" TIMES 20 MILLON EQUALS "PURE EVIL."
YOU CAN'T ARGUE WITH MATH.

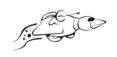

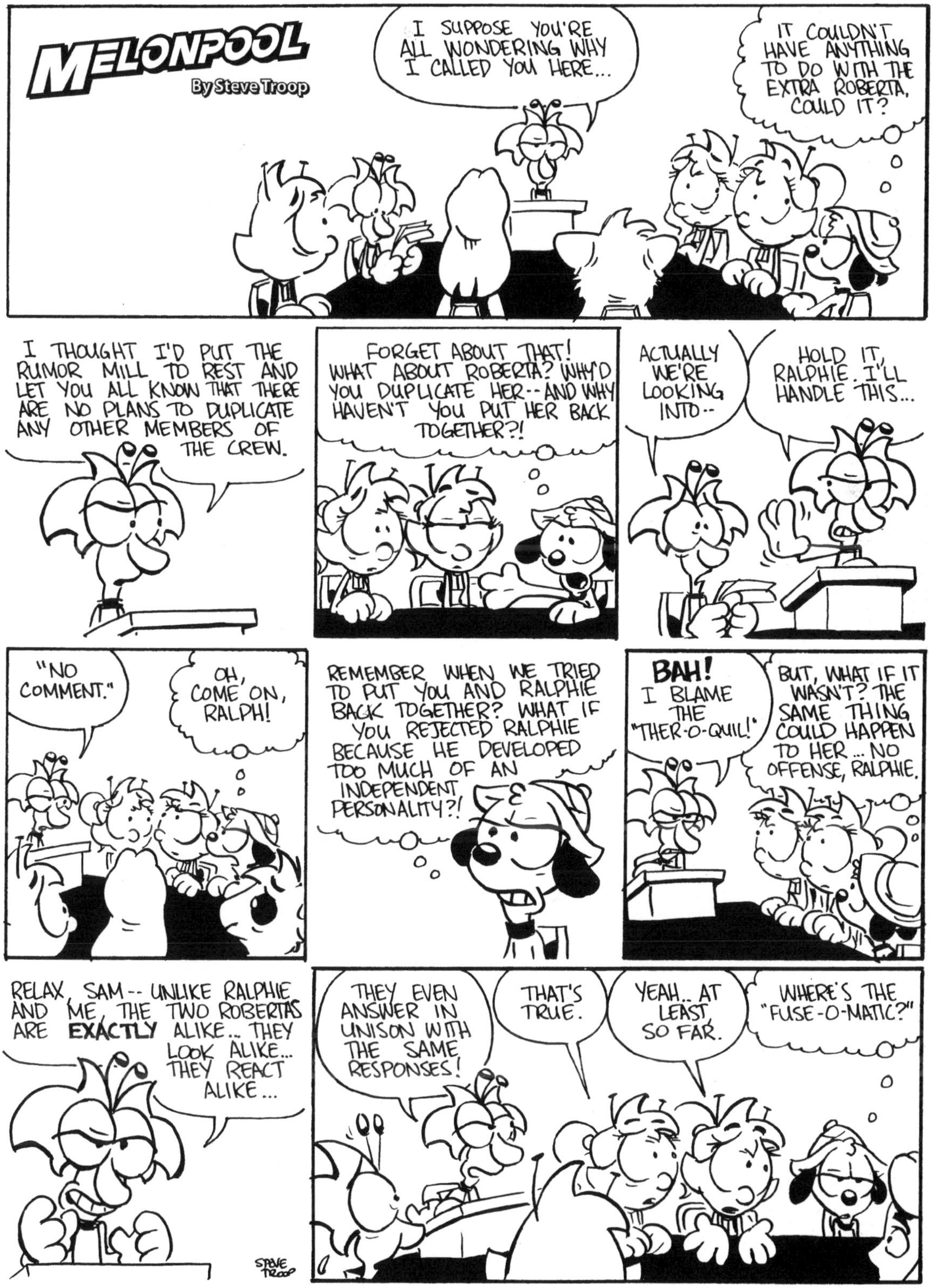
MELONPOOL
By Steve Troop
I SUPPOSE YOU'RE ALL WONDERING WHY I CALLED YOU HERE...
IT COULDN'T HAVE ANYTHING TO DO WITH THE EXTRA ROBERTA, COULD IT?
I THOUGHT I'D PUT THE RUMOR MILL TO REST AND LET YOU ALL KNOW THAT THERE ARE NO PLANS TO DUPLICATE ANY OTHER MEMBERS OF THE CREW.
FORGET ABOUT THAT! WHAT ABOUT ROBERTA? WHY'D YOU DUPLICATE HER--AND WHY HAVEN'T YOU PUT HER BACK TOGETHER?!
ACTUALLY WE'RE LOOKING INTO--
HOLD IT, RALPHIE. I'LL HANDLE THIS...
"NO COMMENT."
OH, COME ON, RALPH!
REMEMBER WHEN WE TRIED TO PUT YOU AND RALPHIE BACK TOGETHER? WHAT IF YOU REJECTED RALPHIE BECAUSE HE DEVELOPED TOO MUCH OF AN INDEPENDENT PERSONALITY?!
BAH! I BLAME THE "THER-O-QUIL!"
BUT, WHAT IF IT WASN'T? THE SAME THING COULD HAPPEN TO HER... NO OFFENSE, RALPHIE.
RELAX, SAM-- UNLIKE RALPHIE AND ME, THE TWO ROBERTAS ARE EXACTLY ALIKE... THEY LOOK ALIKE... THEY REACT ALIKE...
THEY EVEN ANSWER IN UNISON WITH THE SAME RESPONSES!
THAT'S TRUE.
YEAH... AT LEAST SO FAR.
WHERE'S THE "FUSE-O-MATIC?"
STEVE TROOP

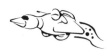

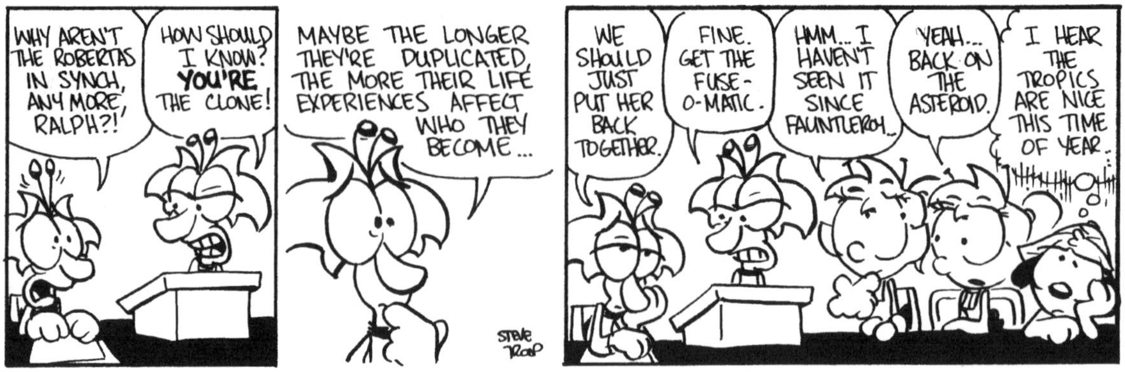
WHY AREN'T THE ROBERTAS IN SYNCH, ANYMORE, RALPH?!
HOW SHOULD I KNOW? YOU'RE THE CLONE!
MAYBE THE LONGER THEY'RE DUPLICATED, THE MORE THEIR LIFE EXPERIENCES AFFECT WHO THEY BECOME...
WE SHOULD JUST PUT HER BACK TOGETHER.
FINE. GET THE FUSE-O-MATIC.
HMM... I HAVEN'T SEEN IT SINCE FAUNTLEROY...
YEAH... BACK ON THE ASTEROID.
I HEAR THE TROPICS ARE NICE THIS TIME OF YEAR...
STEVE TROOP

I like it when Ralph conducts board meetings. Not only is it a good way to get a lot of information out, it's also the perfect opportunity for Ralph to make snide remarks about the rest of the crew or their current situation. Whenever I can, I have Ralph refer to Mayberry as a "puppet," because in certain circles Mayberry is a puppet (like at comic conventions and upcoming motion pictures).

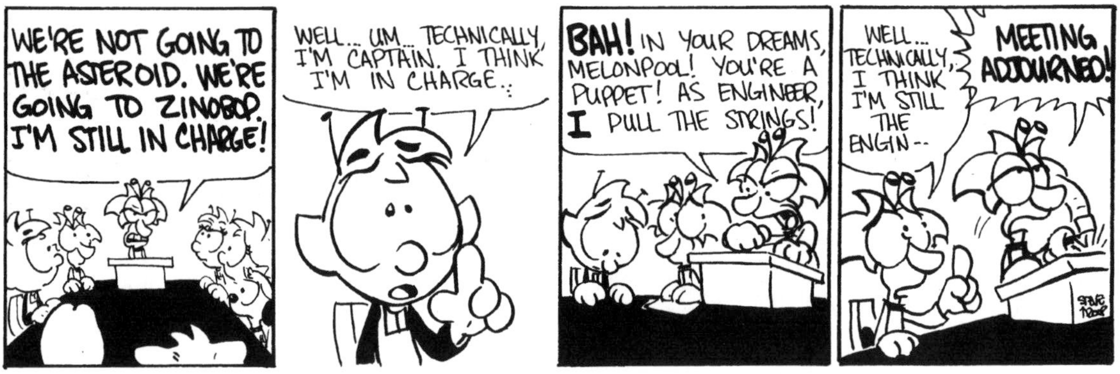
WE'RE NOT GOING TO THE ASTEROID. WE'RE GOING TO ZINOBOP. I'M STILL IN CHARGE!
WELL... UM... TECHNICALLY, I'M CAPTAIN. I THINK I'M IN CHARGE...
BAH! IN YOUR DREAMS, MELONPOOL! YOU'RE A PUPPET! AS ENGINEER, I PULL THE STRINGS!
WELL... TECHNICALLY, I THINK I'M STILL THE ENGIN--
MEETING ADJOURNED!
STEVE TROOP

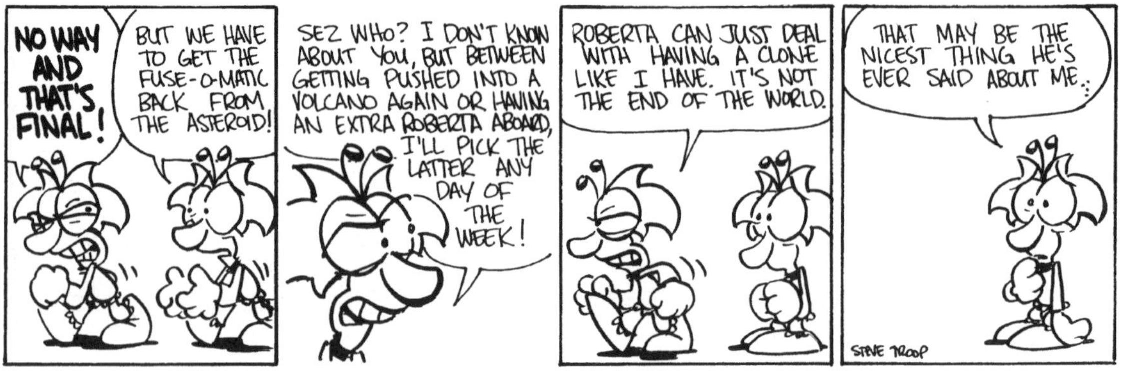
NO WAY AND THAT'S FINAL!
BUT WE HAVE TO GET THE FUSE-O-MATIC BACK FROM THE ASTEROID!
SEZ WHO? I DON'T KNOW ABOUT YOU, BUT BETWEEN GETTING PUSHED INTO A VOLCANO AGAIN OR HAVING AN EXTRA ROBERTA ABOARD, I'LL PICK THE LATTER ANY DAY OF THE WEEK!
ROBERTA CAN JUST DEAL WITH HAVING A CLONE LIKE I HAVE. IT'S NOT THE END OF THE WORLD.
THAT MAY BE THE NICEST THING HE'S EVER SAID ABOUT ME...
STEVE TROOP

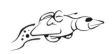

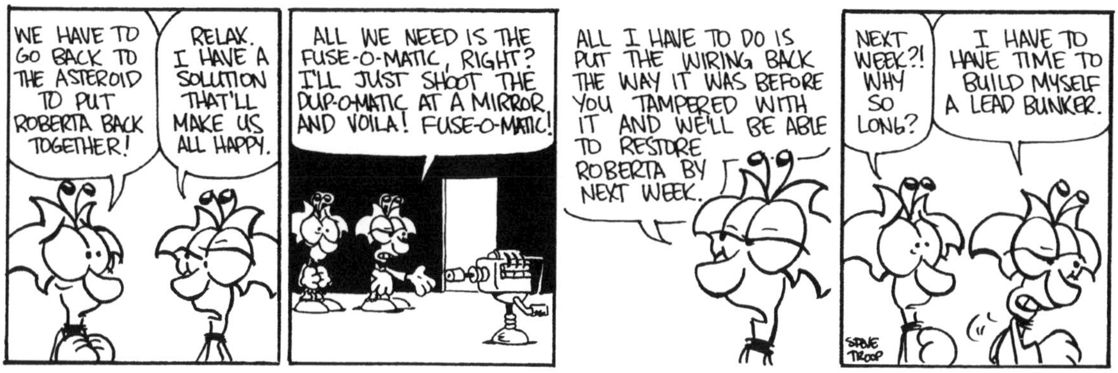
WE HAVE TO GO BACK TO THE ASTEROID TO PUT ROBERTA BACK TOGETHER!
RELAX. I HAVE A SOLUTION THAT'LL MAKE US ALL HAPPY.
ALL WE NEED IS THE FUSE-O-MATIC, RIGHT? I'LL JUST SHOOT THE DUP-O-MATIC AT A MIRROR AND VOILA! FUSE-O-MATIC!
ALL I HAVE TO DO IS PUT THE WIRING BACK THE WAY IT WAS BEFORE YOU TAMPERED WITH IT AND WE'LL BE ABLE TO RESTORE ROBERTA BY NEXT WEEK.
NEXT WEEK?! WHY SO LONG?
I HAVE TO HAVE TIME TO BUILD MYSELF A LEAD BUNKER.
STEVE TROOP

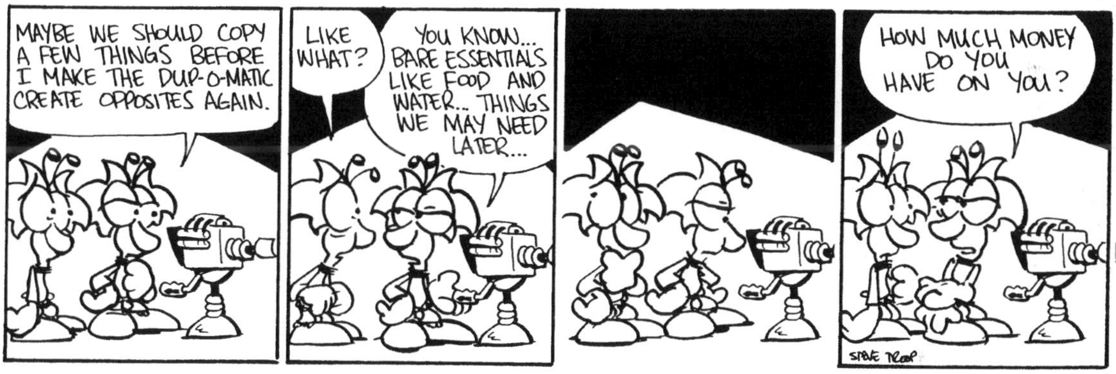
MAYBE WE SHOULD COPY A FEW THINGS BEFORE I MAKE THE DUP-O-MATIC CREATE OPPOSITES AGAIN.
LIKE WHAT?
YOU KNOW... BARE ESSENTIALS LIKE FOOD AND WATER... THINGS WE MAY NEED LATER...
HOW MUCH MONEY DO YOU HAVE ON YOU?
STEVE TROOP

The asteroid that Jalea mentions in the first panel is the same asteroid that the crew of terraformed (or "Zinoformed") to resemble *Gilligan's Island* (see TUM IV). During their almost one-year exile on this asteroid, Mayberry routinely borrowed Sam's Gilligan hat.

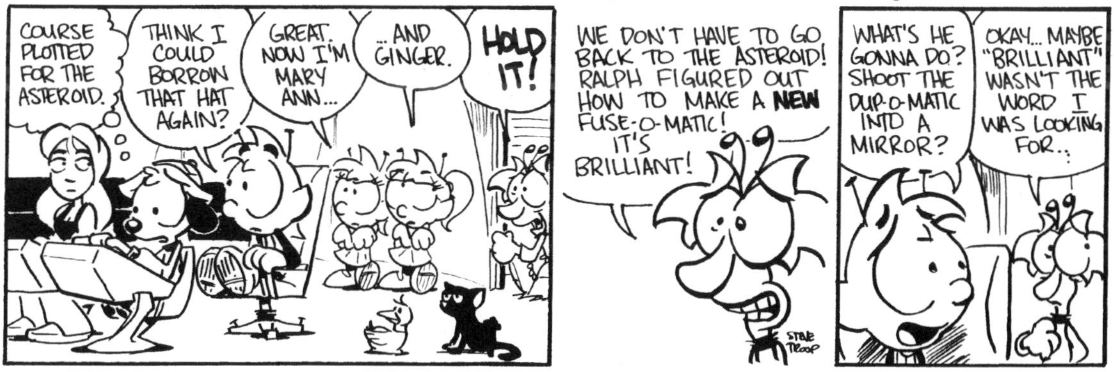
COURSE PLOTTED FOR THE ASTEROID.
THINK I COULD BORROW THAT HAT AGAIN?
GREAT. NOW I'M MARY ANN...
...AND GINGER.
HOLD IT!
WE DON'T HAVE TO GO BACK TO THE ASTEROID! RALPH FIGURED OUT HOW TO MAKE A NEW FUSE-O-MATIC! IT'S BRILLIANT!
WHAT'S HE GONNA DO? SHOOT THE DUP-O-MATIC INTO A MIRROR?
OKAY... MAYBE "BRILLIANT" WASN'T THE WORD I WAS LOOKING FOR...
STEVE TROOP

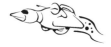

I penciled this strip from left-to-right, top-to-bottom—but I actually inked it top-to-bottom, left-to-right, character-by-character, giving it a very consistent look all the way through.

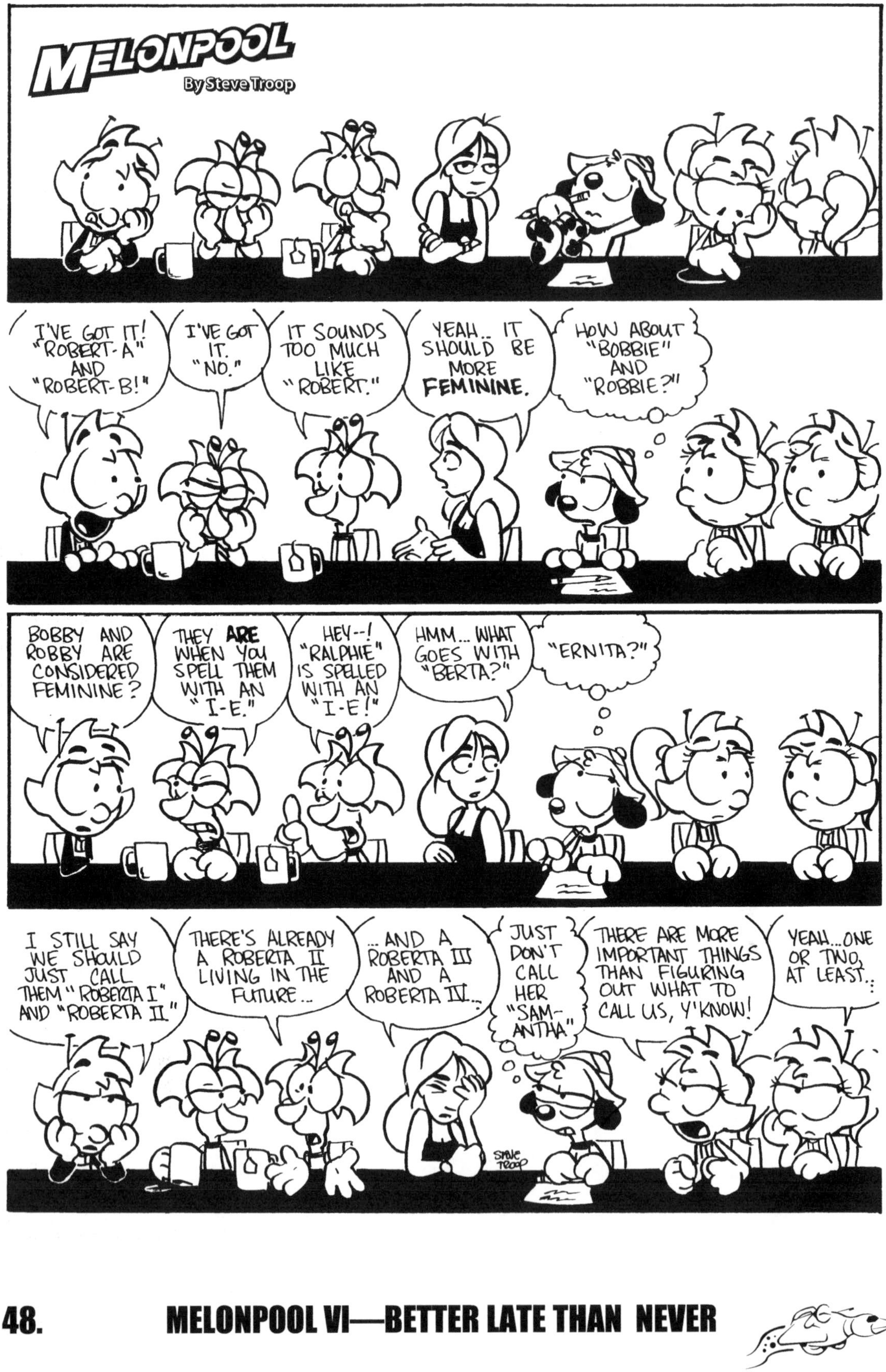
MELONPOOL
By Steve Troop
I'VE GOT IT! "ROBERT-A" AND "ROBERT-B!"
I'VE GOT IT. "NO."
IT SOUNDS TOO MUCH LIKE "ROBERT."
YEAH.. IT SHOULD BE MORE FEMININE.
HOW ABOUT "BOBBIE" AND "ROBBIE?"
BOBBY AND ROBBY ARE CONSIDERED FEMININE?
THEY ARE WHEN YOU SPELL THEM WITH AN "I-E."
HEY--! "RALPHIE" IS SPELLED WITH AN "I-E!"
HMM... WHAT GOES WITH "BERTA?"
"ERNITA?"
I STILL SAY WE SHOULD JUST CALL THEM "ROBERTA I" AND "ROBERTA II"
THERE'S ALREADY A ROBERTA II LIVING IN THE FUTURE...
...AND A ROBERTA III AND A ROBERTA IV...
JUST DON'T CALL HER "SAMANTHA"
THERE ARE MORE IMPORTANT THINGS THAN FIGURING OUT WHAT TO CALL US, Y'KNOW!
YEAH...ONE OR TWO, AT LEAST...
STEVE TROOP

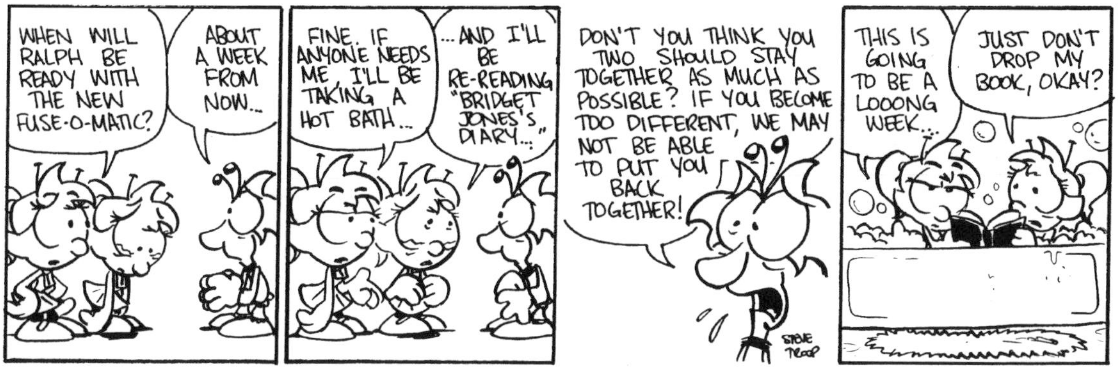
WHEN WILL RALPH BE READY WITH THE NEW FUSE-O-MATIC?
ABOUT A WEEK FROM NOW...
FINE. IF ANYONE NEEDS ME, I'LL BE TAKING A HOT BATH...
...AND I'LL BE RE-READING "BRIDGET JONES'S DIARY..."
DON'T YOU THINK YOU TWO SHOULD STAY TOGETHER AS MUCH AS POSSIBLE? IF YOU BECOME TOO DIFFERENT, WE MAY NOT BE ABLE TO PUT YOU BACK TOGETHER!
STEVE TROOP
THIS IS GOING TO BE A LOOONG WEEK...
JUST DON'T DROP MY BOOK, OKAY?

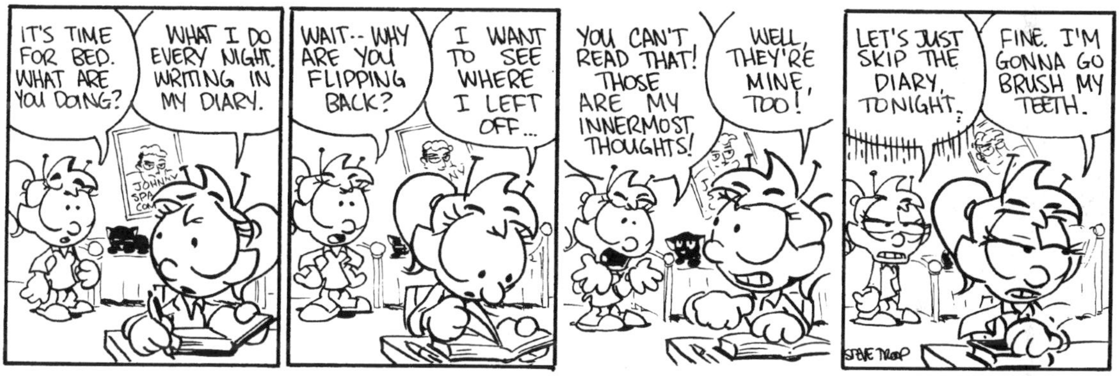
IT'S TIME FOR BED. WHAT ARE YOU DOING?
WHAT I DO EVERY NIGHT. WRITING IN MY DIARY.
WAIT-- WHY ARE YOU FLIPPING BACK?
I WANT TO SEE WHERE I LEFT OFF...
YOU CAN'T READ THAT! THOSE ARE MY INNERMOST THOUGHTS!
WELL, THEY'RE MINE, TOO!
LET'S JUST SKIP THE DIARY, TONIGHT...
FINE. I'M GONNA GO BRUSH MY TEETH.
STEVE TROOP

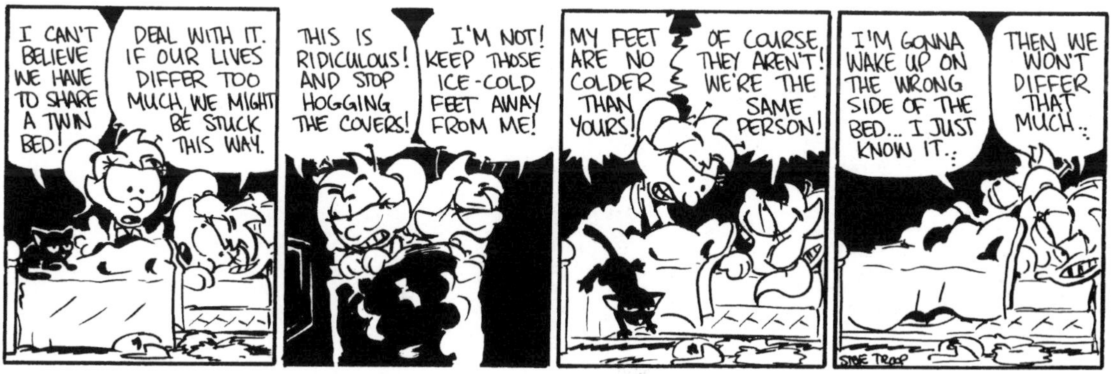
I CAN'T BELIEVE WE HAVE TO SHARE A TWIN BED!
DEAL WITH IT. IF OUR LIVES DIFFER TOO MUCH, WE MIGHT BE STUCK THIS WAY.
THIS IS RIDICULOUS! AND STOP HOGGING THE COVERS!
I'M NOT! KEEP THOSE ICE-COLD FEET AWAY FROM ME!
MY FEET ARE NO COLDER THAN YOURS!
OF COURSE THEY AREN'T! WE'RE THE SAME PERSON!
I'M GONNA WAKE UP ON THE WRONG SIDE OF THE BED... I JUST KNOW IT...
THEN WE WON'T DIFFER THAT MUCH...
STEVE TROOP

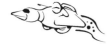

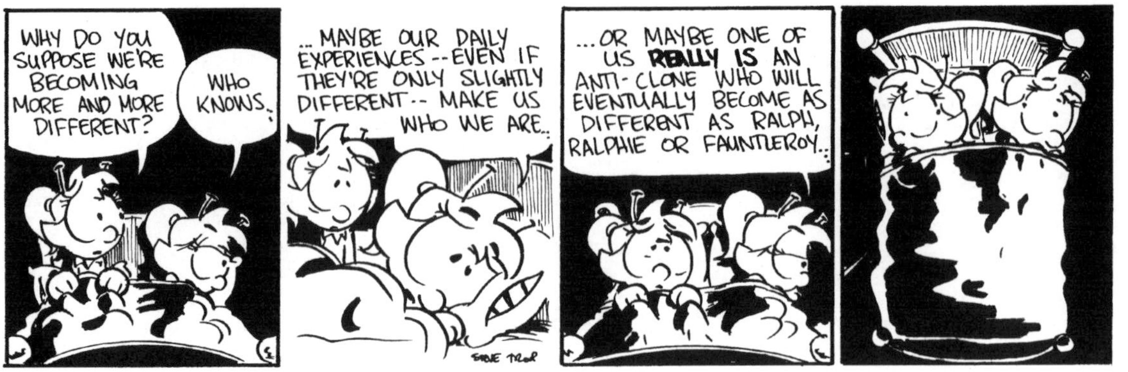
WHY DO YOU SUPPOSE WE'RE BECOMING MORE AND MORE DIFFERENT?
WHO KNOWS..
...MAYBE OUR DAILY EXPERIENCES--EVEN IF THEY'RE ONLY SLIGHTLY DIFFERENT--MAKE US WHO WE ARE..
...OR MAYBE ONE OF US **REALLY IS** AN ANTI-CLONE WHO WILL EVENTUALLY BECOME AS DIFFERENT AS RALPH, RALPHIE OR FAUNTLEROY..

Sometimes, the difference between having to design a lead bunker and not having to design a lead bunker relies completely on the staging.

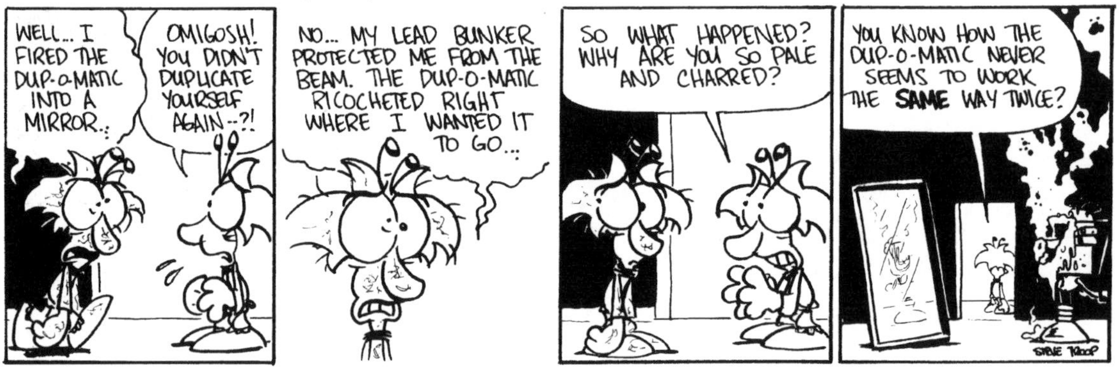
WELL... I FIRED THE DUP-O-MATIC INTO A MIRROR..
OMIGOSH! YOU DIDN'T DUPLICATE YOURSELF AGAIN--?!
NO... MY LEAD BUNKER PROTECTED ME FROM THE BEAM. THE DUP-O-MATIC RICOCHETED RIGHT WHERE I WANTED IT TO GO...
SO WHAT HAPPENED? WHY ARE YOU SO PALE AND CHARRED?
YOU KNOW HOW THE DUP-O-MATIC NEVER SEEMS TO WORK THE **SAME** WAY TWICE?

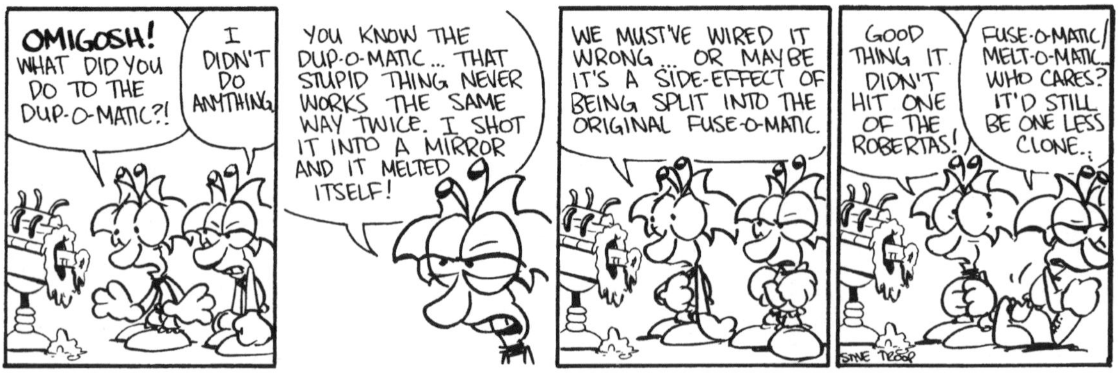
OMIGOSH! WHAT DID YOU DO TO THE DUP-O-MATIC?!
I DIDN'T DO ANYTHING
YOU KNOW THE DUP-O-MATIC... THAT STUPID THING NEVER WORKS THE SAME WAY TWICE. I SHOT IT INTO A MIRROR AND IT MELTED ITSELF!
WE MUST'VE WIRED IT WRONG... OR MAYBE IT'S A SIDE-EFFECT OF BEING SPLIT INTO THE ORIGINAL FUSE-O-MATIC.
GOOD THING IT DIDN'T HIT ONE OF THE ROBERTAS!
FUSE-O-MATIC/ MELT-O-MATIC.. WHO CARES? IT'D STILL BE ONE LESS CLONE..

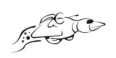

A lot of *Melonpool* readers were surprised to learn that Melotia and the Planet Zinobop were both in the same solar system. To be honest, so was I!

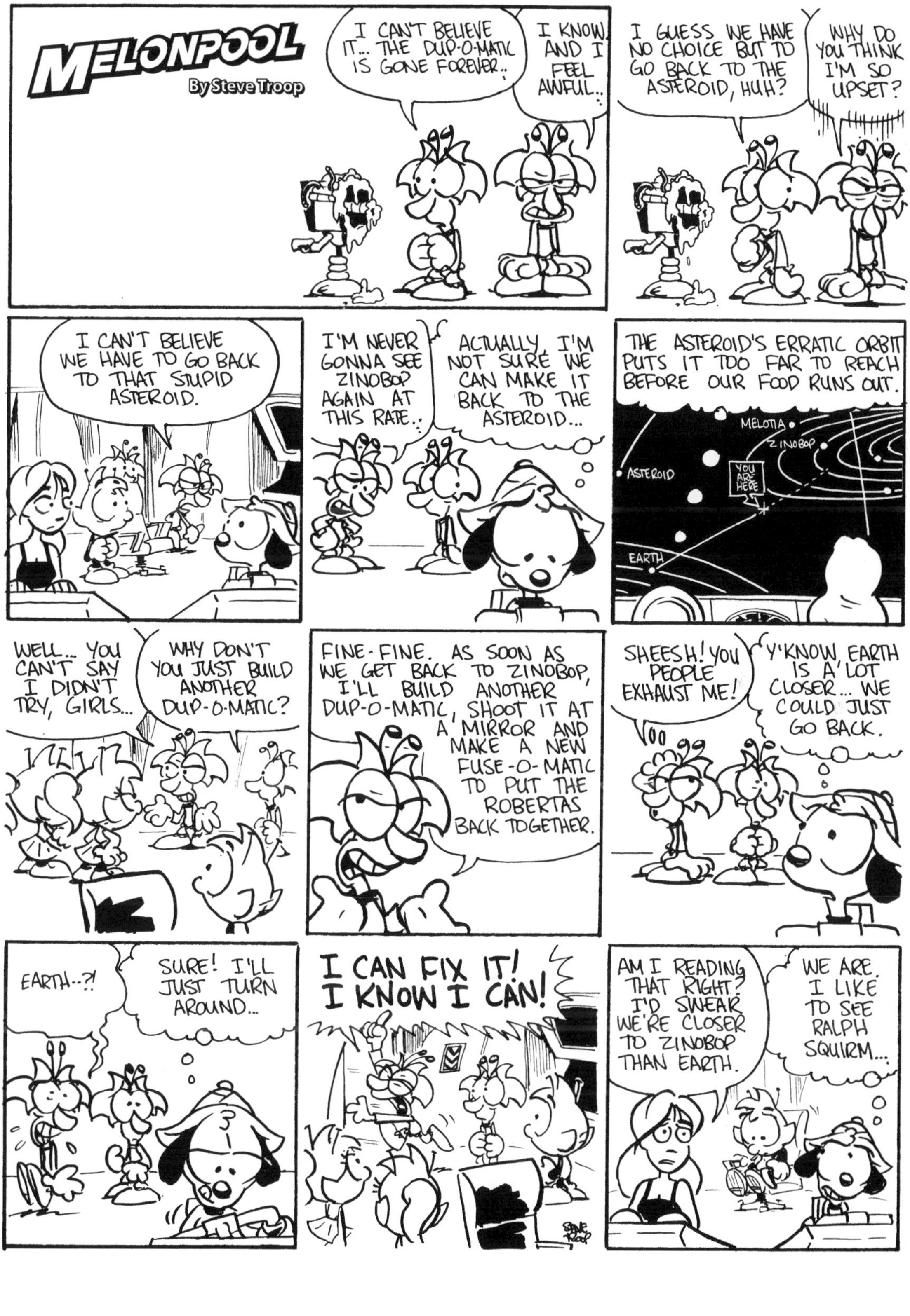
MELONPOOL
By Steve Troop
I CAN'T BELIEVE IT... THE DUP-O-MATIC IS GONE FOREVER...
I KNOW. AND I FEEL AWFUL...
I GUESS WE HAVE NO CHOICE BUT TO GO BACK TO THE ASTEROID, HUH?
WHY DO YOU THINK I'M SO UPSET?
I CAN'T BELIEVE WE HAVE TO GO BACK TO THAT STUPID ASTEROID.
I'M NEVER GONNA SEE ZINOBOP AGAIN AT THIS RATE...
ACTUALLY, I'M NOT SURE WE CAN MAKE IT BACK TO THE ASTEROID...
THE ASTEROID'S ERRATIC ORBIT PUTS IT TOO FAR TO REACH BEFORE OUR FOOD RUNS OUT.
MELOTIA
ZINOBOP
ASTEROID
YOU ARE HERE
EARTH
WELL... YOU CAN'T SAY I DIDN'T TRY, GIRLS...
WHY DON'T YOU JUST BUILD ANOTHER DUP-O-MATIC?
FINE-FINE. AS SOON AS WE GET BACK TO ZINOBOP, I'LL BUILD ANOTHER DUP-O-MATIC, SHOOT IT AT A MIRROR AND MAKE A NEW FUSE-O-MATIC TO PUT THE ROBERTAS BACK TOGETHER.
SHEESH! YOU PEOPLE EXHAUST ME!
Y'KNOW, EARTH IS A LOT CLOSER... WE COULD JUST GO BACK.
EARTH...?!
SURE! I'LL JUST TURN AROUND...
I CAN FIX IT! I KNOW I CAN!
AM I READING THAT RIGHT? I'D SWEAR WE'RE CLOSER TO ZINOBOP THAN EARTH.
WE ARE. I LIKE TO SEE RALPH SQUIRM...

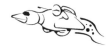

Among the items used for Ralph's makeshift spacesuit: a fish bowl and a vacuum cleaner.

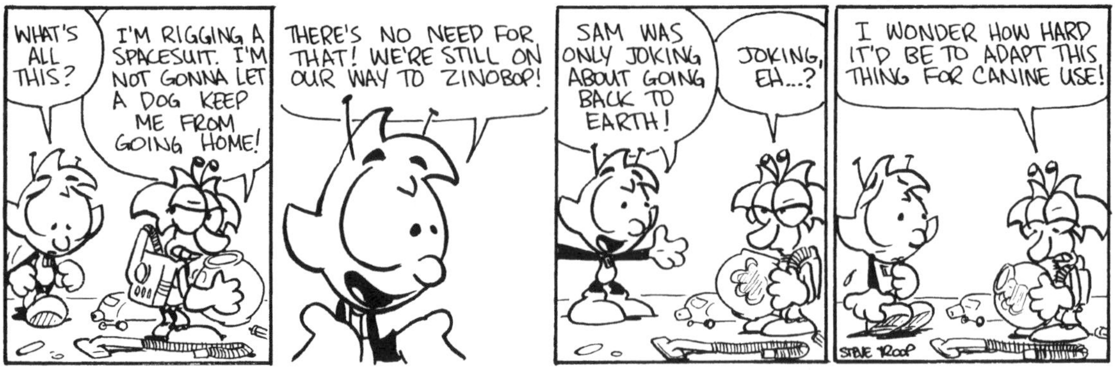
WHAT'S ALL THIS?
I'M RIGGING A SPACESUIT. I'M NOT GONNA LET A DOG KEEP ME FROM GOING HOME!
THERE'S NO NEED FOR THAT! WE'RE STILL ON OUR WAY TO ZINOBOP!
SAM WAS ONLY JOKING ABOUT GOING BACK TO EARTH!
JOKING, EH...?
I WONDER HOW HARD IT'D BE TO ADAPT THIS THING FOR CANINE USE!
STEVE TROOP

Believe it or not, the reason that Ralph cites below for creating Sammy the Hammy and the *Steel Duck* was always what I had in mind. It only took me about eight years to get around to being able to use it!

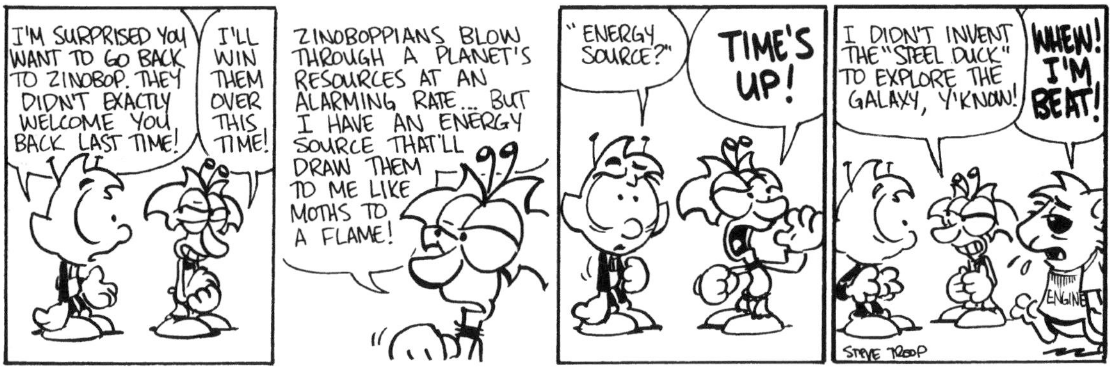
I'M SURPRISED YOU WANT TO GO BACK TO ZINOBOP. THEY DIDN'T EXACTLY WELCOME YOU BACK LAST TIME!
I'LL WIN THEM OVER THIS TIME!
ZINOBOPPIANS BLOW THROUGH A PLANET'S RESOURCES AT AN ALARMING RATE... BUT I HAVE AN ENERGY SOURCE THAT'LL DRAW THEM TO ME LIKE MOTHS TO A FLAME!
"ENERGY SOURCE?"
TIME'S UP!
I DIDN'T INVENT THE "STEEL DUCK" TO EXPLORE THE GALAXY, Y'KNOW!
WHEW! I'M BEAT!
ENGINE
STEVE TROOP

An obvious play on *Star Trek V: The Final Frontier.* More on this later....

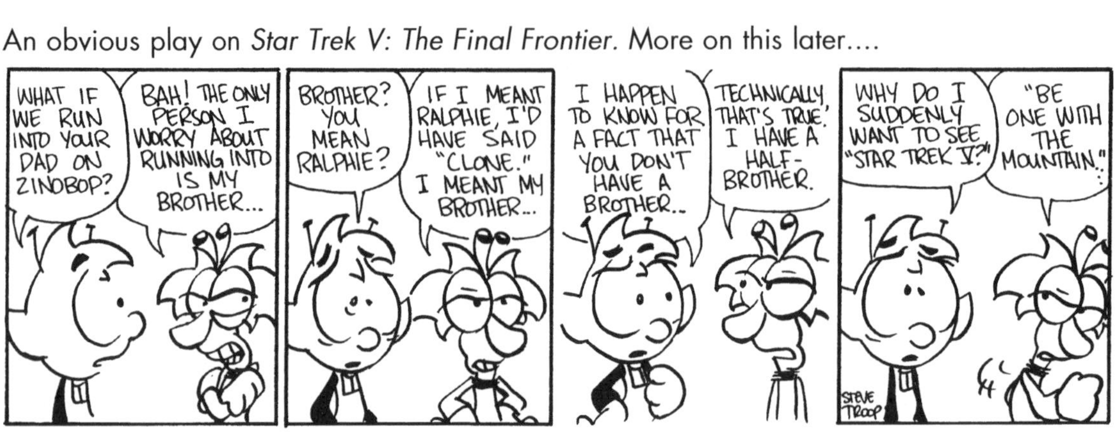
WHAT IF WE RUN INTO YOUR DAD ON ZINOBOP?
BAH! THE ONLY PERSON I WORRY ABOUT RUNNING INTO IS MY BROTHER...
BROTHER? YOU MEAN RALPHIE?
IF I MEANT RALPHIE, I'D HAVE SAID "CLONE." I MEANT MY BROTHER...
I HAPPEN TO KNOW FOR A FACT THAT YOU DON'T HAVE A BROTHER..
TECHNICALLY, THAT'S TRUE. I HAVE A HALF-BROTHER.
WHY DO I SUDDENLY WANT TO SEE "STAR TREK V"?
"BE ONE WITH THE MOUNTAIN."
STEVE TROOP

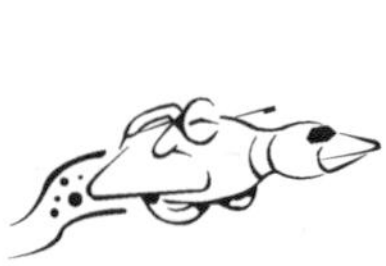

Many people have written me over the years with detailed psychological evaluations on Ralph's screwed up childhood. It's pretty remarkable to have created such a rich and complex character—especially since most of the things he says or does are written without too much thought. Hopefully, that's not a reflection of my screwed-up childhood.

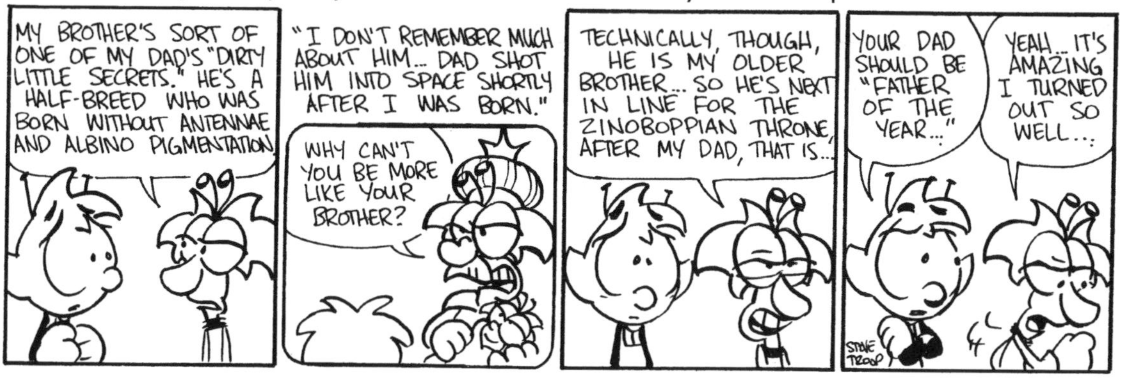
MY BROTHER'S SORT OF ONE OF MY DAD'S "DIRTY LITTLE SECRETS." HE'S A HALF-BREED WHO WAS BORN WITHOUT ANTENNAE AND ALBINO PIGMENTATION.
"I DON'T REMEMBER MUCH ABOUT HIM... DAD SHOT HIM INTO SPACE SHORTLY AFTER I WAS BORN."
WHY CAN'T YOU BE MORE LIKE YOUR BROTHER?
TECHNICALLY, THOUGH, HE IS MY OLDER BROTHER... SO HE'S NEXT IN LINE FOR THE ZINOBOPPIAN THRONE, AFTER MY DAD, THAT IS...
YOUR DAD SHOULD BE "FATHER OF THE YEAR..."
YEAH... IT'S AMAZING I TURNED OUT SO WELL...
STEVE TROOP

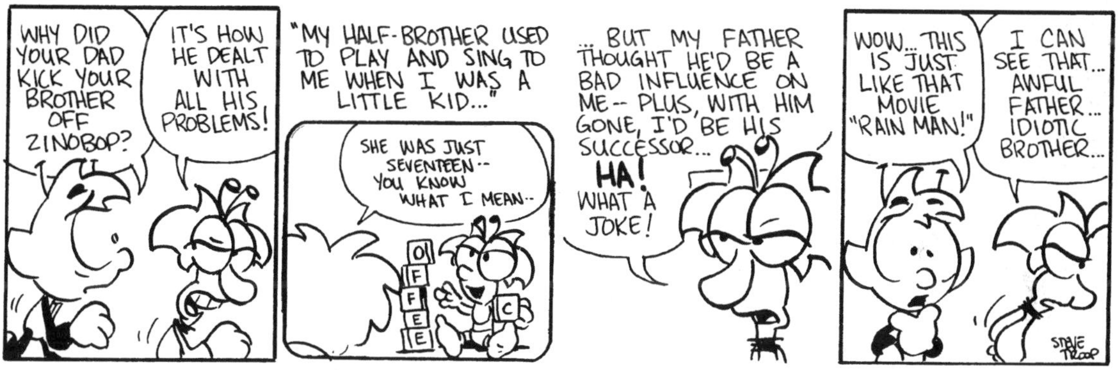
WHY DID YOUR DAD KICK YOUR BROTHER OFF ZINOBOP?
IT'S HOW HE DEALT WITH ALL HIS PROBLEMS!
"MY HALF-BROTHER USED TO PLAY AND SING TO ME WHEN I WAS A LITTLE KID..."
SHE WAS JUST SEVENTEEN -- YOU KNOW WHAT I MEAN --
... BUT MY FATHER THOUGHT HE'D BE A BAD INFLUENCE ON ME -- PLUS, WITH HIM GONE, I'D BE HIS SUCCESSOR... HA! WHAT A JOKE!
WOW... THIS IS JUST LIKE THAT MOVIE "RAIN MAN!"
I CAN SEE THAT... AWFUL FATHER... IDIOTIC BROTHER...
STEVE TROOP

Again... more on this later!

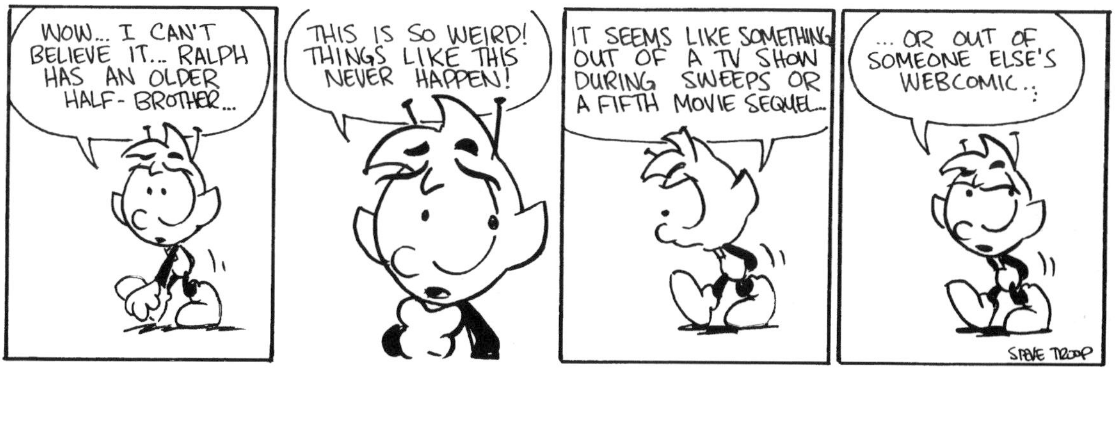
WOW... I CAN'T BELIEVE IT... RALPH HAS AN OLDER HALF-BROTHER...
THIS IS SO WEIRD! THINGS LIKE THIS NEVER HAPPEN!
IT SEEMS LIKE SOMETHING OUT OF A TV SHOW DURING SWEEPS OR A FIFTH MOVIE SEQUEL...
... OR OUT OF SOMEONE ELSE'S WEBCOMIC...
STEVE TROOP

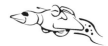

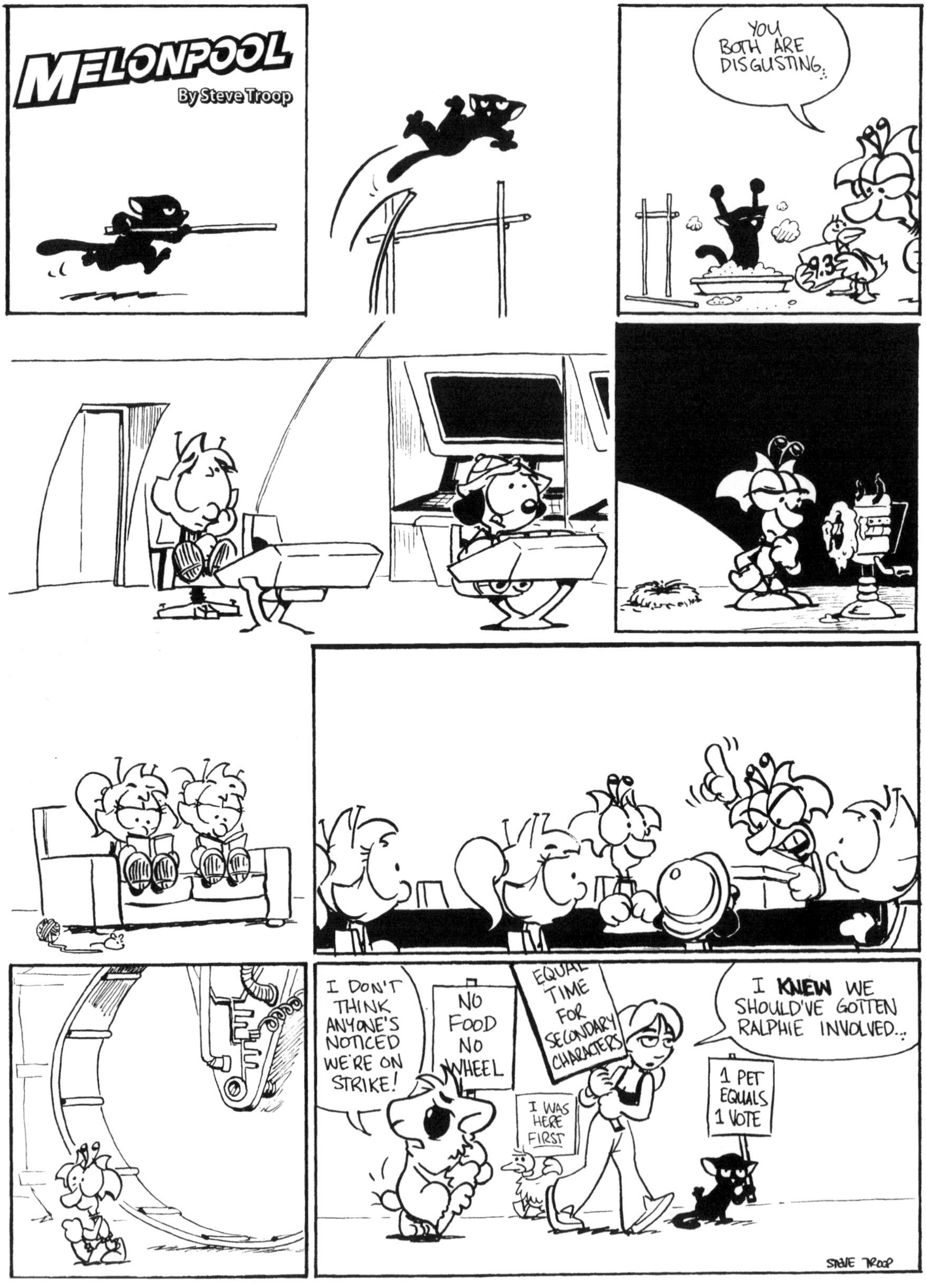
MELONPOOL
By Steve Troop
YOU BOTH ARE DISGUSTING...
9.3
I DON'T THINK ANYONE'S NOTICED WE'RE ON STRIKE!
NO FOOD NO WHEEL
EQUAL TIME FOR SECONDARY CHARACTERS
I WAS HERE FIRST
I KNEW WE SHOULD'VE GOTTEN RALPHIE INVOLVED...
1 PET EQUALS 1 VOTE
STEVE TROOP

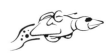

Charles Brubaker, cartoon historian and one of my long-time readers, posted this on the forums after this strip ran:

> I noticed that Melonpool, Ralph and Sam in the flashback panel looks like how they looked 8 years ago. Nice touch.

Silly rabbit. I actually cut and pasted a panel from an earlier strip (See TUM II, page 18).

HMM... MELOTIA AND ZINOBOP ARE BOTH IN THE SAME SOLAR SYSTEM, RIGHT?
YEAH...
IF YOU WERE FLYING TO ZINOBOP FROM MELOTIA, HOW'D YOU CRASH-LAND ON EARTH -- A PLANET 3 LIGHT-YEARS AWAY?
WOW, RALPH -- THIS IS AWESOME! YOU'RE SO LUCKY -- I'D DO ANYTHING TO BE CAPTAIN OF A SPACESHIP!
DID YOU MAKE A WRONG TURN?
IN A MANNER OF SPEAKING...
STEVE TROOP

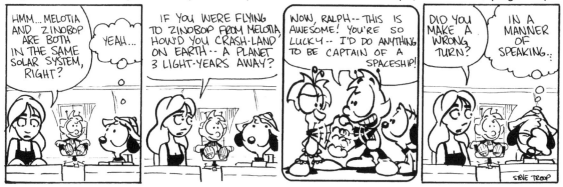

On the other hand, in the last three panels of this strip, I tried to emulate my old art style the best I could. See the difference?

SO IT'S MAYBERRY'S FAULT THAT YOU GUYS CRASHED ON EARTH?
WELL... YES AND NO...
OKAY, RALPH. COURSE LAID IN FOR THE PLANET ZINOBOP...
NOT SO FAST...
THIS IS AN UNTESTED VESSEL WITH A BRAND-NEW ENERGY SOURCE! WE NEED A SHAKEDOWN CRUISE TO WORK OUT THE KINKS, FIRST!
SO... WHERE TO, THEN?
WHO CARES? ASK OUR IDIOT CAPTAIN...
STEVE TROOP

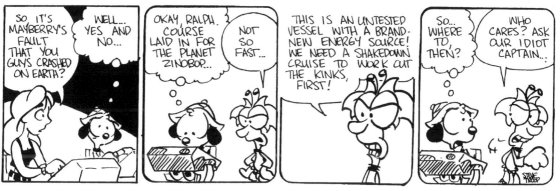

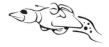

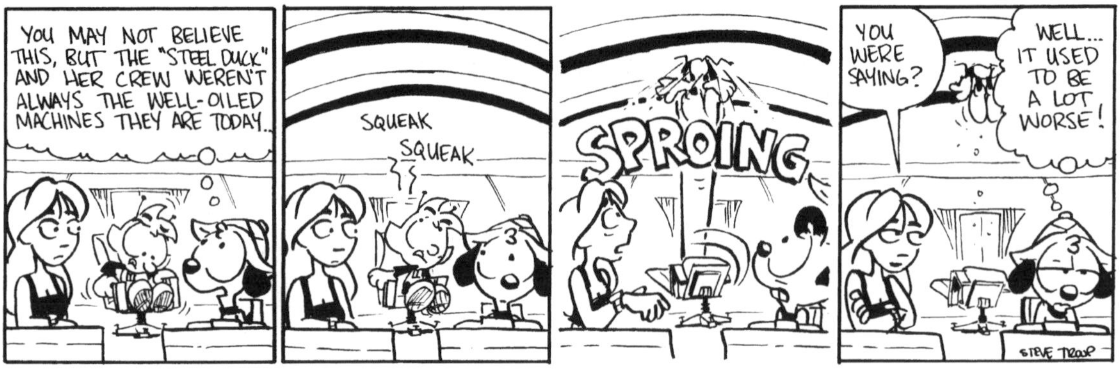
YOU MAY NOT BELIEVE THIS, BUT THE "STEEL DUCK" AND HER CREW WEREN'T ALWAYS THE WELL-OILED MACHINES THEY ARE TODAY...
SQUEAK
SQUEAK
SPROING
YOU WERE SAYING?
WELL... IT USED TO BE A LOT WORSE!
STEVE TROOP

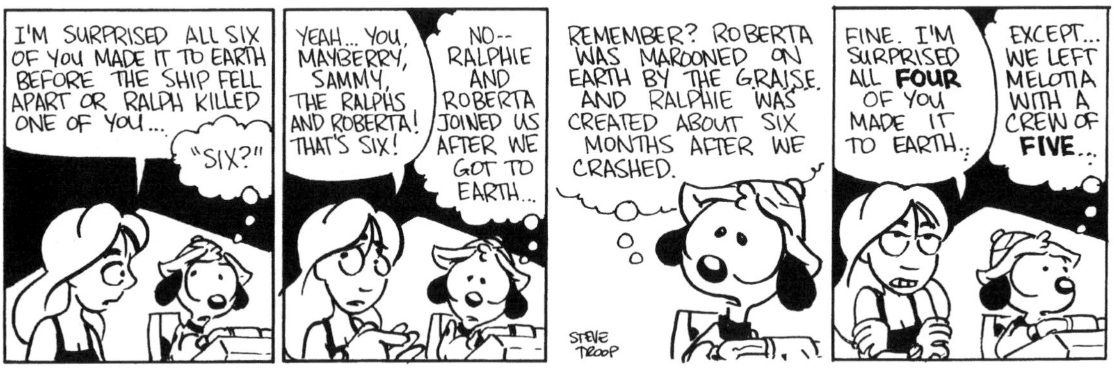
I'M SURPRISED ALL SIX OF YOU MADE IT TO EARTH BEFORE THE SHIP FELL APART OR RALPH KILLED ONE OF YOU...
"SIX?"
YEAH... YOU, MAYBERRY, SAMMY, THE RALPHS AND ROBERTA! THAT'S SIX!
NO-- RALPHIE AND ROBERTA JOINED US AFTER WE GOT TO EARTH...
REMEMBER? ROBERTA WAS MAROONED ON EARTH BY THE GRAISE AND RALPHIE WAS CREATED ABOUT SIX MONTHS AFTER WE CRASHED.
STEVE TROOP
FINE. I'M SURPRISED ALL FOUR OF YOU MADE IT TO EARTH...
EXCEPT... WE LEFT MELOTIA WITH A CREW OF FIVE...

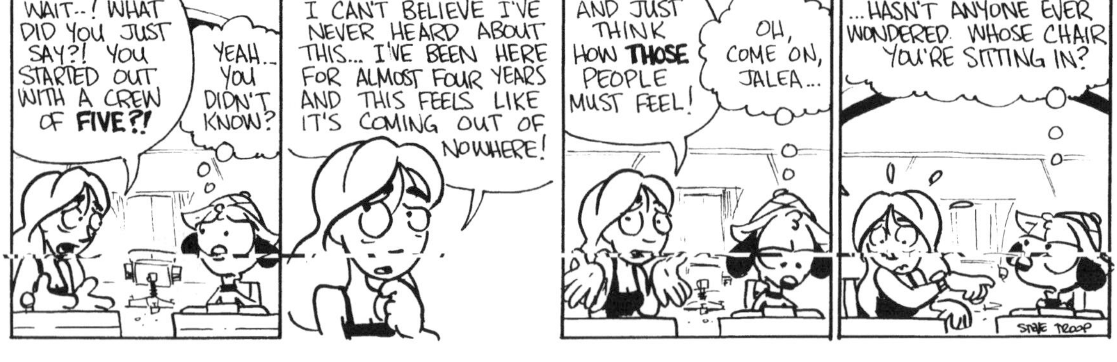
WAIT--! WHAT DID YOU JUST SAY?! YOU STARTED OUT WITH A CREW OF FIVE?!
YEAH... YOU DIDN'T KNOW?
I CAN'T BELIEVE I'VE NEVER HEARD ABOUT THIS... I'VE BEEN HERE FOR ALMOST FOUR YEARS AND THIS FEELS LIKE IT'S COMING OUT OF NOWHERE!
AND JUST THINK HOW THOSE PEOPLE MUST FEEL!
OH, COME ON, JALEA...
...HASN'T ANYONE EVER WONDERED WHOSE CHAIR YOU'RE SITTING IN?
STEVE TROOP

Sam's Novel (TUM I, pages 133–134) was discovered by the rest of the crew when Sam was in his coma (TUM V, pages 48–49).

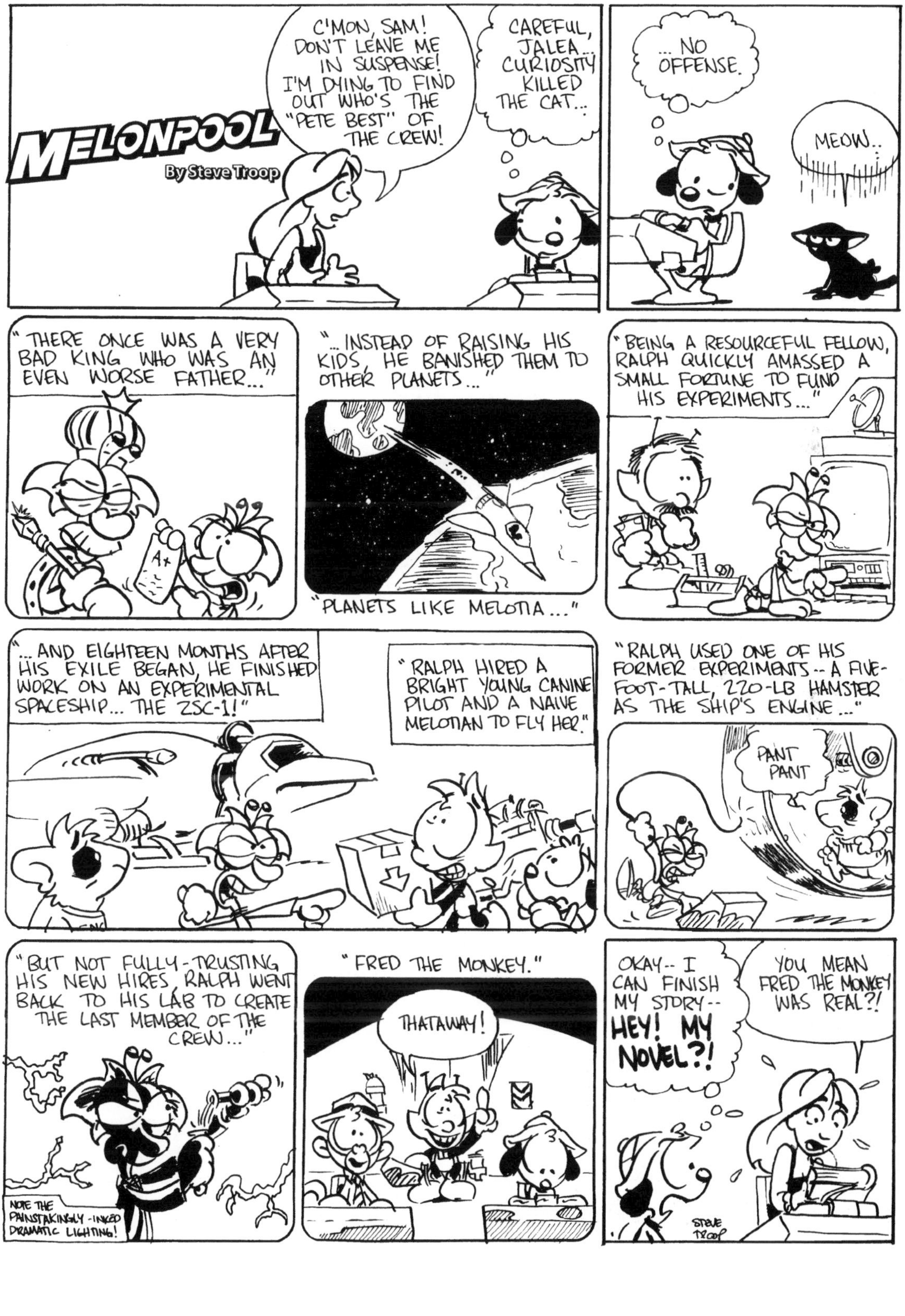
MELONPOOL
By Steve Troop
C'MON, SAM! DON'T LEAVE ME IN SUSPENSE! I'M DYING TO FIND OUT WHO'S THE "PETE BEST" OF THE CREW!
CAREFUL, JALEA... CURIOSITY KILLED THE CAT...
... NO OFFENSE.
MEOW...
"THERE ONCE WAS A VERY BAD KING WHO WAS AN EVEN WORSE FATHER..."
A+
"... INSTEAD OF RAISING HIS KIDS, HE BANISHED THEM TO OTHER PLANETS..."
"PLANETS LIKE MELOTIA..."
"BEING A RESOURCEFUL FELLOW, RALPH QUICKLY AMASSED A SMALL FORTUNE TO FUND HIS EXPERIMENTS..."
"... AND EIGHTEEN MONTHS AFTER HIS EXILE BEGAN, HE FINISHED WORK ON AN EXPERIMENTAL SPACESHIP... THE ZSC-1!"
"RALPH HIRED A BRIGHT YOUNG CANINE PILOT AND A NAIVE MELOTIAN TO FLY HER."
"RALPH USED ONE OF HIS FORMER EXPERIMENTS -- A FIVE-FOOT-TALL, 220-LB HAMSTER AS THE SHIP'S ENGINE..."
PANT PANT
"BUT NOT FULLY-TRUSTING HIS NEW HIRES, RALPH WENT BACK TO HIS LAB TO CREATE THE LAST MEMBER OF THE CREW..."
NOTE THE PAINSTAKINGLY-INKED DRAMATIC LIGHTING!
"FRED THE MONKEY."
THATAWAY!
OKAY-- I CAN FINISH MY STORY-- HEY! MY NOVEL?!
YOU MEAN FRED THE MONKEY WAS REAL?!
STEVE TROOP

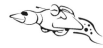

Fred the Monkey was a major character in the *Melonpool* strips I drew in high school in the late '80s. When I revamped the strip in 1996 for the Internet, I decided to eliminate some of the animals to clean house a bit. My semi-evolved simian was cut from the strip, bringing the number of intelligent animals down to a manageable level.

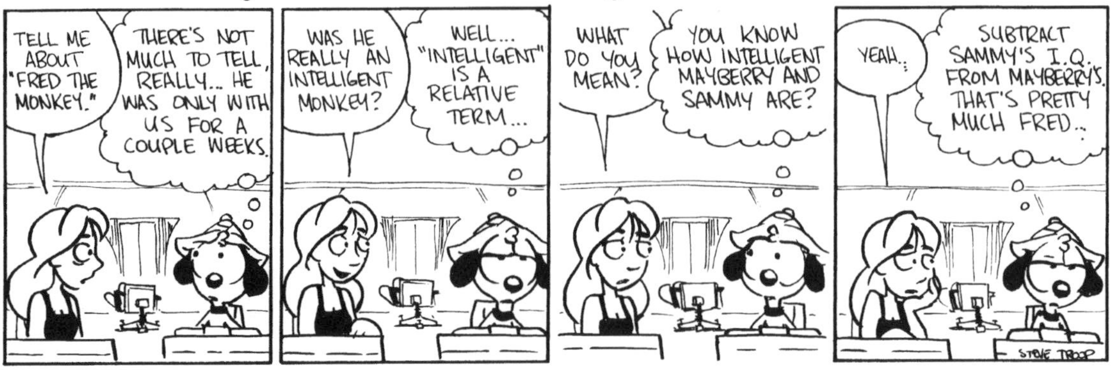
TELL ME ABOUT "FRED THE MONKEY."
THERE'S NOT MUCH TO TELL, REALLY... HE WAS ONLY WITH US FOR A COUPLE WEEKS.
WAS HE REALLY AN INTELLIGENT MONKEY?
WELL... "INTELLIGENT" IS A RELATIVE TERM...
WHAT DO YOU MEAN?
YOU KNOW HOW INTELLIGENT MAYBERRY AND SAMMY ARE?
YEAH...
SUBTRACT SAMMY'S I.Q. FROM MAYBERRY'S. THAT'S PRETTY MUCH FRED...
STEVE TROOP

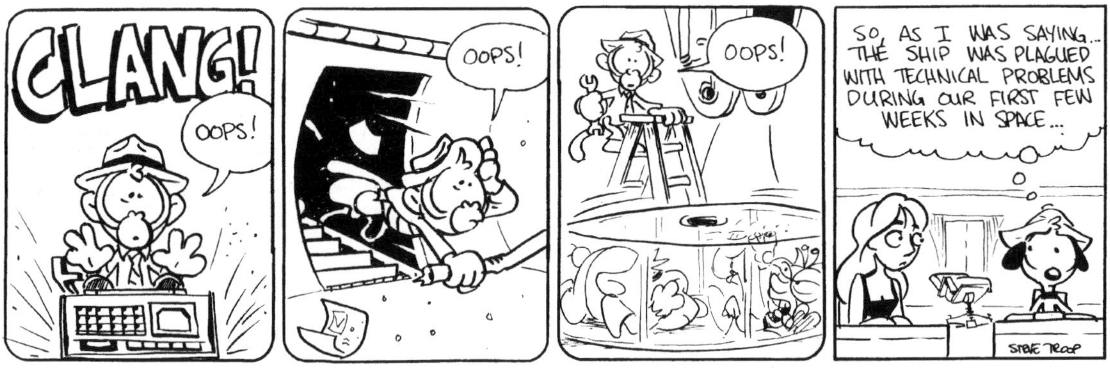
CLANG!
OOPS!
OOPS!
OOPS!
SO, AS I WAS SAYING... THE SHIP WAS PLAGUED WITH TECHNICAL PROBLEMS DURING OUR FIRST FEW WEEKS IN SPACE...
STEVE TROOP

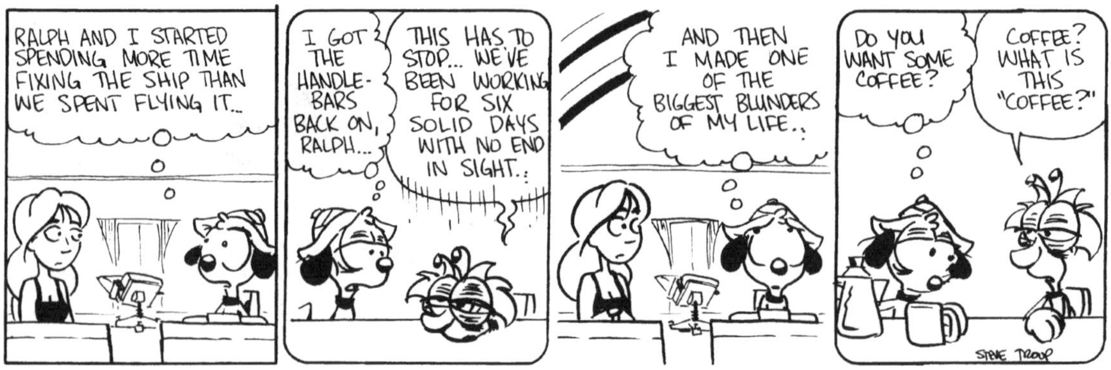
RALPH AND I STARTED SPENDING MORE TIME FIXING THE SHIP THAN WE SPENT FLYING IT...
I GOT THE HANDLE-BARS BACK ON, RALPH...
THIS HAS TO STOP... WE'VE BEEN WORKING FOR SIX SOLID DAYS WITH NO END IN SIGHT...
AND THEN I MADE ONE OF THE BIGGEST BLUNDERS OF MY LIFE...
DO YOU WANT SOME COFFEE?
COFFEE? WHAT IS THIS "COFFEE?"
STEVE TROOP

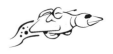

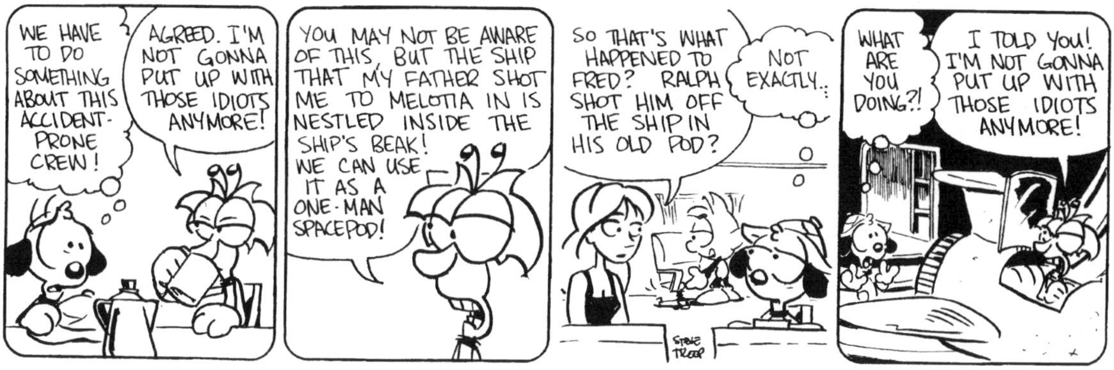
WE HAVE TO DO SOMETHING ABOUT THIS ACCIDENT-PRONE CREW!
AGREED. I'M NOT GONNA PUT UP WITH THOSE IDIOTS ANYMORE!
YOU MAY NOT BE AWARE OF THIS, BUT THE SHIP THAT MY FATHER SHOT ME TO MELOTIA IN IS NESTLED INSIDE THE SHIP'S BEAK! WE CAN USE IT AS A ONE-MAN SPACEPOD!
SO THAT'S WHAT HAPPENED TO FRED? RALPH SHOT HIM OFF THE SHIP IN HIS OLD POD?
NOT EXACTLY...
STEVE TROOP
WHAT ARE YOU DOING?!
I TOLD YOU! I'M NOT GONNA PUT UP WITH THOSE IDIOTS ANYMORE!

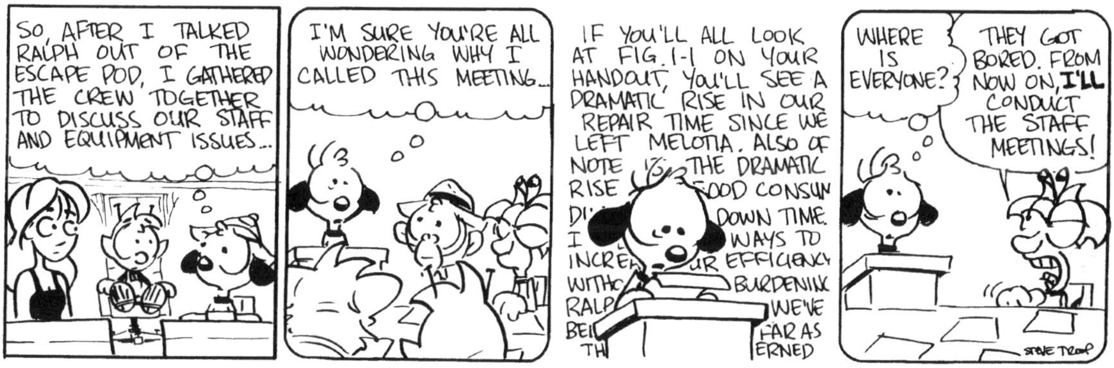
SO, AFTER I TALKED RALPH OUT OF THE ESCAPE POD, I GATHERED THE CREW TOGETHER TO DISCUSS OUR STAFF AND EQUIPMENT ISSUES...
I'M SURE YOU'RE ALL WONDERING WHY I CALLED THIS MEETING...
IF YOU'LL ALL LOOK AT FIG. 1-1 ON YOUR HANDOUT, YOU'LL SEE A DRAMATIC RISE IN OUR REPAIR TIME SINCE WE LEFT MELOTIA. ALSO OF NOTE
THE DRAMATIC
RISE
OOD CONSUM
DOWN TIME.
WAYS TO
EFFICIENCY
BURDENING
WE'VE
FAR AS
ERNED
WHERE IS EVERYONE?
THEY GOT BORED. FROM NOW ON, **I'LL** CONDUCT THE STAFF MEETINGS!
STEVE TROOP

Around this time, cartoonist David McGuire came up with an interesting theory that Sam might not be the intelligent historian with all the common sense. And I quote:

```
> I think Sam's a mutant and a liar.
```

Well, he's no mutant. No comment on the rest.

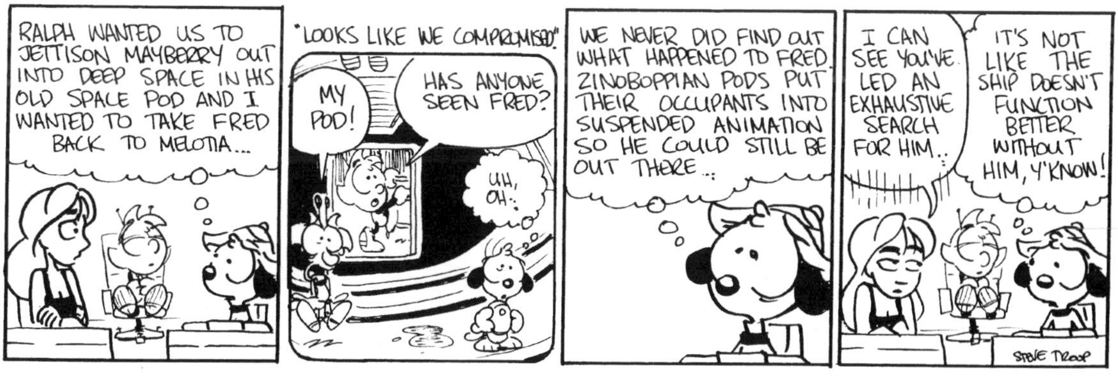
RALPH WANTED US TO JETTISON MAYBERRY OUT INTO DEEP SPACE IN HIS OLD SPACE POD AND I WANTED TO TAKE FRED BACK TO MELOTIA...
"LOOKS LIKE WE COMPROMISED."
MY POD!
HAS ANYONE SEEN FRED?
UH, OH...
WE NEVER DID FIND OUT WHAT HAPPENED TO FRED. ZINOBOPPIAN PODS PUT THEIR OCCUPANTS INTO SUSPENDED ANIMATION SO HE COULD STILL BE OUT THERE...
I CAN SEE YOU'VE LED AN EXHAUSTIVE SEARCH FOR HIM...
IT'S NOT LIKE THE SHIP DOESN'T FUNCTION BETTER WITHOUT HIM, Y'KNOW!
STEVE TROOP

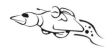

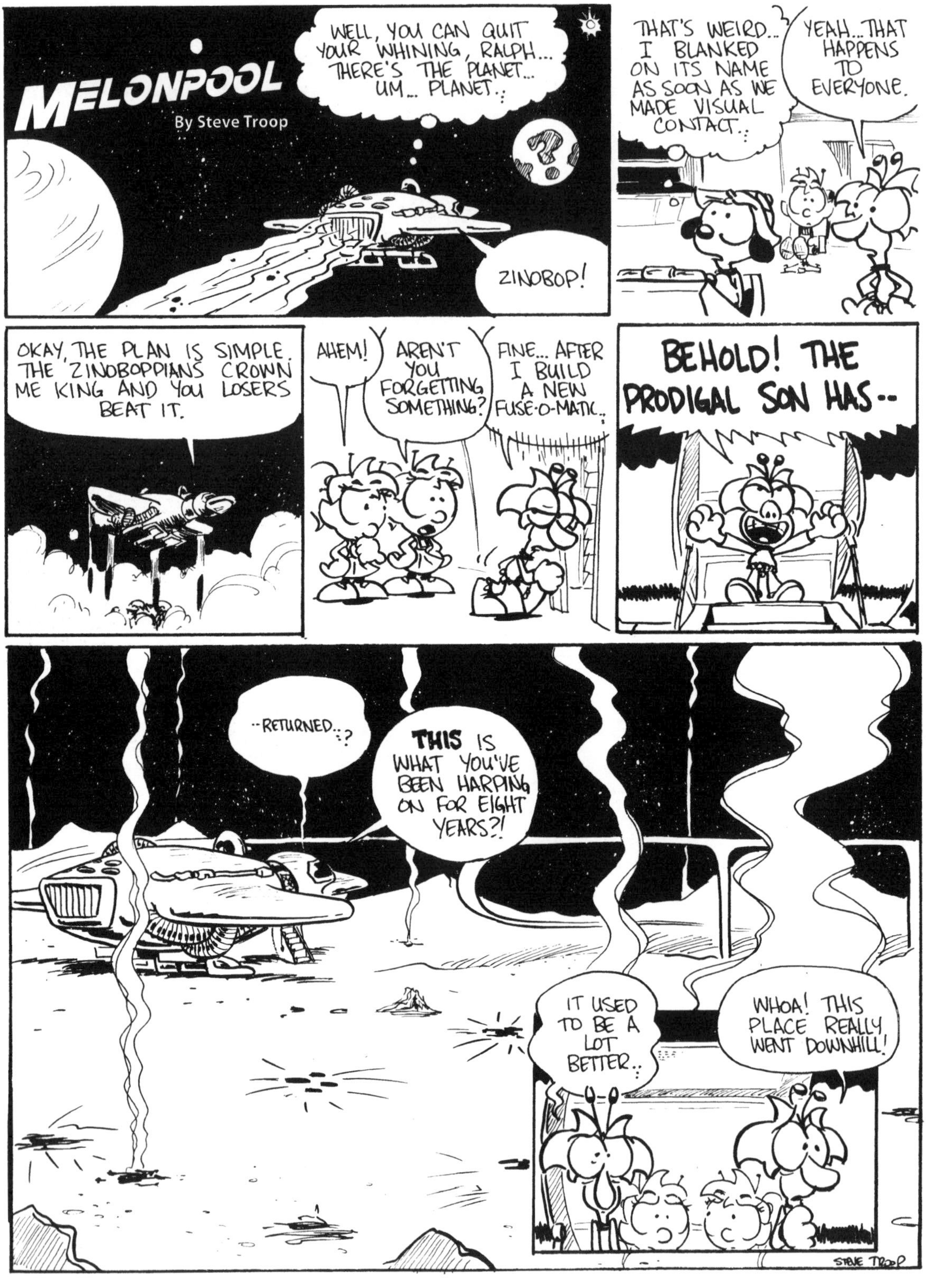
MELONPOOL
By Steve Troop
WELL, YOU CAN QUIT YOUR WHINING, RALPH... THERE'S THE PLANET... UM... PLANET...
ZINOBOP!
THAT'S WEIRD... I BLANKED ON ITS NAME AS SOON AS WE MADE VISUAL CONTACT...
YEAH... THAT HAPPENS TO EVERYONE.
OKAY, THE PLAN IS SIMPLE. THE ZINOBOPPIANS CROWN ME KING AND YOU LOSERS BEAT IT.
AHEM!
AREN'T YOU FORGETTING SOMETHING?
FINE... AFTER I BUILD A NEW FUSE-O-MATIC...
BEHOLD! THE PRODIGAL SON HAS--
--RETURNED...?
THIS IS WHAT YOU'VE BEEN HARPING ON FOR EIGHT YEARS?!
IT USED TO BE A LOT BETTER...
WHOA! THIS PLACE REALLY WENT DOWNHILL!
STEVE TROOP

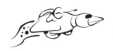

In the first panel, Ralph is making the same weird digging motion that Charlton Heston made when he saw the ruins of the Statue of Liberty at the end of *The Planet of the Apes*.

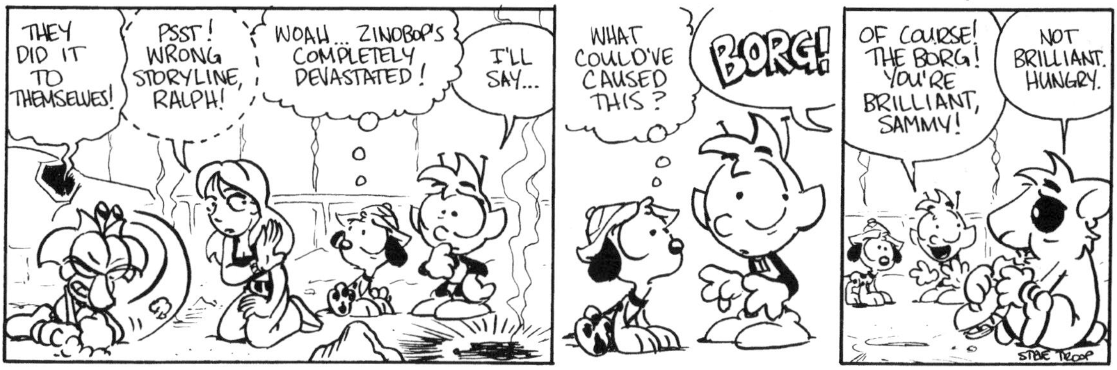
THEY DID IT TO THEMSELVES!
PSST! WRONG STORYLINE, RALPH!
WOAH... ZINOBOP'S COMPLETELY DEVASTATED!
I'LL SAY...
WHAT COULD'VE CAUSED THIS?
BORG!
OF COURSE! THE BORG! YOU'RE BRILLIANT, SAMMY!
NOT BRILLIANT. HUNGRY.

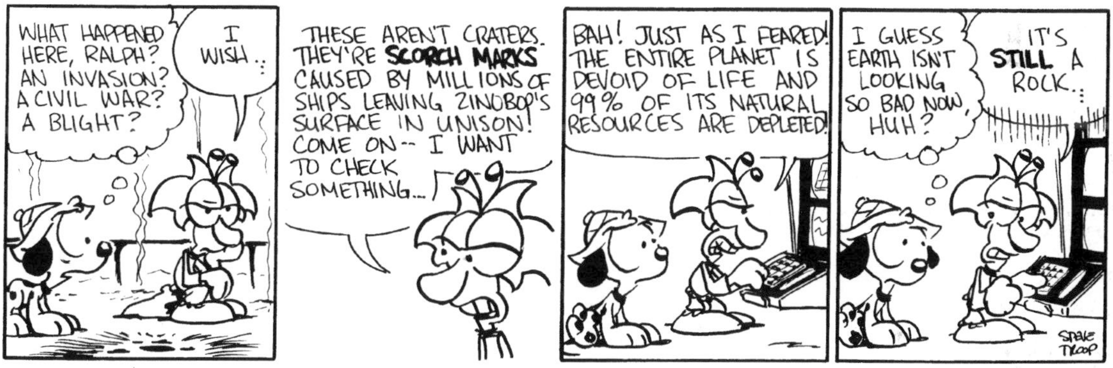
WHAT HAPPENED HERE, RALPH? AN INVASION? A CIVIL WAR? A BLIGHT?
I WISH...
THESE AREN'T CRATERS. THEY'RE SCORCH MARKS CAUSED BY MILLIONS OF SHIPS LEAVING ZINOBOP'S SURFACE IN UNISON! COME ON -- I WANT TO CHECK SOMETHING...
BAH! JUST AS I FEARED! THE ENTIRE PLANET IS DEVOID OF LIFE AND 99% OF ITS NATURAL RESOURCES ARE DEPLETED!
I GUESS EARTH ISN'T LOOKING SO BAD NOW, HUH?
IT'S STILL A ROCK...

When Ralph used Zinoforming to create the *Gilligan's Island* asteroid (See TUM IV, pages 48), he explained that Zinoboppians run through natural resources like other races run through toilet paper. Obviously, I have a habit of paying off the most trivial of throwaway lines. Sam's line in the second panel is a direct lift from an old *Saturday Night Live* sketch with Jane Curtain and Dan Aykroyd.

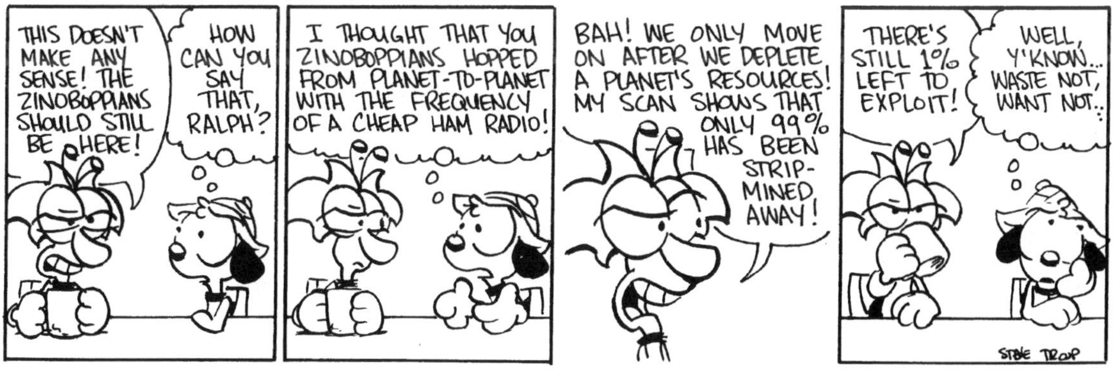
THIS DOESN'T MAKE ANY SENSE! THE ZINOBOPPIANS SHOULD STILL BE HERE!
HOW CAN YOU SAY THAT, RALPH?
I THOUGHT THAT YOU ZINOBOPPIANS HOPPED FROM PLANET-TO-PLANET WITH THE FREQUENCY OF A CHEAP HAM RADIO!
BAH! WE ONLY MOVE ON AFTER WE DEPLETE A PLANET'S RESOURCES! MY SCAN SHOWS THAT ONLY 99% HAS BEEN STRIP-MINED AWAY!
THERE'S STILL 1% LEFT TO EXPLOIT!
WELL, Y'KNOW... WASTE NOT, WANT NOT...

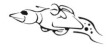

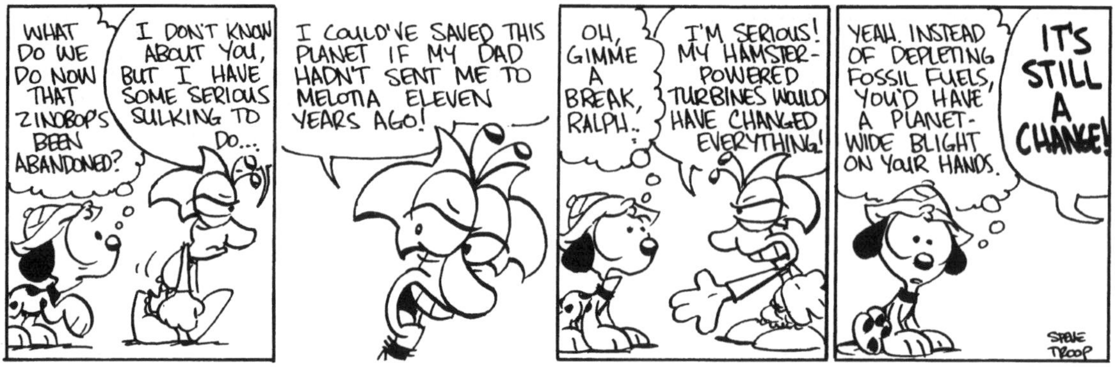
WHAT DO WE DO NOW THAT ZINOBOP'S BEEN ABANDONED?
I DON'T KNOW ABOUT YOU, BUT I HAVE SOME SERIOUS SULKING TO DO...
I COULD'VE SAVED THIS PLANET IF MY DAD HADN'T SENT ME TO MELOTIA ELEVEN YEARS AGO!
OH, GIMME A BREAK, RALPH..
I'M SERIOUS! MY HAMSTER-POWERED TURBINES WOULD HAVE CHANGED EVERYTHING!
YEAH. INSTEAD OF DEPLETING FOSSIL FUELS, YOU'D HAVE A PLANET-WIDE BLIGHT ON YOUR HANDS.
IT'S STILL A CHANGE!
STEVE TROOP

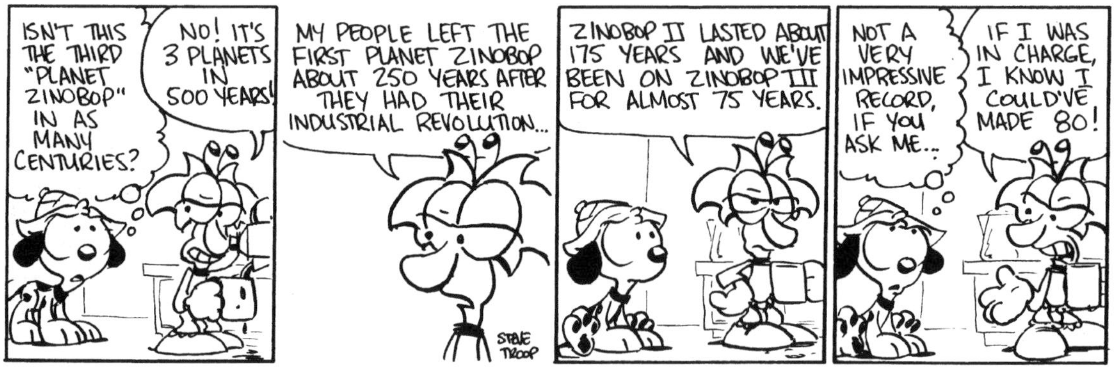
ISN'T THIS THE THIRD "PLANET ZINOBOP" IN AS MANY CENTURIES?
NO! IT'S 3 PLANETS IN 500 YEARS!
MY PEOPLE LEFT THE FIRST PLANET ZINOBOP ABOUT 250 YEARS AFTER THEY HAD THEIR INDUSTRIAL REVOLUTION...
STEVE TROOP
ZINOBOP II LASTED ABOUT 175 YEARS AND WE'VE BEEN ON ZINOBOP III FOR ALMOST 75 YEARS.
NOT A VERY IMPRESSIVE RECORD, IF YOU ASK ME...
IF I WAS IN CHARGE, I KNOW I COULD'VE MADE 80!

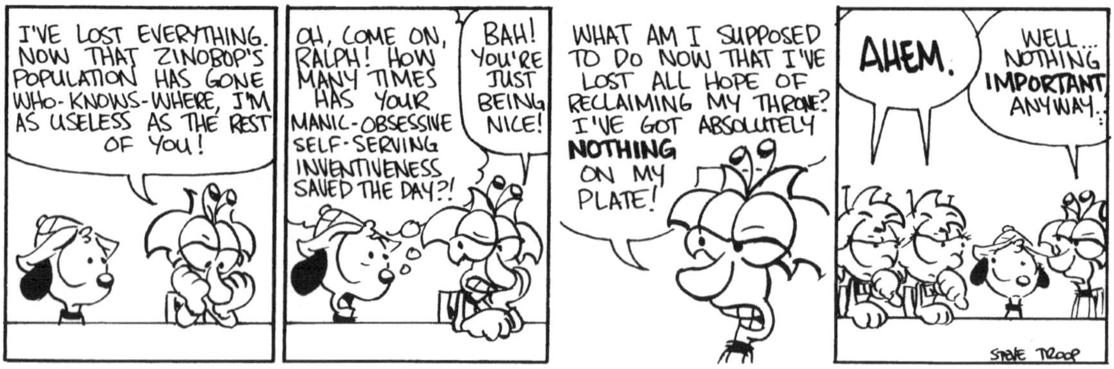
I'VE LOST EVERYTHING. NOW THAT ZINOBOP'S POPULATION HAS GONE WHO-KNOWS-WHERE, I'M AS USELESS AS THE REST OF YOU!
OH, COME ON, RALPH! HOW MANY TIMES HAS YOUR MANIC-OBSESSIVE SELF-SERVING INVENTIVENESS SAVED THE DAY?!
BAH! YOU'RE JUST BEING NICE!
WHAT AM I SUPPOSED TO DO NOW THAT I'VE LOST ALL HOPE OF RECLAIMING MY THRONE? I'VE GOT ABSOLUTELY NOTHING ON MY PLATE!
AHEM.
WELL... NOTHING IMPORTANT, ANYWAY..
STEVE TROOP

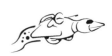

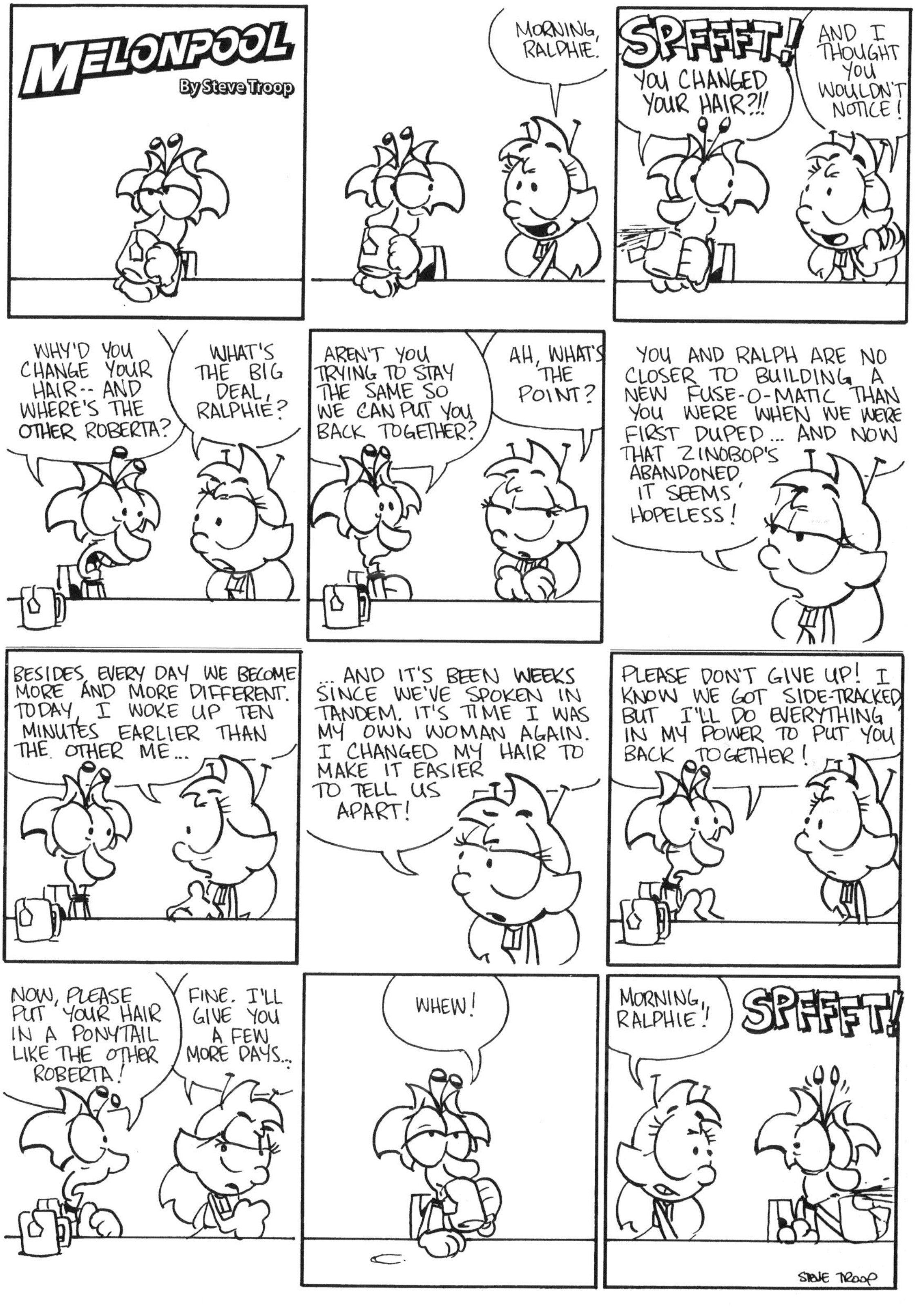
MELONPOOL
By Steve Troop
MORNING, RALPHIE.
SPFFFT!
YOU CHANGED YOUR HAIR?!!
AND I THOUGHT YOU WOULDN'T NOTICE!
WHY'D YOU CHANGE YOUR HAIR-- AND WHERE'S THE OTHER ROBERTA?
WHAT'S THE BIG DEAL, RALPHIE?
AREN'T YOU TRYING TO STAY THE SAME SO WE CAN PUT YOU BACK TOGETHER?
AH, WHAT'S THE POINT?
YOU AND RALPH ARE NO CLOSER TO BUILDING A NEW FUSE-O-MATIC THAN YOU WERE WHEN WE WERE FIRST DUPED... AND NOW THAT ZINOBOP'S ABANDONED IT SEEMS HOPELESS!
BESIDES, EVERY DAY WE BECOME MORE AND MORE DIFFERENT. TODAY, I WOKE UP TEN MINUTES EARLIER THAN THE OTHER ME...
...AND IT'S BEEN WEEKS SINCE WE'VE SPOKEN IN TANDEM. IT'S TIME I WAS MY OWN WOMAN AGAIN. I CHANGED MY HAIR TO MAKE IT EASIER TO TELL US APART!
PLEASE DON'T GIVE UP! I KNOW WE GOT SIDE-TRACKED BUT I'LL DO EVERYTHING IN MY POWER TO PUT YOU BACK TOGETHER!
NOW, PLEASE PUT YOUR HAIR IN A PONYTAIL LIKE THE OTHER ROBERTA!
FINE. I'LL GIVE YOU A FEW MORE DAYS...
WHEW!
MORNING, RALPHIE!
SPFFFT!
STEVE TROOP

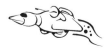

During Melonpool's original eight-year run from 1996–2004, the strip was pretty much the poster child for hiatuses. My worst year was 2001 where I only drew 91 strips. When I came back, I was determined not to have any more of these hiatuses ... with the possible exception of my birthday.

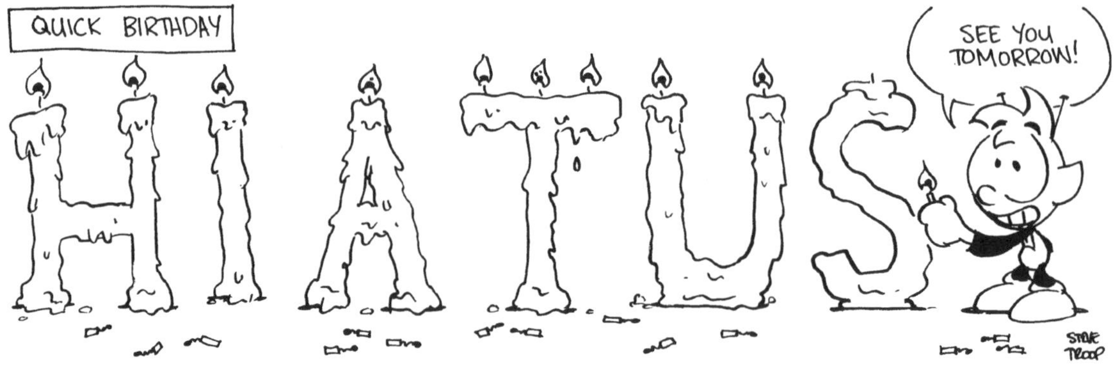
QUICK BIRTHDAY
HIATUS
SEE YOU TOMORROW!
STEVE TROOP

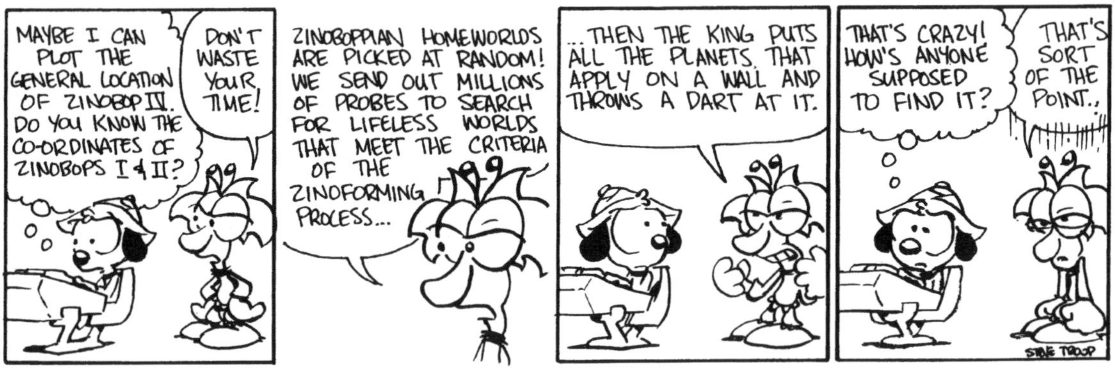
MAYBE I CAN PLOT THE GENERAL LOCATION OF ZINOBOP IV. DO YOU KNOW THE CO-ORDINATES OF ZINOBOPS I & II?
DON'T WASTE YOUR TIME!
ZINOBOPPIAN HOMEWORLDS ARE PICKED AT RANDOM! WE SEND OUT MILLIONS OF PROBES TO SEARCH FOR LIFELESS WORLDS THAT MEET THE CRITERIA OF THE ZINOFORMING PROCESS...
...THEN THE KING PUTS ALL THE PLANETS THAT APPLY ON A WALL AND THROWS A DART AT IT.
THAT'S CRAZY! HOW'S ANYONE SUPPOSED TO FIND IT?
THAT'S SORT OF THE POINT.
STEVE TROOP

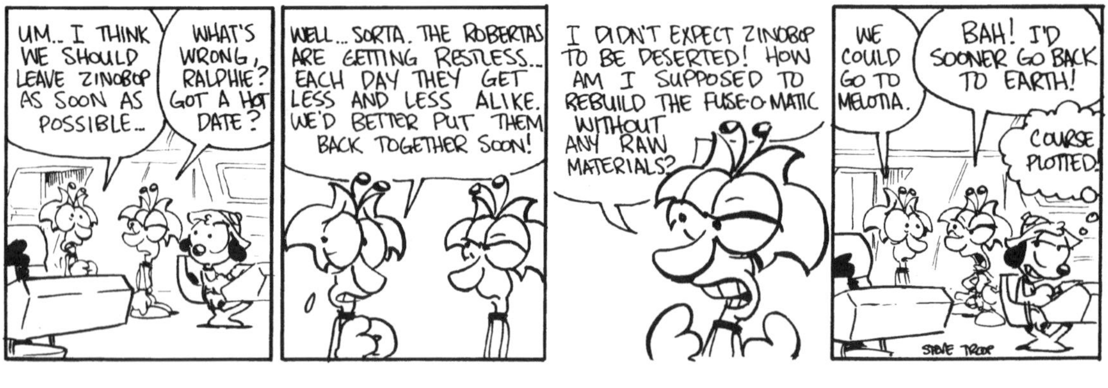
UM.. I THINK WE SHOULD LEAVE ZINOBOP AS SOON AS POSSIBLE..
WHAT'S WRONG, RALPHIE? GOT A HOT DATE?
WELL... SORTA. THE ROBERTAS ARE GETTING RESTLESS.. EACH DAY THEY GET LESS AND LESS ALIKE. WE'D BETTER PUT THEM BACK TOGETHER SOON!
I DIDN'T EXPECT ZINOBOP TO BE DESERTED! HOW AM I SUPPOSED TO REBUILD THE FUSE-O-MATIC WITHOUT ANY RAW MATERIALS?
WE COULD GO TO MELOTIA.
BAH! I'D SOONER GO BACK TO EARTH!
COURSE PLOTTED!
STEVE TROOP

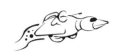

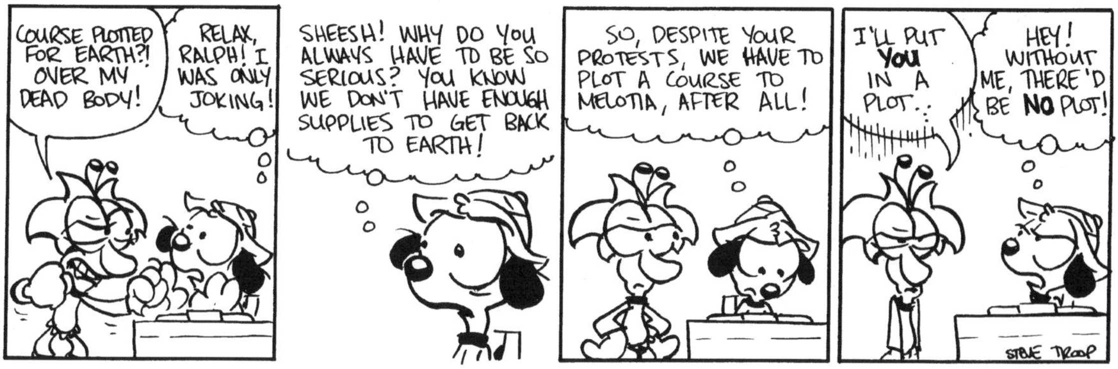
COURSE PLOTTED FOR EARTH?! OVER MY DEAD BODY!
RELAX, RALPH! I WAS ONLY JOKING!
SHEESH! WHY DO YOU ALWAYS HAVE TO BE SO SERIOUS? YOU KNOW WE DON'T HAVE ENOUGH SUPPLIES TO GET BACK TO EARTH!
SO, DESPITE YOUR PROTESTS, WE HAVE TO PLOT A COURSE TO MELOTIA, AFTER ALL!
I'LL PUT **YOU** IN A PLOT...
HEY! WITHOUT ME, THERE'D BE **NO** PLOT!
STEVE TROOP

The only two essential crew positions aboard the Steel Duck are having someone to steer (Sam) and someone to run on the wheel (Sammy). Maybe Ralph wouldn't remind people of how much he didn't need people if he realized that his position wasn't on the list, either.

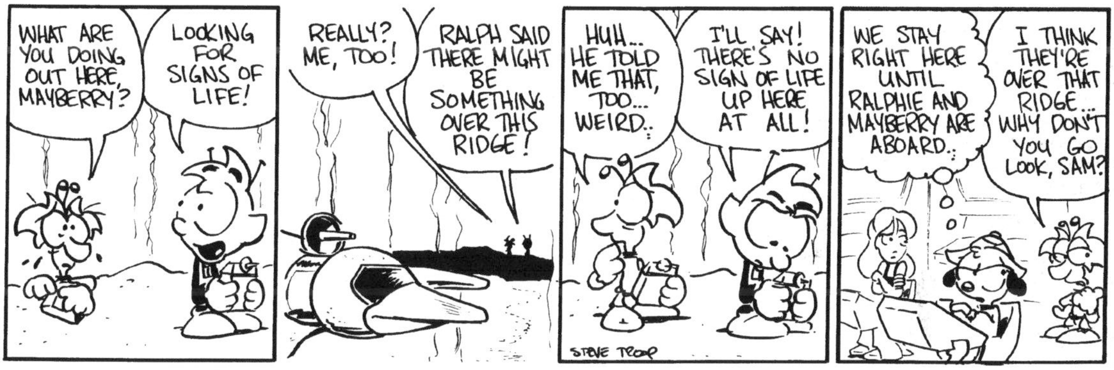
WHAT ARE YOU DOING OUT HERE, MAYBERRY?
LOOKING FOR SIGNS OF LIFE!
REALLY? ME, TOO!
RALPH SAID THERE MIGHT BE SOMETHING OVER THIS RIDGE!
HUH... HE TOLD ME THAT, TOO... WEIRD...
I'LL SAY! THERE'S NO SIGN OF LIFE UP HERE AT ALL!
STEVE TROOP
WE STAY RIGHT HERE UNTIL RALPHIE AND MAYBERRY ARE ABOARD...
I THINK THEY'RE OVER THAT RIDGE... WHY DON'T YOU GO LOOK, SAM?

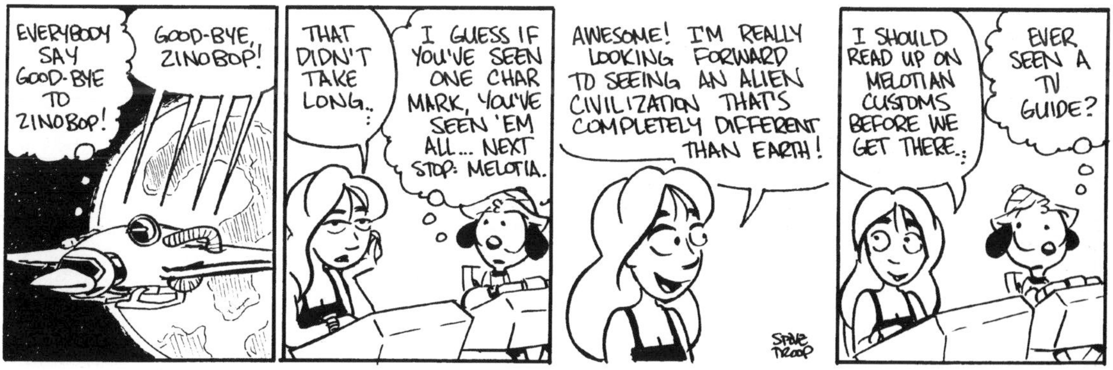
EVERYBODY SAY GOOD-BYE TO ZINOBOP!
GOOD-BYE, ZINOBOP!
THAT DIDN'T TAKE LONG...
I GUESS IF YOU'VE SEEN ONE CHAR MARK, YOU'VE SEEN 'EM ALL... NEXT STOP: MELOTIA.
AWESOME! I'M REALLY LOOKING FORWARD TO SEEING AN ALIEN CIVILIZATION THAT'S COMPLETELY DIFFERENT THAN EARTH!
STEVE TROOP
I SHOULD READ UP ON MELOTIAN CUSTOMS BEFORE WE GET THERE...
EVER SEEN A TV GUIDE?

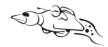

Some readers on the forums began referring to the pigtail Roberta as "Mary Ann Roberta" and the one with her hair down as "Smurfette Roberta." And so did I.

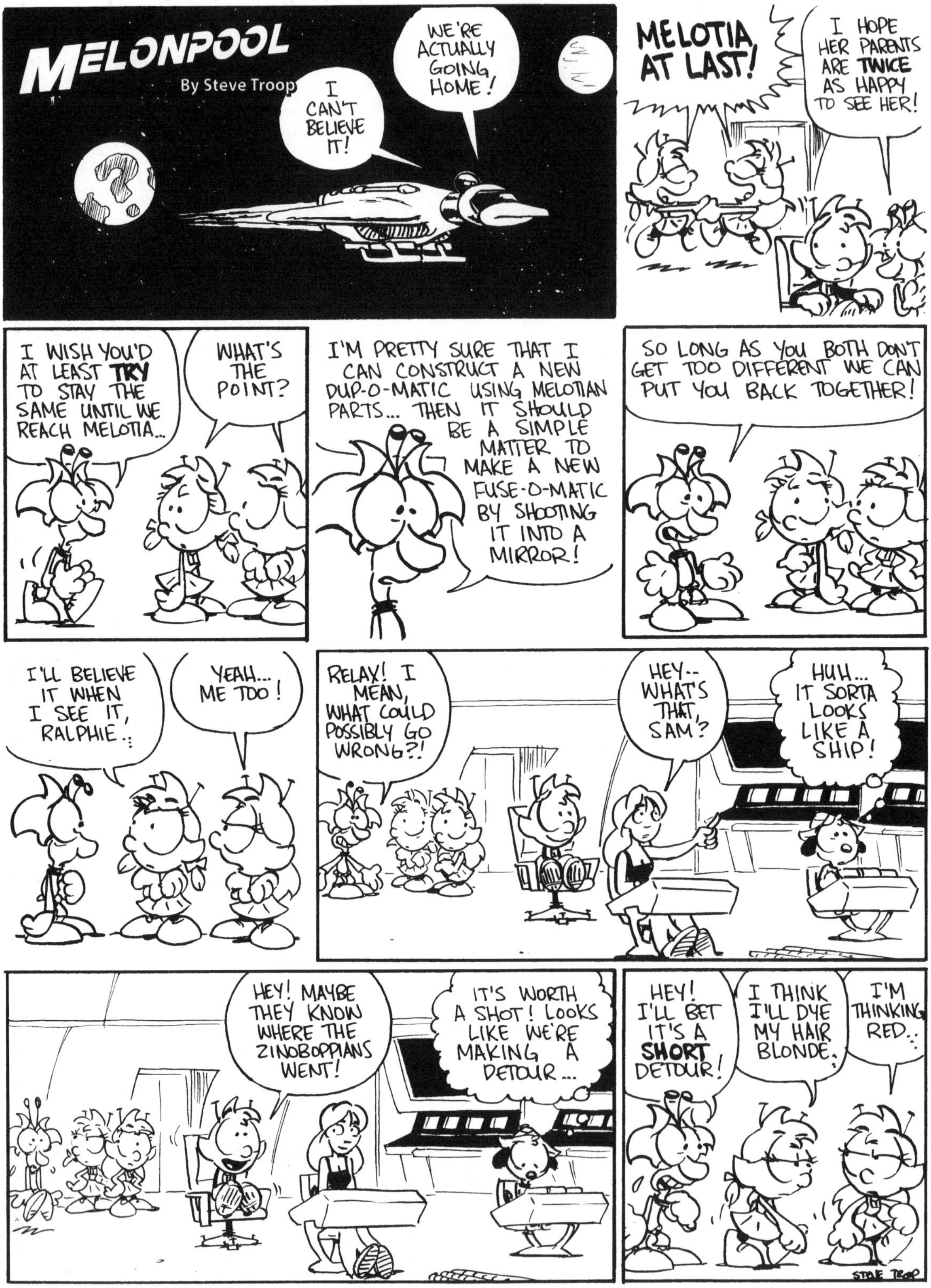
MELONPOOL
By Steve Troop
I CAN'T BELIEVE IT!
WE'RE ACTUALLY GOING HOME!
MELOTIA AT LAST!
I HOPE HER PARENTS ARE TWICE AS HAPPY TO SEE HER!
I WISH YOU'D AT LEAST TRY TO STAY THE SAME UNTIL WE REACH MELOTIA...
WHAT'S THE POINT?
I'M PRETTY SURE THAT I CAN CONSTRUCT A NEW DUP-O-MATIC USING MELOTIAN PARTS... THEN IT SHOULD BE A SIMPLE MATTER TO MAKE A NEW FUSE-O-MATIC BY SHOOTING IT INTO A MIRROR!
SO LONG AS YOU BOTH DON'T GET TOO DIFFERENT WE CAN PUT YOU BACK TOGETHER!
I'LL BELIEVE IT WHEN I SEE IT, RALPHIE...
YEAH... ME TOO!
RELAX! I MEAN, WHAT COULD POSSIBLY GO WRONG?!
HEY-- WHAT'S THAT, SAM?
HUH... IT SORTA LOOKS LIKE A SHIP!
HEY! MAYBE THEY KNOW WHERE THE ZINOBOPPIANS WENT!
IT'S WORTH A SHOT! LOOKS LIKE WE'RE MAKING A DETOUR...
HEY! I'LL BET IT'S A SHORT DETOUR!
I THINK I'LL DYE MY HAIR BLONDE...
I'M THINKING RED...
STEVE TROOP

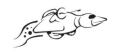

I struggled to come up with the design for the other ship featured in this storyline. After countless attempts, I showed what I was working on to Chris Calvert, a co-worker of mine at the time, and he suggested that I base it on a familiar shape. I won't spoil it for those of you reading this for the first time, but I was a little leery of the design, so I posted a preview on the *Melonpool* forums to see if anyone recognized it. No one did, but the ship was soon dubbed "the rat ship."

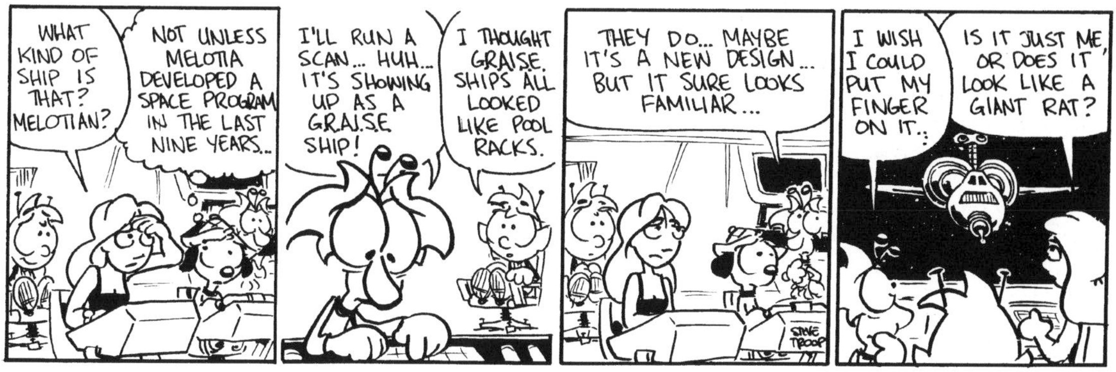

WHAT KIND OF SHIP IS THAT? MELOTIAN?
NOT UNLESS MELOTIA DEVELOPED A SPACE PROGRAM IN THE LAST NINE YEARS...
I'LL RUN A SCAN... HUH... IT'S SHOWING UP AS A G.R.A.I.S.E. SHIP!
I THOUGHT G.R.A.I.S.E. SHIPS ALL LOOKED LIKE POOL RACKS.
THEY DO... MAYBE IT'S A NEW DESIGN... BUT IT SURE LOOKS FAMILIAR...
I WISH I COULD PUT MY FINGER ON IT...
IS IT JUST ME, OR DOES IT LOOK LIKE A GIANT RAT?
STEVE TROOP

"Don't Hate Me, Because I'm Beautiful" was Jalea's hit song back when she was a robotic pop singer on Earth (see TUM III, pages iii, 91).

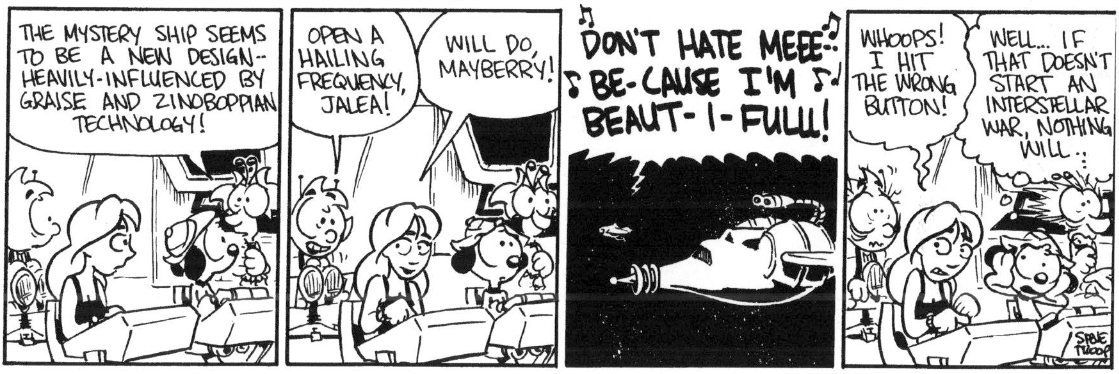

THE MYSTERY SHIP SEEMS TO BE A NEW DESIGN-- HEAVILY-INFLUENCED BY GRAISE AND ZINOBOPPIAN TECHNOLOGY!
OPEN A HAILING FREQUENCY, JALEA!
WILL DO, MAYBERRY!
DON'T HATE MEEE BE-CAUSE I'M BEAUT-I-FULL!
WHOOPS! I HIT THE WRONG BUTTON!
WELL... IF THAT DOESN'T START AN INTERSTELLAR WAR, NOTHING WILL...
STEVE TROOP

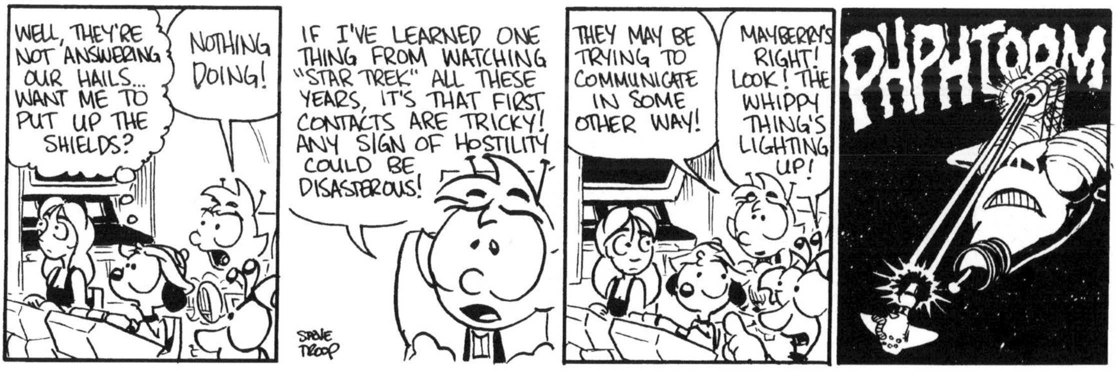

WELL, THEY'RE NOT ANSWERING OUR HAILS... WANT ME TO PUT UP THE SHIELDS?
NOTHING DOING!
IF I'VE LEARNED ONE THING FROM WATCHING "STAR TREK" ALL THESE YEARS, IT'S THAT FIRST CONTACTS ARE TRICKY! ANY SIGN OF HOSTILITY COULD BE DISASTEROUS!
STEVE TROOP
THEY MAY BE TRYING TO COMMUNICATE IN SOME OTHER WAY!
MAYBERRY'S RIGHT! LOOK! THE WHIPPY THING'S LIGHTING UP!
PHPHTOOM

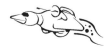

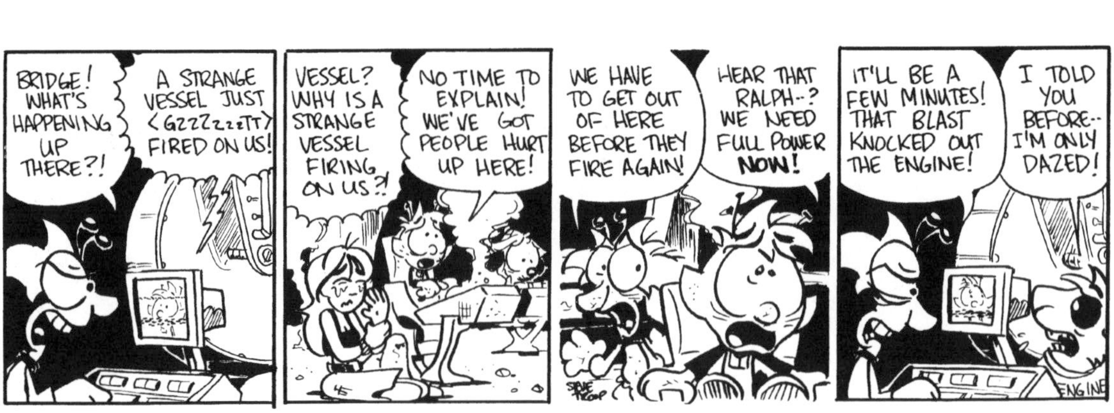
BRIDGE! WHAT'S HAPPENING UP THERE?!
A STRANGE VESSEL JUST <GZZZzzzTT> FIRED ON US!
VESSEL? WHY IS A STRANGE VESSEL FIRING ON US?!
NO TIME TO EXPLAIN! WE'VE GOT PEOPLE HURT UP HERE!
WE HAVE TO GET OUT OF HERE BEFORE THEY FIRE AGAIN!
HEAR THAT RALPH--? WE NEED FULL POWER NOW!
STEVE TROOP
IT'LL BE A FEW MINUTES! THAT BLAST KNOCKED OUT THE ENGINE!
I TOLD YOU BEFORE-- I'M ONLY DAZED!
ENGINE

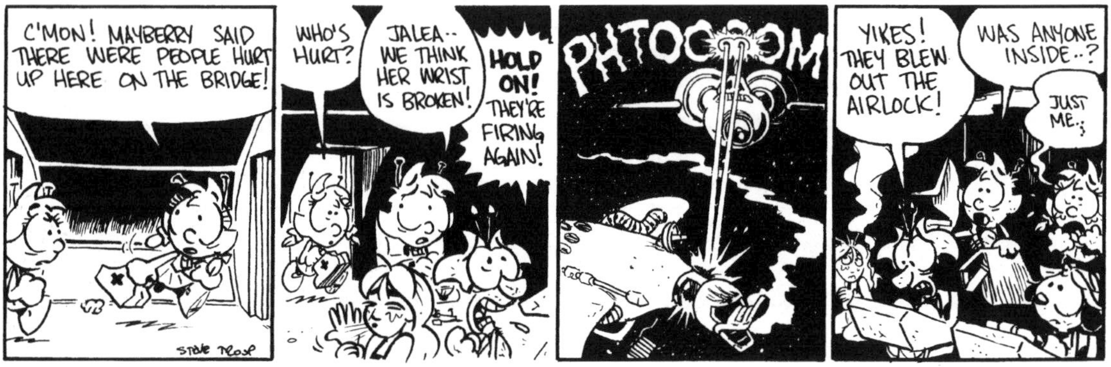
C'MON! MAYBERRY SAID THERE WERE PEOPLE HURT UP HERE ON THE BRIDGE!
STEVE TROOP
WHO'S HURT?
JALEA-- WE THINK HER WRIST IS BROKEN!
HOLD ON! THEY'RE FIRING AGAIN!
PHTOOOOM
YIKES! THEY BLEW OUT THE AIRLOCK!
WAS ANYONE INSIDE--?
JUST ME..;

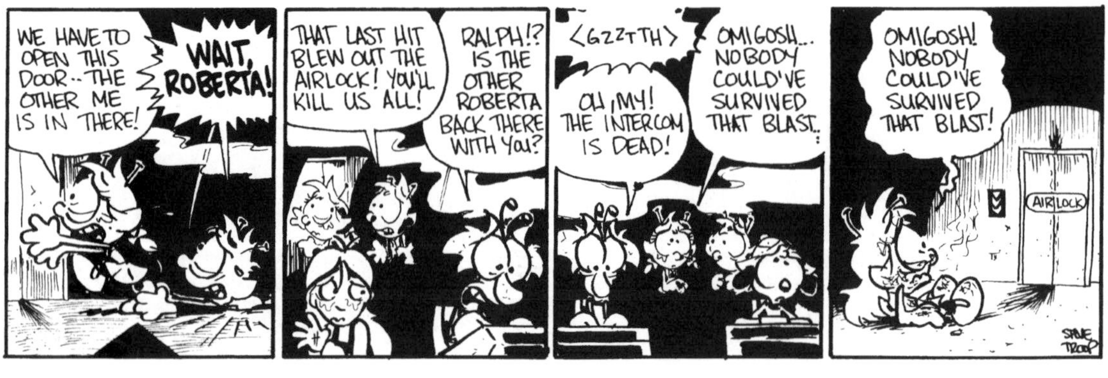
WE HAVE TO OPEN THIS DOOR--THE OTHER ME IS IN THERE!
WAIT, ROBERTA!
THAT LAST HIT BLEW OUT THE AIRLOCK! YOU'LL KILL US ALL!
RALPH!? IS THE OTHER ROBERTA BACK THERE WITH YOU?
<GZZTTH>
OH, MY! THE INTERCOM IS DEAD!
OMIGOSH... NOBODY COULD'VE SURVIVED THAT BLAST..
OMIGOSH! NOBODY COULD'VE SURVIVED THAT BLAST!
AIRLOCK
STEVE TROOP

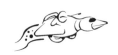

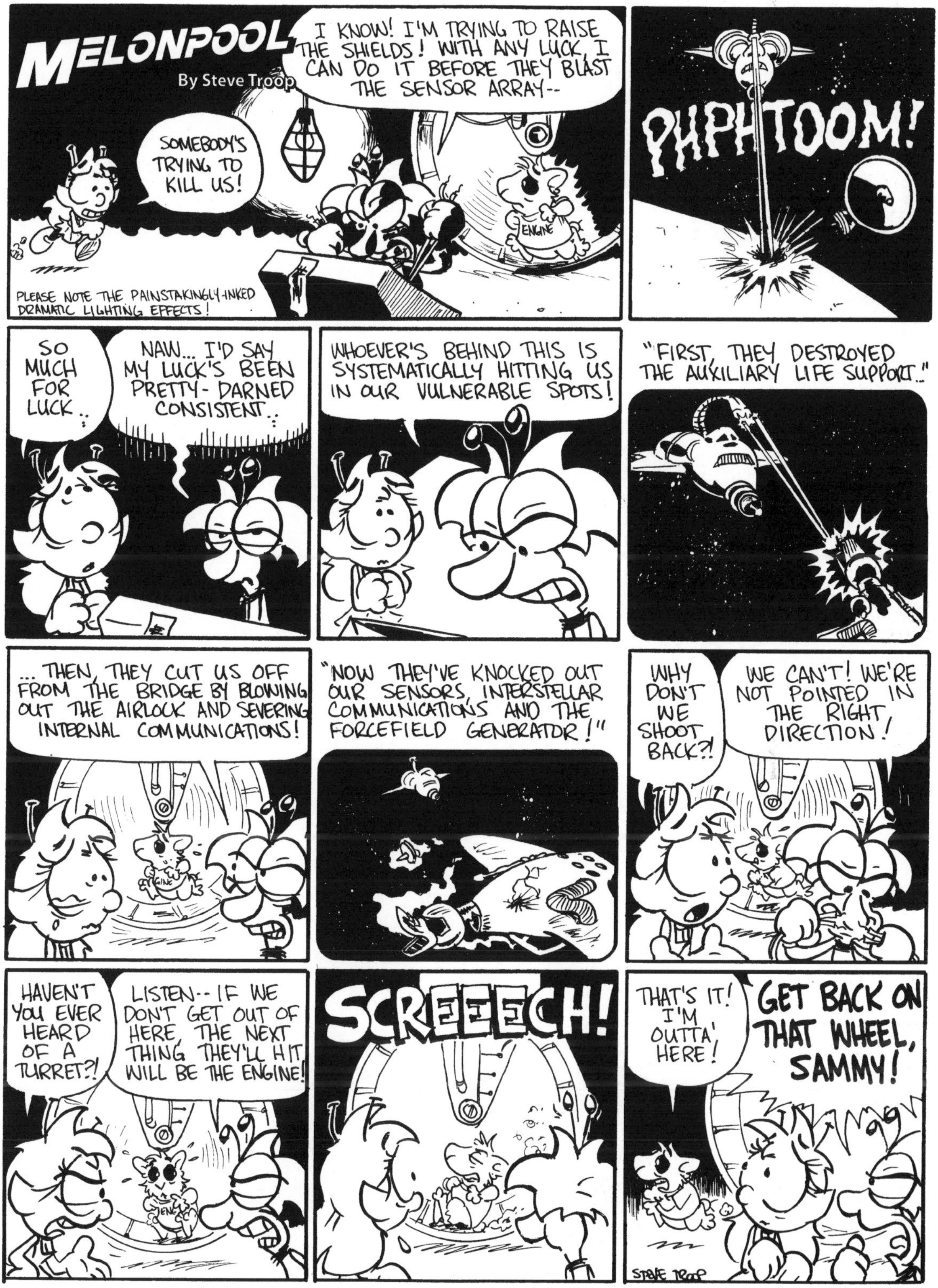
MELONPOOL
By Steve Troop
SOMEBODY'S TRYING TO KILL US!
I KNOW! I'M TRYING TO RAISE THE SHIELDS! WITH ANY LUCK, I CAN DO IT BEFORE THEY BLAST THE SENSOR ARRAY--
ENGINE
PLEASE NOTE THE PAINSTAKINGLY-INKED DRAMATIC LIGHTING EFFECTS!
PHPHTOOM!
SO MUCH FOR LUCK...
NAW... I'D SAY MY LUCK'S BEEN PRETTY-DARNED CONSISTENT...
WHOEVER'S BEHIND THIS IS SYSTEMATICALLY HITTING US IN OUR VULNERABLE SPOTS!
"FIRST, THEY DESTROYED THE AUXILIARY LIFE SUPPORT..."
...THEN, THEY CUT US OFF FROM THE BRIDGE BY BLOWING OUT THE AIRLOCK AND SEVERING INTERNAL COMMUNICATIONS!
"NOW THEY'VE KNOCKED OUT OUR SENSORS, INTERSTELLAR COMMUNICATIONS AND THE FORCEFIELD GENERATOR!"
WHY DON'T WE SHOOT BACK?!
WE CAN'T! WE'RE NOT POINTED IN THE RIGHT DIRECTION!
HAVEN'T YOU EVER HEARD OF A TURRET?!
LISTEN--IF WE DON'T GET OUT OF HERE, THE NEXT THING THEY'LL HIT WILL BE THE ENGINE!
SCREEECH!
THAT'S IT! I'M OUTTA' HERE!
GET BACK ON THAT WHEEL, SAMMY!
STEVE TROOP

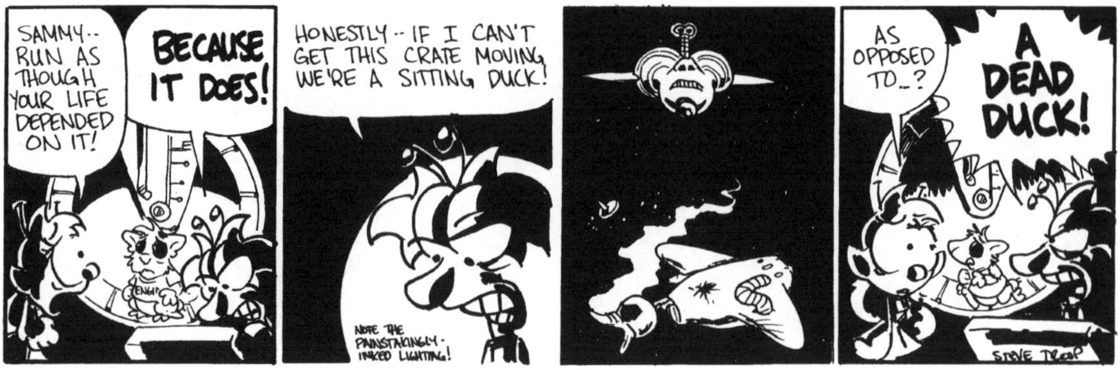
SAMMY.. RUN AS THOUGH YOUR LIFE DEPENDED ON IT!
BECAUSE IT DOES!
HONESTLY.. IF I CAN'T GET THIS CRATE MOVING WE'RE A SITTING DUCK!
NOTE THE PAINSTAKINGLY-INKED LIGHTING!
AS OPPOSED TO...?
A DEAD DUCK!
STEVE TROOP

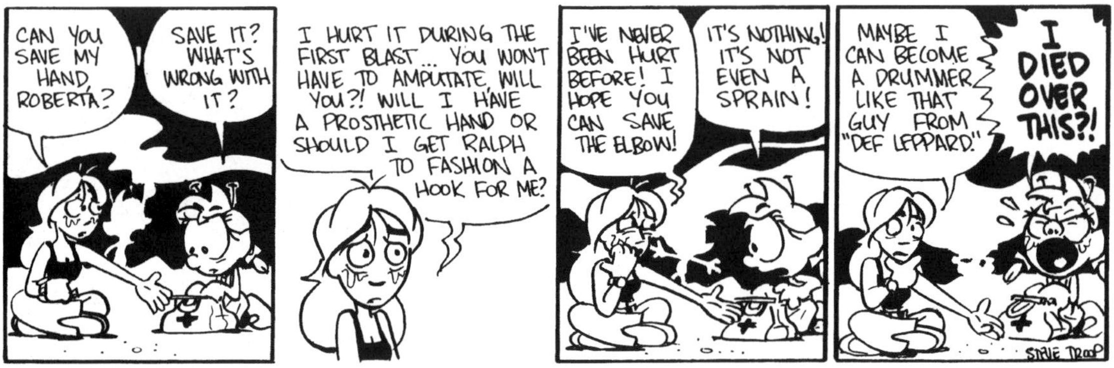
CAN YOU SAVE MY HAND, ROBERTA?
SAVE IT? WHAT'S WRONG WITH IT?
I HURT IT DURING THE FIRST BLAST... YOU WON'T HAVE TO AMPUTATE, WILL YOU?! WILL I HAVE A PROSTHETIC HAND OR SHOULD I GET RALPH TO FASHION A HOOK FOR ME?
I'VE NEVER BEEN HURT BEFORE! I HOPE YOU CAN SAVE THE ELBOW!
IT'S NOTHING! IT'S NOT EVEN A SPRAIN!
MAYBE I CAN BECOME A DRUMMER LIKE THAT GUY FROM "DEF LEPPARD."
I DIED OVER THIS?!
STEVE TROOP

If you're wondering why I haven't been commenting on the last few pages of strips—it's because I'm as wrapped up in the drama as you are! Why did I stop drawing this strip again?

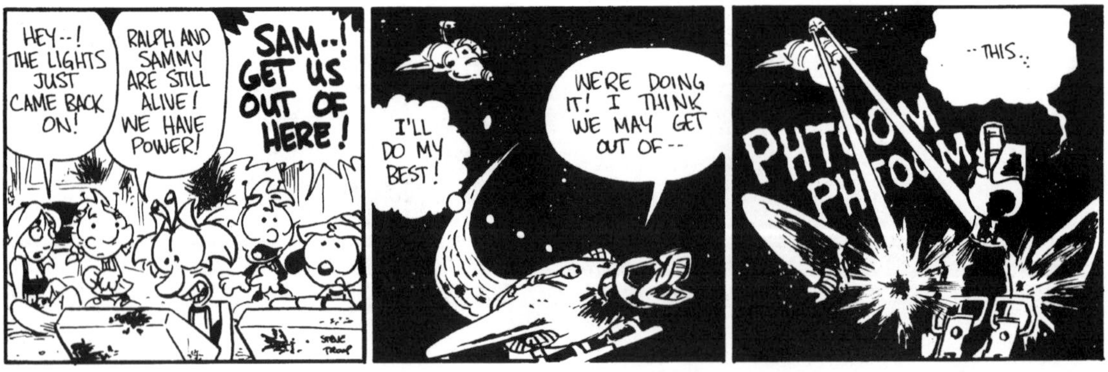
HEY..! THE LIGHTS JUST CAME BACK ON!
RALPH AND SAMMY ARE STILL ALIVE! WE HAVE POWER!
SAM..! GET US OUT OF HERE!
STEVE TROOP
I'LL DO MY BEST!
WE'RE DOING IT! I THINK WE MAY GET OUT OF --
..THIS..
PHTOOM
PHTOOM

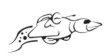

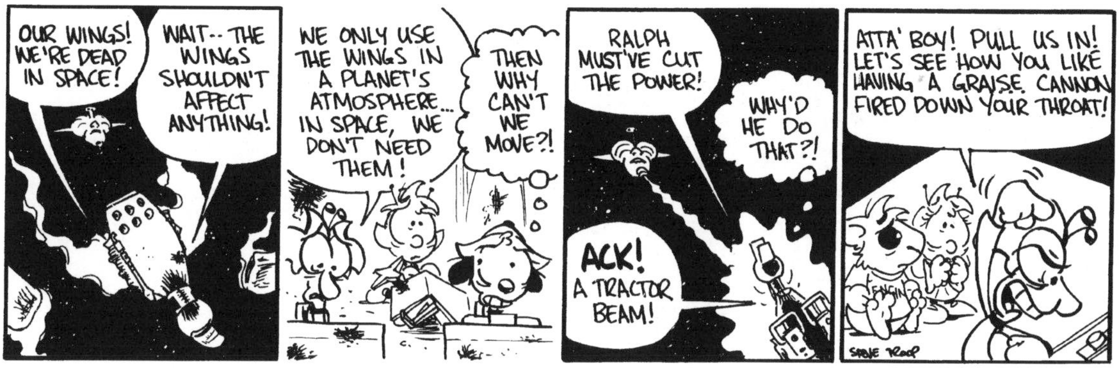
OUR WINGS! WE'RE DEAD IN SPACE!
WAIT-- THE WINGS SHOULDN'T AFFECT ANYTHING!
WE ONLY USE THE WINGS IN A PLANET'S ATMOSPHERE... IN SPACE, WE DON'T NEED THEM!
THEN WHY CAN'T WE MOVE?!
RALPH MUST'VE CUT THE POWER!
WHY'D HE DO THAT?!
ACK! A TRACTOR BEAM!
ATTA' BOY! PULL US IN! LET'S SEE HOW YOU LIKE HAVING A GRAISE CANNON FIRED DOWN YOUR THROAT!
FENGIN
STEVE TROOP

Ralph installed an upgraded GRAISE cannon when he rebuilt the *Steel Duck* aboard the abandoned GRAISE ship near Earth (see TUM V, pages 65–77). This is only the second time he's fired it though. The first time was to help out the cast of *It's Walky* during David Willis's action-packed finale (see TUM V, pages 112–114).

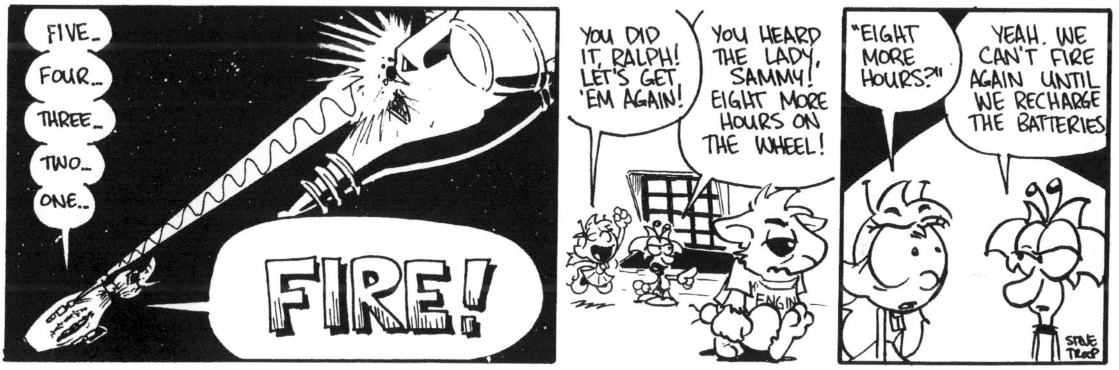
FIVE..
FOUR..
THREE..
TWO..
ONE..
FIRE!
YOU DID IT, RALPH! LET'S GET 'EM AGAIN!
YOU HEARD THE LADY, SAMMY! EIGHT MORE HOURS ON THE WHEEL!
FENGIN
"EIGHT MORE HOURS?"
YEAH. WE CAN'T FIRE AGAIN UNTIL WE RECHARGE THE BATTERIES
STEVE TROOP

Still think the enemy ship looks like a rat? It never will again!

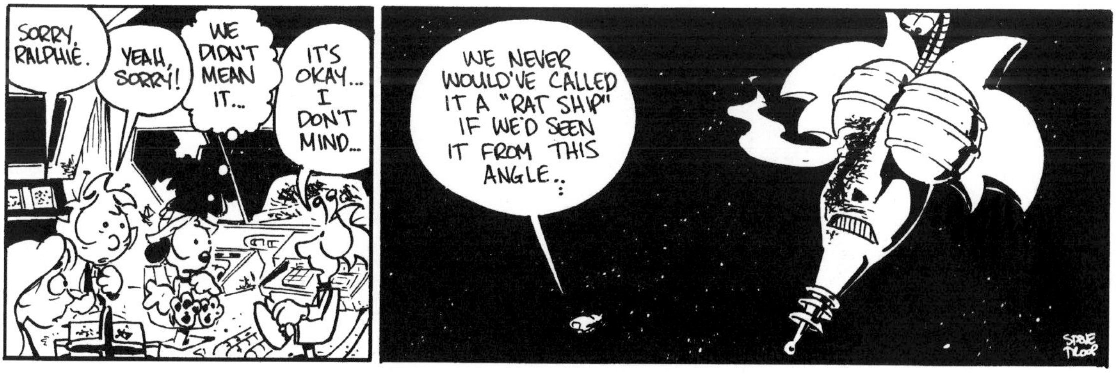
SORRY, RALPHIE.
YEAH, SORRY!
WE DIDN'T MEAN IT...
IT'S OKAY... I DON'T MIND...
WE NEVER WOULD'VE CALLED IT A "RAT SHIP" IF WE'D SEEN IT FROM THIS ANGLE..
STEVE TROOP

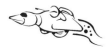

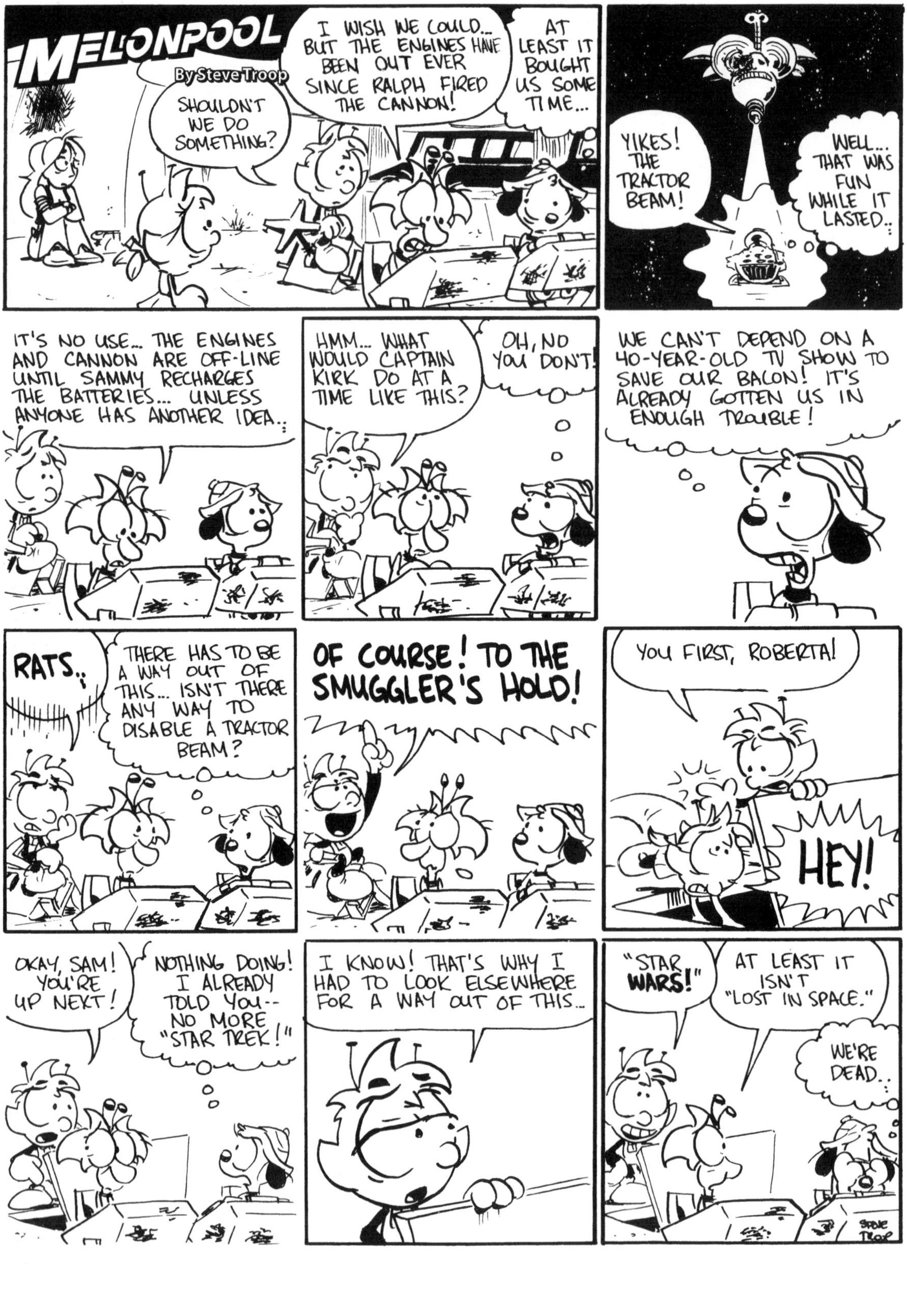
MELONPOOL
By Steve Troop
SHOULDN'T WE DO SOMETHING?
I WISH WE COULD... BUT THE ENGINES HAVE BEEN OUT EVER SINCE RALPH FIRED THE CANNON!
AT LEAST IT BOUGHT US SOME TIME...
YIKES! THE TRACTOR BEAM!
WELL... THAT WAS FUN WHILE IT LASTED..:
IT'S NO USE... THE ENGINES AND CANNON ARE OFF-LINE UNTIL SAMMY RECHARGES THE BATTERIES... UNLESS ANYONE HAS ANOTHER IDEA..:
HMM... WHAT WOULD CAPTAIN KIRK DO AT A TIME LIKE THIS?
OH, NO YOU DON'T!
WE CAN'T DEPEND ON A 40-YEAR-OLD TV SHOW TO SAVE OUR BACON! IT'S ALREADY GOTTEN US IN ENOUGH TROUBLE!
RATS..:
THERE HAS TO BE A WAY OUT OF THIS... ISN'T THERE ANY WAY TO DISABLE A TRACTOR BEAM?
OF COURSE! TO THE SMUGGLER'S HOLD!
YOU FIRST, ROBERTA!
HEY!
OKAY, SAM! YOU'RE UP NEXT!
NOTHING DOING! I ALREADY TOLD YOU-- NO MORE "STAR TREK!"
I KNOW! THAT'S WHY I HAD TO LOOK ELSEWHERE FOR A WAY OUT OF THIS...
"STAR WARS!"
AT LEAST IT ISN'T "LOST IN SPACE."
WE'RE DEAD..:

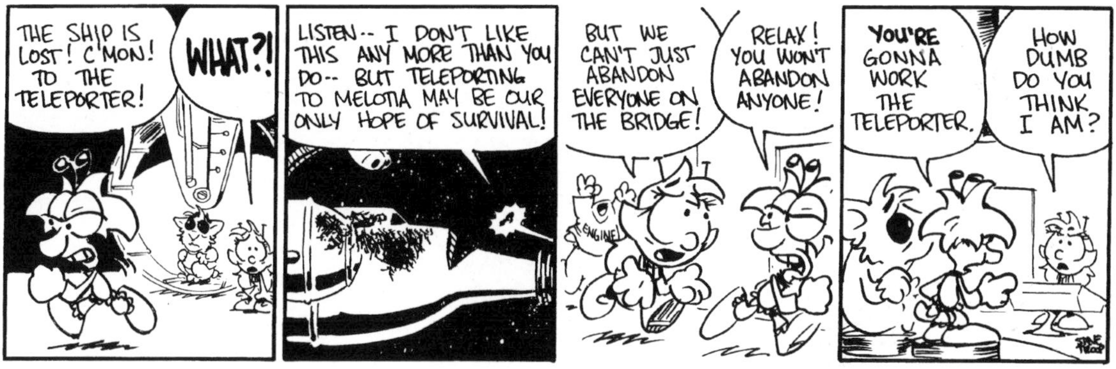
THE SHIP IS LOST! C'MON! TO THE TELEPORTER!
WHAT?!
LISTEN-- I DON'T LIKE THIS ANY MORE THAN YOU DO-- BUT TELEPORTING TO MELOTIA MAY BE OUR ONLY HOPE OF SURVIVAL!
BUT WE CAN'T JUST ABANDON EVERYONE ON THE BRIDGE!
ENGINE
RELAX! YOU WON'T ABANDON ANYONE!
YOU'RE GONNA WORK THE TELEPORTER.
HOW DUMB DO YOU THINK I AM?
STEVE TROOP

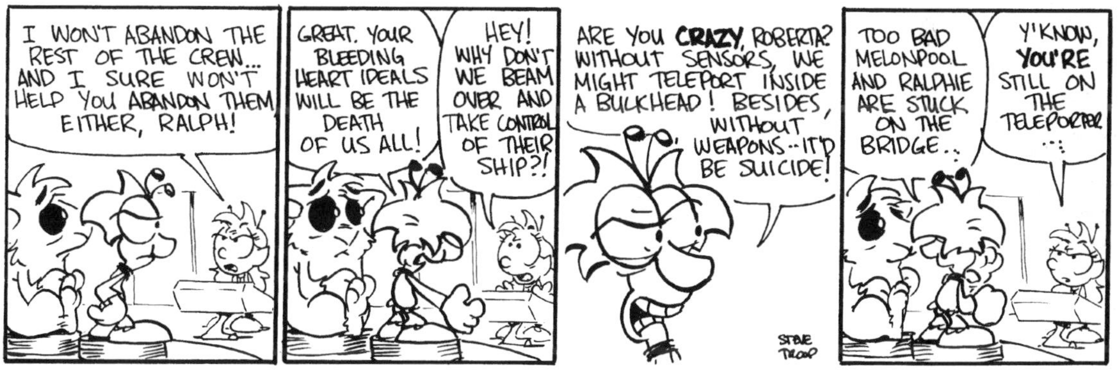
I WON'T ABANDON THE REST OF THE CREW... AND I SURE WON'T HELP YOU ABANDON THEM EITHER, RALPH!
GREAT. YOUR BLEEDING HEART IDEALS WILL BE THE DEATH OF US ALL!
HEY! WHY DON'T WE BEAM OVER AND TAKE CONTROL OF THEIR SHIP?!
ARE YOU CRAZY, ROBERTA? WITHOUT SENSORS, WE MIGHT TELEPORT INSIDE A BULKHEAD! BESIDES, WITHOUT WEAPONS--IT'D BE SUICIDE!
STEVE TROOP
TOO BAD MELONPOOL AND RALPHIE ARE STUCK ON THE BRIDGE..
Y'KNOW, YOU'RE STILL ON THE TELEPORTER ...

Nestled in the bits of wreckage in the second panel are the *Galileo* shuttlecraft from *Star Trek* and part of an X-Wing Fighter from *Star Wars*.

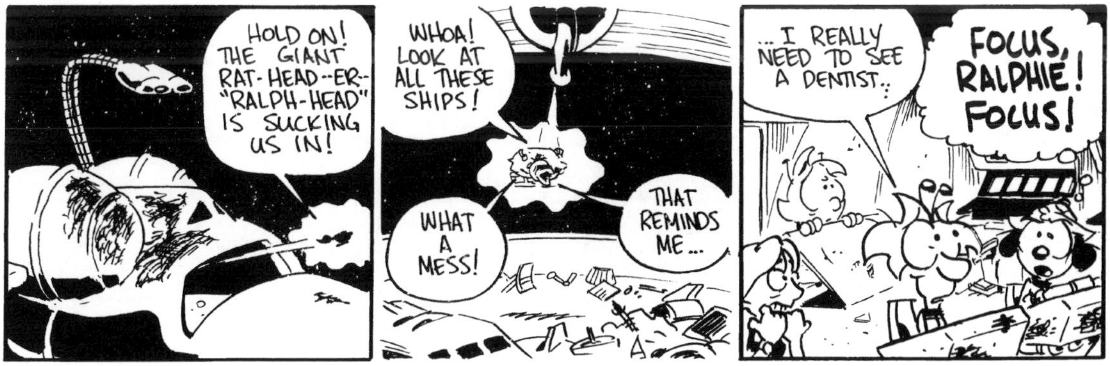
HOLD ON! THE GIANT RAT-HEAD--ER-- "RALPH-HEAD" IS SUCKING US IN!
WHOA! LOOK AT ALL THESE SHIPS!
WHAT A MESS!
THAT REMINDS ME...
...I REALLY NEED TO SEE A DENTIST..
FOCUS, RALPHIE! FOCUS!

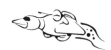

All of the weapons have been used previously in the continuity of *Melonpool*. The garden hose attachment was seen in *The Melonpool Movie* (TUM I, pages 61–64) and on page 104 of The Melonpool Chronicles Revisited; the foolproof alarm clock was first used as a weapon by Ralph and Jalea (TUM IV, page 30 and a board with a nail in it was used countless times in the strip—most notably by Sam on the *Gilligan's Island* asteroid (TUM V, page 33).

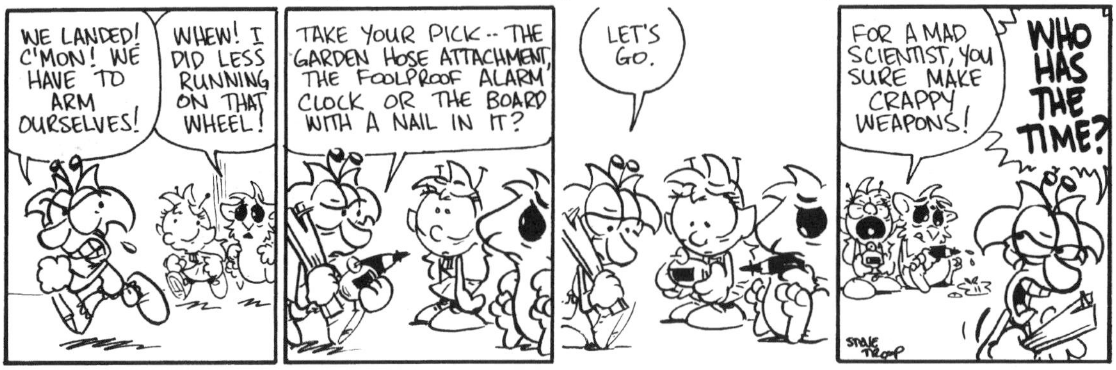
WE LANDED! C'MON! WE HAVE TO ARM OURSELVES!
WHEW! I DID LESS RUNNING ON THAT WHEEL!
TAKE YOUR PICK -- THE GARDEN HOSE ATTACHMENT, THE FOOLPROOF ALARM CLOCK OR THE BOARD WITH A NAIL IN IT?
LET'S GO.
FOR A MAD SCIENTIST, YOU SURE MAKE CRAPPY WEAPONS!
WHO HAS THE TIME?
STEVE TROOP

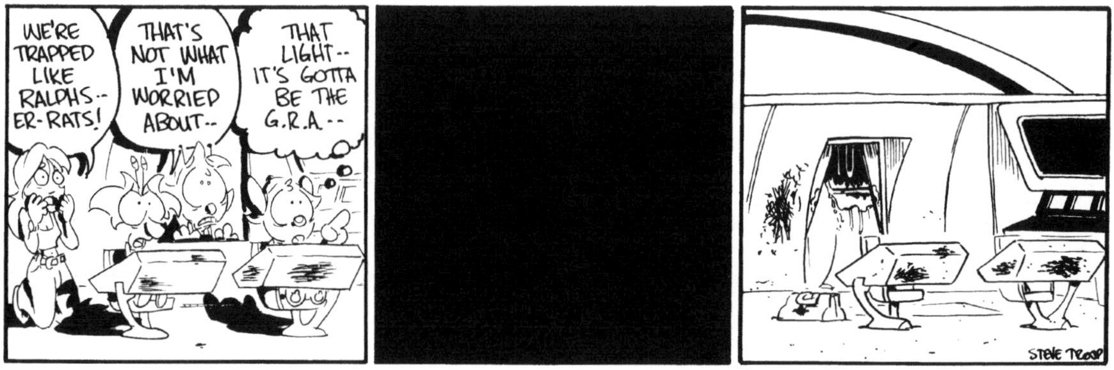
WE'RE TRAPPED LIKE RALPHS -- ER-RATS!
THAT'S NOT WHAT I'M WORRIED ABOUT --
THAT LIGHT -- IT'S GOTTA BE THE G.R.A. --
STEVE TROOP

I painstakingly modeled the background of the strip after the dungeon from the *Gilligan's Island* episode, "The Friendly Physician." Not only is the background more or less accurate, but I placed the *Melonpool* cast in the same spot as their castaway counterpart: Mayberry is Gilligan, Sammy is Skipper, Ralph is Mr. Howell, Ralphie is Mrs. Howell, Jalea is Ginger, Sam is Professor and Roberta is, of course, Mary Ann.

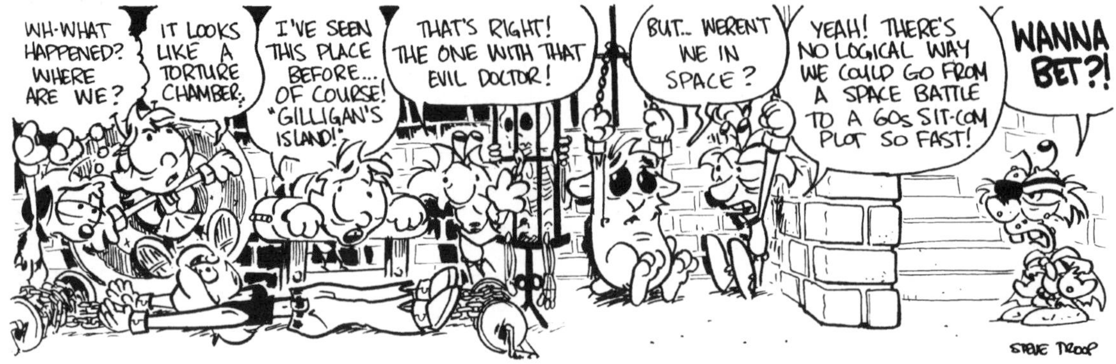
WH-WHAT HAPPENED? WHERE ARE WE?
IT LOOKS LIKE A TORTURE CHAMBER.
I'VE SEEN THIS PLACE BEFORE... OF COURSE! "GILLIGAN'S ISLAND!"
THAT'S RIGHT! THE ONE WITH THAT EVIL DOCTOR!
BUT... WEREN'T WE IN SPACE?
YEAH! THERE'S NO LOGICAL WAY WE COULD GO FROM A SPACE BATTLE TO A 60s SIT-COM PLOT SO FAST!
WANNA BET?!
STEVE TROOP

Everything that Fauntleroy mentions finding on the asteroid is something that was featured in an episode of *Gilligan's Island.* If I know anything, it's useless trivia about '60s TV.

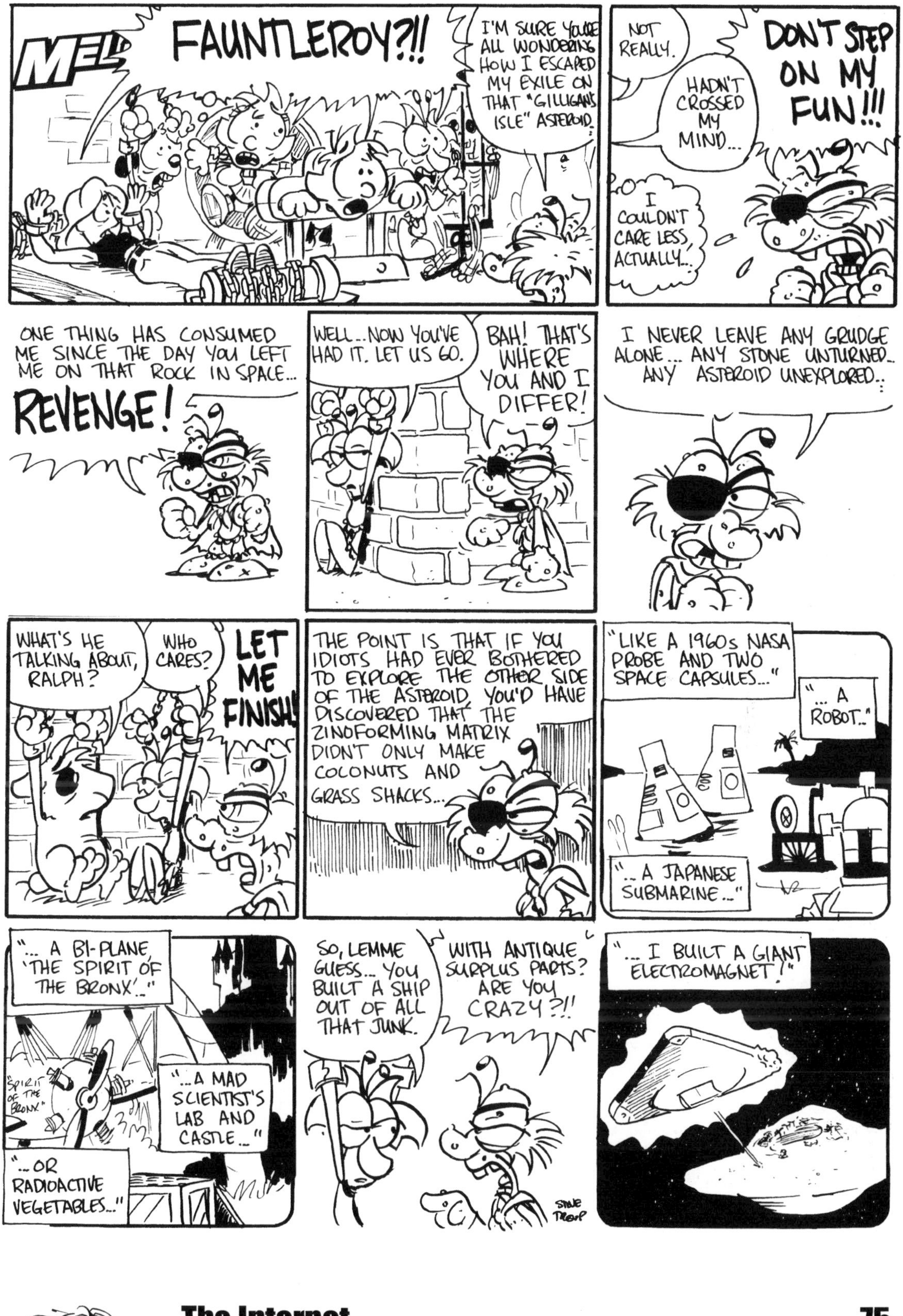
MEL!
FAUNTLEROY?!!
I'M SURE YOU'RE ALL WONDERING HOW I ESCAPED MY EXILE ON THAT "GILLIGAN'S ISLE" ASTEROID.
NOT REALLY.
HADN'T CROSSED MY MIND...
I COULDN'T CARE LESS, ACTUALLY...
DON'T STEP ON MY FUN!!!
ONE THING HAS CONSUMED ME SINCE THE DAY YOU LEFT ME ON THAT ROCK IN SPACE...
REVENGE!
WELL... NOW YOU'VE HAD IT. LET US GO.
BAH! THAT'S WHERE YOU AND I DIFFER!
I NEVER LEAVE ANY GRUDGE ALONE... ANY STONE UNTURNED... ANY ASTEROID UNEXPLORED...
WHAT'S HE TALKING ABOUT, RALPH?
WHO CARES?
LET ME FINISH!
THE POINT IS THAT IF YOU IDIOTS HAD EVER BOTHERED TO EXPLORE THE OTHER SIDE OF THE ASTEROID, YOU'D HAVE DISCOVERED THAT THE ZINOFORMING MATRIX DIDN'T ONLY MAKE COCONUTS AND GRASS SHACKS...
"LIKE A 1960s NASA PROBE AND TWO SPACE CAPSULES..."
"... A ROBOT..."
"... A JAPANESE SUBMARINE..."
"... A BI-PLANE 'THE SPIRIT OF THE BRONX'..."
"SPIRIT OF THE BRONX"
"... A MAD SCIENTIST'S LAB AND CASTLE..."
"... OR RADIOACTIVE VEGETABLES..."
SO, LEMME GUESS... YOU BUILT A SHIP OUT OF ALL THAT JUNK.
WITH ANTIQUE SURPLUS PARTS? ARE YOU CRAZY?!!
"... I BUILT A GIANT ELECTROMAGNET!"
STEVE TROOP

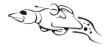

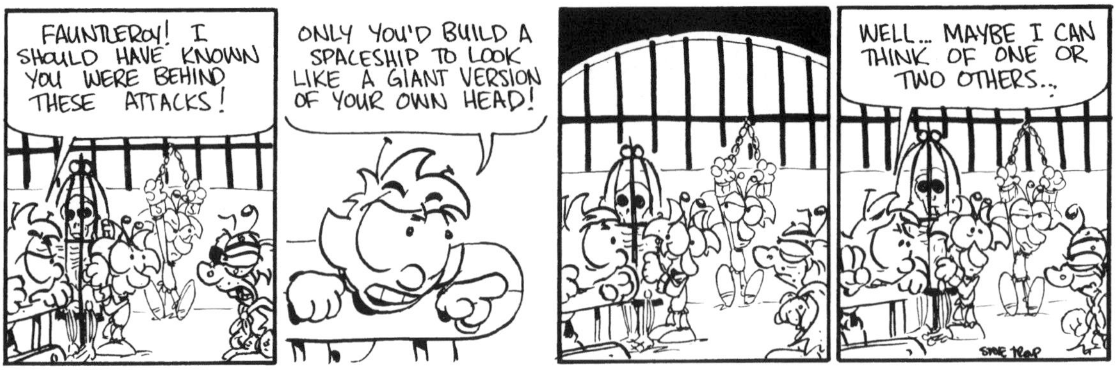
FAUNTLEROY! I SHOULD HAVE KNOWN YOU WERE BEHIND THESE ATTACKS!
ONLY YOU'D BUILD A SPACESHIP TO LOOK LIKE A GIANT VERSION OF YOUR OWN HEAD!
WELL... MAYBE I CAN THINK OF ONE OR TWO OTHERS...
STEVE TROOP

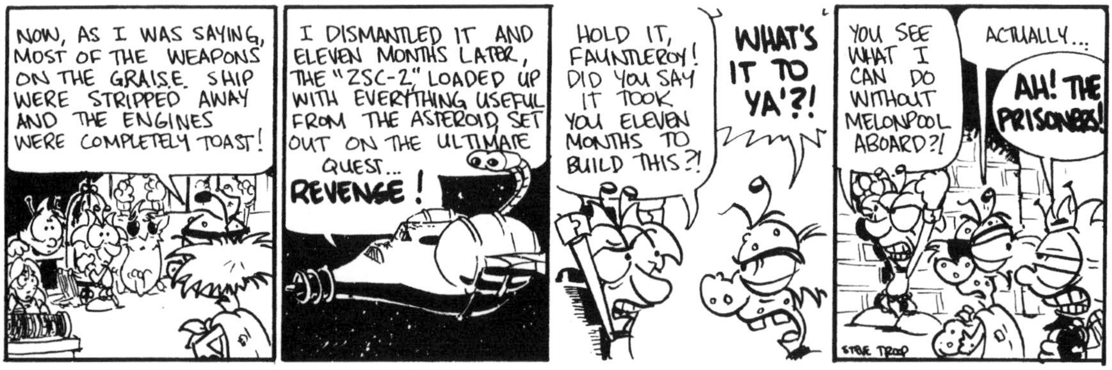
NOW, AS I WAS SAYING, MOST OF THE WEAPONS ON THE GRAISE SHIP WERE STRIPPED AWAY AND THE ENGINES WERE COMPLETELY TOAST!
I DISMANTLED IT AND ELEVEN MONTHS LATER, THE "ZSC-2" LOADED UP WITH EVERYTHING USEFUL FROM THE ASTEROID SET OUT ON THE ULTIMATE QUEST... REVENGE!
HOLD IT, FAUNTLEROY! DID YOU SAY IT TOOK YOU ELEVEN MONTHS TO BUILD THIS?!
WHAT'S IT TO YA'?!
YOU SEE WHAT I CAN DO WITHOUT MELONPOOL ABOARD?!
ACTUALLY...
AH! THE PRISONERS!
STEVE TROOP

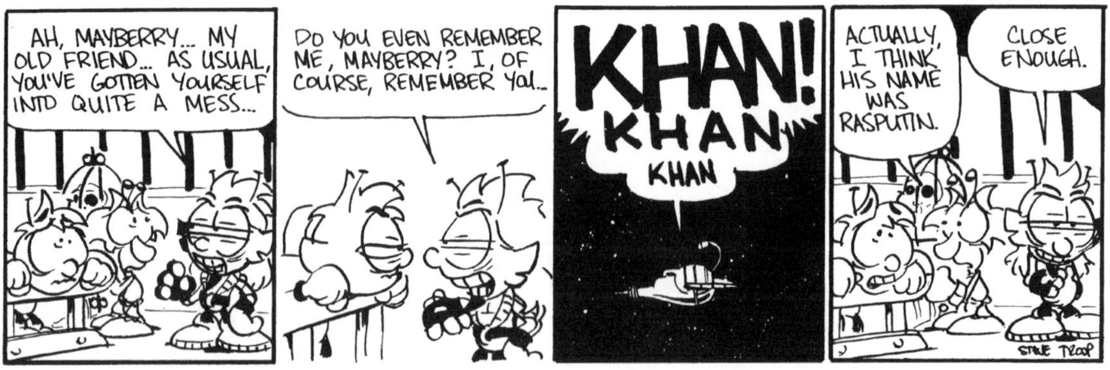
AH, MAYBERRY... MY OLD FRIEND... AS USUAL, YOU'VE GOTTEN YOURSELF INTO QUITE A MESS...
DO YOU EVEN REMEMBER ME, MAYBERRY? I, OF COURSE, REMEMBER YOU...
KHAN!
KHAN
KHAN
ACTUALLY, I THINK HIS NAME WAS RASPUTIN.
CLOSE ENOUGH.
STEVE TROOP

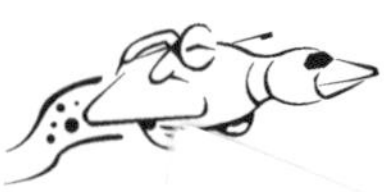

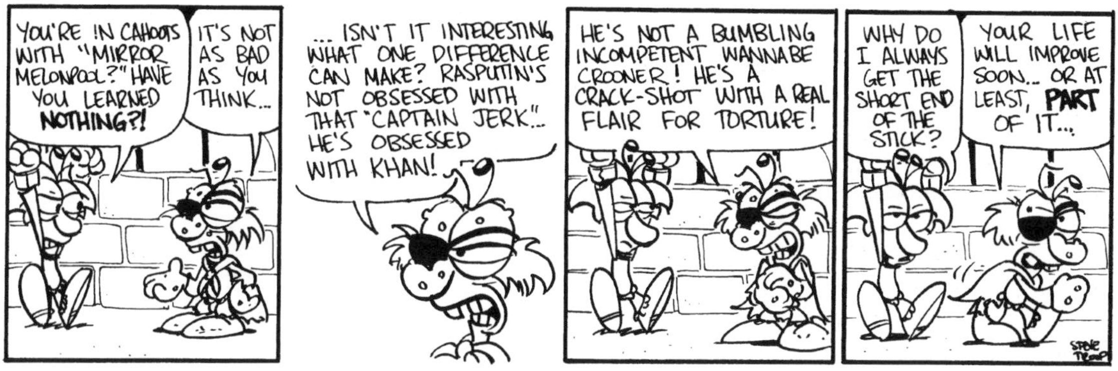
YOU'RE IN CAHOOTS WITH "MIRROR MELONPOOL?" HAVE YOU LEARNED NOTHING?!
IT'S NOT AS BAD AS YOU THINK...
... ISN'T IT INTERESTING WHAT ONE DIFFERENCE CAN MAKE? RASPUTIN'S NOT OBSESSED WITH THAT "CAPTAIN JERK"... HE'S OBSESSED WITH KHAN!
HE'S NOT A BUMBLING INCOMPETENT WANNABE CROONER! HE'S A CRACK-SHOT WITH A REAL FLAIR FOR TORTURE!
WHY DO I ALWAYS GET THE SHORT END OF THE STICK?
YOUR LIFE WILL IMPROVE SOON... OR AT LEAST, PART OF IT...
STEVE TROOP

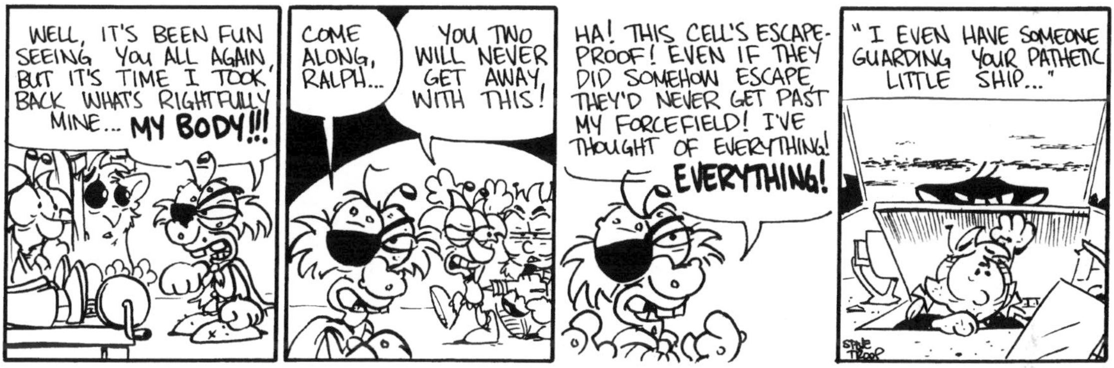
WELL, IT'S BEEN FUN SEEING YOU ALL AGAIN, BUT IT'S TIME I TOOK BACK WHAT'S RIGHTFULLY MINE... MY BODY!!!
COME ALONG, RALPH...
YOU TWO WILL NEVER GET AWAY WITH THIS!
HA! THIS CELL'S ESCAPE-PROOF! EVEN IF THEY DID SOMEHOW ESCAPE, THEY'D NEVER GET PAST MY FORCEFIELD! I'VE THOUGHT OF EVERYTHING! EVERYTHING!
"I EVEN HAVE SOMEONE GUARDING YOUR PATHETIC LITTLE SHIP..."
STEVE TROOP

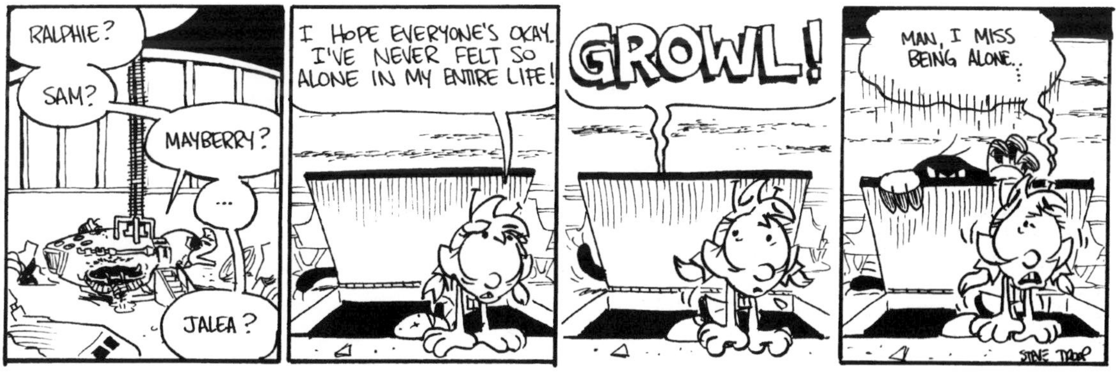
RALPHIE?
SAM?
MAYBERRY?
...
JALEA?
I HOPE EVERYONE'S OKAY. I'VE NEVER FELT SO ALONE IN MY ENTIRE LIFE!
GROWL!
MAN, I MISS BEING ALONE...
STEVE TROOP

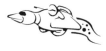

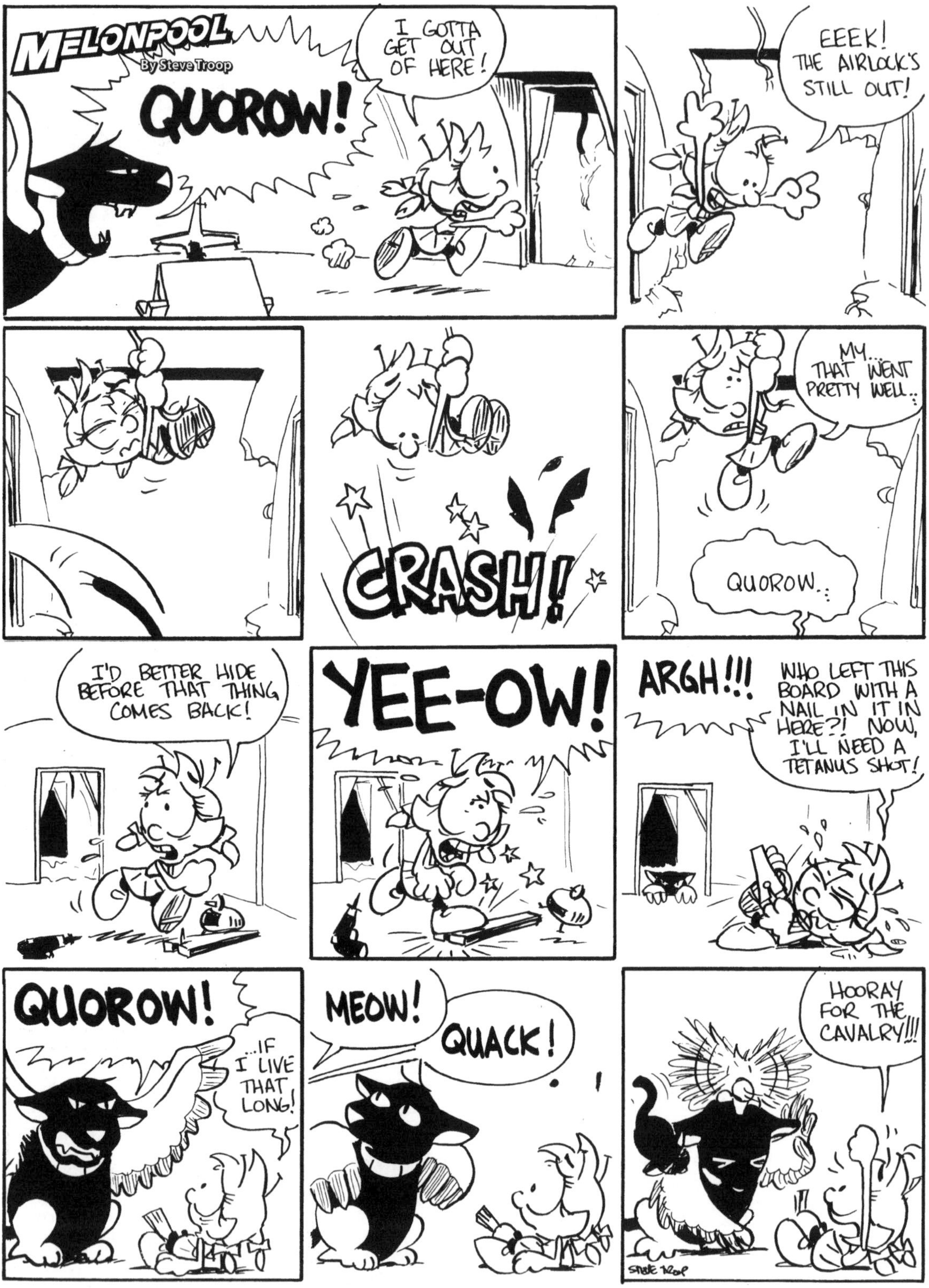

MELONPOOL
By Steve Troop
QUOROW!
I GOTTA GET OUT OF HERE!
EEEK! THE AIRLOCK'S STILL OUT!
CRASH!
MY... THAT WENT PRETTY WELL...
QUOROW...
I'D BETTER HIDE BEFORE THAT THING COMES BACK!
YEE-OW!
ARGH!!!
WHO LEFT THIS BOARD WITH A NAIL IN IT IN HERE?! NOW, I'LL NEED A TETANUS SHOT!
QUOROW!
...IF I LIVE THAT LONG!
MEOW!
QUACK!
HOORAY FOR THE CAVALRY!!!
STEVE TROOP

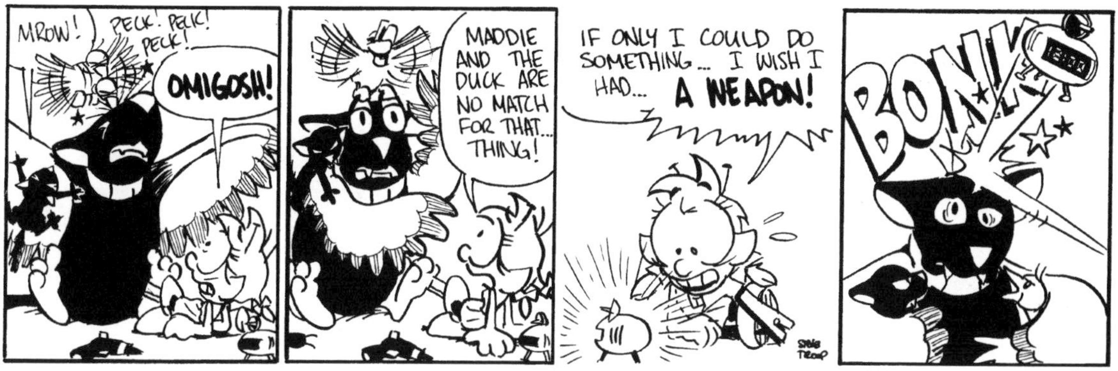
MROW!
PECK! PECK! PECK!
OMIGOSH!
MADDIE AND THE DUCK ARE NO MATCH FOR THAT... THING!
IF ONLY I COULD DO SOMETHING... I WISH I HAD... A WEAPON!
BONK

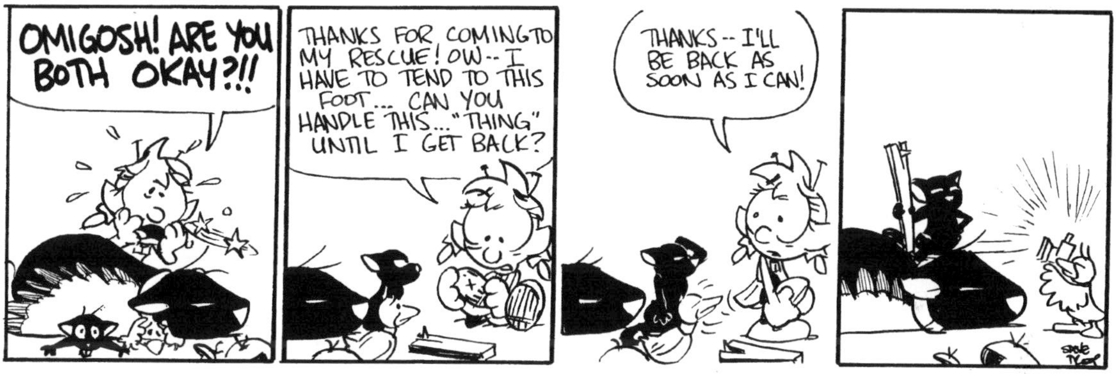
OMIGOSH! ARE YOU BOTH OKAY?!!
THANKS FOR COMING TO MY RESCUE! OW-- I HAVE TO TEND TO THIS FOOT... CAN YOU HANDLE THIS..."THING" UNTIL I GET BACK?
THANKS -- I'LL BE BACK AS SOON AS I CAN!

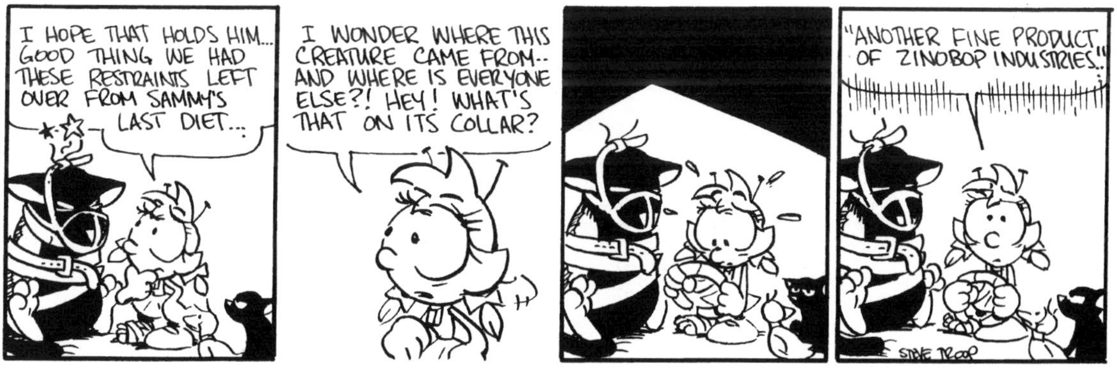
I HOPE THAT HOLDS HIM... GOOD THING WE HAD THESE RESTRAINTS LEFT OVER FROM SAMMY'S LAST DIET...
I WONDER WHERE THIS CREATURE CAME FROM-- AND WHERE IS EVERYONE ELSE?! HEY! WHAT'S THAT ON ITS COLLAR?
"ANOTHER FINE PRODUCT OF ZINOBOP INDUSTRIES."
STEVE TROOP

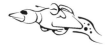

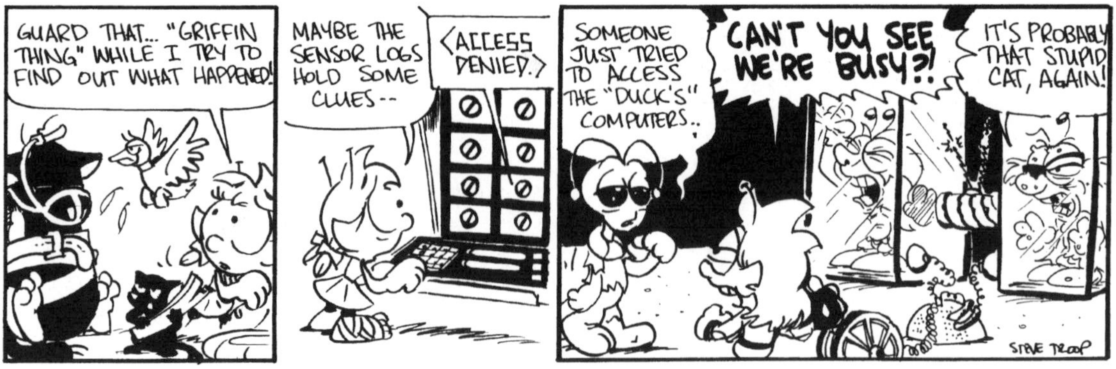
GUARD THAT... "GRIFFIN THING" WHILE I TRY TO FIND OUT WHAT HAPPENED!
MAYBE THE SENSOR LOGS HOLD SOME CLUES--
<ACCESS DENIED.>
SOMEONE JUST TRIED TO ACCESS THE "DUCK'S" COMPUTERS..
CAN'T YOU SEE WE'RE BUSY?!
IT'S PROBABLY THAT STUPID CAT, AGAIN!
STEVE TROOP

The "improvised Cerebral Swapper" was actually in the Gilligan's Island episode "The Friendly Physician," just like the painstakingly-drawn dungeon on page 74.

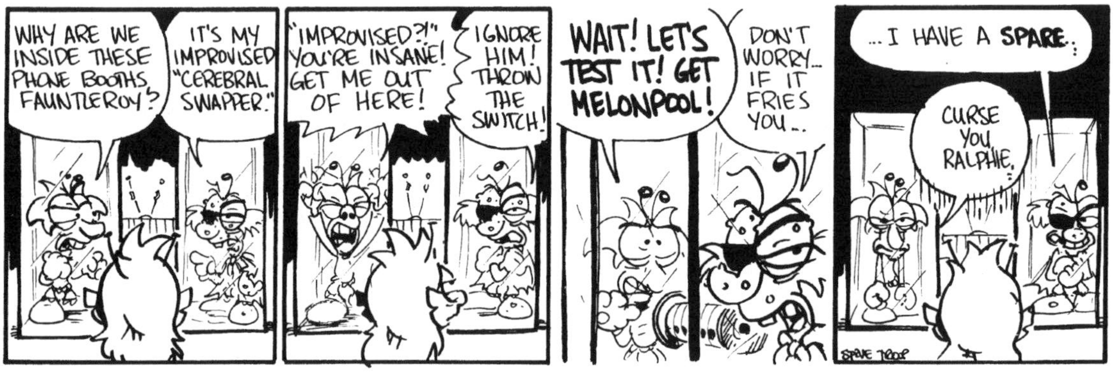
WHY ARE WE INSIDE THESE PHONE BOOTHS, FAUNTLEROY?
IT'S MY IMPROVISED "CEREBRAL SWAPPER."
"IMPROVISED?!" YOU'RE INSANE! GET ME OUT OF HERE!
IGNORE HIM! THROW THE SWITCH!
WAIT! LET'S TEST IT! GET MELONPOOL!
DON'T WORRY... IF IT FRIES YOU...
...I HAVE A SPARE.
CURSE YOU, RALPHIE.
STEVE TROOP

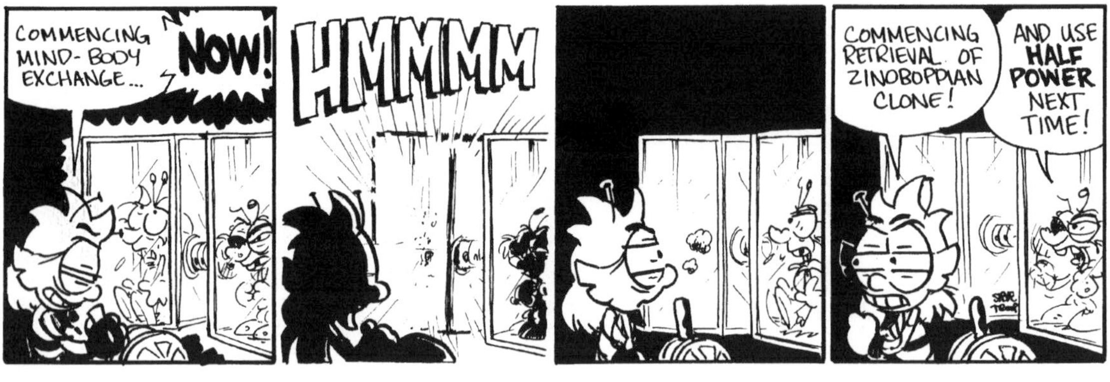
COMMENCING MIND-BODY EXCHANGE...
NOW!
HMMMM
COMMENCING RETRIEVAL OF ZINOBOPPIAN CLONE!
AND USE HALF POWER NEXT TIME!

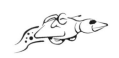

The "Brain Augmentor" was last seen in TUM I, page 141. Ralph never throws anything away—and neither do I, apparently!

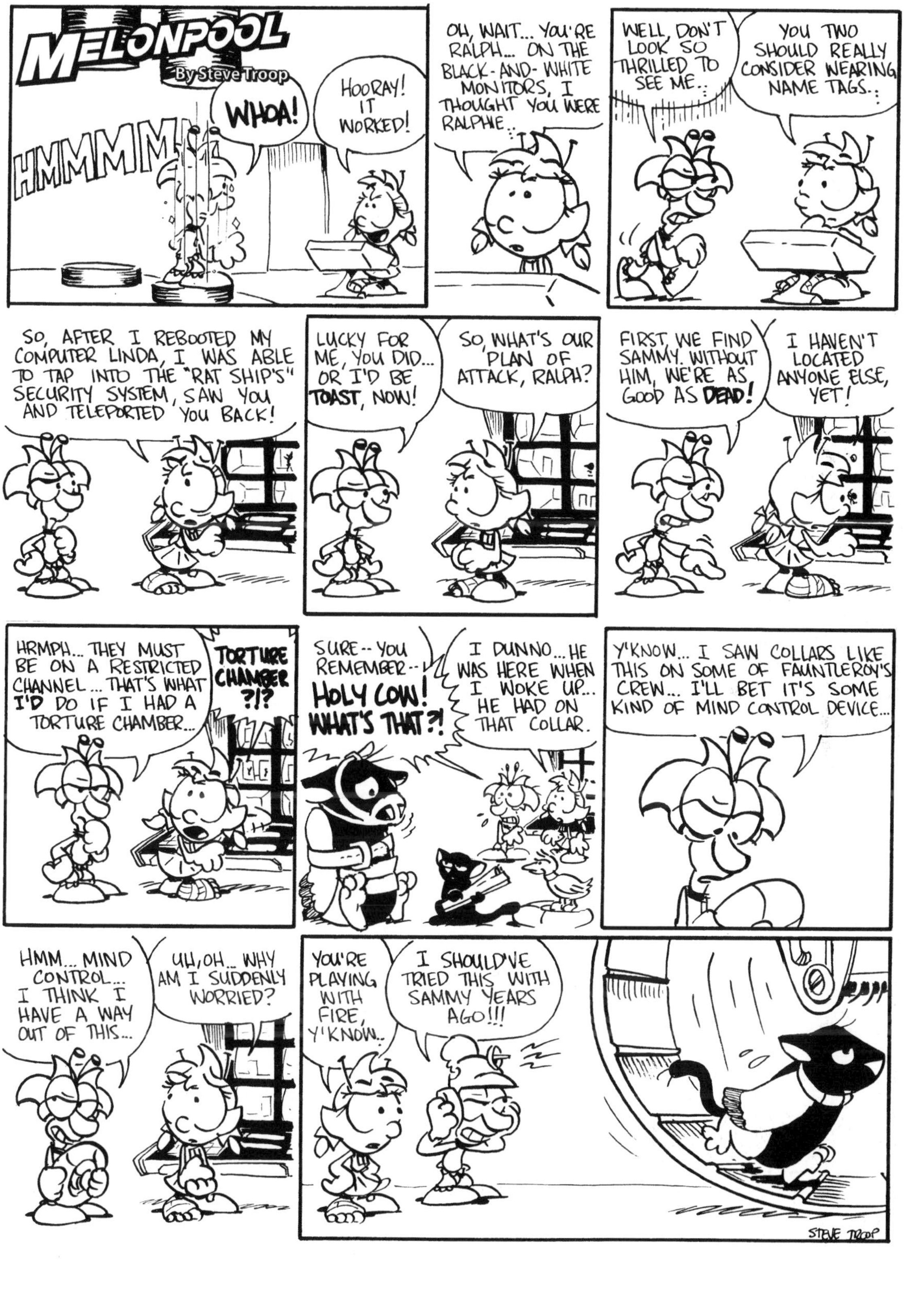

MELONPOOL
By Steve Troop
HMMMM
WHOA!
HOORAY! IT WORKED!
OH, WAIT... YOU'RE RALPH... ON THE BLACK-AND-WHITE MONITORS, I THOUGHT YOU WERE RALPHIE...
WELL, DON'T LOOK SO THRILLED TO SEE ME...
YOU TWO SHOULD REALLY CONSIDER WEARING NAME TAGS...
SO, AFTER I REBOOTED MY COMPUTER LINDA, I WAS ABLE TO TAP INTO THE "RAT SHIP'S" SECURITY SYSTEM, SAW YOU AND TELEPORTED YOU BACK!
LUCKY FOR ME, YOU DID... OR I'D BE TOAST, NOW!
SO, WHAT'S OUR PLAN OF ATTACK, RALPH?
FIRST, WE FIND SAMMY. WITHOUT HIM, WE'RE AS GOOD AS DEAD!
I HAVEN'T LOCATED ANYONE ELSE, YET!
HRMPH... THEY MUST BE ON A RESTRICTED CHANNEL... THAT'S WHAT I'D DO IF I HAD A TORTURE CHAMBER...
TORTURE CHAMBER ?!?
SURE-- YOU REMEMBER--
HOLY COW! WHAT'S THAT?!
I DUNNO... HE WAS HERE WHEN I WOKE UP... HE HAD ON THAT COLLAR.
Y'KNOW... I SAW COLLARS LIKE THIS ON SOME OF FAUNTLEROY'S CREW... I'LL BET IT'S SOME KIND OF MIND CONTROL DEVICE...
HMM... MIND CONTROL... I THINK I HAVE A WAY OUT OF THIS...
UH, OH... WHY AM I SUDDENLY WORRIED?
YOU'RE PLAYING WITH FIRE, Y'KNOW...
I SHOULD'VE TRIED THIS WITH SAMMY YEARS AGO!!!
STEVE TROOP

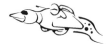

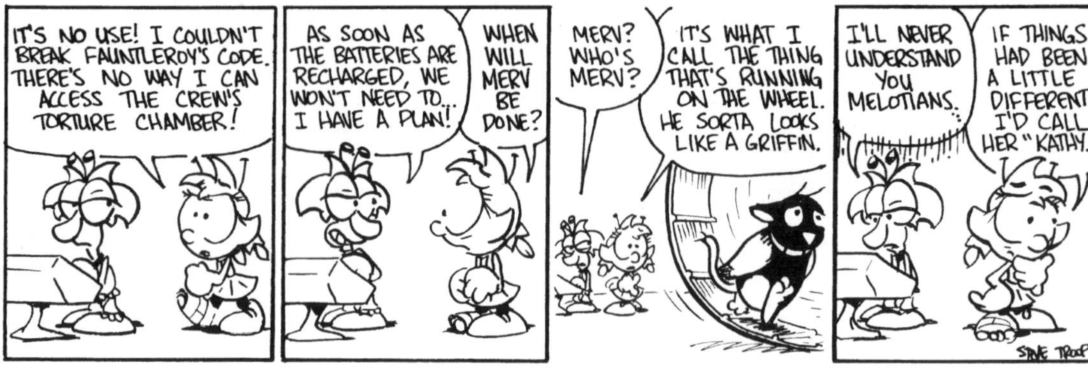
IT'S NO USE! I COULDN'T BREAK FAUNTLEROY'S CODE. THERE'S NO WAY I CAN ACCESS THE CREW'S TORTURE CHAMBER!
AS SOON AS THE BATTERIES ARE RECHARGED, WE WON'T NEED TO... I HAVE A PLAN!
WHEN WILL MERV BE DONE?
MERV? WHO'S MERV?
IT'S WHAT I CALL THE THING THAT'S RUNNING ON THE WHEEL. HE SORTA LOOKS LIKE A GRIFFIN.
I'LL NEVER UNDERSTAND YOU MELOTIANS...
IF THINGS HAD BEEN A LITTLE DIFFERENT, I'D CALL HER "KATHY."
STEVE TROOP

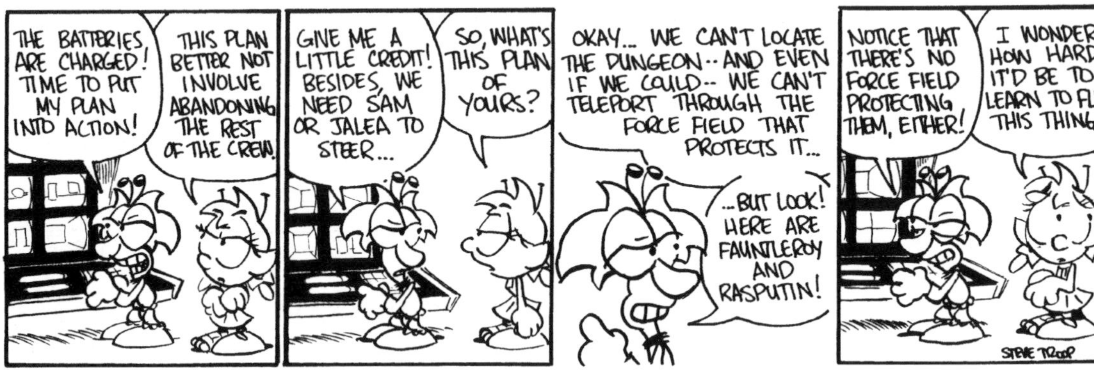
THE BATTERIES ARE CHARGED! TIME TO PUT MY PLAN INTO ACTION!
THIS PLAN BETTER NOT INVOLVE ABANDONING THE REST OF THE CREW!
GIVE ME A LITTLE CREDIT! BESIDES, WE NEED SAM OR JALEA TO STEER...
SO, WHAT'S THIS PLAN OF YOURS?
OKAY... WE CAN'T LOCATE THE DUNGEON -- AND EVEN IF WE COULD -- WE CAN'T TELEPORT THROUGH THE FORCE FIELD THAT PROTECTS IT...
...BUT LOOK! HERE ARE FAUNTLEROY AND RASPUTIN!
NOTICE THAT THERE'S NO FORCE FIELD PROTECTING THEM, EITHER!
I WONDER HOW HARD IT'D BE TO LEARN TO FLY THIS THING...
STEVE TROOP

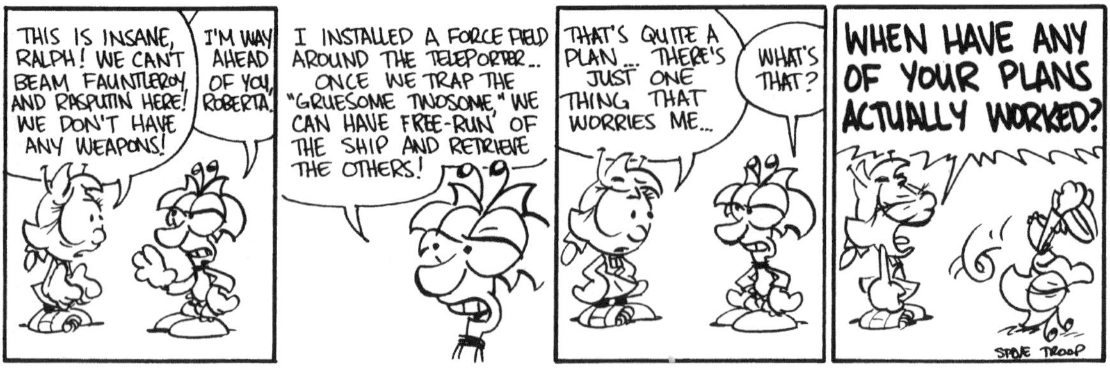
THIS IS INSANE, RALPH! WE CAN'T BEAM FAUNTLEROY AND RASPUTIN HERE! WE DON'T HAVE ANY WEAPONS!
I'M WAY AHEAD OF YOU, ROBERTA.
I INSTALLED A FORCE FIELD AROUND THE TELEPORTER... ONCE WE TRAP THE "GRUESOME TWOSOME," WE CAN HAVE FREE-RUN OF THE SHIP AND RETRIEVE THE OTHERS!
THAT'S QUITE A PLAN... THERE'S JUST ONE THING THAT WORRIES ME...
WHAT'S THAT?
WHEN HAVE ANY OF YOUR PLANS ACTUALLY WORKED?
STEVE TROOP

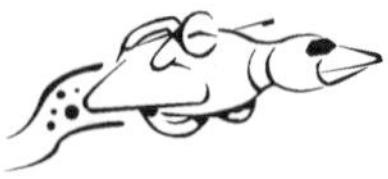

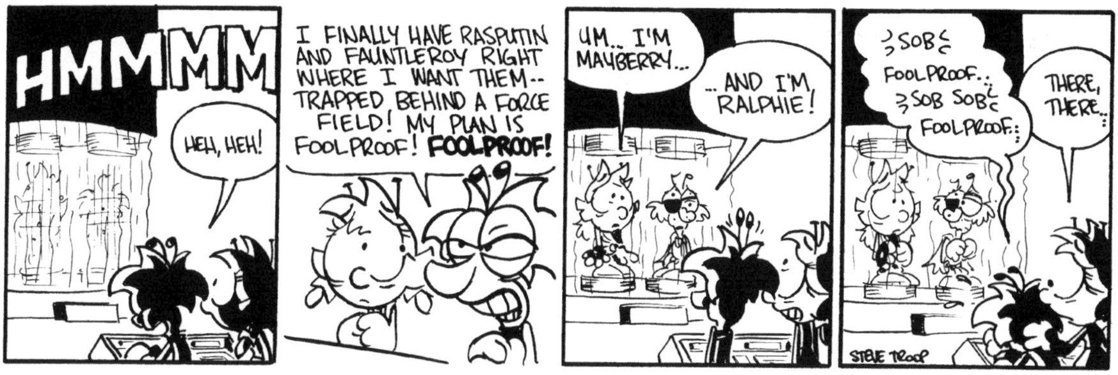
HMMMM
HEH, HEH!
I FINALLY HAVE RASPUTIN AND FAUNTLEROY RIGHT WHERE I WANT THEM-- TRAPPED BEHIND A FORCE FIELD! MY PLAN IS FOOLPROOF! FOOLPROOF!
UM... I'M MAYBERRY...
...AND I'M RALPHIE!
SOB
FOOLPROOF...
SOB SOB
FOOLPROOF...
THERE, THERE...
STEVE TROOP

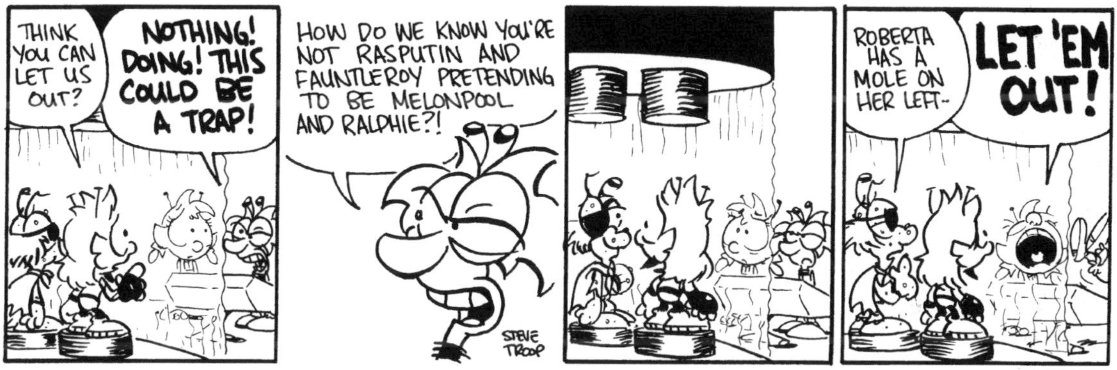
THINK YOU CAN LET US OUT?
NOTHING! DOING! THIS COULD BE A TRAP!
HOW DO WE KNOW YOU'RE NOT RASPUTIN AND FAUNTLEROY PRETENDING TO BE MELONPOOL AND RALPHIE?!
STEVE TROOP
ROBERTA HAS A MOLE ON HER LEFT--
LET 'EM OUT!

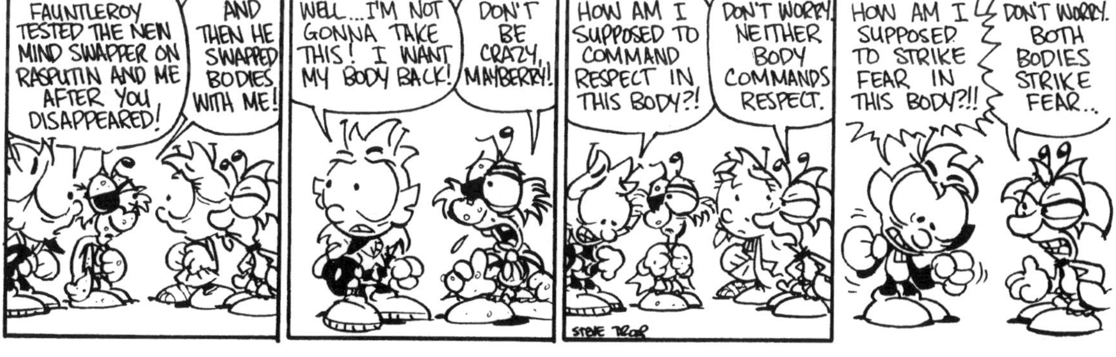
FAUNTLEROY TESTED THE NEW MIND SWAPPER ON RASPUTIN AND ME AFTER YOU DISAPPEARED!
AND THEN HE SWAPPED BODIES WITH ME!
WELL...I'M NOT GONNA TAKE THIS! I WANT MY BODY BACK!
DON'T BE CRAZY, MAYBERRY!
HOW AM I SUPPOSED TO COMMAND RESPECT IN THIS BODY?!
DON'T WORRY! NEITHER BODY COMMANDS RESPECT.
STEVE TROOP
HOW AM I SUPPOSED TO STRIKE FEAR IN THIS BODY?!!
DON'T WORRY. BOTH BODIES STRIKE FEAR...

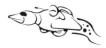

Rasputin Melonpool has the distinction of being the only canon character that was not created by me. Paul Southworth (creator of *Ugly Hill* and *Krazy Larry*) created Rasputin during the **Mirror Melonpool** guest weeks (see TUM III, pages, 113–115; TUM IV, pages 146–148).

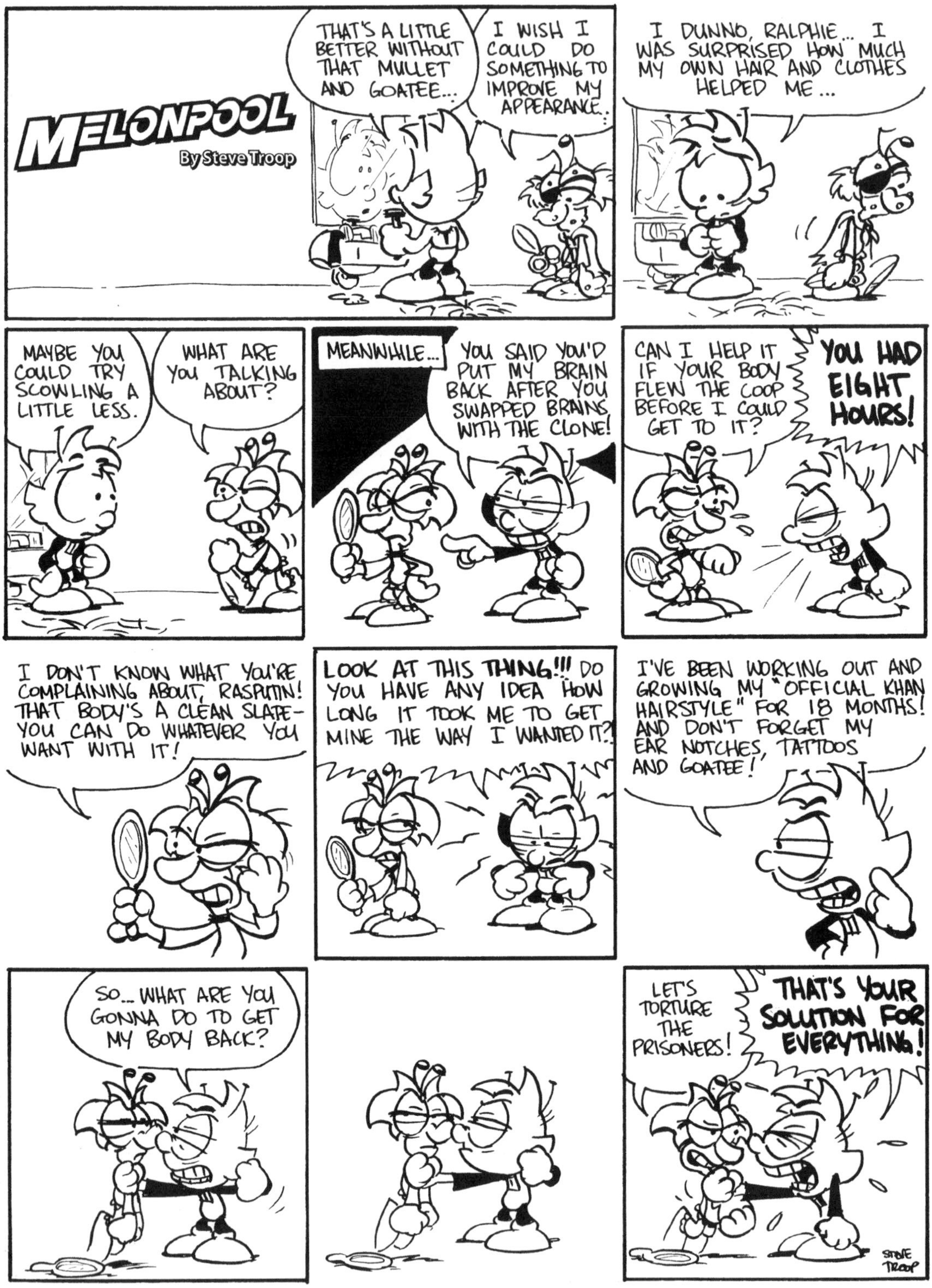

MELONPOOL
By Steve Troop
THAT'S A LITTLE BETTER WITHOUT THAT MULLET AND GOATEE...
I WISH I COULD DO SOMETHING TO IMPROVE MY APPEARANCE...
I DUNNO, RALPHIE... I WAS SURPRISED HOW MUCH MY OWN HAIR AND CLOTHES HELPED ME...
MAYBE YOU COULD TRY SCOWLING A LITTLE LESS.
WHAT ARE YOU TALKING ABOUT?
MEANWHILE...
YOU SAID YOU'D PUT MY BRAIN BACK AFTER YOU SWAPPED BRAINS WITH THE CLONE!
CAN I HELP IT IF YOUR BODY FLEW THE COOP BEFORE I COULD GET TO IT?
YOU HAD EIGHT HOURS!
I DON'T KNOW WHAT YOU'RE COMPLAINING ABOUT, RASPUTIN! THAT BODY'S A CLEAN SLATE-YOU CAN DO WHATEVER YOU WANT WITH IT!
LOOK AT THIS THING!!! DO YOU HAVE ANY IDEA HOW LONG IT TOOK ME TO GET MINE THE WAY I WANTED IT?!
I'VE BEEN WORKING OUT AND GROWING MY "OFFICIAL KHAN HAIRSTYLE" FOR 18 MONTHS! AND DON'T FORGET MY EAR NOTCHES, TATTOOS AND GOATEE!
SO... WHAT ARE YOU GONNA DO TO GET MY BODY BACK?
LET'S TORTURE THE PRISONERS!
THAT'S YOUR SOLUTION FOR EVERYTHING!
STEVE TROOP

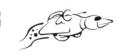

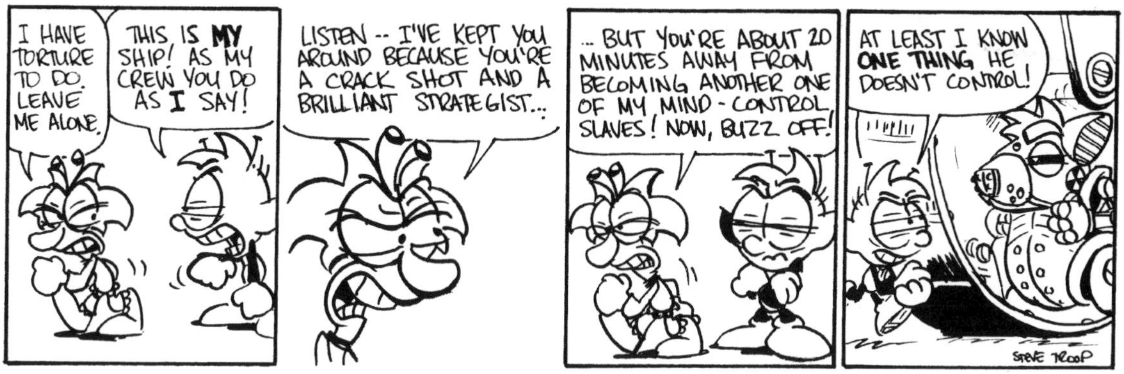
I HAVE TORTURE TO DO. LEAVE ME ALONE.
THIS IS **MY** SHIP! AS MY CREW YOU DO AS **I** SAY!
LISTEN -- I'VE KEPT YOU AROUND BECAUSE YOU'RE A CRACK SHOT AND A BRILLIANT STRATEGIST...
... BUT YOU'RE ABOUT 20 MINUTES AWAY FROM BECOMING ANOTHER ONE OF MY MIND-CONTROL SLAVES! NOW, BUZZ OFF!
AT LEAST I KNOW **ONE THING** HE DOESN'T CONTROL!
STEVE TROOP

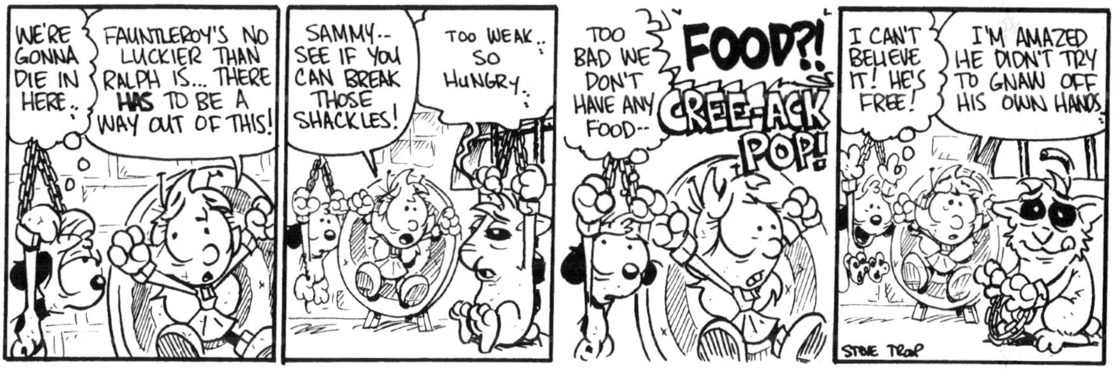
WE'RE GONNA DIE IN HERE...
FAUNTLEROY'S NO LUCKIER THAN RALPH IS... THERE **HAS** TO BE A WAY OUT OF THIS!
SAMMY.. SEE IF YOU CAN BREAK THOSE SHACKLES!
TOO WEAK... SO HUNGRY...
TOO BAD WE DON'T HAVE ANY FOOD--
FOOD?!
CREE-ACK
POP!
I CAN'T BELIEVE IT! HE'S FREE!
I'M AMAZED HE DIDN'T TRY TO GNAW OFF HIS OWN HANDS.
STEVE TROOP

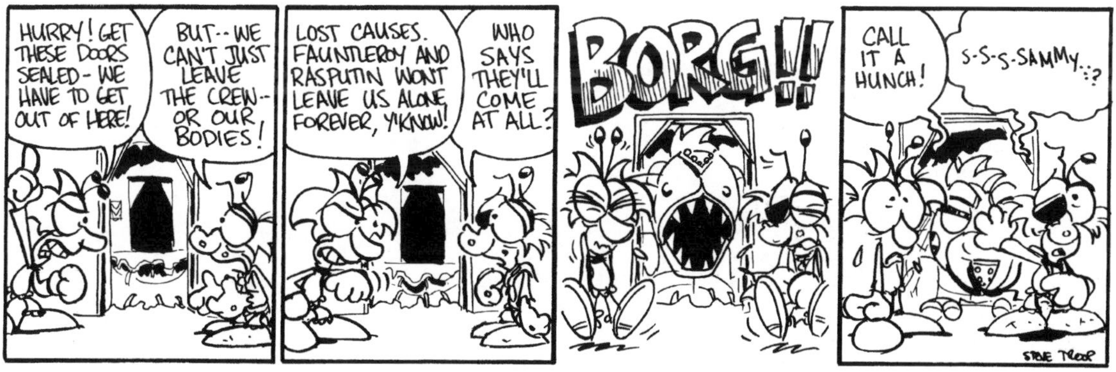
HURRY! GET THESE DOORS SEALED - WE HAVE TO GET OUT OF HERE!
BUT-- WE CAN'T JUST LEAVE THE CREW-- OR OUR BODIES!
LOST CAUSES. FAUNTLEROY AND RASPUTIN WON'T LEAVE US ALONE FOREVER, Y'KNOW!
WHO SAYS THEY'LL COME AT ALL?
BORG!!
CALL IT A HUNCH!
S-S-S-SAMMY...?
STEVE TROOP

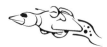

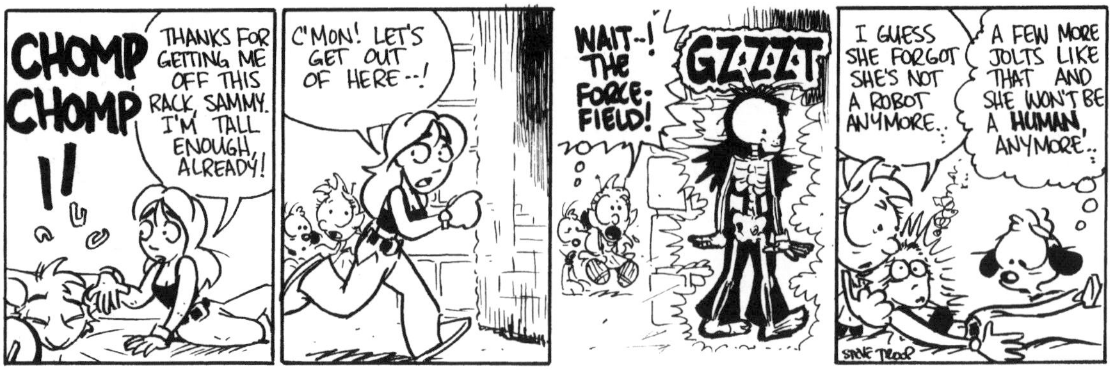
CHOMP CHOMP
THANKS FOR GETTING ME OFF THIS RACK, SAMMY. I'M TALL ENOUGH, ALREADY!
C'MON! LET'S GET OUT OF HERE--!
WAIT--! THE FORCE-FIELD!
GZ-Z-Z-T
I GUESS SHE FORGOT SHE'S NOT A ROBOT ANYMORE..
A FEW MORE JOLTS LIKE THAT AND SHE WON'T BE A **HUMAN**, ANYMORE..
STEVE TROOP

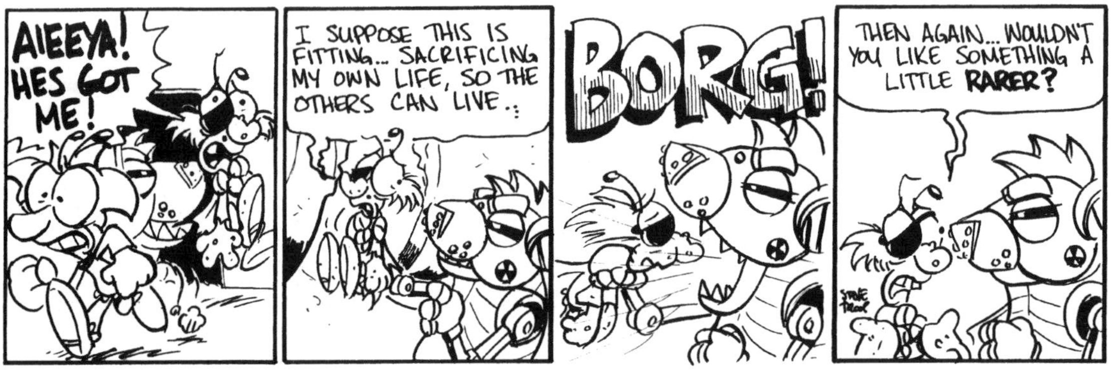
AIEEYA! HES GOT ME!
I SUPPOSE THIS IS FITTING... SACRIFICING MY OWN LIFE, SO THE OTHERS CAN LIVE..
BORG!
THEN AGAIN... WOULDN'T YOU LIKE SOMETHING A LITTLE **RARER?**
STEVE TROOP

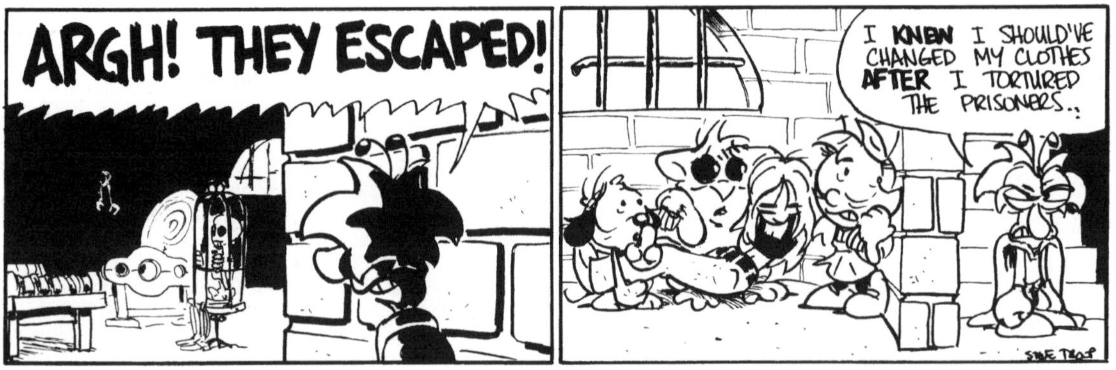
ARGH! THEY ESCAPED!
I **KNEW** I SHOULD'VE CHANGED MY CLOTHES **AFTER** I TORTURED THE PRISONERS..
STEVE TROOP

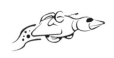

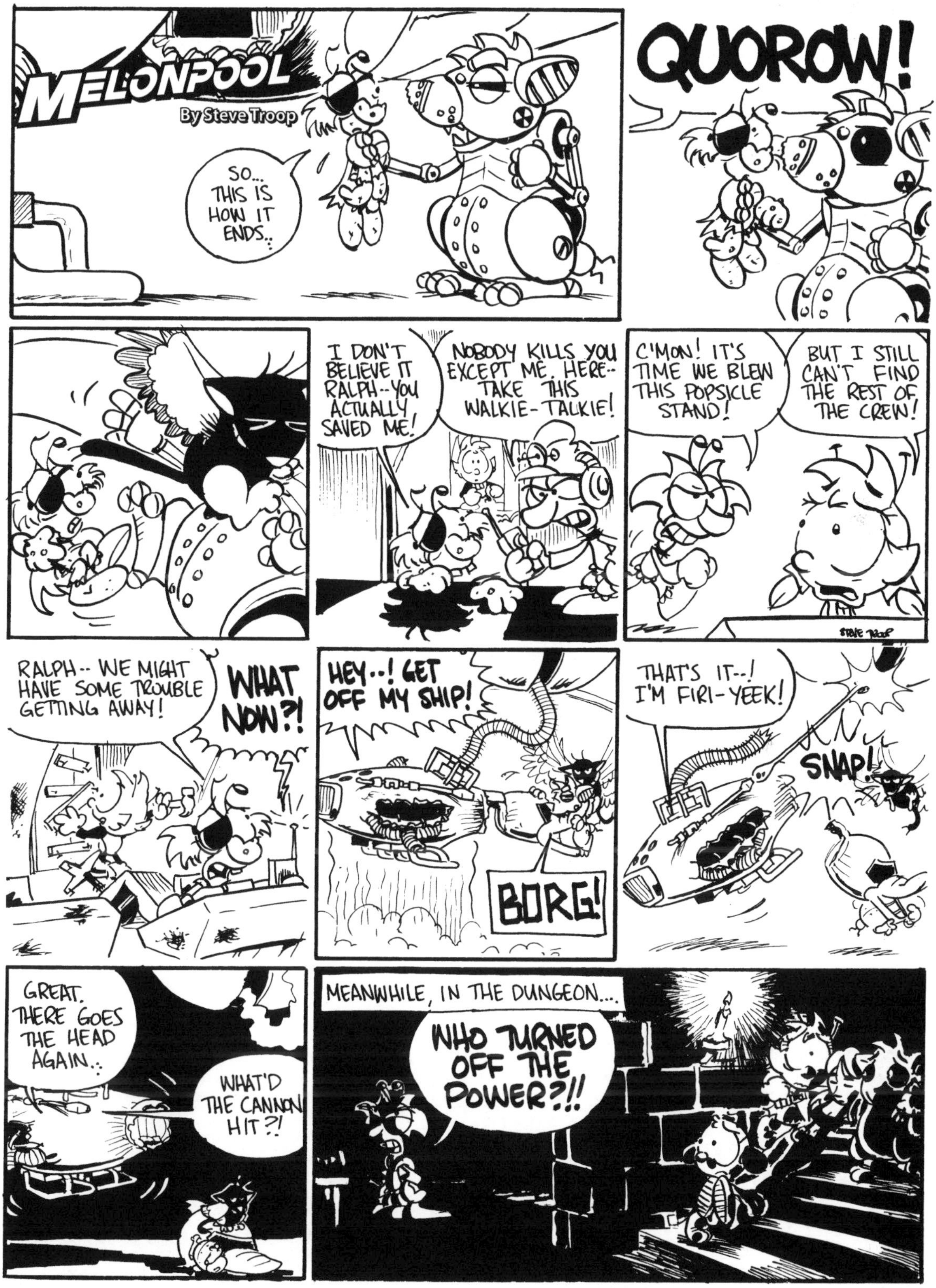
MELONPOOL
By Steve Troop
SO... THIS IS HOW IT ENDS...
QUOROW!
I DON'T BELIEVE IT RALPH--YOU ACTUALLY SAVED ME!
NOBODY KILLS YOU EXCEPT ME. HERE-- TAKE THIS WALKIE-TALKIE!
C'MON! IT'S TIME WE BLEW THIS POPSICLE STAND!
BUT I STILL CAN'T FIND THE REST OF THE CREW!
STEVE TROOP
RALPH-- WE MIGHT HAVE SOME TROUBLE GETTING AWAY!
WHAT NOW?!
HEY--! GET OFF MY SHIP!
BORG!
THAT'S IT--! I'M FIRI-YEEK!
SNAP!
GREAT. THERE GOES THE HEAD AGAIN...
WHAT'D THE CANNON HIT?!
MEANWHILE, IN THE DUNGEON....
WHO TURNED OFF THE POWER?!!

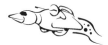

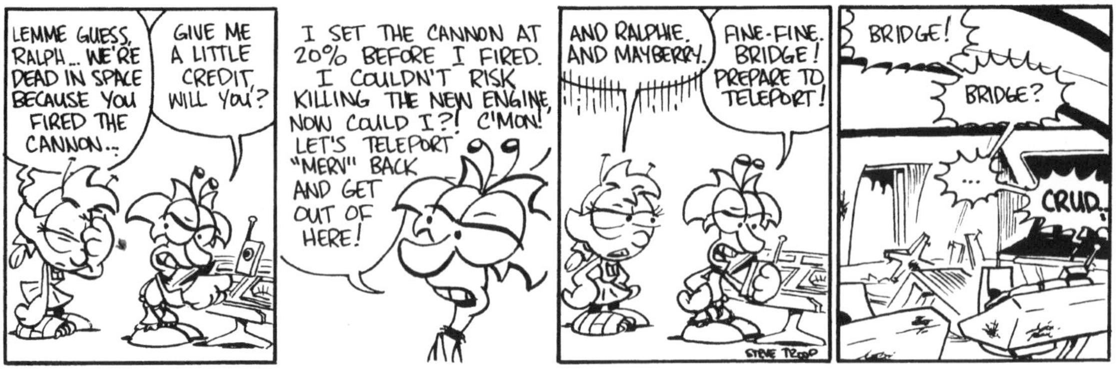
LEMME GUESS, RALPH... WE'RE DEAD IN SPACE BECAUSE YOU FIRED THE CANNON...
GIVE ME A LITTLE CREDIT, WILL YOU?
I SET THE CANNON AT 20% BEFORE I FIRED. I COULDN'T RISK KILLING THE NEW ENGINE, NOW COULD I?! C'MON! LET'S TELEPORT "MERV" BACK AND GET OUT OF HERE!
AND RALPHIE. AND MAYBERRY.
FINE-FINE. BRIDGE! PREPARE TO TELEPORT!
BRIDGE!
BRIDGE?
...
CRUD..

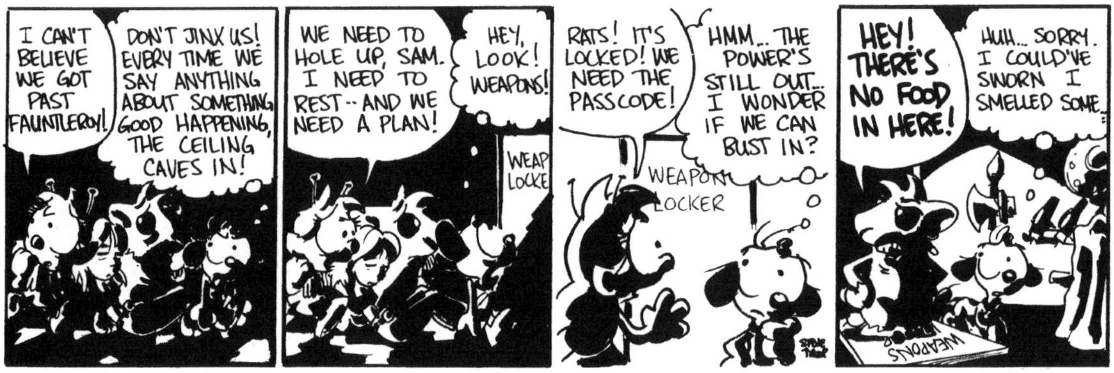
I CAN'T BELIEVE WE GOT PAST FAUNTLEROY!
DON'T JINX US! EVERY TIME WE SAY ANYTHING ABOUT SOMETHING GOOD HAPPENING, THE CEILING CAVES IN!
WE NEED TO HOLE UP, SAM. I NEED TO REST-- AND WE NEED A PLAN!
HEY, LOOK! WEAPONS!
WEAP LOCKE
RATS! IT'S LOCKED! WE NEED THE PASSCODE!
HMM... THE POWER'S STILL OUT... I WONDER IF WE CAN BUST IN?
WEAPON LOCKER
HEY! THERE'S NO FOOD IN HERE!
HUH... SORRY. I COULD'VE SWORN I SMELLED SOME...
WEAPONS

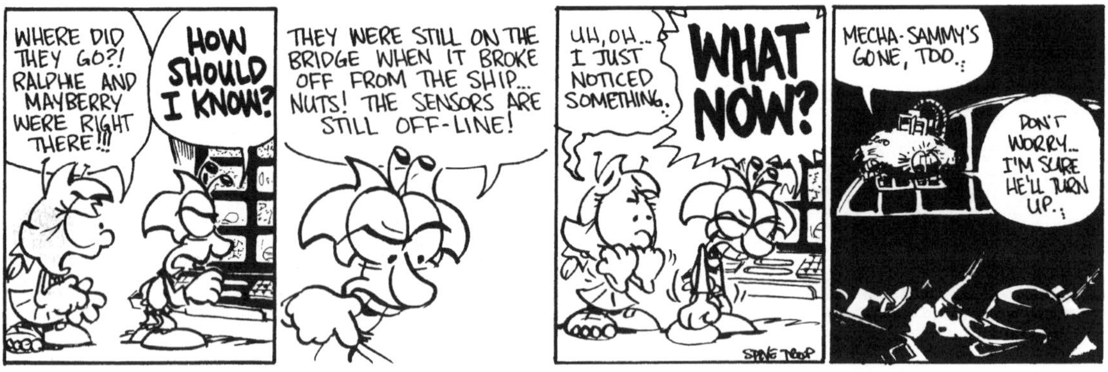
WHERE DID THEY GO?! RALPHIE AND MAYBERRY WERE RIGHT THERE!!!
HOW SHOULD I KNOW?
THEY WERE STILL ON THE BRIDGE WHEN IT BROKE OFF FROM THE SHIP... NUTS! THE SENSORS ARE STILL OFF-LINE!
UH, OH... I JUST NOTICED SOMETHING...
WHAT NOW?
MECHA-SAMMY'S GONE, TOO...
DON'T WORRY... I'M SURE HE'LL TURN UP...

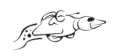

The aliens featured in silhouette are all from other webcomics. Among the refugees depicted here are: a GRAISE (from my comic), a Uryuom (from Dan Shive's *El Goonish Shive*), a grey alien (from Jeff Darlington's *GPF*) and an ALIEN (from David Willis' *It's Walky*).

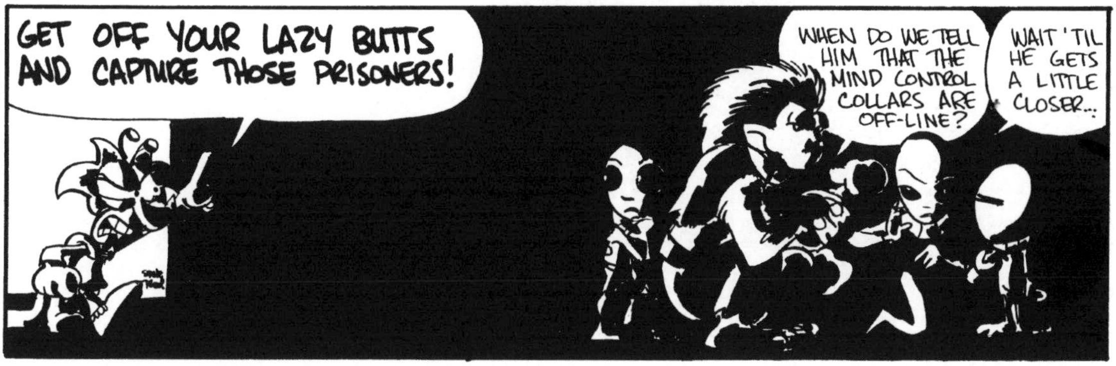
GET OFF YOUR LAZY BUTTS AND CAPTURE THOSE PRISONERS!
WHEN DO WE TELL HIM THAT THE MIND CONTROL COLLARS ARE OFF-LINE?
WAIT 'TIL HE GETS A LITTLE CLOSER...

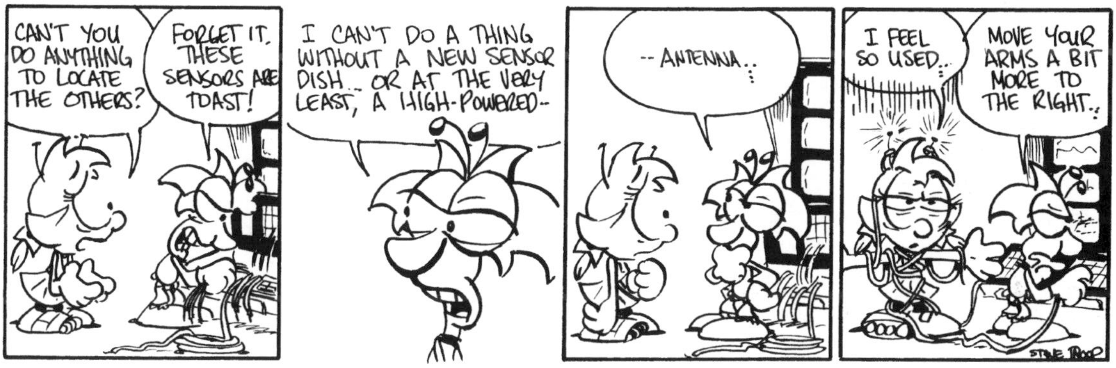
CAN'T YOU DO ANYTHING TO LOCATE THE OTHERS?
FORGET IT. THESE SENSORS ARE TOAST!
I CAN'T DO A THING WITHOUT A NEW SENSOR DISH... OR AT THE VERY LEAST, A HIGH-POWERED--
--ANTENNA...
I FEEL SO USED...
MOVE YOUR ARMS A BIT MORE TO THE RIGHT...
STEVE TROOP

Interesting how all of the weapons in Fauntleroy and Rasputin's cache look like *Star Trek* phasers. Apparently, mirror duplicates don't fall far from the tree....

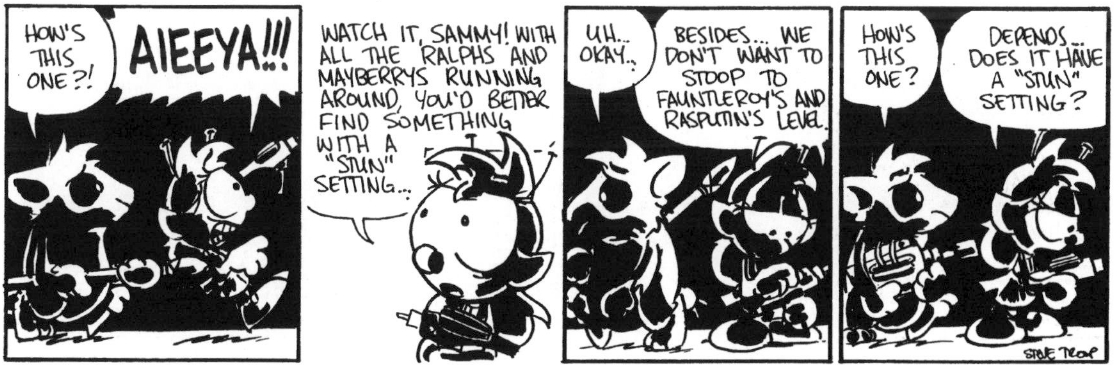
HOW'S THIS ONE?!
AIEEYA!!!
WATCH IT, SAMMY! WITH ALL THE RALPHS AND MAYBERRYS RUNNING AROUND, YOU'D BETTER FIND SOMETHING WITH A "STUN" SETTING...
UH... OKAY...
BESIDES... WE DON'T WANT TO STOOP TO FAUNTLEROY'S AND RASPUTIN'S LEVEL.
HOW'S THIS ONE?
DEPENDS... DOES IT HAVE A "STUN" SETTING?
STEVE TROOP

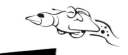

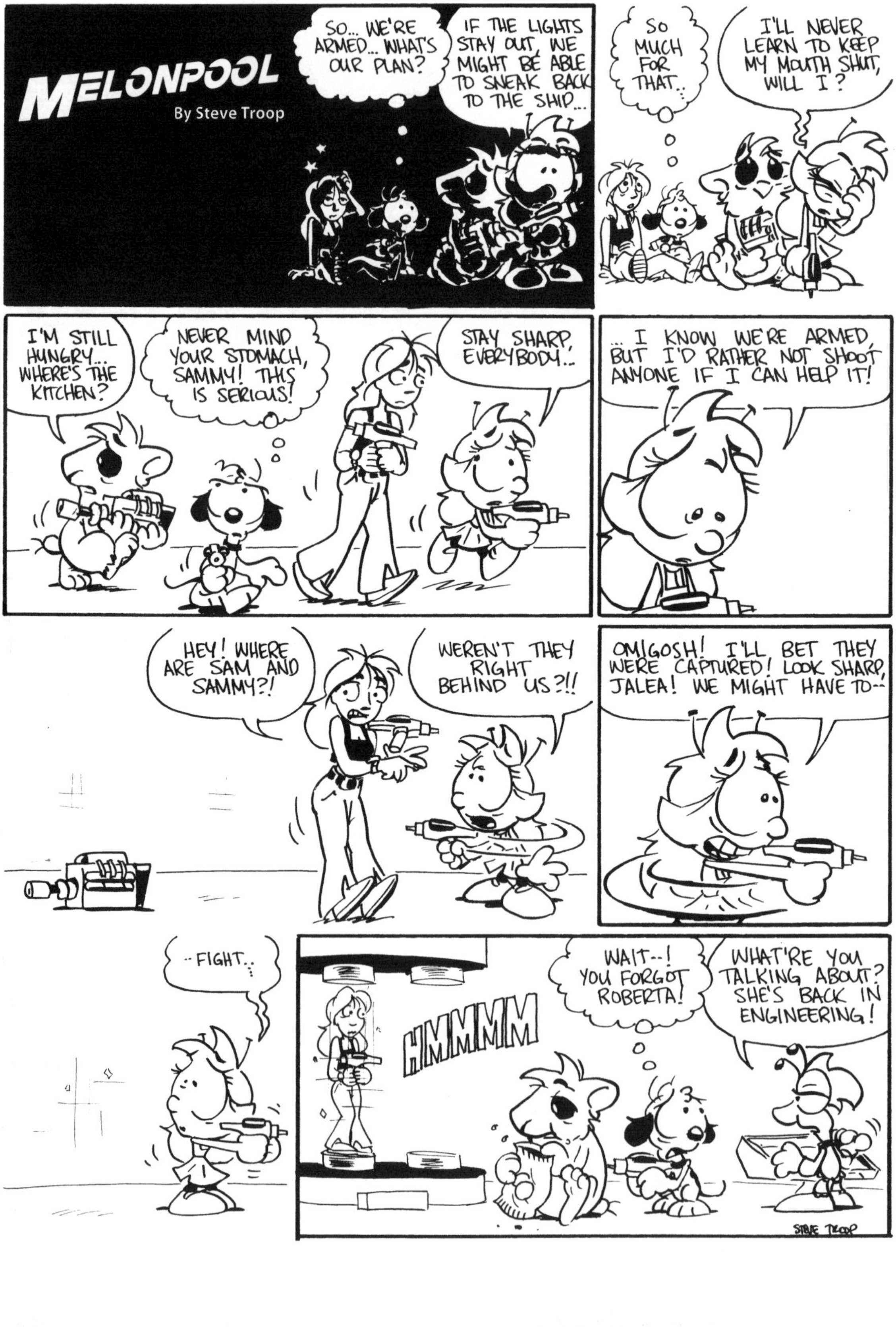
MELONPOOL
By Steve Troop
SO... WE'RE ARMED... WHAT'S OUR PLAN?
IF THE LIGHTS STAY OUT, WE MIGHT BE ABLE TO SNEAK BACK TO THE SHIP...
SO MUCH FOR THAT...
I'LL NEVER LEARN TO KEEP MY MOUTH SHUT, WILL I?
I'M STILL HUNGRY... WHERE'S THE KITCHEN?
NEVER MIND YOUR STOMACH, SAMMY! THIS IS SERIOUS!
STAY SHARP, EVERYBODY...
... I KNOW WE'RE ARMED, BUT I'D RATHER NOT SHOOT ANYONE IF I CAN HELP IT!
HEY! WHERE ARE SAM AND SAMMY?!
WEREN'T THEY RIGHT BEHIND US?!!
OMIGOSH! I'LL BET THEY WERE CAPTURED! LOOK SHARP, JALEA! WE MIGHT HAVE TO--
--FIGHT...
HMMMM
WAIT--! YOU FORGOT ROBERTA!
WHAT'RE YOU TALKING ABOUT? SHE'S BACK IN ENGINEERING!
STEVE TROOP

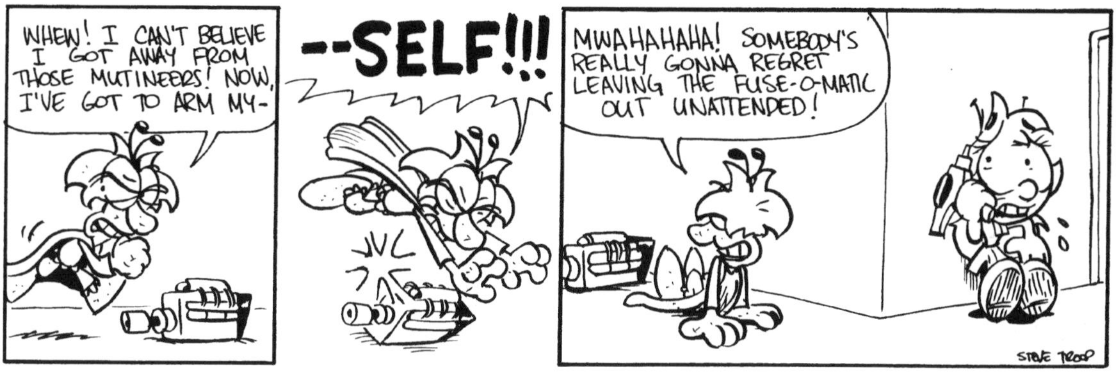
WHEW! I CAN'T BELIEVE I GOT AWAY FROM THOSE MUTINEERS! NOW, I'VE GOT TO ARM MY-
--SELF!!!
MWAHAHAHA! SOMEBODY'S REALLY GONNA REGRET LEAVING THE FUSE-O-MATIC OUT UNATTENDED!
STEVE TROOP

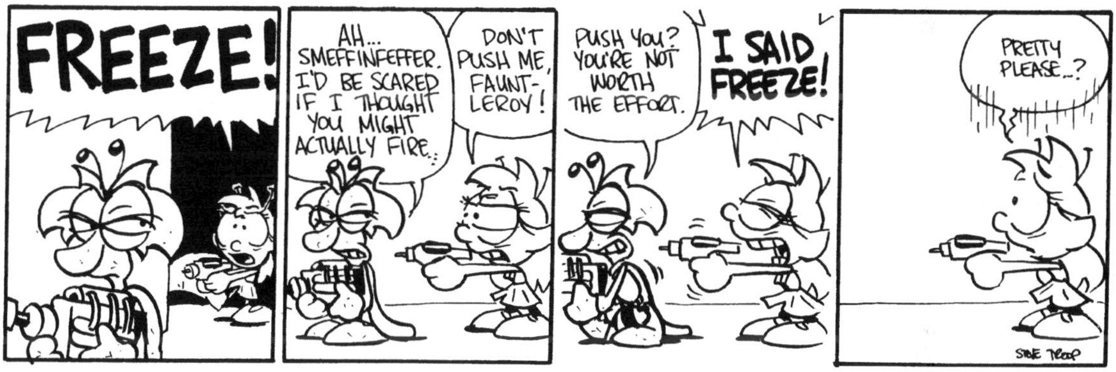
FREEZE!
AH... SMEFFINFEFFER. I'D BE SCARED IF I THOUGHT YOU MIGHT ACTUALLY FIRE...
DON'T PUSH ME, FAUNTLEROY!
PUSH YOU? YOU'RE NOT WORTH THE EFFORT.
I SAID FREEZE!
PRETTY PLEASE...?
STEVE TROOP

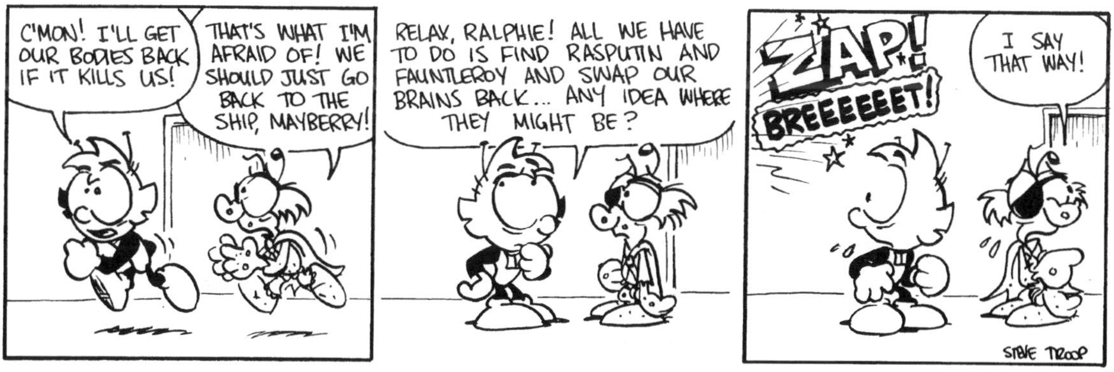
C'MON! I'LL GET OUR BODIES BACK IF IT KILLS US!
THAT'S WHAT I'M AFRAID OF! WE SHOULD JUST GO BACK TO THE SHIP, MAYBERRY!
RELAX, RALPHIE! ALL WE HAVE TO DO IS FIND RASPUTIN AND FAUNTLEROY AND SWAP OUR BRAINS BACK... ANY IDEA WHERE THEY MIGHT BE?
ZAP!
BREEEEEET!
I SAY THAT WAY!
STEVE TROOP

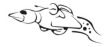

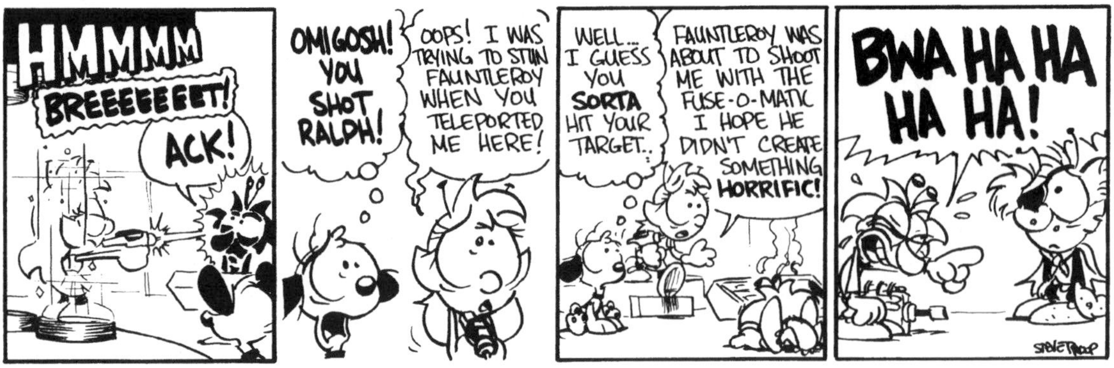
HMMMM
BREEEEEEET!
ACK!
OMIGOSH! YOU SHOT RALPH!
OOPS! I WAS TRYING TO STUN FAUNTLEROY WHEN YOU TELEPORTED ME HERE!
WELL... I GUESS YOU SORTA HIT YOUR TARGET..
FAUNTLEROY WAS ABOUT TO SHOOT ME WITH THE FUSE-O-MATIC I HOPE HE DIDN'T CREATE SOMETHING HORRIFIC!
BWA HA HA HA HA!
STEVE TROOP

Don't worry—this is just my 2005 April Fool's strip. Lyman, formerly of *Garfield,* figured prominently in the **Times, They are a Changin'** storyline (see TUM IV, pages 106–143). That storyline was so popular that, for a time, Wikipedia cited *Melonpool* as the reason Lyman disappeared from Garfield without explanation.

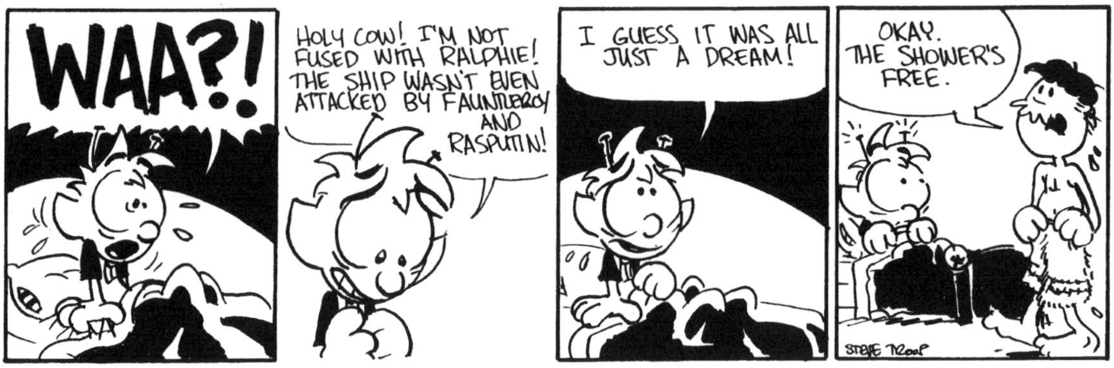
WAA?!
HOLY COW! I'M NOT FUSED WITH RALPHIE! THE SHIP WASN'T EVEN ATTACKED BY FAUNTLEROY AND RASPUTIN!
I GUESS IT WAS ALL JUST A DREAM!
OKAY. THE SHOWER'S FREE.
STEVE TROOP

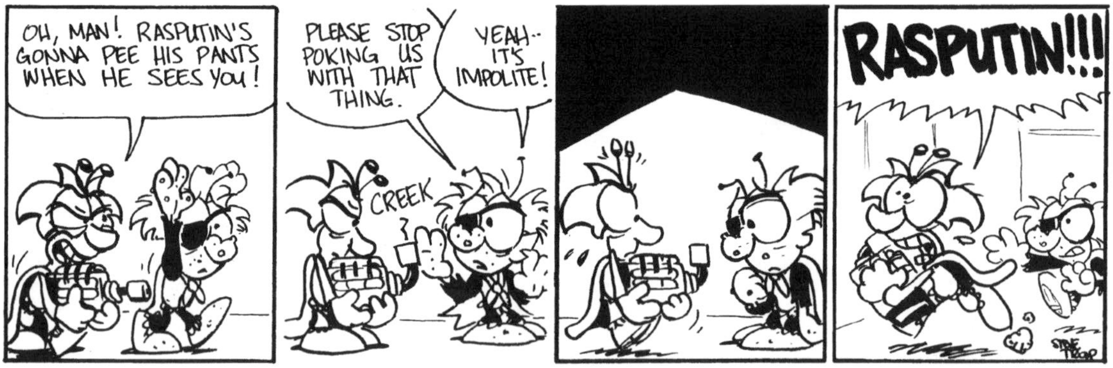
OH, MAN! RASPUTIN'S GONNA PEE HIS PANTS WHEN HE SEES YOU!
PLEASE STOP POKING US WITH THAT THING.
YEAH.. IT'S IMPOLITE!
CREEK
RASPUTIN!!!

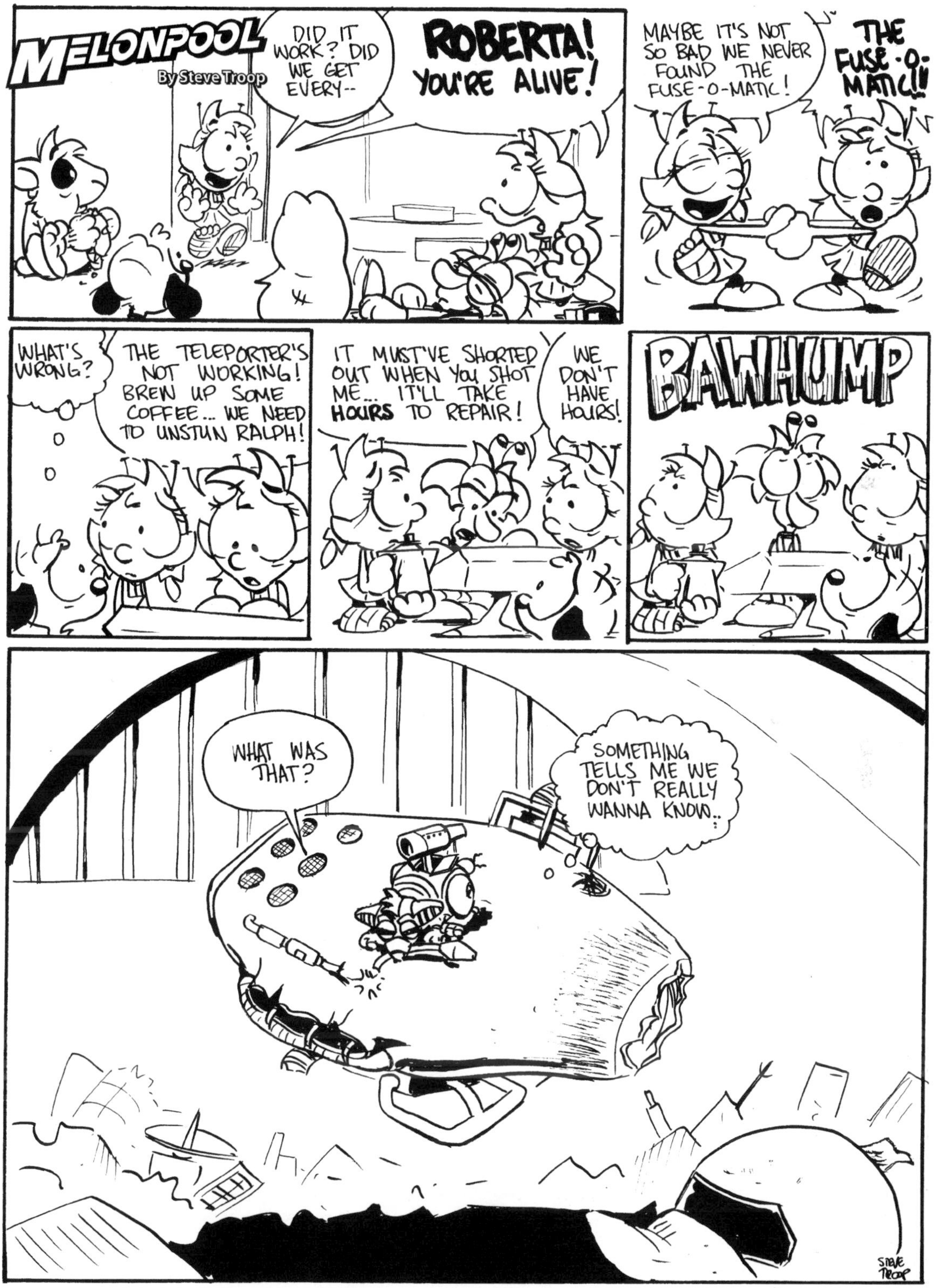

MELONPOOL
By Steve Troop
DID IT WORK? DID WE GET EVERY--
ROBERTA! YOU'RE ALIVE!
MAYBE IT'S NOT SO BAD WE NEVER FOUND THE FUSE-O-MATIC!
THE FUSE-O-MATIC!!
WHAT'S WRONG?
THE TELEPORTER'S NOT WORKING! BREW UP SOME COFFEE... WE NEED TO UNSTUN RALPH!
IT MUST'VE SHORTED OUT WHEN YOU SHOT ME... IT'LL TAKE HOURS TO REPAIR!
WE DON'T HAVE HOURS!
BAWHUMP
WHAT WAS THAT?
SOMETHING TELLS ME WE DON'T REALLY WANNA KNOW..
STEVE TROOP

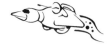

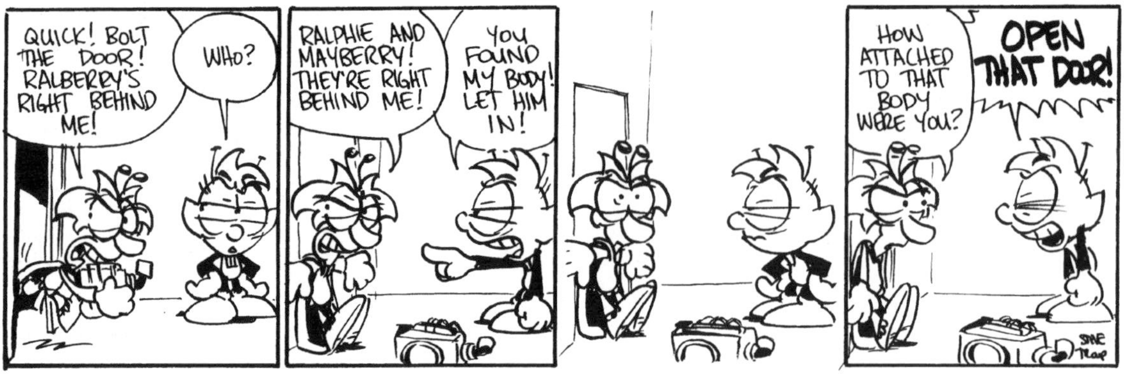
QUICK! BOLT THE DOOR! RALBERRY'S RIGHT BEHIND ME!
WHO?
RALPHIE AND MAYBERRY! THEY'RE RIGHT BEHIND ME!
YOU FOUND MY BODY! LET HIM IN!
HOW ATTACHED TO THAT BODY WERE YOU?
OPEN THAT DOOR!
STEVE TROOP

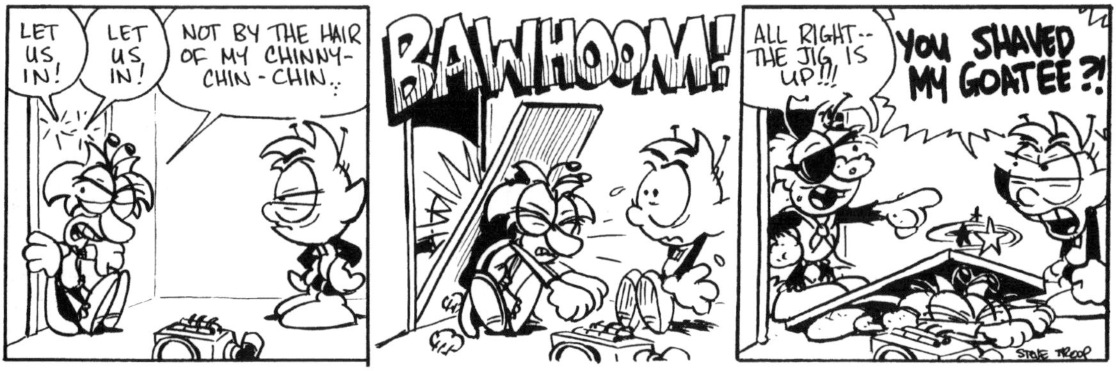
LET US IN!
LET US IN!
NOT BY THE HAIR OF MY CHINNY-CHIN-CHIN...
BAWHOOM!
ALL RIGHT-- THE JIG IS UP!!!
YOU SHAVED MY GOATEE ?!
STEVE TROOP

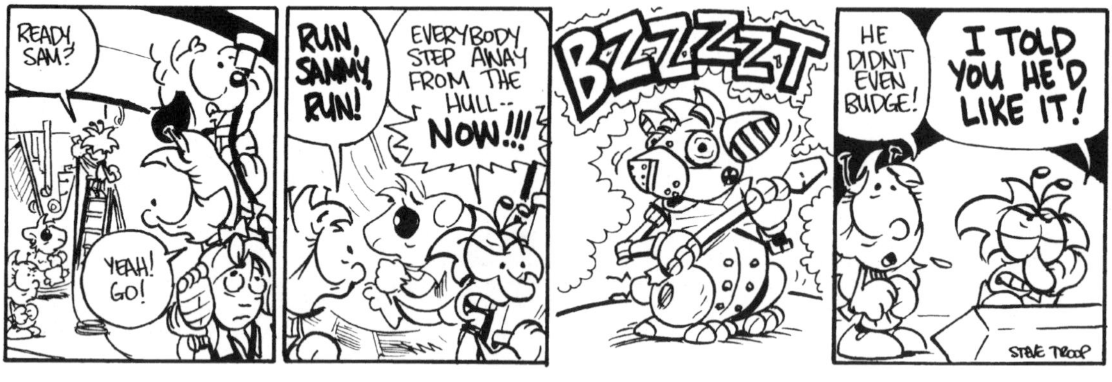
READY, SAM?
YEAH! GO!
RUN, SAMMY, RUN!
EVERYBODY STEP AWAY FROM THE HULL-- NOW!!!
BZZZZZT
HE DIDN'T EVEN BUDGE!
I TOLD YOU HE'D LIKE IT!
STEVE TROOP

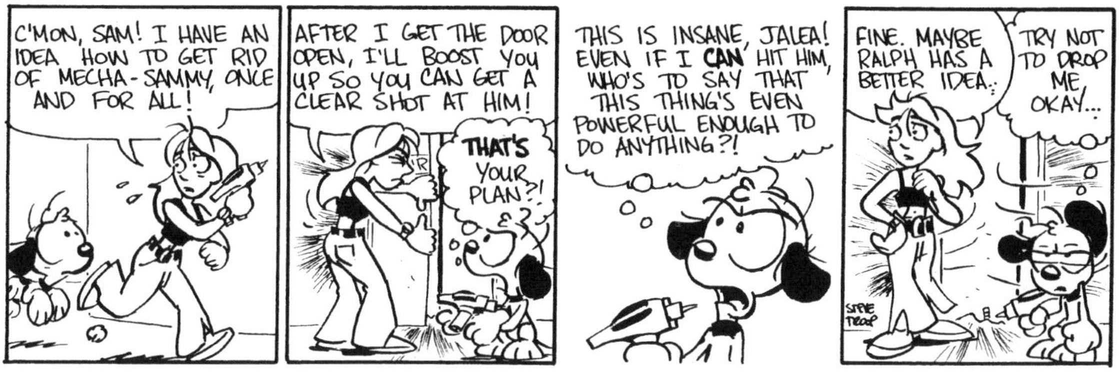
C'MON, SAM! I HAVE AN IDEA HOW TO GET RID OF MECHA-SAMMY, ONCE AND FOR ALL!
AFTER I GET THE DOOR OPEN, I'LL BOOST YOU UP SO YOU CAN GET A CLEAR SHOT AT HIM!
THAT'S YOUR PLAN?!
THIS IS INSANE, JALEA! EVEN IF I CAN HIT HIM, WHO'S TO SAY THAT THIS THING'S EVEN POWERFUL ENOUGH TO DO ANYTHING?!
FINE. MAYBE RALPH HAS A BETTER IDEA...
TRY NOT TO DROP ME, OKAY...
STEVE TROOP

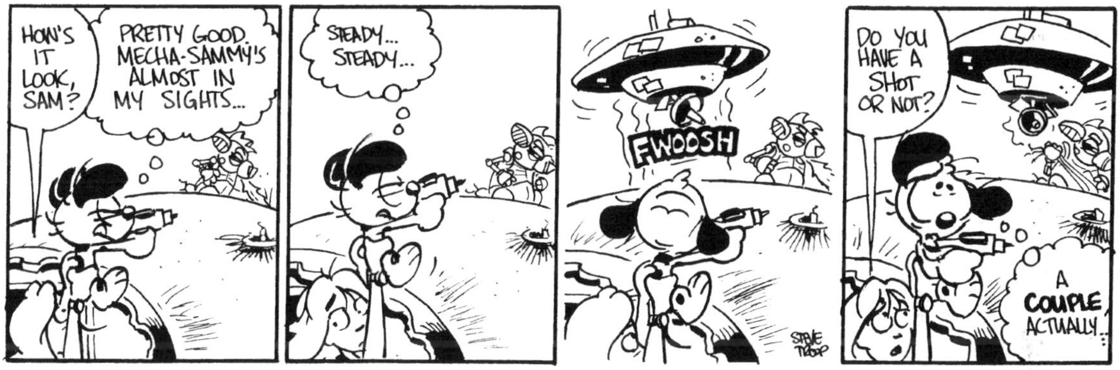
HOW'S IT LOOK, SAM?
PRETTY GOOD. MECHA-SAMMY'S ALMOST IN MY SIGHTS...
STEADY... STEADY...
FWOOSH
STEVE TROOP
DO YOU HAVE A SHOT OR NOT?
A COUPLE, ACTUALLY...

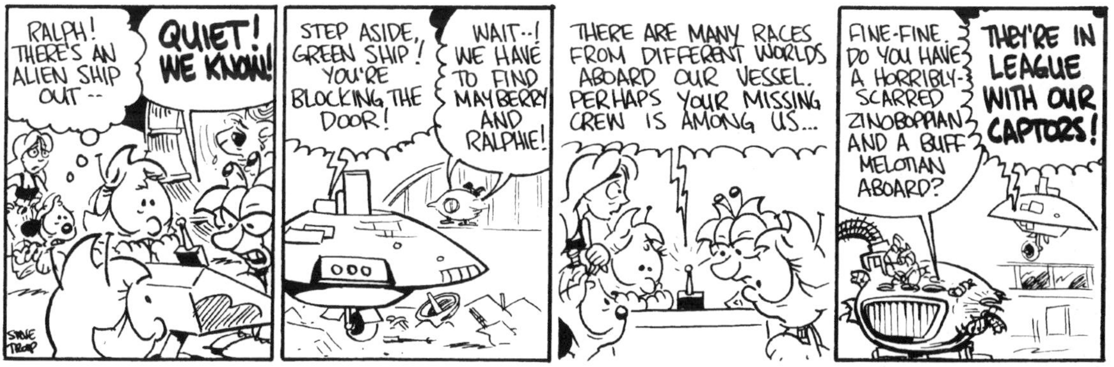
RALPH! THERE'S AN ALIEN SHIP OUT --
QUIET! WE KNOW!
STEVE TROOP
STEP ASIDE, GREEN SHIP! YOU'RE BLOCKING THE DOOR!
WAIT--! WE HAVE TO FIND MAYBERRY AND RALPHIE!
THERE ARE MANY RACES FROM DIFFERENT WORLDS ABOARD OUR VESSEL. PERHAPS YOUR MISSING CREW IS AMONG US...
FINE-FINE. DO YOU HAVE A HORRIBLY-SCARRED ZINOBOPPIAN AND A BUFF MELOTIAN ABOARD?
THEY'RE IN LEAGUE WITH OUR CAPTORS!

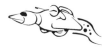

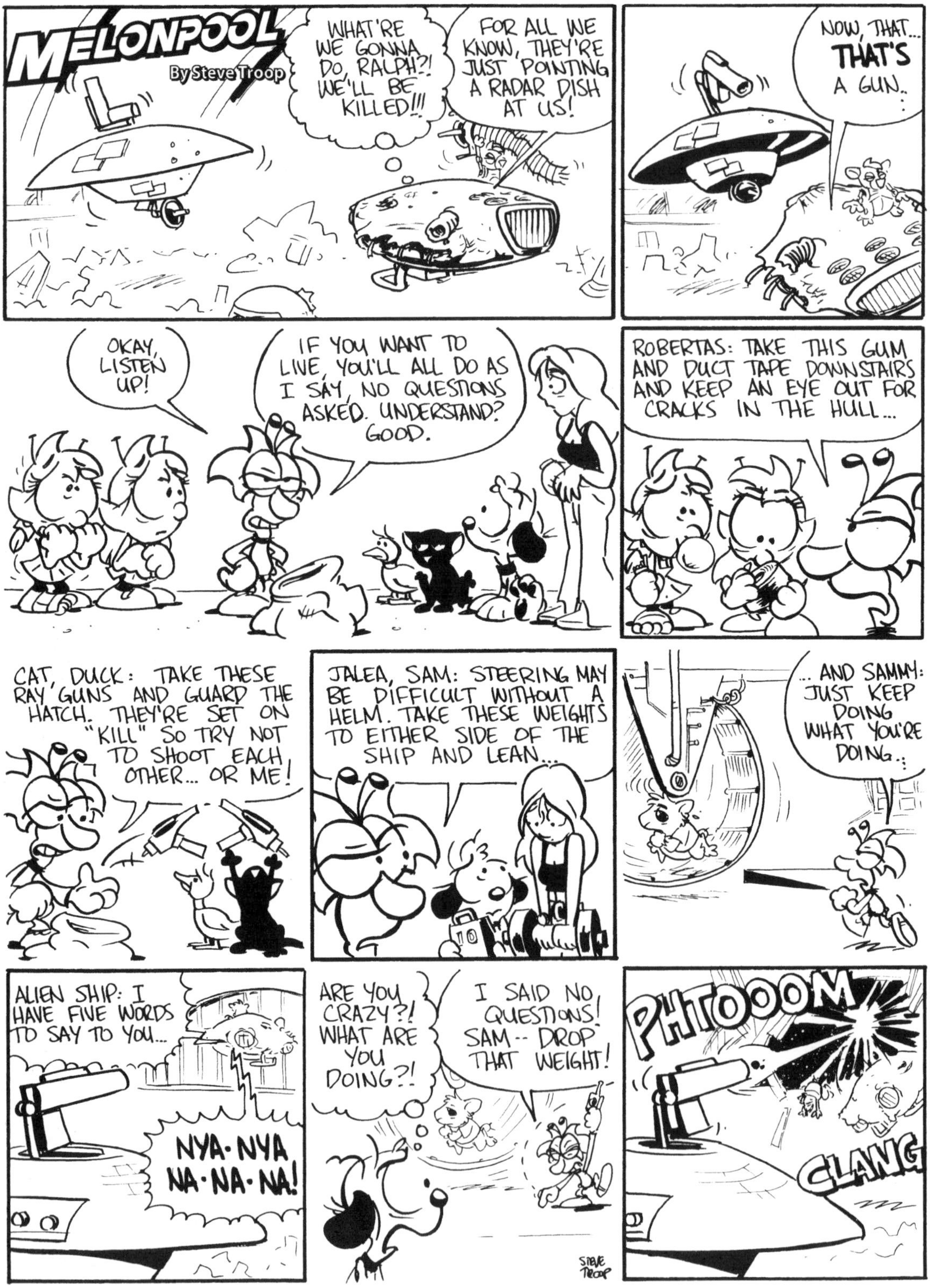
MELONPOOL
By Steve Troop
WHAT'RE WE GONNA DO, RALPH?! WE'LL BE KILLED!!!
FOR ALL WE KNOW, THEY'RE JUST POINTING A RADAR DISH AT US!
NOW, THAT... THAT'S A GUN...
OKAY, LISTEN UP!
IF YOU WANT TO LIVE, YOU'LL ALL DO AS I SAY, NO QUESTIONS ASKED. UNDERSTAND? GOOD.
ROBERTAS: TAKE THIS GUM AND DUCT TAPE DOWNSTAIRS AND KEEP AN EYE OUT FOR CRACKS IN THE HULL...
CAT, DUCK: TAKE THESE RAY GUNS AND GUARD THE HATCH. THEY'RE SET ON "KILL" SO TRY NOT TO SHOOT EACH OTHER... OR ME!
JALEA, SAM: STEERING MAY BE DIFFICULT WITHOUT A HELM. TAKE THESE WEIGHTS TO EITHER SIDE OF THE SHIP AND LEAN...
10
... AND SAMMY: JUST KEEP DOING WHAT YOU'RE DOING...
ALIEN SHIP: I HAVE FIVE WORDS TO SAY TO YOU...
NYA-NYA NA-NA-NA!
ARE YOU CRAZY?! WHAT ARE YOU DOING?!
I SAID NO QUESTIONS! SAM -- DROP THAT WEIGHT!
STEVE TROOP
PHTOOOM
CLANG

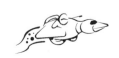

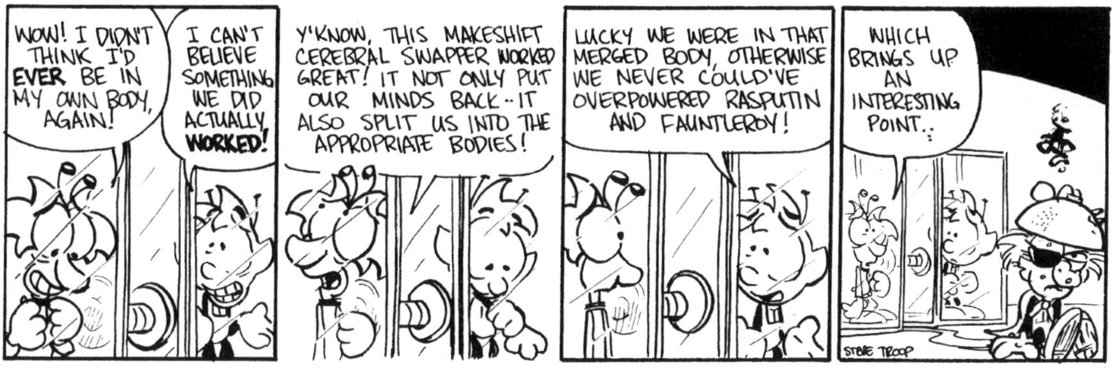
WOW! I DIDN'T THINK I'D EVER BE IN MY OWN BODY, AGAIN!
I CAN'T BELIEVE SOMETHING WE DID ACTUALLY WORKED!
Y'KNOW, THIS MAKESHIFT CEREBRAL SWAPPER WORKED GREAT! IT NOT ONLY PUT OUR MINDS BACK -- IT ALSO SPLIT US INTO THE APPROPRIATE BODIES!
LUCKY WE WERE IN THAT MERGED BODY, OTHERWISE WE NEVER COULD'VE OVERPOWERED RASPUTIN AND FAUNTLEROY!
WHICH BRINGS UP AN INTERESTING POINT...
STEVE TROOP

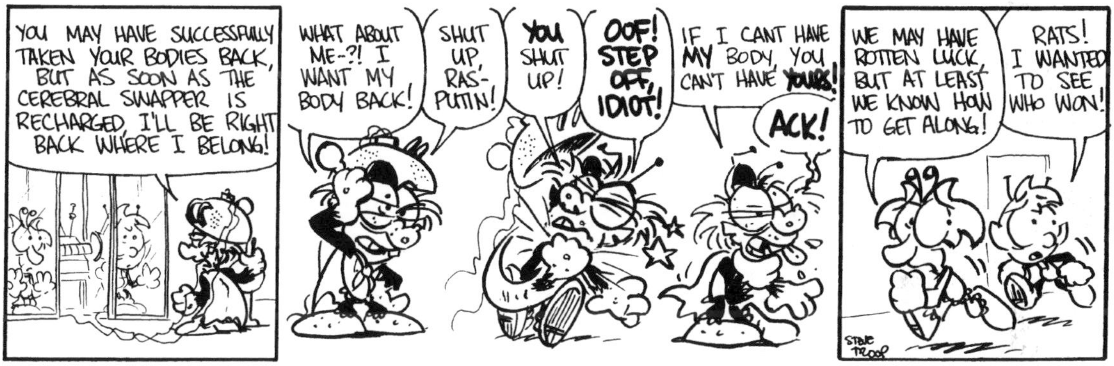
YOU MAY HAVE SUCCESSFULLY TAKEN YOUR BODIES BACK, BUT AS SOON AS THE CEREBRAL SWAPPER IS RECHARGED, I'LL BE RIGHT BACK WHERE I BELONG!
WHAT ABOUT ME--?! I WANT MY BODY BACK!
SHUT UP, RAS-PUTIN!
YOU SHUT UP!
OOF! STEP OFF, IDIOT!
IF I CANT HAVE MY BODY, YOU CAN'T HAVE YOURS!
ACK!
WE MAY HAVE ROTTEN LUCK, BUT AT LEAST WE KNOW HOW TO GET ALONG!
RATS! I WANTED TO SEE WHO WON!
STEVE TROOP

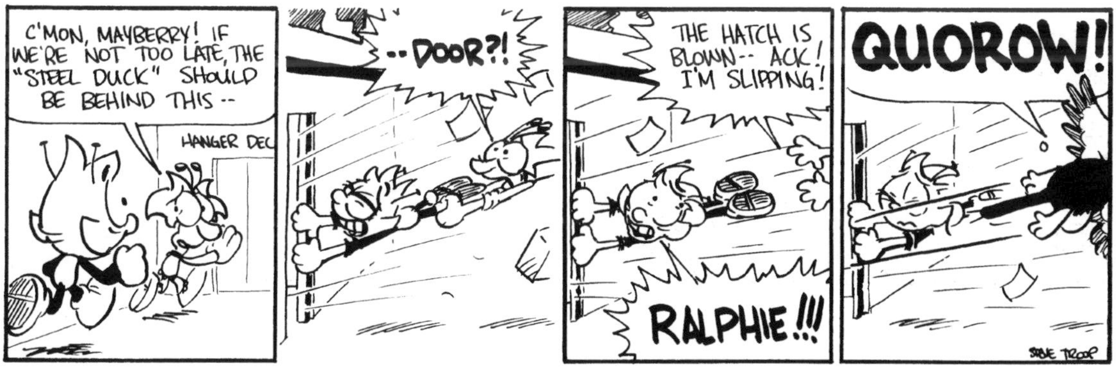
C'MON, MAYBERRY! IF WE'RE NOT TOO LATE, THE "STEEL DUCK" SHOULD BE BEHIND THIS --
HANGER DEC
-- DOOR?!
THE HATCH IS BLOWN -- ACK! I'M SLIPPING!
RALPHIE!!!
QUOROW!
STEVE TROOP

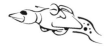

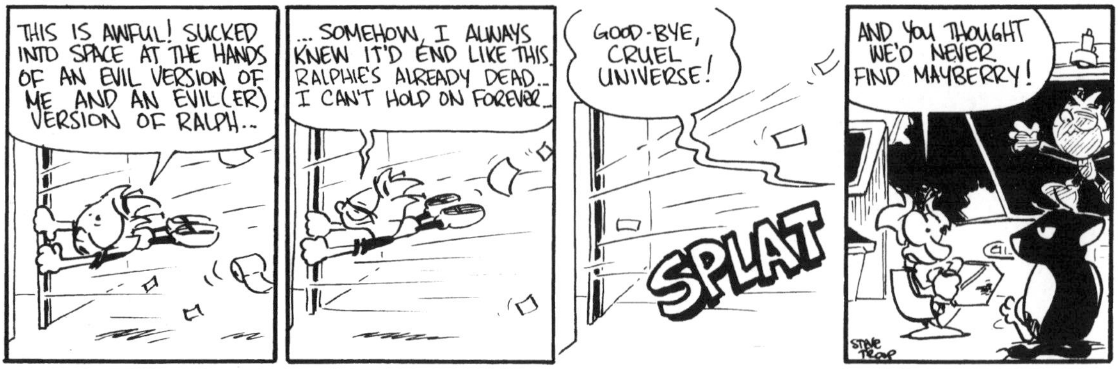
THIS IS AWFUL! SUCKED INTO SPACE AT THE HANDS OF AN EVIL VERSION OF ME AND AN EVIL(ER) VERSION OF RALPH...
... SOMEHOW, I ALWAYS KNEW IT'D END LIKE THIS. RALPHIE'S ALREADY DEAD... I CAN'T HOLD ON FOREVER...
GOOD-BYE, CRUEL UNIVERSE!
SPLAT
AND YOU THOUGHT WE'D NEVER FIND MAYBERRY!
STEVE TROOP

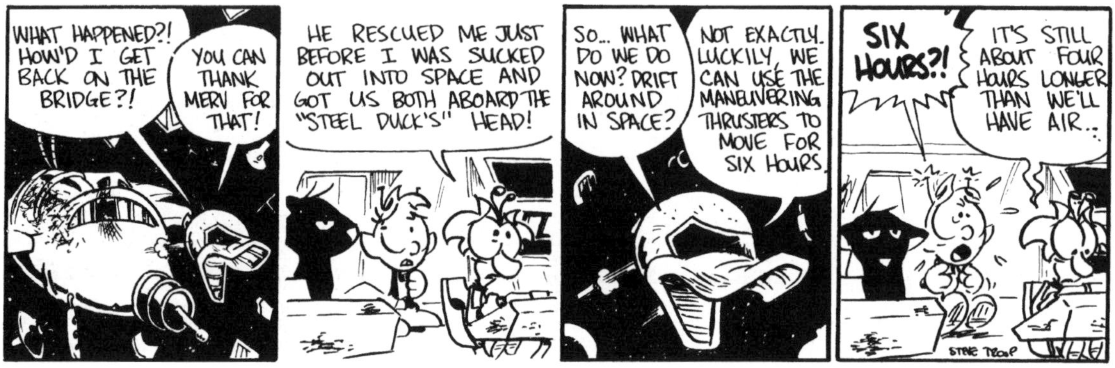
WHAT HAPPENED?! HOW'D I GET BACK ON THE BRIDGE?!
YOU CAN THANK MERV FOR THAT!
HE RESCUED ME JUST BEFORE I WAS SUCKED OUT INTO SPACE AND GOT US BOTH ABOARD THE "STEEL DUCK'S" HEAD!
SO... WHAT DO WE DO NOW? DRIFT AROUND IN SPACE?
NOT EXACTLY. LUCKILY, WE CAN USE THE MANEUVERING THRUSTERS TO MOVE FOR SIX HOURS.
SIX HOURS?!
IT'S STILL ABOUT FOUR HOURS LONGER THAN WE'LL HAVE AIR...
STEVE TROOP

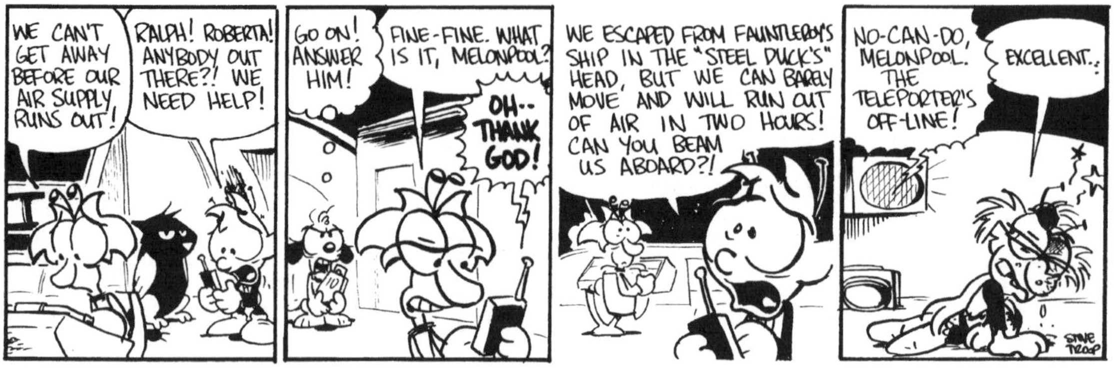
WE CAN'T GET AWAY BEFORE OUR AIR SUPPLY RUNS OUT!
RALPH! ROBERTA! ANYBODY OUT THERE?! WE NEED HELP!
GO ON! ANSWER HIM!
FINE-FINE. WHAT IS IT, MELONPOOL?
OH... THANK GOD!
WE ESCAPED FROM FAUNTLEROY'S SHIP IN THE "STEEL DUCK'S" HEAD, BUT WE CAN BARELY MOVE AND WILL RUN OUT OF AIR IN TWO HOURS! CAN YOU BEAM US ABOARD?!
NO-CAN-DO, MELONPOOL. THE TELEPORTER'S OFF-LINE!
EXCELLENT...
STEVE TROOP

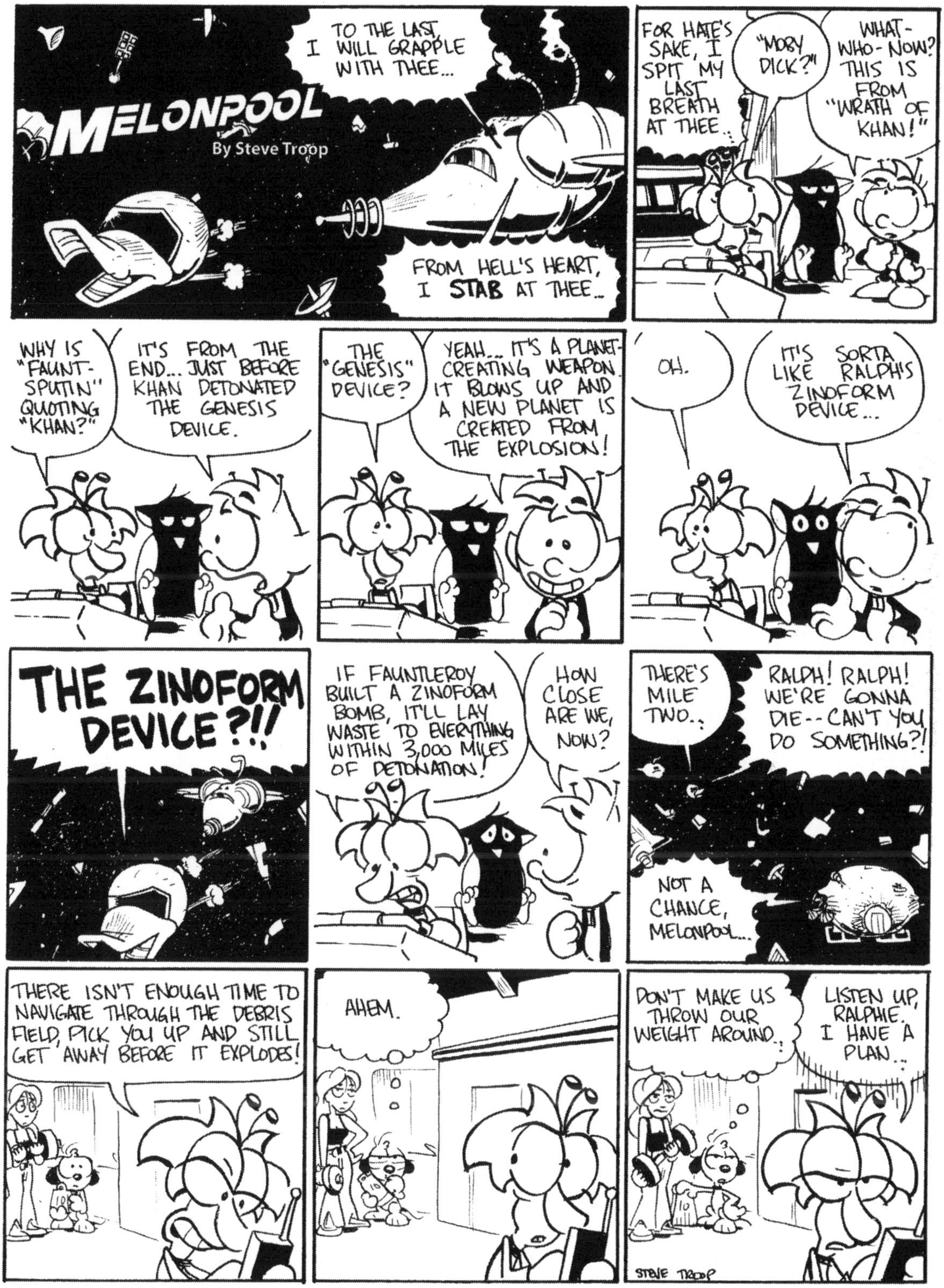
MELONPOOL
By Steve Troop
TO THE LAST, I WILL GRAPPLE WITH THEE...
FROM HELL'S HEART, I STAB AT THEE...
FOR HATE'S SAKE, I SPIT MY LAST BREATH AT THEE...
"MOBY DICK?"
WHAT-WHO-NOW? THIS IS FROM "WRATH OF KHAN!"
WHY IS "FAUNT-SPUTIN" QUOTING "KHAN?"
IT'S FROM THE END... JUST BEFORE KHAN DETONATED THE GENESIS DEVICE.
THE "GENESIS" DEVICE?
YEAH... IT'S A PLANET-CREATING WEAPON. IT BLOWS UP AND A NEW PLANET IS CREATED FROM THE EXPLOSION!
OH.
IT'S SORTA LIKE RALPH'S ZINOFORM DEVICE...
THE ZINOFORM DEVICE?!!
IF FAUNTLEROY BUILT A ZINOFORM BOMB, IT'LL LAY WASTE TO EVERYTHING WITHIN 3,000 MILES OF DETONATION!
HOW CLOSE ARE WE, NOW?
THERE'S MILE TWO...
RALPH! RALPH! WE'RE GONNA DIE--CAN'T YOU DO SOMETHING?!
NOT A CHANCE, MELONPOOL...
THERE ISN'T ENOUGH TIME TO NAVIGATE THROUGH THE DEBRIS FIELD, PICK YOU UP AND STILL GET AWAY BEFORE IT EXPLODES!
AHEM.
DON'T MAKE US THROW OUR WEIGHT AROUND...
LISTEN UP, RALPHIE. I HAVE A PLAN...
STEVE TROOP

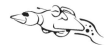

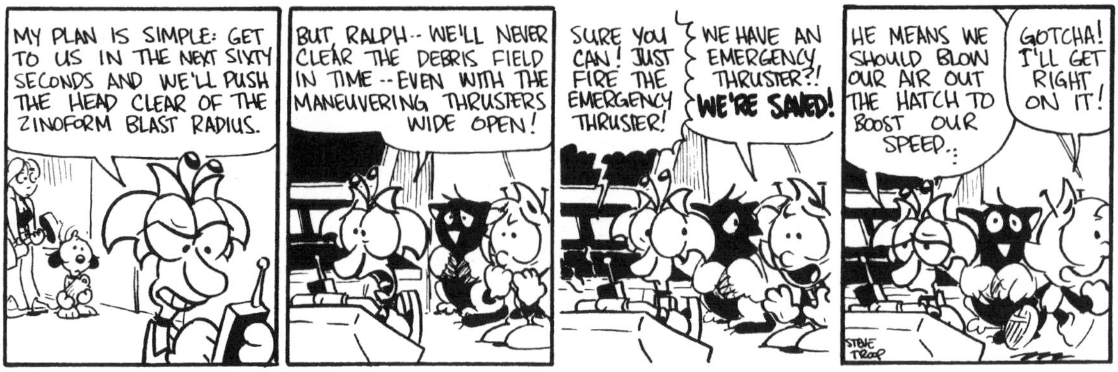
MY PLAN IS SIMPLE: GET TO US IN THE NEXT SIXTY SECONDS AND WE'LL PUSH THE HEAD CLEAR OF THE ZINOFORM BLAST RADIUS.
BUT, RALPH-- WE'LL NEVER CLEAR THE DEBRIS FIELD IN TIME --EVEN WITH THE MANEUVERING THRUSTERS WIDE OPEN!
SURE YOU CAN! JUST FIRE THE EMERGENCY THRUSTER!
WE HAVE AN EMERGENCY THRUSTER?! WE'RE SAVED!
HE MEANS WE SHOULD BLOW OUR AIR OUT THE HATCH TO BOOST OUR SPEED...
GOTCHA! I'LL GET RIGHT ON IT!
STEVE TROOP

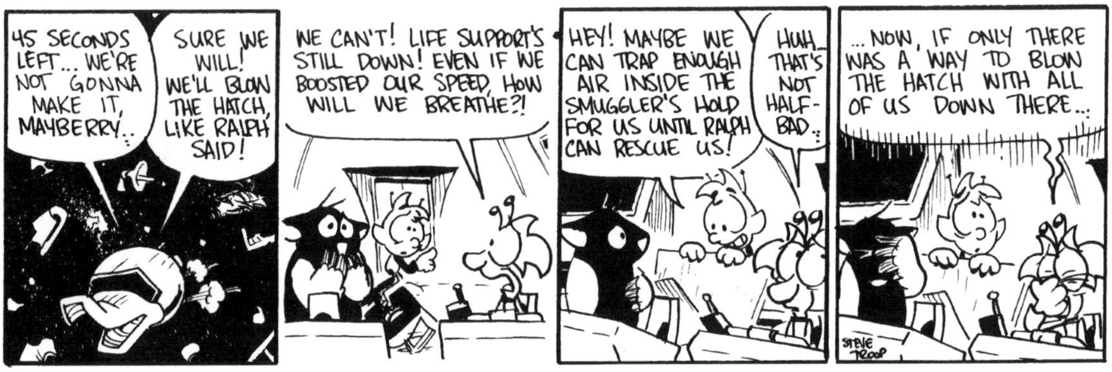
45 SECONDS LEFT... WE'RE NOT GONNA MAKE IT, MAYBERRY...
SURE WE WILL! WE'LL BLOW THE HATCH, LIKE RALPH SAID!
WE CAN'T! LIFE SUPPORT'S STILL DOWN! EVEN IF WE BOOSTED OUR SPEED, HOW WILL WE BREATHE?!
HEY! MAYBE WE CAN TRAP ENOUGH AIR INSIDE THE SMUGGLER'S HOLD FOR US UNTIL RALPH CAN RESCUE US!
HUH. THAT'S NOT HALF-BAD...
...NOW, IF ONLY THERE WAS A WAY TO BLOW THE HATCH WITH ALL OF US DOWN THERE...
STEVE TROOP

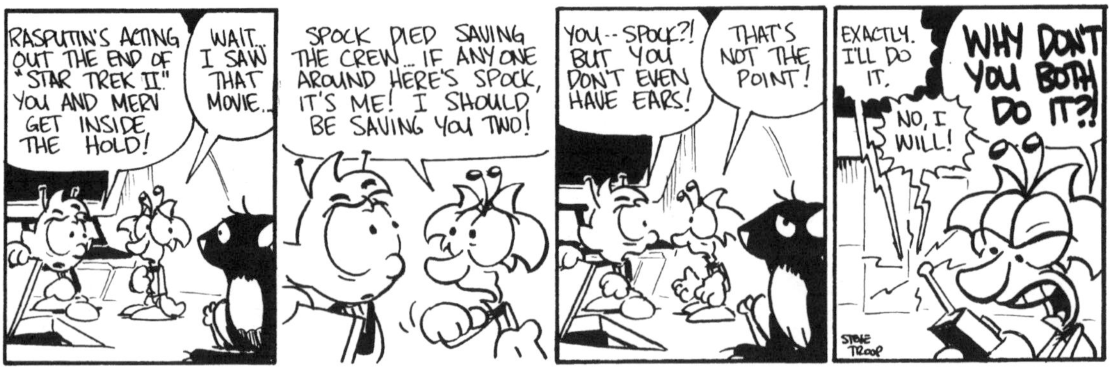
RASPUTIN'S ACTING OUT THE END OF "STAR TREK II." YOU AND MERV GET INSIDE THE HOLD!
WAIT... I SAW THAT MOVIE...
SPOCK DIED SAVING THE CREW... IF ANYONE AROUND HERE'S SPOCK, IT'S ME! I SHOULD BE SAVING YOU TWO!
YOU-- SPOCK?! BUT YOU DON'T EVEN HAVE EARS!
THAT'S NOT THE POINT!
EXACTLY. I'LL DO IT.
NO, I WILL!
WHY DON'T YOU BOTH DO IT?!
STEVE TROOP

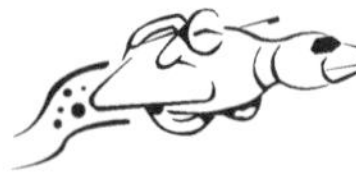

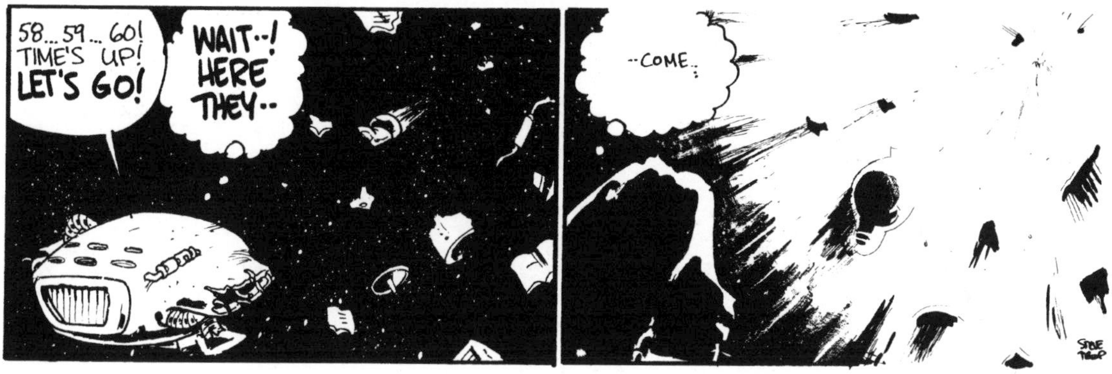
58... 59... 60! TIME'S UP! LET'S GO!
WAIT..! HERE THEY..
--COME..
STEVE TROOP

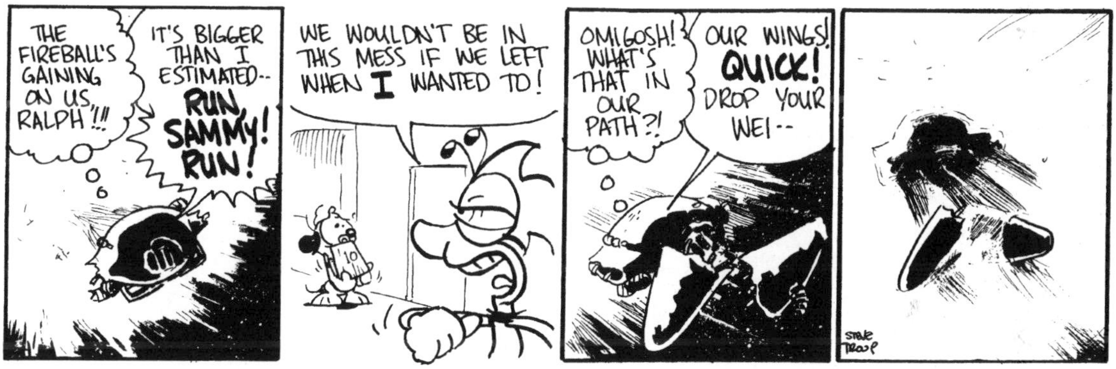
THE FIREBALL'S GAINING ON US, RALPH'!!!
IT'S BIGGER THAN I ESTIMATED-- RUN, SAMMY! RUN!
WE WOULDN'T BE IN THIS MESS IF WE LEFT WHEN I WANTED TO!
OMIGOSH! WHAT'S THAT IN OUR PATH?!
OUR WINGS! QUICK! DROP YOUR WEI--
STEVE TROOP

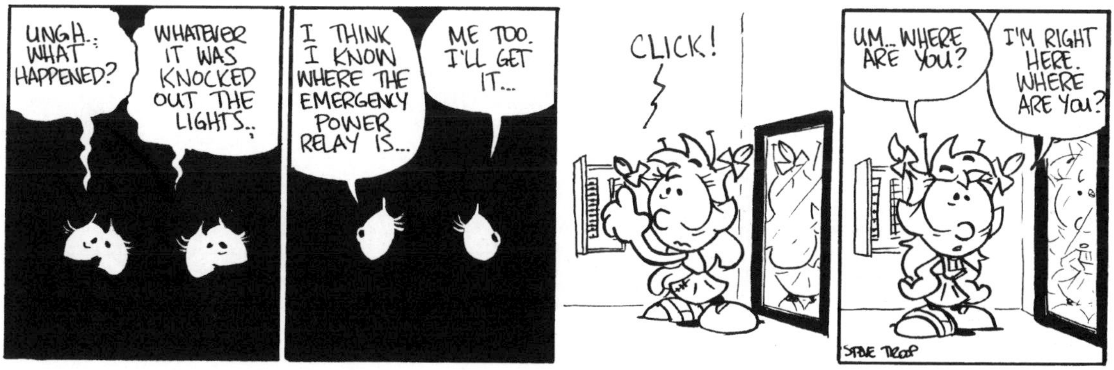
UNGH.. WHAT HAPPENED?
WHATEVER IT WAS KNOCKED OUT THE LIGHTS..
I THINK I KNOW WHERE THE EMERGENCY POWER RELAY IS...
ME TOO. I'LL GET IT...
CLICK!
UM... WHERE ARE YOU?
I'M RIGHT HERE. WHERE ARE YOU?
STEVE TROOP

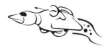

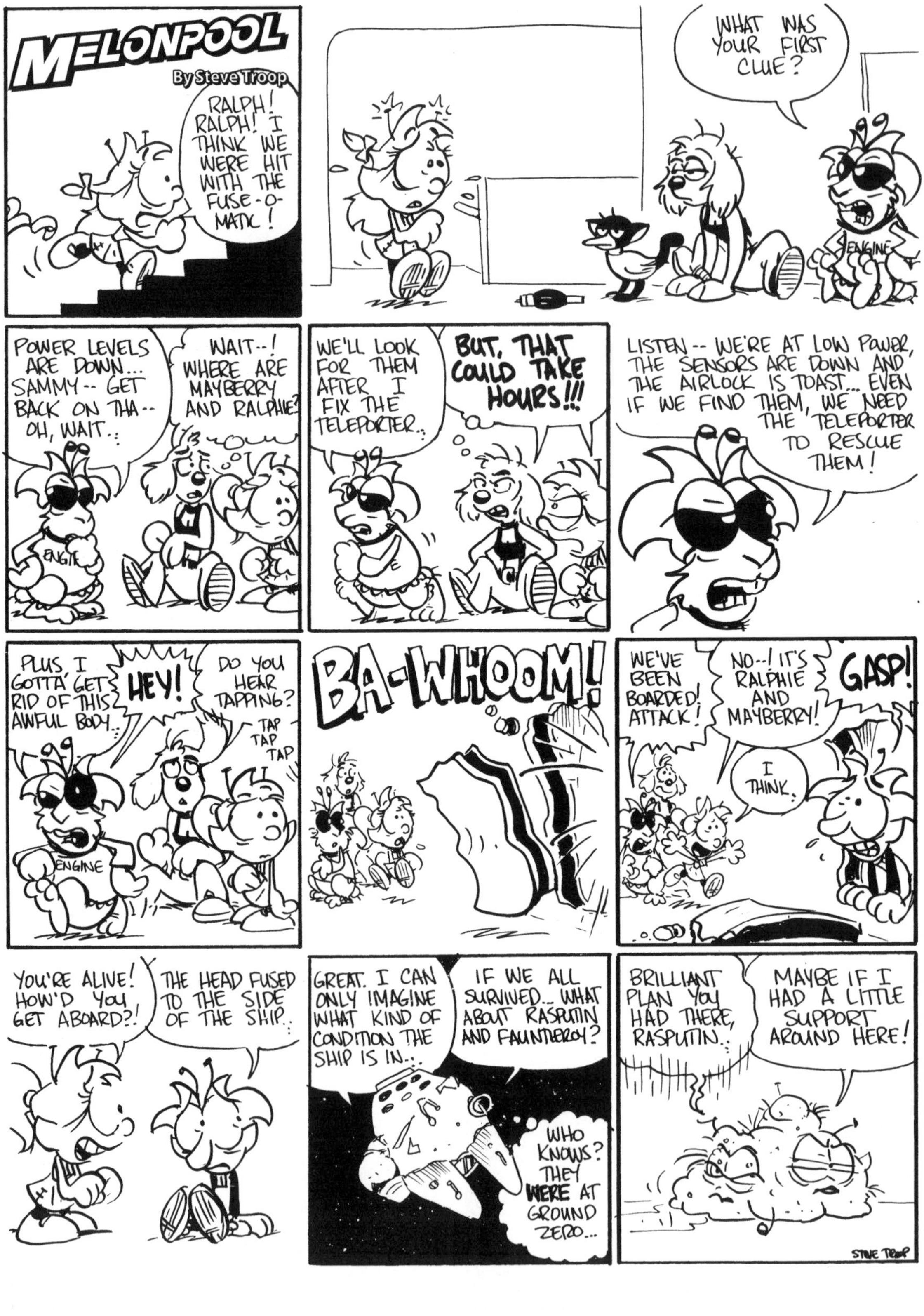
MELONPOOL
By Steve Troop
RALPH! RALPH! I THINK WE WERE HIT WITH THE FUSE-O-MATIC!
WHAT WAS YOUR FIRST CLUE?
ENGINE
POWER LEVELS ARE DOWN... SAMMY -- GET BACK ON THA-- OH, WAIT...
WAIT--! WHERE ARE MAYBERRY AND RALPHIE?
ENGINE
WE'LL LOOK FOR THEM AFTER I FIX THE TELEPORTER...
BUT, THAT COULD TAKE HOURS!!!
LISTEN -- WE'RE AT LOW POWER, THE SENSORS ARE DOWN AND THE AIRLOCK IS TOAST... EVEN IF WE FIND THEM, WE NEED THE TELEPORTER TO RESCUE THEM!
PLUS, I GOTTA GET RID OF THIS AWFUL BODY...
HEY!
DO YOU HEAR TAPPING?
TAP TAP TAP
ENGINE
BA-WHOOM!
WE'VE BEEN BOARDED! ATTACK!
NO--! IT'S RALPHIE AND MAYBERRY!
GASP!
I THINK...
YOU'RE ALIVE! HOW'D YOU GET ABOARD?!
THE HEAD FUSED TO THE SIDE OF THE SHIP...
GREAT. I CAN ONLY IMAGINE WHAT KIND OF CONDITION THE SHIP IS IN...
IF WE ALL SURVIVED... WHAT ABOUT RASPUTIN AND FAUNTLEROY?
WHO KNOWS? THEY WERE AT GROUND ZERO...
BRILLIANT PLAN YOU HAD THERE, RASPUTIN...
MAYBE IF I HAD A LITTLE SUPPORT AROUND HERE!
STEVE TROOP

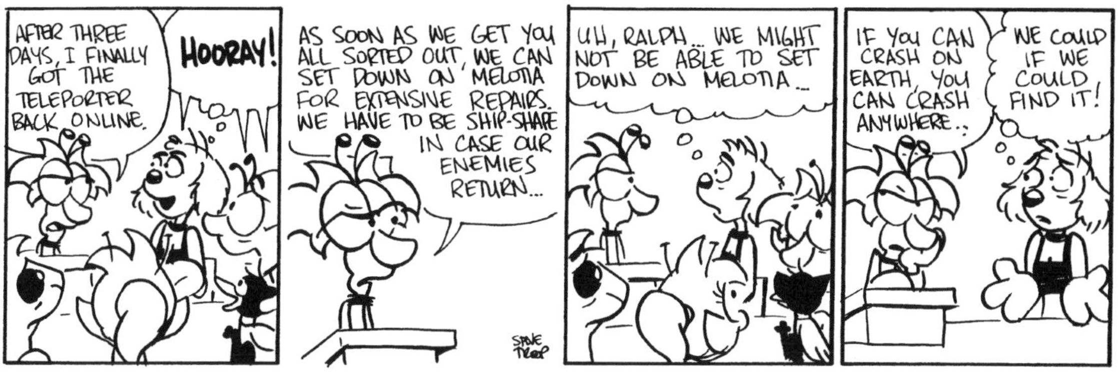
AFTER THREE DAYS, I FINALLY GOT THE TELEPORTER BACK ONLINE.
HOORAY!
AS SOON AS WE GET YOU ALL SORTED OUT, WE CAN SET DOWN ON MELOTIA FOR EXTENSIVE REPAIRS. WE HAVE TO BE SHIP-SHAPE IN CASE OUR ENEMIES RETURN...
STEVE TROOP
UH, RALPH... WE MIGHT NOT BE ABLE TO SET DOWN ON MELOTIA...
IF YOU CAN CRASH ON EARTH, YOU CAN CRASH ANYWHERE...
WE COULD IF WE COULD FIND IT!

Much like Mayberry, Orion's Belt is the only constellation I can pick out of the night's sky.

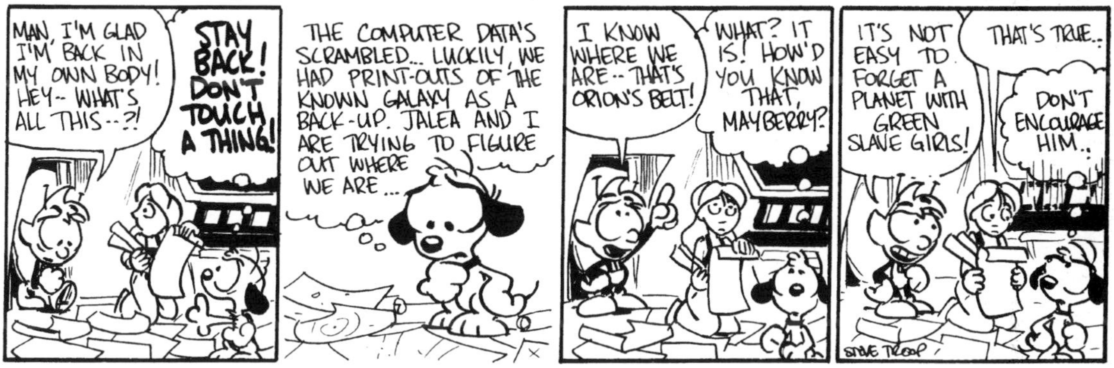
MAN, I'M GLAD I'M BACK IN MY OWN BODY! HEY-- WHAT'S ALL THIS--?!
STAY BACK! DON'T TOUCH A THING!
THE COMPUTER DATA'S SCRAMBLED... LUCKILY, WE HAD PRINT-OUTS OF THE KNOWN GALAXY AS A BACK-UP. JALEA AND I ARE TRYING TO FIGURE OUT WHERE WE ARE...
I KNOW WHERE WE ARE-- THAT'S ORION'S BELT!
WHAT? IT IS! HOW'D YOU KNOW THAT, MAYBERRY?
IT'S NOT EASY TO FORGET A PLANET WITH GREEN SLAVE GIRLS!
THAT'S TRUE...
DON'T ENCOURAGE HIM...
STEVE TROOP

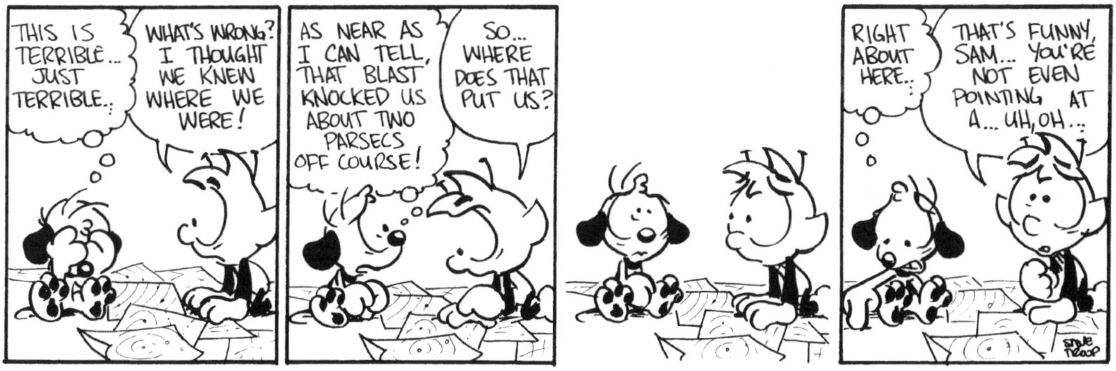
THIS IS TERRIBLE... JUST TERRIBLE...
WHAT'S WRONG? I THOUGHT WE KNEW WHERE WE WERE!
AS NEAR AS I CAN TELL, THAT BLAST KNOCKED US ABOUT TWO PARSECS OFF COURSE!
SO... WHERE DOES THAT PUT US?
RIGHT ABOUT HERE...
THAT'S FUNNY, SAM... YOU'RE NOT EVEN POINTING AT A... UH, OH...
STEVE TROOP

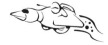

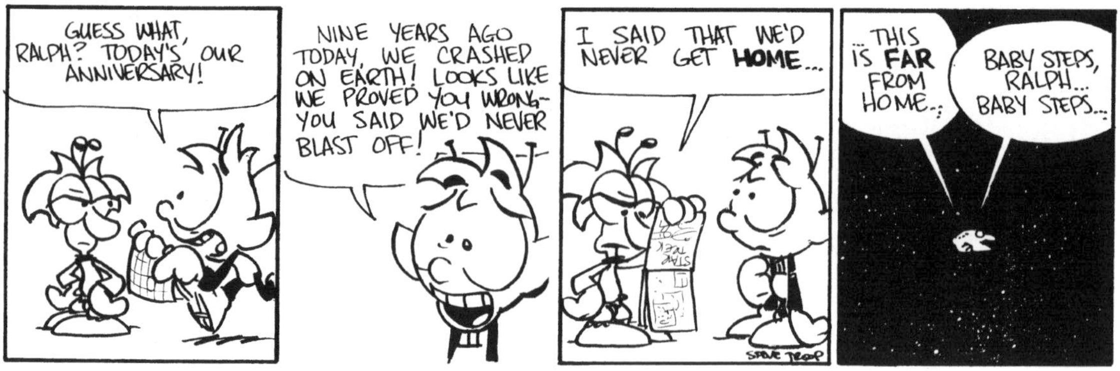
GUESS WHAT, RALPH? TODAY'S OUR ANNIVERSARY!
NINE YEARS AGO TODAY, WE CRASHED ON EARTH! LOOKS LIKE WE PROVED YOU WRONG-- YOU SAID WE'D NEVER BLAST OFF!
I SAID THAT WE'D NEVER GET **HOME**...
...THIS IS **FAR** FROM HOME...
BABY STEPS, RALPH... BABY STEPS...
STEVE TROOP

For those of you who haven't figured it out, Merv was the product of the egg that the fused-together Sammy-Maddie-Quack laid during the **Double Trouble** storyline (TUM V, page 25). QUOROW is "Quack," "Borg" and "Meow" all merged together.

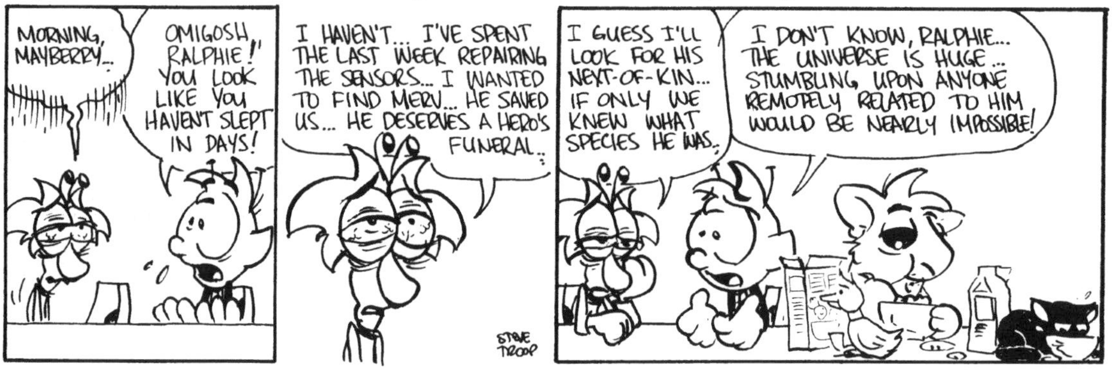
MORNING, MAYBERRY...
OMIGOSH, RALPHIE! YOU LOOK LIKE YOU HAVEN'T SLEPT IN DAYS!
I HAVEN'T... I'VE SPENT THE LAST WEEK REPAIRING THE SENSORS... I WANTED TO FIND MERV... HE SAVED US... HE DESERVES A HERO'S FUNERAL...
STEVE TROOP
I GUESS I'LL LOOK FOR HIS NEXT-OF-KIN... IF ONLY WE KNEW WHAT SPECIES HE WAS...
I DON'T KNOW, RALPHIE... THE UNIVERSE IS HUGE... STUMBLING UPON ANYONE REMOTELY RELATED TO HIM WOULD BE NEARLY IMPOSSIBLE!

Nobody ever noticed it, but the design of the Space Station is identical to the body of Crow from *Mystery Science Theater 3000* (see TUM V, page 151).

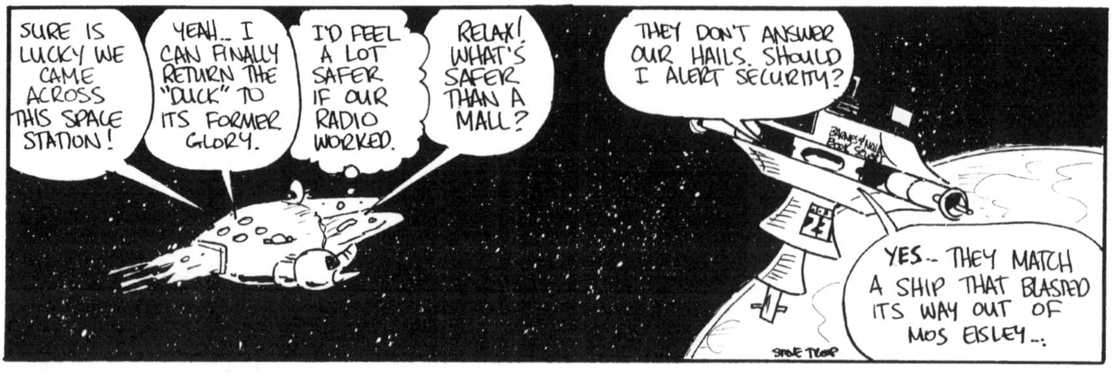
SURE IS LUCKY WE CAME ACROSS THIS SPACE STATION!
YEAH... I CAN FINALLY RETURN THE "DUCK" TO ITS FORMER GLORY.
I'D FEEL A LOT SAFER IF OUR RADIO WORKED.
RELAX! WHAT'S SAFER THAN A MALL?
THEY DON'T ANSWER OUR HAILS. SHOULD I ALERT SECURITY?
YES... THEY MATCH A SHIP THAT BLASTED ITS WAY OUT OF MOS EISLEY...
STEVE TROOP

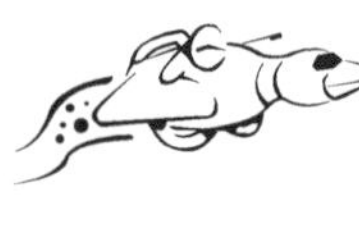

Because most of *Melonpool's* adventures took place on Earth, I hadn't designed any new aliens since 1992. These guys may be lame, but at least none of them look like Calvin or a Muppet!

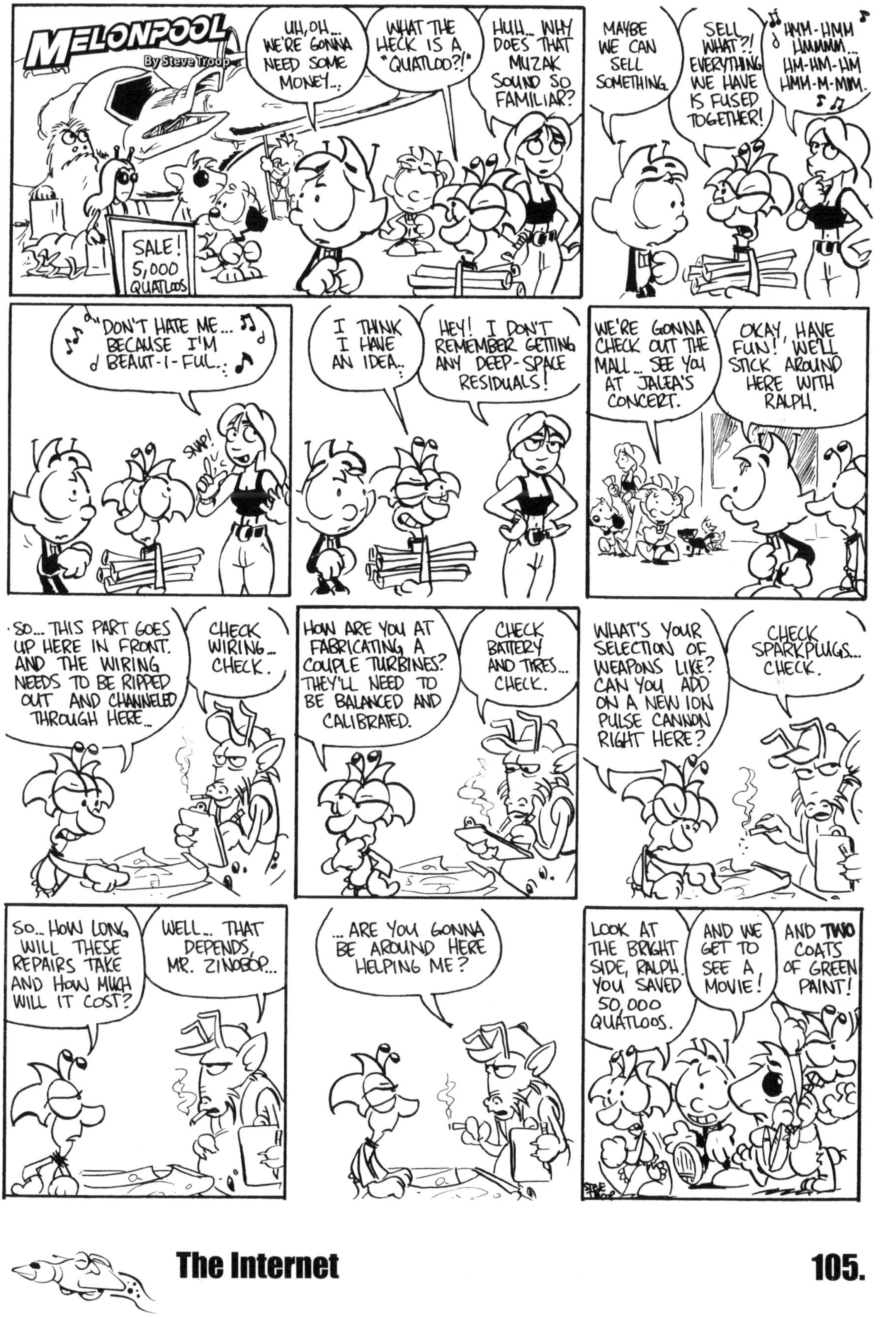
MELONPOOL
By Steve Troop
SALE! 5,000 QUATLOOS
UH, OH... WE'RE GONNA NEED SOME MONEY...
WHAT THE HECK IS A "QUATLOO?!"
HUH... WHY DOES THAT MUZAK SOUND SO FAMILIAR?
MAYBE WE CAN SELL SOMETHING.
SELL WHAT?! EVERYTHING WE HAVE IS FUSED TOGETHER!
HMM-HMM HMMMM... HM-HM-HM HMM-M-MM.
"DON'T HATE ME... BECAUSE I'M BEAUT-I-FUL..."
SNAP!
I THINK I HAVE AN IDEA...
HEY! I DON'T REMEMBER GETTING ANY DEEP-SPACE RESIDUALS!
WE'RE GONNA CHECK OUT THE MALL... SEE YOU AT JALEA'S CONCERT.
OKAY, HAVE FUN! WE'LL STICK AROUND HERE WITH RALPH.
SO... THIS PART GOES UP HERE IN FRONT. AND THE WIRING NEEDS TO BE RIPPED OUT AND CHANNELED THROUGH HERE...
CHECK WIRING... CHECK.
HOW ARE YOU AT FABRICATING A COUPLE TURBINES? THEY'LL NEED TO BE BALANCED AND CALIBRATED.
CHECK BATTERY AND TIRES... CHECK.
WHAT'S YOUR SELECTION OF WEAPONS LIKE? CAN YOU ADD ON A NEW ION PULSE CANNON RIGHT HERE?
CHECK SPARKPLUGS... CHECK.
SO... HOW LONG WILL THESE REPAIRS TAKE AND HOW MUCH WILL IT COST?
WELL... THAT DEPENDS, MR. ZINOBOP...
...ARE YOU GONNA BE AROUND HERE HELPING ME?
LOOK AT THE BRIGHT SIDE, RALPH. YOU SAVED 50,000 QUATLOOS.
AND WE GET TO SEE A MOVIE!
AND TWO COATS OF GREEN PAINT!
STEVE TROOP

The Zortic/Melonpool Crossover shows how two seemingly similar ideas can lead to entirely different results. Both parts of the crossover are included (along with commentary by both strips' creators) below.

MARK MEKKES: I wrote the first rough draft for this crossover (based on Steve's ideas). It was a huge, rambling epic that would have dragged on forever. Fortunately, Steve was able to cut out the extraneous stuff and piece together the remains into a tight, energetic story that really highlighted the characters, yet somehow kept all of the fun and flavor of what I had written.

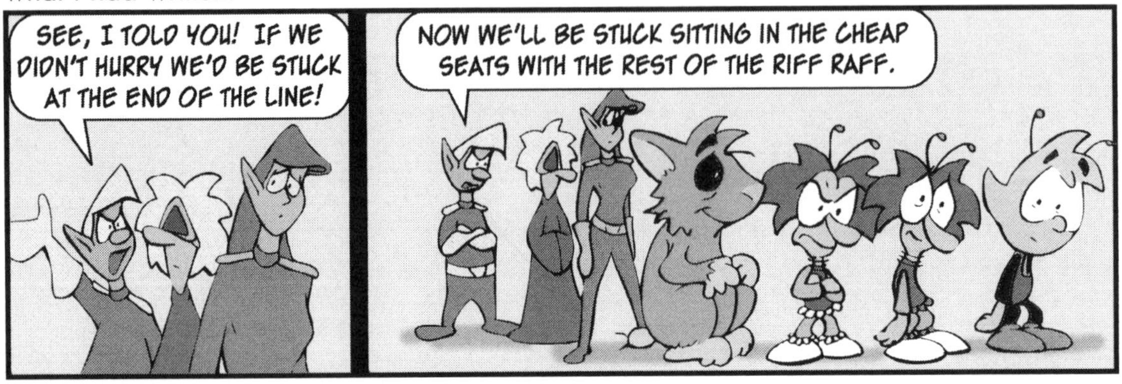
SEE, I TOLD YOU! IF WE DIDN'T HURRY WE'D BE STUCK AT THE END OF THE LINE!
NOW WE'LL BE STUCK SITTING IN THE CHEAP SEATS WITH THE REST OF THE RIFF RAFF.

STEVE TROOP: I first heard of *Zortic* about three years into my initial run when Mark Mekkes e-mailed me. He'd been drawing his comic for about a year at that time and had been inundated with people asking about my strip. Granted—there are some startling similarities—but we both figure we're ripping off *My Favorite Martian* more than each other, so we become friends instead of fighting to the death.

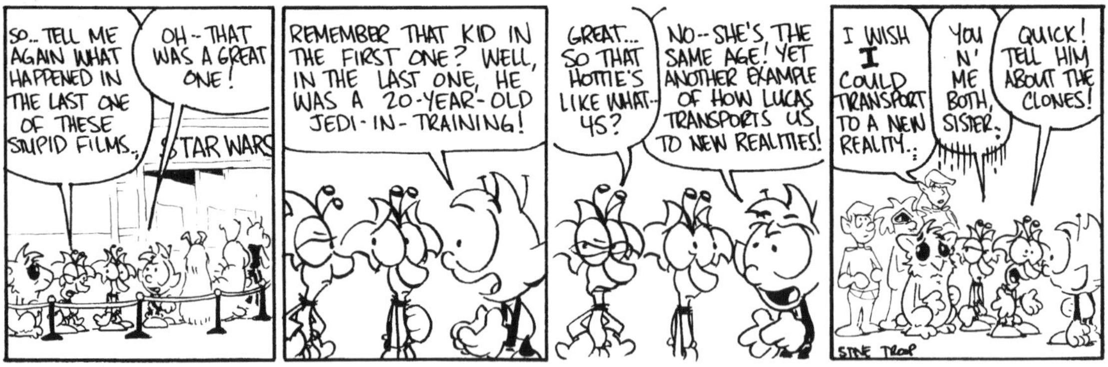
SO... TELL ME AGAIN WHAT HAPPENED IN THE LAST ONE OF THESE STUPID FILMS..
OH -- THAT WAS A GREAT ONE!
STAR WARS
REMEMBER THAT KID IN THE FIRST ONE? WELL, IN THE LAST ONE, HE WAS A 20-YEAR-OLD JEDI-IN-TRAINING!
GREAT... SO THAT HOTTIE'S LIKE WHAT -- 45?
NO -- SHE'S THE SAME AGE! YET ANOTHER EXAMPLE OF HOW LUCAS TRANSPORTS US TO NEW REALITIES!
I WISH I COULD TRANSPORT TO A NEW REALITY..
YOU N' ME BOTH, SISTER.
QUICK! TELL HIM ABOUT THE CLONES!
STEVE TROOP

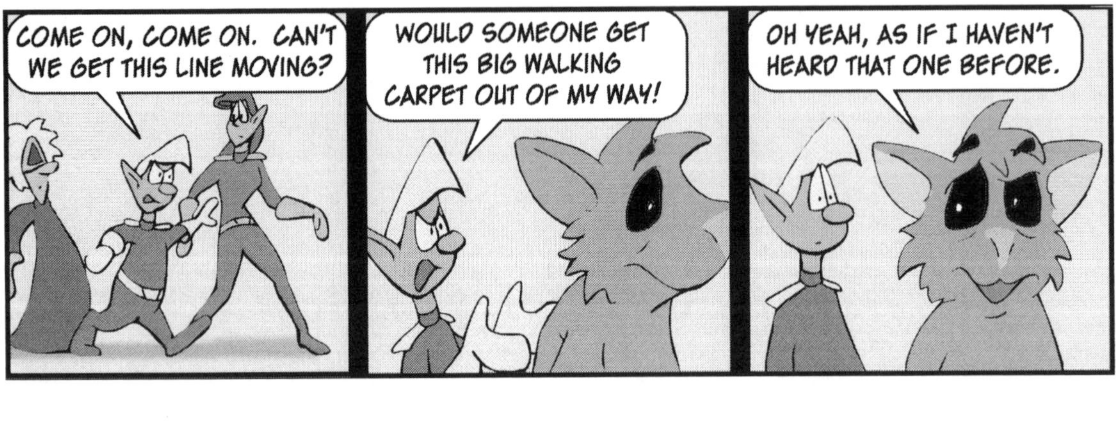
COME ON, COME ON. CAN'T WE GET THIS LINE MOVING?
WOULD SOMEONE GET THIS BIG WALKING CARPET OUT OF MY WAY!
OH YEAH, AS IF I HAVEN'T HEARD THAT ONE BEFORE.

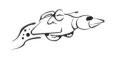

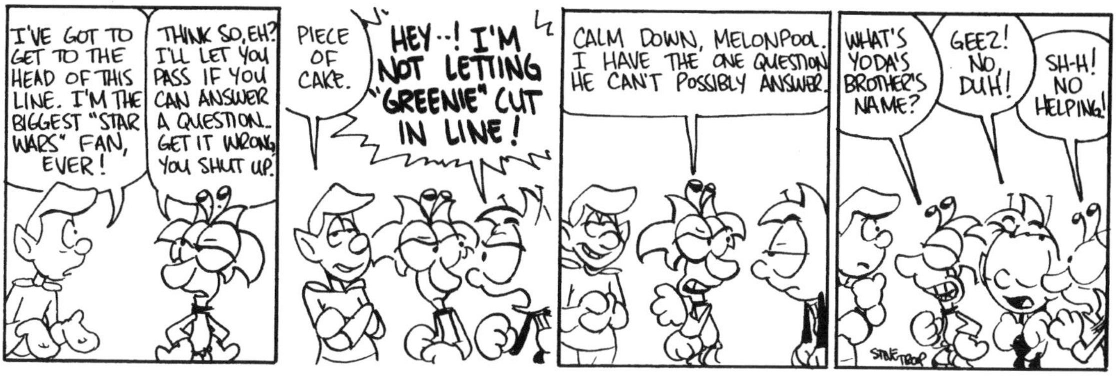
I'VE GOT TO GET TO THE HEAD OF THIS LINE. I'M THE BIGGEST "STAR WARS" FAN, EVER!
THINK SO, EH? I'LL LET YOU PASS IF YOU CAN ANSWER A QUESTION.. GET IT WRONG, YOU SHUT UP.
PIECE OF CAKE.
HEY..! I'M NOT LETTING "GREENIE" CUT IN LINE!
CALM DOWN, MELONPOOL. I HAVE THE ONE QUESTION HE CAN'T POSSIBLY ANSWER.
WHAT'S YODA'S BROTHER'S NAME?
GEEZ! NO, DUH!
SH-H! NO HELPING!
STEVE TROOP

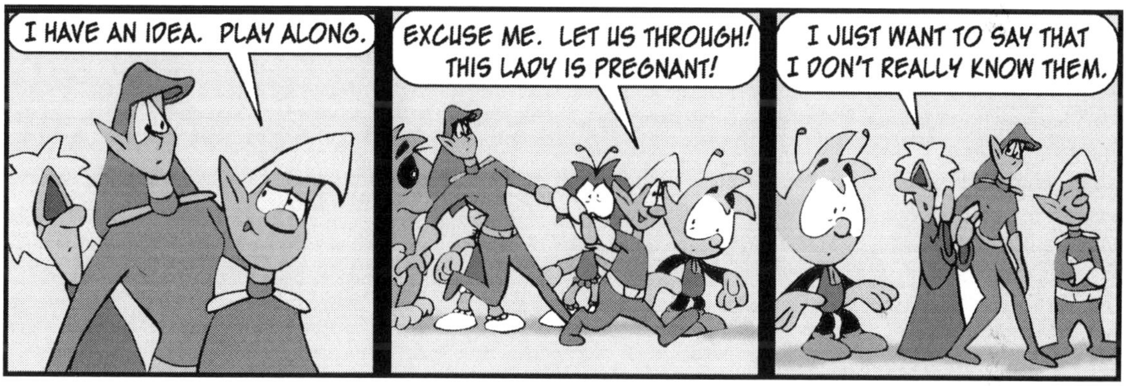
I HAVE AN IDEA. PLAY ALONG.
EXCUSE ME. LET US THROUGH! THIS LADY IS PREGNANT!
I JUST WANT TO SAY THAT I DON'T REALLY KNOW THEM.

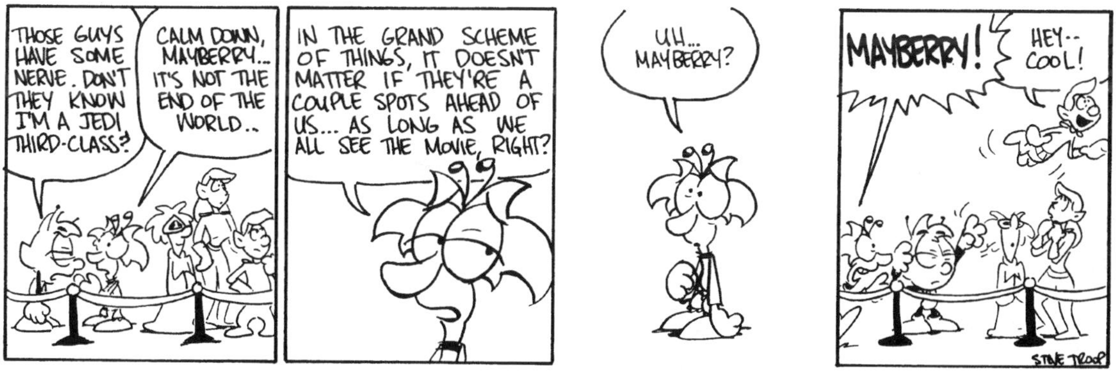
THOSE GUYS HAVE SOME NERVE. DON'T THEY KNOW I'M A JEDI THIRD-CLASS?!
CALM DOWN, MAYBERRY... IT'S NOT THE END OF THE WORLD..
IN THE GRAND SCHEME OF THINGS, IT DOESN'T MATTER IF THEY'RE A COUPLE SPOTS AHEAD OF US... AS LONG AS WE ALL SEE THE MOVIE, RIGHT?
UH... MAYBERRY?
MAYBERRY!
HEY.. COOL!
STEVE TROOP

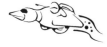

MEKKES: I had always sworn that I was going to leave Splink's past a mystery—I wanted him to be an enigma. But when Steve came up with this idea, it was just too perfect. Our ability to think alike was obvious; so much of what we had done had already paralleled one another by accident. So I thought this was an ideal way to capitalize on that.

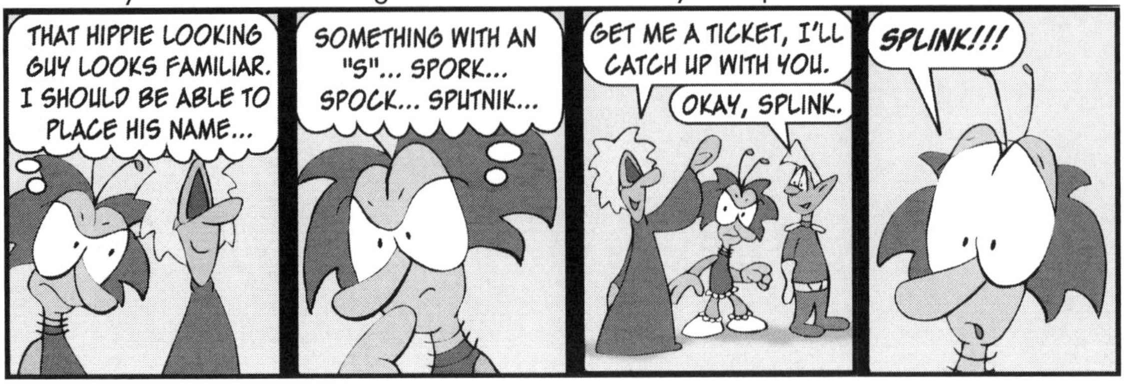
THAT HIPPIE LOOKING GUY LOOKS FAMILIAR. I SHOULD BE ABLE TO PLACE HIS NAME...
SOMETHING WITH AN "S"... SPORK... SPOCK... SPUTNIK...
GET ME A TICKET, I'LL CATCH UP WITH YOU.
OKAY, SPLINK.
SPLINK!!!

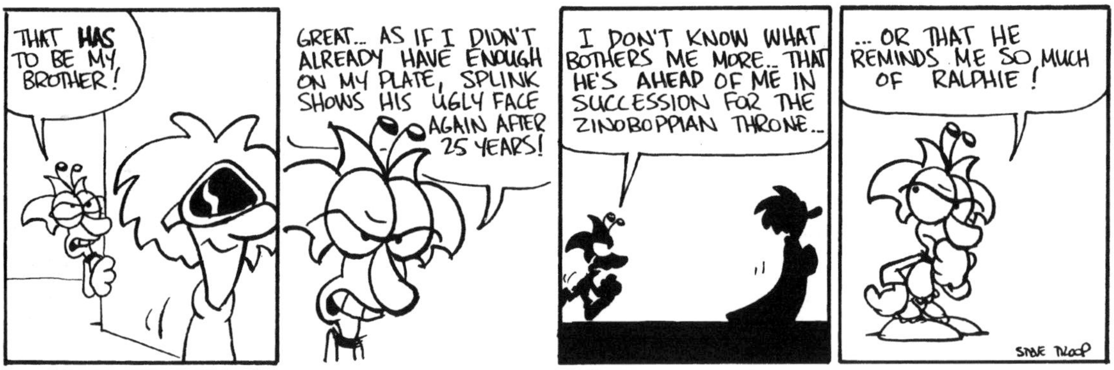
THAT HAS TO BE MY BROTHER!
GREAT... AS IF I DIDN'T ALREADY HAVE ENOUGH ON MY PLATE, SPLINK SHOWS HIS UGLY FACE AGAIN AFTER 25 YEARS!
I DON'T KNOW WHAT BOTHERS ME MORE... THAT HE'S AHEAD OF ME IN SUCCESSION FOR THE ZINOBOPPIAN THRONE...
... OR THAT HE REMINDS ME SO MUCH OF RALPHIE!

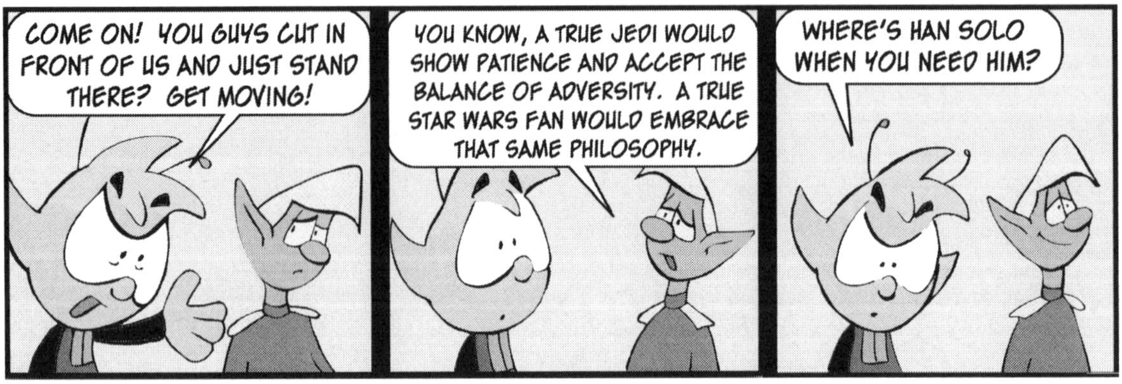
COME ON! YOU GUYS CUT IN FRONT OF US AND JUST STAND THERE? GET MOVING!
YOU KNOW, A TRUE JEDI WOULD SHOW PATIENCE AND ACCEPT THE BALANCE OF ADVERSITY. A TRUE STAR WARS FAN WOULD EMBRACE THAT SAME PHILOSOPHY.
WHERE'S HAN SOLO WHEN YOU NEED HIM?

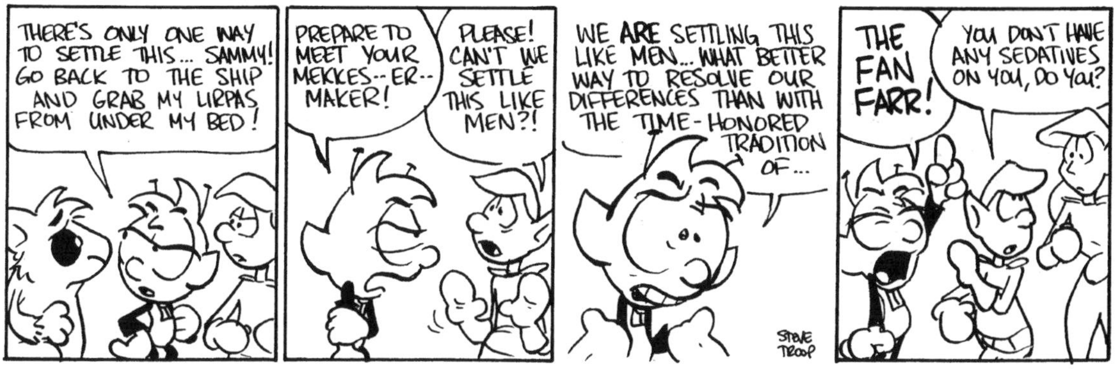
THERE'S ONLY ONE WAY TO SETTLE THIS... SAMMY! GO BACK TO THE SHIP AND GRAB MY LIRPAS FROM UNDER MY BED!
PREPARE TO MEET YOUR MEKKES--ER--MAKER!
PLEASE! CAN'T WE SETTLE THIS LIKE MEN?!
WE ARE SETTLING THIS LIKE MEN... WHAT BETTER WAY TO RESOLVE OUR DIFFERENCES THAN WITH THE TIME-HONORED TRADITION OF...
THE FAN FARR!
YOU DON'T HAVE ANY SEDATIVES ON YOU, DO YOU?
STEVE TROOP

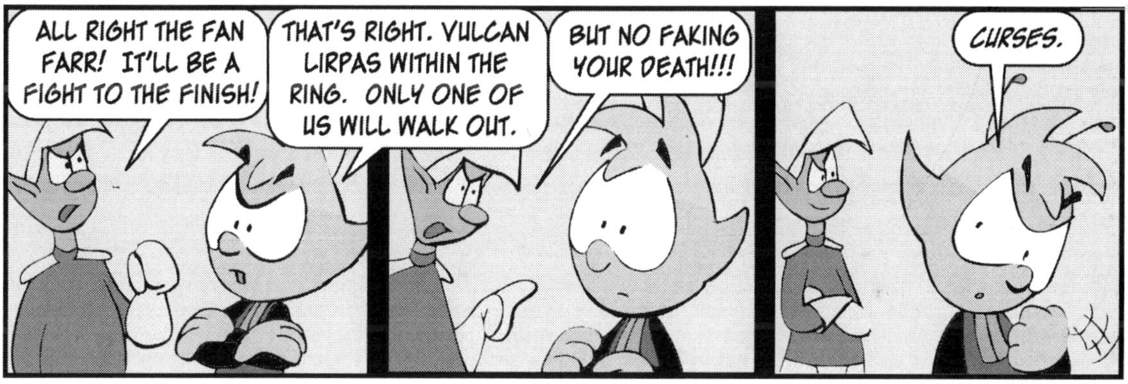
ALL RIGHT THE FAN FARR! IT'LL BE A FIGHT TO THE FINISH!
THAT'S RIGHT. VULCAN LIRPAS WITHIN THE RING. ONLY ONE OF US WILL WALK OUT.
BUT NO FAKING YOUR DEATH!!!
CURSES.

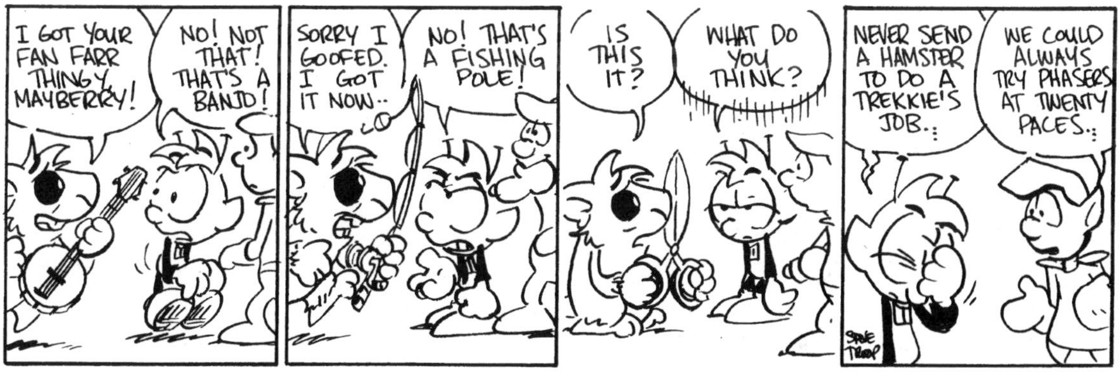
I GOT YOUR FAN FARR THINGY, MAYBERRY!
NO! NOT THAT! THAT'S A BANJO!
SORRY I GOOFED. I GOT IT NOW..
NO! THAT'S A FISHING POLE!
IS THIS IT?
WHAT DO YOU THINK?
NEVER SEND A HAMSTER TO DO A TREKKIE'S JOB..
WE COULD ALWAYS TRY PHASERS AT TWENTY PACES..
STEVE TROOP

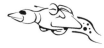

MEKKES: Drawing our characters together was a huge challenge. They're similar enough that I kept finding myself wanting to draw them the same, especially the difference in proportions during the fight scenes. It really became a great study in the subtle differences of our styles.

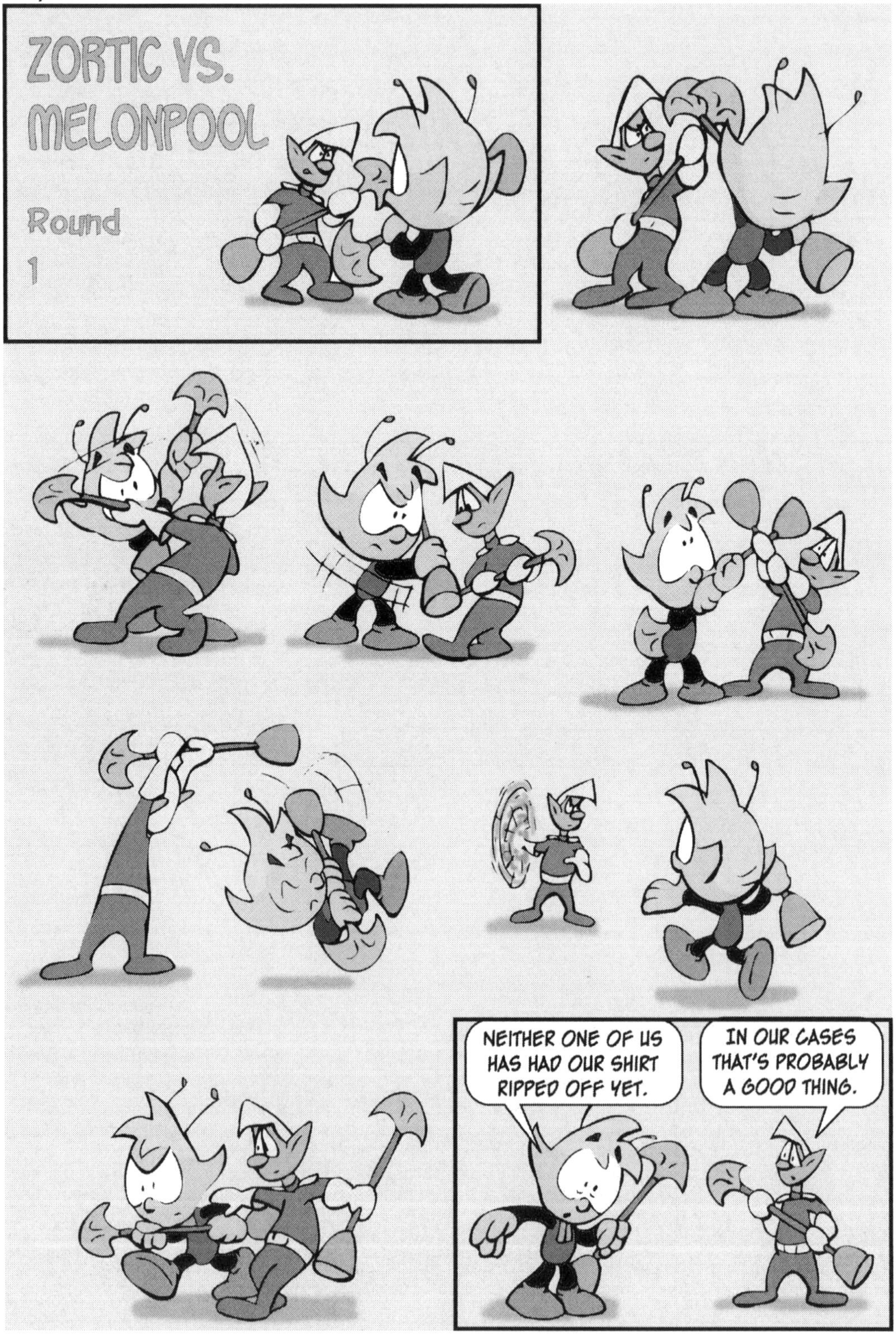

ZORTIC VS. MELONPOOL
Round 1
NEITHER ONE OF US HAS HAD OUR SHIRT RIPPED OFF YET.
IN OUR CASES THAT'S PROBABLY A GOOD THING.

TROOP: I think the nerd quotient of *Melonpool* is high enough that 90% of its fan base can recognize the "Amok Time" theme, even when written out phonetically between panels.

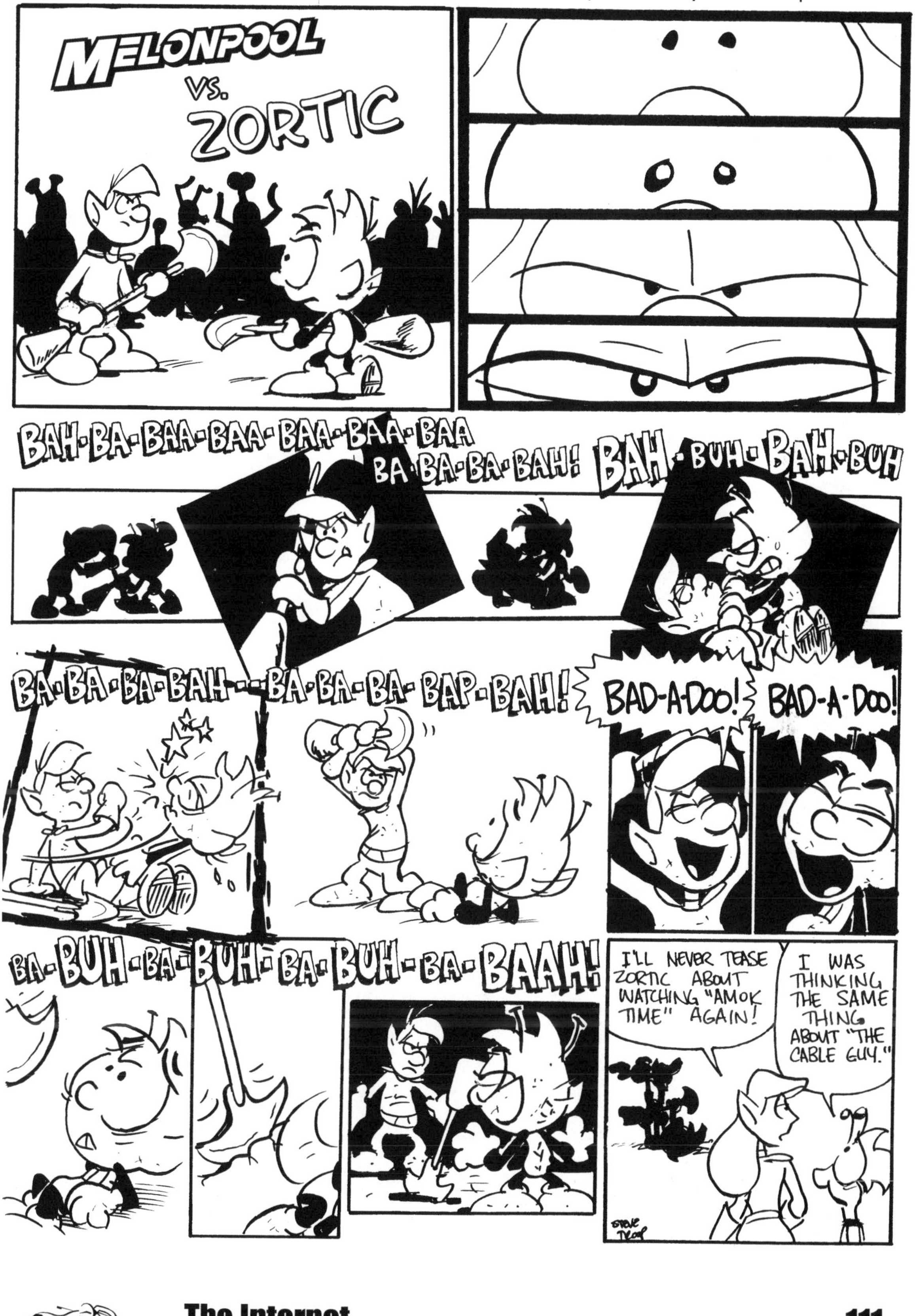

MELONPOOL VS. ZORTIC
BAH-BA-BAA-BAA-BAA-BAA-BAA
BA-BA-BA-BAH! BAH-BUH-BAH-BUH
BA-BA-BA-BAH---BA-BA-BA-BAP-BAH!
BAD-A-DOO!
BAD-A-DOO!
BA-BUH-BA-BUH-BA-BUH-BA-BAAH!
I'LL NEVER TEASE ZORTIC ABOUT WATCHING "AMOK TIME" AGAIN!
I WAS THINKING THE SAME THING ABOUT "THE CABLE GUY."

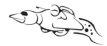

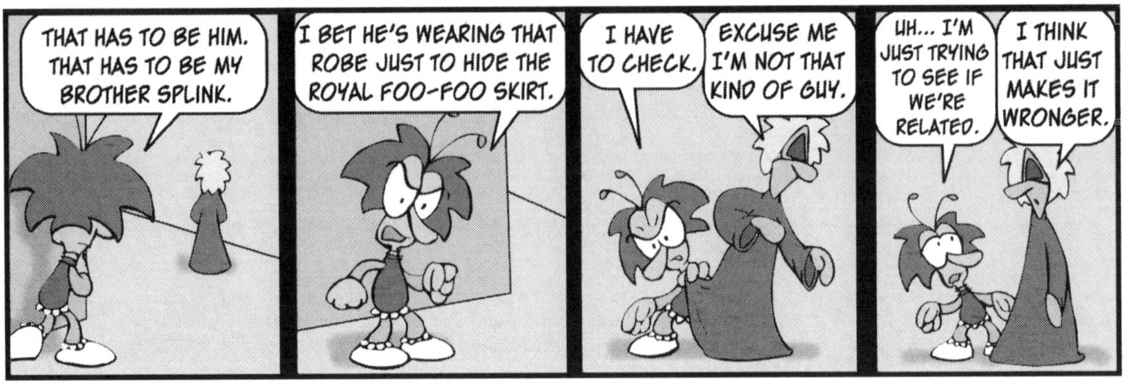
THAT HAS TO BE HIM. THAT HAS TO BE MY BROTHER SPLINK.
I BET HE'S WEARING THAT ROBE JUST TO HIDE THE ROYAL FOO-FOO SKIRT.
I HAVE TO CHECK.
EXCUSE ME I'M NOT THAT KIND OF GUY.
UH... I'M JUST TRYING TO SEE IF WE'RE RELATED.
I THINK THAT JUST MAKES IT WRONGER.

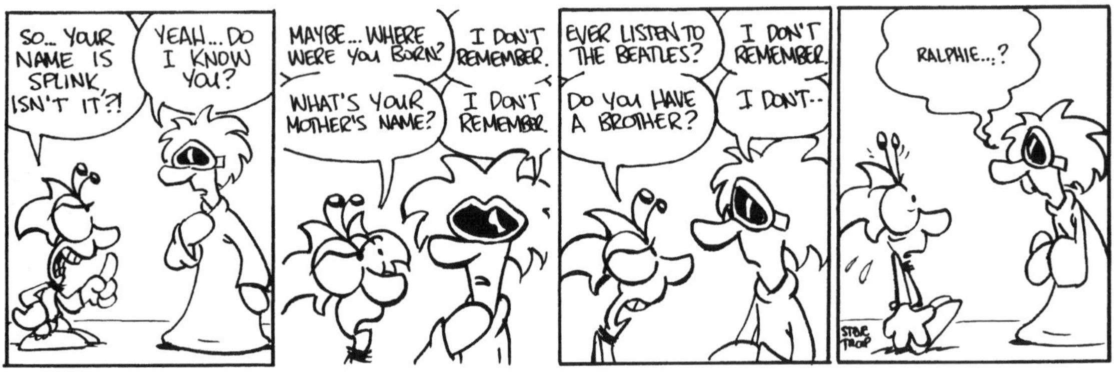
SO... YOUR NAME IS SPLINK, ISN'T IT?!
YEAH... DO I KNOW YOU?
MAYBE... WHERE WERE YOU BORN?
I DON'T REMEMBER.
WHAT'S YOUR MOTHER'S NAME?
I DON'T REMEMBER
EVER LISTEN TO THE BEATLES?
I DON'T REMEMBER.
DO YOU HAVE A BROTHER?
I DON'T--
RALPHIE...?

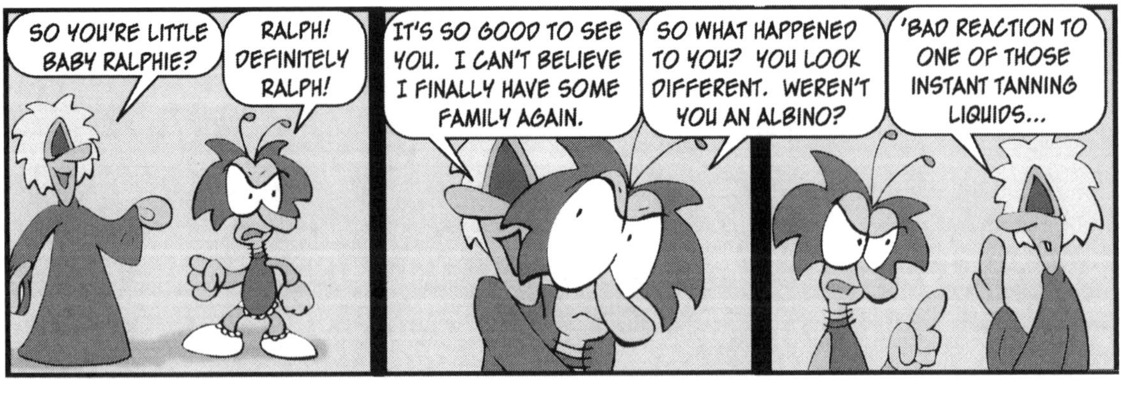
SO YOU'RE LITTLE BABY RALPHIE?
RALPH! DEFINITELY RALPH!
IT'S SO GOOD TO SEE YOU. I CAN'T BELIEVE I FINALLY HAVE SOME FAMILY AGAIN.
SO WHAT HAPPENED TO YOU? YOU LOOK DIFFERENT. WEREN'T YOU AN ALBINO?
'BAD REACTION TO ONE OF THOSE INSTANT TANNING LIQUIDS...

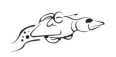

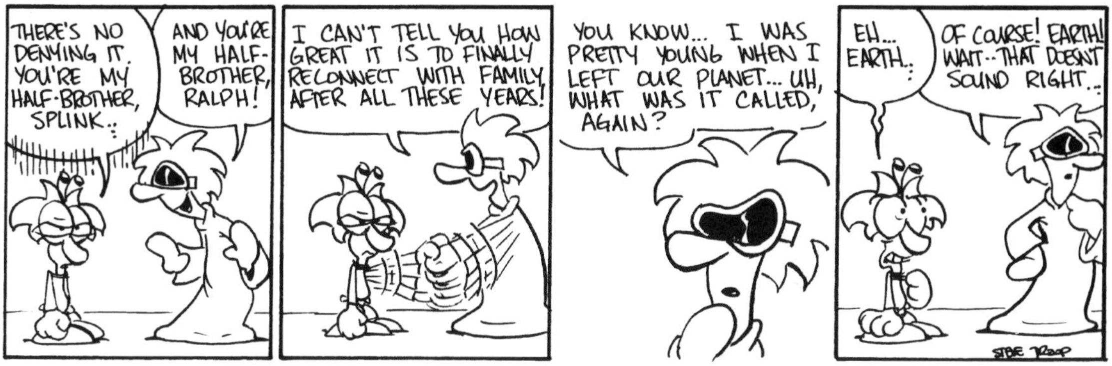
THERE'S NO DENYING IT. YOU'RE MY HALF-BROTHER, SPLINK..
AND YOU'RE MY HALF-BROTHER, RALPH!
I CAN'T TELL YOU HOW GREAT IT IS TO FINALLY RECONNECT WITH FAMILY AFTER ALL THESE YEARS!
YOU KNOW... I WAS PRETTY YOUNG WHEN I LEFT OUR PLANET... UH, WHAT WAS IT CALLED, AGAIN?
EH... EARTH..
OF COURSE! EARTH! WAIT.. THAT DOESN'T SOUND RIGHT..
STEVE TROOP

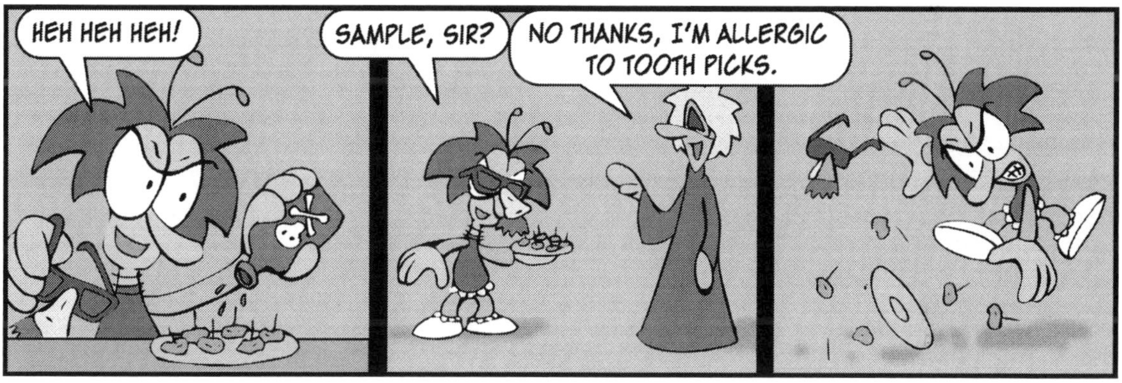
HEH HEH HEH!
SAMPLE, SIR?
NO THANKS, I'M ALLERGIC TO TOOTH PICKS.

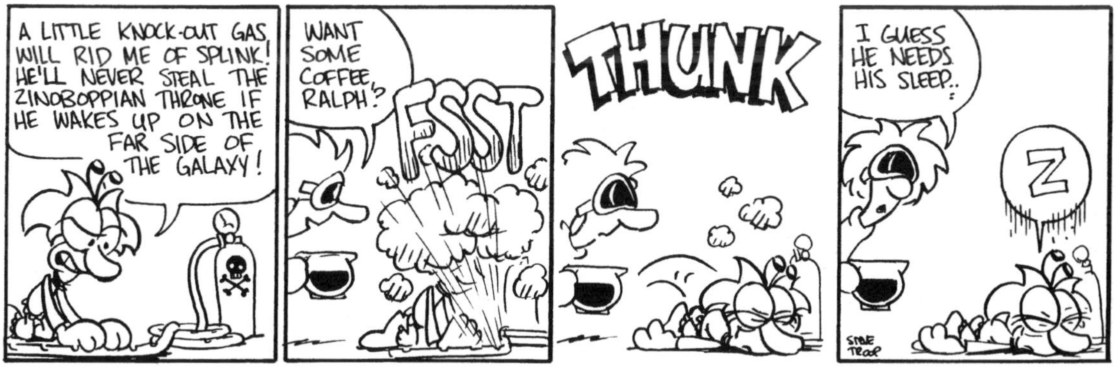
A LITTLE KNOCK-OUT GAS WILL RID ME OF SPLINK! HE'LL NEVER STEAL THE ZINOBOPPIAN THRONE IF HE WAKES UP ON THE FAR SIDE OF THE GALAXY!
WANT SOME COFFEE, RALPH?
FSST
THUNK
I GUESS HE NEEDS HIS SLEEP..
Z
STEVE TROOP

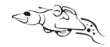

MEKKES: Having characters fight each other in a crossover is really overdone, but for Melonpool and Zortic, it just seemed necessary. I think that fans of both strips have always kind of taken sides and perceived the other comic as a rip-off of their favorite title. Steve and I have always kind of played that off as a friendly rivalry. Besides that, we both deal with a lot of popular references and icons, so starting with the expected fight was perfectly natural.

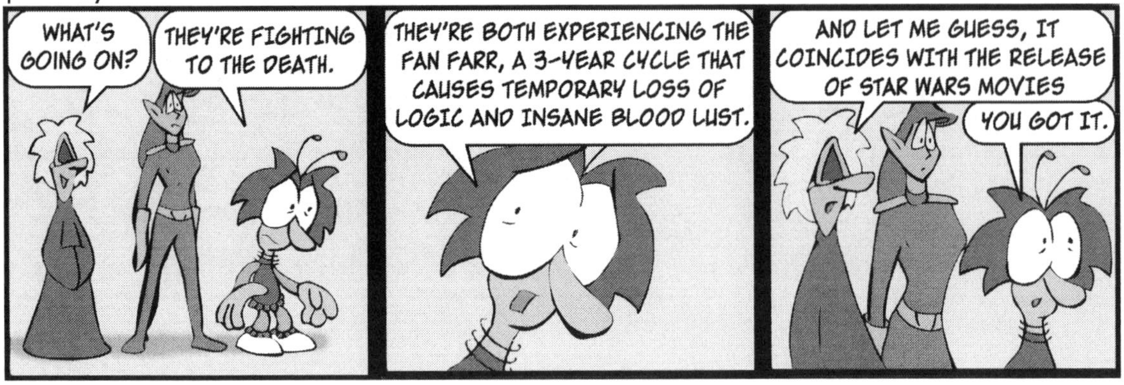
WHAT'S GOING ON?
THEY'RE FIGHTING TO THE DEATH.
THEY'RE BOTH EXPERIENCING THE FAN FARR, A 3-YEAR CYCLE THAT CAUSES TEMPORARY LOSS OF LOGIC AND INSANE BLOOD LUST.
AND LET ME GUESS, IT COINCIDES WITH THE RELEASE OF STAR WARS MOVIES
YOU GOT IT.

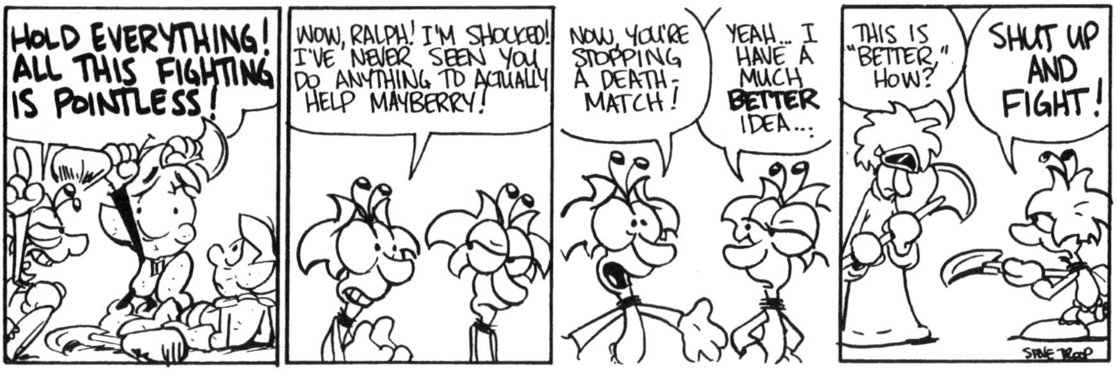
HOLD EVERYTHING! ALL THIS FIGHTING IS POINTLESS!
WOW, RALPH! I'M SHOCKED! I'VE NEVER SEEN YOU DO ANYTHING TO ACTUALLY HELP MAYBERRY!
NOW, YOU'RE STOPPING A DEATH-MATCH!
YEAH... I HAVE A MUCH **BETTER** IDEA...
THIS IS "BETTER," HOW?
SHUT UP AND FIGHT!
STEVE TROOP

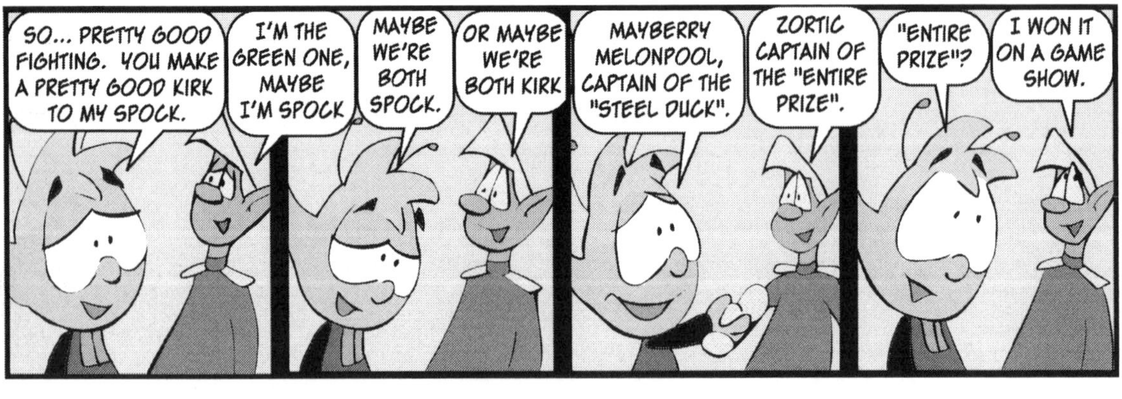
SO... PRETTY GOOD FIGHTING. YOU MAKE A PRETTY GOOD KIRK TO MY SPOCK.
I'M THE GREEN ONE, MAYBE I'M SPOCK
MAYBE WE'RE BOTH SPOCK.
OR MAYBE WE'RE BOTH KIRK
MAYBERRY MELONPOOL, CAPTAIN OF THE "STEEL DUCK".
ZORTIC CAPTAIN OF THE "ENTIRE PRIZE".
"ENTIRE PRIZE"?
I WON IT ON A GAME SHOW.

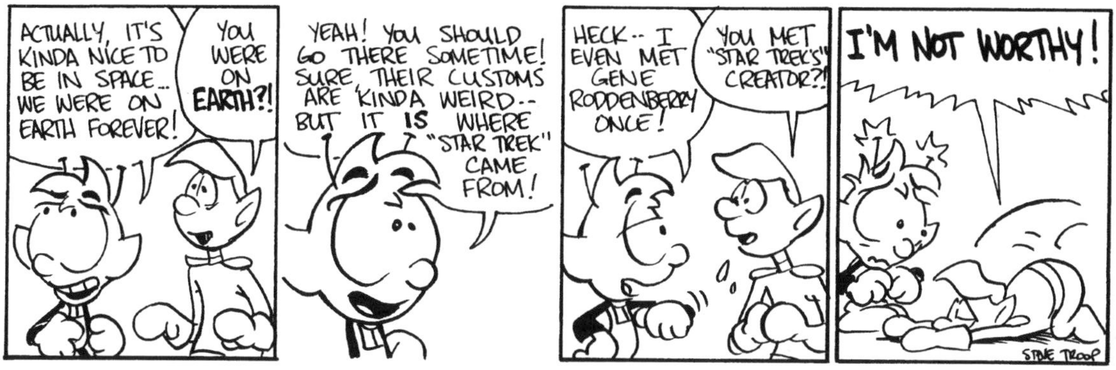
ACTUALLY, IT'S KINDA NICE TO BE IN SPACE... WE WERE ON EARTH FOREVER!
YOU WERE ON EARTH?!
YEAH! YOU SHOULD GO THERE SOMETIME! SURE, THEIR CUSTOMS ARE KINDA WEIRD-- BUT IT IS WHERE "STAR TREK" CAME FROM!
HECK-- I EVEN MET GENE RODDENBERRY ONCE!
YOU MET "STAR TREK'S" CREATOR?!
I'M NOT WORTHY!
STEVE TROOP

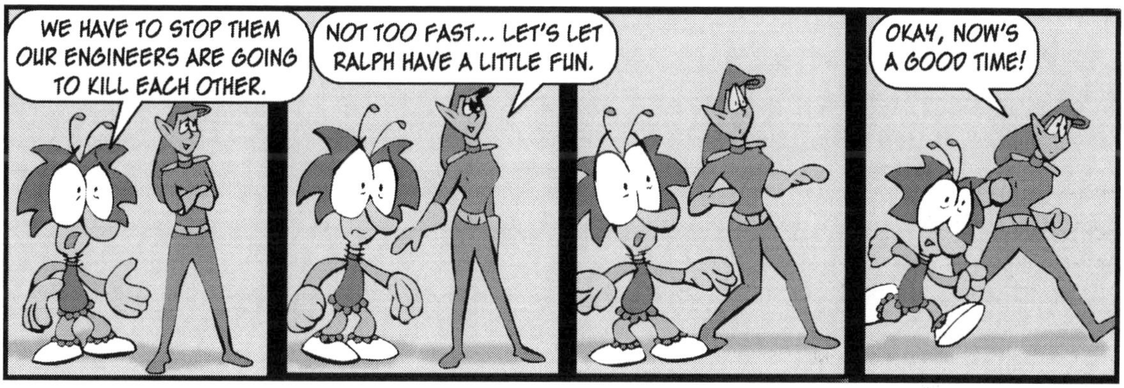
WE HAVE TO STOP THEM OUR ENGINEERS ARE GOING TO KILL EACH OTHER.
NOT TOO FAST... LET'S LET RALPH HAVE A LITTLE FUN.
OKAY, NOW'S A GOOD TIME!

TROOP: I'm particularly proud of the artwork in the first panel. Mark and I both have had a hard time convincing our fans that neither one of us had any knowledge of the other while creating our strips—even more so when they see Ralph and Splink next to one another.

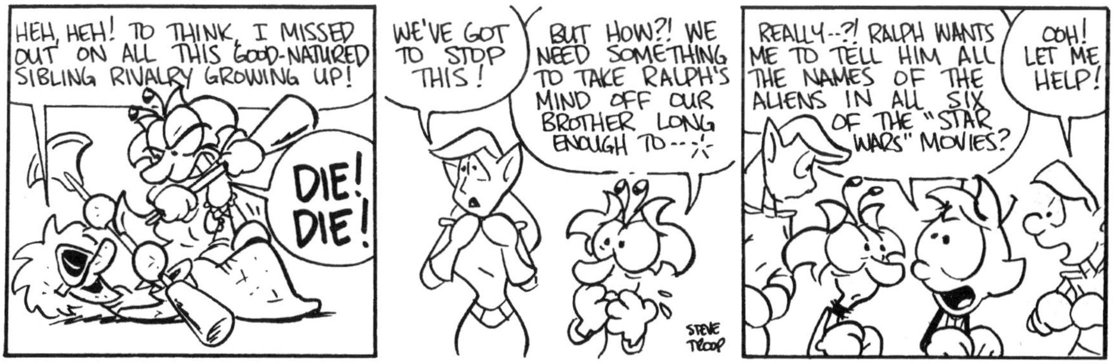
HEH, HEH! TO THINK, I MISSED OUT ON ALL THIS GOOD-NATURED SIBLING RIVALRY GROWING UP!
DIE! DIE!
WE'VE GOT TO STOP THIS!
BUT HOW?! WE NEED SOMETHING TO TAKE RALPH'S MIND OFF OUR BROTHER LONG ENOUGH TO--
STEVE TROOP
REALLY--?! RALPH WANTS ME TO TELL HIM ALL THE NAMES OF THE ALIENS IN ALL SIX OF THE "STAR WARS" MOVIES?
OOH! LET ME HELP!

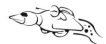

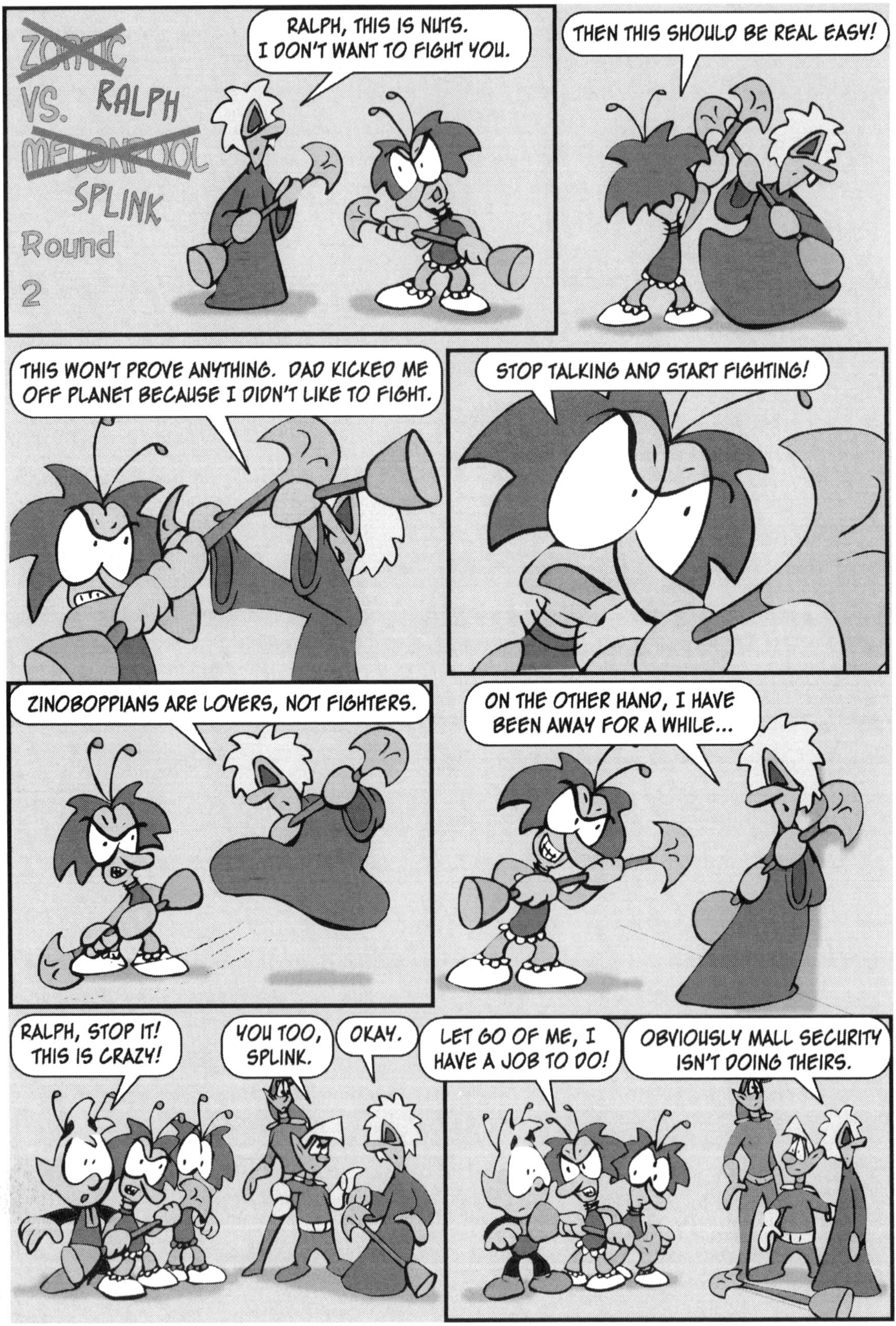
ZORTIC VS. MELONPOOL
RALPH
SPLINK
Round 2
RALPH, THIS IS NUTS. I DON'T WANT TO FIGHT YOU.
THEN THIS SHOULD BE REAL EASY!
THIS WON'T PROVE ANYTHING. DAD KICKED ME OFF PLANET BECAUSE I DIDN'T LIKE TO FIGHT.
STOP TALKING AND START FIGHTING!
ZINOBOPPIANS ARE LOVERS, NOT FIGHTERS.
ON THE OTHER HAND, I HAVE BEEN AWAY FOR A WHILE...
RALPH, STOP IT! THIS IS CRAZY!
YOU TOO, SPLINK.
OKAY.
LET GO OF ME, I HAVE A JOB TO DO!
OBVIOUSLY MALL SECURITY ISN'T DOING THEIRS.

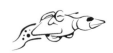

MEKKES: Steve and I both grew up on opposite sides of the country, but both watched a lot of the same shows. Obviously, we also developed many of the same creative instincts. Every time I read this strip, I can't help but think that's what Steve is trying to say here.

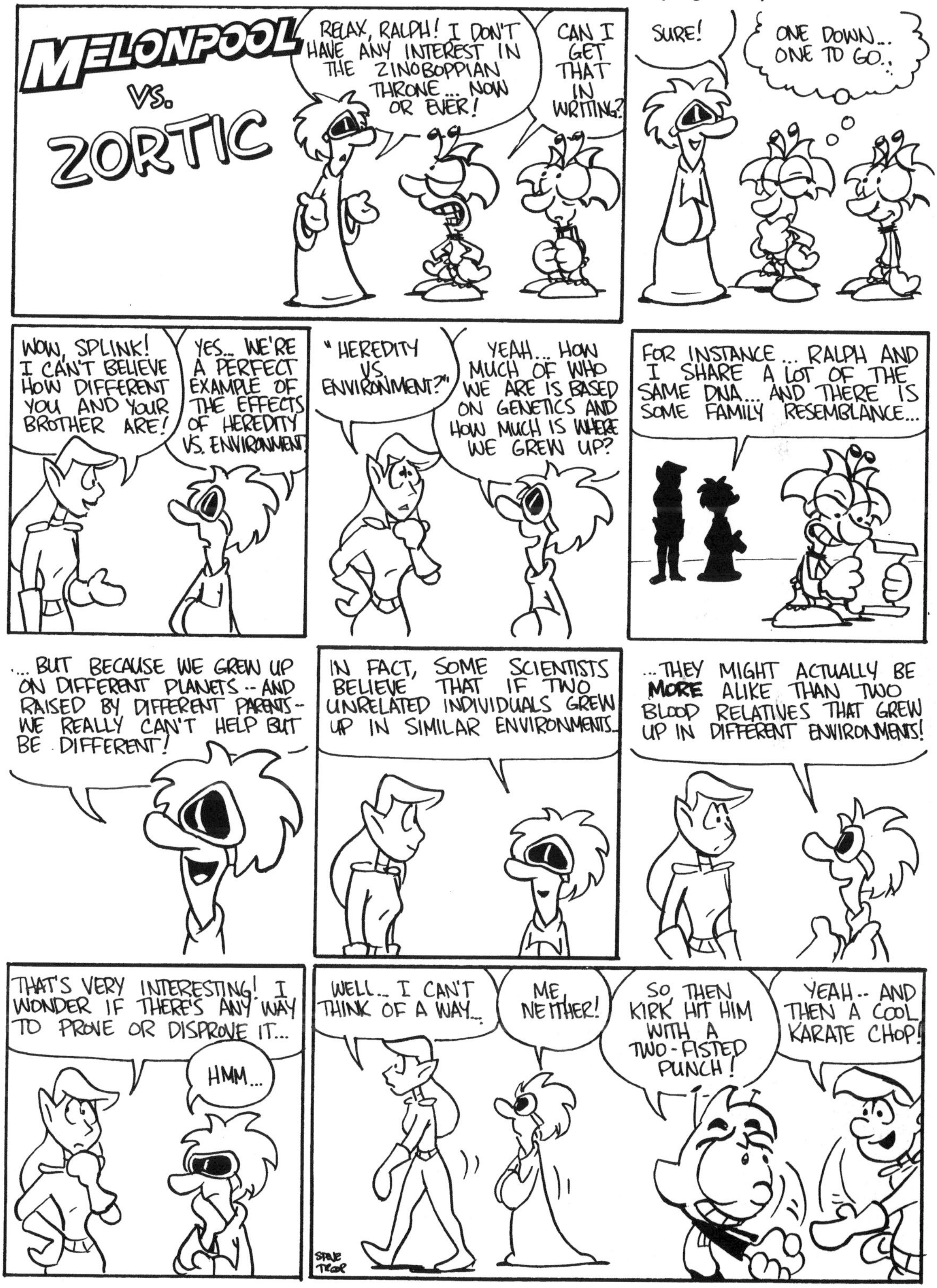

MELONPOOL VS. ZORTIC
RELAX, RALPH! I DON'T HAVE ANY INTEREST IN THE ZINOBOPPIAN THRONE... NOW OR EVER!
CAN I GET THAT IN WRITING?
SURE!
ONE DOWN... ONE TO GO...
WOW, SPLINK! I CAN'T BELIEVE HOW DIFFERENT YOU AND YOUR BROTHER ARE!
YES... WE'RE A PERFECT EXAMPLE OF THE EFFECTS OF HEREDITY VS. ENVIRONMENT!
"HEREDITY VS. ENVIRONMENT?"
YEAH... HOW MUCH OF WHO WE ARE IS BASED ON GENETICS AND HOW MUCH IS WHERE WE GREW UP?
FOR INSTANCE... RALPH AND I SHARE A LOT OF THE SAME DNA... AND THERE IS SOME FAMILY RESEMBLANCE...
... BUT BECAUSE WE GREW UP ON DIFFERENT PLANETS -- AND RAISED BY DIFFERENT PARENTS -- WE REALLY CAN'T HELP BUT BE DIFFERENT!
IN FACT, SOME SCIENTISTS BELIEVE THAT IF TWO UNRELATED INDIVIDUALS GREW UP IN SIMILAR ENVIRONMENTS...
... THEY MIGHT ACTUALLY BE MORE ALIKE THAN TWO BLOOD RELATIVES THAT GREW UP IN DIFFERENT ENVIRONMENTS!
THAT'S VERY INTERESTING! I WONDER IF THERE'S ANY WAY TO PROVE OR DISPROVE IT...
HMM...
WELL... I CAN'T THINK OF A WAY...
ME NEITHER!
SO THEN KIRK HIT HIM WITH A TWO-FISTED PUNCH!
YEAH -- AND THEN A COOL KARATE CHOP!
STEVE TROOP

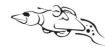

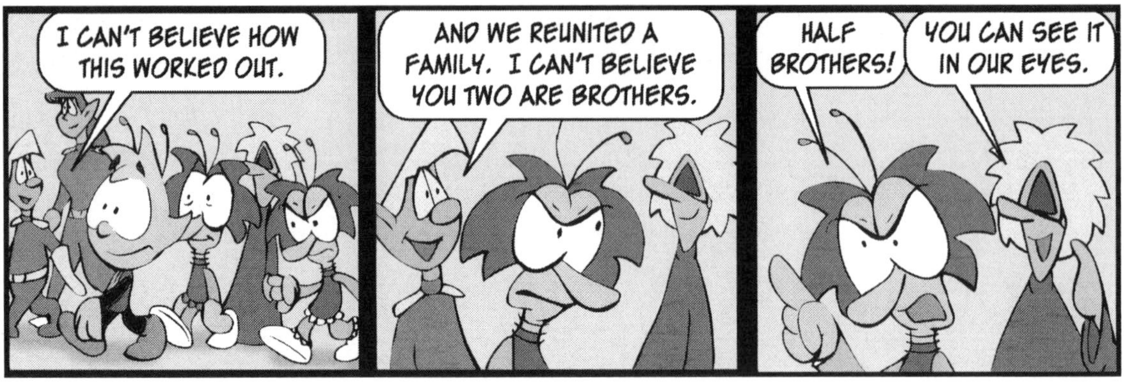
I CAN'T BELIEVE HOW THIS WORKED OUT.
AND WE REUNITED A FAMILY. I CAN'T BELIEVE YOU TWO ARE BROTHERS.
HALF BROTHERS!
YOU CAN SEE IT IN OUR EYES.

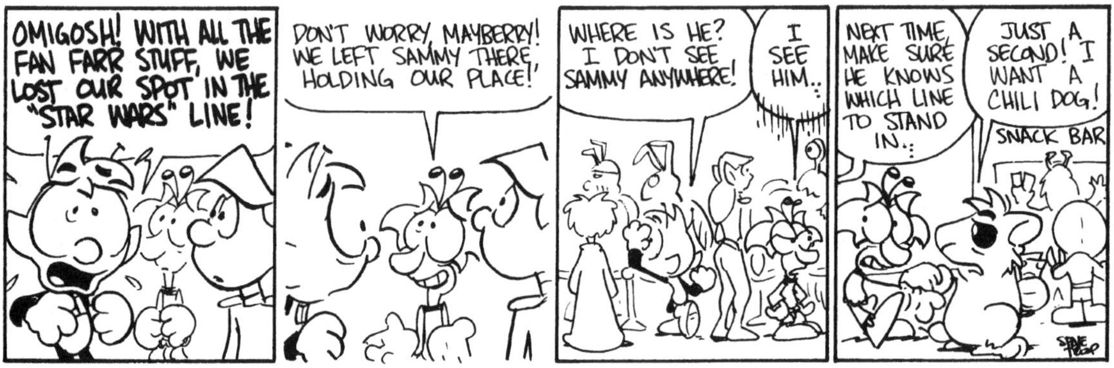
OMIGOSH! WITH ALL THE FAN FARR STUFF, WE LOST OUR SPOT IN THE "STAR WARS" LINE!
DON'T WORRY, MAYBERRY! WE LEFT SAMMY THERE, HOLDING OUR PLACE!
WHERE IS HE? I DON'T SEE SAMMY ANYWHERE!
I SEE HIM...
NEXT TIME, MAKE SURE HE KNOWS WHICH LINE TO STAND IN...
JUST A SECOND! I WANT A CHILI DOG!
SNACK BAR

MEKKES: It's hard to see, but several reoccurring Zortic characters are in line in the distance , including Chubby the Lump, Red Bimbo (Zoie's mother) and Junior (Zortic's father).

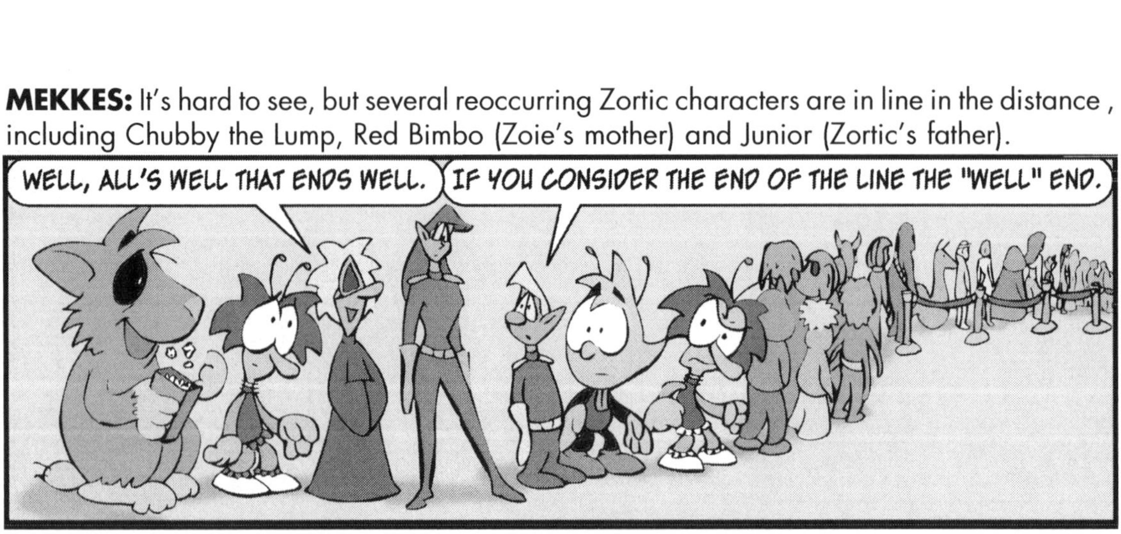
WELL, ALL'S WELL THAT ENDS WELL.
IF YOU CONSIDER THE END OF THE LINE THE "WELL" END.

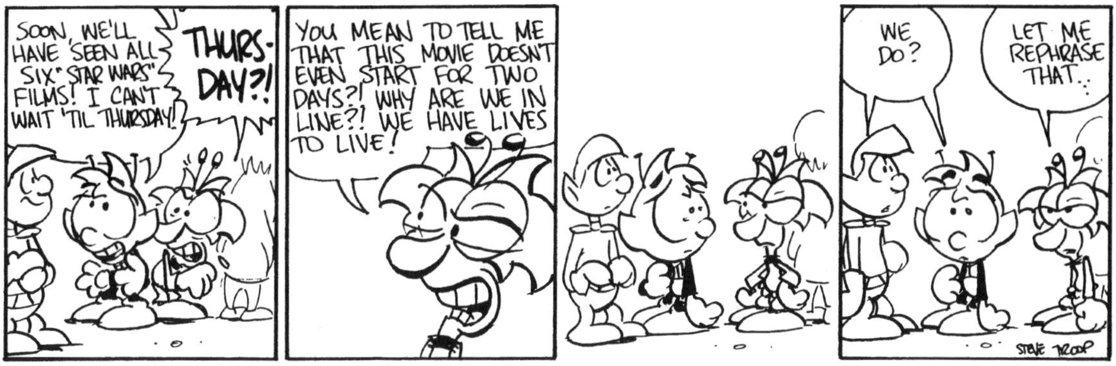
SOON, WE'LL HAVE SEEN ALL SIX "STAR WARS" FILMS! I CAN'T WAIT 'TIL THURSDAY!
THURS-DAY?!
YOU MEAN TO TELL ME THAT THIS MOVIE DOESN'T EVEN START FOR TWO DAYS?! WHY ARE WE IN LINE?! WE HAVE LIVES TO LIVE!
WE DO?
LET ME REPHRASE THAT...
STEVE TROOP

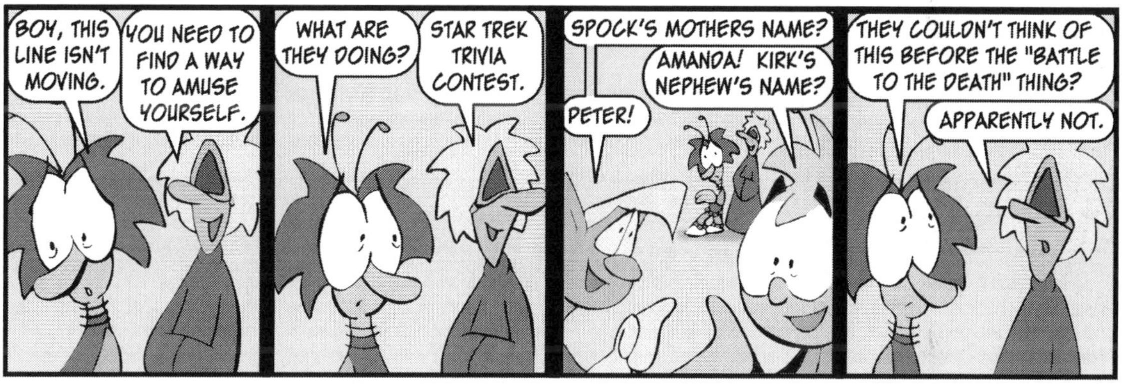
BOY, THIS LINE ISN'T MOVING.
YOU NEED TO FIND A WAY TO AMUSE YOURSELF.
WHAT ARE THEY DOING?
STAR TREK TRIVIA CONTEST.
SPOCK'S MOTHERS NAME?
PETER!
AMANDA! KIRK'S NEPHEW'S NAME?
THEY COULDN'T THINK OF THIS BEFORE THE "BATTLE TO THE DEATH" THING?
APPARENTLY NOT.

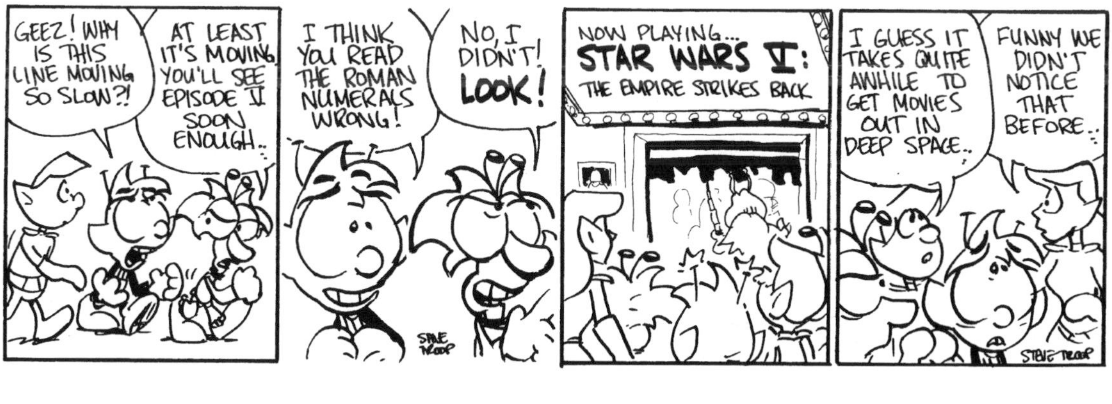
GEEZ! WHY IS THIS LINE MOVING SO SLOW?!
AT LEAST IT'S MOVING. YOU'LL SEE EPISODE VI SOON ENOUGH...
I THINK YOU READ THE ROMAN NUMERALS WRONG!
NO, I DIDN'T! LOOK!
STEVE TROOP
NOW PLAYING...
STAR WARS V: THE EMPIRE STRIKES BACK
I GUESS IT TAKES QUITE AWHILE TO GET MOVIES OUT IN DEEP SPACE...
FUNNY WE DIDN'T NOTICE THAT BEFORE...
STEVE TROOP

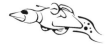

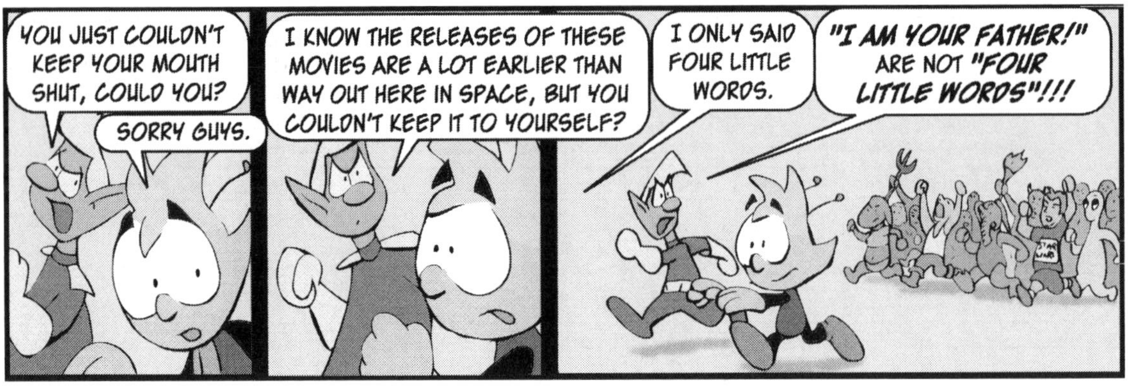
YOU JUST COULDN'T KEEP YOUR MOUTH SHUT, COULD YOU?
SORRY GUYS.
I KNOW THE RELEASES OF THESE MOVIES ARE A LOT EARLIER THAN WAY OUT HERE IN SPACE, BUT YOU COULDN'T KEEP IT TO YOURSELF?
I ONLY SAID FOUR LITTLE WORDS.
"I AM YOUR FATHER!" ARE NOT "FOUR LITTLE WORDS"!!!

TROOP: I'm particularly proud of the dramatic camera angle I used in this strip. One of the drawbacks to my four-panel format is that it doesn't really lend itself to dramatic camera angles... at least, usually.

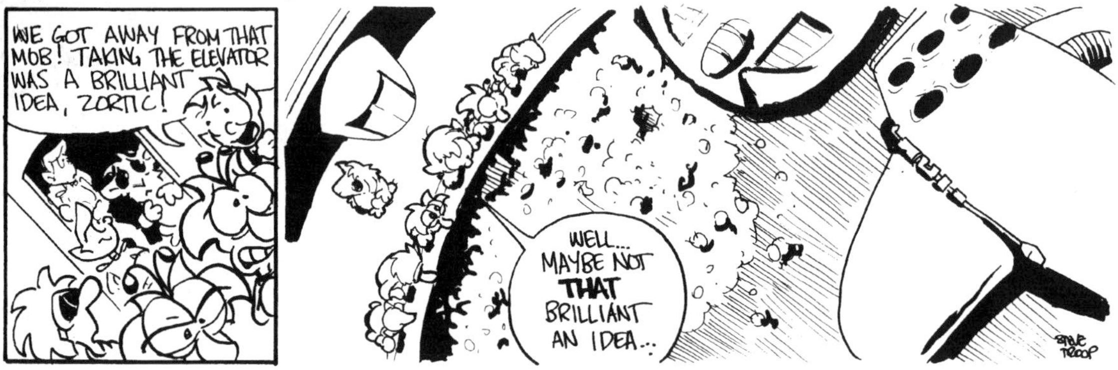
WE GOT AWAY FROM THAT MOB! TAKING THE ELEVATOR WAS A BRILLIANT IDEA, ZORTIC!
WELL... MAYBE NOT THAT BRILLIANT AN IDEA...
STEVE TROOP

MEKKES: In the initial draft, in order to force the gang to turn over Splink, Ralph had developed an electromagnetic pulse device that would have completely erased every copy of the digitally produced *Star Wars* prequels, which ultimately started a riot... In hindsight, that probably really wasn't that significant of a threat...

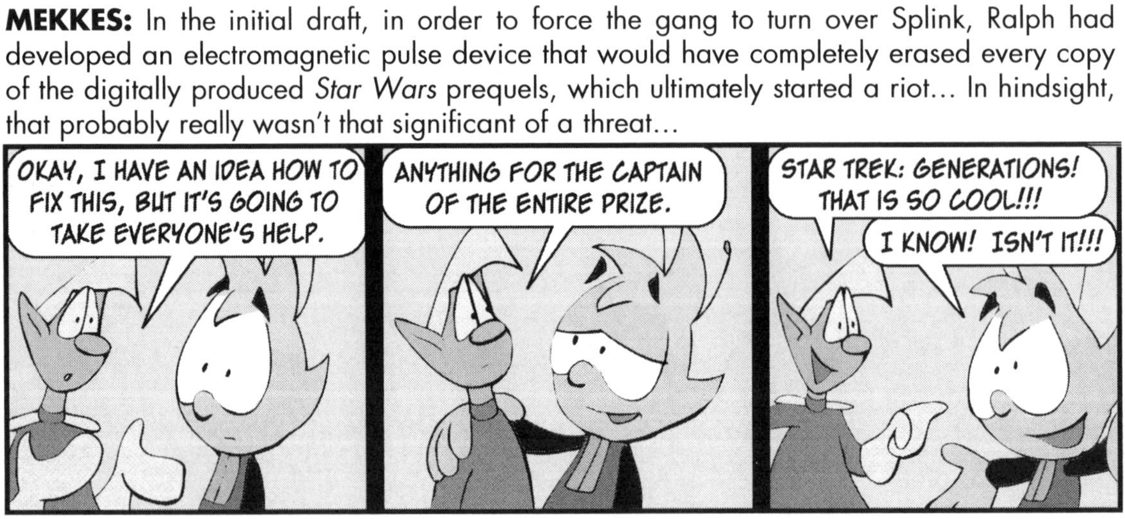
OKAY, I HAVE AN IDEA HOW TO FIX THIS, BUT IT'S GOING TO TAKE EVERYONE'S HELP.
ANYTHING FOR THE CAPTAIN OF THE ENTIRE PRIZE.
STAR TREK: GENERATIONS! THAT IS SO COOL!!!
I KNOW! ISN'T IT!!!

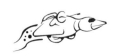

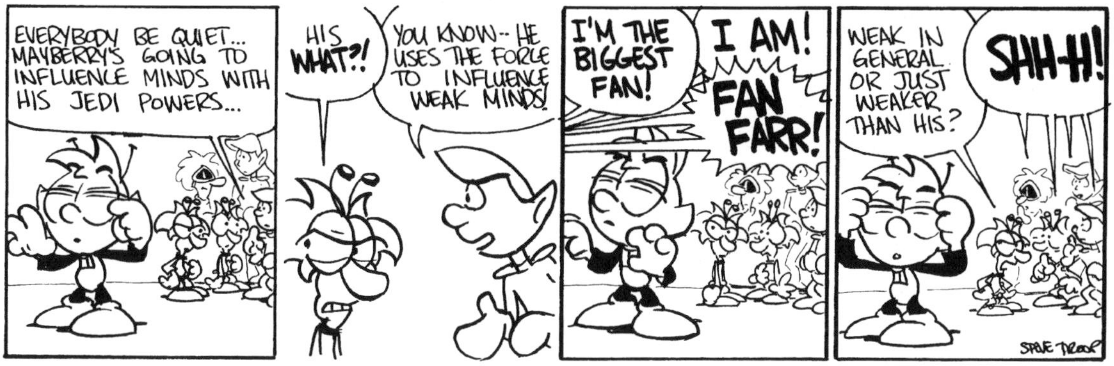
EVERYBODY BE QUIET... MAYBERRY'S GOING TO INFLUENCE MINDS WITH HIS JEDI POWERS...
HIS WHAT?!
YOU KNOW-- HE USES THE FORCE TO INFLUENCE WEAK MINDS!
I'M THE BIGGEST FAN!
I AM!
FAN FARR!
WEAK IN GENERAL OR JUST WEAKER THAN HIS?
SHH-H!
STEVE TROOP

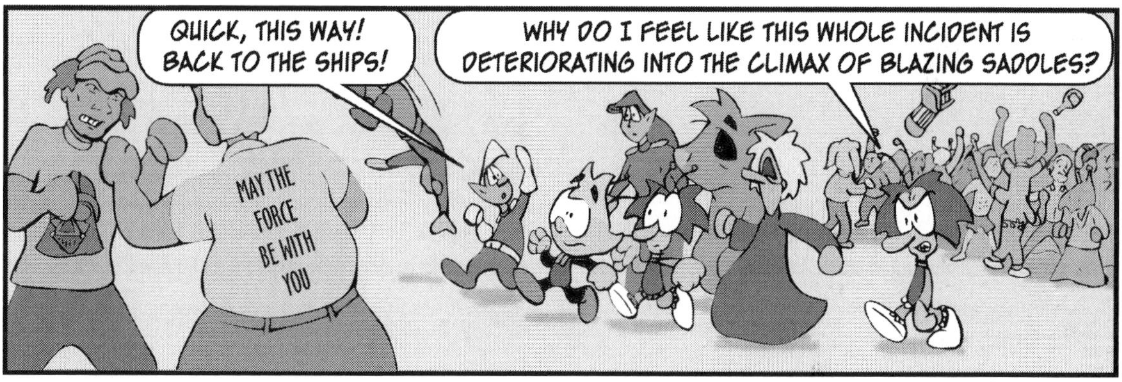
QUICK, THIS WAY! BACK TO THE SHIPS!
WHY DO I FEEL LIKE THIS WHOLE INCIDENT IS DETERIORATING INTO THE CLIMAX OF BLAZING SADDLES?
MAY THE FORCE BE WITH YOU

TROOP: Mark actually used this strip as the basis for another *Zortic/Melonpool* crossover after I had removed the *Melonpool* archives from the Internet. While I didn't have anything to do with the artwork of that story, I did help Mark with a few gags and continuity issues—which is why I've included it in the section called **Zortic to the Rescue!** (see pages 179–196).

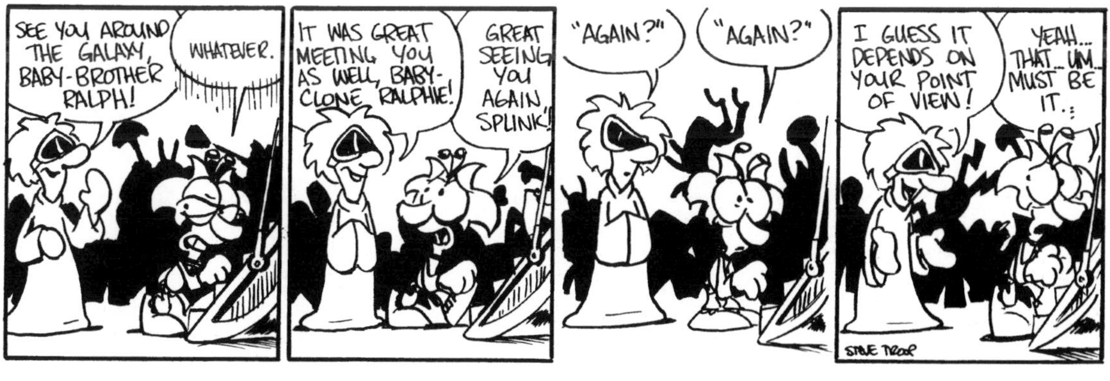
SEE YOU AROUND THE GALAXY, BABY-BROTHER RALPH!
WHATEVER.
IT WAS GREAT MEETING YOU AS WELL, BABY-CLONE RALPHIE!
GREAT SEEING YOU AGAIN, SPLINK!
"AGAIN?"
"AGAIN?"
I GUESS IT DEPENDS ON YOUR POINT OF VIEW!
YEAH... THAT... UM... MUST BE IT...
STEVE TROOP

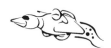

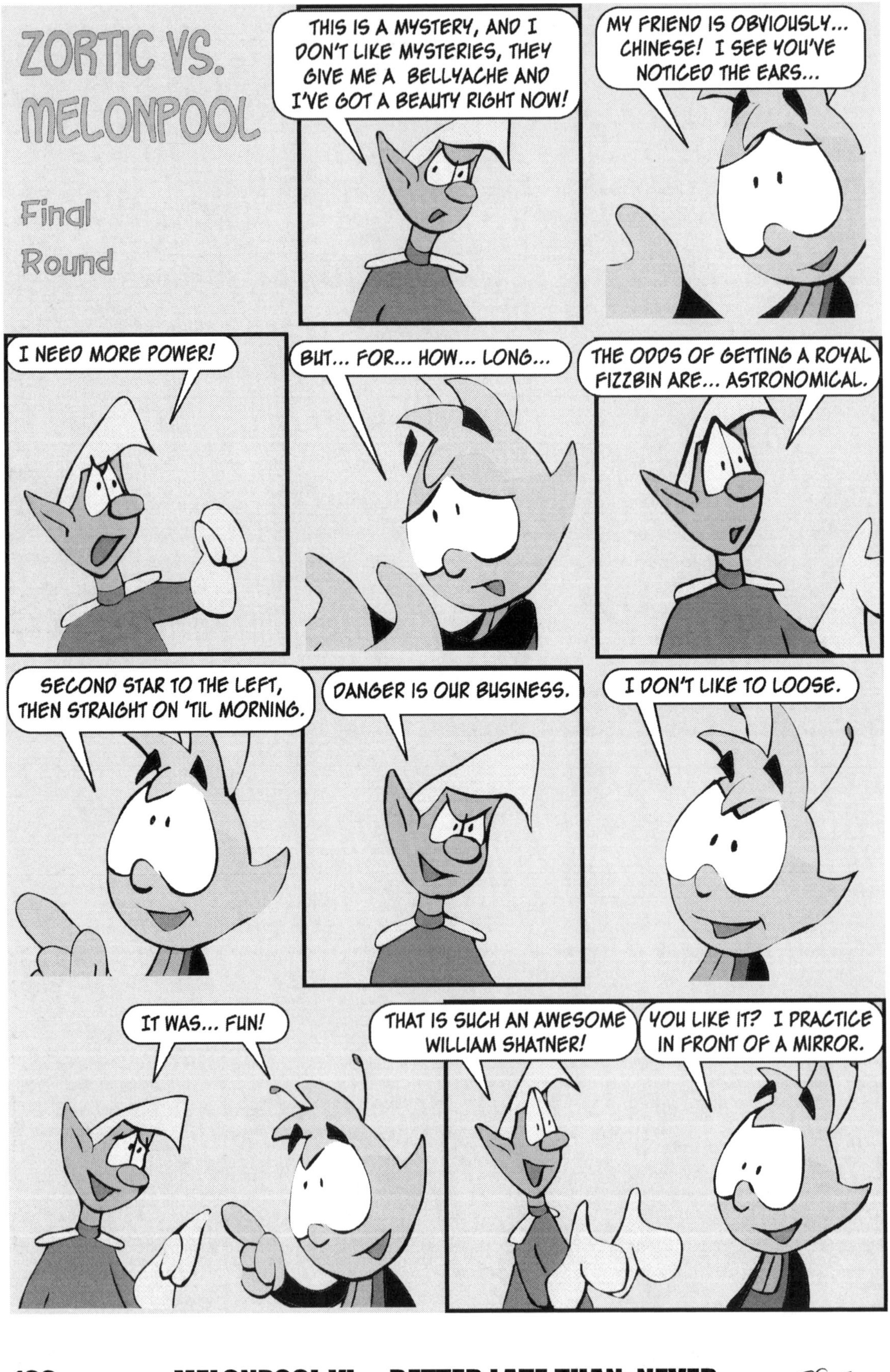
ZORTIC VS. MELONPOOL
Final Round
THIS IS A MYSTERY, AND I DON'T LIKE MYSTERIES, THEY GIVE ME A BELLYACHE AND I'VE GOT A BEAUTY RIGHT NOW!
MY FRIEND IS OBVIOUSLY... CHINESE! I SEE YOU'VE NOTICED THE EARS...
I NEED MORE POWER!
BUT... FOR... HOW... LONG...
THE ODDS OF GETTING A ROYAL FIZZBIN ARE... ASTRONOMICAL.
SECOND STAR TO THE LEFT, THEN STRAIGHT ON 'TIL MORNING.
DANGER IS OUR BUSINESS.
I DON'T LIKE TO LOOSE.
IT WAS... FUN!
THAT IS SUCH AN AWESOME WILLIAM SHATNER!
YOU LIKE IT? I PRACTICE IN FRONT OF A MIRROR.

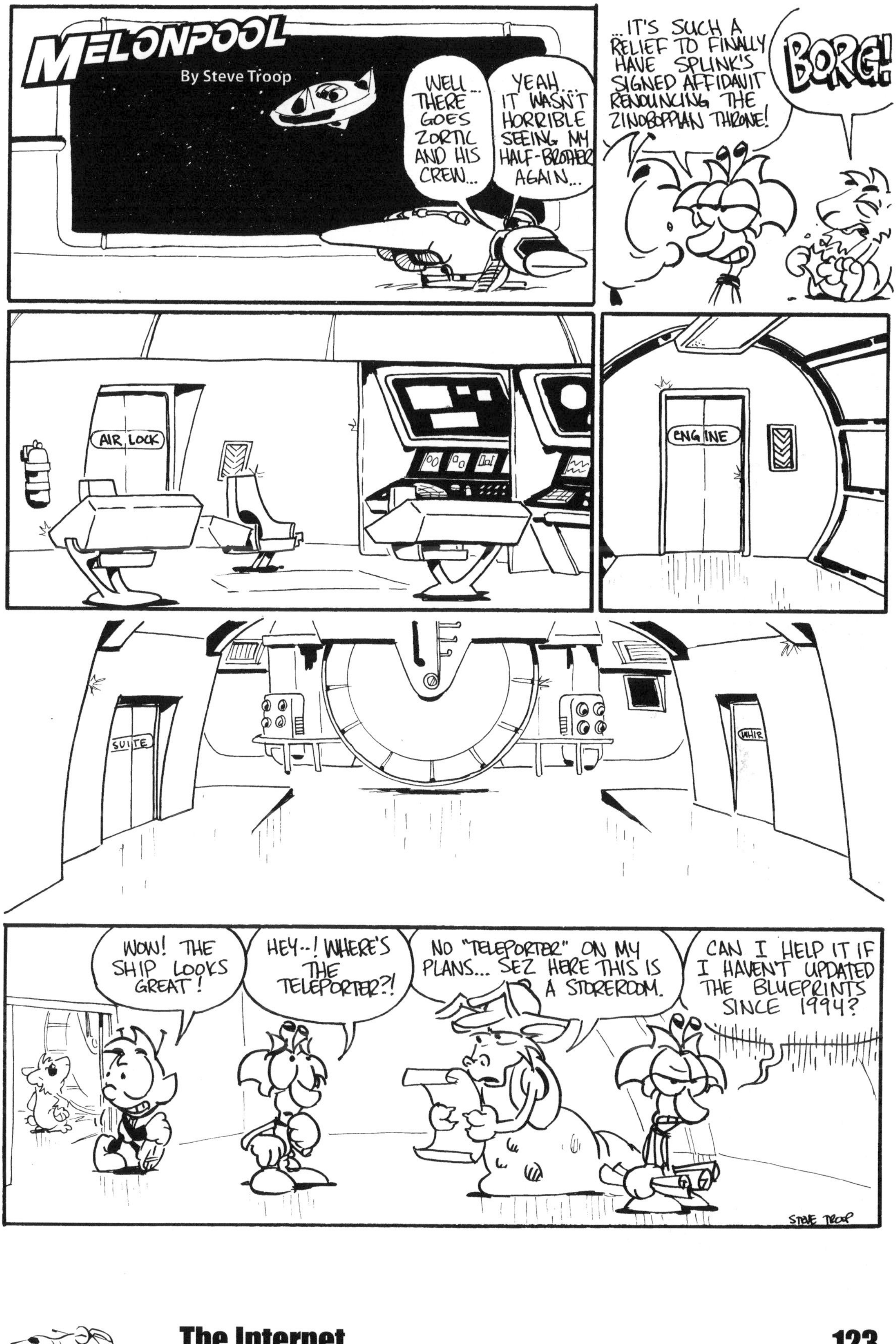
MELONPOOL
By Steve Troop
WELL... THERE GOES ZORTIC AND HIS CREW...
YEAH... IT WASN'T HORRIBLE SEEING MY HALF-BROTHER AGAIN...
...IT'S SUCH A RELIEF TO FINALLY HAVE SPLINK'S SIGNED AFFIDAVIT RENOUNCING THE ZINOBOPPIAN THRONE!
BORG!
AIR LOCK
ENGINE
SUITE
WOW! THE SHIP LOOKS GREAT!
HEY--! WHERE'S THE TELEPORTER?!
NO "TELEPORTER" ON MY PLANS... SEZ HERE THIS IS A STOREROOM.
CAN I HELP IT IF I HAVEN'T UPDATED THE BLUEPRINTS SINCE 1994?
STEVE TROOP

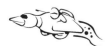

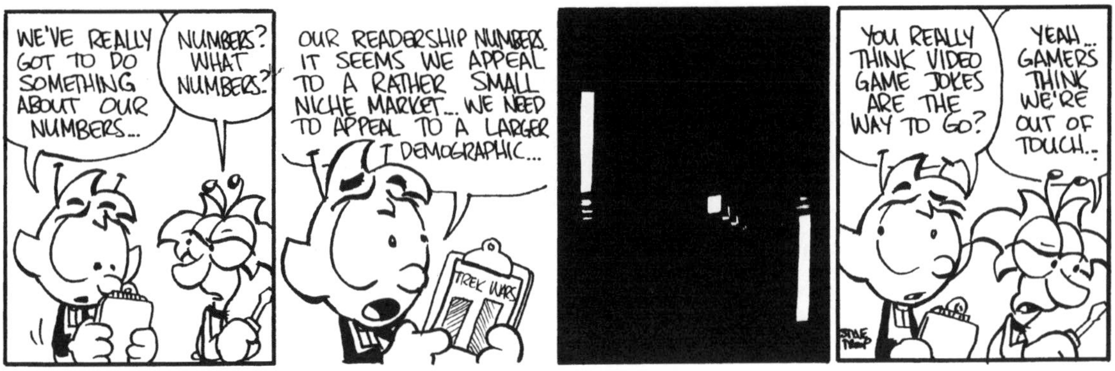
WE'VE REALLY GOT TO DO SOMETHING ABOUT OUR NUMBERS...
NUMBERS? WHAT NUMBERS?
OUR READERSHIP NUMBERS. IT SEEMS WE APPEAL TO A RATHER SMALL NICHE MARKET... WE NEED TO APPEAL TO A LARGER DEMOGRAPHIC...
TREK WARS
YOU REALLY THINK VIDEO GAME JOKES ARE THE WAY TO GO?
YEAH... GAMERS THINK WE'RE OUT OF TOUCH...
STEVE TROOP

Panels 2, 3 and 4 feature cameos of some of the most popular girls in webcomics (at least, as of 2005), alongside some of the nerdiest characters in webcomics. There's Jade and Francis from *PVP* in the second panel, Monique and Slick (technically not a nerd—but rather nerdy, nevertheless) from *Sinfest* in the third and Nick and Ki from *General Protection Fault*.

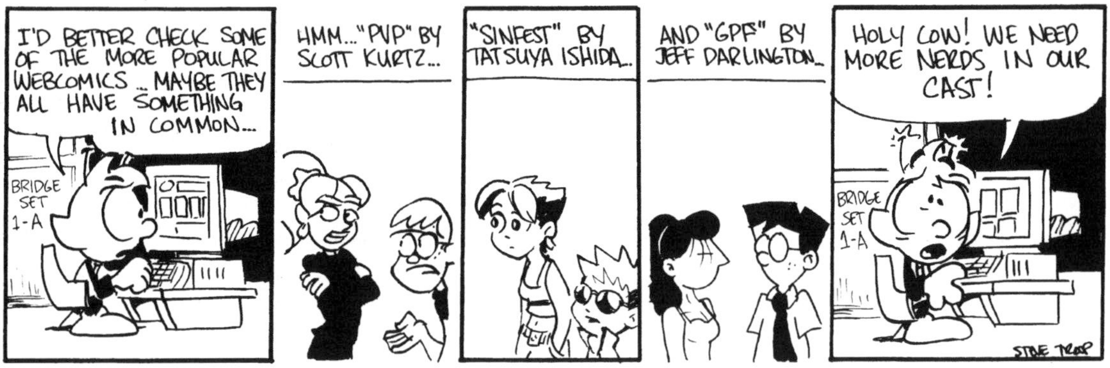
I'D BETTER CHECK SOME OF THE MORE POPULAR WEBCOMICS... MAYBE THEY ALL HAVE SOMETHING IN COMMON...
BRIDGE SET 1-A
HMM..."PVP" BY SCOTT KURTZ...
"SINFEST" BY TATSUYA ISHIDA...
AND "GPF" BY JEFF DARLINGTON...
HOLY COW! WE NEED MORE NERDS IN OUR CAST!
BRIDGE SET 1-A
STEVE TROOP

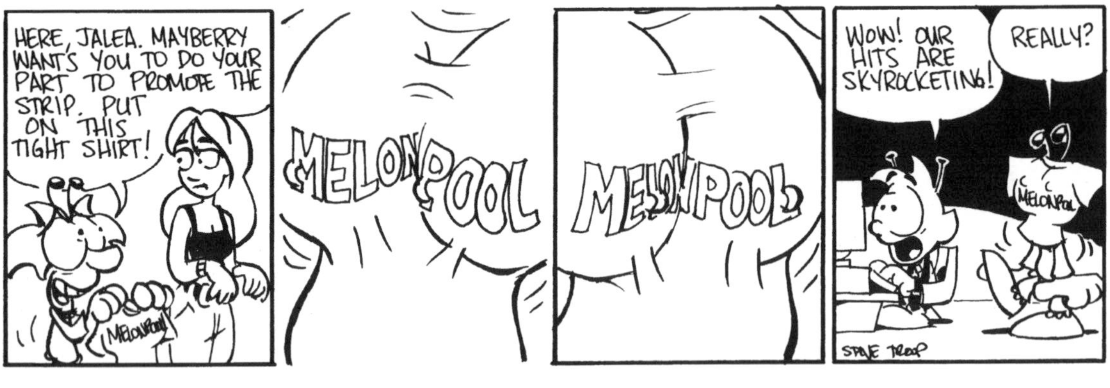
HERE, JALEA. MAYBERRY WANTS YOU TO DO YOUR PART TO PROMOTE THE STRIP. PUT ON THIS TIGHT SHIRT!
MELONPOOL
MELONPOOL
MELONPOOL
WOW! OUR HITS ARE SKYROCKETING!
REALLY?
MELONPOOL
STEVE TROOP

At the time this strip ran, the three most popular blogs about webcomics were Websnark, Comixpedia and Digital Strips. Interestingly enough, *Melonpool* got mentioned on all three sites when this strip ran—a trifecta!

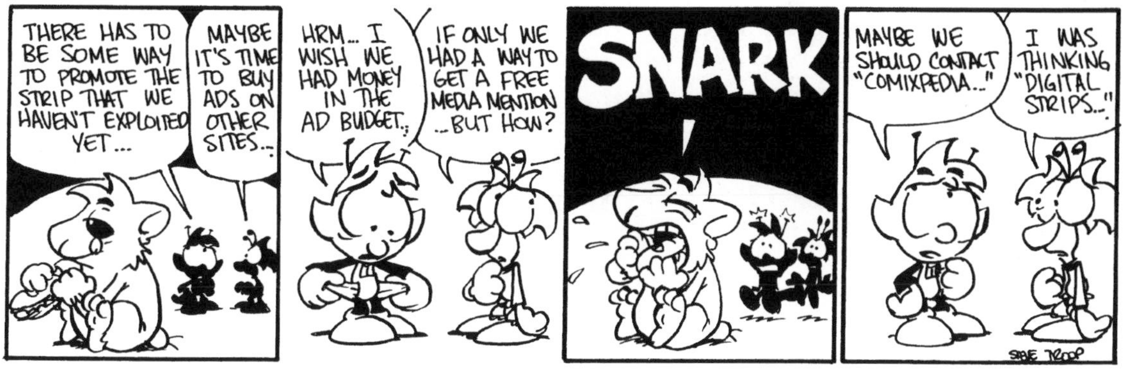

THERE HAS TO BE SOME WAY TO PROMOTE THE STRIP THAT WE HAVEN'T EXPLOITED YET...
MAYBE IT'S TIME TO BUY ADS ON OTHER SITES...
HRM... I WISH WE HAD MONEY IN THE AD BUDGET...
IF ONLY WE HAD A WAY TO GET A FREE MEDIA MENTION ...BUT HOW?
SNARK
MAYBE WE SHOULD CONTACT "COMIXPEDIA..."
I WAS THINKING "DIGITAL STRIPS..."
STEVE TROOP

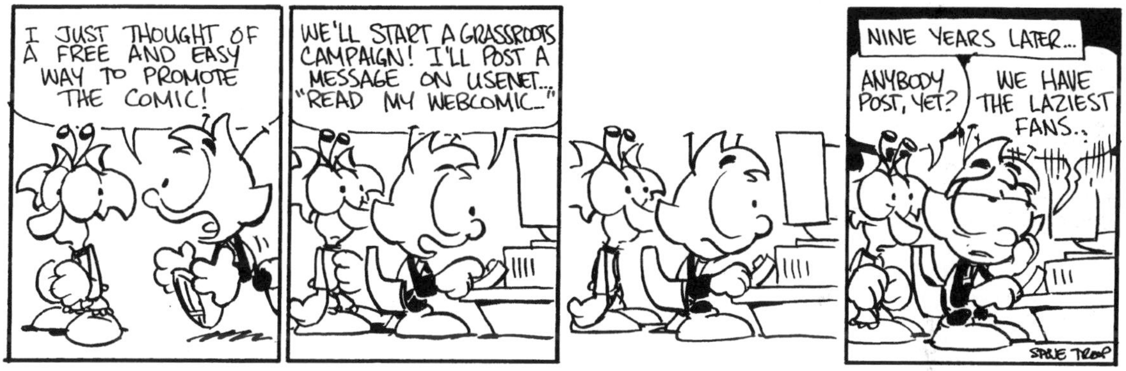

I JUST THOUGHT OF A FREE AND EASY WAY TO PROMOTE THE COMIC!
WE'LL START A GRASSROOTS CAMPAIGN! I'LL POST A MESSAGE ON USENET... "READ MY WEBCOMIC..."
NINE YEARS LATER...
ANYBODY POST, YET?
WE HAVE THE LAZIEST FANS...
STEVE TROOP

Wapsi Square by Paul Taylor was also one of the founding members of Blank Label Comics and had a very successful run of "eight-ball" T-shirts around the time this strip ran. I always thought about doing a parody of his design by making an infinity symbol version, but this strip was about as close as I ever got.

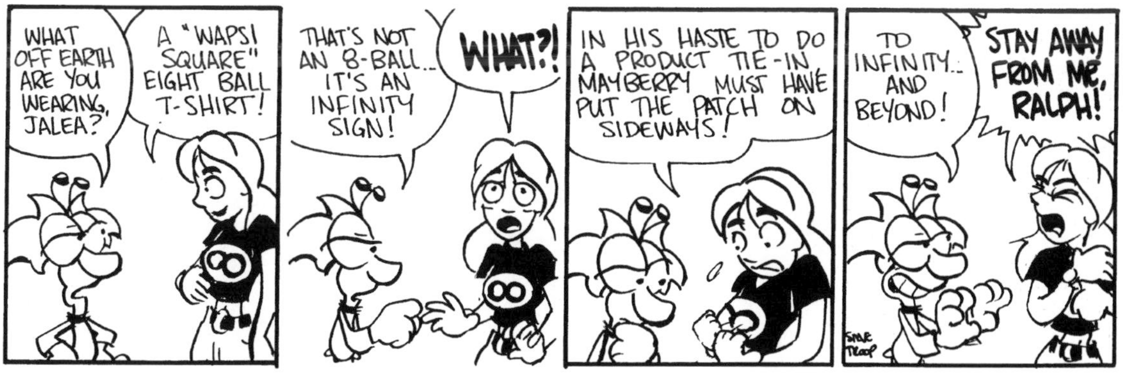

WHAT OFF EARTH ARE YOU WEARING, JALEA?
A "WAPSI SQUARE" EIGHT BALL T-SHIRT!
THAT'S NOT AN 8-BALL... IT'S AN INFINITY SIGN!
WHAT?!
IN HIS HASTE TO DO A PRODUCT TIE-IN MAYBERRY MUST HAVE PUT THE PATCH ON SIDEWAYS!
TO INFINITY... AND BEYOND!
STAY AWAY FROM ME, RALPH!
STEVE TROOP

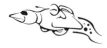

This strip is a follow-up to other "behind the scenes" adventures in webcomics, as seen in TUM I, page 126 and TUM II page 160.

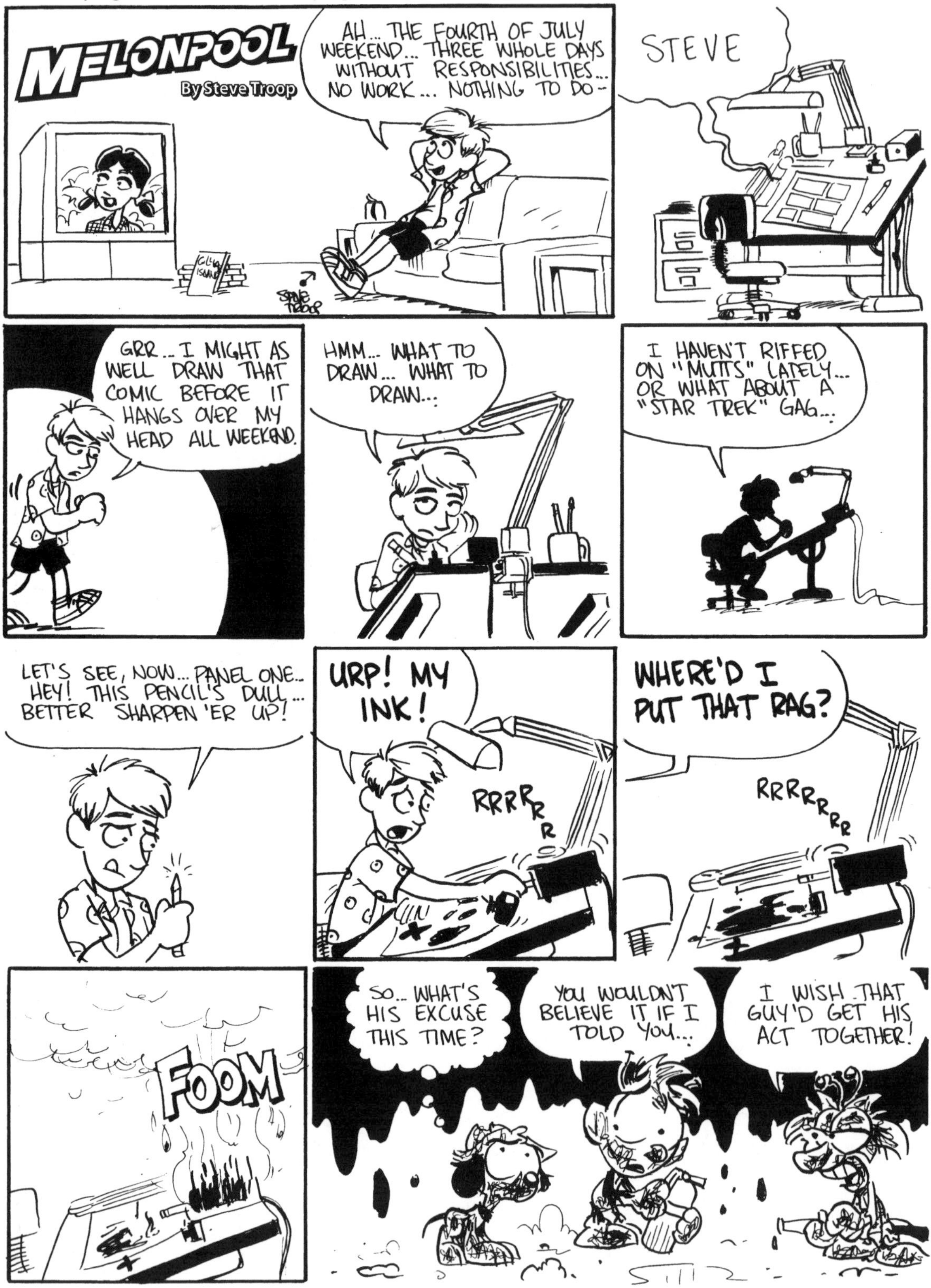
MELONPOOL
By Steve Troop
AH... THE FOURTH OF JULY WEEKEND... THREE WHOLE DAYS WITHOUT RESPONSIBILITIES... NO WORK... NOTHING TO DO--
STEVE
GRR... I MIGHT AS WELL DRAW THAT COMIC BEFORE IT HANGS OVER MY HEAD ALL WEEKEND.
HMM... WHAT TO DRAW... WHAT TO DRAW...
I HAVEN'T RIFFED ON "MUTTS" LATELY... OR WHAT ABOUT A "STAR TREK" GAG...
LET'S SEE, NOW... PANEL ONE.. HEY! THIS PENCIL'S DULL... BETTER SHARPEN 'ER UP!
URP! MY INK!
RRRRRR
WHERE'D I PUT THAT RAG?
RRRRRRRR
FOOM
SO... WHAT'S HIS EXCUSE THIS TIME?
YOU WOULDN'T BELIEVE IT IF I TOLD YOU...
I WISH THAT GUY'D GET HIS ACT TOGETHER!

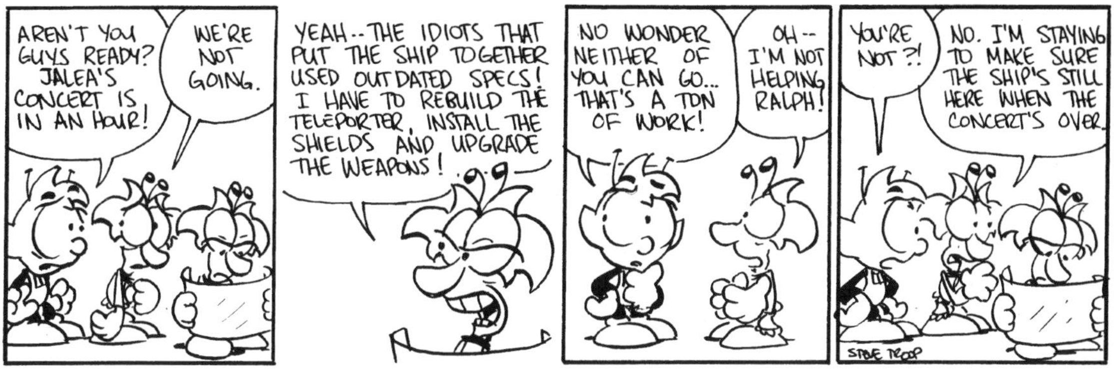

AREN'T YOU GUYS READY? JALEA'S CONCERT IS IN AN HOUR!
WE'RE NOT GOING.
YEAH--THE IDIOTS THAT PUT THE SHIP TOGETHER USED OUTDATED SPECS! I HAVE TO REBUILD THE TELEPORTER, INSTALL THE SHIELDS AND UPGRADE THE WEAPONS!
NO WONDER NEITHER OF YOU CAN GO... THAT'S A TON OF WORK!
OH-- I'M NOT HELPING RALPH!
YOU'RE NOT?!
NO. I'M STAYING TO MAKE SURE THE SHIP'S STILL HERE WHEN THE CONCERT'S OVER.
STEVE TROOP

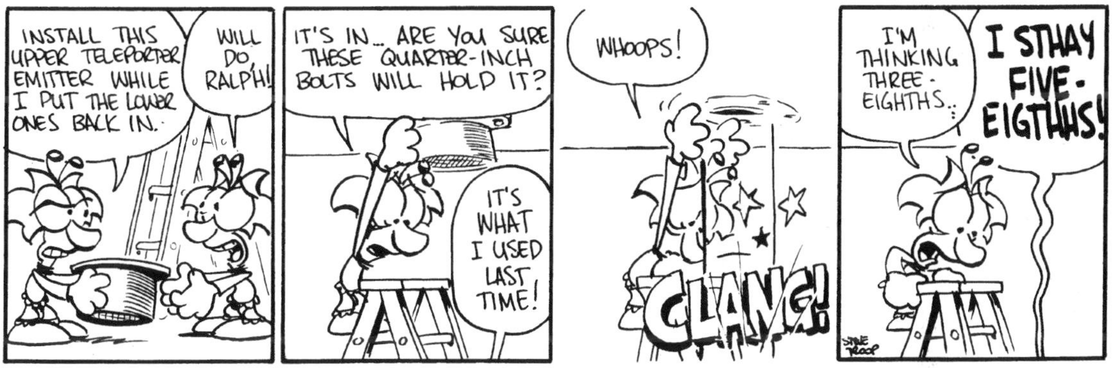

INSTALL THIS UPPER TELEPORTER EMITTER WHILE I PUT THE LOWER ONES BACK IN.
WILL DO, RALPH!
IT'S IN... ARE YOU SURE THESE QUARTER-INCH BOLTS WILL HOLD IT?
IT'S WHAT I USED LAST TIME!
WHOOPS!
CLANG!
I'M THINKING THREE-EIGHTHS...
I STHAY FIVE-EIGTHHS!
STEVE TROOP

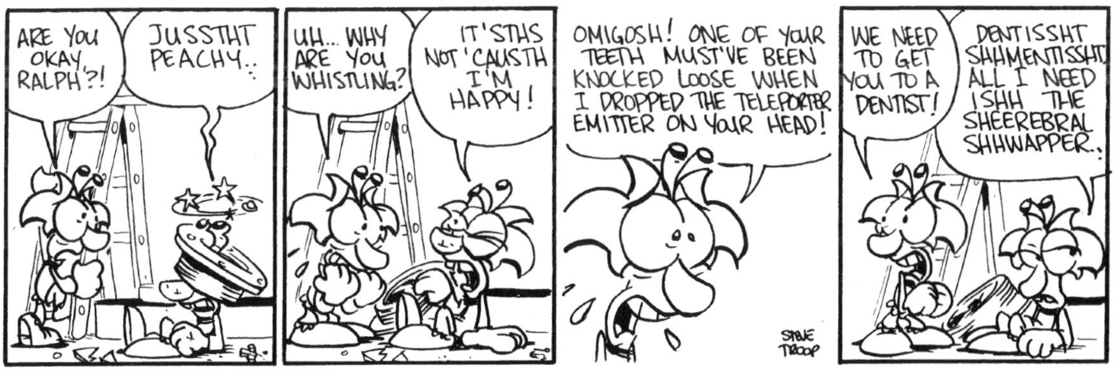

ARE YOU OKAY, RALPH?!
JUSSTHT PEACHY...
UH... WHY ARE YOU WHISTLING?
IT'STHS NOT 'CAUSTH I'M HAPPY!
OMIGOSH! ONE OF YOUR TEETH MUST'VE BEEN KNOCKED LOOSE WHEN I DROPPED THE TELEPORTER EMITTER ON YOUR HEAD!
STEVE TROOP
WE NEED TO GET YOU TO A DENTIST!
DENTISSHT SHHMENTISSHT! ALL I NEED ISHH THE SHEEREBRAL SHHWAPPER...

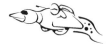

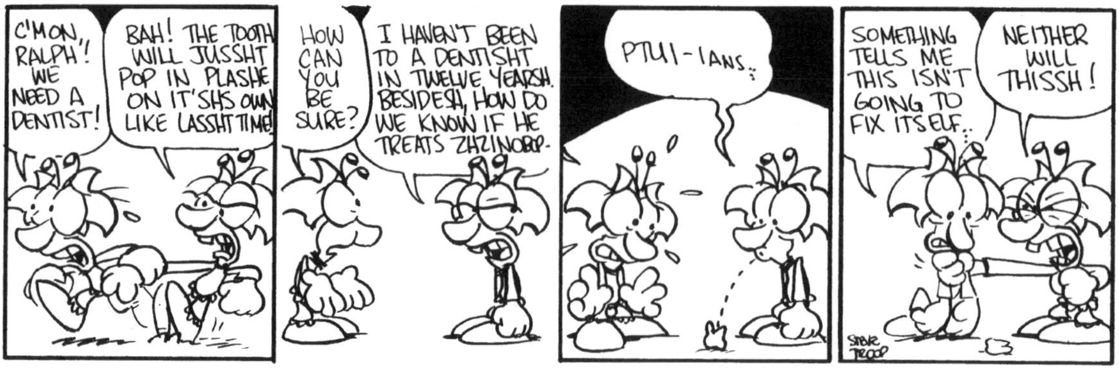
C'MON, RALPH! WE NEED A DENTIST!
BAH! THE TOOTH WILL JUSSHT POP IN PLASHE ON IT'SHS OWN LIKE LASSHT TIME!
HOW CAN YOU BE SURE?
I HAVEN'T BEEN TO A DENTISHT IN TWELVE YEARSH. BESIDESH, HOW DO WE KNOW IF HE TREATS ZHZINORP-
PTUI-IANS..
SOMETHING TELLS ME THIS ISN'T GOING TO FIX ITSELF..
NEITHER WILL THISSH!
STEVE TROOP

This series of strips is based on some abandoned ideas from the Palomar *Telescope* era of *Melonpool.* As originally scripted, Ralph's nose was bitten off by a snapping turtle and the crew had to scramble for a way to re-attach it. I never drew it, but once some story idea enters my mind, I never truly abandon things—it just sort of evolves.

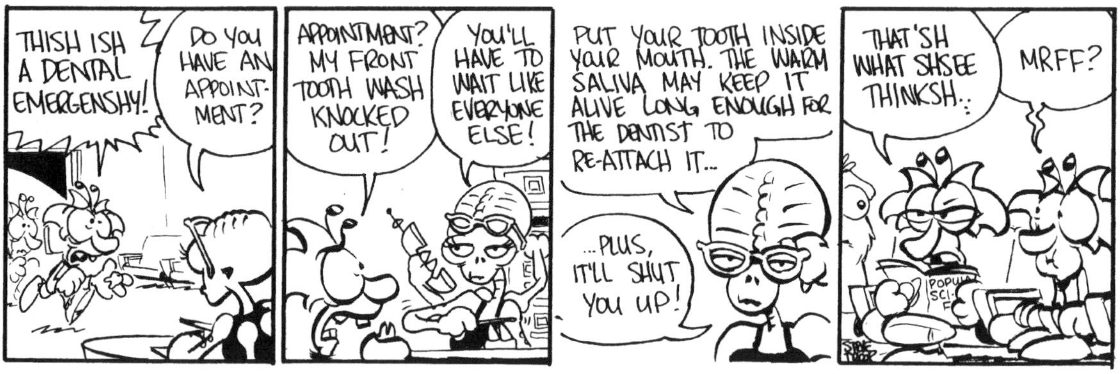
THISH ISH A DENTAL EMERGENSHY!
DO YOU HAVE AN APPOINTMENT?
APPOINTMENT? MY FRONT TOOTH WASH KNOCKED OUT!
YOU'LL HAVE TO WAIT LIKE EVERYONE ELSE!
PUT YOUR TOOTH INSIDE YOUR MOUTH. THE WARM SALIVA MAY KEEP IT ALIVE LONG ENOUGH FOR THE DENTIST TO RE-ATTACH IT...
...PLUS, IT'LL SHUT YOU UP!
THAT'SH WHAT SHSEE THINKSH..
MRFF?
STEVE TROOP

Is it just me, or do all of my throwaway aliens look like Muppets or undersea creatures?

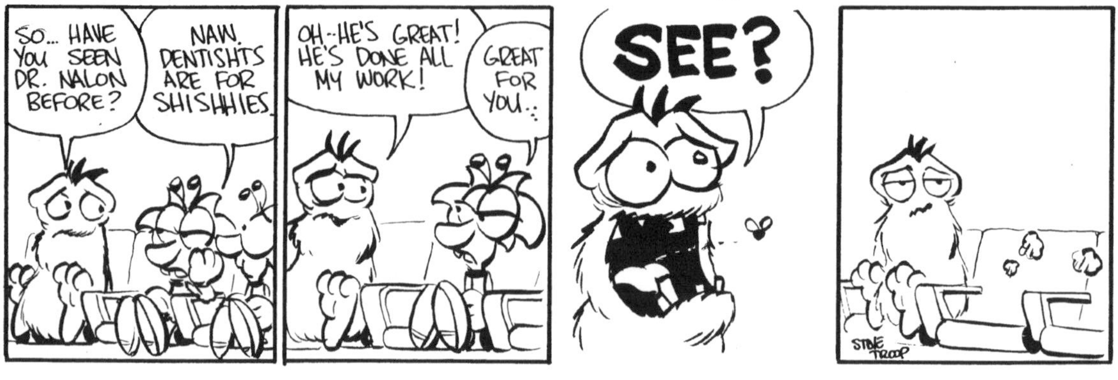
SO... HAVE YOU SEEN DR. NALON BEFORE?
NAW. DENTISHTS ARE FOR SHISHHIES
OH--HE'S GREAT! HE'S DONE ALL MY WORK!
GREAT FOR YOU..
SEE?
STEVE TROOP

Ralph's dentist was loosely based on the dentist I was seeing at the time. My real dentist was a little slimier, now that I think about it....

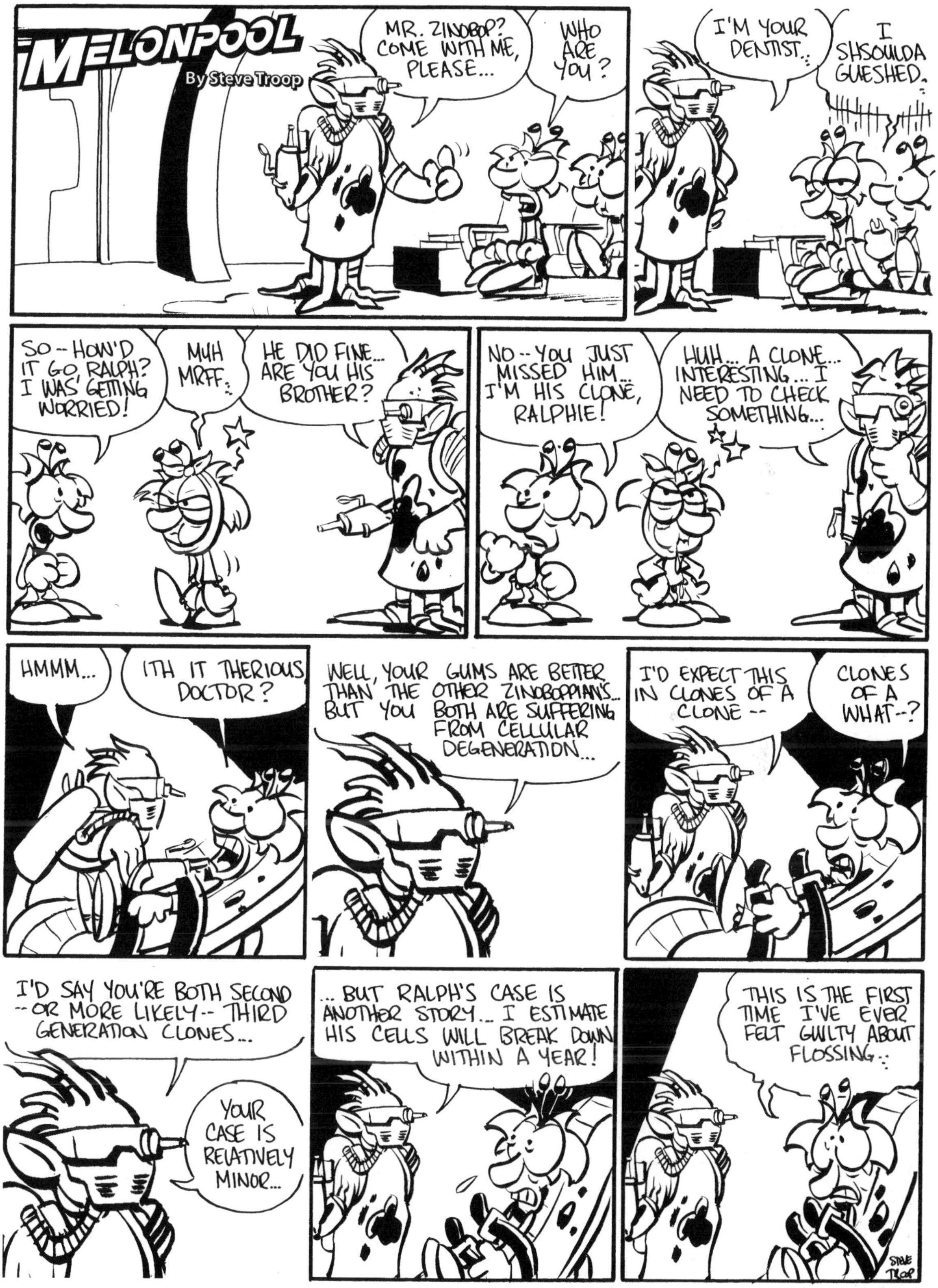

MELONPOOL
By Steve Troop
MR. ZINDBOP? COME WITH ME, PLEASE...
WHO ARE YOU?
I'M YOUR DENTIST.
I SHSOULDA GUESHED.
SO -- HOW'D IT GO, RALPH? I WAS GETTING WORRIED!
MUH MRFF.
HE DID FINE... ARE YOU HIS BROTHER?
NO -- YOU JUST MISSED HIM... I'M HIS CLONE, RALPHIE!
HUH... A CLONE... INTERESTING... I NEED TO CHECK SOMETHING...
HMMM...
ITH IT THERIOUS, DOCTOR?
WELL, YOUR GUMS ARE BETTER THAN THE OTHER ZINDBOPPIAN'S... BUT YOU BOTH ARE SUFFERING FROM CELLULAR DEGENERATION...
I'D EXPECT THIS IN CLONES OF A CLONE --
CLONES OF A WHAT--?
I'D SAY YOU'RE BOTH SECOND -- OR MORE LIKELY -- THIRD GENERATION CLONES...
YOUR CASE IS RELATIVELY MINOR...
... BUT RALPH'S CASE IS ANOTHER STORY... I ESTIMATE HIS CELLS WILL BREAK DOWN WITHIN A YEAR!
THIS IS THE FIRST TIME I'VE EVER FELT GUILTY ABOUT FLOSSING.
STEVE TROOP

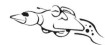

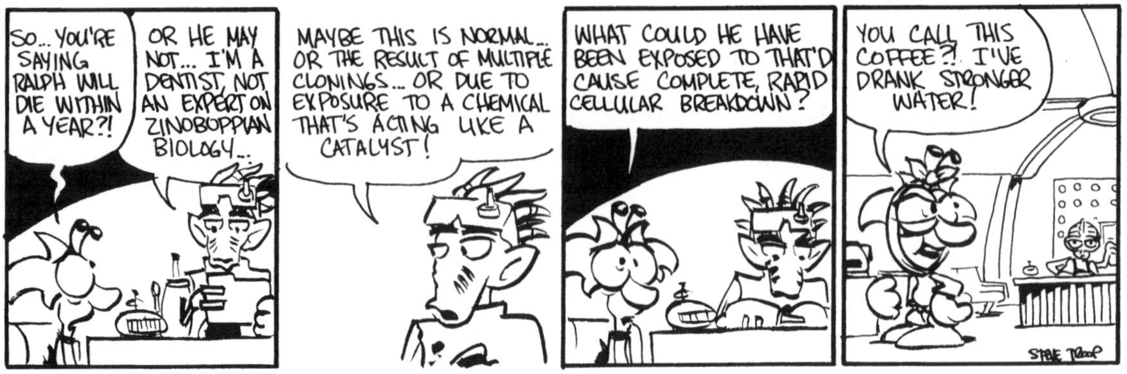
SO... YOU'RE SAYING RALPH WILL DIE WITHIN A YEAR?!
OR HE MAY NOT... I'M A DENTIST, NOT AN EXPERT ON ZINOBOPPIAN BIOLOGY...
MAYBE THIS IS NORMAL... OR THE RESULT OF MULTIPLE CLONINGS... OR DUE TO EXPOSURE TO A CHEMICAL THAT'S ACTING LIKE A CATALYST!
WHAT COULD HE HAVE BEEN EXPOSED TO THAT'D CAUSE COMPLETE, RAPID CELLULAR BREAKDOWN?
YOU CALL THIS COFFEE?! I'VE DRANK STRONGER WATER!
STEVE TROOP

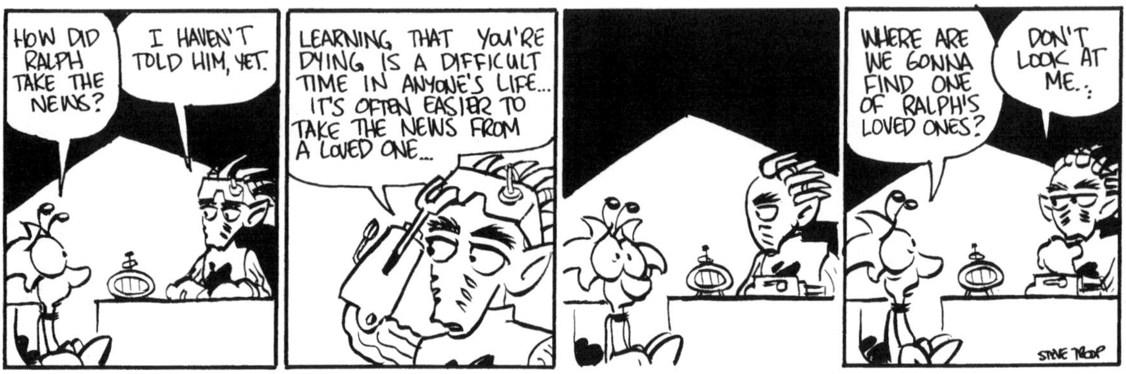
HOW DID RALPH TAKE THE NEWS?
I HAVEN'T TOLD HIM, YET.
LEARNING THAT YOU'RE DYING IS A DIFFICULT TIME IN ANYONE'S LIFE... IT'S OFTEN EASIER TO TAKE THE NEWS FROM A LOVED ONE...
WHERE ARE WE GONNA FIND ONE OF RALPH'S LOVED ONES?
DON'T LOOK AT ME..
STEVE TROOP

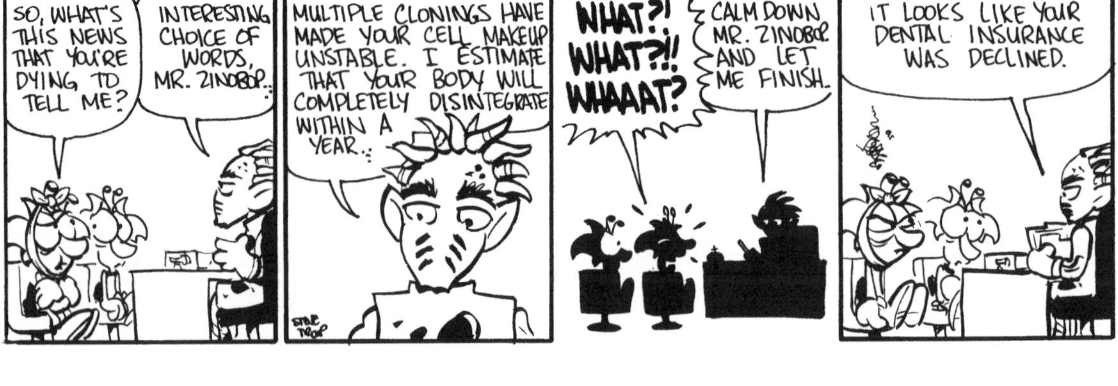
SO, WHAT'S THIS NEWS THAT YOU'RE DYING TO TELL ME?
INTERESTING CHOICE OF WORDS, MR. ZINOBOP..
MULTIPLE CLONINGS HAVE MADE YOUR CELL MAKEUP UNSTABLE. I ESTIMATE THAT YOUR BODY WILL COMPLETELY DISINTEGRATE WITHIN A YEAR..
STEVE TROOP
WHAT?! WHAT?!! WHAAAT?
CALM DOWN MR. ZINOBOP AND LET ME FINISH.
IT LOOKS LIKE YOUR DENTAL INSURANCE WAS DECLINED.

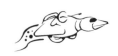

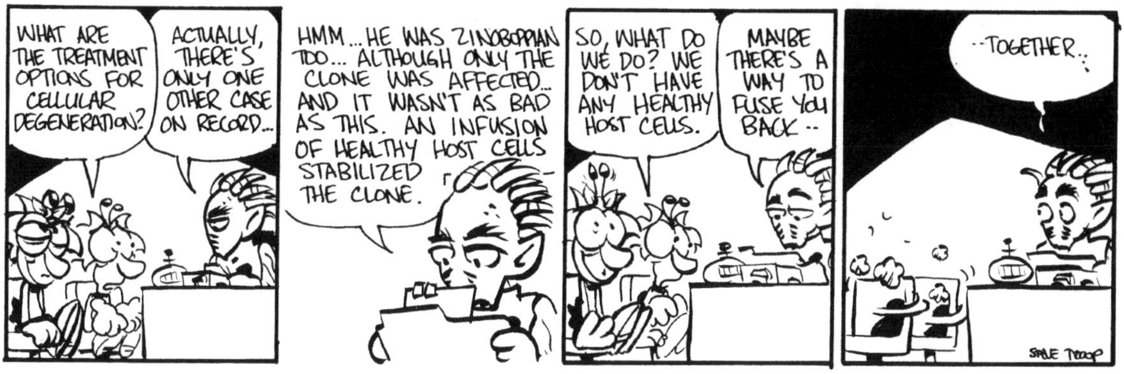
WHAT ARE THE TREATMENT OPTIONS FOR CELLULAR DEGENERATION?
ACTUALLY, THERE'S ONLY ONE OTHER CASE ON RECORD...
HMM... HE WAS ZINOBOPPIAN TOO... ALTHOUGH ONLY THE CLONE WAS AFFECTED... AND IT WASN'T AS BAD AS THIS. AN INFUSION OF HEALTHY HOST CELLS STABILIZED THE CLONE.
SO, WHAT DO WE DO? WE DON'T HAVE ANY HEALTHY HOST CELLS.
MAYBE THERE'S A WAY TO FUSE YOU BACK --
-- TOGETHER...
STEVE TROOP

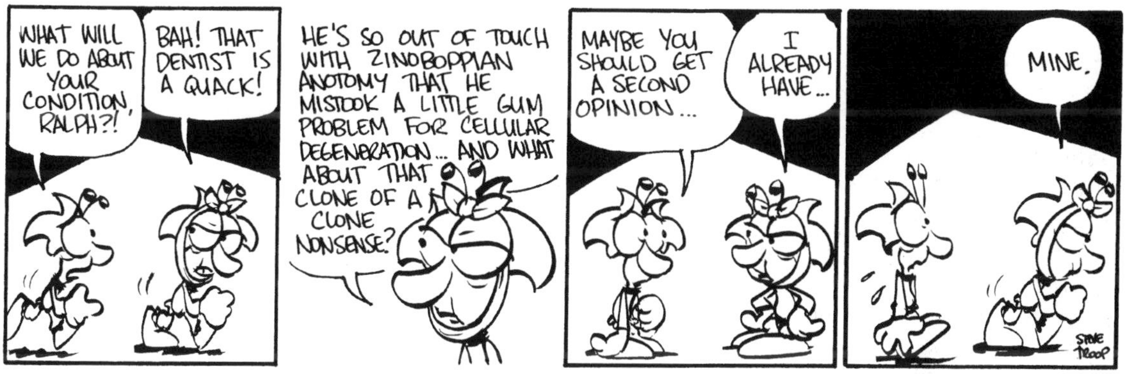
WHAT WILL WE DO ABOUT YOUR CONDITION, RALPH?!
BAH! THAT DENTIST IS A QUACK!
HE'S SO OUT OF TOUCH WITH ZINOBOPPIAN ANOTOMY THAT HE MISTOOK A LITTLE GUM PROBLEM FOR CELLULAR DEGENERATION... AND WHAT ABOUT THAT CLONE OF A CLONE NONSENSE?
MAYBE YOU SHOULD GET A SECOND OPINION...
I ALREADY HAVE...
MINE.
STEVE TROOP

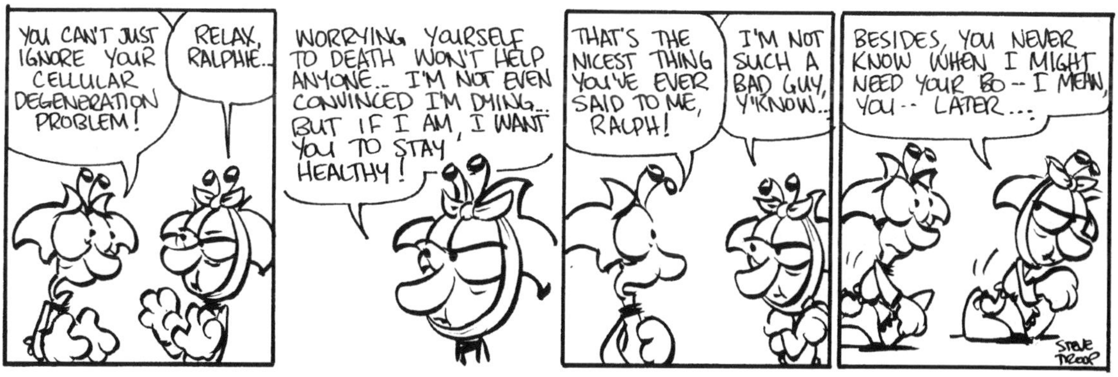
YOU CAN'T JUST IGNORE YOUR CELLULAR DEGENERATION PROBLEM!
RELAX, RALPHIE...
WORRYING YOURSELF TO DEATH WON'T HELP ANYONE... I'M NOT EVEN CONVINCED I'M DYING... BUT IF I AM, I WANT YOU TO STAY HEALTHY!
THAT'S THE NICEST THING YOU'VE EVER SAID TO ME, RALPH!
I'M NOT SUCH A BAD GUY, Y'KNOW...
BESIDES, YOU NEVER KNOW WHEN I MIGHT NEED YOUR BO -- I MEAN, YOU -- LATER...
STEVE TROOP

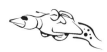

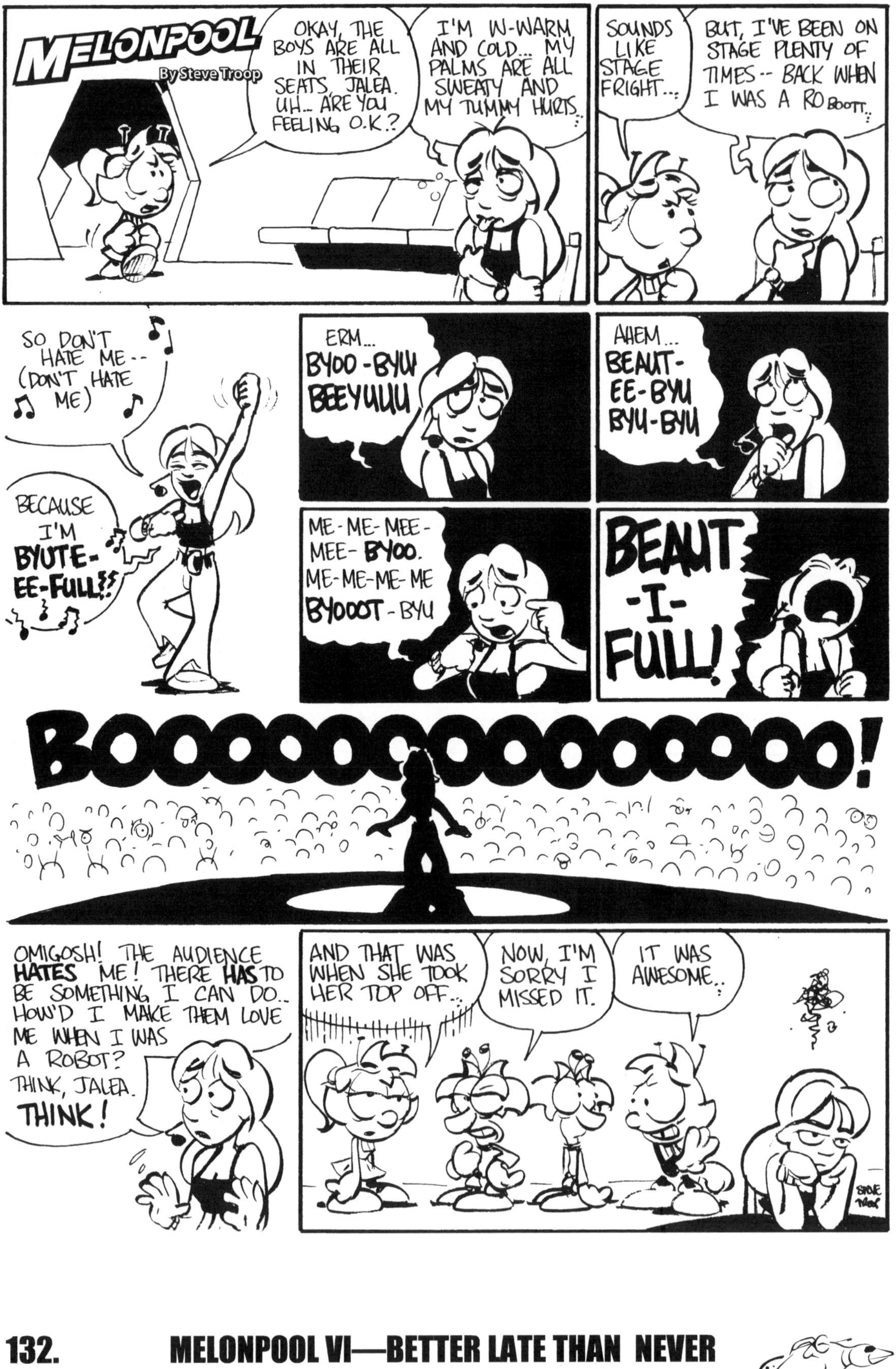
MELONPOOL
By Steve Troop
OKAY, THE BOYS ARE ALL IN THEIR SEATS, JALEA. UH... ARE YOU FEELING O.K.?
I'M W-WARM AND COLD... MY PALMS ARE ALL SWEATY AND MY TUMMY HURTS...
SOUNDS LIKE STAGE FRIGHT...
BUT, I'VE BEEN ON STAGE PLENTY OF TIMES -- BACK WHEN I WAS A RO BOOTT...
SO DON'T HATE ME -- (DON'T HATE ME)
BECAUSE I'M BYUTE-EE-FULL!?!
ERM... BYOO-BYU BEEYUUU
AHEM... BEAUT-EE-BYU BYU-BYU
ME-ME-MEE-MEE- BYOO. ME-ME-ME-ME BYOOOT-BYU
BEAUT -I- FULL!
BOOOOOOOOOOOOOO!
OMIGOSH! THE AUDIENCE HATES ME! THERE HAS TO BE SOMETHING I CAN DO.. HOW'D I MAKE THEM LOVE ME WHEN I WAS A ROBOT? THINK, JALEA. THINK!
AND THAT WAS WHEN SHE TOOK HER TOP OFF...
NOW, I'M SORRY I MISSED IT.
IT WAS AWESOME...

This strip references Ashley Simpson's infamous *Saturday Night Live* performance where she was caught lipsynching to a pre-recorded track.

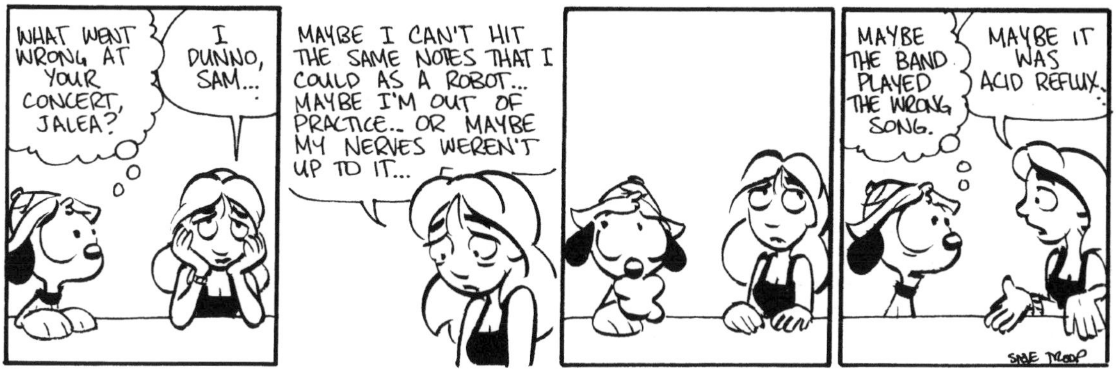
WHAT WENT WRONG AT YOUR CONCERT, JALEA?
I DUNNO, SAM...
MAYBE I CAN'T HIT THE SAME NOTES THAT I COULD AS A ROBOT... MAYBE I'M OUT OF PRACTICE... OR MAYBE MY NERVES WEREN'T UP TO IT...
MAYBE THE BAND PLAYED THE WRONG SONG.
MAYBE IT WAS ACID REFLUX...
STEVE TROOP

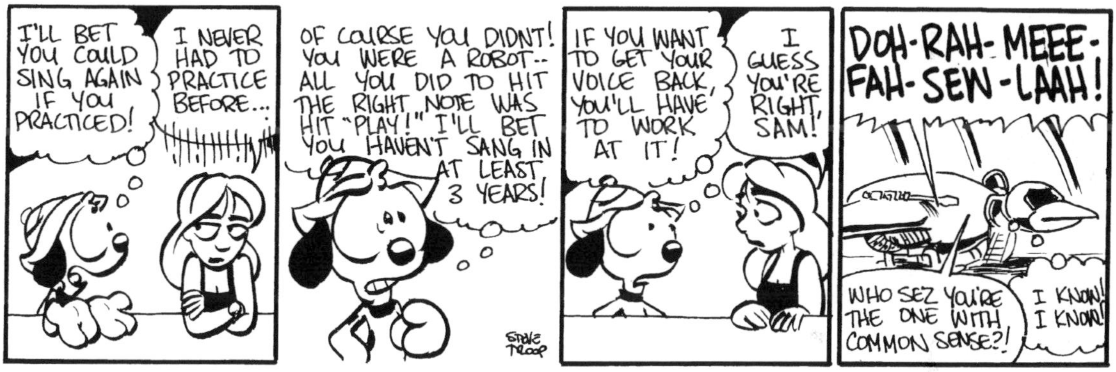
I'LL BET YOU COULD SING AGAIN IF YOU PRACTICED!
I NEVER HAD TO PRACTICE BEFORE...
OF COURSE YOU DIDN'T! YOU WERE A ROBOT-- ALL YOU DID TO HIT THE RIGHT NOTE WAS HIT "PLAY!" I'LL BET YOU HAVEN'T SANG IN AT LEAST 3 YEARS!
STEVE TROOP
IF YOU WANT TO GET YOUR VOICE BACK, YOU'LL HAVE TO WORK AT IT!
I GUESS YOU'RE RIGHT, SAM!
DOH-RAH-MEEE-FAH-SEW-LAAH!
WHO SEZ YOU'RE THE ONE WITH COMMON SENSE?!
I KNOW! I KNOW!

James Doohan died on July 17, 2005, after a long battle with Alzheimer's disease. I usually don't do obituary strips, but somehow, the original cast of *Star Trek* seems to warrant them (See TUM II, page 141). I don't know what adventures Doohan had in the *Melonpool* universe, but DeForest Kelley ended up as Ralph's guardian angel (see TUM II, pages 179183).

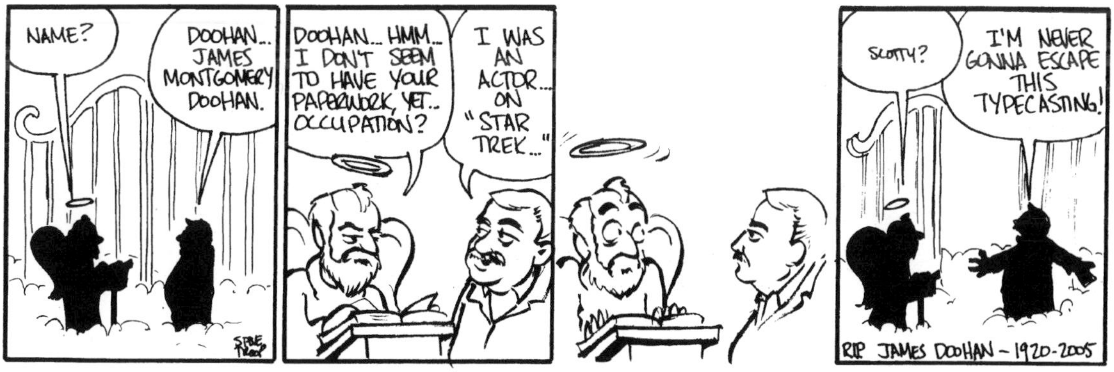
NAME?
DOOHAN... JAMES MONTGOMERY DOOHAN.
STEVE TROOP
DOOHAN... HMM... I DON'T SEEM TO HAVE YOUR PAPERWORK, YET... OCCUPATION?
I WAS AN ACTOR... ON "STAR TREK..."
SCOTTY?
I'M NEVER GONNA ESCAPE THIS TYPECASTING!
RIP JAMES DOOHAN – 1920-2005

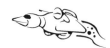

This strip was based on something that Paul Taylor (creator of *Wapsi Square*) drew as *Melonpool* banner ad concept. I liked it so much, I redrew it as part of the actual continuity.

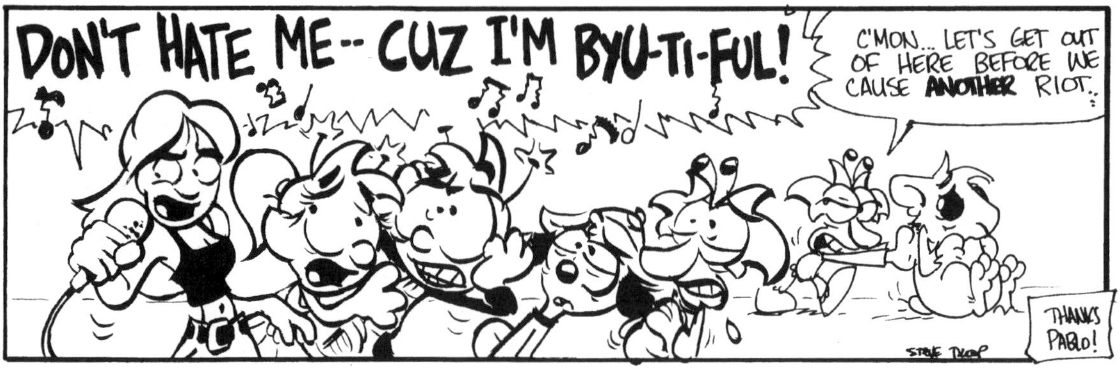
DON'T HATE ME-- CUZ I'M BYU-TI-FUL!
C'MON... LET'S GET OUT OF HERE BEFORE WE CAUSE ANOTHER RIOT...
THANKS PABLO!
STEVE TROOP

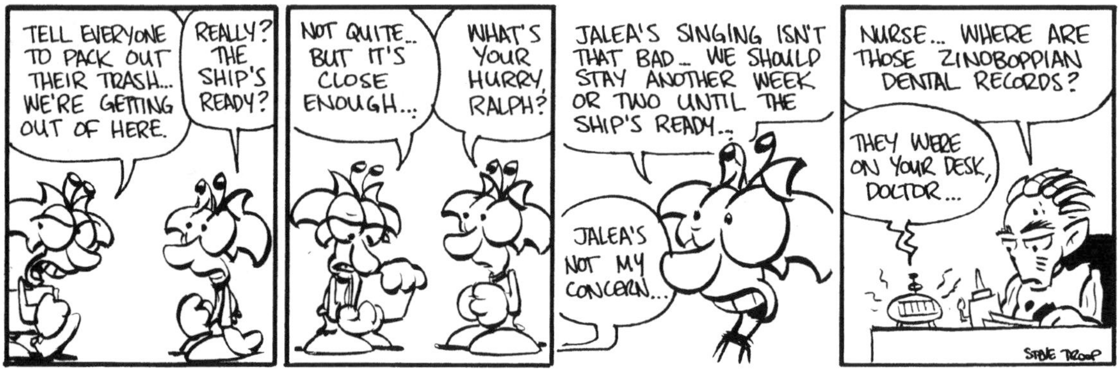
TELL EVERYONE TO PACK OUT THEIR TRASH... WE'RE GETTING OUT OF HERE.
REALLY? THE SHIP'S READY?
NOT QUITE... BUT IT'S CLOSE ENOUGH...
WHAT'S YOUR HURRY, RALPH?
JALEA'S SINGING ISN'T THAT BAD... WE SHOULD STAY ANOTHER WEEK OR TWO UNTIL THE SHIP'S READY...
JALEA'S NOT MY CONCERN...
NURSE... WHERE ARE THOSE ZINOBOPPIAN DENTAL RECORDS?
THEY WERE ON YOUR DESK, DOCTOR...
STEVE TROOP

This would have been a set up for a later storyline if I had continued the *Melonpool* webcomic. Maybe I'll make it into a puppet movie, instead.

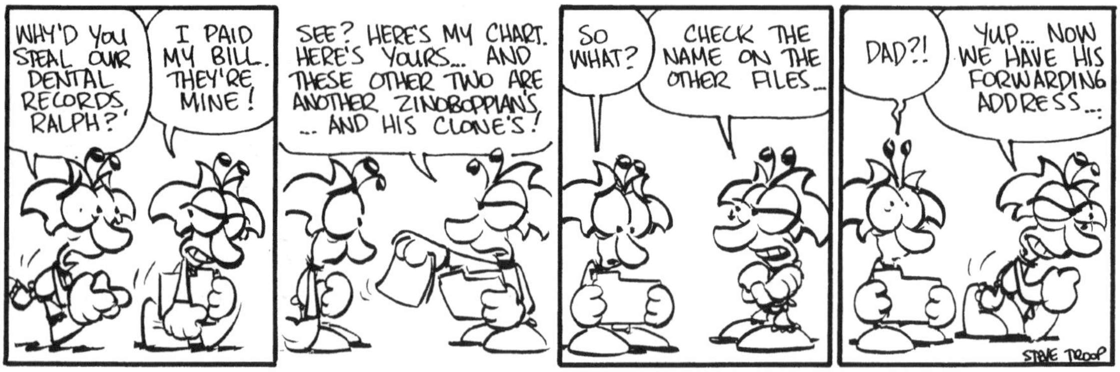
WHY'D YOU STEAL OUR DENTAL RECORDS, RALPH?
I PAID MY BILL. THEY'RE MINE!
SEE? HERE'S MY CHART. HERE'S YOURS... AND THESE OTHER TWO ARE ANOTHER ZINOBOPPIAN'S ... AND HIS CLONE'S!
SO WHAT?
CHECK THE NAME ON THE OTHER FILES...
DAD?!
YUP... NOW WE HAVE HIS FORWARDING ADDRESS...
STEVE TROOP

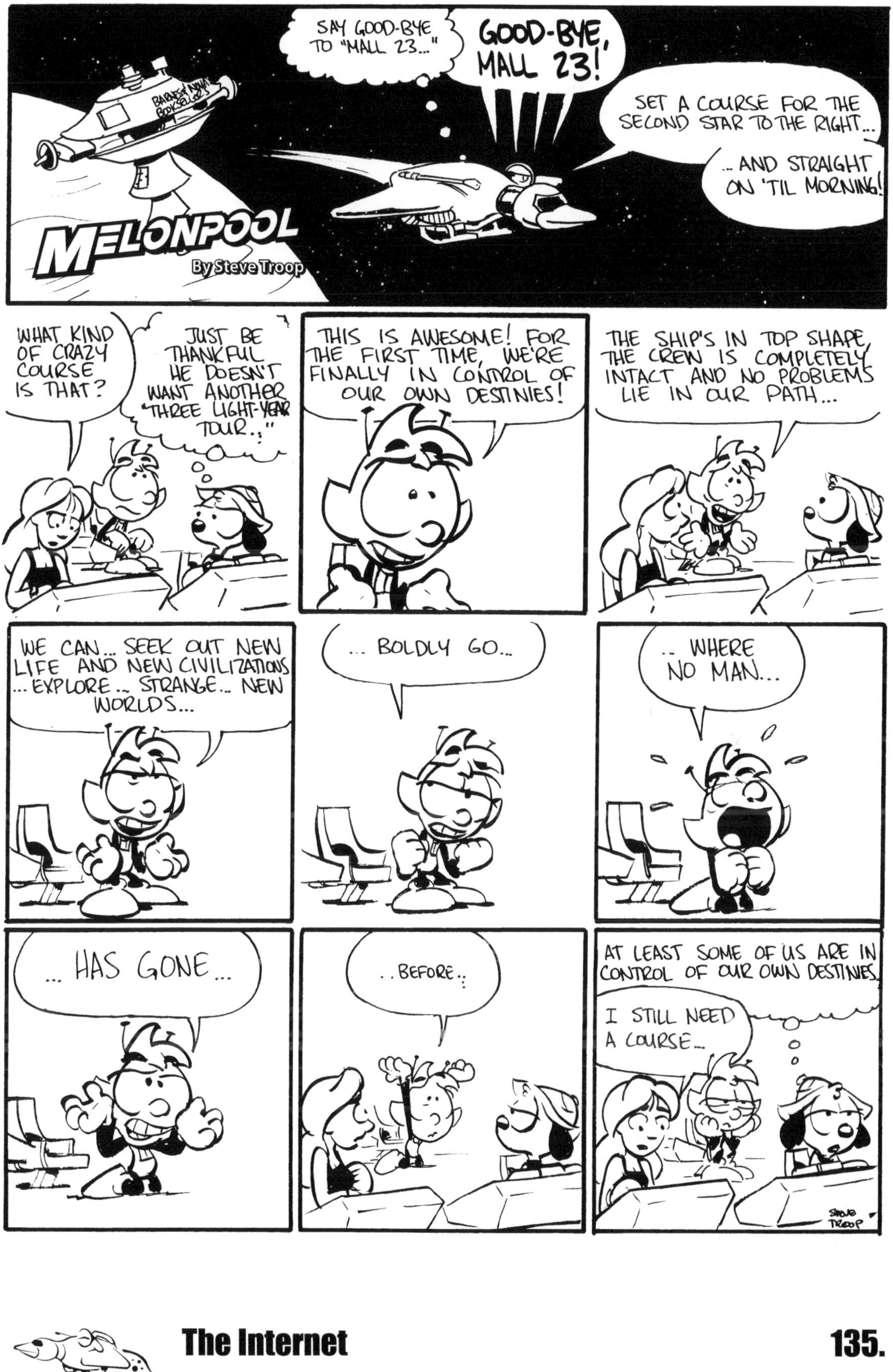
SAY GOOD-BYE TO "MALL 23..."
GOOD-BYE, MALL 23!
SET A COURSE FOR THE SECOND STAR TO THE RIGHT...
... AND STRAIGHT ON 'TIL MORNING!
MELONPOOL
By Steve Troop
WHAT KIND OF CRAZY COURSE IS THAT?
JUST BE THANKFUL HE DOESN'T WANT ANOTHER "THREE LIGHT-YEAR TOUR..."
THIS IS AWESOME! FOR THE FIRST TIME, WE'RE FINALLY IN CONTROL OF OUR OWN DESTINIES!
THE SHIP'S IN TOP SHAPE, THE CREW IS COMPLETELY INTACT AND NO PROBLEMS LIE IN OUR PATH...
WE CAN... SEEK OUT NEW LIFE AND NEW CIVILIZATIONS ... EXPLORE... STRANGE... NEW WORLDS...
... BOLDLY GO...
.. WHERE NO MAN...
... HAS GONE...
.. BEFORE..
AT LEAST SOME OF US ARE IN CONTROL OF OUR OWN DESTINIES.
I STILL NEED A COURSE...
STEVE TROOP

Crazy, super complicated time travel storylines is probably what *Melonpool* was most known for during its initial run. Often. I would spend years plotting out the crazy alternate timelines in my sketchbooks until I got them coherent enough to put into the strip. **Infinite Ralphie** was no exception—and was one of the first ideas I fleshed out when I decided to bring the strip back.

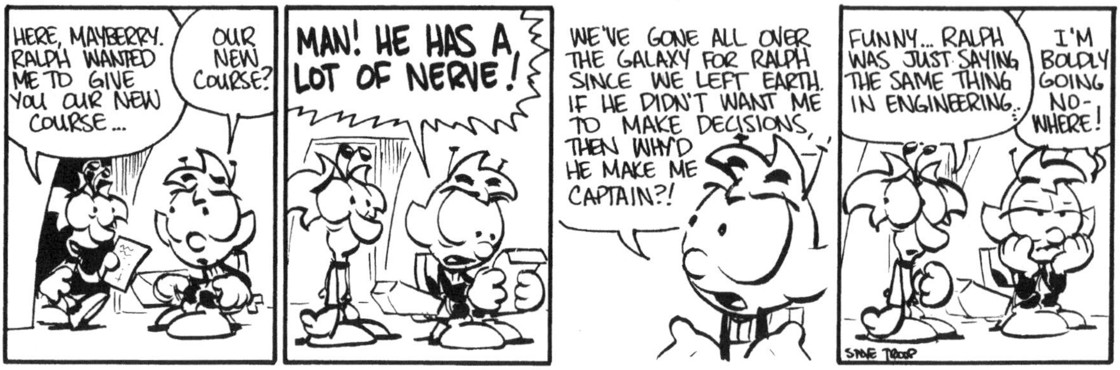
HERE, MAYBERRY. RALPH WANTED ME TO GIVE YOU OUR NEW COURSE...
OUR NEW COURSE?
MAN! HE HAS A LOT OF NERVE!
WE'VE GONE ALL OVER THE GALAXY FOR RALPH SINCE WE LEFT EARTH. IF HE DIDN'T WANT ME TO MAKE DECISIONS, THEN WHY'D HE MAKE ME CAPTAIN?!
FUNNY... RALPH WAS JUST SAYING THE SAME THING IN ENGINEERING...
I'M BOLDLY GOING NO-WHERE!
STEVE TROOP

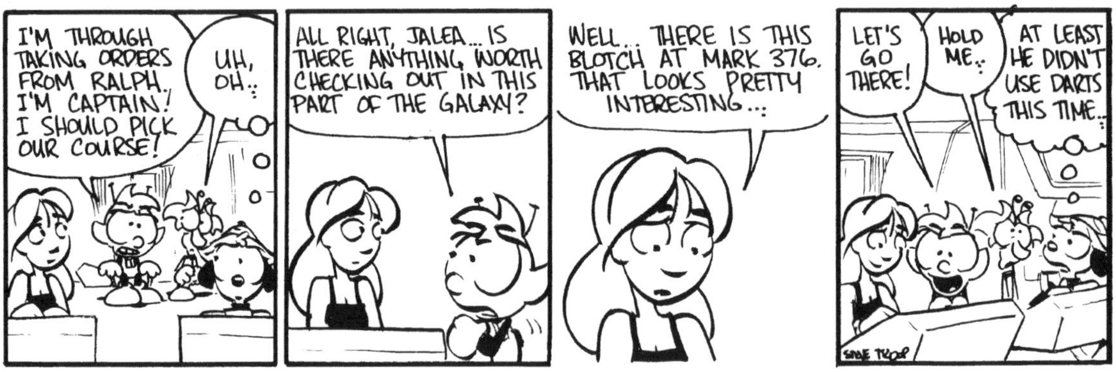
I'M THROUGH TAKING ORDERS FROM RALPH. I'M CAPTAIN! I SHOULD PICK OUR COURSE!
UH, OH...
ALL RIGHT, JALEA... IS THERE ANYTHING WORTH CHECKING OUT IN THIS PART OF THE GALAXY?
WELL... THERE IS THIS BLOTCH AT MARK 376. THAT LOOKS PRETTY INTERESTING...
LET'S GO THERE!
HOLD ME...
AT LEAST HE DIDN'T USE DARTS THIS TIME...
STEVE TROOP

Sometimes, plot expositions can be funny. And sometimes, it turns out like this one.

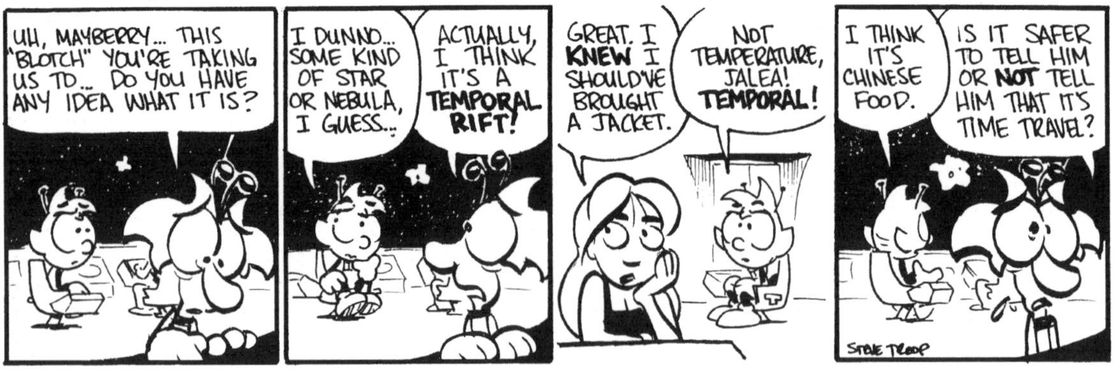
UH, MAYBERRY... THIS "BLOTCH" YOU'RE TAKING US TO... DO YOU HAVE ANY IDEA WHAT IT IS?
I DUNNO... SOME KIND OF STAR OR NEBULA, I GUESS...
ACTUALLY, I THINK IT'S A TEMPORAL RIFT!
GREAT. I KNEW I SHOULD'VE BROUGHT A JACKET.
NOT TEMPERATURE, JALEA! TEMPORAL!
I THINK IT'S CHINESE FOOD.
IS IT SAFER TO TELL HIM OR NOT TELL HIM THAT IT'S TIME TRAVEL?
STEVE TROOP

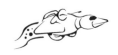

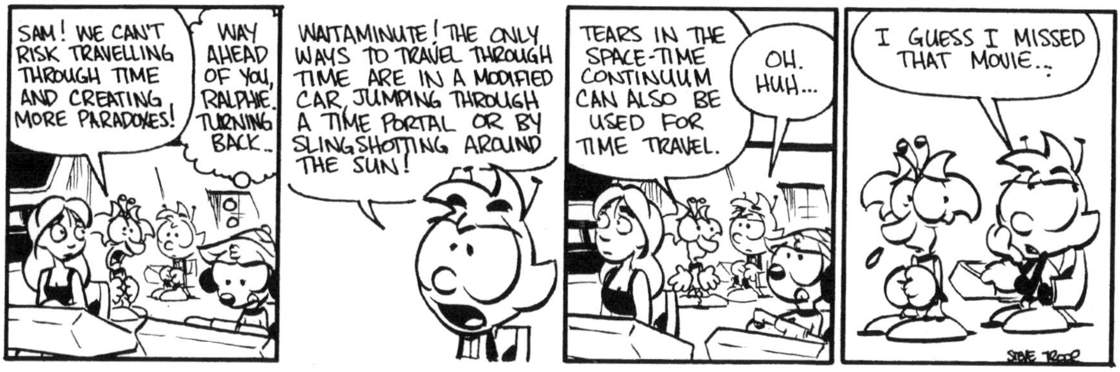
SAM! WE CAN'T RISK TRAVELLING THROUGH TIME AND CREATING MORE PARADOXES!
WAY AHEAD OF YOU, RALPHIE. TURNING BACK..
WAITAMINUTE! THE ONLY WAYS TO TRAVEL THROUGH TIME ARE IN A MODIFIED CAR, JUMPING THROUGH A TIME PORTAL OR BY SLINGSHOTTING AROUND THE SUN!
TEARS IN THE SPACE-TIME CONTINUUM CAN ALSO BE USED FOR TIME TRAVEL.
OH. HUH...
I GUESS I MISSED THAT MOVIE..

You may not have noticed it, but in most of Sam's appearances since being caught in the two-year time loop (TUM V, pages 87–111), I've drawn a little bag under his eyes—a small indication that he's growing older as the strip progresses.

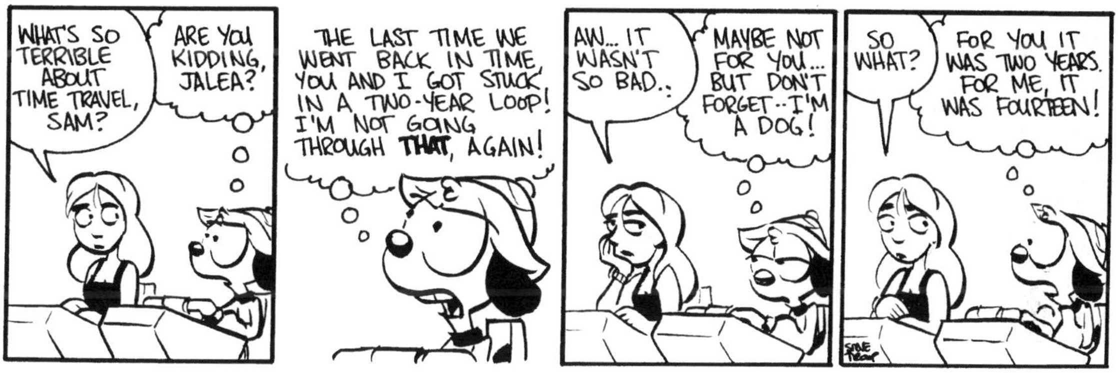
WHAT'S SO TERRIBLE ABOUT TIME TRAVEL, SAM?
ARE YOU KIDDING, JALEA?
THE LAST TIME WE WENT BACK IN TIME, YOU AND I GOT STUCK IN A TWO-YEAR LOOP! I'M NOT GOING THROUGH THAT, AGAIN!
AW... IT WASN'T SO BAD..
MAYBE NOT FOR YOU... BUT DON'T FORGET--I'M A DOG!
SO WHAT?
FOR YOU IT WAS TWO YEARS. FOR ME, IT WAS FOURTEEN!

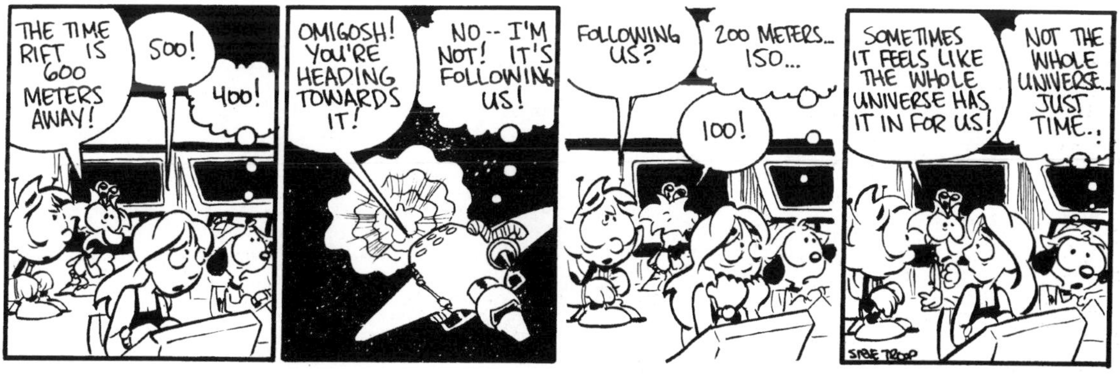
THE TIME RIFT IS 600 METERS AWAY!
500!
400!
OMIGOSH! YOU'RE HEADING TOWARDS IT!
NO-- I'M NOT! IT'S FOLLOWING US!
FOLLOWING US?
200 METERS... 150...
100!
SOMETIMES IT FEELS LIKE THE WHOLE UNIVERSE HAS IT IN FOR US!
NOT THE WHOLE UNIVERSE.. JUST TIME..

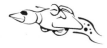

They say that my parents' generation never forgot where they were when JFK was assassinated and that people of my generation will never forget what they were doing when the Twin Towers came down. I drew this strip in the waiting room of the hospital the day my grandmother was diagnosed with terminal stomach cancer. Kind of sad that it will always remind me of that.

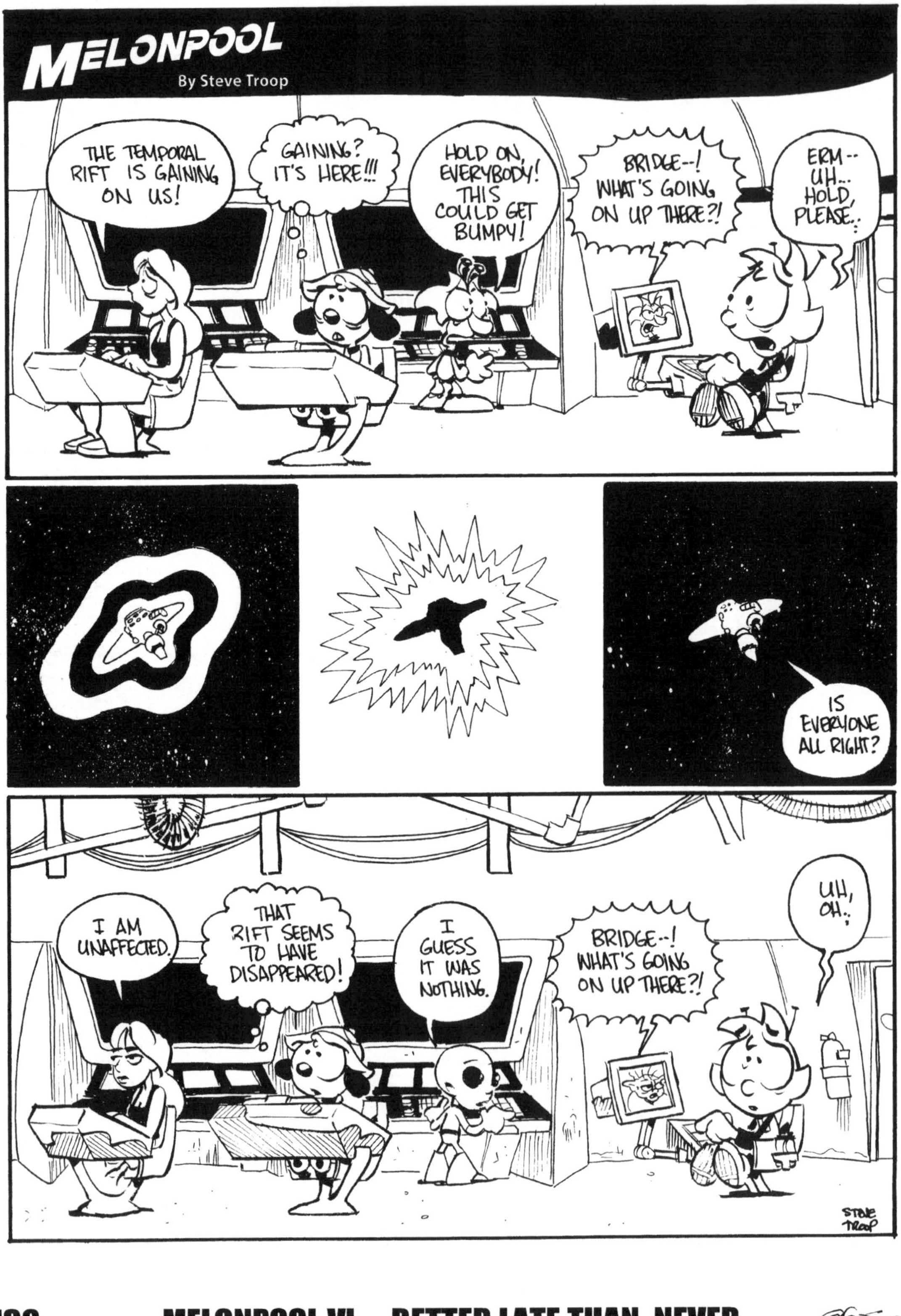

MELONPOOL
By Steve Troop
THE TEMPORAL RIFT IS GAINING ON US!
GAINING? IT'S HERE!!!
HOLD ON, EVERYBODY! THIS COULD GET BUMPY!
BRIDGE--! WHAT'S GOING ON UP THERE?!
ERM-- UH... HOLD, PLEASE..
IS EVERYONE ALL RIGHT?
I AM UNAFFECTED.
THAT RIFT SEEMS TO HAVE DISAPPEARED!
I GUESS IT WAS NOTHING.
BRIDGE--! WHAT'S GOING ON UP THERE?!
UH, OH..
STEVE TROOP

Some *Melonpool* fans started accidentally referring to "Sitch" as "Stitch" in the forums. Actually, like all of the GRAISE who have been referred to by name, Sitch is named after a prominent UFO investigator. In this case, he was named after Zecharia Sitchin.

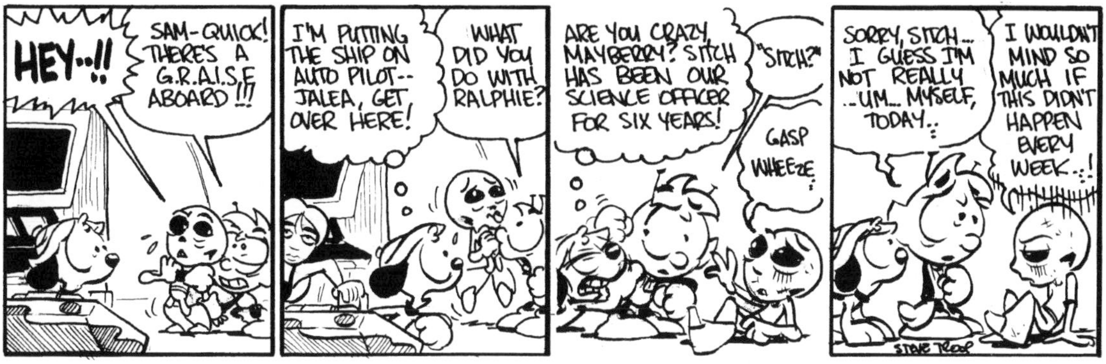
HEY..!!
SAM-QUICK! THERE'S A G.R.A.I.S.E ABOARD!!!
I'M PUTTING THE SHIP ON AUTO PILOT-- JALEA, GET OVER HERE!
WHAT DID YOU DO WITH RALPHIE?
ARE YOU CRAZY, MAYBERRY? SITCH HAS BEEN OUR SCIENCE OFFICER FOR SIX YEARS!
"SITCH?"
GASP WHEEZE
SORRY, SITCH... I GUESS I'M NOT REALLY ..UM... MYSELF, TODAY..
I WOULDN'T MIND SO MUCH IF THIS DIDN'T HAPPEN EVERY WEEK..!
STEVE TROOP

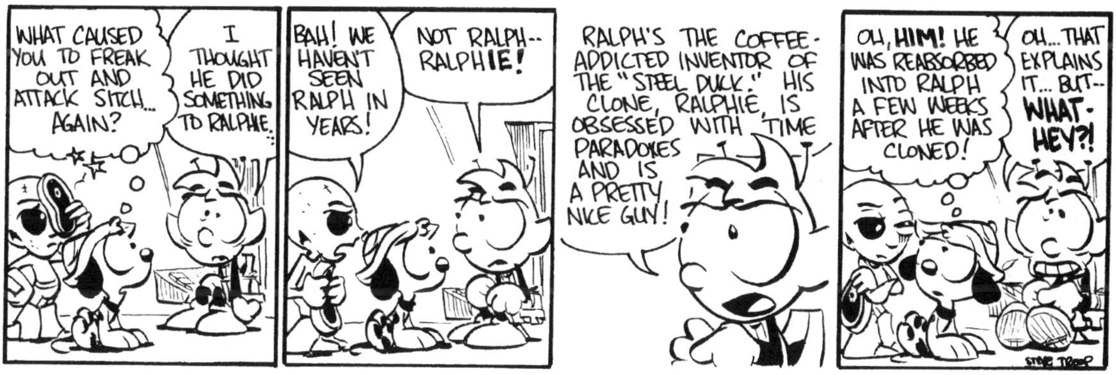
WHAT CAUSED YOU TO FREAK OUT AND ATTACK SITCH... AGAIN?
I THOUGHT HE DID SOMETHING TO RALPHIE.
BAH! WE HAVEN'T SEEN RALPH IN YEARS!
NOT RALPH-- RALPHIE!
RALPH'S THE COFFEE-ADDICTED INVENTOR OF THE "STEEL DUCK." HIS CLONE, RALPHIE, IS OBSESSED WITH TIME PARADOXES AND IS A PRETTY NICE GUY!
OH, HIM! HE WAS REABSORBED INTO RALPH A FEW WEEKS AFTER HE WAS CLONED!
OH... THAT EXPLAINS IT... BUT-- WHAT-HEY?!
STEVE TROOP

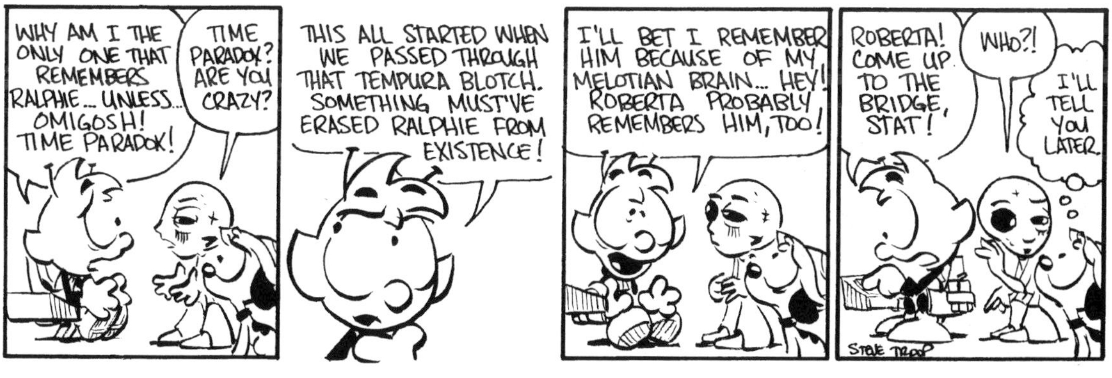
WHY AM I THE ONLY ONE THAT REMEMBERS RALPHIE... UNLESS... OMIGOSH! TIME PARADOX!
TIME PARADOX? ARE YOU CRAZY?
THIS ALL STARTED WHEN WE PASSED THROUGH THAT TEMPURA BLOTCH. SOMETHING MUST'VE ERASED RALPHIE FROM EXISTENCE!
I'LL BET I REMEMBER HIM BECAUSE OF MY MELOTIAN BRAIN... HEY! ROBERTA PROBABLY REMEMBERS HIM, TOO!
ROBERTA! COME UP TO THE BRIDGE, STAT!
WHO?!
I'LL TELL YOU LATER.
STEVE TROOP

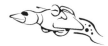

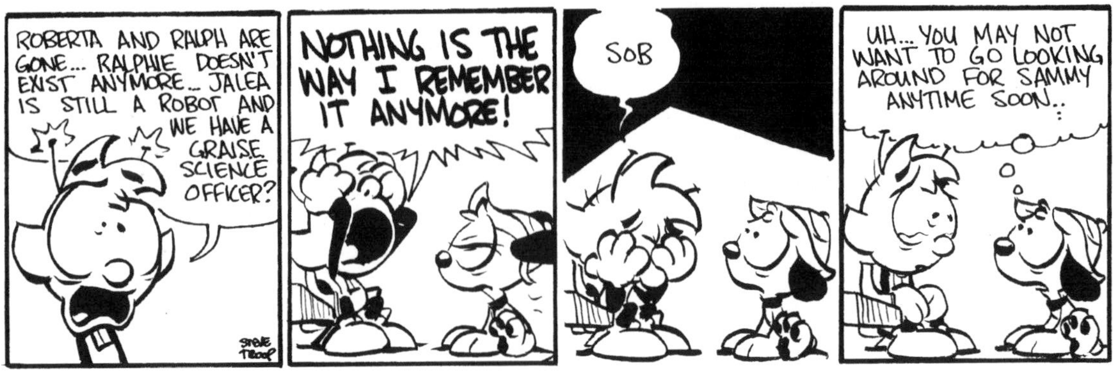
ROBERTA AND RALPH ARE GONE... RALPHIE DOESN'T EXIST ANYMORE... JALEA IS STILL A ROBOT AND WE HAVE A GRAISE SCIENCE OFFICER?
STEVE TROOP
NOTHING IS THE WAY I REMEMBER IT ANYMORE!
SOB
UH... YOU MAY NOT WANT TO GO LOOKING AROUND FOR SAMMY ANYTIME SOON...

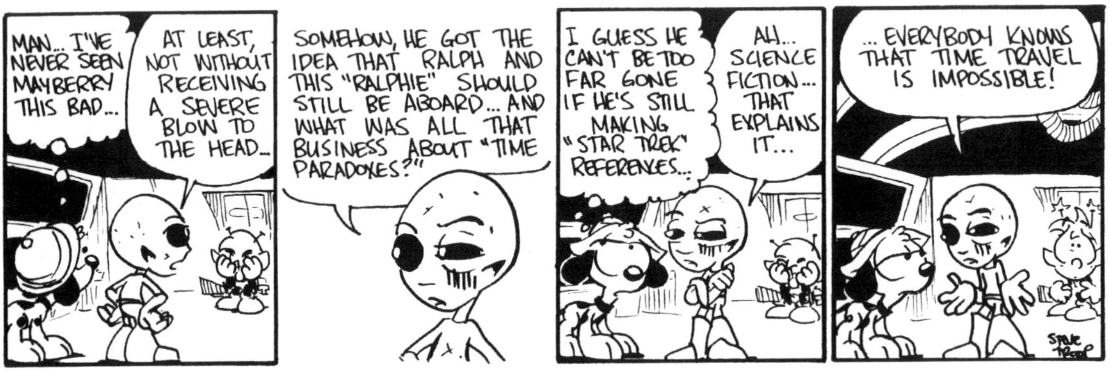
MAN... I'VE NEVER SEEN MAYBERRY THIS BAD...
AT LEAST, NOT WITHOUT RECEIVING A SEVERE BLOW TO THE HEAD...
SOMEHOW, HE GOT THE IDEA THAT RALPH AND THIS "RALPHIE" SHOULD STILL BE ABOARD... AND WHAT WAS ALL THAT BUSINESS ABOUT "TIME PARADOXES?"
I GUESS HE CAN'T BE TOO FAR GONE IF HE'S STILL MAKING "STAR TREK" REFERENCES...
AH... SCIENCE FICTION... THAT EXPLAINS IT...
... EVERYBODY KNOWS THAT TIME TRAVEL IS IMPOSSIBLE!
STEVE TROOP

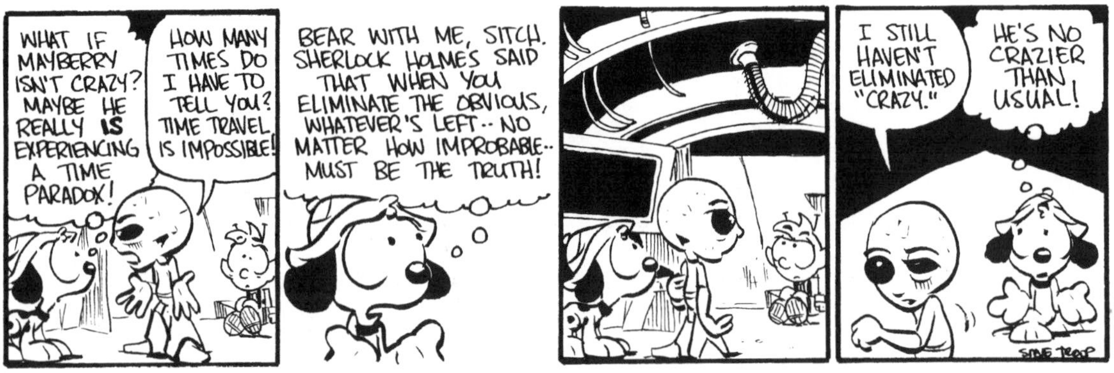
WHAT IF MAYBERRY ISN'T CRAZY? MAYBE HE REALLY IS EXPERIENCING A TIME PARADOX!
HOW MANY TIMES DO I HAVE TO TELL YOU? TIME TRAVEL IS IMPOSSIBLE!
BEAR WITH ME, SITCH. SHERLOCK HOLMES SAID THAT WHEN YOU ELIMINATE THE OBVIOUS, WHATEVER'S LEFT -- NO MATTER HOW IMPROBABLE -- MUST BE THE TRUTH!
I STILL HAVEN'T ELIMINATED "CRAZY."
HE'S NO CRAZIER THAN USUAL!
STEVE TROOP

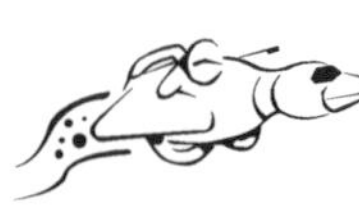

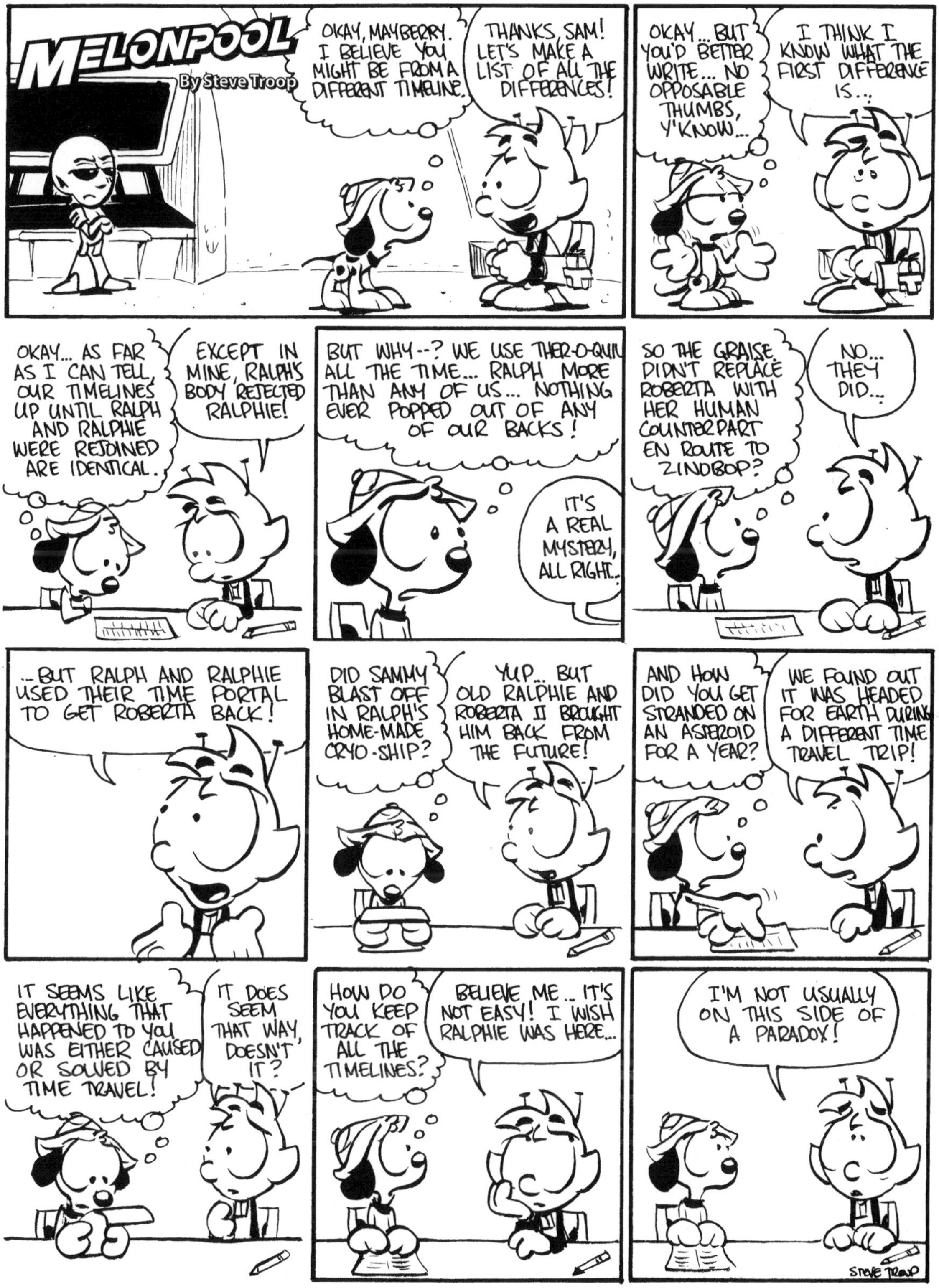

MELONPOOL
By Steve Troop
OKAY, MAYBERRY. I BELIEVE YOU MIGHT BE FROM A DIFFERENT TIMELINE.
THANKS, SAM! LET'S MAKE A LIST OF ALL THE DIFFERENCES!
OKAY... BUT YOU'D BETTER WRITE... NO OPPOSABLE THUMBS, Y'KNOW...
I THINK I KNOW WHAT THE FIRST DIFFERENCE IS...
OKAY... AS FAR AS I CAN TELL, OUR TIMELINES UP UNTIL RALPH AND RALPHIE WERE REJOINED ARE IDENTICAL.
EXCEPT IN MINE, RALPH'S BODY REJECTED RALPHIE!
BUT WHY--? WE USE THER-O-QUIN ALL THE TIME... RALPH MORE THAN ANY OF US... NOTHING EVER POPPED OUT OF ANY OF OUR BACKS!
IT'S A REAL MYSTERY, ALL RIGHT...
SO THE GRAISE DIDN'T REPLACE ROBERTA WITH HER HUMAN COUNTERPART EN ROUTE TO ZINDBOP?
NO... THEY DID...
...BUT RALPH AND RALPHIE USED THEIR TIME PORTAL TO GET ROBERTA BACK!
DID SAMMY BLAST OFF IN RALPH'S HOME-MADE CRYO-SHIP?
YUP... BUT OLD RALPHIE AND ROBERTA II BROUGHT HIM BACK FROM THE FUTURE!
AND HOW DID YOU GET STRANDED ON AN ASTEROID FOR A YEAR?
WE FOUND OUT IT WAS HEADED FOR EARTH DURING A DIFFERENT TIME TRAVEL TRIP!
IT SEEMS LIKE EVERYTHING THAT HAPPENED TO YOU WAS EITHER CAUSED OR SOLVED BY TIME TRAVEL!
IT DOES SEEM THAT WAY, DOESN'T IT?
HOW DO YOU KEEP TRACK OF ALL THE TIMELINES?
BELIEVE ME... IT'S NOT EASY! I WISH RALPHIE WAS HERE...
I'M NOT USUALLY ON THIS SIDE OF A PARADOX!
STEVE TROOP

In the original timeline, Ralph and Ralphie sent themselves back in time to keep the GRAISE from replacing Roberta with a human named Rebecca Smith-Pheiffer and leaving Sammy a huge blob after force feeding him (see TUM II, pages 98–114).

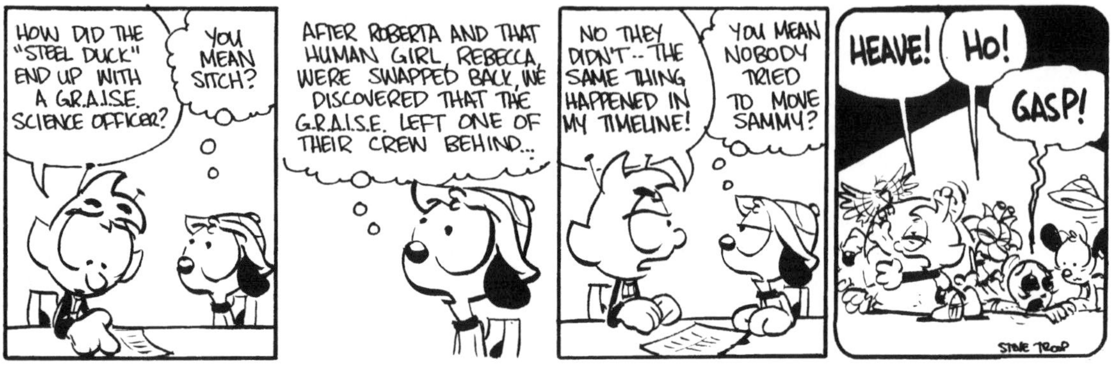
HOW DID THE "STEEL DUCK" END UP WITH A G.R.A.I.S.E. SCIENCE OFFICER?
YOU MEAN SITCH?
AFTER ROBERTA AND THAT HUMAN GIRL, REBECCA, WERE SWAPPED BACK, WE DISCOVERED THAT THE G.R.A.I.S.E. LEFT ONE OF THEIR CREW BEHIND...
NO THEY DIDN'T-- THE SAME THING HAPPENED IN MY TIMELINE!
YOU MEAN NOBODY TRIED TO MOVE SAMMY?
HEAVE!
HO!
GASP!
STEVE TROOP

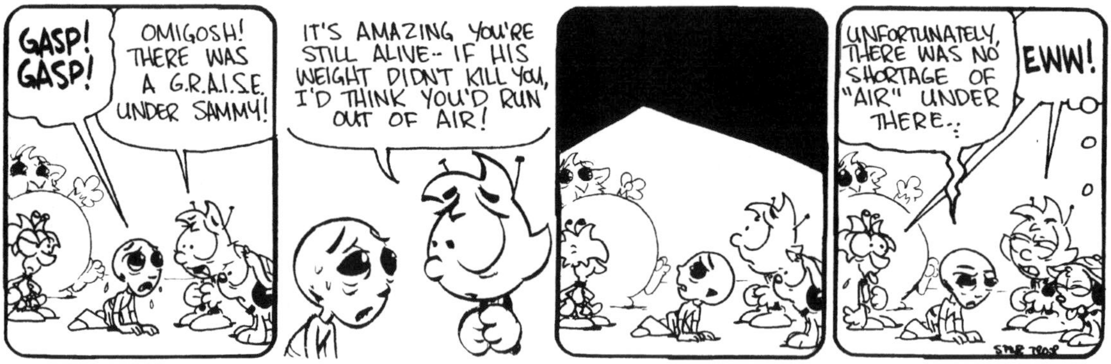
GASP! GASP!
OMIGOSH! THERE WAS A G.R.A.I.S.E. UNDER SAMMY!
IT'S AMAZING YOU'RE STILL ALIVE-- IF HIS WEIGHT DIDN'T KILL YOU, I'D THINK YOU'D RUN OUT OF AIR!
UNFORTUNATELY, THERE WAS NO SHORTAGE OF "AIR" UNDER THERE...
EWW!
STEVE TROOP

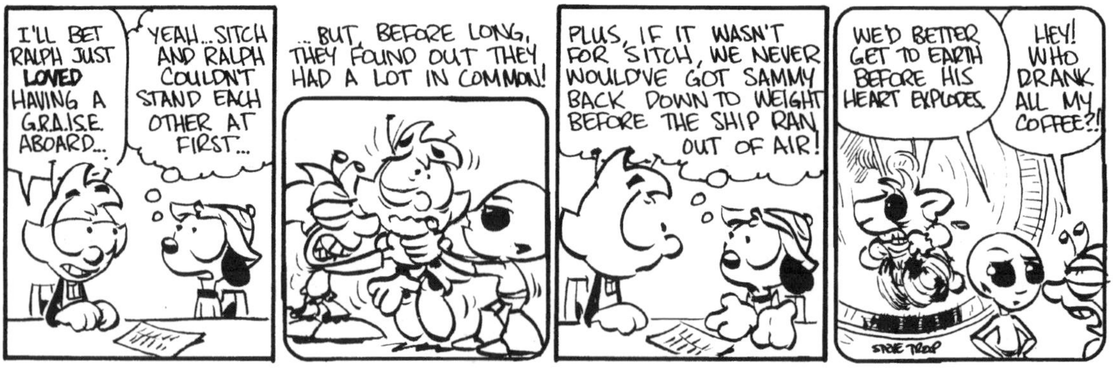
I'LL BET RALPH JUST **LOVED** HAVING A G.R.A.I.S.E. ABOARD...
YEAH...SITCH AND RALPH COULDN'T STAND EACH OTHER AT FIRST...
...BUT, BEFORE LONG, THEY FOUND OUT THEY HAD A LOT IN COMMON!
PLUS, IF IT WASN'T FOR SITCH, WE NEVER WOULD'VE GOT SAMMY BACK DOWN TO WEIGHT BEFORE THE SHIP RAN OUT OF AIR!
WE'D BETTER GET TO EARTH BEFORE HIS HEART EXPLODES.
HEY! WHO DRANK ALL MY COFFEE?!
STEVE TROOP

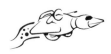

In the original timeline, Ralph built a one-man cryogenic space pod to send himself back to Zinobop. Since it was made out of a refrigerator, Sammy accidentally blasted himself off instead, creating a 138-year time loop (see TUM III, pages 25–55). The loop was fixed by Old Ralphie and Roberta II, who had settled in 2182 at the end of the original **Time Travel Saga** (See TUM I, pages 148–167), which in this continuity, never happened!

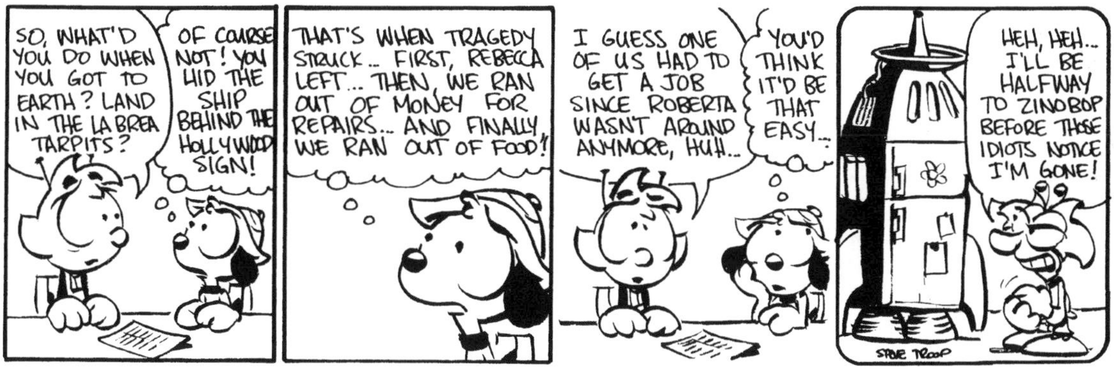
SO, WHAT'D YOU DO WHEN YOU GOT TO EARTH? LAND IN THE LA BREA TARPITS?
OF COURSE NOT! YOU HID THE SHIP BEHIND THE HOLLYWOOD SIGN!
THAT'S WHEN TRAGEDY STRUCK... FIRST, REBECCA LEFT... THEN, WE RAN OUT OF MONEY FOR REPAIRS... AND FINALLY, WE RAN OUT OF FOOD!
I GUESS ONE OF US HAD TO GET A JOB SINCE ROBERTA WASN'T AROUND ANYMORE, HUH...
YOU'D THINK IT'D BE THAT EASY...
HEH, HEH... I'LL BE HALFWAY TO ZINOBOP BEFORE THOSE IDIOTS NOTICE I'M GONE!
STEVE TROOP

From Mayberry's point of view. Ralph and No-da went to Las Vegas and made a ton of money using the grey side of the force—only to lose it all when No-da got drunk on all of the free cocktails (see TUM II, pages 134–138).

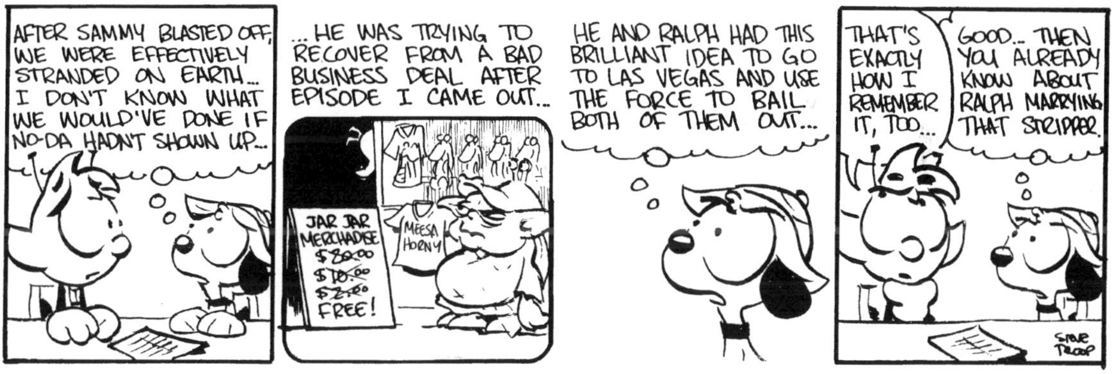
AFTER SAMMY BLASTED OFF, WE WERE EFFECTIVELY STRANDED ON EARTH... I DON'T KNOW WHAT WE WOULD'VE DONE IF NO-DA HADN'T SHOWN UP...
...HE WAS TRYING TO RECOVER FROM A BAD BUSINESS DEAL AFTER EPISODE I CAME OUT...
JAR JAR MERCHANDISE $80.00 $10.00 $2.00 FREE!
MEESA HORNY
HE AND RALPH HAD THIS BRILLIANT IDEA TO GO TO LAS VEGAS AND USE THE FORCE TO BAIL BOTH OF THEM OUT...
THAT'S EXACTLY HOW I REMEMBER IT, TOO...
GOOD... THEN YOU ALREADY KNOW ABOUT RALPH MARRYING THAT STRIPPER.
STEVE TROOP

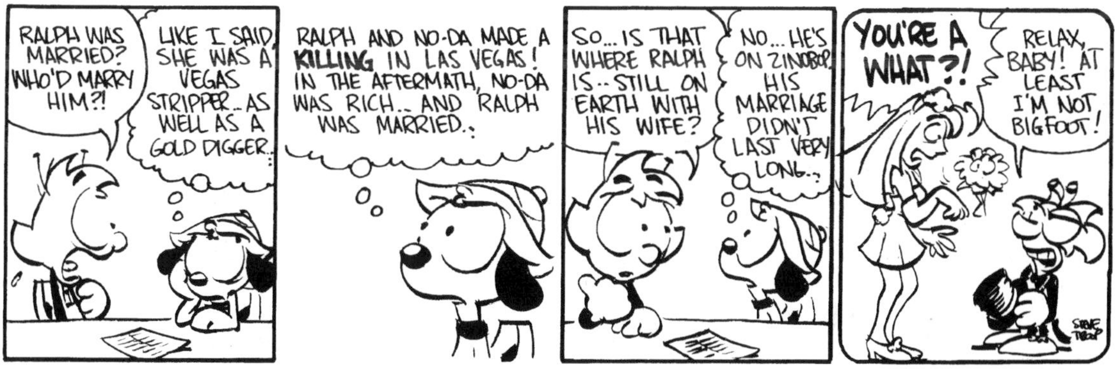
RALPH WAS MARRIED? WHO'D MARRY HIM?!
LIKE I SAID, SHE WAS A VEGAS STRIPPER... AS WELL AS A GOLD DIGGER...
RALPH AND NO-DA MADE A KILLING IN LAS VEGAS! IN THE AFTERMATH, NO-DA WAS RICH... AND RALPH WAS MARRIED...
SO... IS THAT WHERE RALPH IS... STILL ON EARTH WITH HIS WIFE?
NO... HE'S ON ZINOBOP. HIS MARRIAGE DIDN'T LAST VERY LONG...
YOU'RE A WHAT?!
RELAX, BABY! AT LEAST I'M NOT BIGFOOT!
STEVE TROOP

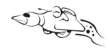

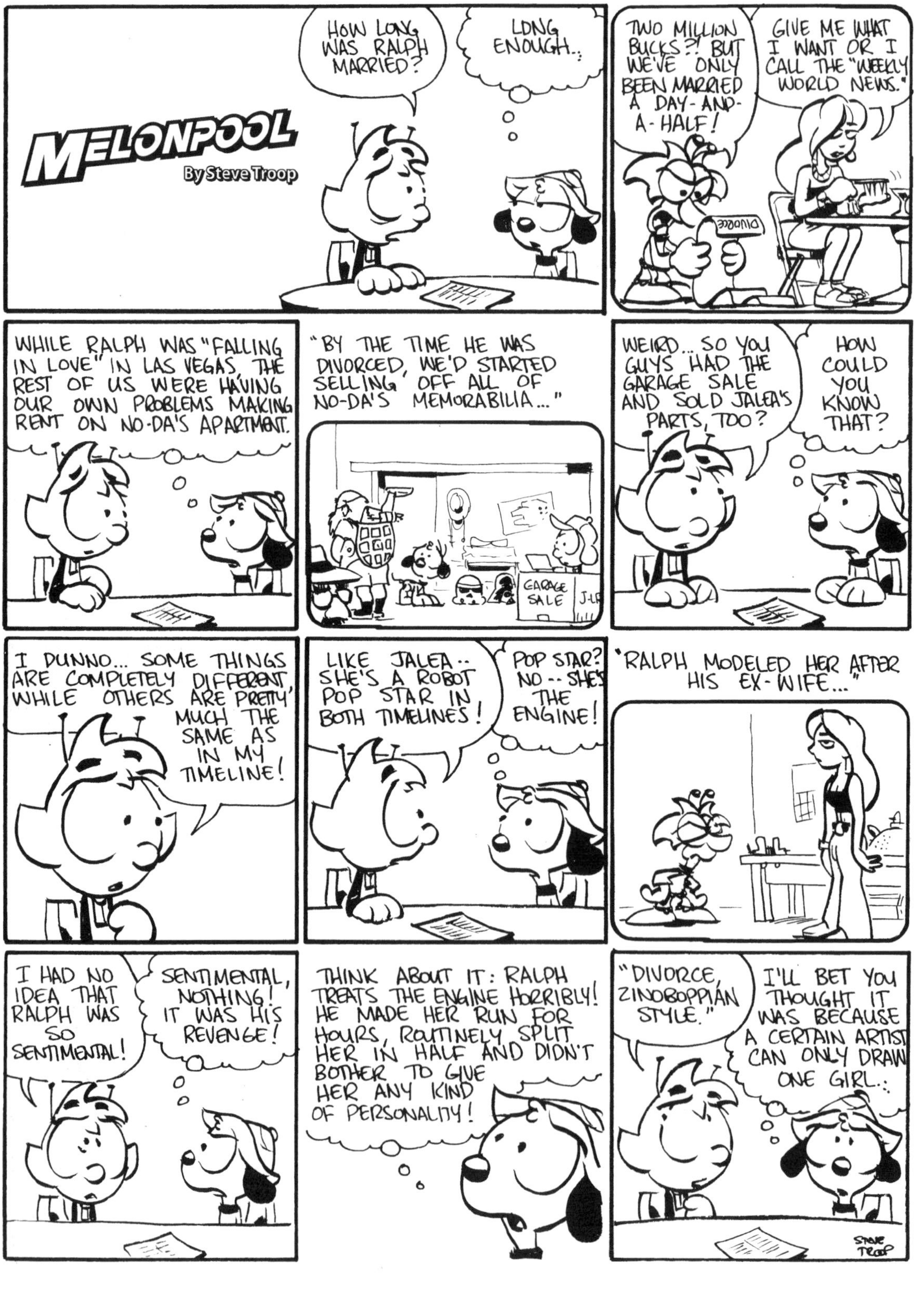
MELONPOOL
By Steve Troop
HOW LONG WAS RALPH MARRIED?
LONG ENOUGH...
TWO MILLION BUCKS?! BUT WE'VE ONLY BEEN MARRIED A DAY-AND-A-HALF!
GIVE ME WHAT I WANT OR I CALL THE "WEEKLY WORLD NEWS."
DIVORCE
WHILE RALPH WAS "FALLING IN LOVE" IN LAS VEGAS, THE REST OF US WERE HAVING OUR OWN PROBLEMS MAKING RENT ON NO-DA'S APARTMENT.
"BY THE TIME HE WAS DIVORCED, WE'D STARTED SELLING OFF ALL OF NO-DA'S MEMORABILIA..."
GARAGE SALE
WEIRD... SO YOU GUYS HAD THE GARAGE SALE AND SOLD JALEA'S PARTS, TOO?
HOW COULD YOU KNOW THAT?
I DUNNO... SOME THINGS ARE COMPLETELY DIFFERENT, WHILE OTHERS ARE PRETTY MUCH THE SAME AS IN MY TIMELINE!
LIKE JALEA.. SHE'S A ROBOT POP STAR IN BOTH TIMELINES!
POP STAR? NO -- SHE'S THE ENGINE!
"RALPH MODELED HER AFTER HIS EX-WIFE..."
I HAD NO IDEA THAT RALPH WAS SO SENTIMENTAL!
SENTIMENTAL, NOTHING! IT WAS HIS REVENGE!
THINK ABOUT IT: RALPH TREATS THE ENGINE HORRIBLY! HE MADE HER RUN FOR HOURS, ROUTINELY SPLIT HER IN HALF AND DIDN'T BOTHER TO GIVE HER ANY KIND OF PERSONALITY!
"DIVORCE, ZINOBOPPIAN STYLE."
I'LL BET YOU THOUGHT IT WAS BECAUSE A CERTAIN ARTIST CAN ONLY DRAW ONE GIRL...
STEVE TROOP

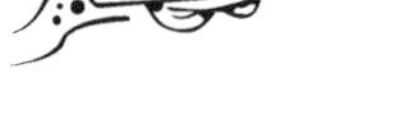

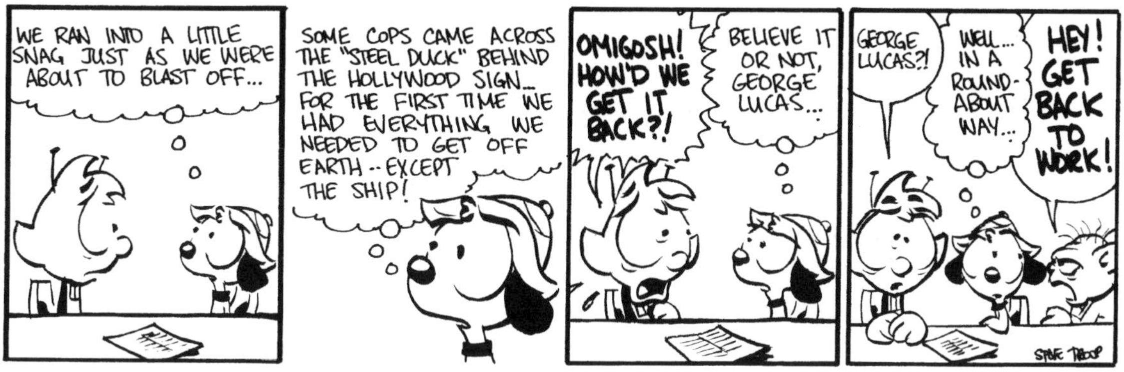
WE RAN INTO A LITTLE SNAG JUST AS WE WERE ABOUT TO BLAST OFF...
SOME COPS CAME ACROSS THE "STEEL DUCK" BEHIND THE HOLLYWOOD SIGN... FOR THE FIRST TIME WE HAD EVERYTHING WE NEEDED TO GET OFF EARTH -- EXCEPT THE SHIP!
OMIGOSH! HOW'D WE GET IT BACK?!
BELIEVE IT OR NOT, GEORGE LUCAS...
GEORGE LUCAS?!
WELL... IN A ROUND-ABOUT WAY...
HEY! GET BACK TO WORK!
STEVE TROOP

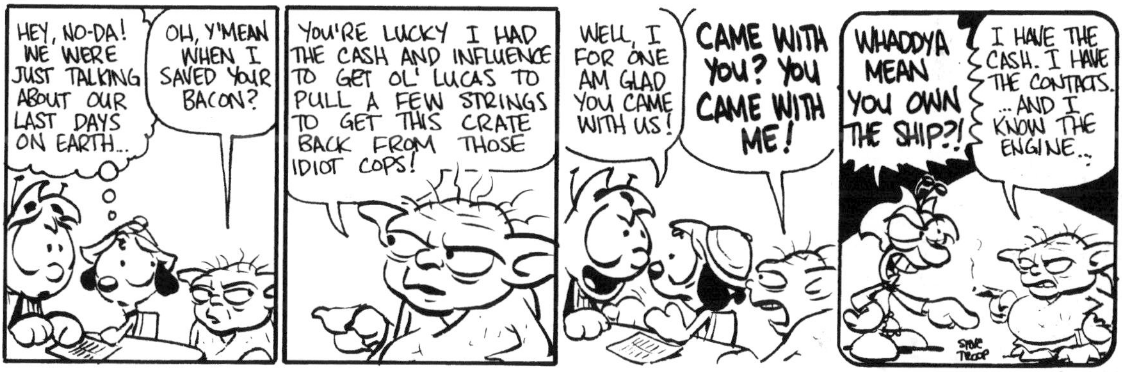
HEY, NO-DA! WE WERE JUST TALKING ABOUT OUR LAST DAYS ON EARTH...
OH, Y'MEAN WHEN I SAVED YOUR BACON?
YOU'RE LUCKY I HAD THE CASH AND INFLUENCE TO GET OL' LUCAS TO PULL A FEW STRINGS TO GET THIS CRATE BACK FROM THOSE IDIOT COPS!
WELL, I FOR ONE AM GLAD YOU CAME WITH US!
CAME WITH YOU? YOU CAME WITH ME!
WHADDYA MEAN YOU OWN THE SHIP?!
I HAVE THE CASH. I HAVE THE CONTACTS. ...AND I KNOW THE ENGINE...
STEVE TROOP

In the original timeline, Mayberry and Ralph briefly teleported into the middle of the Zinoboppian revolution (TUM IV, pages 149–154).

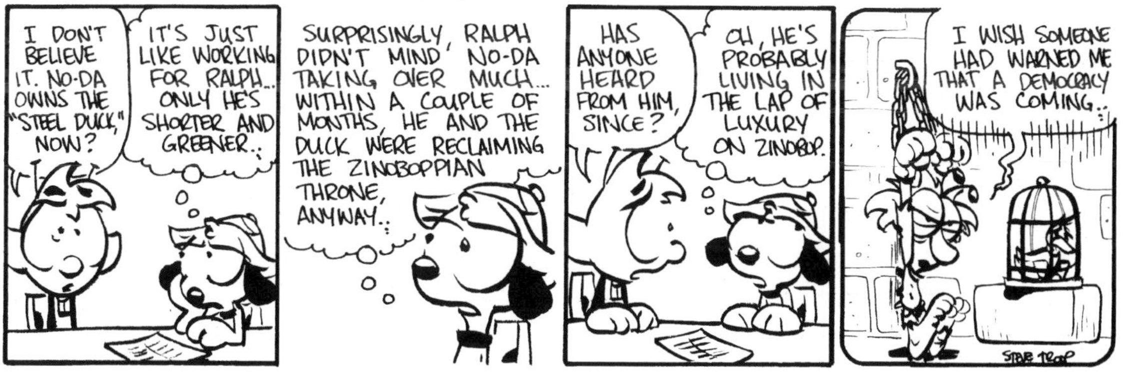
I DON'T BELIEVE IT. NO-DA OWNS THE "STEEL DUCK," NOW?
IT'S JUST LIKE WORKING FOR RALPH... ONLY HE'S SHORTER AND GREENER...
SURPRISINGLY, RALPH DIDN'T MIND NO-DA TAKING OVER MUCH... WITHIN A COUPLE OF MONTHS, HE AND THE DUCK WERE RECLAIMING THE ZINOBOPPIAN THRONE, ANYWAY...
HAS ANYONE HEARD FROM HIM, SINCE?
OH, HE'S PROBABLY LIVING IN THE LAP OF LUXURY ON ZINOBOP.
I WISH SOMEONE HAD WARNED ME THAT A DEMOCRACY WAS COMING...
STEVE TROOP

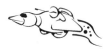

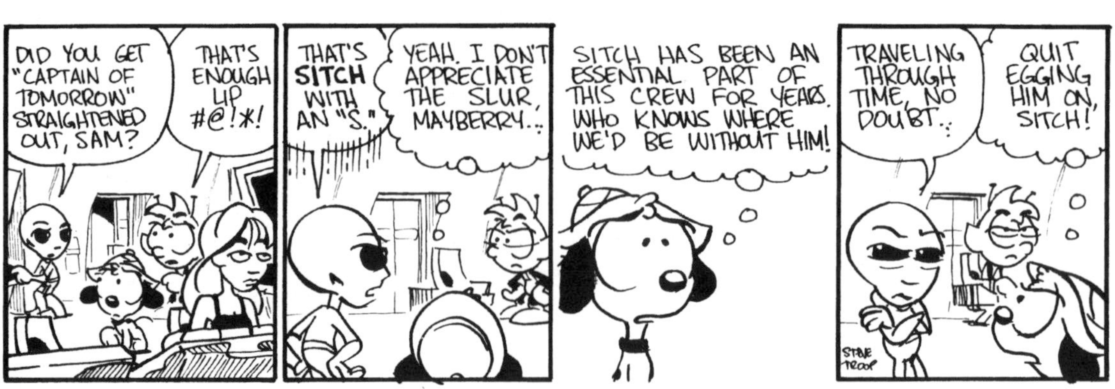
DID YOU GET "CAPTAIN OF TOMORROW" STRAIGHTENED OUT, SAM?
THAT'S ENOUGH UP #@!*!
THAT'S SITCH WITH AN "S."
YEAH. I DON'T APPRECIATE THE SLUR, MAYBERRY...
SITCH HAS BEEN AN ESSENTIAL PART OF THIS CREW FOR YEARS. WHO KNOWS WHERE WE'D BE WITHOUT HIM!
TRAVELING THROUGH TIME, NO DOUBT...
QUIT EGGING HIM ON, SITCH!
STEVE TROOP

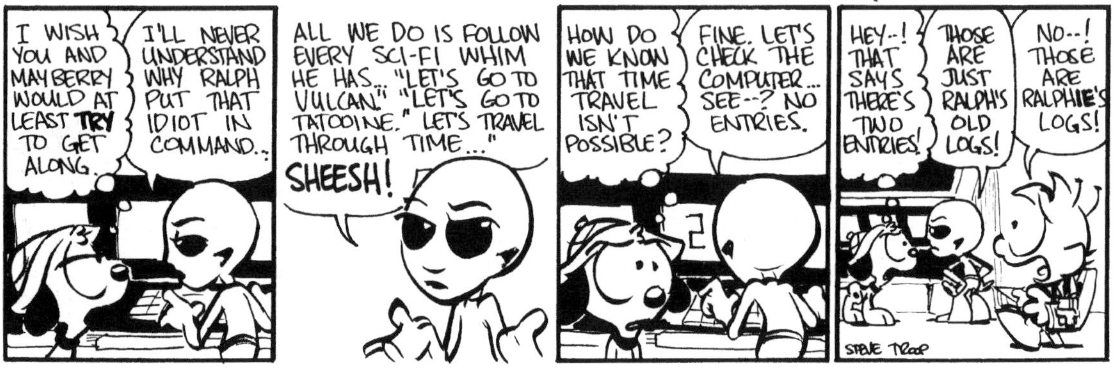
I WISH YOU AND MAYBERRY WOULD AT LEAST TRY TO GET ALONG.
I'LL NEVER UNDERSTAND WHY RALPH PUT THAT IDIOT IN COMMAND...
ALL WE DO IS FOLLOW EVERY SCI-FI WHIM HE HAS... "LET'S GO TO VULCAN." "LET'S GO TO TATOOINE." LET'S TRAVEL THROUGH TIME..."
SHEESH!
HOW DO WE KNOW THAT TIME TRAVEL ISN'T POSSIBLE?
FINE. LET'S CHECK THE COMPUTER... SEE--? NO ENTRIES.
HEY--! THAT SAYS THERE'S TWO ENTRIES!
THOSE ARE JUST RALPH'S OLD LOGS!
NO--! THOSE ARE RALPHIE'S LOGS!
STEVE TROOP

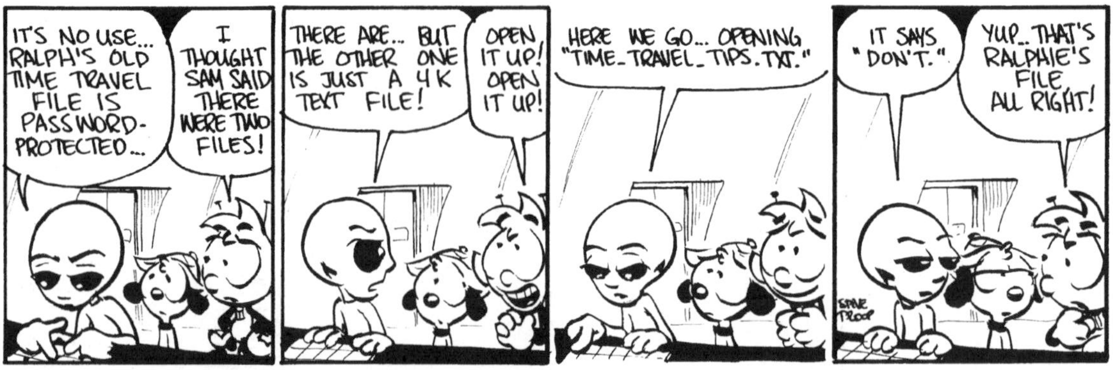
IT'S NO USE... RALPH'S OLD TIME TRAVEL FILE IS PASSWORD-PROTECTED...
I THOUGHT SAM SAID THERE WERE TWO FILES!
THERE ARE... BUT THE OTHER ONE IS JUST A 4K TEXT FILE!
OPEN IT UP! OPEN IT UP!
HERE WE GO... OPENING "TIME_TRAVEL_TIPS.TXT."
IT SAYS "DON'T."
YUP... THAT'S RALPHIE'S FILE ALL RIGHT!
STEVE TROOP

I still think this was a fun way to get a lot of exposition out of the way.

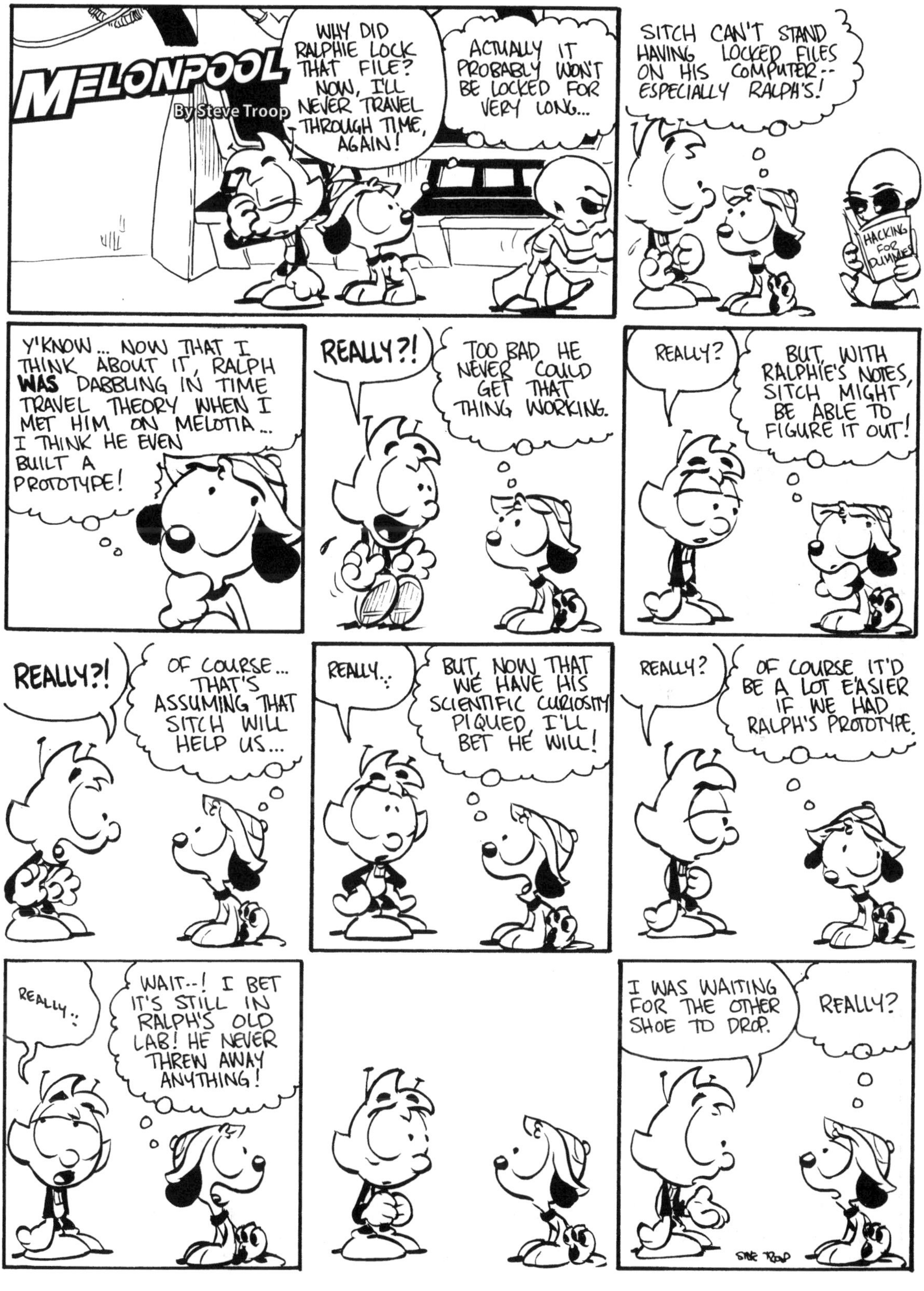

MELONPOOL
By Steve Troop
WHY DID RALPHIE LOCK THAT FILE? NOW, I'LL NEVER TRAVEL THROUGH TIME, AGAIN!
ACTUALLY IT PROBABLY WON'T BE LOCKED FOR VERY LONG...
SITCH CAN'T STAND HAVING LOCKED FILES ON HIS COMPUTER-- ESPECIALLY RALPH'S!
HACKING FOR DUMMIES
Y'KNOW... NOW THAT I THINK ABOUT IT, RALPH WAS DABBLING IN TIME TRAVEL THEORY WHEN I MET HIM ON MELOTIA... I THINK HE EVEN BUILT A PROTOTYPE!
REALLY?!
TOO BAD HE NEVER COULD GET THAT THING WORKING.
REALLY?
BUT, WITH RALPHIE'S NOTES, SITCH MIGHT BE ABLE TO FIGURE IT OUT!
REALLY?!
OF COURSE... THAT'S ASSUMING THAT SITCH WILL HELP US...
REALLY...
BUT, NOW THAT WE HAVE HIS SCIENTIFIC CURIOSITY PIQUED, I'LL BET HE WILL!
REALLY?
OF COURSE IT'D BE A LOT EASIER IF WE HAD RALPH'S PROTOTYPE.
REALLY...
WAIT--! I BET IT'S STILL IN RALPH'S OLD LAB! HE NEVER THREW AWAY ANYTHING!
I WAS WAITING FOR THE OTHER SHOE TO DROP.
REALLY?

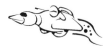

Among the items locked away in Ralph's store room are: the Dup-o-matic (see TUM I, pages 142–144), the Fuse-o-matic (see TUM I, pages 172–182), the Cerebral Swappers (see TUM I, pages 82–83) and the Foolproof Alarm Clock (see TUM I, page 68). I never realized before now how many crazy inventions I put into *Melonpool* during that first year!

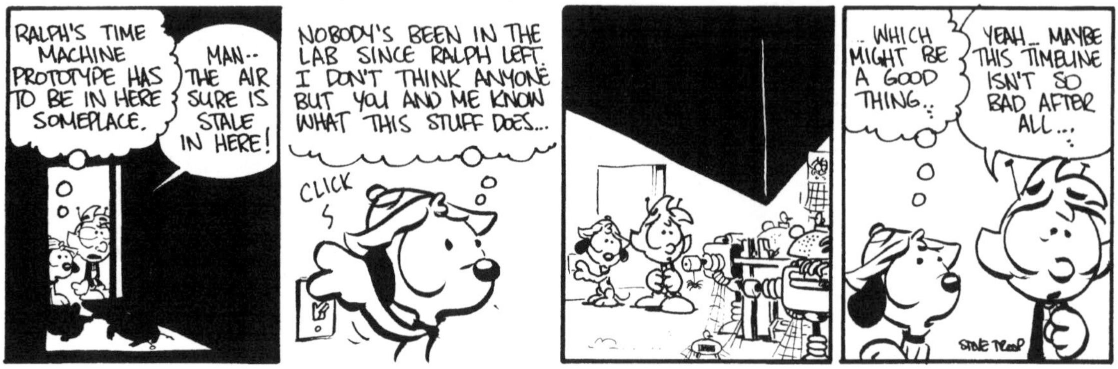
RALPH'S TIME MACHINE PROTOTYPE HAS TO BE IN HERE SOMEPLACE.
MAN-- THE AIR SURE IS STALE IN HERE!
NOBODY'S BEEN IN THE LAB SINCE RALPH LEFT. I DON'T THINK ANYONE BUT YOU AND ME KNOW WHAT THIS STUFF DOES...
CLICK
..WHICH MIGHT BE A GOOD THING..
YEAH... MAYBE THIS TIMELINE ISN'T SO BAD AFTER ALL...
STEVE TROOP

The Time Portal Prototype was used during **the GRAISE Saga** (TUM II, page 104) and **Times, They are A-Changing** (TUM IV, pages 106–143).

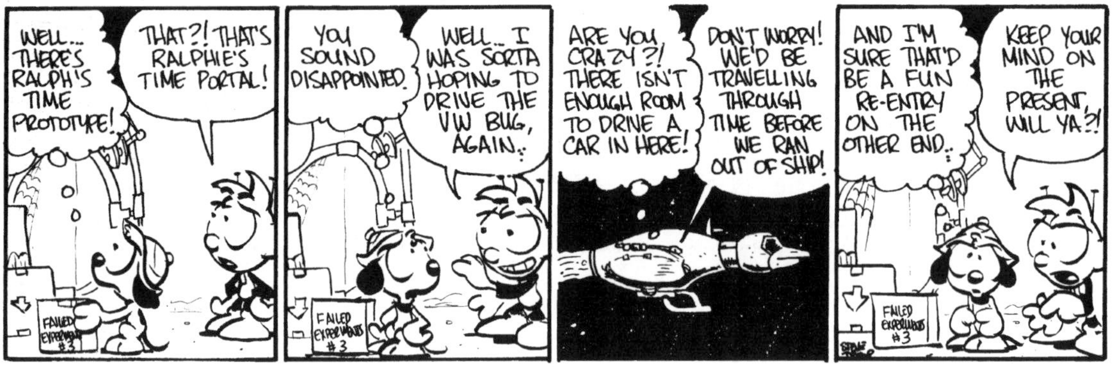
WELL... THERE'S RALPH'S TIME PROTOTYPE!
THAT?! THAT'S RALPHIE'S TIME PORTAL!
FAILED EXPERIMENTS #3
YOU SOUND DISAPPOINTED.
WELL... I WAS SORTA HOPING TO DRIVE THE VW BUG, AGAIN...
FAILED EXPERIMENTS #3
ARE YOU CRAZY?! THERE ISN'T ENOUGH ROOM TO DRIVE A CAR IN HERE!
DON'T WORRY! WE'D BE TRAVELLING THROUGH TIME BEFORE WE RAN OUT OF SHIP!
AND I'M SURE THAT'D BE A FUN RE-ENTRY ON THE OTHER END...
KEEP YOUR MIND ON THE PRESENT, WILL YA?!
FAILED EXPERIMENTS #3

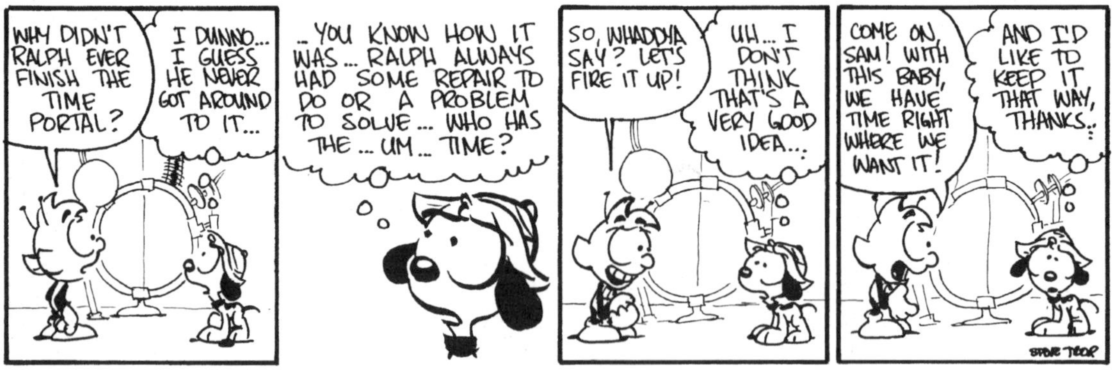
WHY DIDN'T RALPH EVER FINISH THE TIME PORTAL?
I DUNNO... I GUESS HE NEVER GOT AROUND TO IT...
..YOU KNOW HOW IT WAS... RALPH ALWAYS HAD SOME REPAIR TO DO OR A PROBLEM TO SOLVE... WHO HAS THE... UM... TIME?
SO, WHADDYA SAY? LET'S FIRE IT UP!
UH... I DON'T THINK THAT'S A VERY GOOD IDEA...
COME ON, SAM! WITH THIS BABY, WE HAVE TIME RIGHT WHERE WE WANT IT!
AND I'D LIKE TO KEEP IT THAT WAY, THANKS...
STEVE TROOP

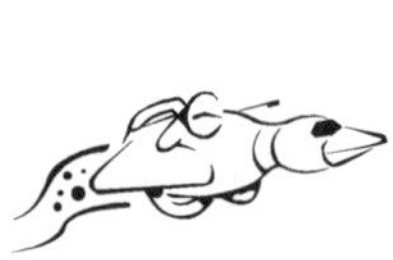

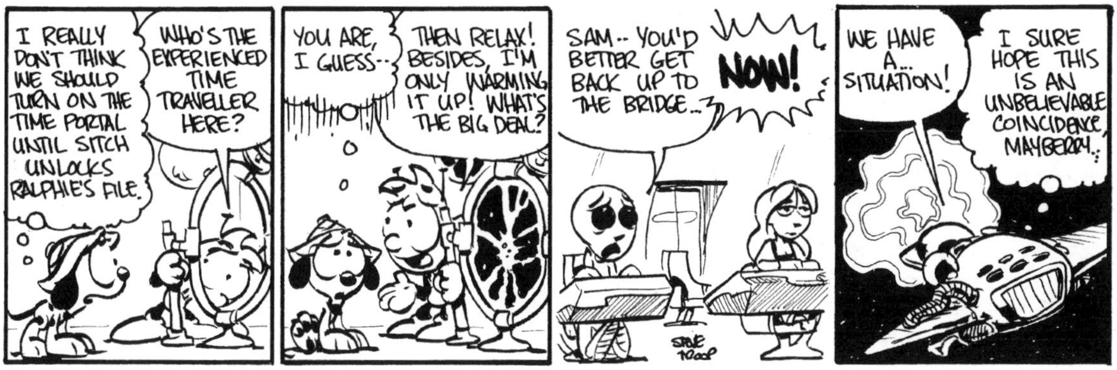
I REALLY DON'T THINK WE SHOULD TURN ON THE TIME PORTAL UNTIL SITCH UNLOCKS RALPHIE'S FILE.
WHO'S THE EXPERIENCED TIME TRAVELLER HERE?
YOU ARE, I GUESS--
THEN RELAX! BESIDES, I'M ONLY WARMING IT UP! WHAT'S THE BIG DEAL?
SAM-- YOU'D BETTER GET BACK UP TO THE BRIDGE...
NOW!
STEVE TROOP
WE HAVE A... SITUATION!
I SURE HOPE THIS IS AN UNBELIEVABLE COINCIDENCE, MAYBERRY...

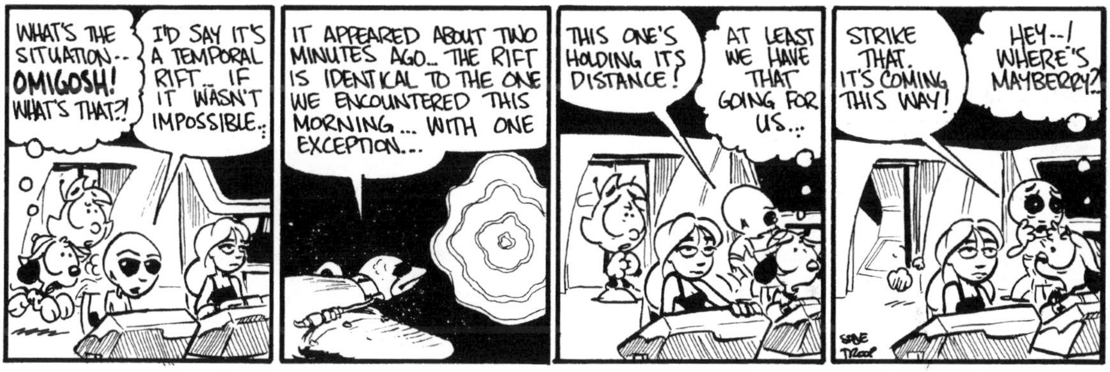
WHAT'S THE SITUATION-- OMIGOSH! WHAT'S THAT?!
I'D SAY IT'S A TEMPORAL RIFT... IF IT WASN'T IMPOSSIBLE...
IT APPEARED ABOUT TWO MINUTES AGO... THE RIFT IS IDENTICAL TO THE ONE WE ENCOUNTERED THIS MORNING... WITH ONE EXCEPTION...
THIS ONE'S HOLDING IT'S DISTANCE!
AT LEAST WE HAVE THAT GOING FOR US...
STRIKE THAT. IT'S COMING THIS WAY!
HEY--! WHERE'S MAYBERRY?
STEVE TROOP

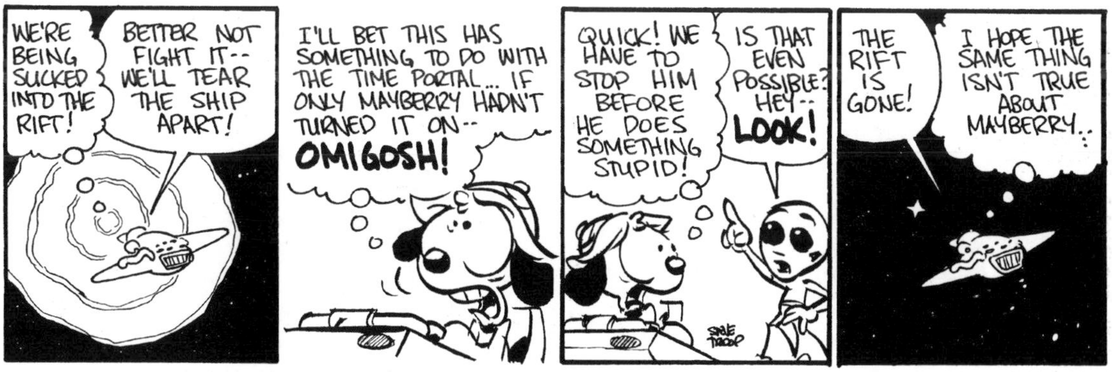
WE'RE BEING SUCKED INTO THE RIFT!
BETTER NOT FIGHT IT-- WE'LL TEAR THE SHIP APART!
I'LL BET THIS HAS SOMETHING TO DO WITH THE TIME PORTAL... IF ONLY MAYBERRY HADN'T TURNED IT ON-- OMIGOSH!
QUICK! WE HAVE TO STOP HIM BEFORE HE DOES SOMETHING STUPID!
IS THAT EVEN POSSIBLE? HEY-- LOOK!
STEVE TROOP
THE RIFT IS GONE!
I HOPE THE SAME THING ISN'T TRUE ABOUT MAYBERRY...

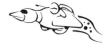

December 30, 1996 was the date that the original **Time Travel Saga** began (TUM I, pages 148–167).

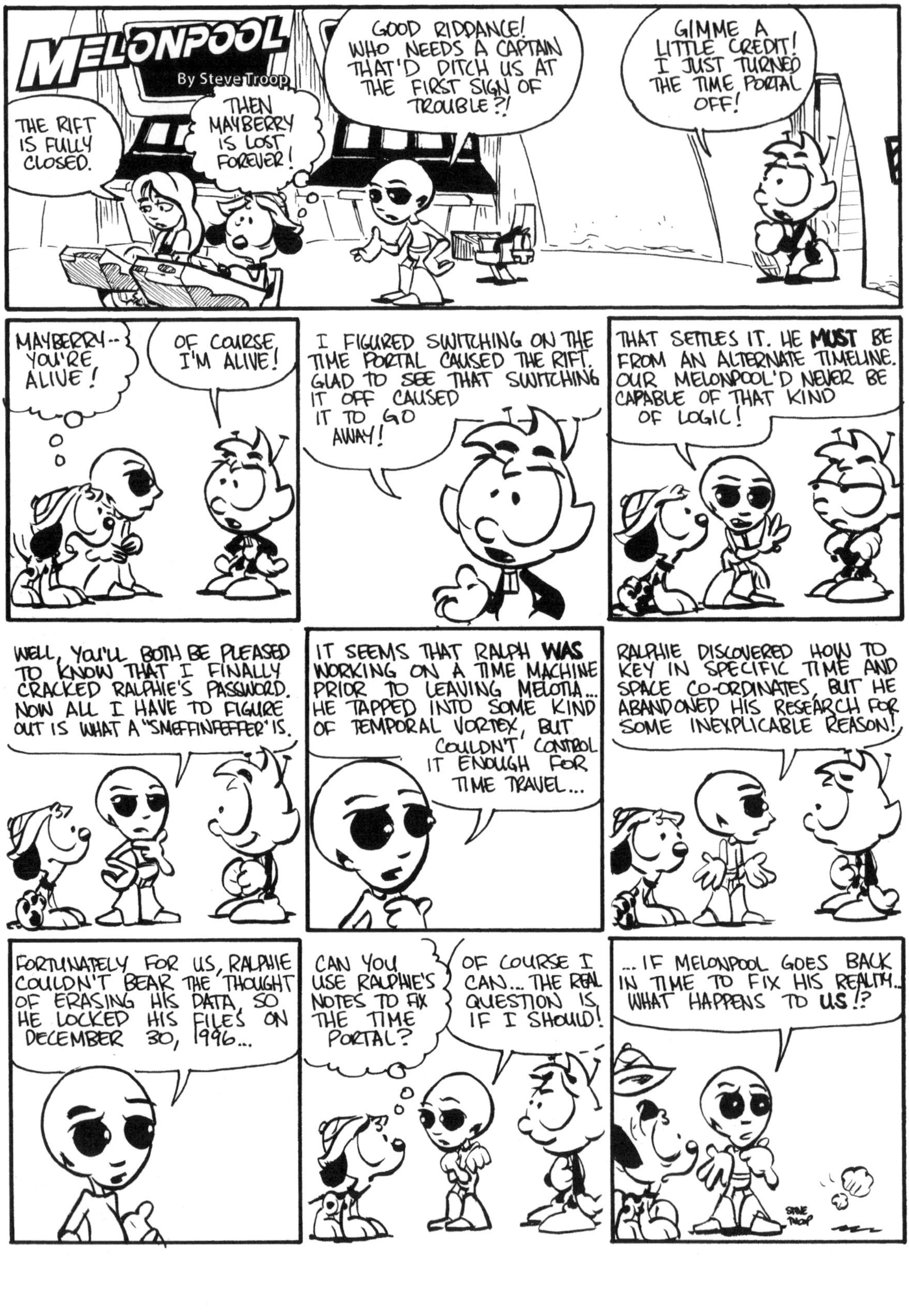

MELONPOOL
By Steve Troop
THE RIFT IS FULLY CLOSED.
THEN MAYBERRY IS LOST FOREVER!
GOOD RIDDANCE! WHO NEEDS A CAPTAIN THAT'D DITCH US AT THE FIRST SIGN OF TROUBLE?!
GIMME A LITTLE CREDIT! I JUST TURNED THE TIME PORTAL OFF!
MAYBERRY-- YOU'RE ALIVE!
OF COURSE, I'M ALIVE!
I FIGURED SWITCHING ON THE TIME PORTAL CAUSED THE RIFT. GLAD TO SEE THAT SWITCHING IT OFF CAUSED IT TO GO AWAY!
THAT SETTLES IT. HE MUST BE FROM AN ALTERNATE TIMELINE. OUR MELONPOOL'D NEVER BE CAPABLE OF THAT KIND OF LOGIC!
WELL, YOU'LL BOTH BE PLEASED TO KNOW THAT I FINALLY CRACKED RALPHIE'S PASSWORD. NOW ALL I HAVE TO FIGURE OUT IS WHAT A "SMEFFINPEFFER" IS.
IT SEEMS THAT RALPH WAS WORKING ON A TIME MACHINE PRIOR TO LEAVING MELOTIA... HE TAPPED INTO SOME KIND OF TEMPORAL VORTEX, BUT COULDN'T CONTROL IT ENOUGH FOR TIME TRAVEL...
RALPHIE DISCOVERED HOW TO KEY IN SPECIFIC TIME AND SPACE CO-ORDINATES, BUT HE ABANDONED HIS RESEARCH FOR SOME INEXPLICABLE REASON!
FORTUNATELY FOR US, RALPHIE COULDN'T BEAR THE THOUGHT OF ERASING HIS DATA, SO HE LOCKED HIS FILES ON DECEMBER 30, 1996...
CAN YOU USE RALPHIE'S NOTES TO FIX THE TIME PORTAL?
OF COURSE I CAN... THE REAL QUESTION IS IF I SHOULD!
...IF MELONPOOL GOES BACK IN TIME TO FIX HIS REALITY... WHAT HAPPENS TO US!?
STEVE TROOP

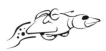

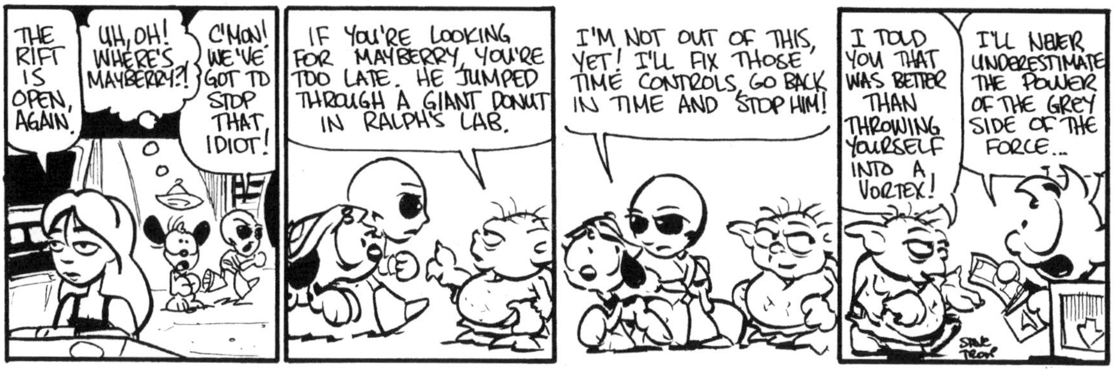
THE RIFT IS OPEN, AGAIN.
UH, OH! WHERE'S MAYBERRY?!
C'MON! WE'VE GOT TO STOP THAT IDIOT!
IF YOU'RE LOOKING FOR MAYBERRY, YOU'RE TOO LATE. HE JUMPED THROUGH A GIANT DONUT IN RALPH'S LAB.
I'M NOT OUT OF THIS, YET! I'LL FIX THOSE TIME CONTROLS, GO BACK IN TIME AND STOP HIM!
I TOLD YOU THAT WAS BETTER THAN THROWING YOURSELF INTO A VORTEX!
I'LL NEVER UNDERESTIMATE THE POWER OF THE GREY SIDE OF THE FORCE...

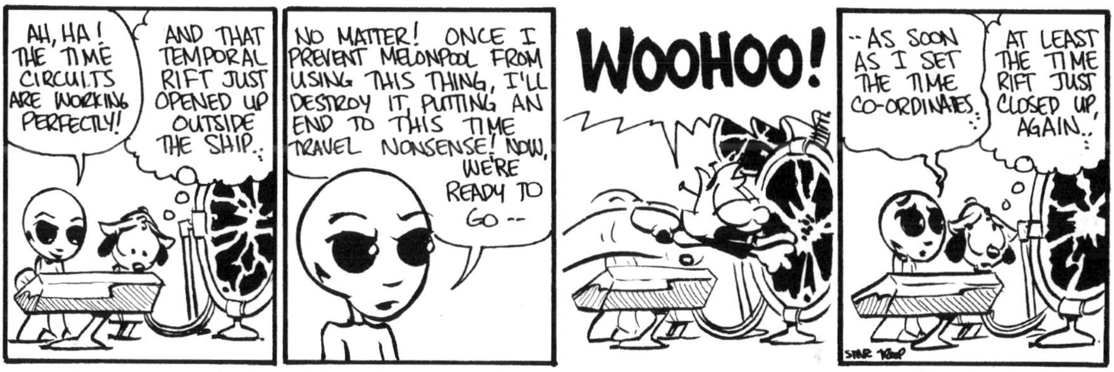
AH, HA! THE TIME CIRCUITS ARE WORKING PERFECTLY!
AND THAT TEMPORAL RIFT JUST OPENED UP OUTSIDE THE SHIP...
NO MATTER! ONCE I PREVENT MELONPOOL FROM USING THIS THING, I'LL DESTROY IT, PUTTING AN END TO THIS TIME TRAVEL NONSENSE! NOW, WE'RE READY TO GO --
WOOHOO!
--AS SOON AS I SET THE TIME CO-ORDINATES...
AT LEAST THE TIME RIFT JUST CLOSED UP, AGAIN...

I typically write time travel storylines by combing through the old TUMs and making lists of plot threads that have been left dangling until I have a story that works within the continuity. A plus is that sometimes I can even plug a plot hole or two along the way.

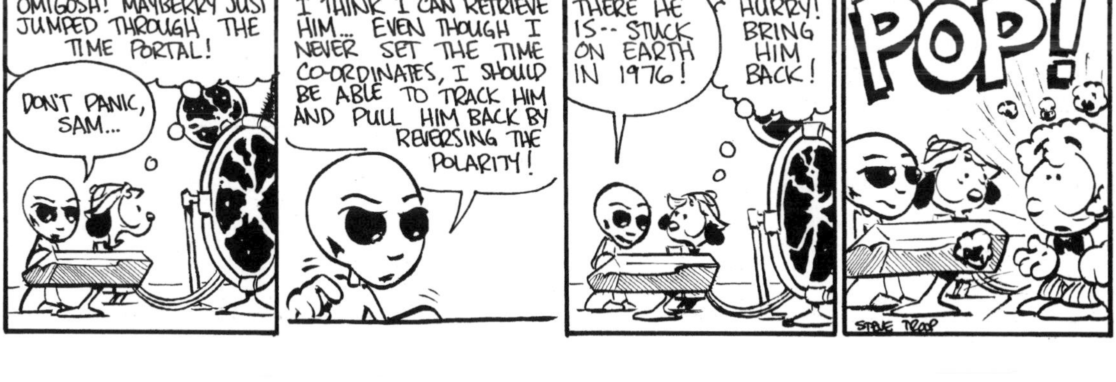
OMIGOSH! MAYBERRY JUST JUMPED THROUGH THE TIME PORTAL!
DON'T PANIC, SAM...
I THINK I CAN RETRIEVE HIM... EVEN THOUGH I NEVER SET THE TIME CO-ORDINATES, I SHOULD BE ABLE TO TRACK HIM AND PULL HIM BACK BY REVERSING THE POLARITY!
THERE HE IS-- STUCK ON EARTH IN 1976!
HURRY! BRING HIM BACK!
POP!

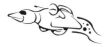

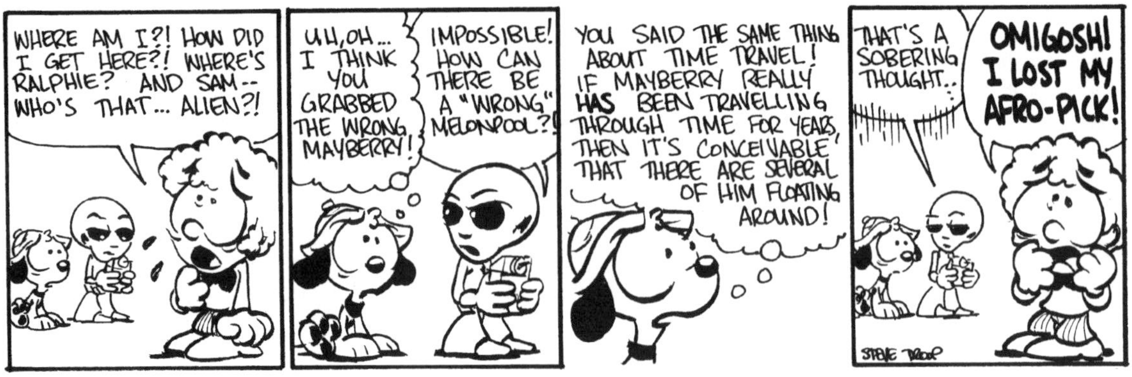
WHERE AM I?! HOW DID I GET HERE?! WHERE'S RALPHIE? AND SAM-- WHO'S THAT... ALIEN?!
UH, OH... I THINK YOU GRABBED THE WRONG MAYBERRY!
IMPOSSIBLE! HOW CAN THERE BE A "WRONG" MELONPOOL?!
YOU SAID THE SAME THING ABOUT TIME TRAVEL! IF MAYBERRY REALLY HAS BEEN TRAVELLING THROUGH TIME FOR YEARS, THEN IT'S CONCEIVABLE THAT THERE ARE SEVERAL OF HIM FLOATING AROUND!
THAT'S A SOBERING THOUGHT..
OMIGOSH! I LOST MY AFRO-PICK!
STEVE TROOP

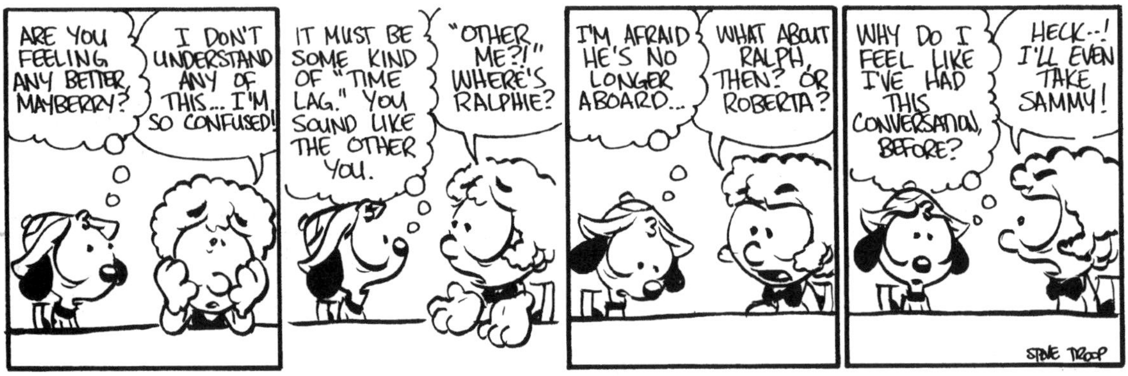
ARE YOU FEELING ANY BETTER, MAYBERRY?
I DON'T UNDERSTAND ANY OF THIS... I'M SO CONFUSED!
IT MUST BE SOME KIND OF "TIME LAG." YOU SOUND LIKE THE OTHER YOU.
"OTHER ME?!" WHERE'S RALPHIE?
I'M AFRAID HE'S NO LONGER ABOARD...
WHAT ABOUT RALPH, THEN? OR ROBERTA?
WHY DO I FEEL LIKE I'VE HAD THIS CONVERSATION, BEFORE?
HECK--! I'LL EVEN TAKE SAMMY!
STEVE TROOP

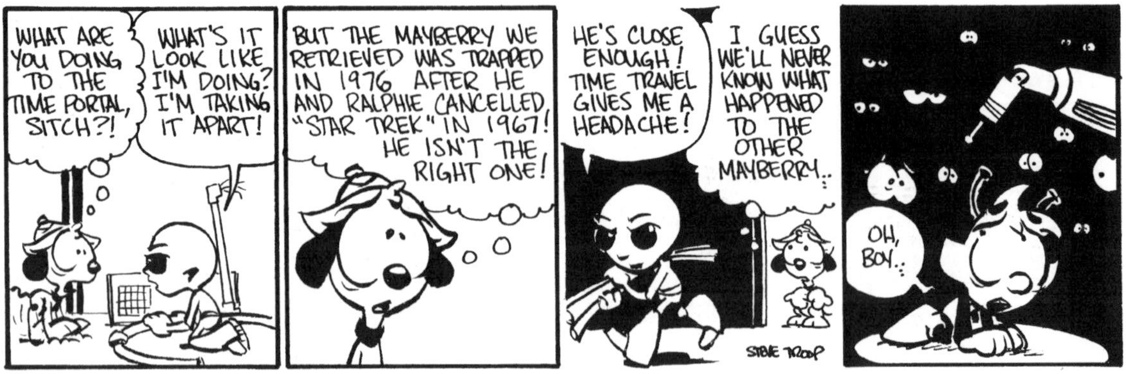
WHAT ARE YOU DOING TO THE TIME PORTAL, SITCH?!
WHAT'S IT LOOK LIKE I'M DOING? I'M TAKING IT APART!
BUT THE MAYBERRY WE RETRIEVED WAS TRAPPED IN 1976 AFTER HE AND RALPHIE CANCELLED "STAR TREK" IN 1967! HE ISN'T THE RIGHT ONE!
HE'S CLOSE ENOUGH! TIME TRAVEL GIVES ME A HEADACHE!
I GUESS WE'LL NEVER KNOW WHAT HAPPENED TO THE OTHER MAYBERRY..
STEVE TROOP
OH, BOY..

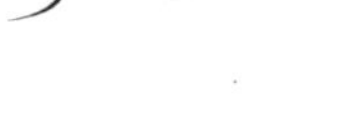

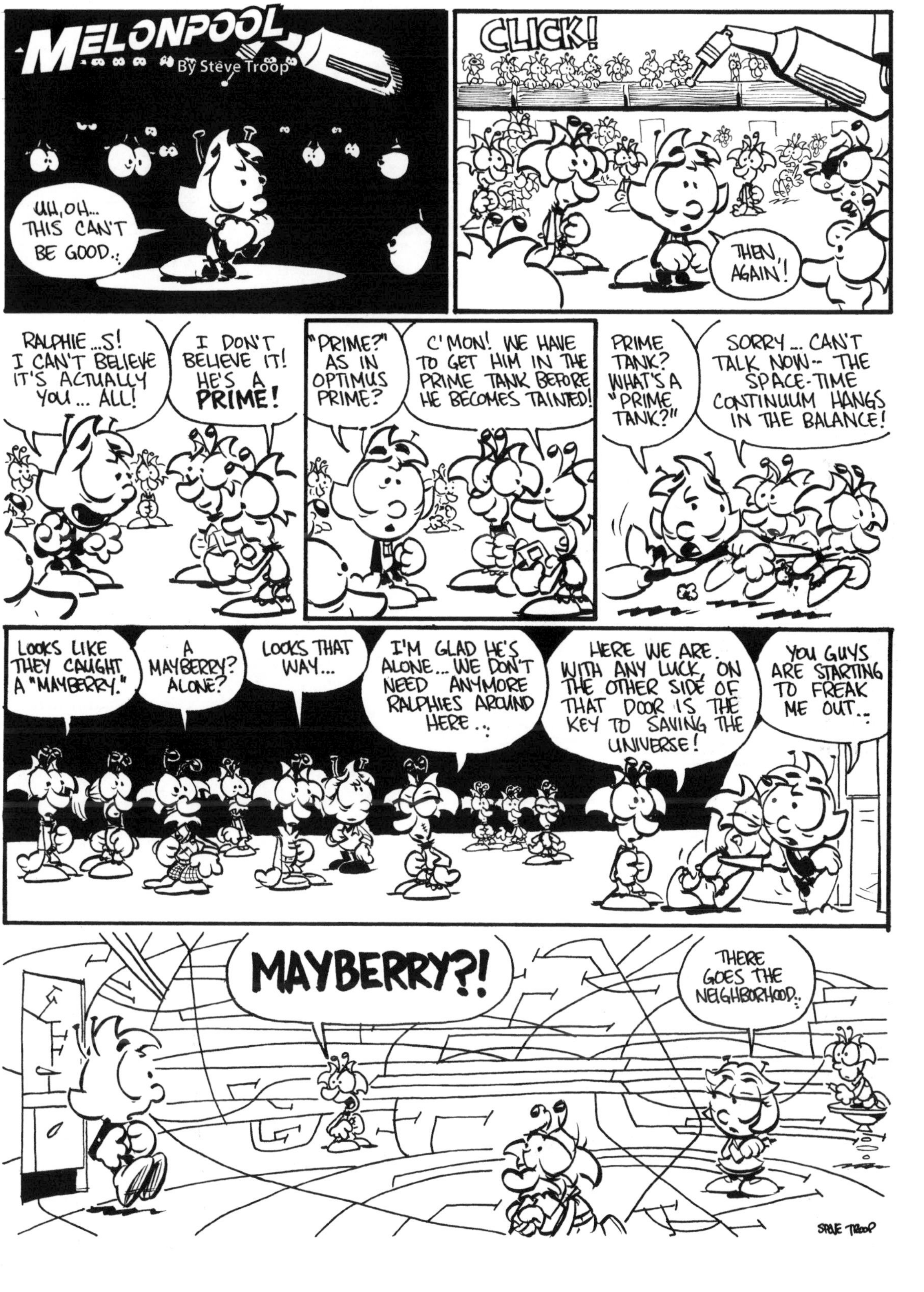
MELONPOOL
By Steve Troop
UH, OH... THIS CAN'T BE GOOD...
CLICK!
THEN, AGAIN!
RALPHIE...S! I CAN'T BELIEVE IT'S ACTUALLY YOU... ALL!
I DON'T BELIEVE IT! HE'S A PRIME!
"PRIME?" AS IN OPTIMUS PRIME?
C'MON! WE HAVE TO GET HIM IN THE PRIME TANK BEFORE HE BECOMES TAINTED!
PRIME TANK? WHAT'S A "PRIME TANK?"
SORRY... CAN'T TALK NOW-- THE SPACE-TIME CONTINUUM HANGS IN THE BALANCE!
LOOKS LIKE THEY CAUGHT A "MAYBERRY."
A MAYBERRY? ALONE?
LOOKS THAT WAY...
I'M GLAD HE'S ALONE... WE DON'T NEED ANYMORE RALPHIES AROUND HERE...
HERE WE ARE. WITH ANY LUCK, ON THE OTHER SIDE OF THAT DOOR IS THE KEY TO SAVING THE UNIVERSE!
YOU GUYS ARE STARTING TO FREAK ME OUT...
MAYBERRY?!
THERE GOES THE NEIGHBORHOOD...
STEVE TROOP

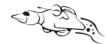

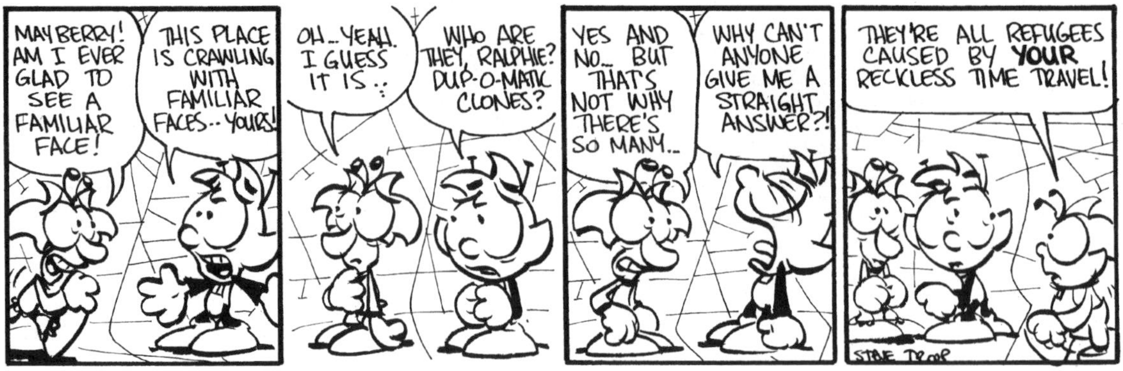
MAYBERRY! AM I EVER GLAD TO SEE A FAMILIAR FACE!
THIS PLACE IS CRAWLING WITH FAMILIAR FACES... YOURS!
OH... YEAH. I GUESS IT IS...
WHO ARE THEY, RALPHIE? DUP-O-MATIC CLONES?
YES AND NO... BUT THAT'S NOT WHY THERE'S SO MANY...
WHY CAN'T ANYONE GIVE ME A STRAIGHT ANSWER?!
THEY'RE ALL REFUGEES CAUSED BY **YOUR** RECKLESS TIME TRAVEL!
STEVE TROOP

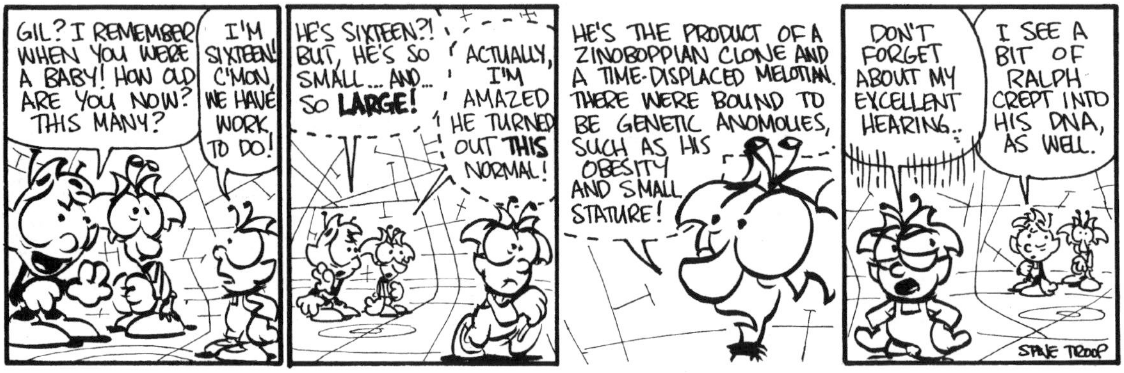
GIL? I REMEMBER WHEN YOU WERE A BABY! HOW OLD ARE YOU NOW? THIS MANY?
I'M SIXTEEN! C'MON, WE HAVE WORK TO DO!
HE'S SIXTEEN?! BUT, HE'S SO SMALL... AND... SO **LARGE!**
ACTUALLY, I'M AMAZED HE TURNED OUT **THIS** NORMAL!
HE'S THE PRODUCT OF A ZINOBOPPIAN CLONE AND A TIME-DISPLACED MELOTIAN. THERE WERE BOUND TO BE GENETIC ANOMOLIES, SUCH AS HIS OBESITY AND SMALL STATURE!
DON'T FORGET ABOUT MY EXCELLENT HEARING...
I SEE A BIT OF RALPH CREPT INTO HIS DNA, AS WELL.
STEVE TROOP

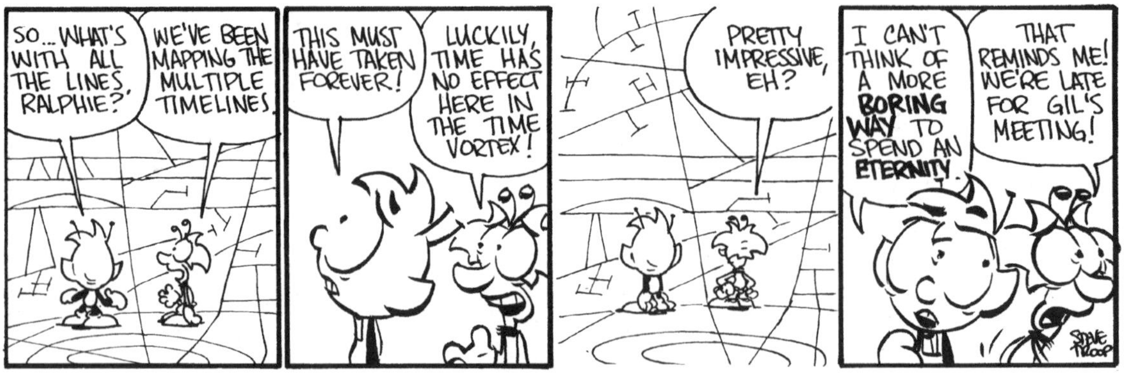
SO... WHAT'S WITH ALL THE LINES, RALPHIE?
WE'VE BEEN MAPPING THE MULTIPLE TIMELINES.
THIS MUST HAVE TAKEN FOREVER!
LUCKILY, TIME HAS NO EFFECT HERE IN THE TIME VORTEX!
PRETTY IMPRESSIVE, EH?
I CAN'T THINK OF A MORE **BORING WAY** TO SPEND AN **ETERNITY**.
THAT REMINDS ME! WE'RE LATE FOR GIL'S MEETING!
STEVE TROOP

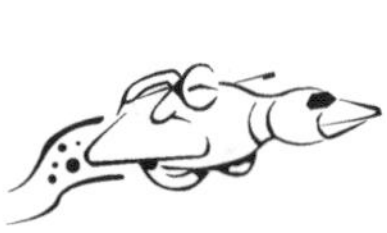

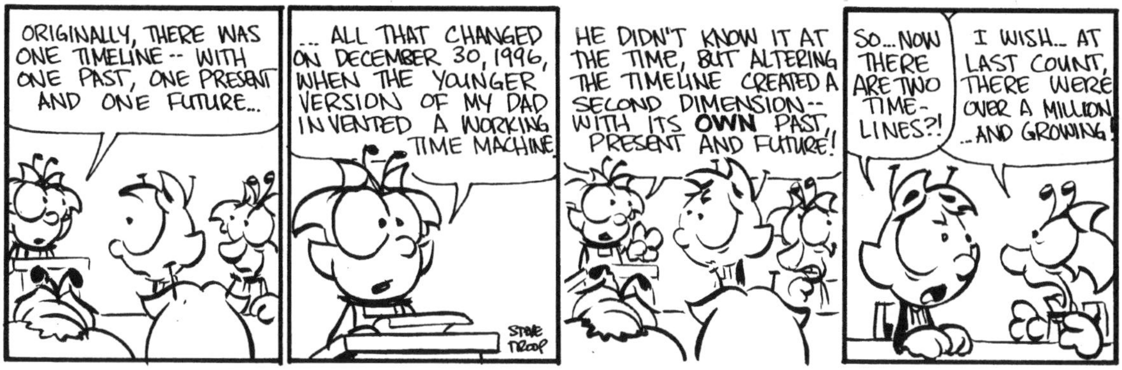
ORIGINALLY, THERE WAS ONE TIMELINE -- WITH ONE PAST, ONE PRESENT AND ONE FUTURE...
... ALL THAT CHANGED ON DECEMBER 30, 1996, WHEN THE YOUNGER VERSION OF MY DAD INVENTED A WORKING TIME MACHINE.
STEVE TROOP
HE DIDN'T KNOW IT AT THE TIME, BUT ALTERING THE TIMELINE CREATED A SECOND DIMENSION -- WITH ITS OWN PAST, PRESENT AND FUTURE!
SO... NOW THERE ARE TWO TIME-LINES?!
I WISH... AT LAST COUNT, THERE WERE OVER A MILLION ...AND GROWING!

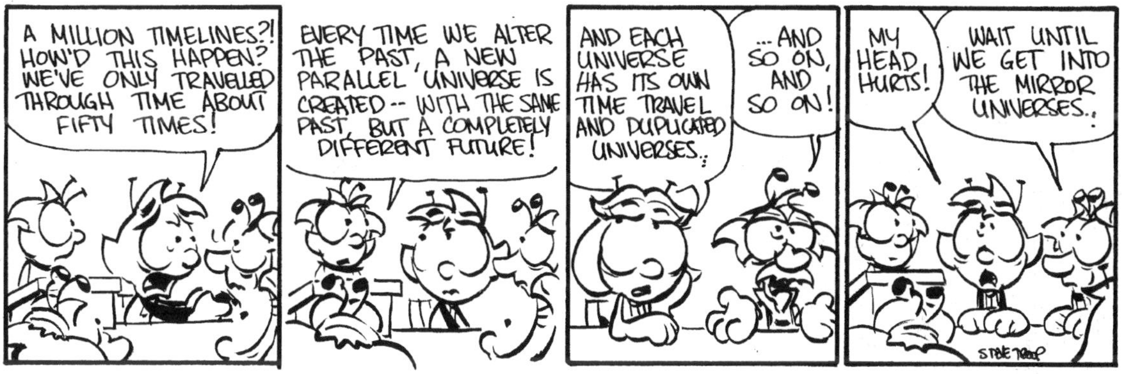
A MILLION TIMELINES?! HOW'D THIS HAPPEN? WE'VE ONLY TRAVELLED THROUGH TIME ABOUT FIFTY TIMES!
EVERY TIME WE ALTER THE PAST, A NEW PARALLEL UNIVERSE IS CREATED -- WITH THE SAME PAST, BUT A COMPLETELY DIFFERENT FUTURE!
AND EACH UNIVERSE HAS ITS OWN TIME TRAVEL AND DUPLICATED UNIVERSES...
...AND SO ON, AND SO ON!
MY HEAD HURTS!
WAIT UNTIL WE GET INTO THE MIRROR UNIVERSES...
STEVE TROOP

The events Mayberry and Ralphie speak about appear on page 165 of TUM I. It's pretty neat how one throwaway comic lead to so many ideas.

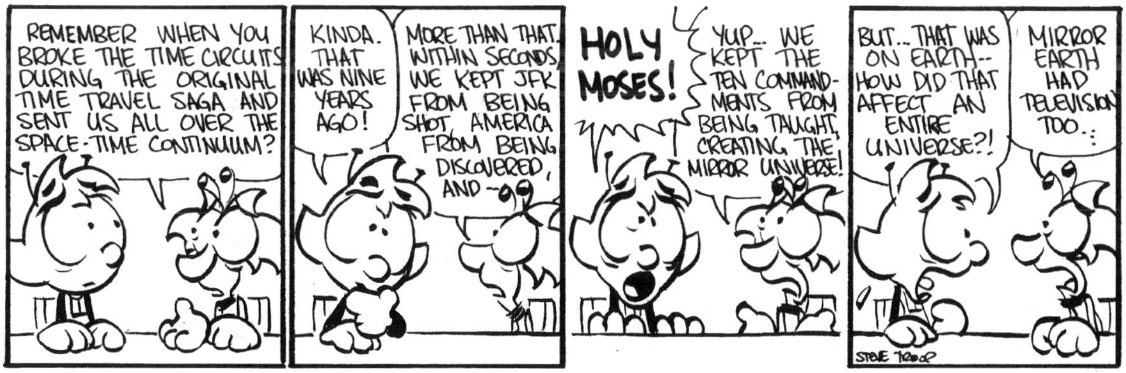
REMEMBER WHEN YOU BROKE THE TIME CIRCUITS DURING THE ORIGINAL TIME TRAVEL SAGA AND SENT US ALL OVER THE SPACE-TIME CONTINUUM?
KINDA. THAT WAS NINE YEARS AGO!
MORE THAN THAT. WITHIN SECONDS, WE KEPT JFK FROM BEING SHOT, AMERICA FROM BEING DISCOVERED, AND --
HOLY MOSES!
YUP... WE KEPT THE TEN COMMANDMENTS FROM BEING TAUGHT, CREATING THE MIRROR UNIVERSE!
BUT... THAT WAS ON EARTH -- HOW DID THAT AFFECT AN ENTIRE UNIVERSE?!
MIRROR EARTH HAD TELEVISION TOO...
STEVE TROOP

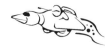

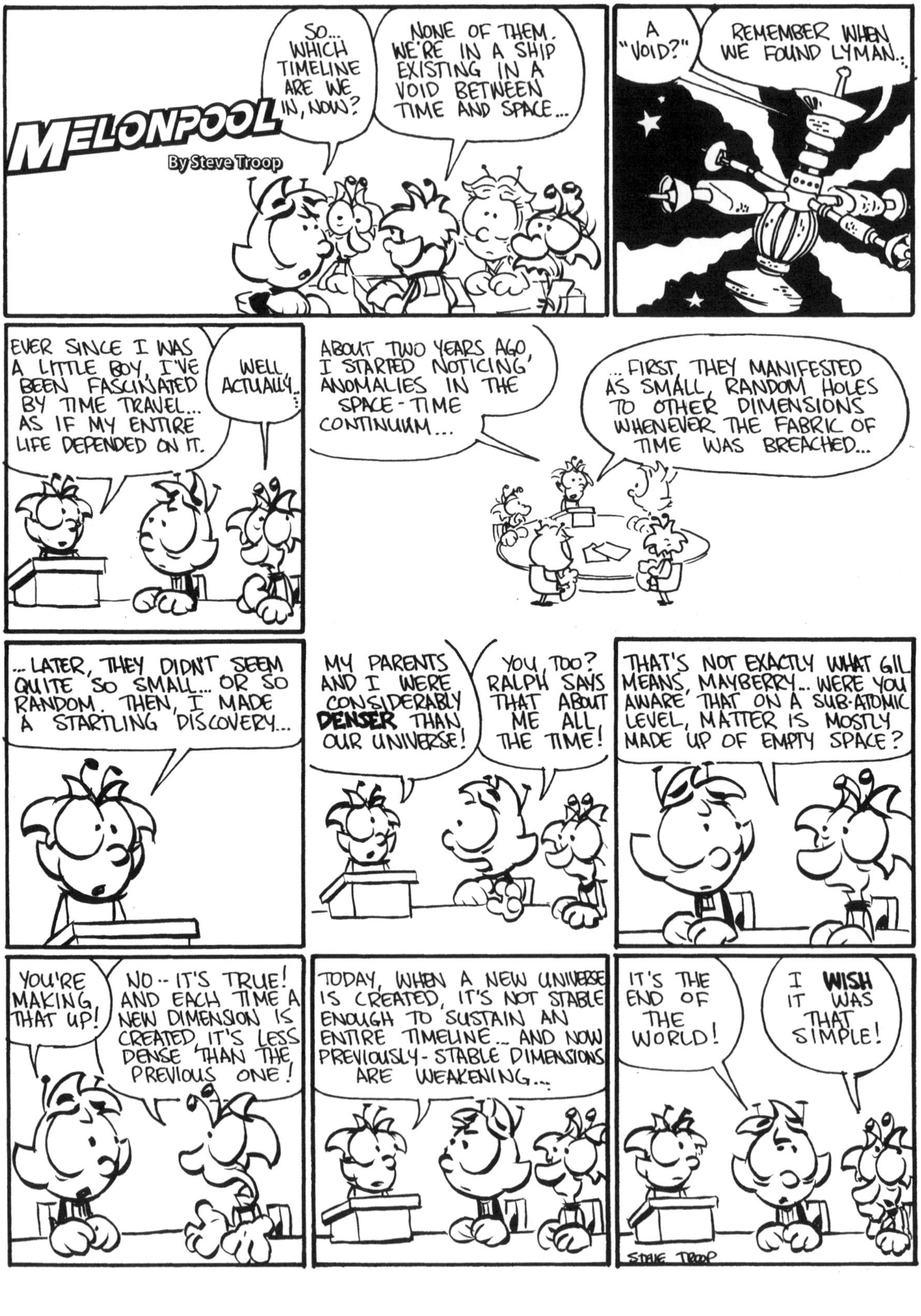
MELONPOOL
By Steve Troop
SO... WHICH TIMELINE ARE WE IN, NOW?
NONE OF THEM. WE'RE IN A SHIP EXISTING IN A VOID BETWEEN TIME AND SPACE...
A "VOID?"
REMEMBER WHEN WE FOUND LYMAN...
EVER SINCE I WAS A LITTLE BOY, I'VE BEEN FASCINATED BY TIME TRAVEL... AS IF MY ENTIRE LIFE DEPENDED ON IT.
WELL, ACTUALLY...
ABOUT TWO YEARS AGO, I STARTED NOTICING ANOMALIES IN THE SPACE-TIME CONTINUUM...
...FIRST, THEY MANIFESTED AS SMALL, RANDOM HOLES TO OTHER DIMENSIONS WHENEVER THE FABRIC OF TIME WAS BREACHED...
...LATER, THEY DIDN'T SEEM QUITE SO SMALL... OR SO RANDOM. THEN, I MADE A STARTLING DISCOVERY...
MY PARENTS AND I WERE CONSIDERABLY DENSER THAN OUR UNIVERSE!
YOU, TOO? RALPH SAYS THAT ABOUT ME ALL THE TIME!
THAT'S NOT EXACTLY WHAT GIL MEANS, MAYBERRY... WERE YOU AWARE THAT ON A SUB-ATOMIC LEVEL, MATTER IS MOSTLY MADE UP OF EMPTY SPACE?
YOU'RE MAKING THAT UP!
NO-- IT'S TRUE! AND EACH TIME A NEW DIMENSION IS CREATED, IT'S LESS DENSE THAN THE PREVIOUS ONE!
TODAY, WHEN A NEW UNIVERSE IS CREATED, IT'S NOT STABLE ENOUGH TO SUSTAIN AN ENTIRE TIMELINE... AND NOW PREVIOUSLY-STABLE DIMENSIONS ARE WEAKENING...
IT'S THE END OF THE WORLD!
I WISH IT WAS THAT SIMPLE!
STEVE TROOP

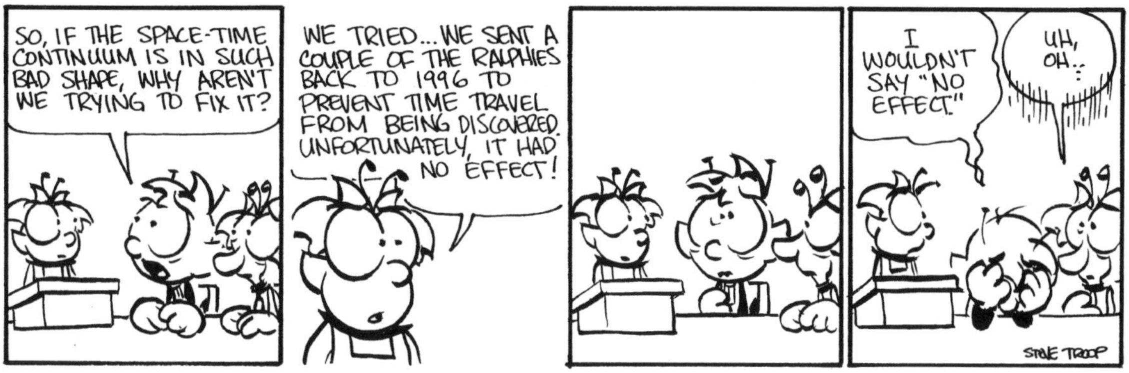
SO, IF THE SPACE-TIME CONTINUUM IS IN SUCH BAD SHAPE, WHY AREN'T WE TRYING TO FIX IT?
WE TRIED... WE SENT A COUPLE OF THE RALPHIES BACK TO 1996 TO PREVENT TIME TRAVEL FROM BEING DISCOVERED. UNFORTUNATELY, IT HAD NO EFFECT!
I WOULDN'T SAY "NO EFFECT."
UH, OH...
STEVE TROOP

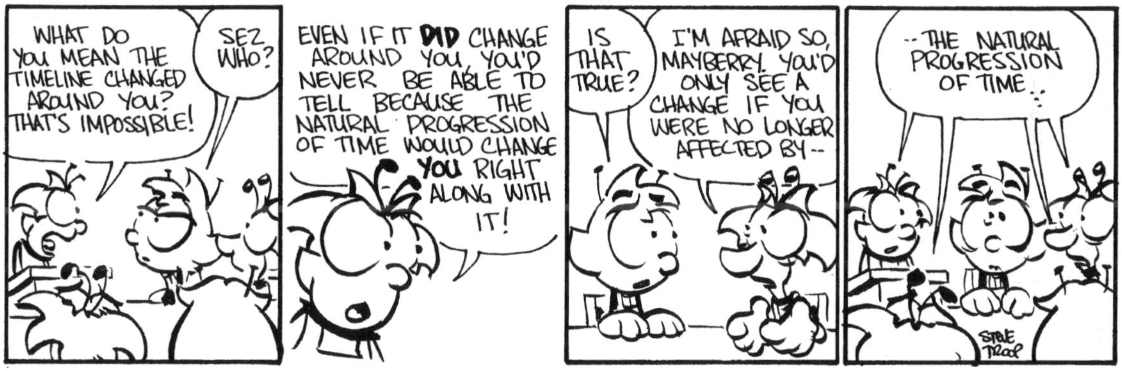
WHAT DO YOU MEAN THE TIMELINE CHANGED AROUND YOU? THAT'S IMPOSSIBLE!
SEZ WHO?
EVEN IF IT DID CHANGE AROUND YOU, YOU'D NEVER BE ABLE TO TELL BECAUSE THE NATURAL PROGRESSION OF TIME WOULD CHANGE YOU RIGHT ALONG WITH IT!
IS THAT TRUE?
I'M AFRAID SO, MAYBERRY. YOU'D ONLY SEE A CHANGE IF YOU WERE NO LONGER AFFECTED BY--
--THE NATURAL PROGRESSION OF TIME...
STEVE TROOP

Sherwood Schwartz, the creator of *Gilligan's Island*, used to tell about how they showed a scene where the Professor demonstrated how to recharge batteries using copper pennies, aluminum foil and sea water to one group of teenagers. Meanwhile, the same experiment was demonstrated by a live instructor to another group of teenagers. A week later, the two groups were tested and the group that watched the *Gilligan* clip understood the concept two-to-one!

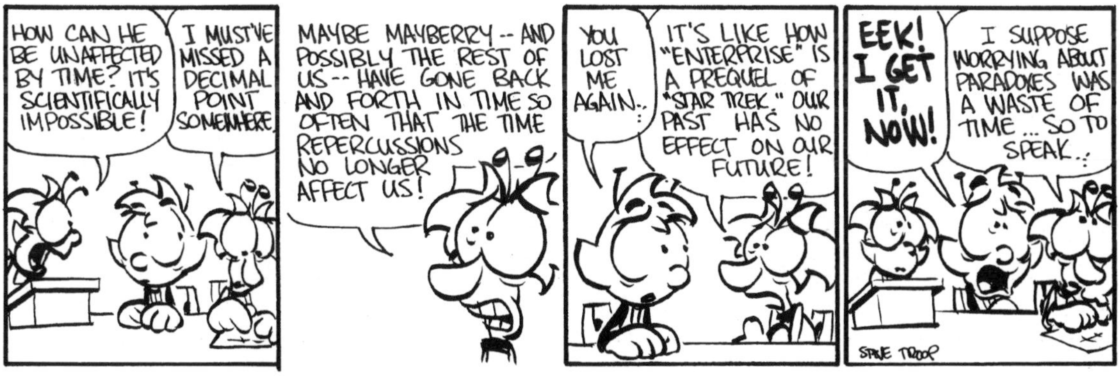
HOW CAN HE BE UNAFFECTED BY TIME? IT'S SCIENTIFICALLY IMPOSSIBLE!
I MUST'VE MISSED A DECIMAL POINT SOMEWHERE.
MAYBE MAYBERRY -- AND POSSIBLY THE REST OF US -- HAVE GONE BACK AND FORTH IN TIME SO OFTEN THAT THE TIME REPERCUSSIONS NO LONGER AFFECT US!
YOU LOST ME AGAIN...
IT'S LIKE HOW "ENTERPRISE" IS A PREQUEL OF "STAR TREK." OUR PAST HAS NO EFFECT ON OUR FUTURE!
EEK! I GET IT, NOW!
I SUPPOSE WORRYING ABOUT PARADOXES WAS A WASTE OF TIME... SO TO SPEAK...
STEVE TROOP

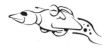

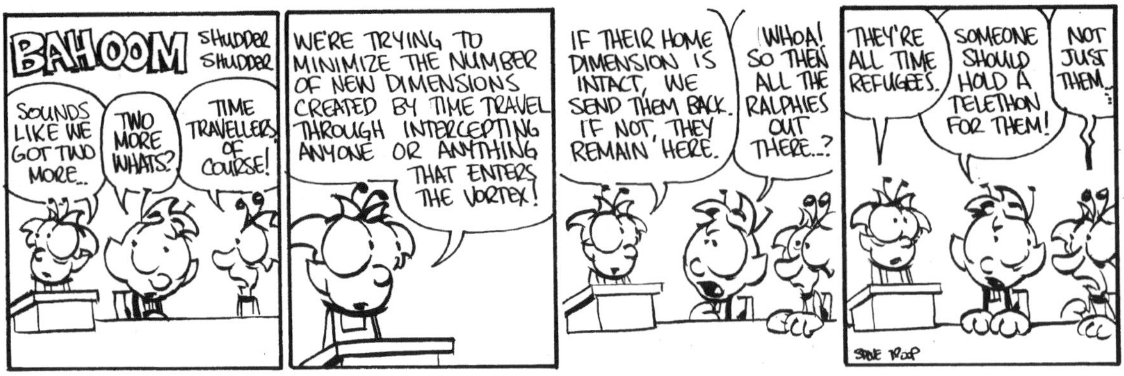
BAHOOM
SHUDDER SHUDDER
SOUNDS LIKE WE GOT TWO MORE...
TWO MORE WHATS?
TIME TRAVELLERS, OF COURSE!
WE'RE TRYING TO MINIMIZE THE NUMBER OF NEW DIMENSIONS CREATED BY TIME TRAVEL THROUGH INTERCEPTING ANYONE OR ANYTHING THAT ENTERS THE VORTEX!
IF THEIR HOME DIMENSION IS INTACT, WE SEND THEM BACK. IF NOT, THEY REMAIN HERE.
WHOA! SO THEN ALL THE RALPHIES OUT THERE...?
THEY'RE ALL TIME REFUGEES.
SOMEONE SHOULD HOLD A TELETHON FOR THEM!
NOT JUST THEM...
STEVE TROOP

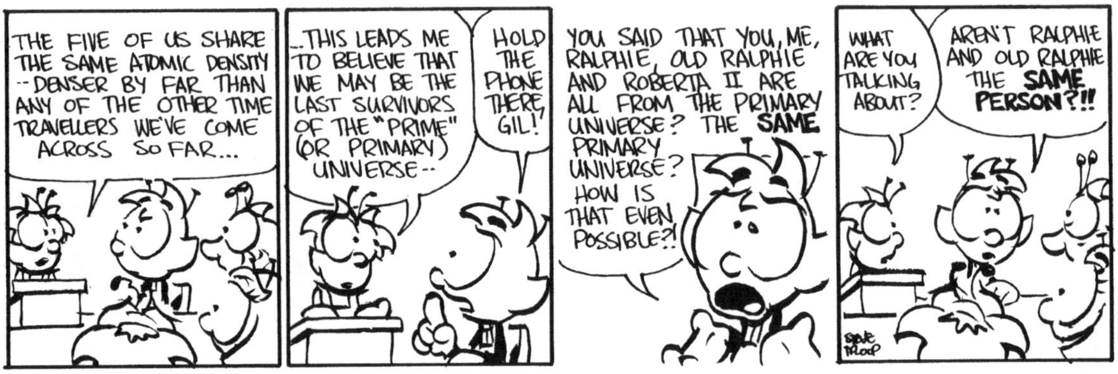
THE FIVE OF US SHARE THE SAME ATOMIC DENSITY --DENSER BY FAR THAN ANY OF THE OTHER TIME TRAVELLERS WE'VE COME ACROSS SO FAR...
...THIS LEADS ME TO BELIEVE THAT WE MAY BE THE LAST SURVIVORS OF THE "PRIME" (OR PRIMARY) UNIVERSE--
HOLD THE PHONE THERE, GIL!
YOU SAID THAT YOU, ME, RALPHIE, OLD RALPHIE AND ROBERTA II ARE ALL FROM THE PRIMARY UNIVERSE? THE SAME PRIMARY UNIVERSE? HOW IS THAT EVEN POSSIBLE?!
WHAT ARE YOU TALKING ABOUT?
AREN'T RALPHIE AND OLD RALPHIE THE SAME PERSON?!!
STEVE TROOP

The battle cry that all of the Mayberry's chant was the exact same line that Mayberry said in the *Melonpool Movie* while watching *Star Trek* on the main viewscreen.

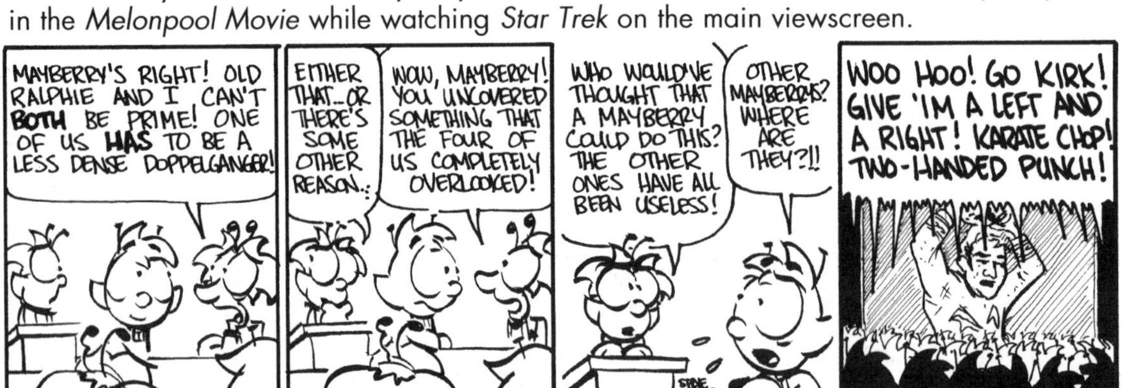
MAYBERRY'S RIGHT! OLD RALPHIE AND I CAN'T BOTH BE PRIME! ONE OF US HAS TO BE A LESS DENSE DOPPELGANGER!
EITHER THAT...OR THERE'S SOME OTHER REASON...
WOW, MAYBERRY! YOU UNCOVERED SOMETHING THAT THE FOUR OF US COMPLETELY OVERLOOKED!
WHO WOULD'VE THOUGHT THAT A MAYBERRY COULD DO THIS? THE OTHER ONES HAVE ALL BEEN USELESS!
OTHER MAYBERRYS? WHERE ARE THEY?!!
STEVE TROOP
WOO HOO! GO KIRK! GIVE 'IM A LEFT AND A RIGHT! KARATE CHOP! TWO-HANDED PUNCH!

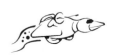

Alternate Ralphies designed by Teague Tyselling (TUM V, pages 57–59) and Yamcha Kibiki (See pages 197–199) appear as well as a Splink from *Zortic* (references too numerous to mention).

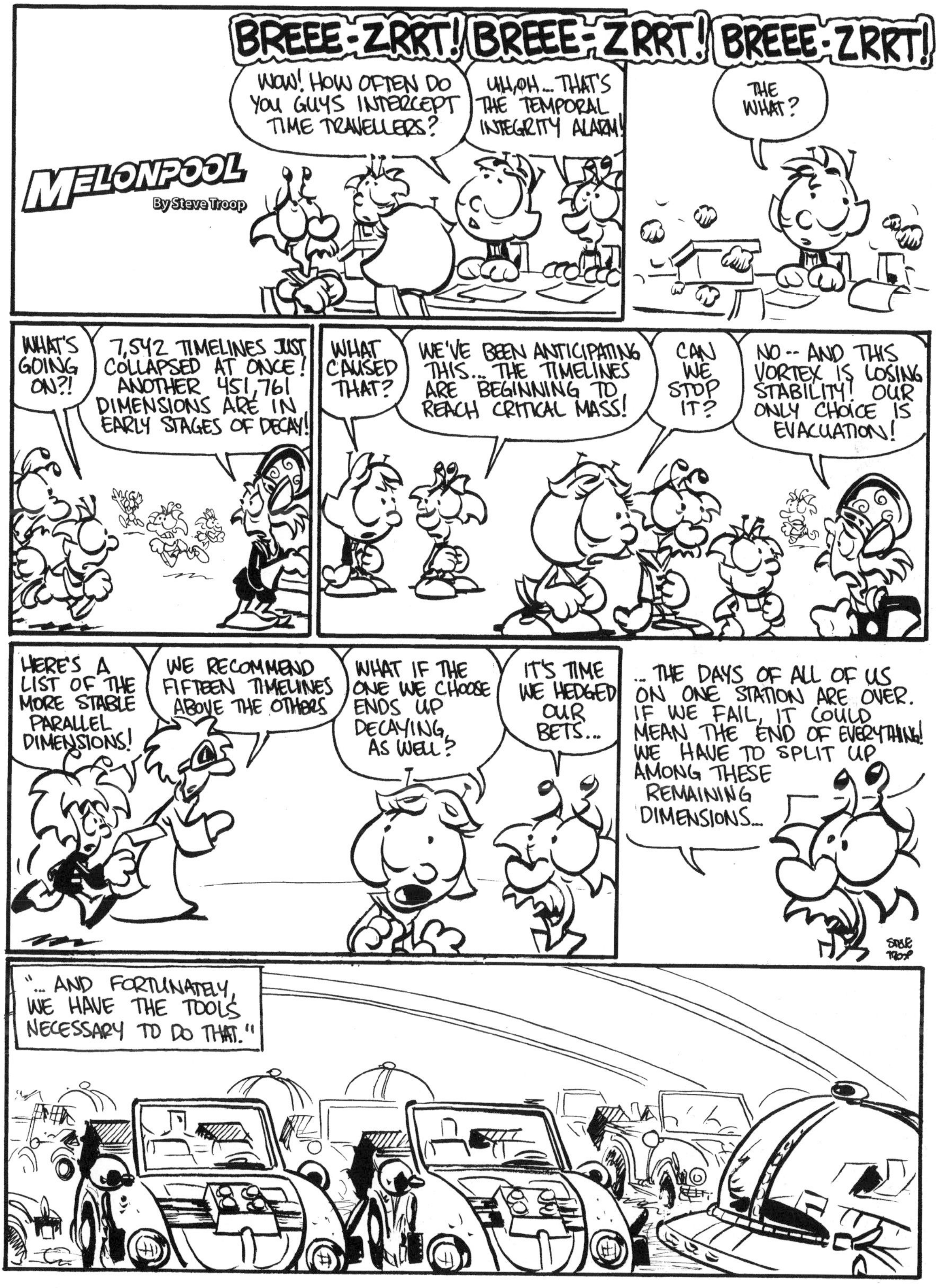
MELONPOOL
By Steve Troop
BREEE-ZRRT! BREEE-ZRRT! BREEE-ZRRT!
WOW! HOW OFTEN DO YOU GUYS INTERCEPT TIME TRAVELLERS?
UH, OH... THAT'S THE TEMPORAL INTEGRITY ALARM!
THE WHAT?
WHAT'S GOING ON?!
7,542 TIMELINES JUST COLLAPSED AT ONCE! ANOTHER 451,761 DIMENSIONS ARE IN EARLY STAGES OF DECAY!
WHAT CAUSED THAT?
WE'VE BEEN ANTICIPATING THIS... THE TIMELINES ARE BEGINNING TO REACH CRITICAL MASS!
CAN WE STOP IT?
NO -- AND THIS VORTEX IS LOSING STABILITY! OUR ONLY CHOICE IS EVACUATION!
HERE'S A LIST OF THE MORE STABLE PARALLEL DIMENSIONS!
WE RECOMMEND FIFTEEN TIMELINES ABOVE THE OTHERS
WHAT IF THE ONE WE CHOOSE ENDS UP DECAYING, AS WELL?
IT'S TIME WE HEDGED OUR BETS...
... THE DAYS OF ALL OF US ON ONE STATION ARE OVER. IF WE FAIL, IT COULD MEAN THE END OF EVERYTHING! WE HAVE TO SPLIT UP AMONG THESE REMAINING DIMENSIONS...
STEVE TROOP
"... AND FORTUNATELY, WE HAVE THE TOOLS NECESSARY TO DO THAT."

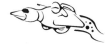

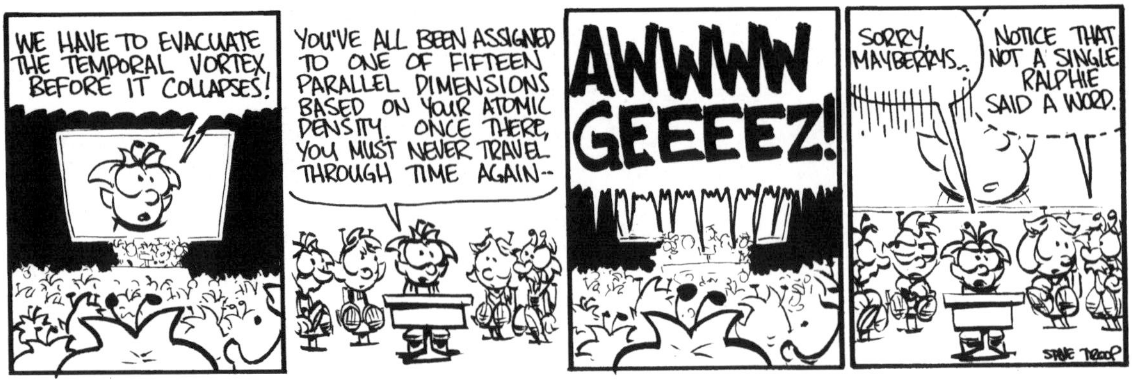
WE HAVE TO EVACUATE THE TEMPORAL VORTEX BEFORE IT COLLAPSES!
YOU'VE ALL BEEN ASSIGNED TO ONE OF FIFTEEN PARALLEL DIMENSIONS BASED ON YOUR ATOMIC DENSITY. ONCE THERE, YOU MUST NEVER TRAVEL THROUGH TIME AGAIN--
AWWWW GEEEEZ!
SORRY, MAYBERRYS...
NOTICE THAT NOT A SINGLE RALPHIE SAID A WORD.
STEVE TROOP

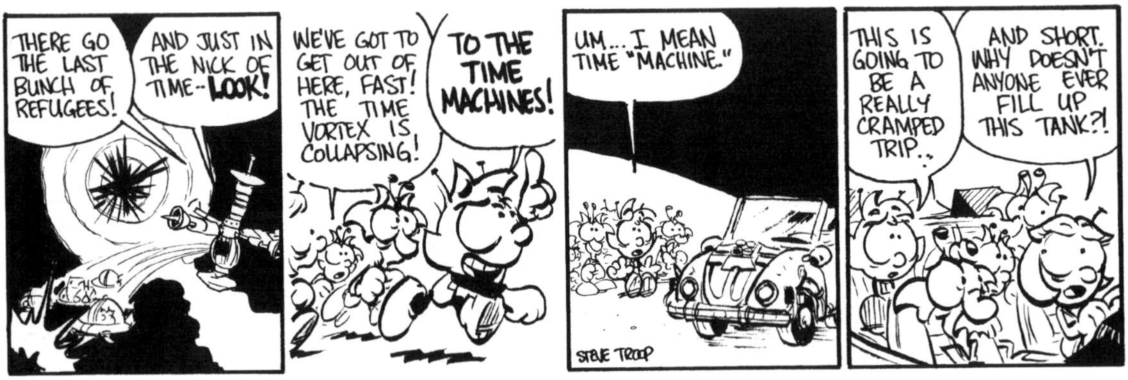
THERE GO THE LAST BUNCH OF REFUGEES!
AND JUST IN THE NICK OF TIME--LOOK!
WE'VE GOT TO GET OUT OF HERE, FAST! THE TIME VORTEX IS COLLAPSING!
TO THE TIME MACHINES!
UM... I MEAN TIME "MACHINE."
STEVE TROOP
THIS IS GOING TO BE A REALLY CRAMPED TRIP...
AND SHORT. WHY DOESN'T ANYONE EVER FILL UP THIS TANK?!

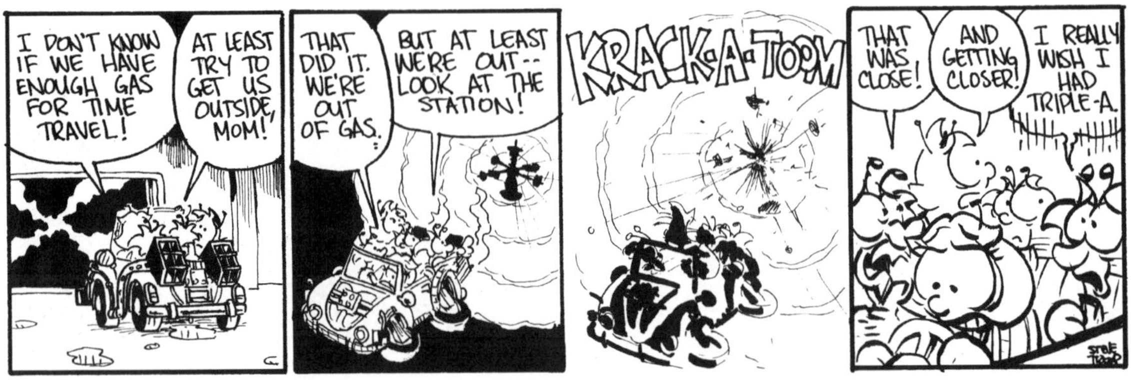
I DON'T KNOW IF WE HAVE ENOUGH GAS FOR TIME TRAVEL!
AT LEAST TRY TO GET US OUTSIDE, MOM!
THAT DID IT. WE'RE OUT OF GAS.
BUT AT LEAST WE'RE OUT-- LOOK AT THE STATION!
KRACK-A-TOOM
THAT WAS CLOSE!
AND GETTING CLOSER!
I REALLY WISH I HAD TRIPLE-A.
STEVE TROOP

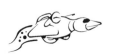

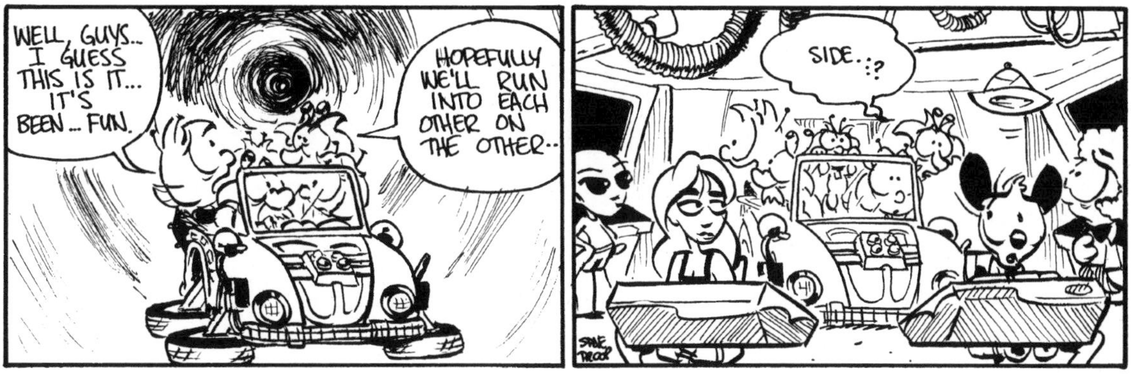
WELL, GUYS... I GUESS THIS IS IT... IT'S BEEN... FUN.
HOPEFULLY WE'LL RUN INTO EACH OTHER ON THE OTHER..
SIDE..:?
STEVE TROOP

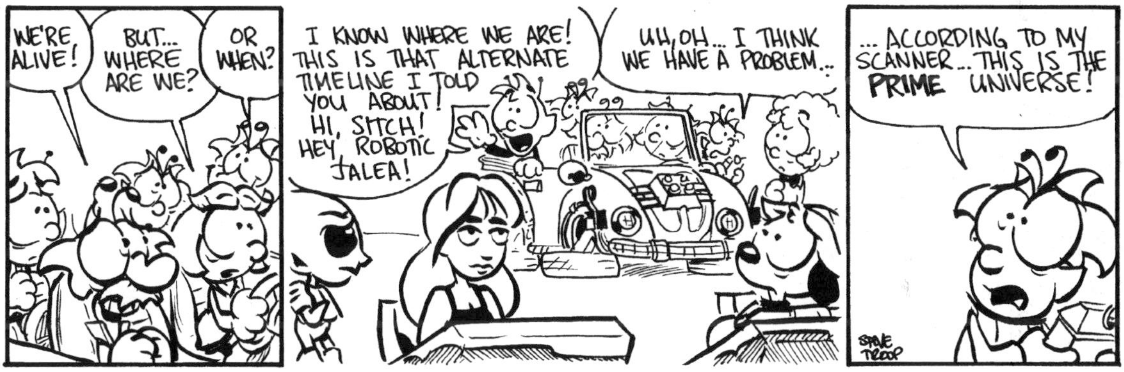
WE'RE ALIVE!
BUT... WHERE ARE WE?
OR WHEN?
I KNOW WHERE WE ARE! THIS IS THAT ALTERNATE TIMELINE I TOLD YOU ABOUT! HI, SITCH! HEY, ROBOTIC JALEA!
UH, OH... I THINK WE HAVE A PROBLEM...
...ACCORDING TO MY SCANNER... THIS IS THE PRIME UNIVERSE!
STEVE TROOP

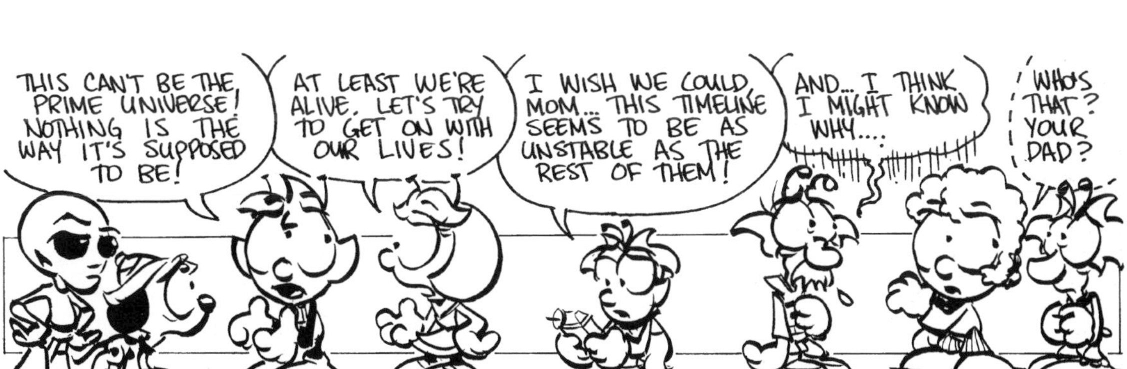
THIS CAN'T BE THE PRIME UNIVERSE! NOTHING IS THE WAY IT'S SUPPOSED TO BE!
AT LEAST WE'RE ALIVE. LET'S TRY TO GET ON WITH OUR LIVES!
I WISH WE COULD, MOM... THIS TIMELINE SEEMS TO BE AS UNSTABLE AS THE REST OF THEM!
AND... I THINK I MIGHT KNOW WHY....
WHO'S THAT? YOUR DAD?
STEVE TROOP

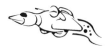

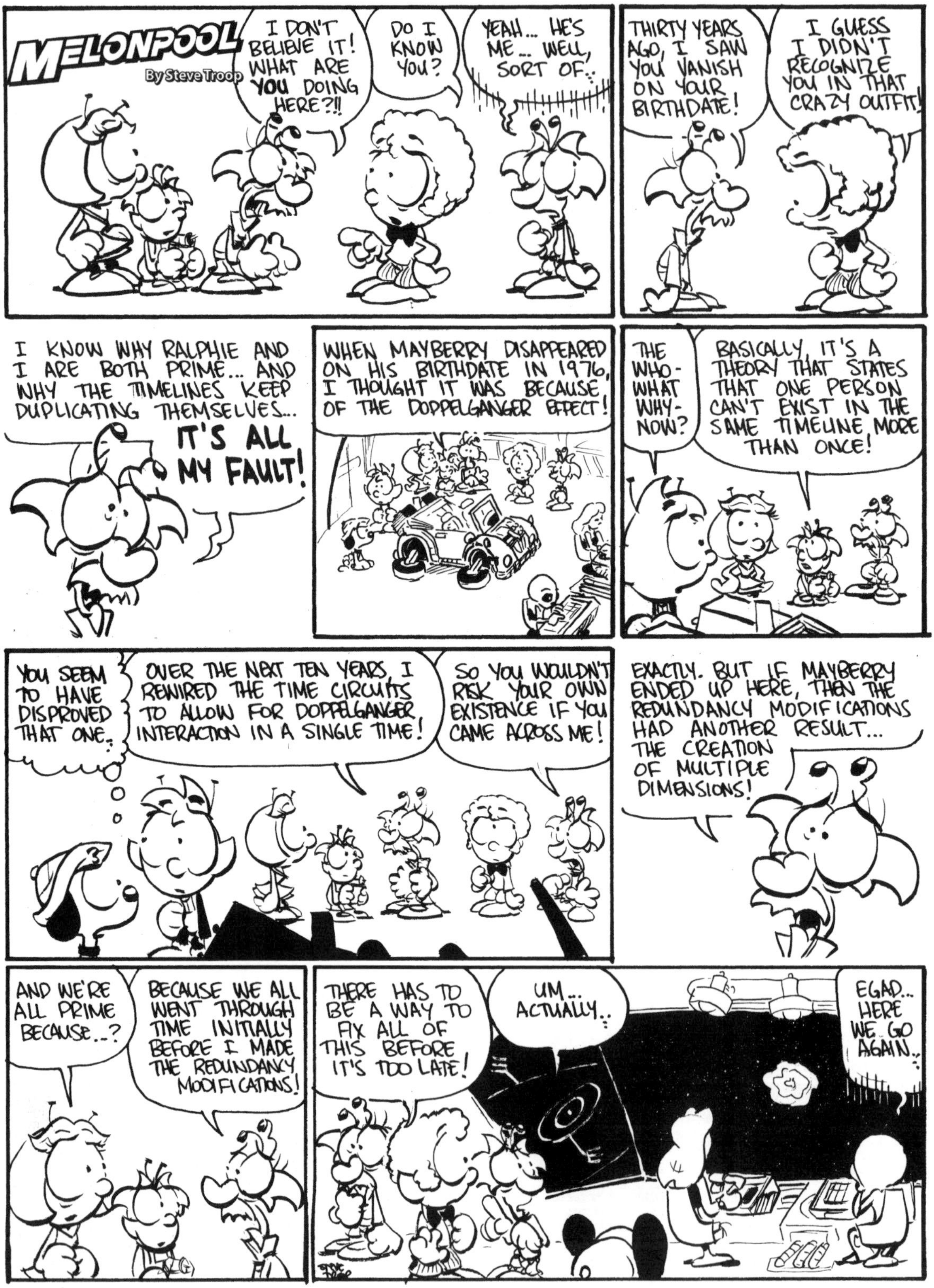
MELONPOOL
By Steve Troop
I DON'T BELIEVE IT! WHAT ARE YOU DOING HERE?!!
DO I KNOW YOU?
YEAH... HE'S ME... WELL, SORT OF...
THIRTY YEARS AGO, I SAW YOU VANISH ON YOUR BIRTHDATE!
I GUESS I DIDN'T RECOGNIZE YOU IN THAT CRAZY OUTFIT!
I KNOW WHY RALPHIE AND I ARE BOTH PRIME... AND WHY THE TIMELINES KEEP DUPLICATING THEMSELVES...
IT'S ALL MY FAULT!
WHEN MAYBERRY DISAPPEARED ON HIS BIRTHDATE IN 1976, I THOUGHT IT WAS BECAUSE OF THE DOPPELGANGER EFFECT!
THE WHO-WHAT WHY-NOW?
BASICALLY, IT'S A THEORY THAT STATES THAT ONE PERSON CAN'T EXIST IN THE SAME TIMELINE MORE THAN ONCE!
YOU SEEM TO HAVE DISPROVED THAT ONE...
OVER THE NEXT TEN YEARS, I REWIRED THE TIME CIRCUITS TO ALLOW FOR DOPPELGANGER INTERACTION IN A SINGLE TIME!
SO YOU WOULDN'T RISK YOUR OWN EXISTENCE IF YOU CAME ACROSS ME!
EXACTLY. BUT IF MAYBERRY ENDED UP HERE, THEN THE REDUNDANCY MODIFICATIONS HAD ANOTHER RESULT... THE CREATION OF MULTIPLE DIMENSIONS!
AND WE'RE ALL PRIME BECAUSE...?
BECAUSE WE ALL WENT THROUGH TIME INITIALLY BEFORE I MADE THE REDUNDANCY MODIFICATIONS!
THERE HAS TO BE A WAY TO FIX ALL OF THIS BEFORE IT'S TOO LATE!
UM... ACTUALLY...
EGAD... HERE WE GO AGAIN...

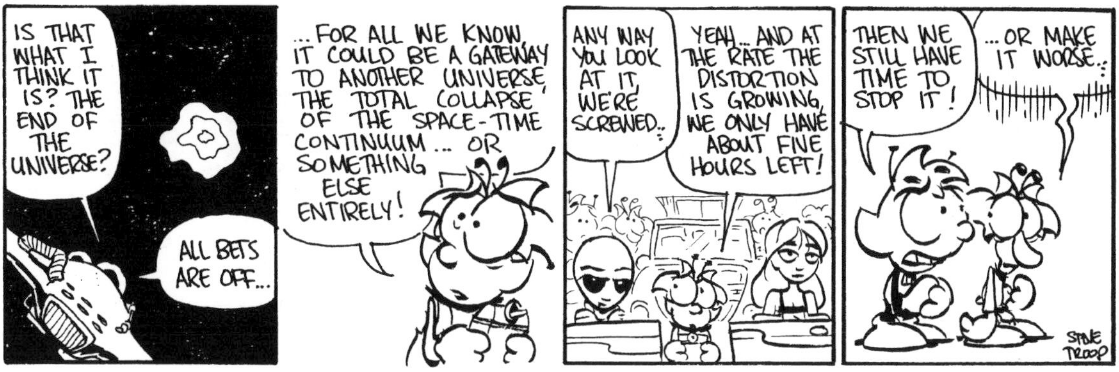
IS THAT WHAT I THINK IT IS? THE END OF THE UNIVERSE?
ALL BETS ARE OFF...
...FOR ALL WE KNOW, IT COULD BE A GATEWAY TO ANOTHER UNIVERSE, THE TOTAL COLLAPSE OF THE SPACE-TIME CONTINUUM... OR SOMETHING ELSE ENTIRELY!
ANY WAY YOU LOOK AT IT, WE'RE SCREWED.
YEAH... AND AT THE RATE THE DISTORTION IS GROWING, WE ONLY HAVE ABOUT FIVE HOURS LEFT!
THEN WE STILL HAVE TIME TO STOP IT!
...OR MAKE IT WORSE.
STEVE TROOP

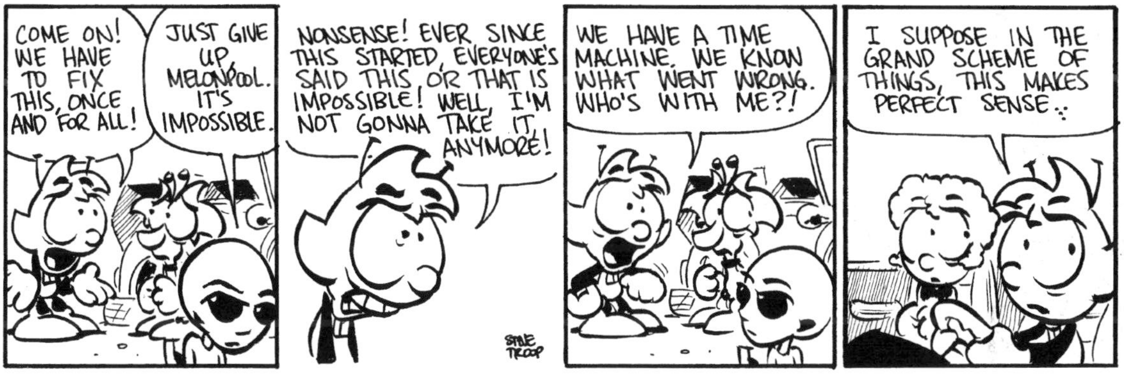
COME ON! WE HAVE TO FIX THIS, ONCE AND FOR ALL!
JUST GIVE UP, MELONPOOL. IT'S IMPOSSIBLE.
NONSENSE! EVER SINCE THIS STARTED, EVERYONE'S SAID THIS OR THAT IS IMPOSSIBLE! WELL, I'M NOT GONNA TAKE IT ANYMORE!
STEVE TROOP
WE HAVE A TIME MACHINE. WE KNOW WHAT WENT WRONG. WHO'S WITH ME?!
I SUPPOSE IN THE GRAND SCHEME OF THINGS, THIS MAKES PERFECT SENSE.

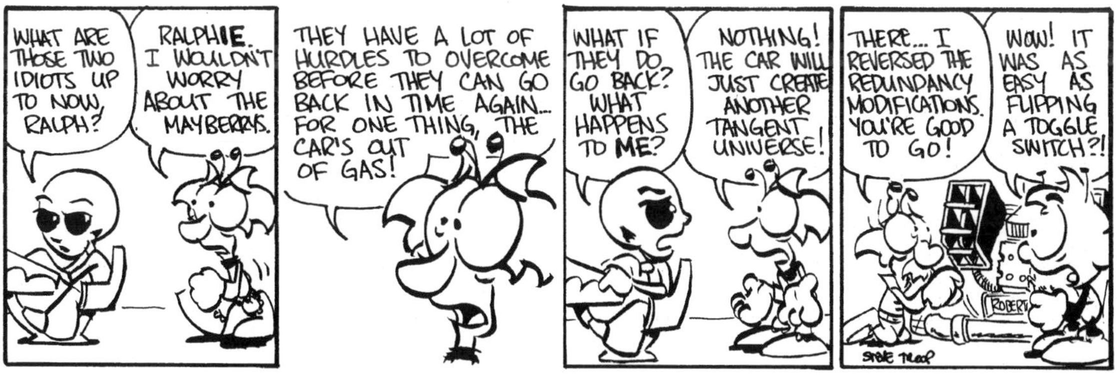
WHAT ARE THOSE TWO IDIOTS UP TO NOW, RALPH?
RALPHIE. I WOULDN'T WORRY ABOUT THE MAYBERRYS.
THEY HAVE A LOT OF HURDLES TO OVERCOME BEFORE THEY CAN GO BACK IN TIME AGAIN... FOR ONE THING, THE CAR'S OUT OF GAS!
WHAT IF THEY DO GO BACK? WHAT HAPPENS TO ME?
NOTHING! THE CAR WILL JUST CREATE ANOTHER TANGENT UNIVERSE!
THERE... I REVERSED THE REDUNDANCY MODIFICATIONS. YOU'RE GOOD TO GO!
WOW! IT WAS AS EASY AS FLIPPING A TOGGLE SWITCH?!
ROBERT
STEVE TROOP

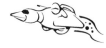

The comic that the third frame was taken from can be seen on TUM I, page 131.

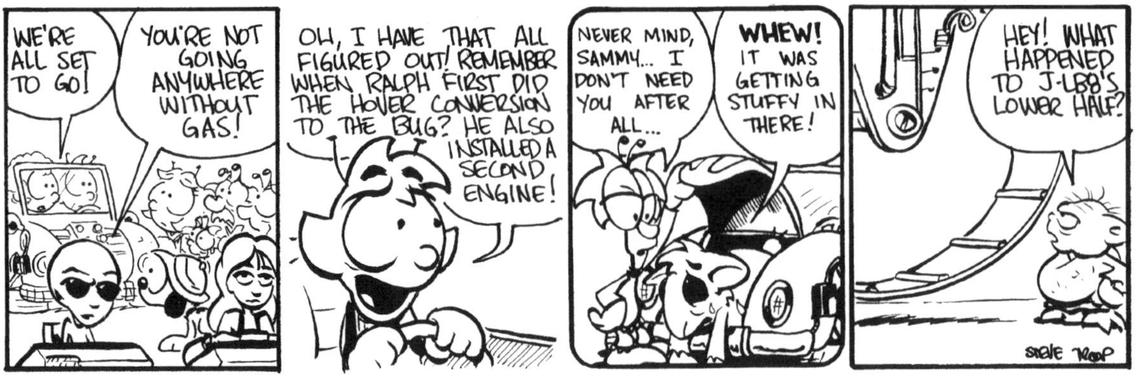
WE'RE ALL SET TO GO!
YOU'RE NOT GOING ANYWHERE WITHOUT GAS!
OH, I HAVE THAT ALL FIGURED OUT! REMEMBER WHEN RALPH FIRST DID THE HOVER CONVERSION TO THE BUG? HE ALSO INSTALLED A SECOND ENGINE!
NEVER MIND, SAMMY... I DON'T NEED YOU AFTER ALL...
WHEW! IT WAS GETTING STUFFY IN THERE!
HEY! WHAT HAPPENED TO J-LB8'S LOWER HALF?
STEVE TROOP

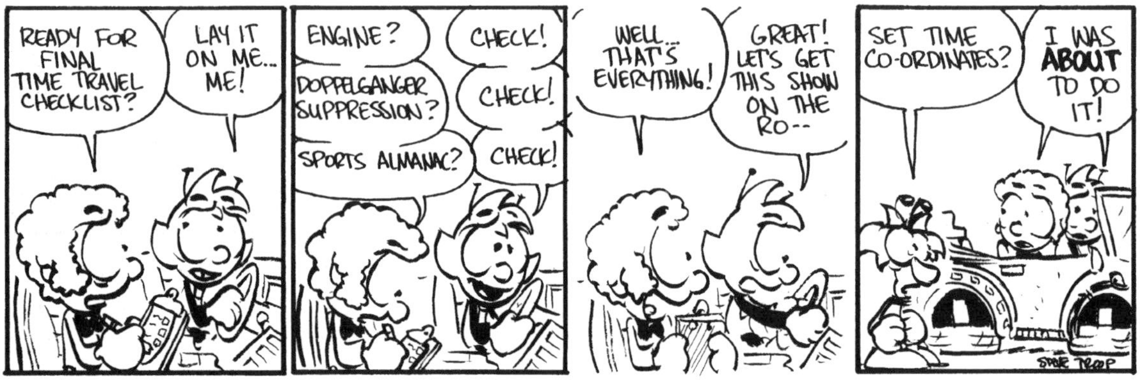
READY FOR FINAL TIME TRAVEL CHECKLIST?
LAY IT ON ME... ME!
ENGINE?
CHECK!
DOPPELGANGER SUPPRESSION?
CHECK!
SPORTS ALMANAC?
CHECK!
WELL... THAT'S EVERYTHING!
GREAT! LET'S GET THIS SHOW ON THE RO--
SET TIME CO-ORDINATES?
I WAS ABOUT TO DO IT!
STEVE TROOP

One of the things that's always bothered me about most (non-*Melonpool*) time travel storylines is the tendency for time travelers to travel both through space and time. If someone travels back from 1996 San Francisco, then he should arrive in 1964 San Francisco—not France or New York or wherever the story should take place. When *Melonpool* travels through time and space, at least I try to explain it.

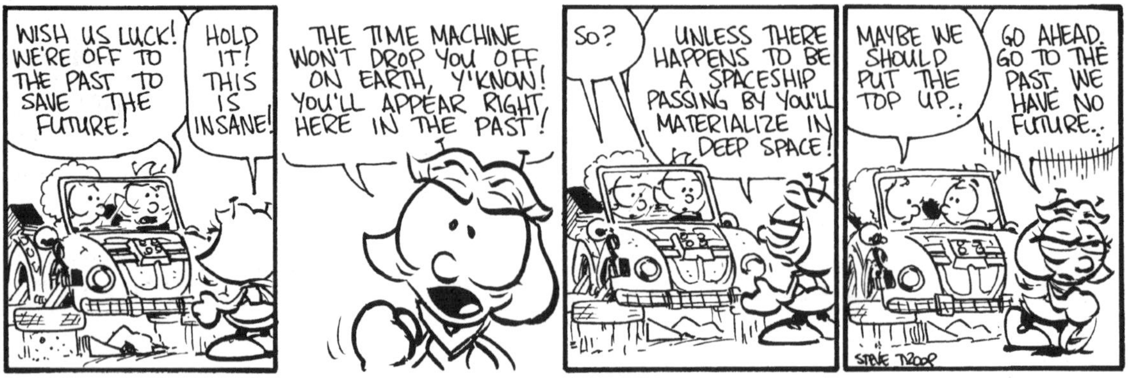
WISH US LUCK! WE'RE OFF TO THE PAST TO SAVE THE FUTURE!
HOLD IT! THIS IS INSANE!
THE TIME MACHINE WON'T DROP YOU OFF ON EARTH, Y'KNOW! YOU'LL APPEAR RIGHT HERE IN THE PAST!
SO?
UNLESS THERE HAPPENS TO BE A SPACESHIP PASSING BY YOU'LL MATERIALIZE IN DEEP SPACE!
MAYBE WE SHOULD PUT THE TOP UP..
GO AHEAD. GO TO THE PAST. WE HAVE NO FUTURE..
STEVE TROOP

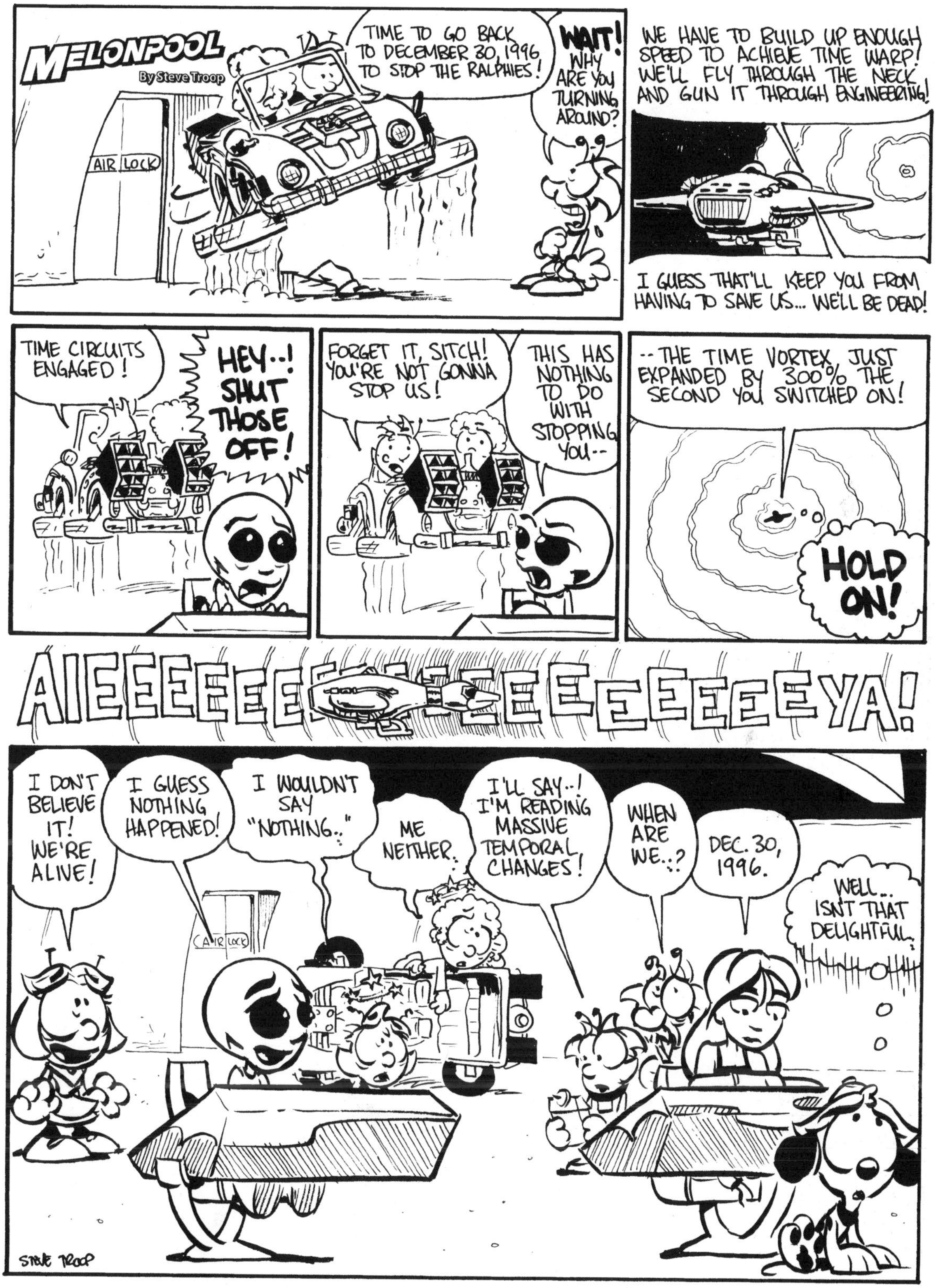
MELONPOOL
By Steve Troop
TIME TO GO BACK TO DECEMBER 30, 1996 TO STOP THE RALPHIES!
WAIT! WHY ARE YOU TURNING AROUND?
AIR LOCK
WE HAVE TO BUILD UP ENOUGH SPEED TO ACHIEVE TIME WARP! WE'LL FLY THROUGH THE NECK AND GUN IT THROUGH ENGINEERING!
I GUESS THAT'LL KEEP YOU FROM HAVING TO SAVE US... WE'LL BE DEAD!
TIME CIRCUITS ENGAGED!
HEY..! SHUT THOSE OFF!
FORGET IT, SITCH! YOU'RE NOT GONNA STOP US!
THIS HAS NOTHING TO DO WITH STOPPING YOU--
--THE TIME VORTEX JUST EXPANDED BY 300% THE SECOND YOU SWITCHED ON!
HOLD ON!
AIEEEEEEEEEEEEEEEEEYA!
I DON'T BELIEVE IT! WE'RE ALIVE!
I GUESS NOTHING HAPPENED!
I WOULDN'T SAY "NOTHING.."
ME NEITHER..
I'LL SAY..! I'M READING MASSIVE TEMPORAL CHANGES!
WHEN ARE WE..?
DEC. 30, 1996.
WELL... ISN'T THAT DELIGHTFUL..
AIR LOCK
STEVE TROOP

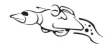

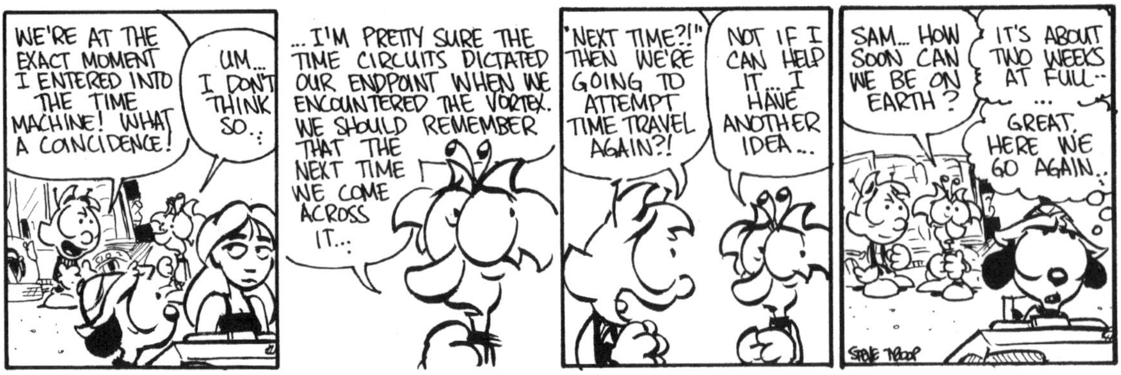
WE'RE AT THE EXACT MOMENT I ENTERED INTO THE TIME MACHINE! WHAT A COINCIDENCE!
UM... I DON'T THINK SO...
...I'M PRETTY SURE THE TIME CIRCUITS DICTATED OUR ENDPOINT WHEN WE ENCOUNTERED THE VORTEX. WE SHOULD REMEMBER THAT THE NEXT TIME WE COME ACROSS IT...
"NEXT TIME?!" THEN WE'RE GOING TO ATTEMPT TIME TRAVEL AGAIN?!
NOT IF I CAN HELP IT... I HAVE ANOTHER IDEA...
SAM... HOW SOON CAN WE BE ON EARTH?
IT'S ABOUT TWO WEEKS AT FULL...
... GREAT. HERE WE GO AGAIN...
STEVE TROOP

In both timelines, Jalea started out life as a protocol droid similar to C-3PO named J-LB8 (See TUM III, pages 78–91). J-LB8 had a rather checkered past, and was disassembled sometime in the mid-1980s. Ralph found most of her parts and rebuilt her as a pop star robot, but her original *Star Wars* past always has a way of catching up with her....

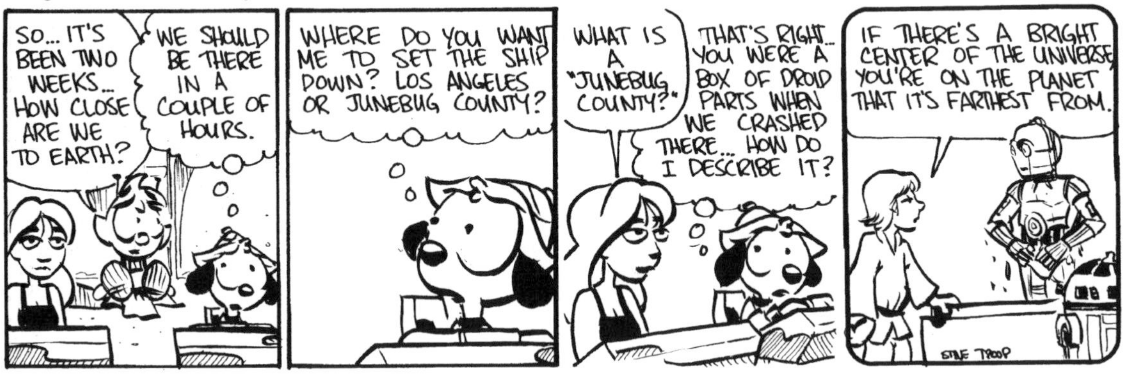
SO... IT'S BEEN TWO WEEKS... HOW CLOSE ARE WE TO EARTH?
WE SHOULD BE THERE IN A COUPLE OF HOURS.
WHERE DO YOU WANT ME TO SET THE SHIP DOWN? LOS ANGELES OR JUNEBUG COUNTY?
WHAT IS A "JUNEBUG COUNTY?"
THAT'S RIGHT... YOU WERE A BOX OF DROID PARTS WHEN WE CRASHED THERE... HOW DO I DESCRIBE IT?
IF THERE'S A BRIGHT CENTER OF THE UNIVERSE, YOU'RE ON THE PLANET THAT IT'S FARTHEST FROM.
STEVE TROOP

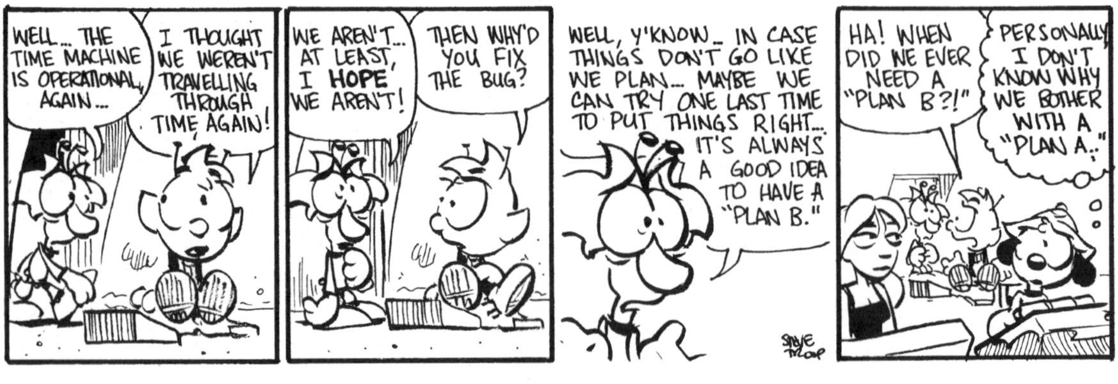
WELL... THE TIME MACHINE IS OPERATIONAL AGAIN...
I THOUGHT WE WEREN'T TRAVELLING THROUGH TIME AGAIN!
WE AREN'T... AT LEAST, I **HOPE** WE AREN'T!
THEN WHY'D YOU FIX THE BUG?
WELL, Y'KNOW... IN CASE THINGS DON'T GO LIKE WE PLAN... MAYBE WE CAN TRY ONE LAST TIME TO PUT THINGS RIGHT... IT'S ALWAYS A GOOD IDEA TO HAVE A "PLAN B."
STEVE TROOP
HA! WHEN DID WE EVER NEED A "PLAN B?!"
PERSONALLY, I DON'T KNOW WHY WE BOTHER WITH A "PLAN A."

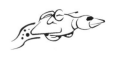

The *Steel Duck* crash landed in Junebug County on April 28, 1996 and remained there for the first few years of the strip (see TUM I; TUM II, pages 8–89).

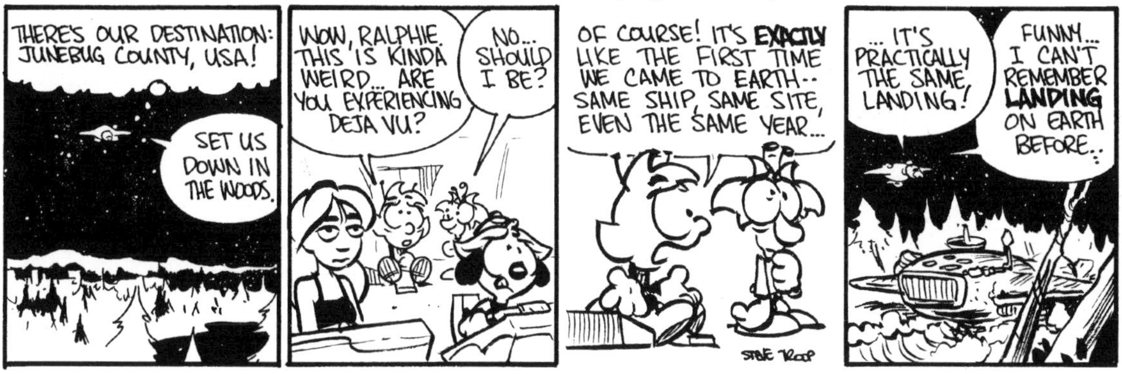
THERE'S OUR DESTINATION: JUNEBUG COUNTY, USA!
SET US DOWN IN THE WOODS.
WOW, RALPHIE. THIS IS KINDA WEIRD... ARE YOU EXPERIENCING DEJA VU?
NO... SHOULD I BE?
OF COURSE! IT'S EXACTLY LIKE THE FIRST TIME WE CAME TO EARTH -- SAME SHIP, SAME SITE, EVEN THE SAME YEAR...
... IT'S PRACTICALLY THE SAME LANDING!
FUNNY... I CAN'T REMEMBER LANDING ON EARTH BEFORE...
STEVE TROOP

This strip references the second strip on page 67 of TUM I.

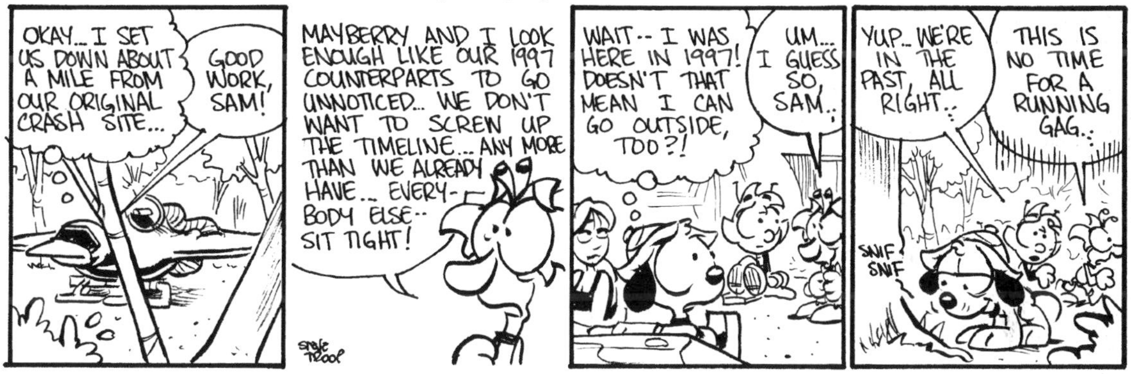
OKAY... I SET US DOWN ABOUT A MILE FROM OUR ORIGINAL CRASH SITE...
GOOD WORK, SAM!
MAYBERRY AND I LOOK ENOUGH LIKE OUR 1997 COUNTERPARTS TO GO UNNOTICED... WE DON'T WANT TO SCREW UP THE TIMELINE... ANY MORE THAN WE ALREADY HAVE... EVERYBODY ELSE -- SIT TIGHT!
STEVE TROOP
WAIT -- I WAS HERE IN 1997! DOESN'T THAT MEAN I CAN GO OUTSIDE, TOO?!
UM... I GUESS SO, SAM...
YUP... WE'RE IN THE PAST, ALL RIGHT...
THIS IS NO TIME FOR A RUNNING GAG...
SNIF SNIF

The next sequence of strips hook up to the **Ralphie Resolution** storyline (see TUM I, pages 172–182).

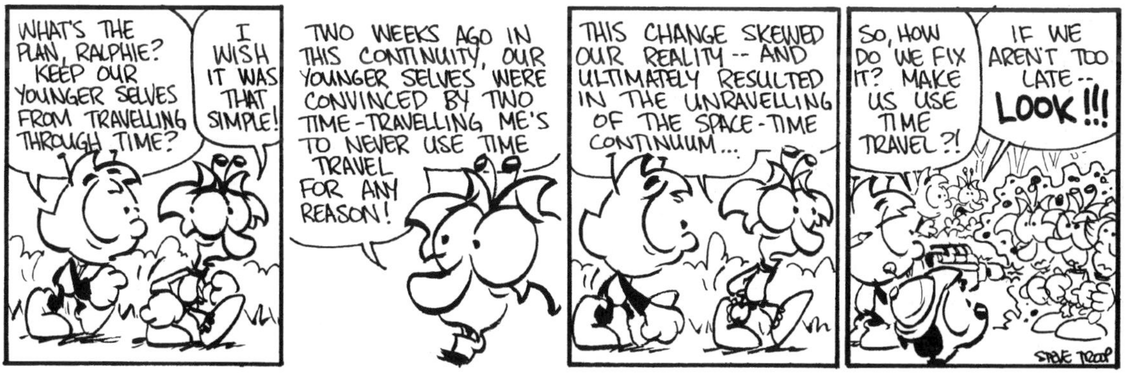
WHAT'S THE PLAN, RALPHIE? KEEP OUR YOUNGER SELVES FROM TRAVELLING THROUGH TIME?
I WISH IT WAS THAT SIMPLE!
TWO WEEKS AGO IN THIS CONTINUITY, OUR YOUNGER SELVES WERE CONVINCED BY TWO TIME-TRAVELLING ME'S TO NEVER USE TIME TRAVEL FOR ANY REASON!
THIS CHANGE SKEWED OUR REALITY -- AND ULTIMATELY RESULTED IN THE UNRAVELLING OF THE SPACE-TIME CONTINUUM...
SO, HOW DO WE FIX IT? MAKE US USE TIME TRAVEL?!
IF WE AREN'T TOO LATE -- LOOK!!!
STEVE TROOP

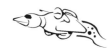

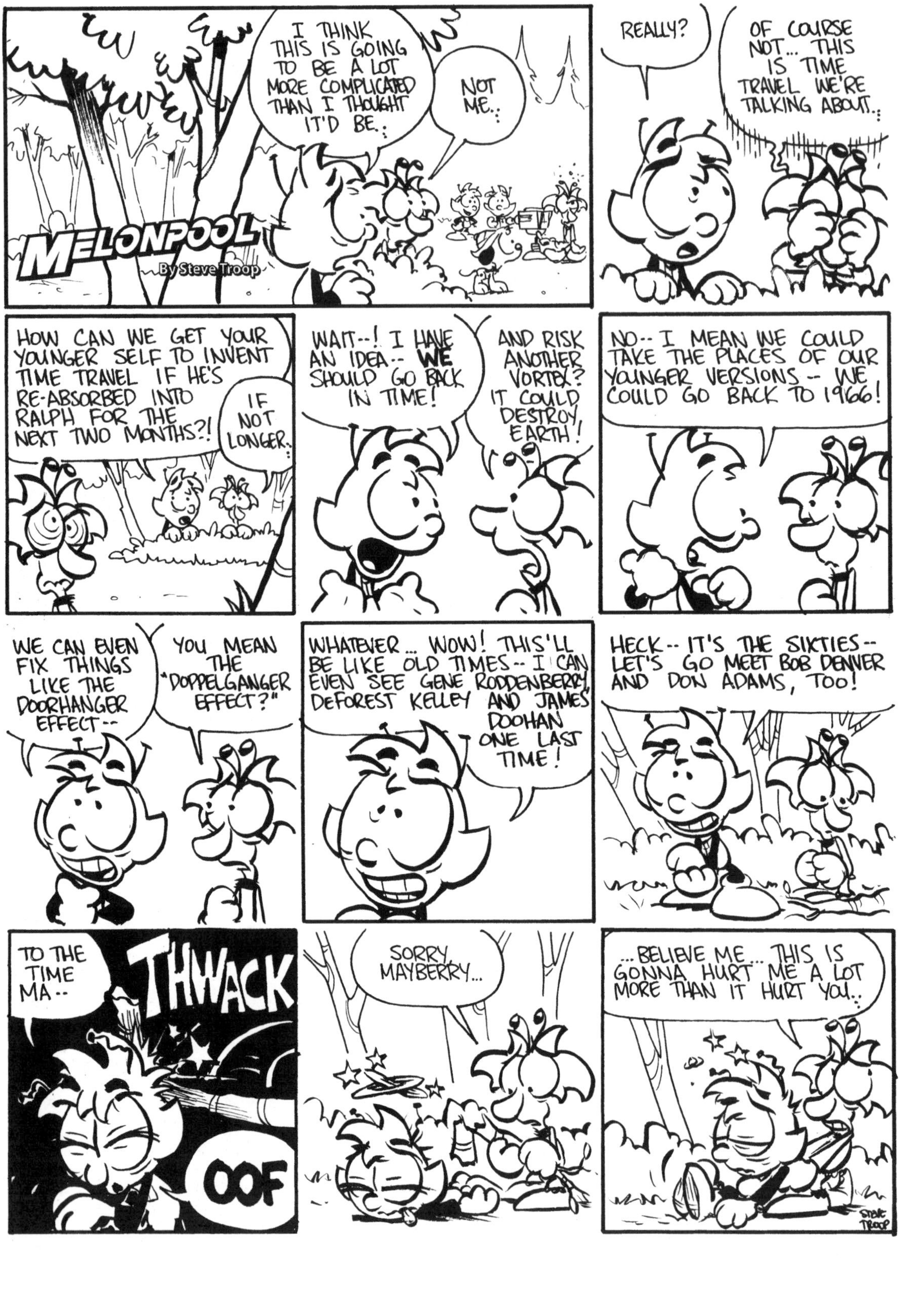
MELONPOOL
By Steve Troop
I THINK THIS IS GOING TO BE A LOT MORE COMPLICATED THAN I THOUGHT IT'D BE...
NOT ME...
REALLY?
OF COURSE NOT... THIS IS TIME TRAVEL WE'RE TALKING ABOUT...
HOW CAN WE GET YOUR YOUNGER SELF TO INVENT TIME TRAVEL IF HE'S RE-ABSORBED INTO RALPH FOR THE NEXT TWO MONTHS?!
IF NOT LONGER...
WAIT--! I HAVE AN IDEA-- WE SHOULD GO BACK IN TIME!
AND RISK ANOTHER VORTEX? IT COULD DESTROY EARTH!
NO-- I MEAN WE COULD TAKE THE PLACES OF OUR YOUNGER VERSIONS -- WE COULD GO BACK TO 1966!
WE CAN EVEN FIX THINGS LIKE THE DOORHANGER EFFECT--
YOU MEAN THE "DOPPELGANGER EFFECT?"
WHATEVER... WOW! THIS'LL BE LIKE OLD TIMES-- I CAN EVEN SEE GENE RODDENBERRY, DEFOREST KELLEY AND JAMES DOOHAN ONE LAST TIME!
HECK-- IT'S THE SIXTIES-- LET'S GO MEET BOB DENVER AND DON ADAMS, TOO!
TO THE TIME MA--
THWACK
OOF
SORRY MAYBERRY...
...BELIEVE ME... THIS IS GONNA HURT ME A LOT MORE THAN IT HURT YOU...
STEVE TROOP

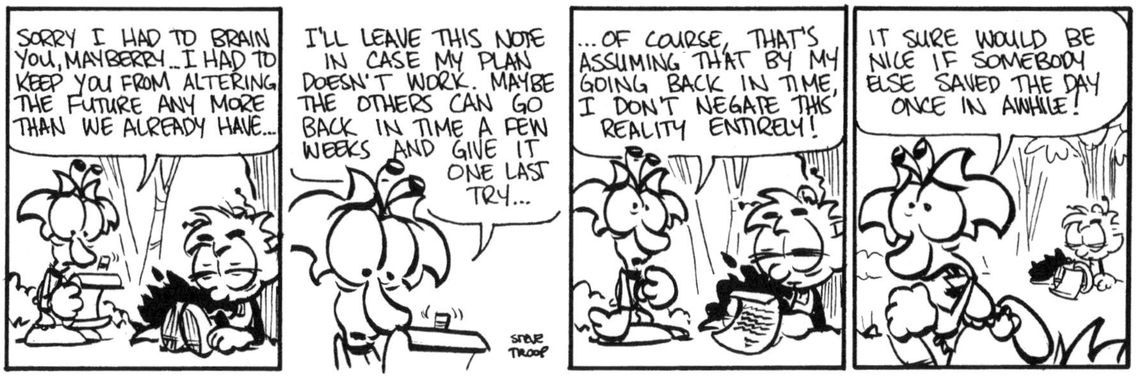
SORRY I HAD TO BRAIN YOU, MAYBERRY... I HAD TO KEEP YOU FROM ALTERING THE FUTURE ANY MORE THAN WE ALREADY HAVE...
I'LL LEAVE THIS NOTE IN CASE MY PLAN DOESN'T WORK. MAYBE THE OTHERS CAN GO BACK IN TIME A FEW WEEKS AND GIVE IT ONE LAST TRY...
STEVE TROOP
...OF COURSE, THAT'S ASSUMING THAT BY MY GOING BACK IN TIME, I DON'T NEGATE THIS REALITY ENTIRELY!
IT SURE WOULD BE NICE IF SOMEBODY ELSE SAVED THE DAY ONCE IN AWHILE!

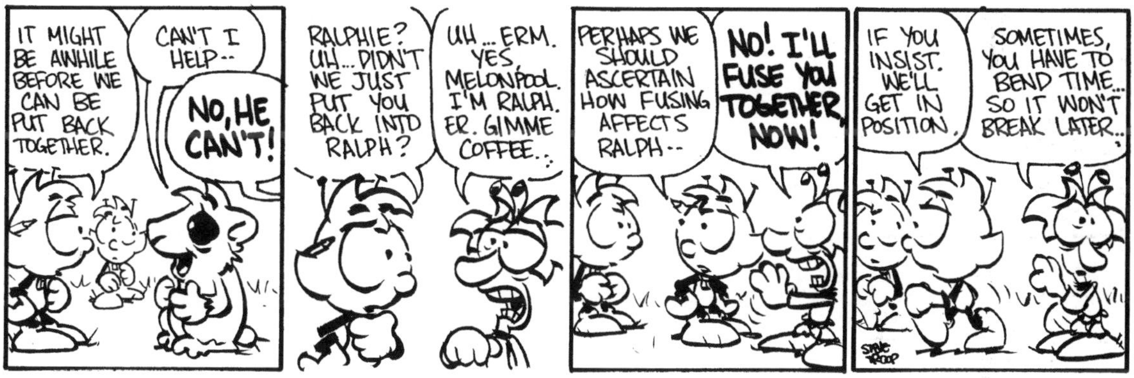
IT MIGHT BE AWHILE BEFORE WE CAN BE PUT BACK TOGETHER.
CAN'T I HELP--
NO, HE CAN'T!
RALPHIE? UH... DIDN'T WE JUST PUT YOU BACK INTO RALPH?
UH... ERM. YES, MELONPOOL. I'M RALPH. ER. GIMME COFFEE...
PERHAPS WE SHOULD ASCERTAIN HOW FUSING AFFECTS RALPH--
NO! I'LL FUSE YOU TOGETHER, NOW!
IF YOU INSIST. WE'LL GET IN POSITION.
SOMETIMES, YOU HAVE TO BEND TIME... SO IT WON'T BREAK LATER...
STEVE TROOP

This strip hooks up with the bottom strip on page 148 of TUM I. Mayberry likes to use time machines for just about everything—including his breakfast choices!

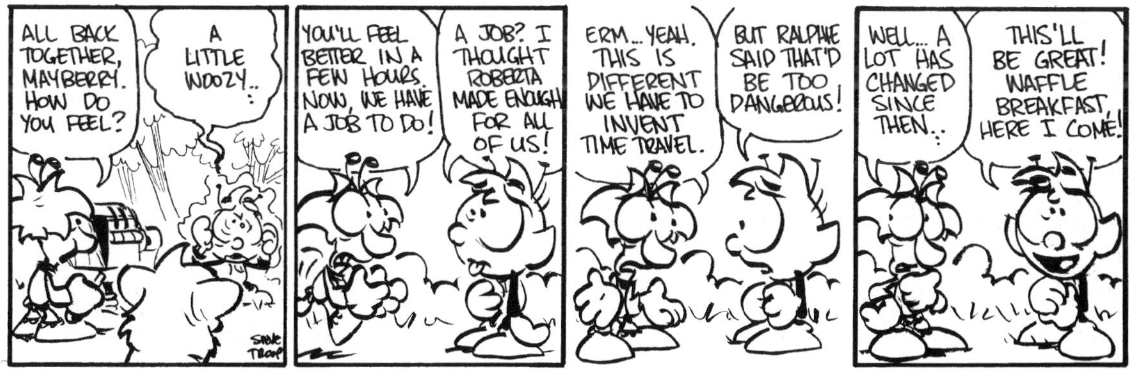
ALL BACK TOGETHER, MAYBERRY. HOW DO YOU FEEL?
A LITTLE WOOZY...
STEVE TROOP
YOU'LL FEEL BETTER IN A FEW HOURS. NOW, WE HAVE A JOB TO DO!
A JOB? I THOUGHT ROBERTA MADE ENOUGH FOR ALL OF US!
ERM... YEAH. THIS IS DIFFERENT. WE HAVE TO INVENT TIME TRAVEL.
BUT RALPHIE SAID THAT'D BE TOO DANGEROUS!
WELL... A LOT HAS CHANGED SINCE THEN...
THIS'LL BE GREAT! WAFFLE BREAKFAST, HERE I COME!

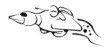

The next batch of strips hook up to the original **Time Travel Saga** (see TUM I, pages 148–165).

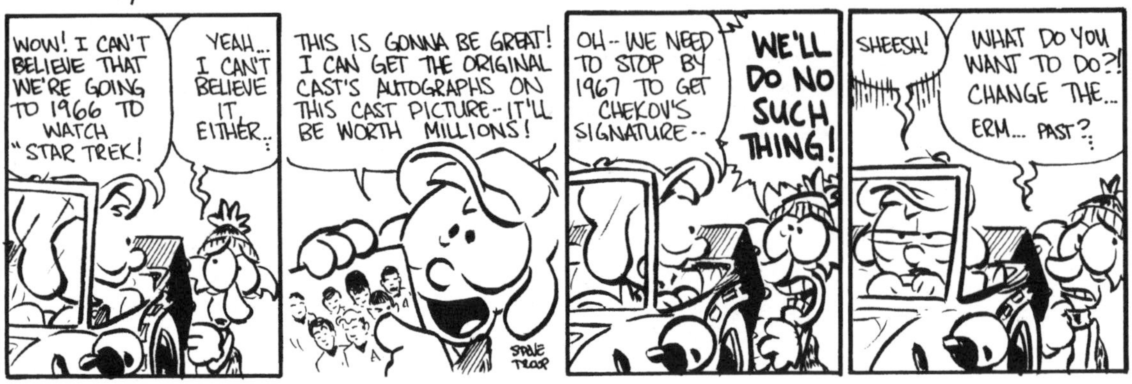
WOW! I CAN'T BELIEVE THAT WE'RE GOING TO 1966 TO WATCH "STAR TREK!
YEAH... I CAN'T BELIEVE IT, EITHER...
THIS IS GONNA BE GREAT! I CAN GET THE ORIGINAL CAST'S AUTOGRAPHS ON THIS CAST PICTURE--IT'LL BE WORTH MILLIONS!
OH--WE NEED TO STOP BY 1967 TO GET CHEKOV'S SIGNATURE--
WE'LL DO NO SUCH THING!
SHEESH!
WHAT DO YOU WANT TO DO?! CHANGE THE... ERM... PAST?...
STEVE TROOP

The first three panels are direct lifts from the original **Time Travel Saga** in TUM I (second strip on page 151; second strip on page 157; and third strip on page 158). If you haven't figured it out already, Mayberry causes a lot of problems for Ralphie whenever they travel through time!

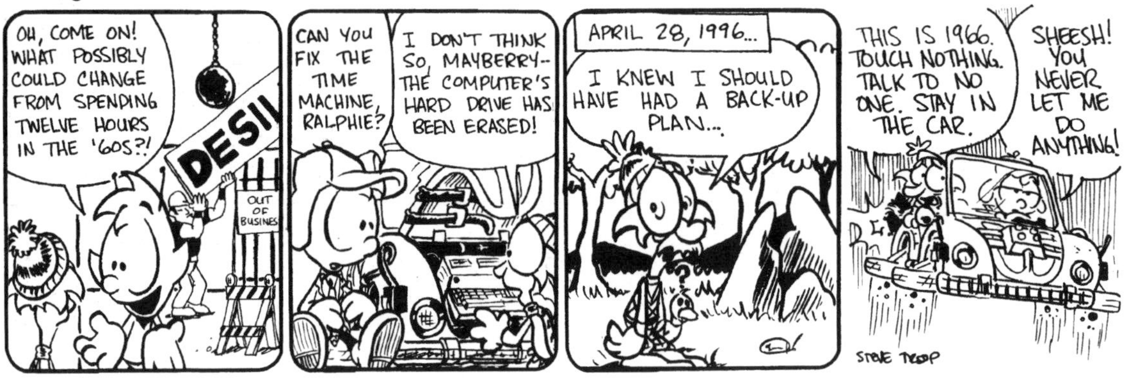
OH, COME ON! WHAT POSSIBLY COULD CHANGE FROM SPENDING TWELVE HOURS IN THE '60S?!
DESI
OUT OF BUSINES
CAN YOU FIX THE TIME MACHINE, RALPHIE?
I DON'T THINK SO, MAYBERRY--THE COMPUTER'S HARD DRIVE HAS BEEN ERASED!
APRIL 28, 1996...
I KNEW I SHOULD HAVE HAD A BACK-UP PLAN...
THIS IS 1966. TOUCH NOTHING. TALK TO NO ONE. STAY IN THE CAR.
SHEESH! YOU NEVER LET ME DO ANYTHING!
STEVE TROOP

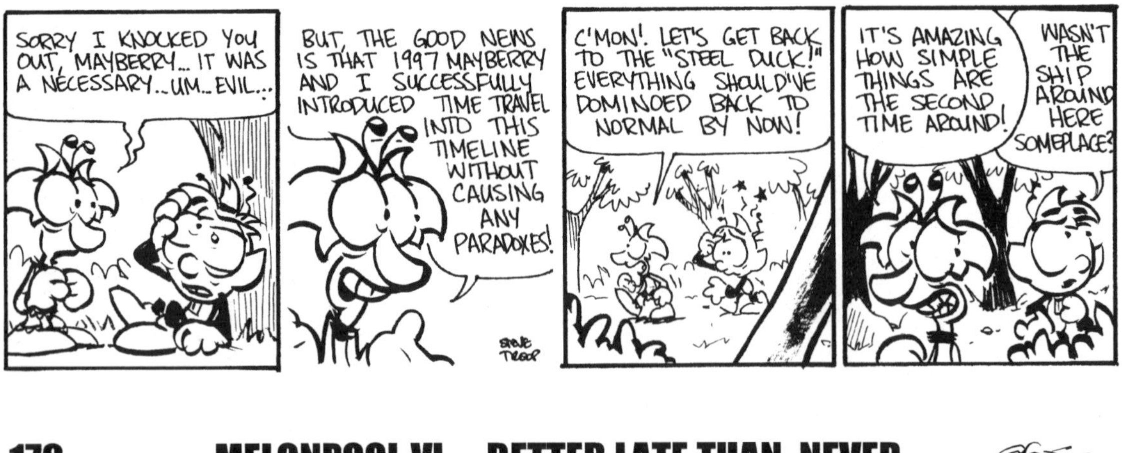
SORRY I KNOCKED YOU OUT, MAYBERRY... IT WAS A NECESSARY...UM...EVIL...
BUT, THE GOOD NEWS IS THAT 1997 MAYBERRY AND I SUCCESSFULLY INTRODUCED TIME TRAVEL INTO THIS TIMELINE WITHOUT CAUSING ANY PARADOXES!
STEVE TROOP
C'MON! LET'S GET BACK TO THE "STEEL DUCK!" EVERYTHING SHOULD'VE DOMINOED BACK TO NORMAL BY NOW!
IT'S AMAZING HOW SIMPLE THINGS ARE THE SECOND TIME AROUND!
WASN'T THE SHIP AROUND HERE SOMEPLACE?

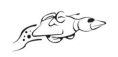

Zinoboppians freeze solid whenever something happens that they can't deal with. The last time it happened was during the **Loose Ends** storyline (see TUM III, pages 133–150).

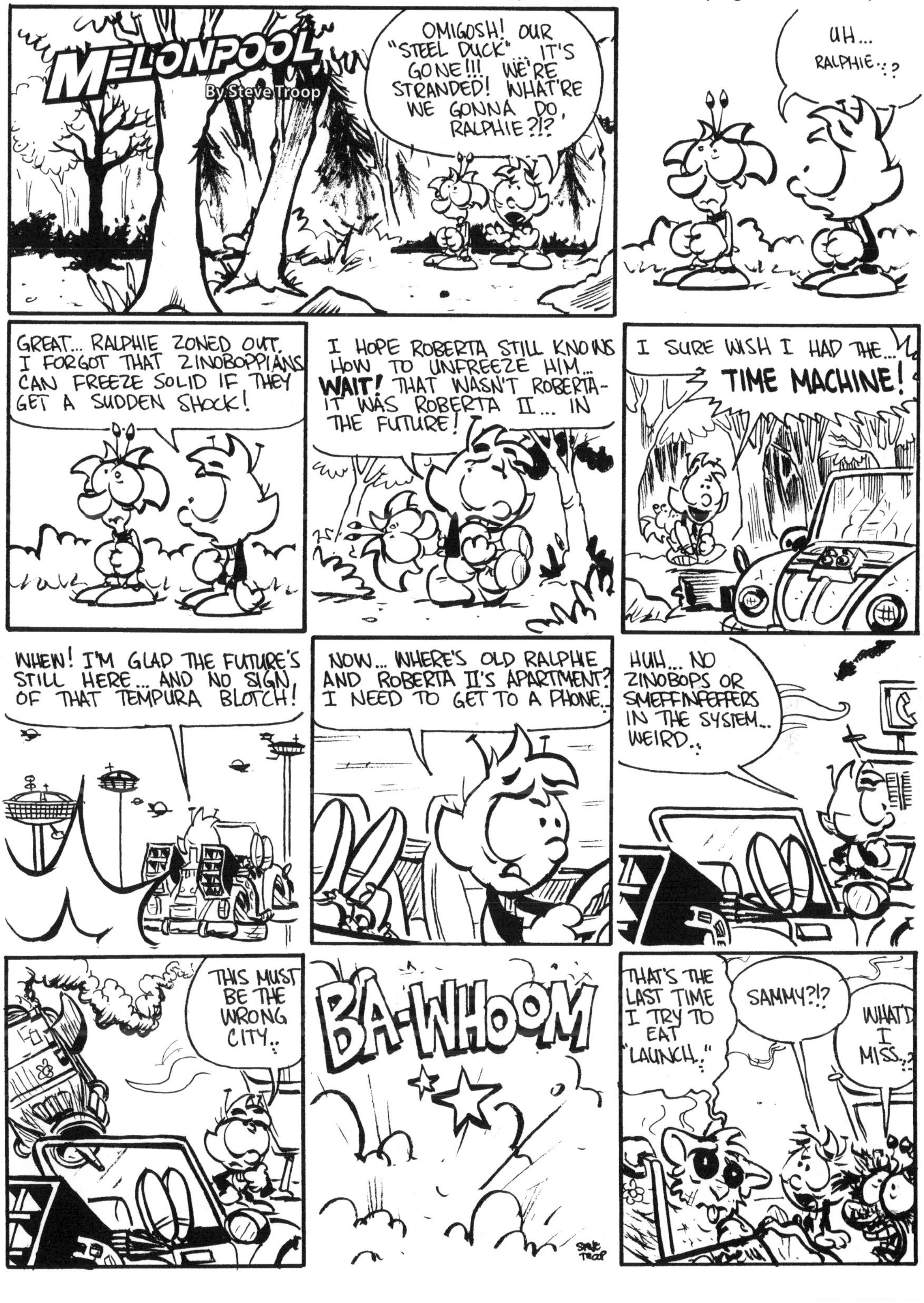

MELONPOOL
By Steve Troop
OMIGOSH! OUR "STEEL DUCK"... IT'S GONE!!! WE'RE STRANDED! WHAT'RE WE GONNA DO, RALPHIE?!?
UH... RALPHIE..?
GREAT... RALPHIE ZONED OUT. I FORGOT THAT ZINOBOPPIANS CAN FREEZE SOLID IF THEY GET A SUDDEN SHOCK!
I HOPE ROBERTA STILL KNOWS HOW TO UNFREEZE HIM... WAIT! THAT WASN'T ROBERTA- IT WAS ROBERTA II... IN THE FUTURE!
I SURE WISH I HAD THE... TIME MACHINE!
WHEW! I'M GLAD THE FUTURE'S STILL HERE... AND NO SIGN OF THAT TEMPURA BLOTCH!
NOW... WHERE'S OLD RALPHIE AND ROBERTA II'S APARTMENT? I NEED TO GET TO A PHONE..
HUH... NO ZINOBOPS OR SMEFFINFEFFERS IN THE SYSTEM... WEIRD..
THIS MUST BE THE WRONG CITY..
BA-WHOOM
THAT'S THE LAST TIME I TRY TO EAT "LAUNCH."
SAMMY?!?
WHAT'D I MISS..?
STEVE TROOP

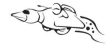

This next sequence hooks up to the **Sammy to the Future** storyline (TUM III, 26–55). Something tells me the reason that *Melonpool* wasn't more popular may have been because it was a tad to self-referential for most of the general population....

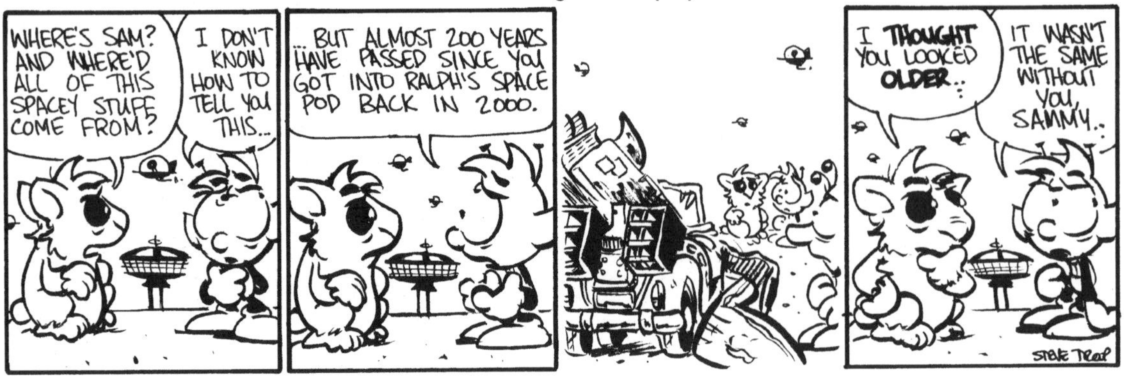
WHERE'S SAM? AND WHERE'D ALL OF THIS SPACEY STUFF COME FROM?
I DON'T KNOW HOW TO TELL YOU THIS...
... BUT ALMOST 200 YEARS HAVE PASSED SINCE YOU GOT INTO RALPH'S SPACE POD BACK IN 2000.
I **THOUGHT** YOU LOOKED **OLDER**...
IT WASN'T THE SAME WITHOUT YOU, SAMMY...
STEVE TROOP

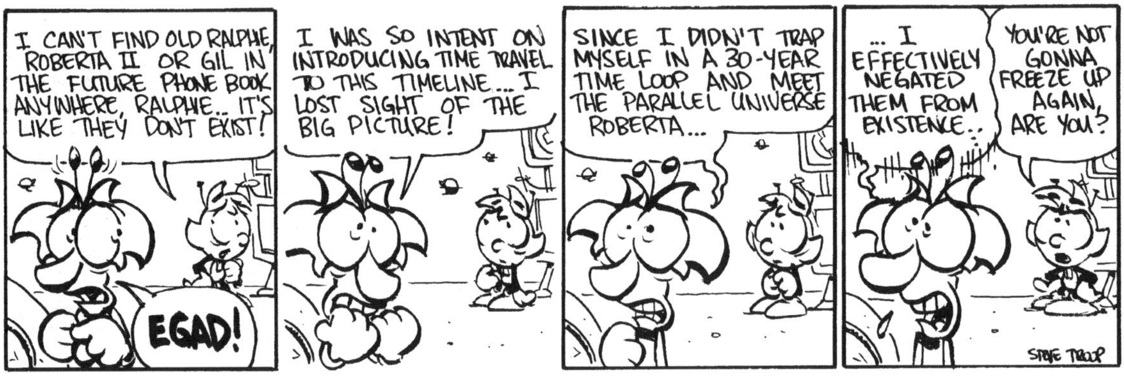
I CAN'T FIND OLD RALPHIE, ROBERTA II OR GIL IN THE FUTURE PHONE BOOK ANYWHERE, RALPHIE... IT'S LIKE THEY DON'T EXIST!
EGAD!
I WAS SO INTENT ON INTRODUCING TIME TRAVEL TO THIS TIMELINE.... I LOST SIGHT OF THE BIG PICTURE!
SINCE I DIDN'T TRAP MYSELF IN A 30-YEAR TIME LOOP AND MEET THE PARALLEL UNIVERSE ROBERTA...
... I EFFECTIVELY NEGATED THEM FROM EXISTENCE...
YOU'RE NOT GONNA FREEZE UP AGAIN, ARE YOU?
STEVE TROOP

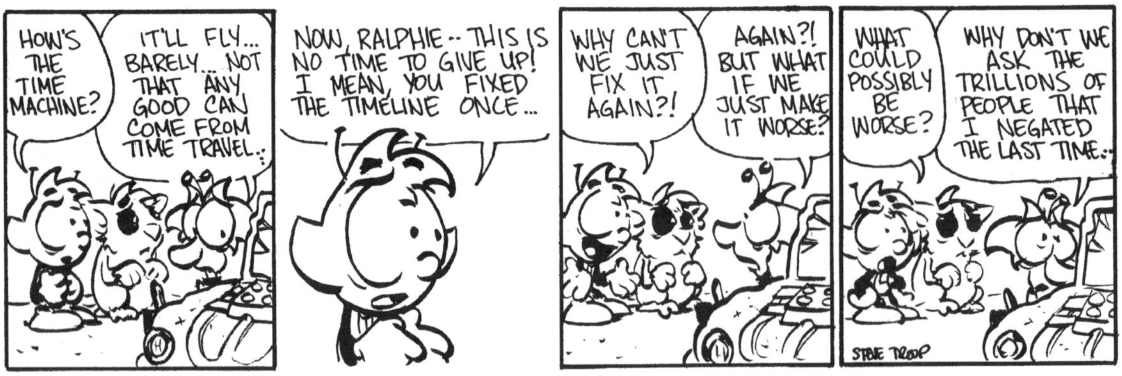
HOW'S THE TIME MACHINE?
IT'LL FLY... BARELY... NOT THAT ANY GOOD CAN COME FROM TIME TRAVEL...
NOW, RALPHIE -- THIS IS NO TIME TO GIVE UP! I MEAN, YOU FIXED THE TIMELINE ONCE...
WHY CAN'T WE JUST FIX IT AGAIN?!
AGAIN?! BUT WHAT IF WE JUST MAKE IT WORSE?
WHAT COULD POSSIBLY BE WORSE?
WHY DON'T WE ASK THE TRILLIONS OF PEOPLE THAT I NEGATED THE LAST TIME...
STEVE TROOP

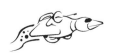

This strip hooks up to two strips from TUM III—the first strip on page 23 and the second strip on page 44. Sometimes time travel comics save me time by simple fact that I can reuse entire panels!

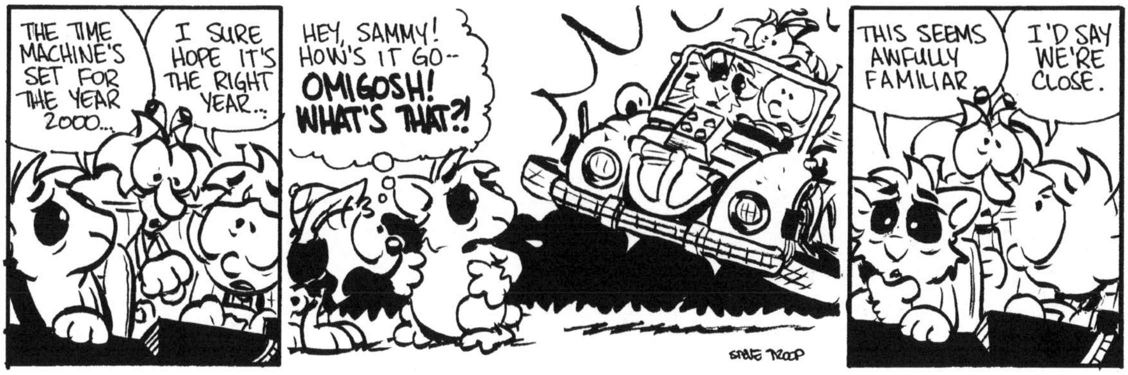
THE TIME MACHINE'S SET FOR THE YEAR 2000...
I SURE HOPE IT'S THE RIGHT YEAR...
HEY, SAMMY! HOW'S IT GO-- OMIGOSH! WHAT'S THAT?!
THIS SEEMS AWFULLY FAMILIAR...
I'D SAY WE'RE CLOSE.
STEVE TROOP

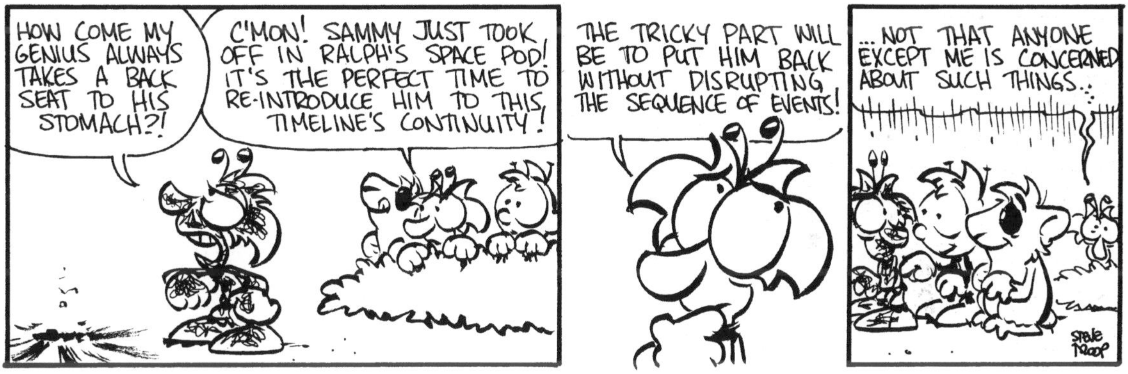
HOW COME MY GENIUS ALWAYS TAKES A BACK SEAT TO HIS STOMACH?!
C'MON! SAMMY JUST TOOK OFF IN RALPH'S SPACE POD! IT'S THE PERFECT TIME TO RE-INTRODUCE HIM TO THIS TIMELINE'S CONTINUITY!
THE TRICKY PART WILL BE TO PUT HIM BACK WITHOUT DISRUPTING THE SEQUENCE OF EVENTS!
...NOT THAT ANYONE EXCEPT ME IS CONCERNED ABOUT SUCH THINGS...
STEVE TROOP

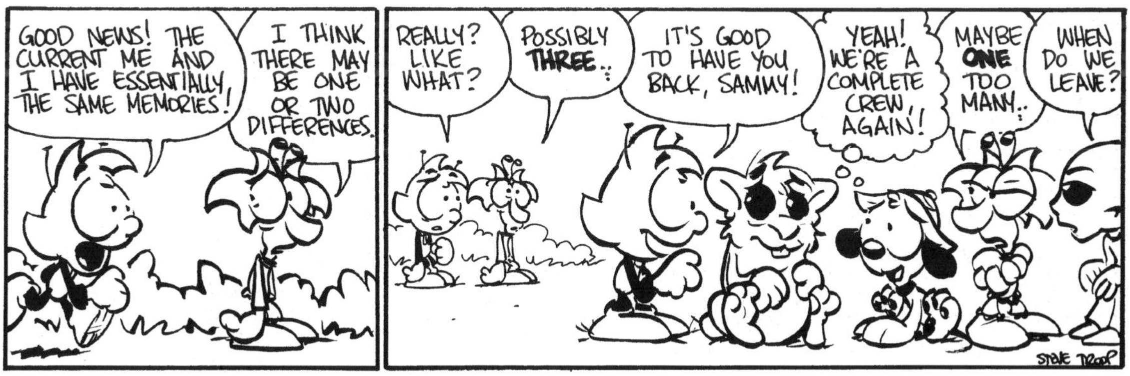
GOOD NEWS! THE CURRENT ME AND I HAVE ESSENTIALLY THE SAME MEMORIES!
I THINK THERE MAY BE ONE OR TWO DIFFERENCES.
REALLY? LIKE WHAT?
POSSIBLY THREE...
IT'S GOOD TO HAVE YOU BACK, SAMMY!
YEAH! WE'RE A COMPLETE CREW, AGAIN!
MAYBE ONE TOO MANY...
WHEN DO WE LEAVE?
STEVE TROOP

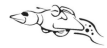

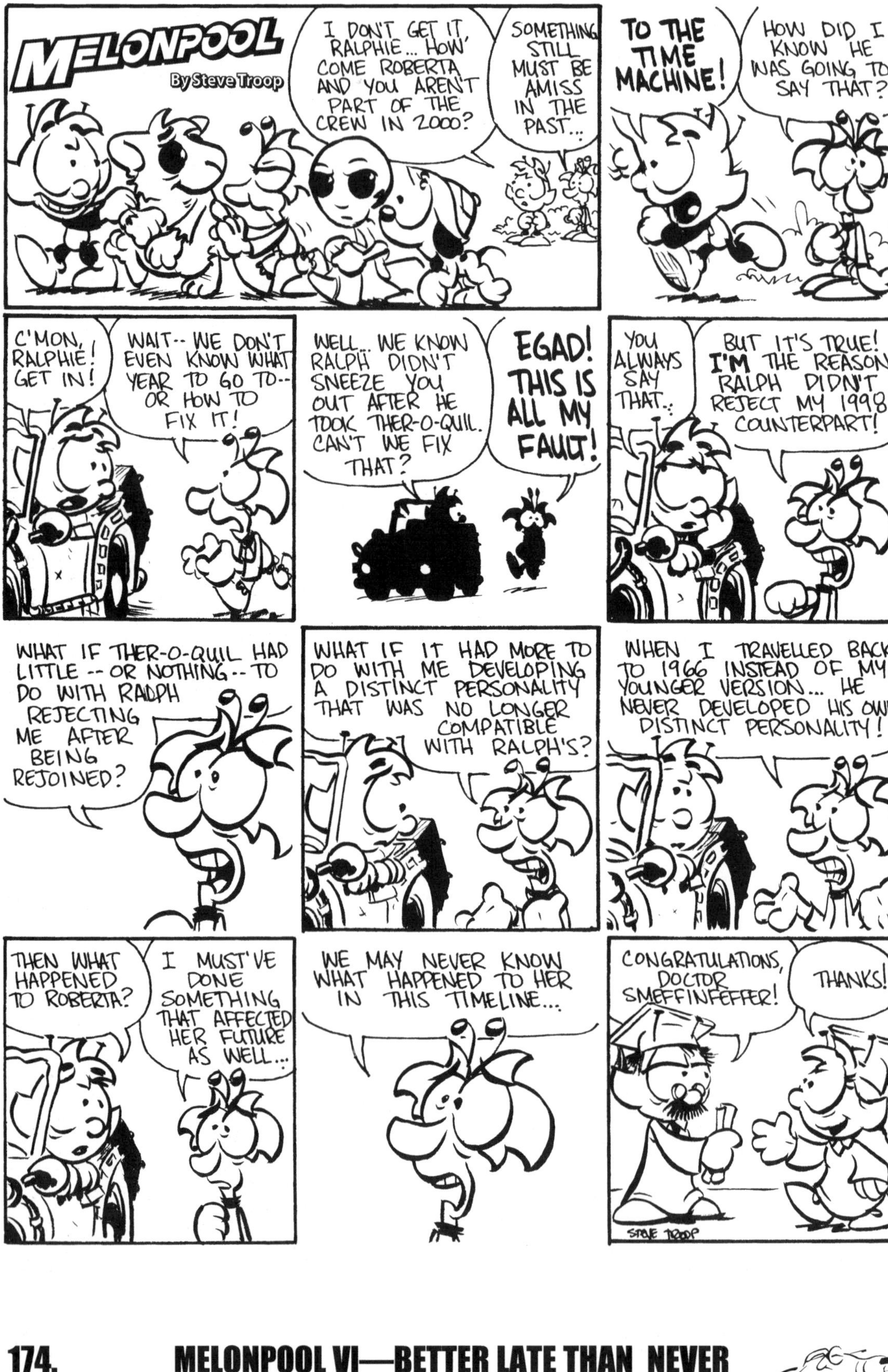
MELONPOOL
By Steve Troop
I DON'T GET IT, RALPHIE... HOW COME ROBERTA AND YOU AREN'T PART OF THE CREW IN 2000?
SOMETHING STILL MUST BE AMISS IN THE PAST...
TO THE TIME MACHINE!
HOW DID I KNOW HE WAS GOING TO SAY THAT?
C'MON, RALPHIE! GET IN!
WAIT-- WE DON'T EVEN KNOW WHAT YEAR TO GO TO-- OR HOW TO FIX IT!
WELL... WE KNOW RALPH DIDN'T SNEEZE YOU OUT AFTER HE TOOK THER-O-QUIL. CAN'T WE FIX THAT?
EGAD! THIS IS ALL MY FAULT!
YOU ALWAYS SAY THAT...
BUT IT'S TRUE! I'M THE REASON RALPH DIDN'T REJECT MY 1998 COUNTERPART!
WHAT IF THER-O-QUIL HAD LITTLE -- OR NOTHING -- TO DO WITH RALPH REJECTING ME AFTER BEING REJOINED?
WHAT IF IT HAD MORE TO DO WITH ME DEVELOPING A DISTINCT PERSONALITY THAT WAS NO LONGER COMPATIBLE WITH RALPH'S?
WHEN I TRAVELLED BACK TO 1966 INSTEAD OF MY YOUNGER VERSION... HE NEVER DEVELOPED HIS OWN DISTINCT PERSONALITY!
THEN WHAT HAPPENED TO ROBERTA?
I MUST'VE DONE SOMETHING THAT AFFECTED HER FUTURE AS WELL...
WE MAY NEVER KNOW WHAT HAPPENED TO HER IN THIS TIMELINE...
CONGRATULATIONS, DOCTOR SMEFFINFEFFER!
THANKS!
STEVE TROOP

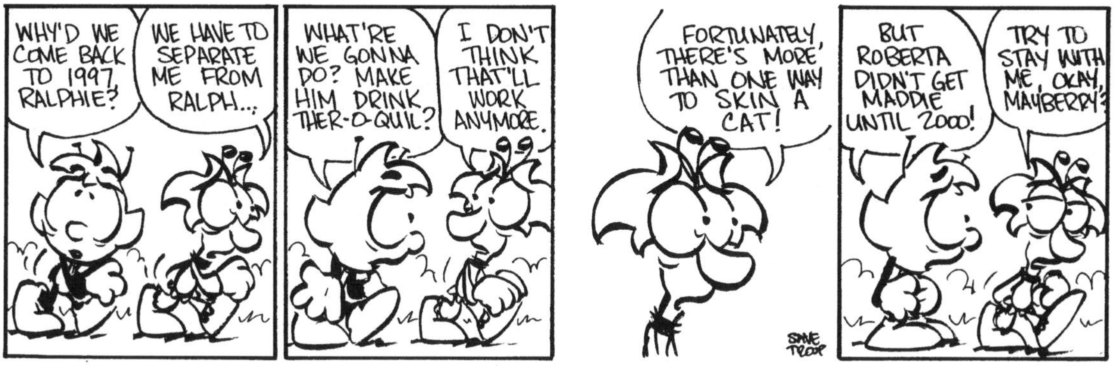

WHY'D WE COME BACK TO 1997, RALPHIE?
WE HAVE TO SEPARATE ME FROM RALPH...
WHAT'RE WE GONNA DO? MAKE HIM DRINK THER-O-QUIL?
I DON'T THINK THAT'LL WORK ANYMORE.
FORTUNATELY, THERE'S MORE THAN ONE WAY TO SKIN A CAT!
BUT ROBERTA DIDN'T GET MADDIE UNTIL 2000!
TRY TO STAY WITH ME, OKAY, MAYBERRY?

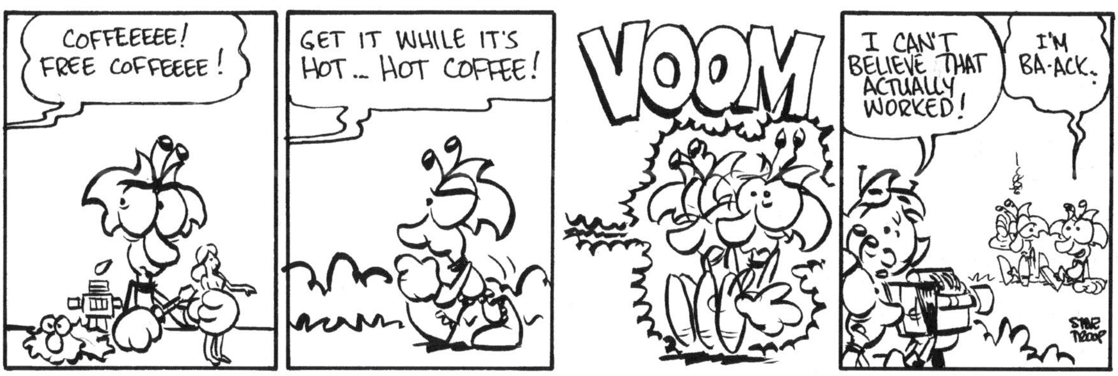

COFFEEEEEE! FREE COFFEEEEE!
GET IT WHILE IT'S HOT... HOT COFFEE!
VOOM
I CAN'T BELIEVE THAT ACTUALLY WORKED!
I'M BA-ACK...

In the original timeline, Roberta was recaptured by the GRAISE when the *Steel Duck* encountered them in 1999. Ralphie and Ralph went back in time and rescued her, but if Ralphie never existed, then that never would have happened, causing Roberta to be returned to Melotia by the GRAISE. And you wonder why I keep such copious notes!

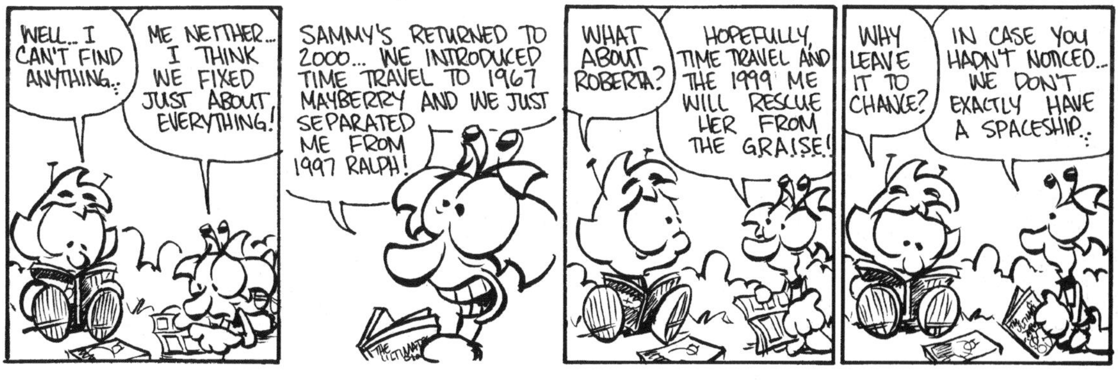

WELL... I CAN'T FIND ANYTHING...
ME NEITHER... I THINK WE FIXED JUST ABOUT EVERYTHING!
SAMMY'S RETURNED TO 2000... WE INTRODUCED TIME TRAVEL TO 1967 MAYBERRY AND WE JUST SEPARATED ME FROM 1997 RALPH!
WHAT ABOUT ROBERTA?
HOPEFULLY, TIME TRAVEL AND THE 1999 ME WILL RESCUE HER FROM THE GRAISE!
WHY LEAVE IT TO CHANCE?
IN CASE YOU HADN'T NOTICED... WE DON'T EXACTLY HAVE A SPACESHIP...

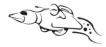

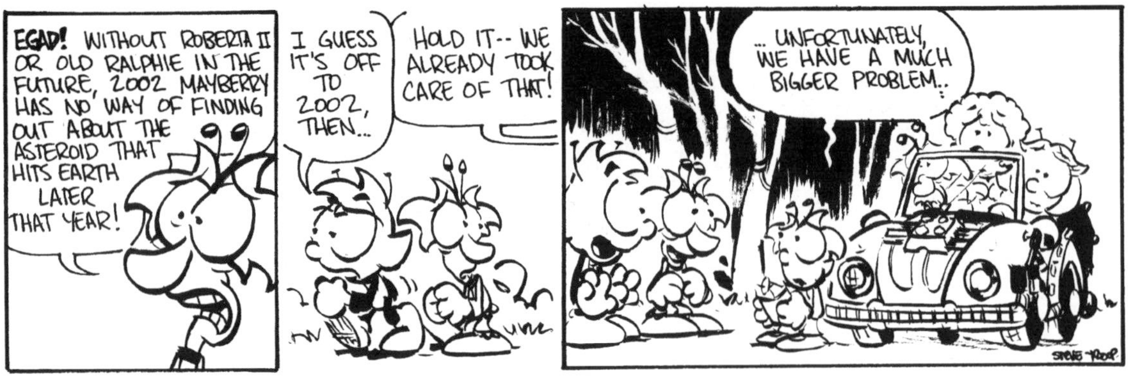
EGAD! WITHOUT ROBERTA II OR OLD RALPHIE IN THE FUTURE, 2002 MAYBERRY HAS NO WAY OF FINDING OUT ABOUT THE ASTEROID THAT HITS EARTH LATER THAT YEAR!
I GUESS IT'S OFF TO 2002, THEN...
HOLD IT-- WE ALREADY TOOK CARE OF THAT!
... UNFORTUNATELY, WE HAVE A MUCH BIGGER PROBLEM...
STEVE TROOP

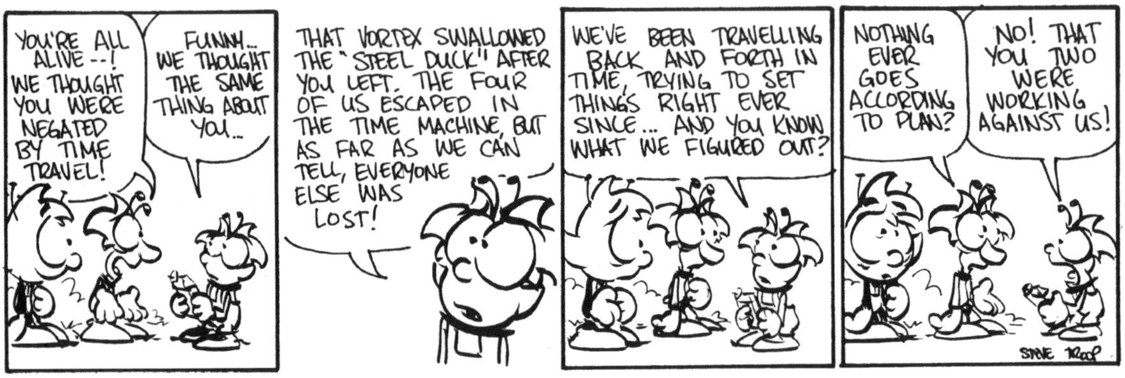
YOU'RE ALL ALIVE--! WE THOUGHT YOU WERE NEGATED BY TIME TRAVEL!
FUNNY... WE THOUGHT THE SAME THING ABOUT YOU...
THAT VORTEX SWALLOWED THE "STEEL DUCK" AFTER YOU LEFT. THE FOUR OF US ESCAPED IN THE TIME MACHINE, BUT AS FAR AS WE CAN TELL, EVERYONE ELSE WAS LOST!
WE'VE BEEN TRAVELLING BACK AND FORTH IN TIME, TRYING TO SET THINGS RIGHT EVER SINCE... AND YOU KNOW WHAT WE FIGURED OUT?
NOTHING EVER GOES ACCORDING TO PLAN?
NO! THAT YOU TWO WERE WORKING AGAINST US!
STEVE TROOP

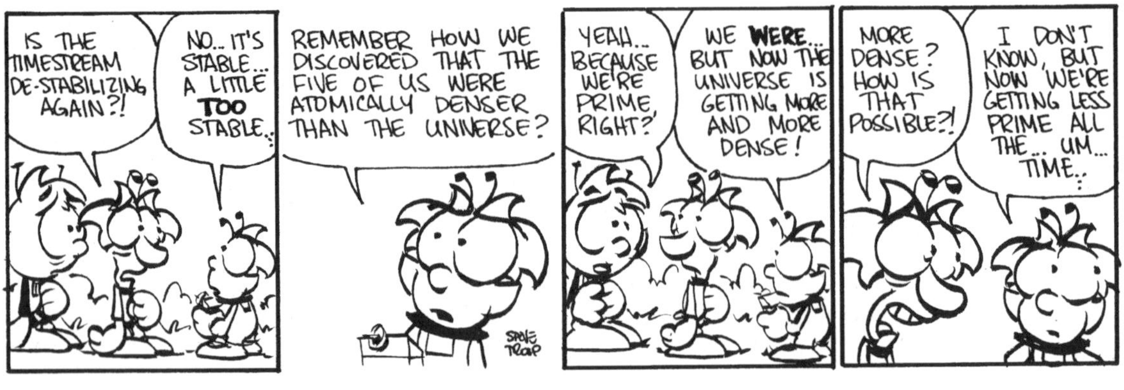
IS THE TIMESTREAM DE-STABILIZING AGAIN?!
NO... IT'S STABLE... A LITTLE TOO STABLE...
REMEMBER HOW WE DISCOVERED THAT THE FIVE OF US WERE ATOMICALLY DENSER THAN THE UNIVERSE?
STEVE TROOP
YEAH... BECAUSE WE'RE PRIME, RIGHT?
WE WERE... BUT NOW THE UNIVERSE IS GETTING MORE AND MORE DENSE!
MORE DENSE? HOW IS THAT POSSIBLE?!
I DON'T KNOW, BUT NOW WE'RE GETTING LESS PRIME ALL THE... UM... TIME...

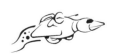

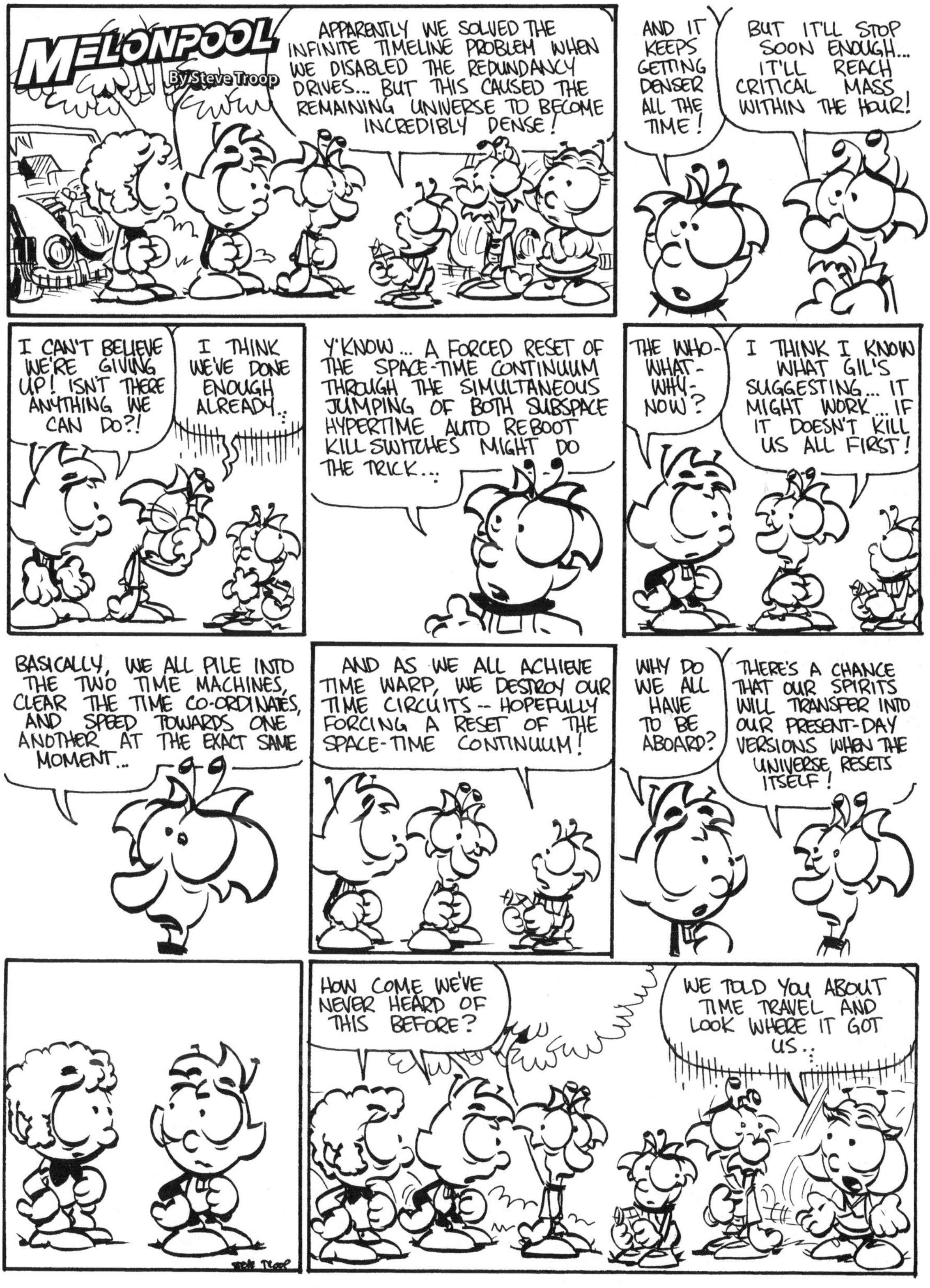
MELONPOOL
By Steve Troop
APPARENTLY WE SOLVED THE INFINITE TIMELINE PROBLEM WHEN WE DISABLED THE REDUNDANCY DRIVES... BUT THIS CAUSED THE REMAINING UNIVERSE TO BECOME INCREDIBLY DENSE!
AND IT KEEPS GETTING DENSER ALL THE TIME!
BUT IT'LL STOP SOON ENOUGH... IT'LL REACH CRITICAL MASS WITHIN THE HOUR!
I CAN'T BELIEVE WE'RE GIVING UP! ISN'T THERE ANYTHING WE CAN DO?!
I THINK WE'VE DONE ENOUGH ALREADY...
Y'KNOW... A FORCED RESET OF THE SPACE-TIME CONTINUUM THROUGH THE SIMULTANEOUS JUMPING OF BOTH SUBSPACE HYPERTIME AUTO REBOOT KILLSWITCHES MIGHT DO THE TRICK...
THE WHO-WHAT-WHY-NOW?
I THINK I KNOW WHAT GIL'S SUGGESTING... IT MIGHT WORK... IF IT DOESN'T KILL US ALL FIRST!
BASICALLY, WE ALL PILE INTO THE TWO TIME MACHINES, CLEAR THE TIME CO-ORDINATES, AND SPEED TOWARDS ONE ANOTHER AT THE EXACT SAME MOMENT...
AND AS WE ALL ACHIEVE TIME WARP, WE DESTROY OUR TIME CIRCUITS -- HOPEFULLY FORCING A RESET OF THE SPACE-TIME CONTINUUM!
WHY DO WE ALL HAVE TO BE ABOARD?
THERE'S A CHANCE THAT OUR SPIRITS WILL TRANSFER INTO OUR PRESENT-DAY VERSIONS WHEN THE UNIVERSE RESETS ITSELF!
HOW COME WE'VE NEVER HEARD OF THIS BEFORE?
WE TOLD YOU ABOUT TIME TRAVEL AND LOOK WHERE IT GOT US...

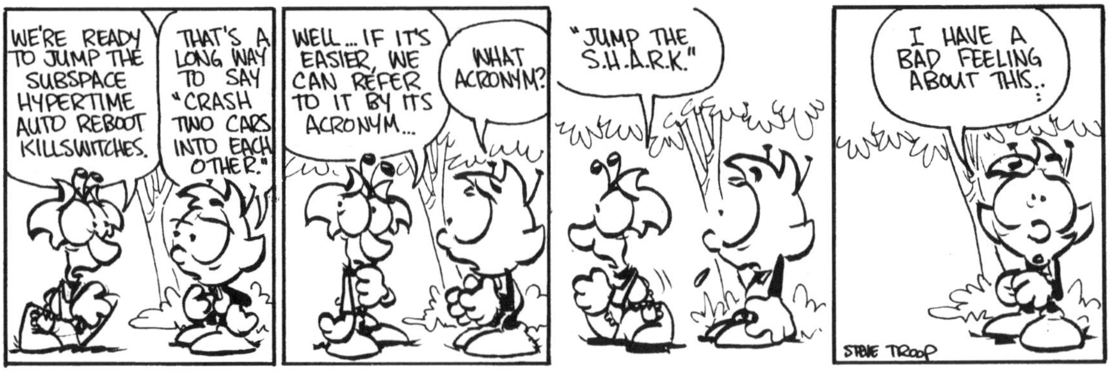
WE'RE READY TO JUMP THE SUBSPACE HYPERTIME AUTO REBOOT KILLSWITCHES.
THAT'S A LONG WAY TO SAY "CRASH TWO CARS INTO EACH OTHER."
WELL... IF IT'S EASIER, WE CAN REFER TO IT BY ITS ACRONYM...
WHAT ACRONYM?
"JUMP THE S.H.A.R.K."
I HAVE A BAD FEELING ABOUT THIS..
STEVE TROOP

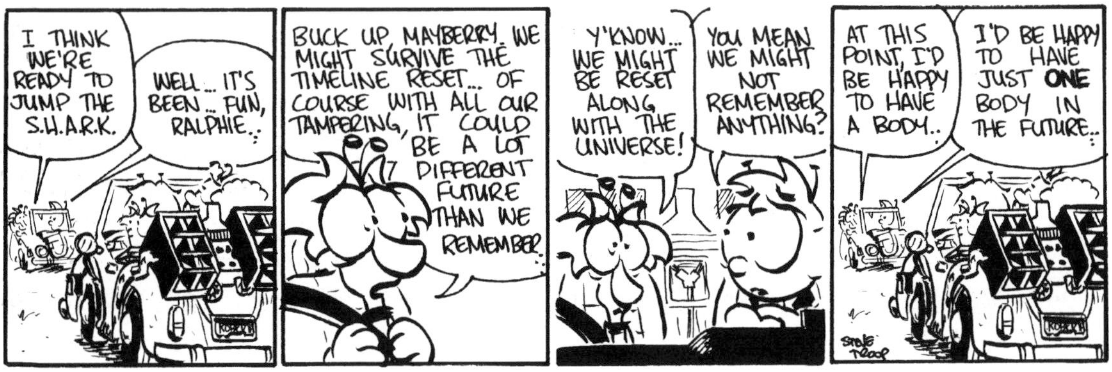
I THINK WE'RE READY TO JUMP THE S.H.A.R.K.
WELL... IT'S BEEN... FUN, RALPHIE..
BUCK UP, MAYBERRY. WE MIGHT SURVIVE THE TIMELINE RESET... OF COURSE WITH ALL OUR TAMPERING, IT COULD BE A LOT DIFFERENT FUTURE THAN WE REMEMBER.
Y'KNOW... WE MIGHT BE RESET ALONG WITH THE UNIVERSE!
YOU MEAN WE MIGHT NOT REMEMBER ANYTHING?
AT THIS POINT, I'D BE HAPPY TO HAVE A BODY..
I'D BE HAPPY TO HAVE JUST **ONE** BODY IN THE FUTURE..
STEVE TROOP

Come on. Secretly you always knew it'd end this way....

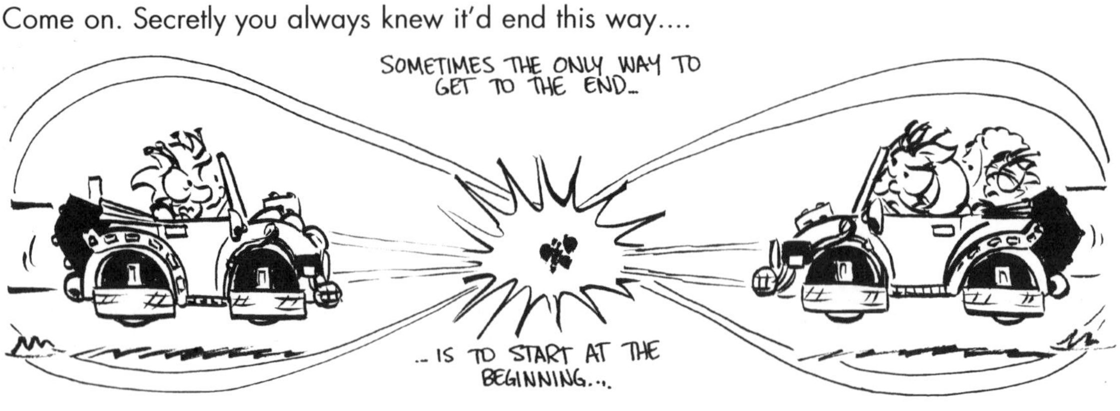
SOMETIMES THE ONLY WAY TO GET TO THE END...
... IS TO START AT THE BEGINNING....

ZORTIC TO THE RESCUE!

So, that's the way Melonpool ended.

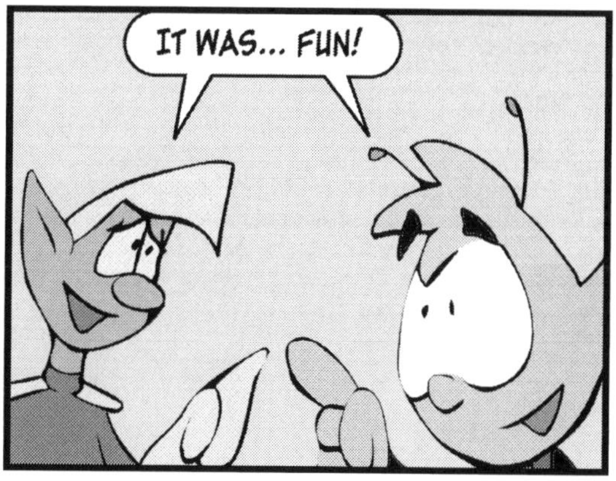
IT WAS... FUN!

Well, not exactly. The day after the last daily strip ran, Melonpool came back as a full-color comic book page-syle stand-alone comic, completely independent of the first nine years of the strip. What's more, I was able to re-introduce each character, to attract new readers. And surprisingly, it worked!

But the new readers didn't come because of the new comic. They came because of the old comic—or the lack of it. As part of the reboot, I also purged the Internet of all nine years of the original strip.

I removed the old strips for two reasons: First, at over 2,000 strips, my archives had reached critical mass. My readership had been stuck at around 1,500 readers for about four years and I could never attract any more. Second, the sales of the first five Melonpool books had stalled out. I figured that anyone who really wanted to read the old strips could always buy the books. A win-win situation.

Sure enough, the first day over 8,000 people visited the site—most to post on the forum about what a jerk I was to take away their free content (which 6,500 of them had never read). Over the next few weeks, I endured hacking attempts to "free" the missing strips, Internet protests and petitions to get me to put them back up. As a side note, at the end of the first month, I had 4,000 regular readers.

And then, my grandmother passed away, I lost my job and broke up with my girlfriend. I stopped updating the strip and quickly lost any of the momentum I had built up. The site didn't update for about eight months... until Mark Mekkes contacted me with an idea... an idea that got me excited about Melonpool again.

It seems that in all the years he had been drawing Zortic, Mark had never done a time travel story. He had an idea where his characters could travel back in time and fix my strip's timeline. I helped with the plotting and suggested a few of the gags. On the day that Zortic fixed the timeline, all of the Melonpool strips went back online—where they remain to this day.

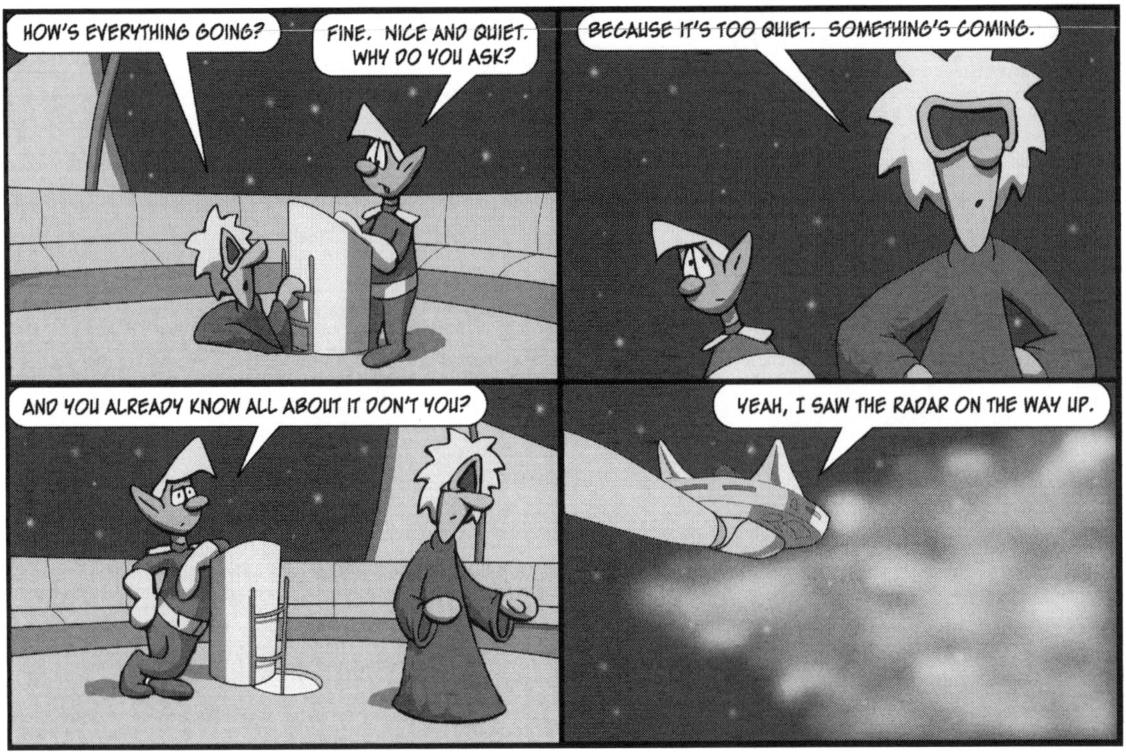
HOW'S EVERYTHING GOING?
FINE. NICE AND QUIET. WHY DO YOU ASK?
BECAUSE IT'S TOO QUIET. SOMETHING'S COMING.
AND YOU ALREADY KNOW ALL ABOUT IT DON'T YOU?
YEAH, I SAW THE RADAR ON THE WAY UP.

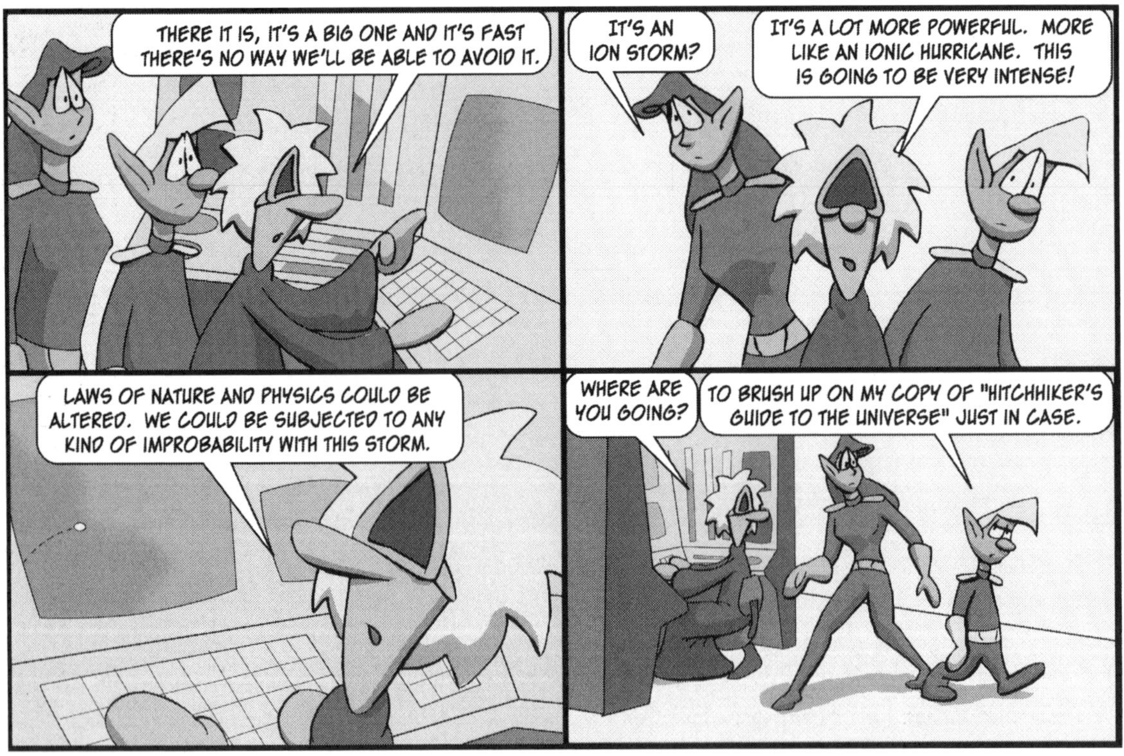
THERE IT IS, IT'S A BIG ONE AND IT'S FAST THERE'S NO WAY WE'LL BE ABLE TO AVOID IT.
IT'S AN ION STORM?
IT'S A LOT MORE POWERFUL. MORE LIKE AN IONIC HURRICANE. THIS IS GOING TO BE VERY INTENSE!
LAWS OF NATURE AND PHYSICS COULD BE ALTERED. WE COULD BE SUBJECTED TO ANY KIND OF IMPROBABILITY WITH THIS STORM.
WHERE ARE YOU GOING?
TO BRUSH UP ON MY COPY OF "HITCHHIKER'S GUIDE TO THE UNIVERSE" JUST IN CASE.

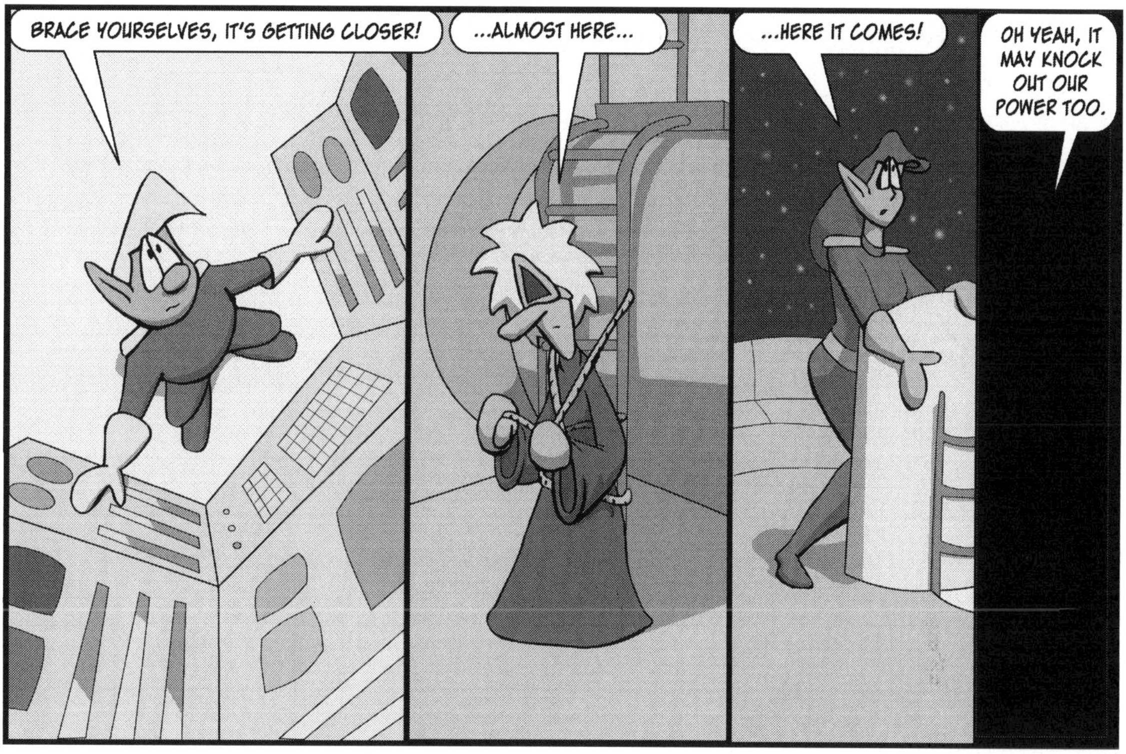
BRACE YOURSELVES, IT'S GETTING CLOSER!
...ALMOST HERE...
...HERE IT COMES!
OH YEAH, IT MAY KNOCK OUT OUR POWER TOO.

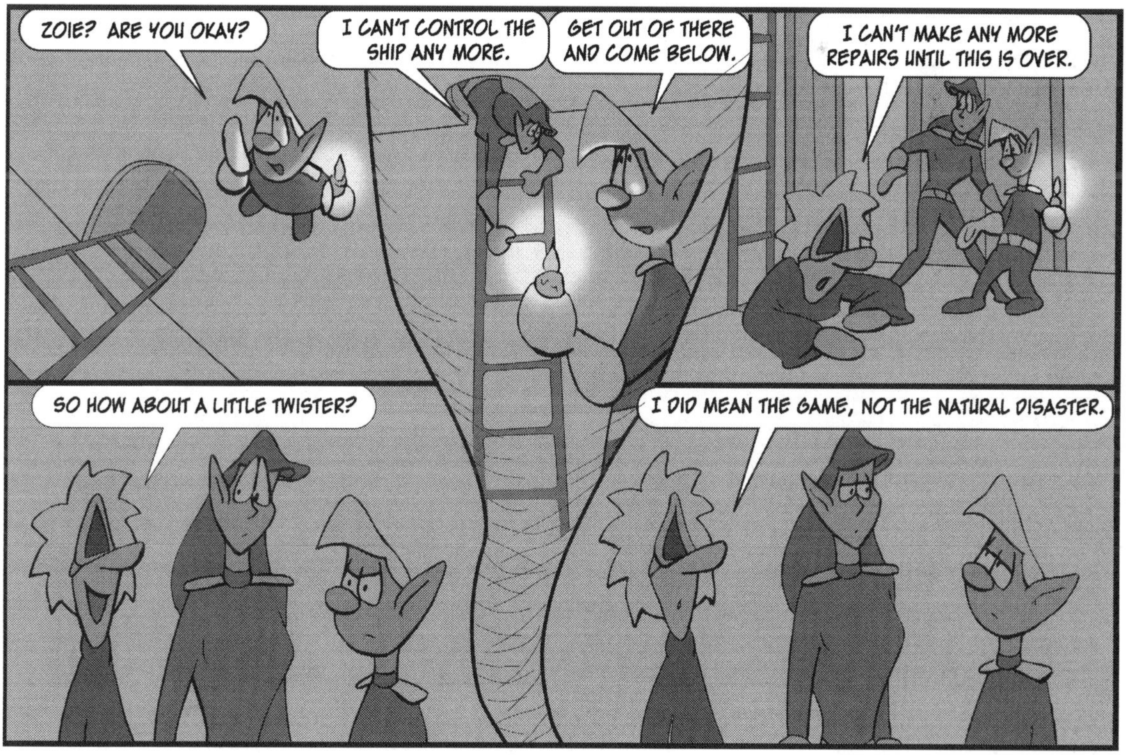
ZOIE? ARE YOU OKAY?
I CAN'T CONTROL THE SHIP ANY MORE.
GET OUT OF THERE AND COME BELOW.
I CAN'T MAKE ANY MORE REPAIRS UNTIL THIS IS OVER.
SO HOW ABOUT A LITTLE TWISTER?
I DID MEAN THE GAME, NOT THE NATURAL DISASTER.

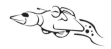

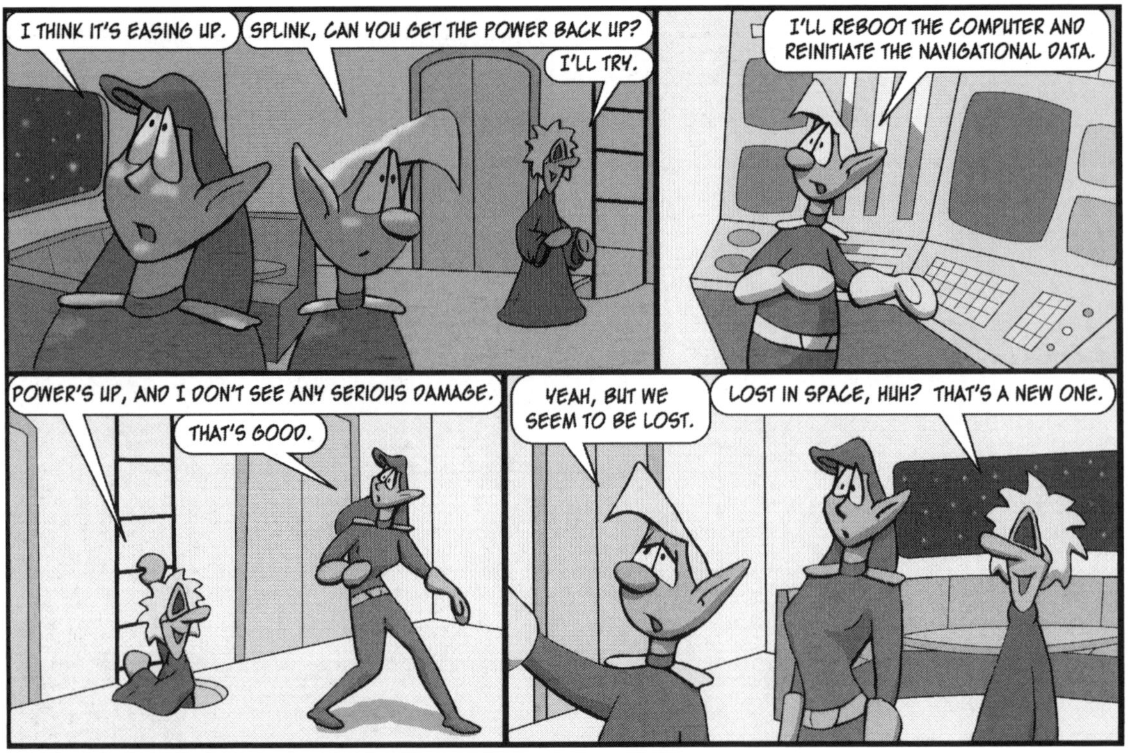
I THINK IT'S EASING UP.
SPLINK, CAN YOU GET THE POWER BACK UP?
I'LL TRY.
I'LL REBOOT THE COMPUTER AND REINITIATE THE NAVIGATIONAL DATA.
POWER'S UP, AND I DON'T SEE ANY SERIOUS DAMAGE.
THAT'S GOOD.
YEAH, BUT WE SEEM TO BE LOST.
LOST IN SPACE, HUH? THAT'S A NEW ONE.

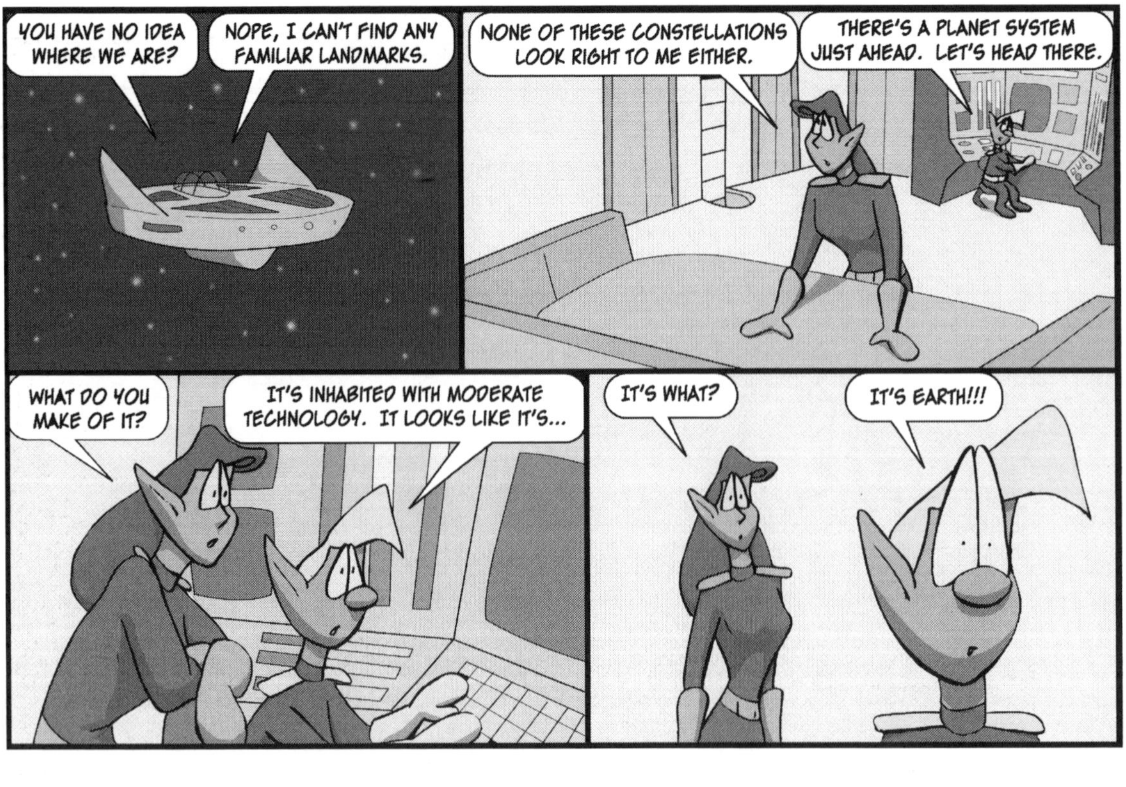
YOU HAVE NO IDEA WHERE WE ARE?
NOPE, I CAN'T FIND ANY FAMILIAR LANDMARKS.
NONE OF THESE CONSTELLATIONS LOOK RIGHT TO ME EITHER.
THERE'S A PLANET SYSTEM JUST AHEAD. LET'S HEAD THERE.
WHAT DO YOU MAKE OF IT?
IT'S INHABITED WITH MODERATE TECHNOLOGY. IT LOOKS LIKE IT'S...
IT'S WHAT?
IT'S EARTH!!!

182. MELONPOOL VI—BETTER LATE THAN NEVER

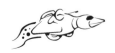

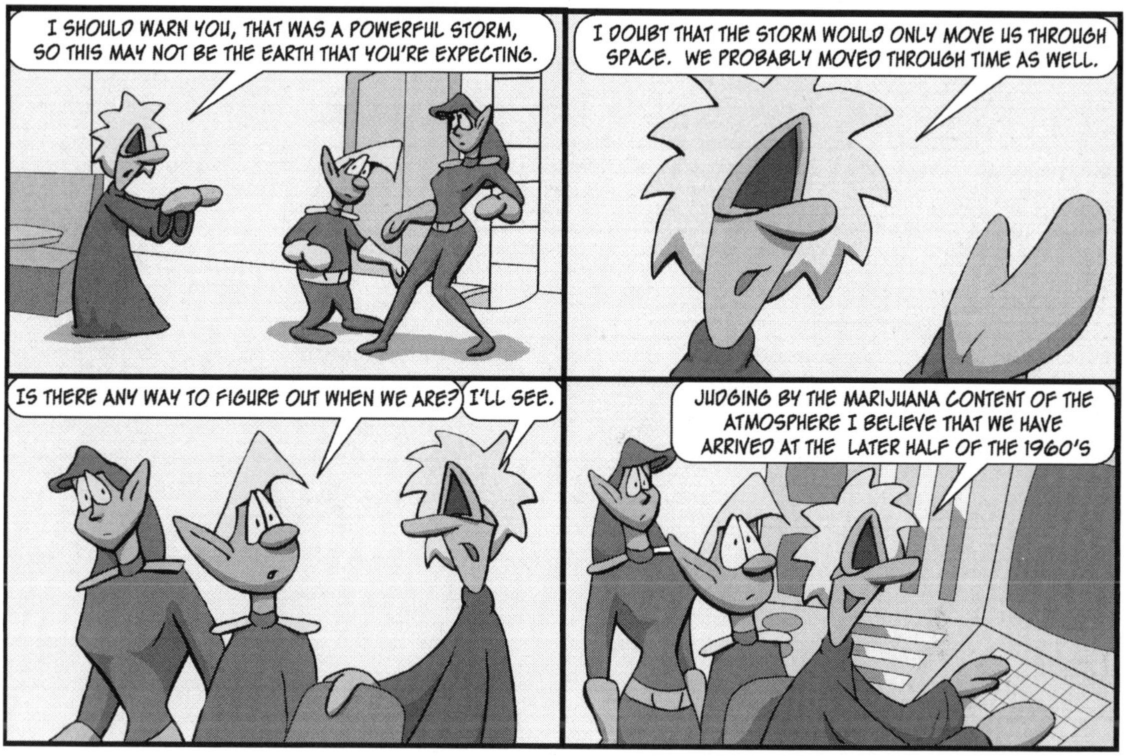
I SHOULD WARN YOU, THAT WAS A POWERFUL STORM, SO THIS MAY NOT BE THE EARTH THAT YOU'RE EXPECTING.
I DOUBT THAT THE STORM WOULD ONLY MOVE US THROUGH SPACE. WE PROBABLY MOVED THROUGH TIME AS WELL.
IS THERE ANY WAY TO FIGURE OUT WHEN WE ARE?
I'LL SEE.
JUDGING BY THE MARIJUANA CONTENT OF THE ATMOSPHERE I BELIEVE THAT WE HAVE ARRIVED AT THE LATER HALF OF THE 1960'S

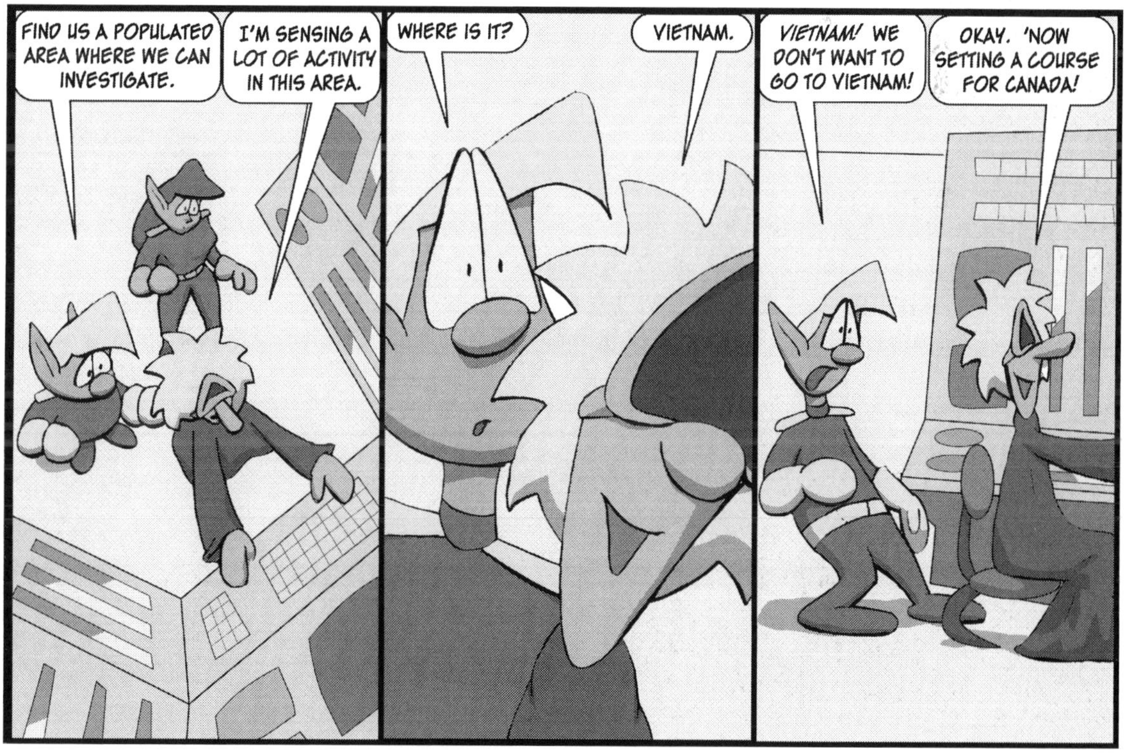
FIND US A POPULATED AREA WHERE WE CAN INVESTIGATE.
I'M SENSING A LOT OF ACTIVITY IN THIS AREA.
WHERE IS IT?
VIETNAM.
VIETNAM! WE DON'T WANT TO GO TO VIETNAM!
OKAY. 'NOW SETTING A COURSE FOR CANADA!

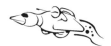

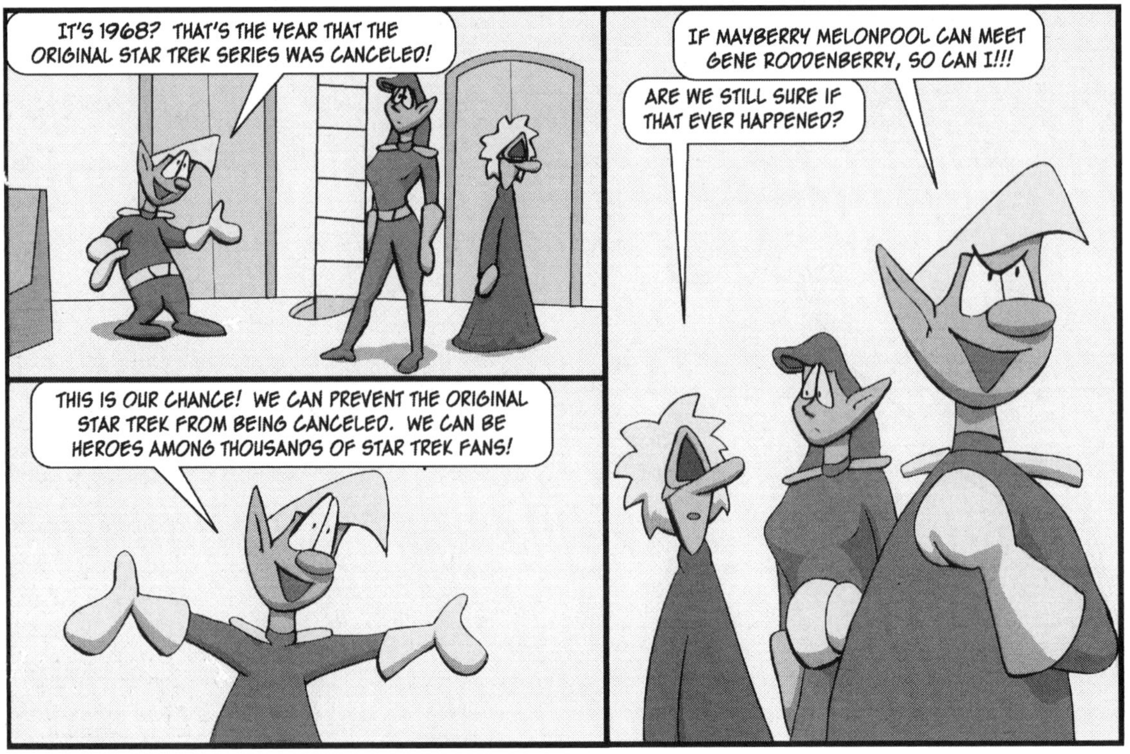
IT'S 1968? THAT'S THE YEAR THAT THE ORIGINAL STAR TREK SERIES WAS CANCELED!
THIS IS OUR CHANCE! WE CAN PREVENT THE ORIGINAL STAR TREK FROM BEING CANCELED. WE CAN BE HEROES AMONG THOUSANDS OF STAR TREK FANS!
IF MAYBERRY MELONPOOL CAN MEET GENE RODDENBERRY, SO CAN I!!!
ARE WE STILL SURE IF THAT EVER HAPPENED?

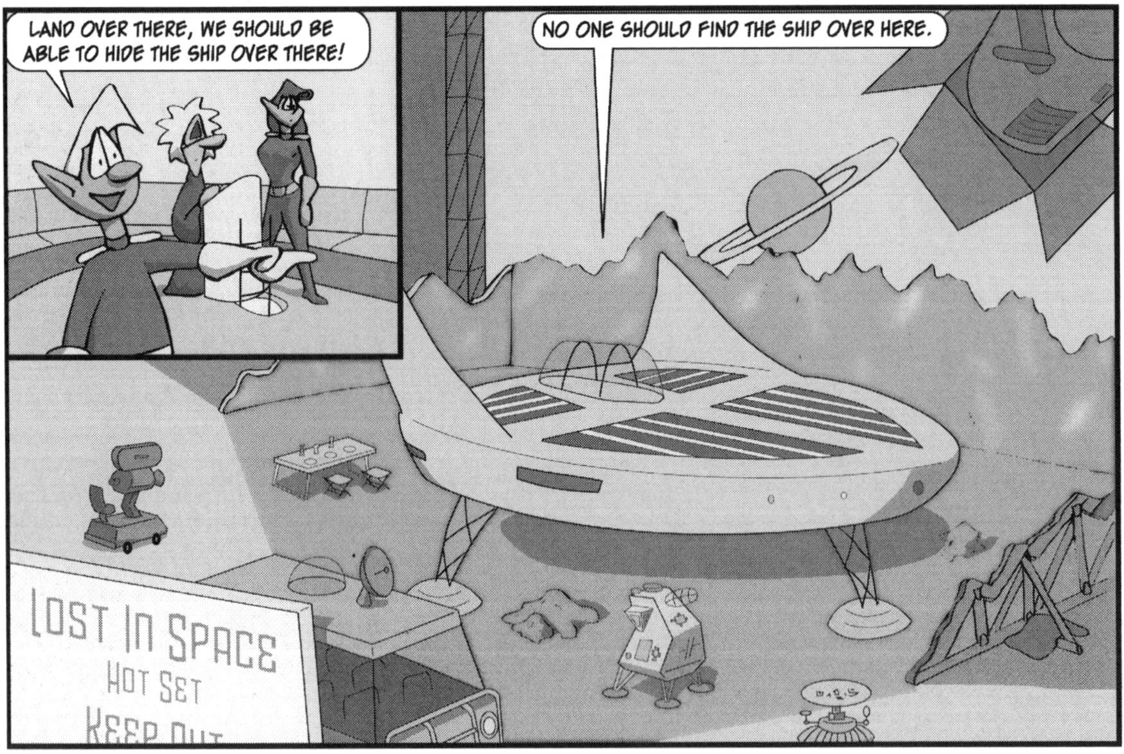
LAND OVER THERE, WE SHOULD BE ABLE TO HIDE THE SHIP OVER THERE!
NO ONE SHOULD FIND THE SHIP OVER HERE.
LOST IN SPACE
HOT SET

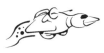

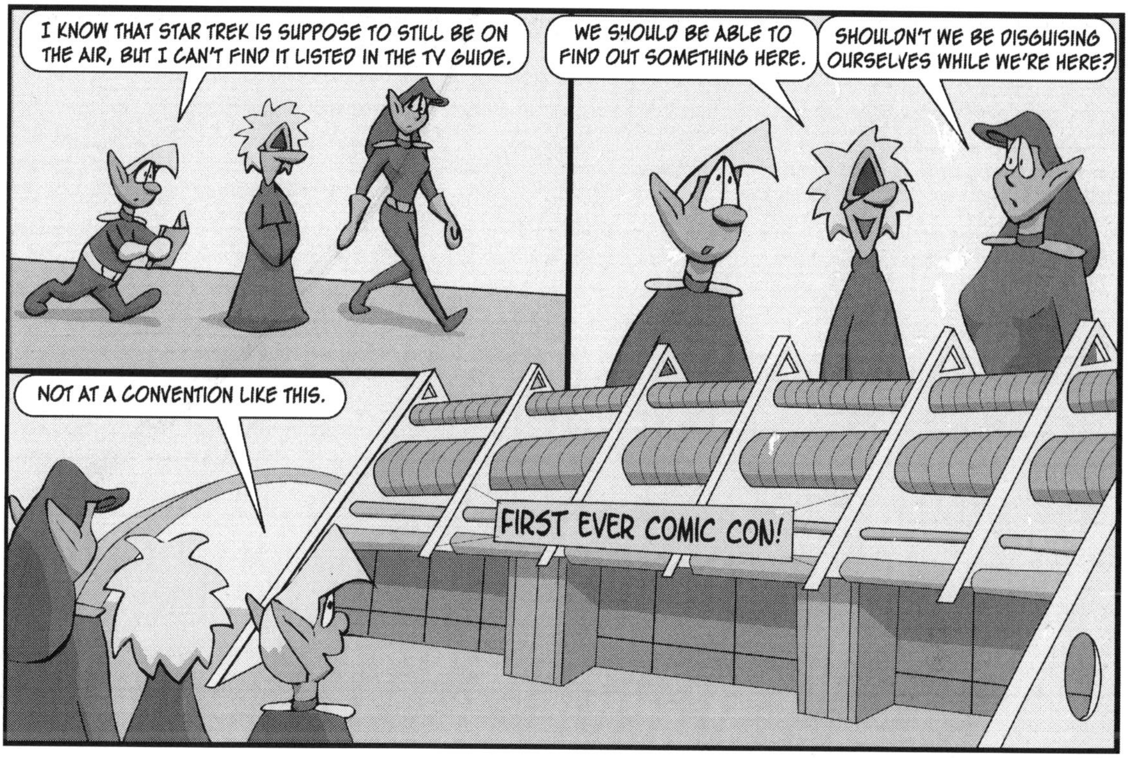
I KNOW THAT STAR TREK IS SUPPOSE TO STILL BE ON THE AIR, BUT I CAN'T FIND IT LISTED IN THE TV GUIDE.
WE SHOULD BE ABLE TO FIND OUT SOMETHING HERE.
SHOULDN'T WE BE DISGUISING OURSELVES WHILE WE'RE HERE?
NOT AT A CONVENTION LIKE THIS.
FIRST EVER COMIC CON!

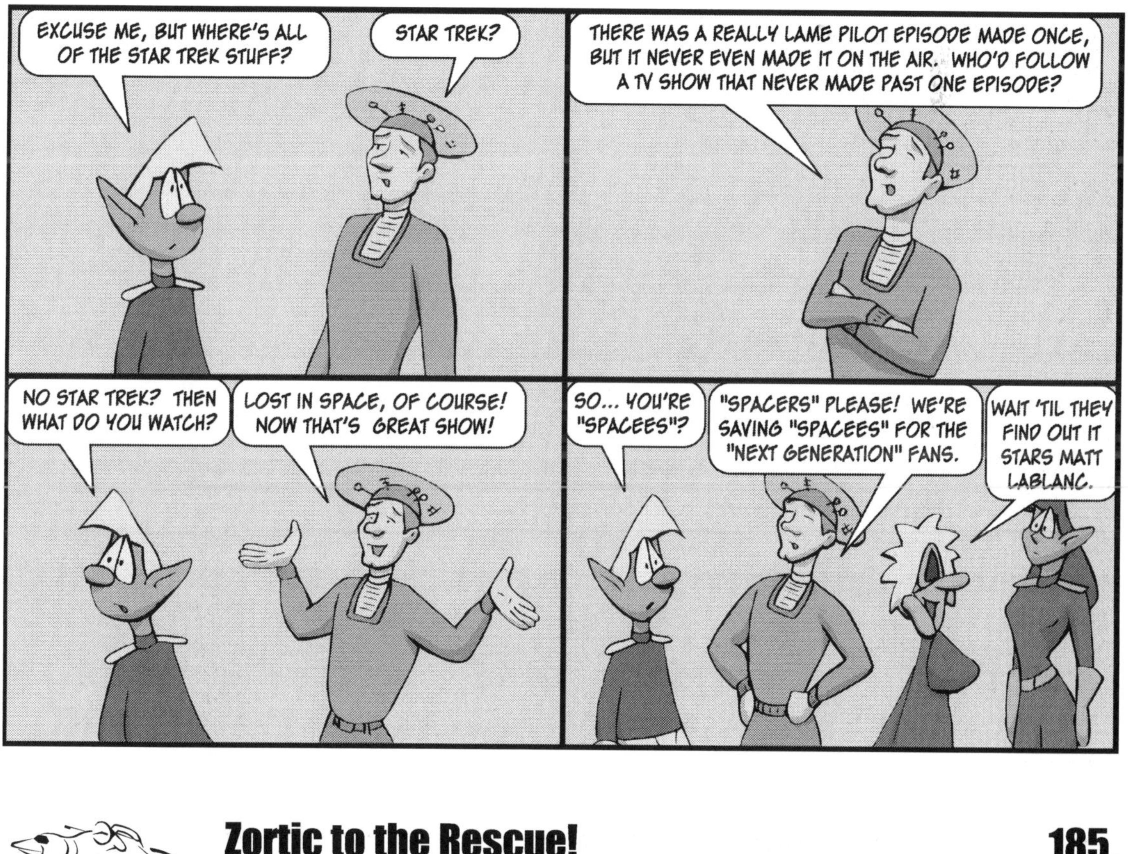
EXCUSE ME, BUT WHERE'S ALL OF THE STAR TREK STUFF?
STAR TREK?
THERE WAS A REALLY LAME PILOT EPISODE MADE ONCE, BUT IT NEVER EVEN MADE IT ON THE AIR. WHO'D FOLLOW A TV SHOW THAT NEVER MADE PAST ONE EPISODE?
NO STAR TREK? THEN WHAT DO YOU WATCH?
LOST IN SPACE, OF COURSE! NOW THAT'S GREAT SHOW!
SO... YOU'RE "SPACEES"?
"SPACERS" PLEASE! WE'RE SAVING "SPACEES" FOR THE "NEXT GENERATION" FANS.
WAIT 'TIL THEY FIND OUT IT STARS MATT LABLANC.

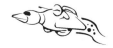

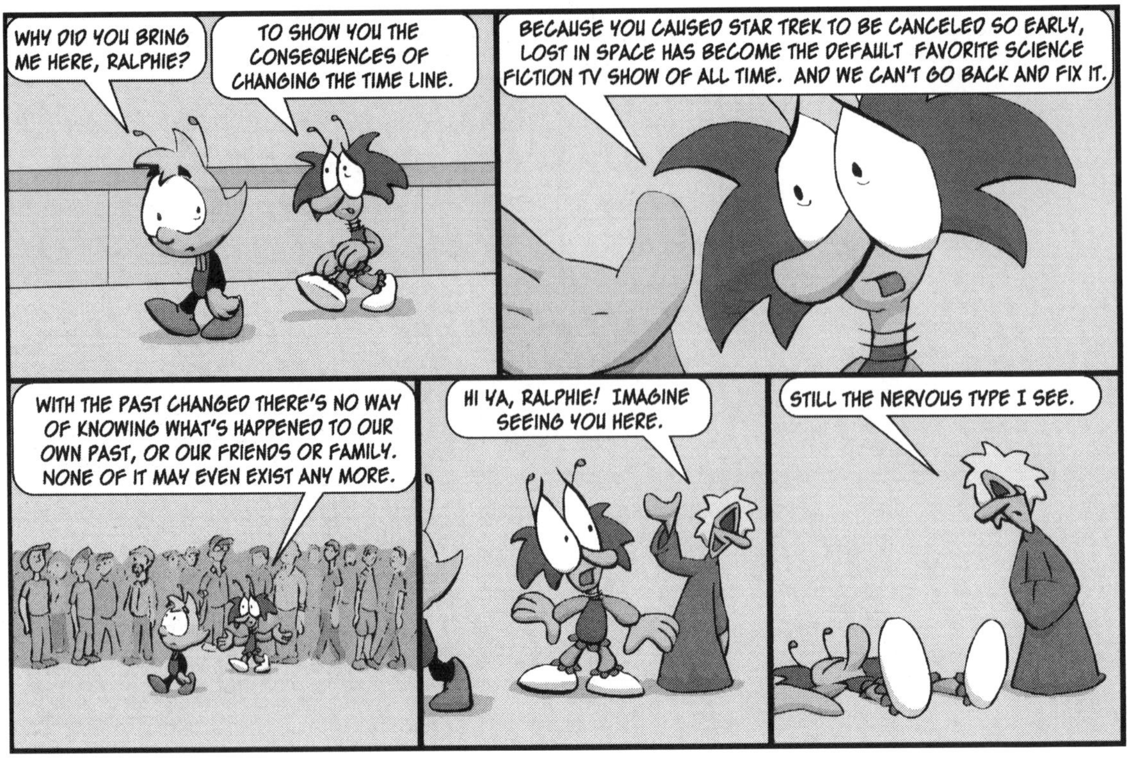
WHY DID YOU BRING ME HERE, RALPHIE?
TO SHOW YOU THE CONSEQUENCES OF CHANGING THE TIME LINE.
BECAUSE YOU CAUSED STAR TREK TO BE CANCELED SO EARLY, LOST IN SPACE HAS BECOME THE DEFAULT FAVORITE SCIENCE FICTION TV SHOW OF ALL TIME. AND WE CAN'T GO BACK AND FIX IT.
WITH THE PAST CHANGED THERE'S NO WAY OF KNOWING WHAT'S HAPPENED TO OUR OWN PAST, OR OUR FRIENDS OR FAMILY. NONE OF IT MAY EVEN EXIST ANY MORE.
HI YA, RALPHIE! IMAGINE SEEING YOU HERE.
STILL THE NERVOUS TYPE I SEE.

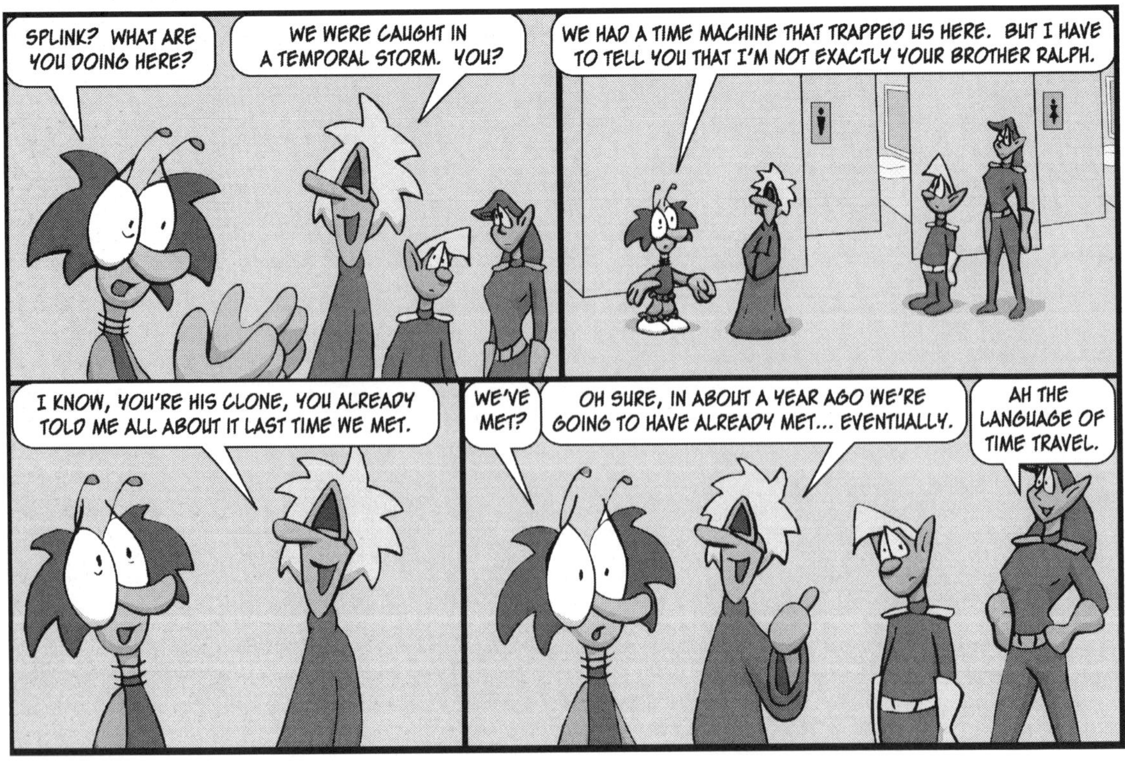
SPLINK? WHAT ARE YOU DOING HERE?
WE WERE CAUGHT IN A TEMPORAL STORM. YOU?
WE HAD A TIME MACHINE THAT TRAPPED US HERE. BUT I HAVE TO TELL YOU THAT I'M NOT EXACTLY YOUR BROTHER RALPH.
I KNOW, YOU'RE HIS CLONE, YOU ALREADY TOLD ME ALL ABOUT IT LAST TIME WE MET.
WE'VE MET?
OH SURE, IN ABOUT A YEAR AGO WE'RE GOING TO HAVE ALREADY MET... EVENTUALLY.
AH THE LANGUAGE OF TIME TRAVEL.

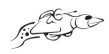

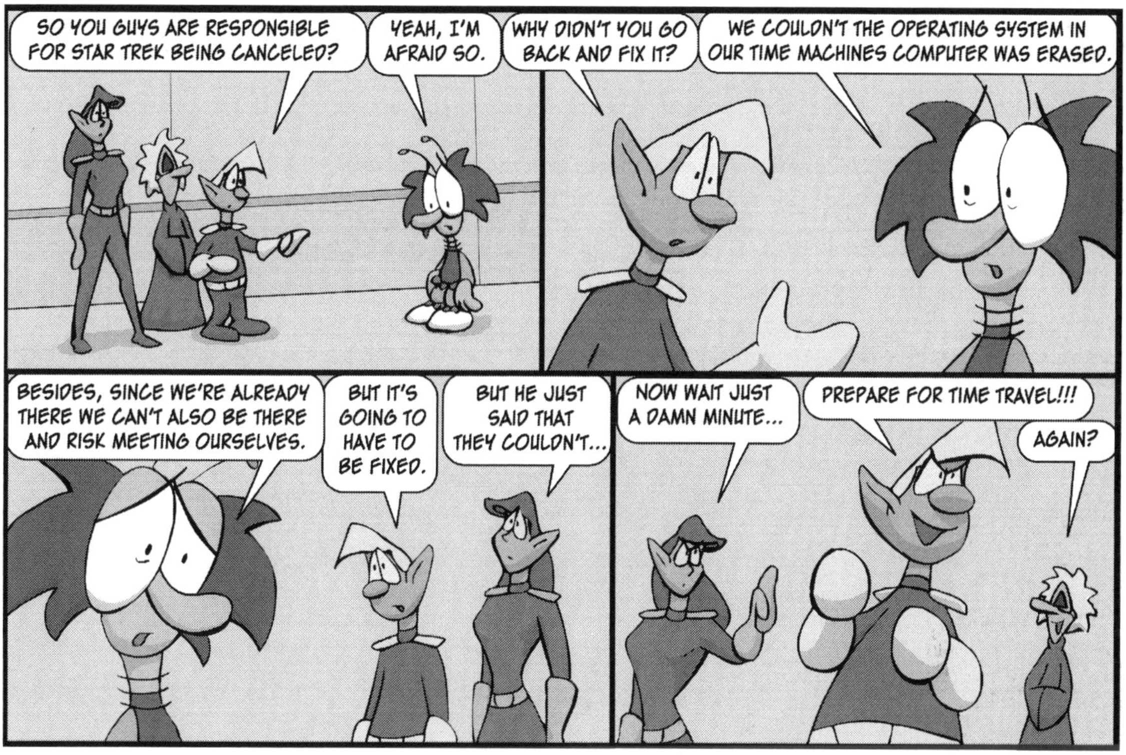
SO YOU GUYS ARE RESPONSIBLE FOR STAR TREK BEING CANCELED?
YEAH, I'M AFRAID SO.
WHY DIDN'T YOU GO BACK AND FIX IT?
WE COULDN'T THE OPERATING SYSTEM IN OUR TIME MACHINES COMPUTER WAS ERASED.
BESIDES, SINCE WE'RE ALREADY THERE WE CAN'T ALSO BE THERE AND RISK MEETING OURSELVES.
BUT IT'S GOING TO HAVE TO BE FIXED.
BUT HE JUST SAID THAT THEY COULDN'T...
NOW WAIT JUST A DAMN MINUTE...
PREPARE FOR TIME TRAVEL!!!
AGAIN?

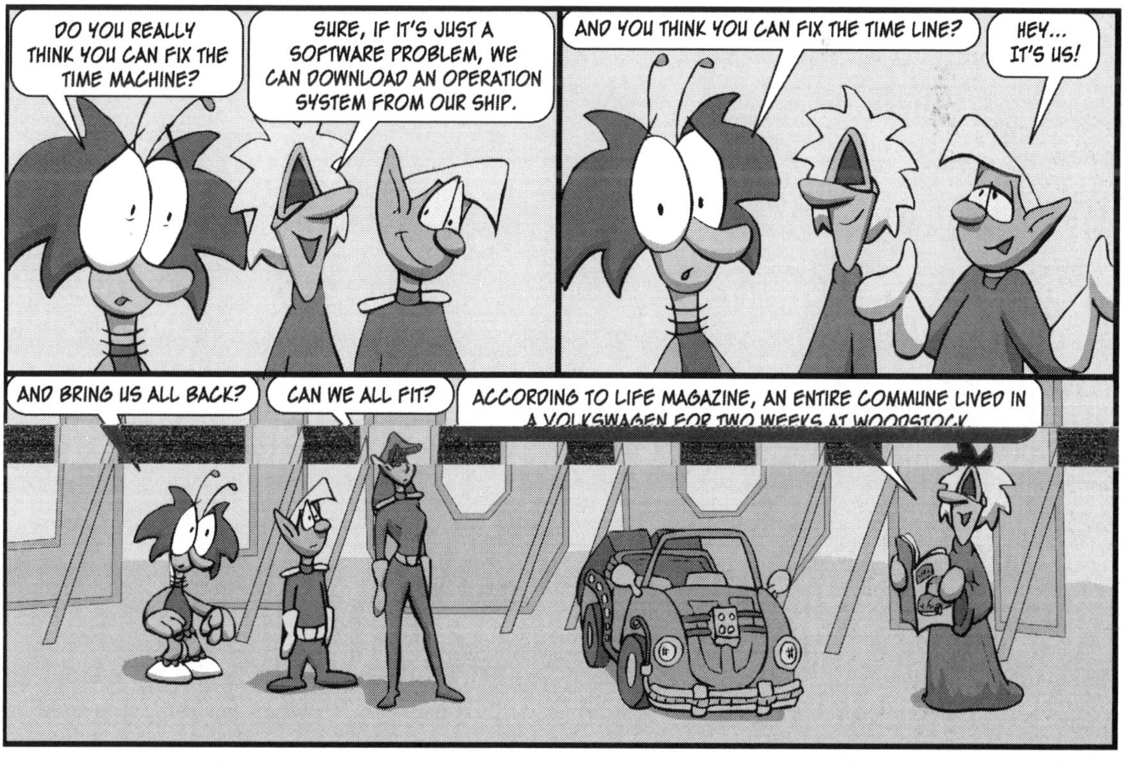
DO YOU REALLY THINK YOU CAN FIX THE TIME MACHINE?
SURE, IF IT'S JUST A SOFTWARE PROBLEM, WE CAN DOWNLOAD AN OPERATION SYSTEM FROM OUR SHIP.
AND YOU THINK YOU CAN FIX THE TIME LINE?
HEY... IT'S US!
AND BRING US ALL BACK?
CAN WE ALL FIT?
ACCORDING TO LIFE MAGAZINE, AN ENTIRE COMMUNE LIVED IN A VOLKSWAGEN FOR TWO WEEKS AT WOODSTOCK.

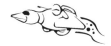

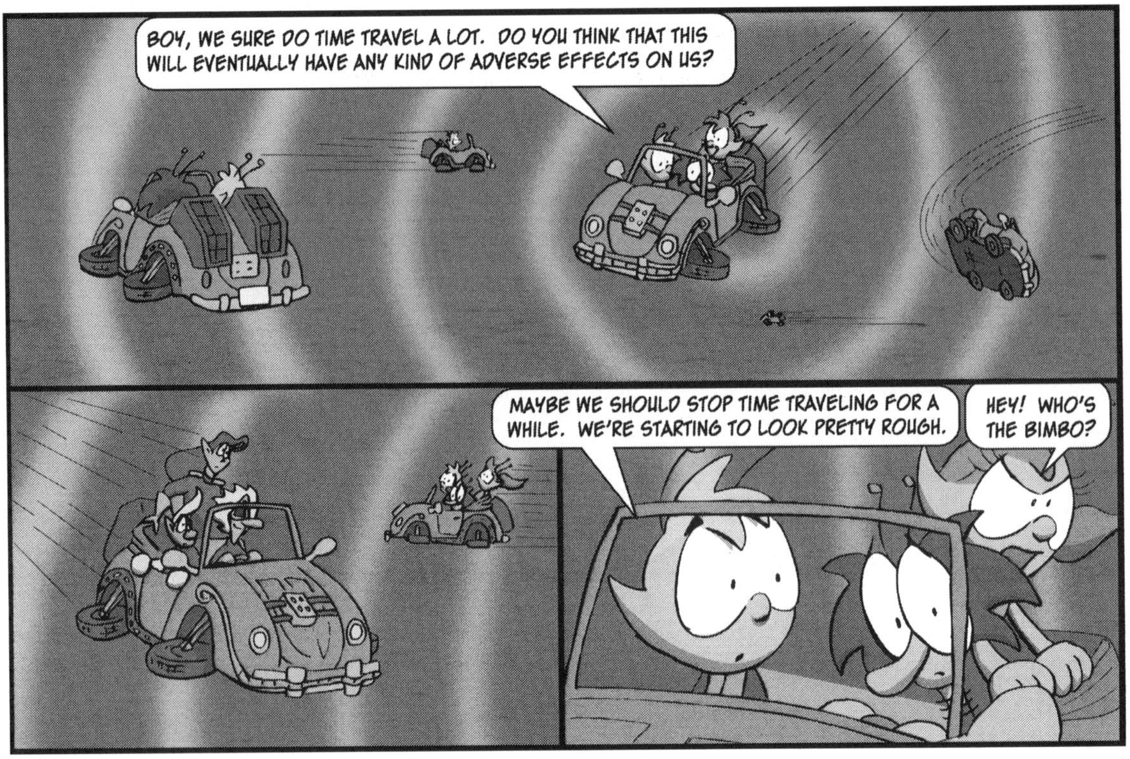
BOY, WE SURE DO TIME TRAVEL A LOT. DO YOU THINK THAT THIS WILL EVENTUALLY HAVE ANY KIND OF ADVERSE EFFECTS ON US?
MAYBE WE SHOULD STOP TIME TRAVELING FOR A WHILE. WE'RE STARTING TO LOOK PRETTY ROUGH.
HEY! WHO'S THE BIMBO?

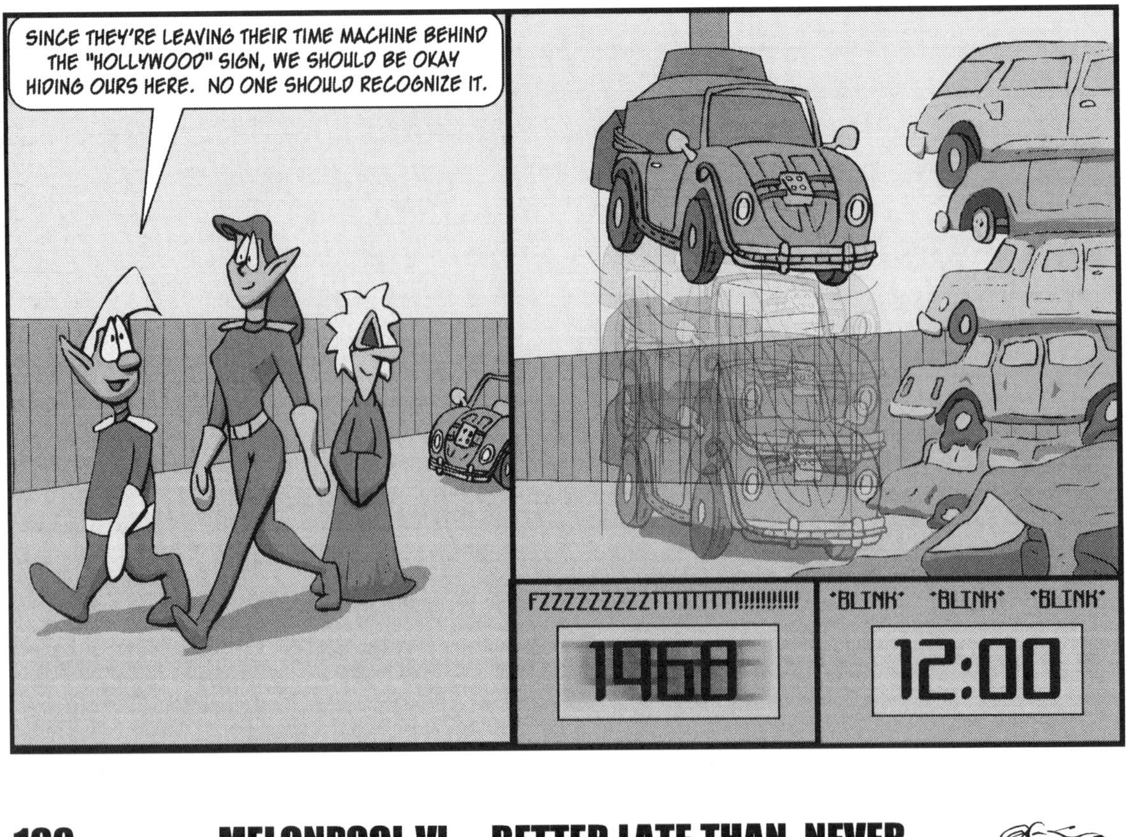
SINCE THEY'RE LEAVING THEIR TIME MACHINE BEHIND THE "HOLLYWOOD" SIGN, WE SHOULD BE OKAY HIDING OURS HERE. NO ONE SHOULD RECOGNIZE IT.
FZZZZZZZZZTTTTTTTT!!!!!!!!!!!
1968
BLINK *BLINK* *BLINK*
12:00

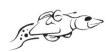

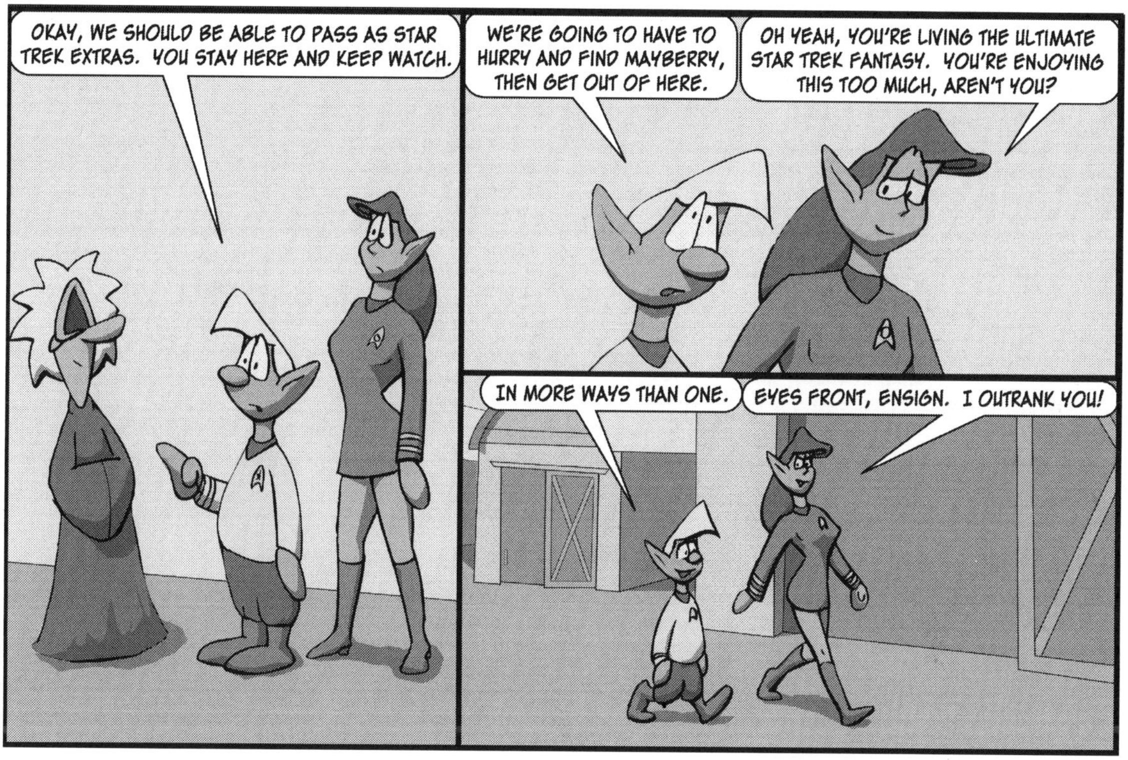
OKAY, WE SHOULD BE ABLE TO PASS AS STAR TREK EXTRAS. YOU STAY HERE AND KEEP WATCH.
WE'RE GOING TO HAVE TO HURRY AND FIND MAYBERRY, THEN GET OUT OF HERE.
OH YEAH, YOU'RE LIVING THE ULTIMATE STAR TREK FANTASY. YOU'RE ENJOYING THIS TOO MUCH, AREN'T YOU?
IN MORE WAYS THAN ONE.
EYES FRONT, ENSIGN. I OUTRANK YOU!

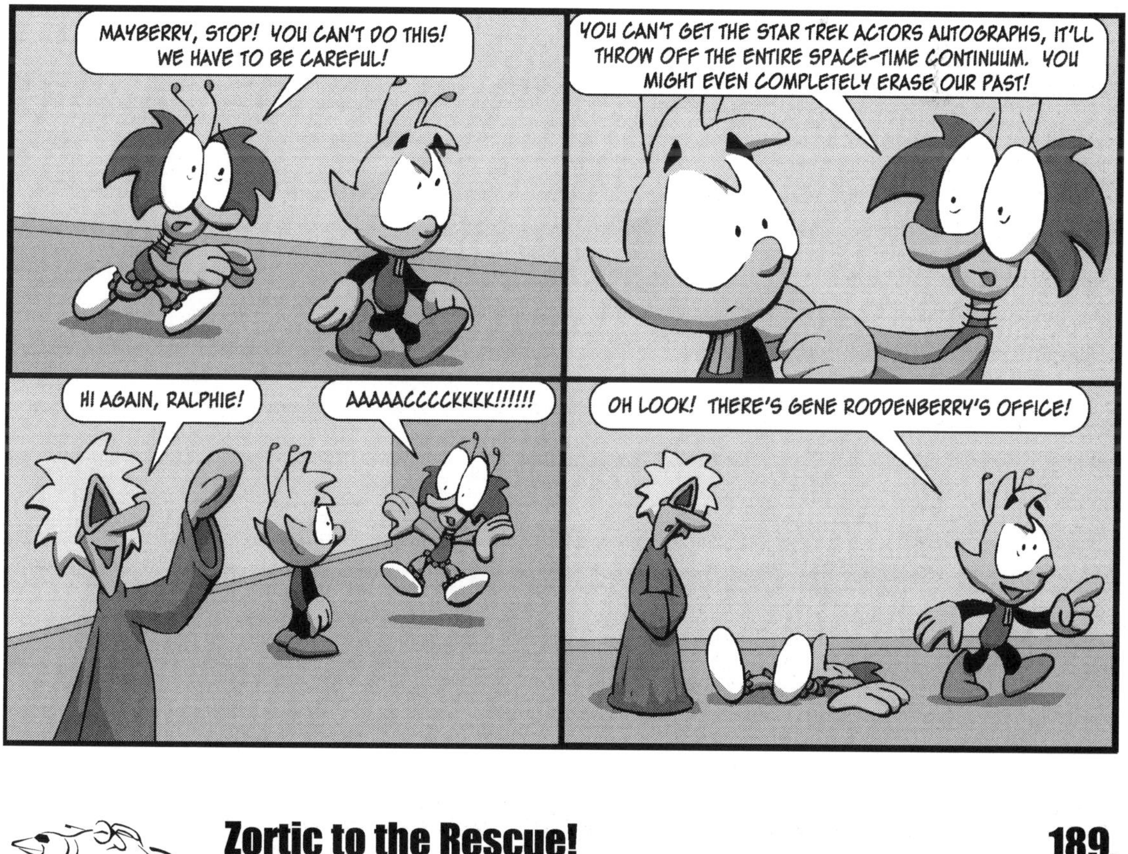
MAYBERRY, STOP! YOU CAN'T DO THIS! WE HAVE TO BE CAREFUL!
YOU CAN'T GET THE STAR TREK ACTORS AUTOGRAPHS, IT'LL THROW OFF THE ENTIRE SPACE-TIME CONTINUUM. YOU MIGHT EVEN COMPLETELY ERASE OUR PAST!
HI AGAIN, RALPHIE!
AAAAACCCCKKKK!!!!!!
OH LOOK! THERE'S GENE RODDENBERRY'S OFFICE!

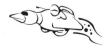

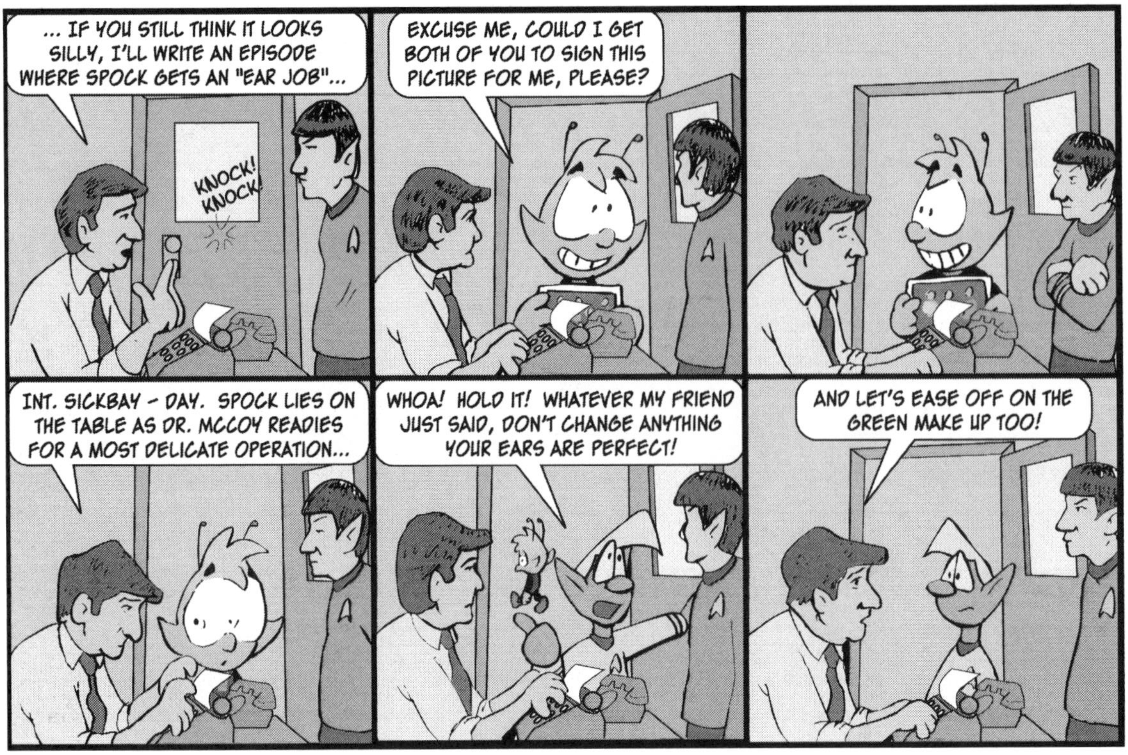
... IF YOU STILL THINK IT LOOKS SILLY, I'LL WRITE AN EPISODE WHERE SPOCK GETS AN "EAR JOB"...
KNOCK! KNOCK!
EXCUSE ME, COULD I GET BOTH OF YOU TO SIGN THIS PICTURE FOR ME, PLEASE?
INT. SICKBAY - DAY. SPOCK LIES ON THE TABLE AS DR. MCCOY READIES FOR A MOST DELICATE OPERATION...
WHOA! HOLD IT! WHATEVER MY FRIEND JUST SAID, DON'T CHANGE ANYTHING YOUR EARS ARE PERFECT!
AND LET'S EASE OFF ON THE GREEN MAKE UP TOO!

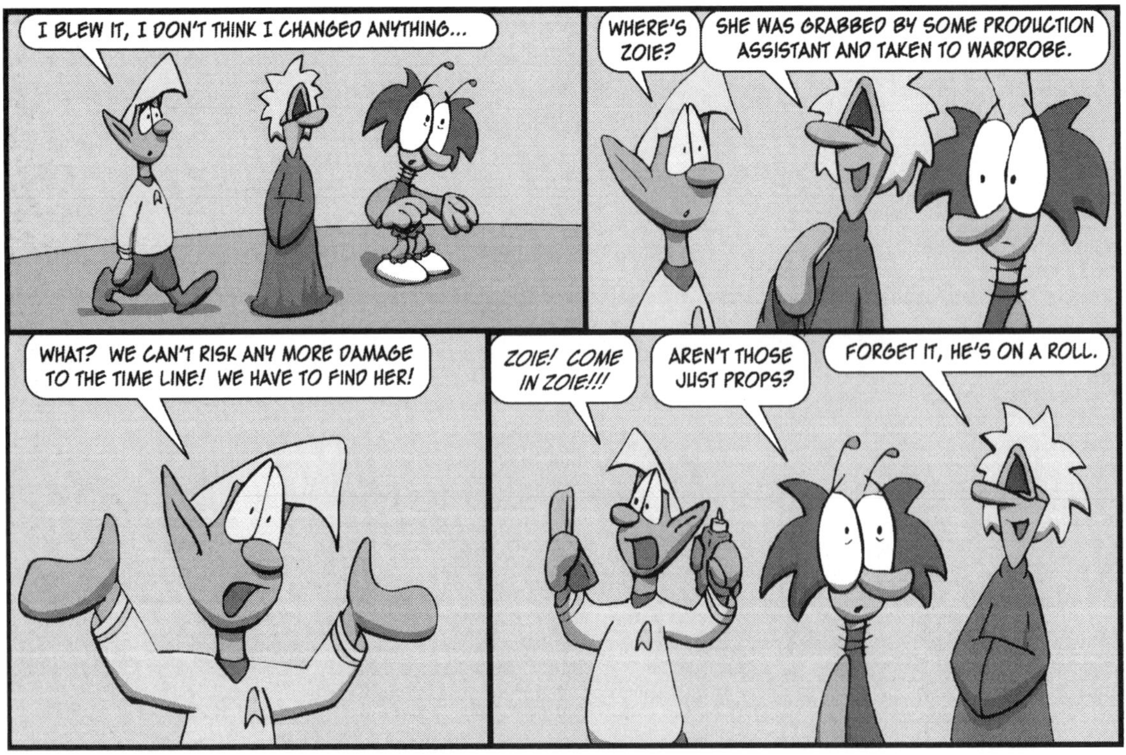
I BLEW IT, I DON'T THINK I CHANGED ANYTHING...
WHERE'S ZOIE?
SHE WAS GRABBED BY SOME PRODUCTION ASSISTANT AND TAKEN TO WARDROBE.
WHAT? WE CAN'T RISK ANY MORE DAMAGE TO THE TIME LINE! WE HAVE TO FIND HER!
ZOIE! COME IN ZOIE!!!
AREN'T THOSE JUST PROPS?
FORGET IT, HE'S ON A ROLL.

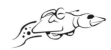

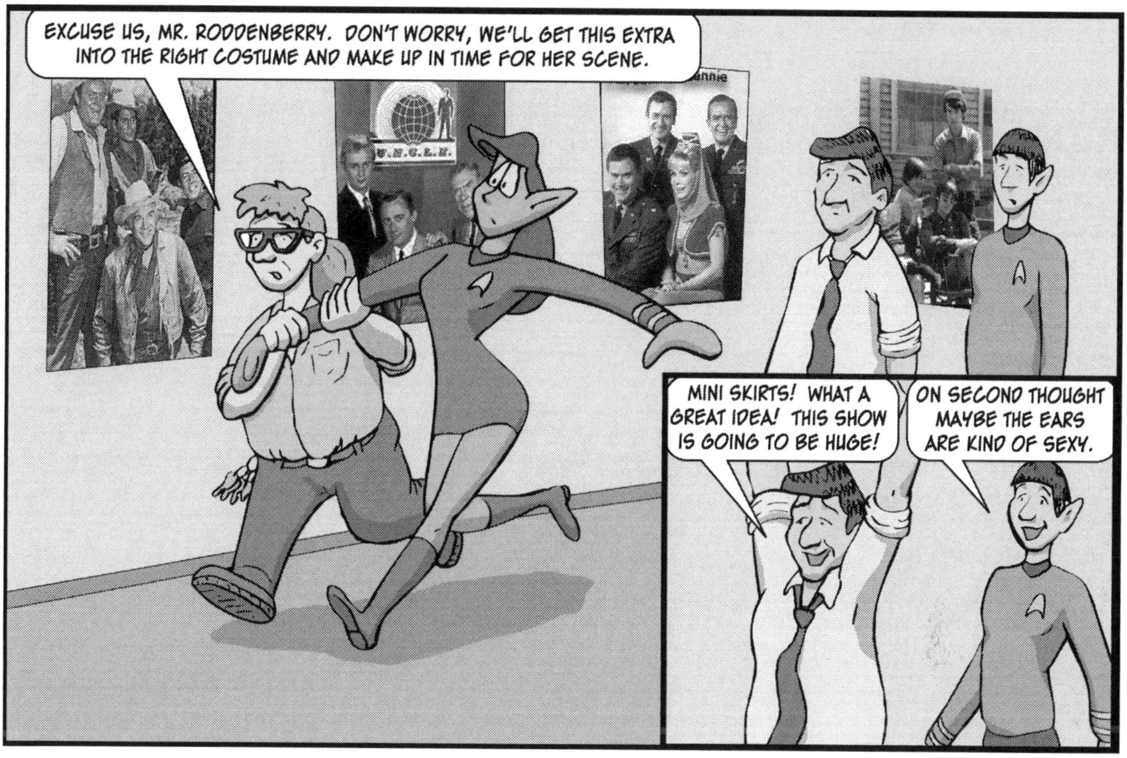
EXCUSE US, MR. RODDENBERRY. DON'T WORRY, WE'LL GET THIS EXTRA INTO THE RIGHT COSTUME AND MAKE UP IN TIME FOR HER SCENE.
U.N.C.L.E.
MINI SKIRTS! WHAT A GREAT IDEA! THIS SHOW IS GOING TO BE HUGE!
ON SECOND THOUGHT MAYBE THE EARS ARE KIND OF SEXY.

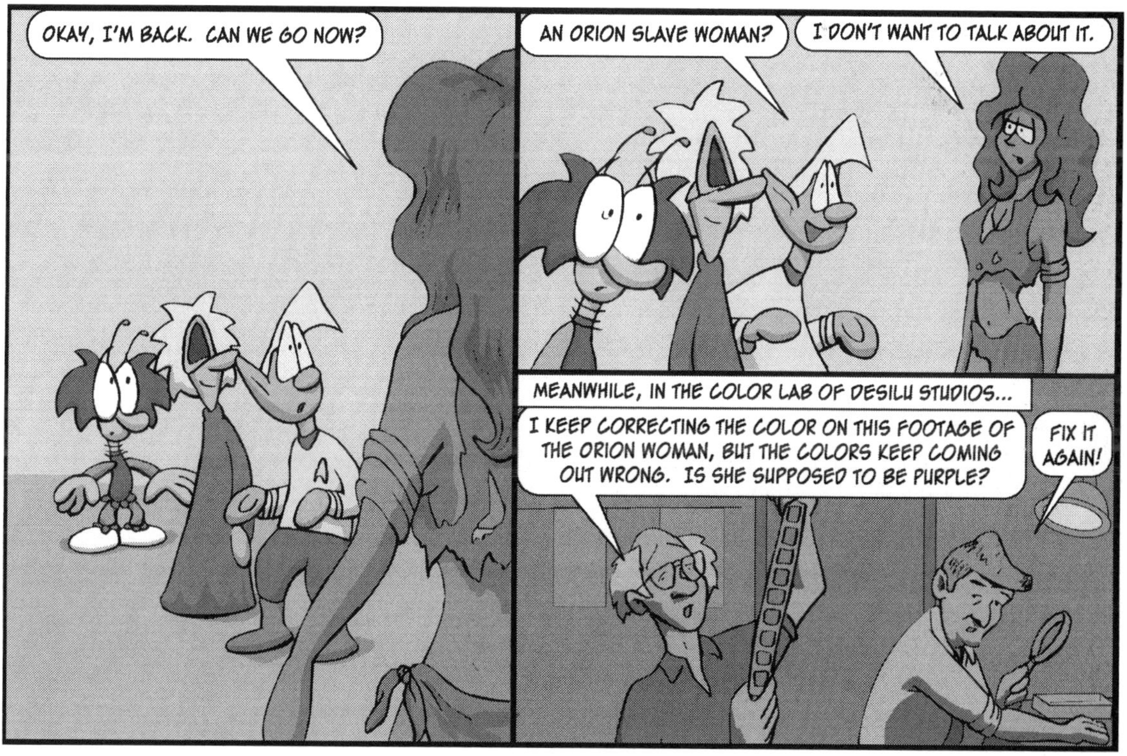
OKAY, I'M BACK. CAN WE GO NOW?
AN ORION SLAVE WOMAN?
I DON'T WANT TO TALK ABOUT IT.
MEANWHILE, IN THE COLOR LAB OF DESILU STUDIOS...
I KEEP CORRECTING THE COLOR ON THIS FOOTAGE OF THE ORION WOMAN, BUT THE COLORS KEEP COMING OUT WRONG. IS SHE SUPPOSED TO BE PURPLE?
FIX IT AGAIN!

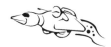

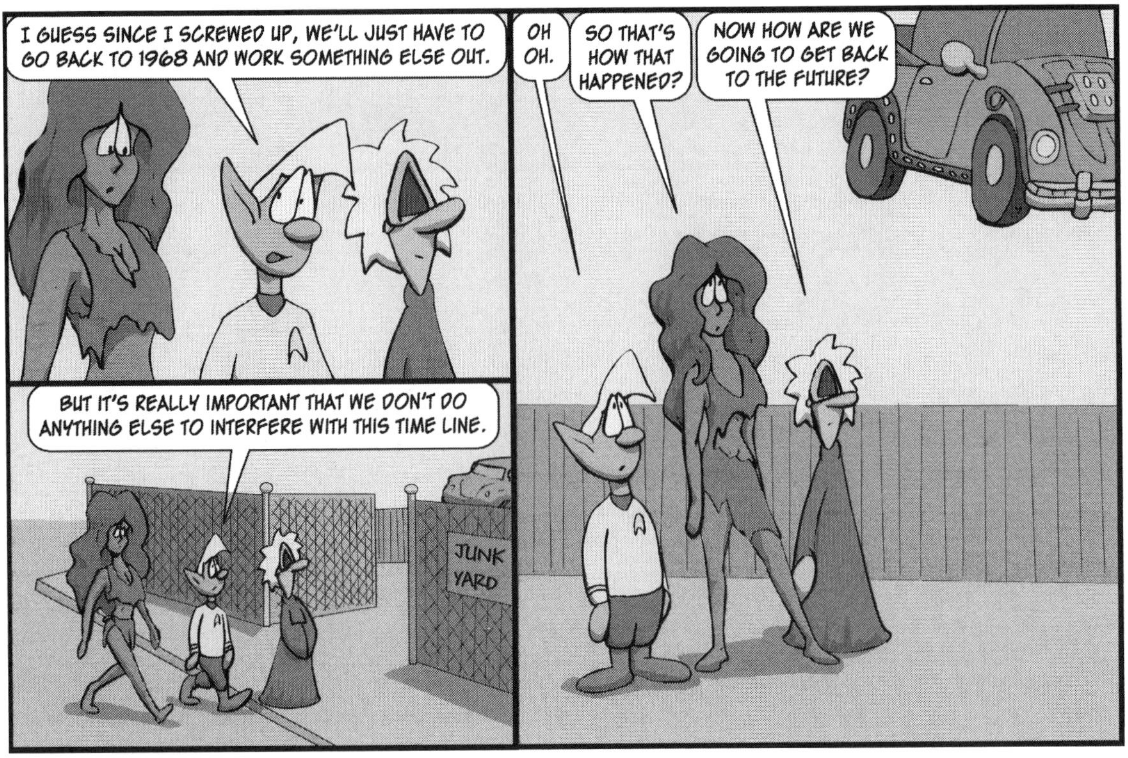
I GUESS SINCE I SCREWED UP, WE'LL JUST HAVE TO GO BACK TO 1968 AND WORK SOMETHING ELSE OUT.
BUT IT'S REALLY IMPORTANT THAT WE DON'T DO ANYTHING ELSE TO INTERFERE WITH THIS TIME LINE.
JUNK YARD
OH OH.
SO THAT'S HOW THAT HAPPENED?
NOW HOW ARE WE GOING TO GET BACK TO THE FUTURE?

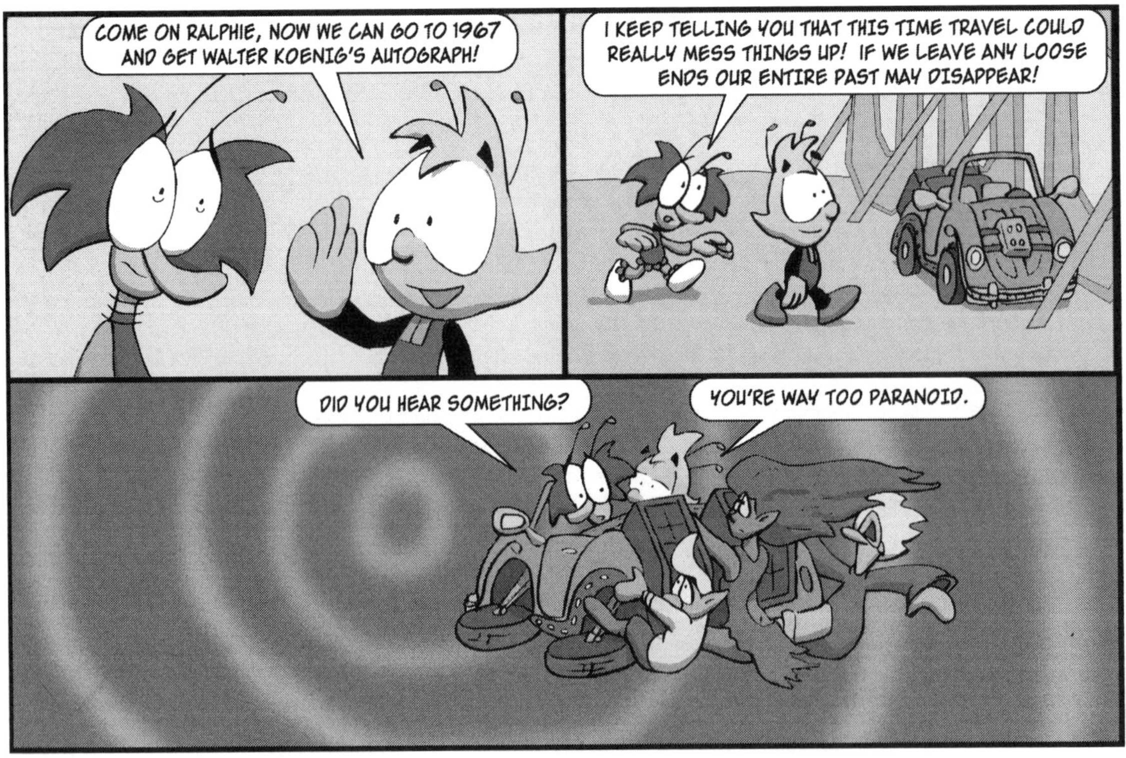
COME ON RALPHIE, NOW WE CAN GO TO 1967 AND GET WALTER KOENIG'S AUTOGRAPH!
I KEEP TELLING YOU THAT THIS TIME TRAVEL COULD REALLY MESS THINGS UP! IF WE LEAVE ANY LOOSE ENDS OUR ENTIRE PAST MAY DISAPPEAR!
DID YOU HEAR SOMETHING?
YOU'RE WAY TOO PARANOID.

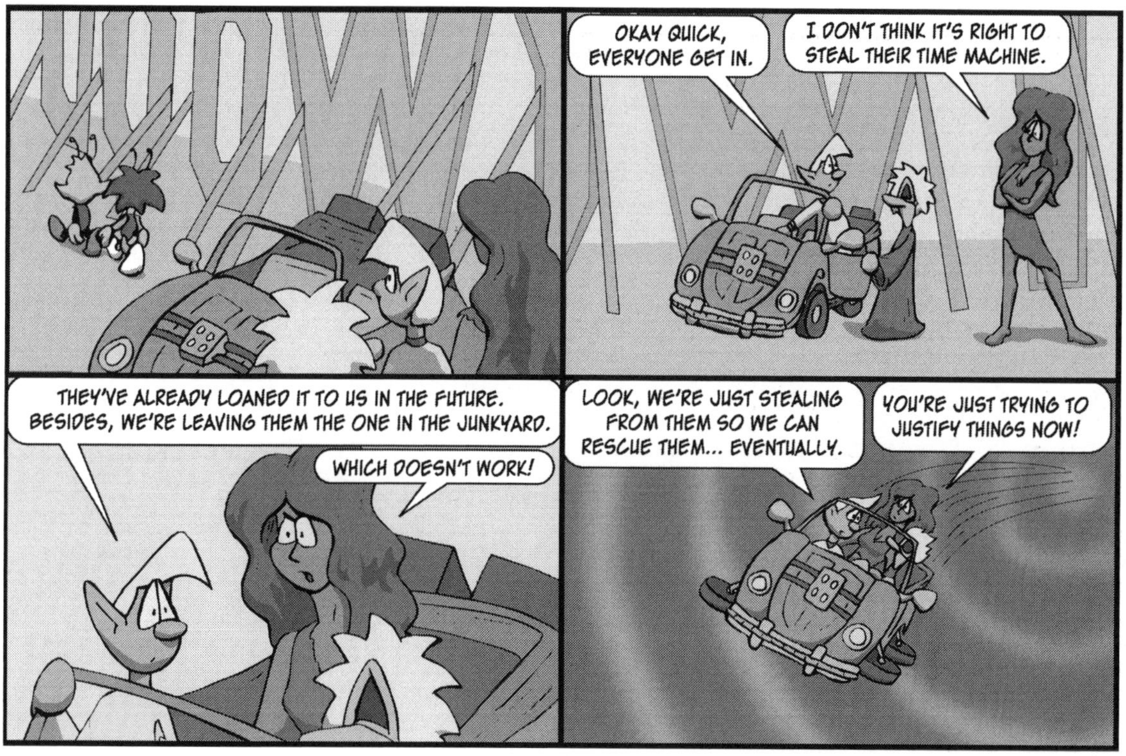
OKAY QUICK, EVERYONE GET IN.
I DON'T THINK IT'S RIGHT TO STEAL THEIR TIME MACHINE.
THEY'VE ALREADY LOANED IT TO US IN THE FUTURE. BESIDES, WE'RE LEAVING THEM THE ONE IN THE JUNKYARD.
WHICH DOESN'T WORK!
LOOK, WE'RE JUST STEALING FROM THEM SO WE CAN RESCUE THEM... EVENTUALLY.
YOU'RE JUST TRYING TO JUSTIFY THINGS NOW!

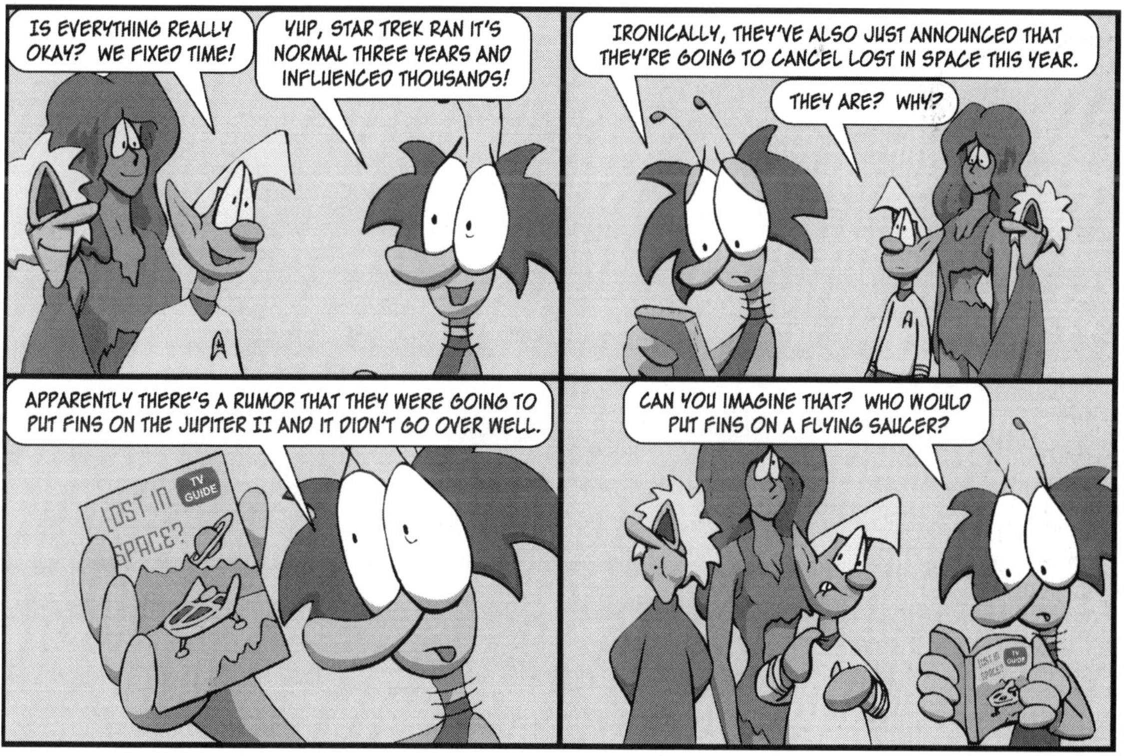
IS EVERYTHING REALLY OKAY? WE FIXED TIME!
YUP, STAR TREK RAN IT'S NORMAL THREE YEARS AND INFLUENCED THOUSANDS!
IRONICALLY, THEY'VE ALSO JUST ANNOUNCED THAT THEY'RE GOING TO CANCEL LOST IN SPACE THIS YEAR.
THEY ARE? WHY?
APPARENTLY THERE'S A RUMOR THAT THEY WERE GOING TO PUT FINS ON THE JUPITER II AND IT DIDN'T GO OVER WELL.
LOST IN SPACE?
TV GUIDE
CAN YOU IMAGINE THAT? WHO WOULD PUT FINS ON A FLYING SAUCER?

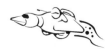

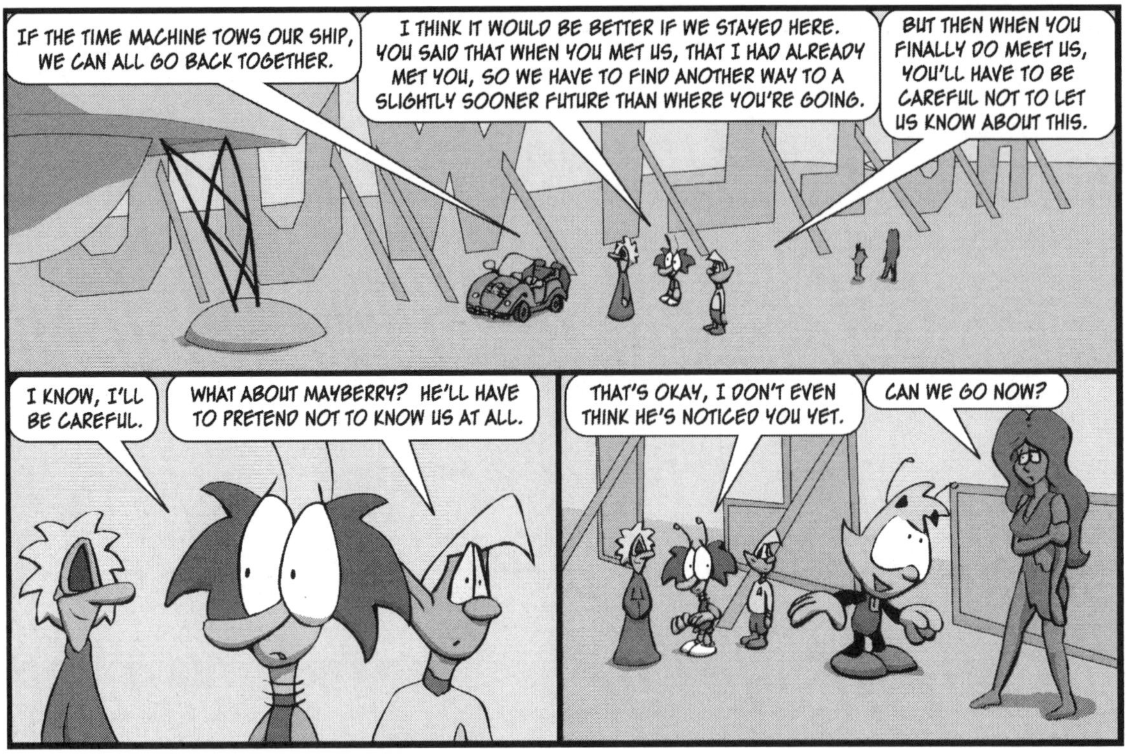
IF THE TIME MACHINE TOWS OUR SHIP, WE CAN ALL GO BACK TOGETHER.
I THINK IT WOULD BE BETTER IF WE STAYED HERE. YOU SAID THAT WHEN YOU MET US, THAT I HAD ALREADY MET YOU, SO WE HAVE TO FIND ANOTHER WAY TO A SLIGHTLY SOONER FUTURE THAN WHERE YOU'RE GOING.
BUT THEN WHEN YOU FINALLY DO MEET US, YOU'LL HAVE TO BE CAREFUL NOT TO LET US KNOW ABOUT THIS.
I KNOW, I'LL BE CAREFUL.
WHAT ABOUT MAYBERRY? HE'LL HAVE TO PRETEND NOT TO KNOW US AT ALL.
THAT'S OKAY, I DON'T EVEN THINK HE'S NOTICED YOU YET.
CAN WE GO NOW?

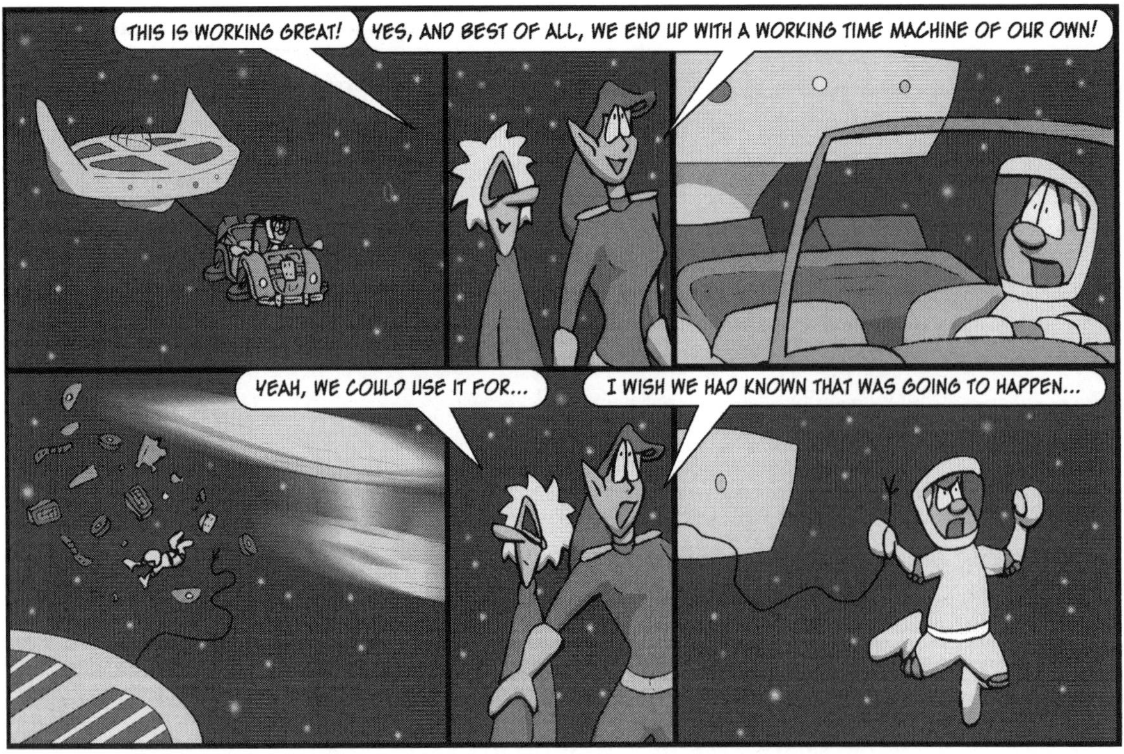
THIS IS WORKING GREAT!
YES, AND BEST OF ALL, WE END UP WITH A WORKING TIME MACHINE OF OUR OWN!
YEAH, WE COULD USE IT FOR...
I WISH WE HAD KNOWN THAT WAS GOING TO HAPPEN...

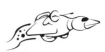

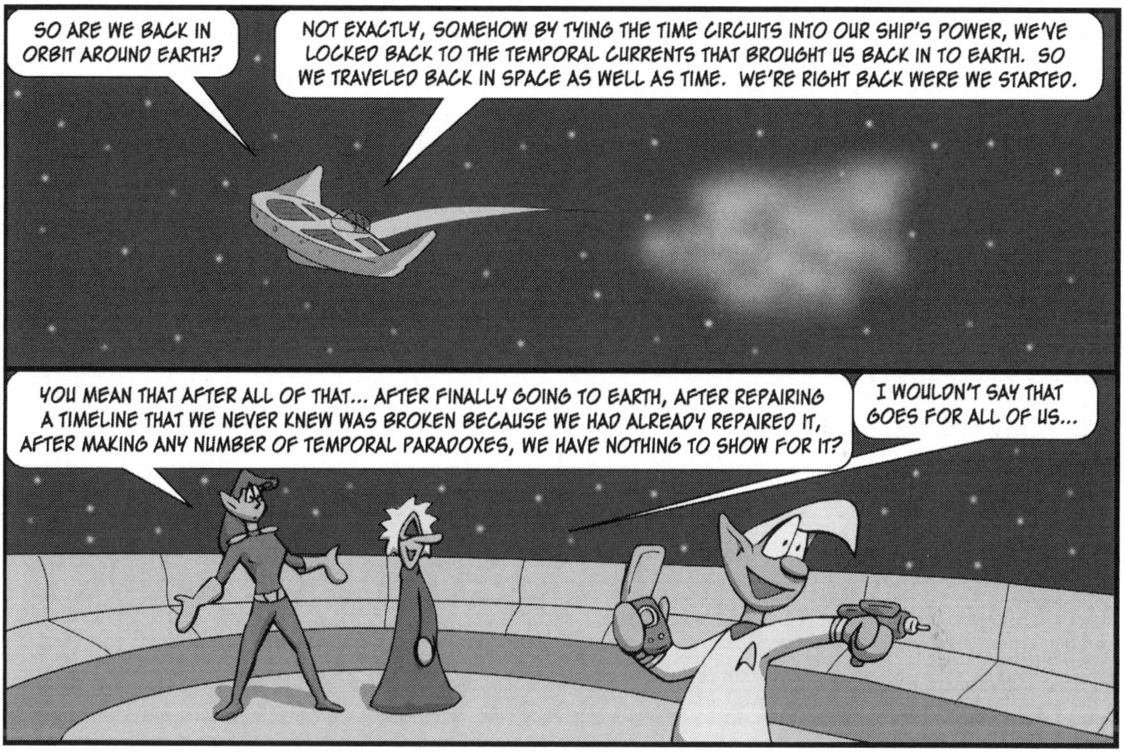
SO ARE WE BACK IN ORBIT AROUND EARTH?
NOT EXACTLY, SOMEHOW BY TYING THE TIME CIRCUITS INTO OUR SHIP'S POWER, WE'VE LOCKED BACK TO THE TEMPORAL CURRENTS THAT BROUGHT US BACK IN TO EARTH. SO WE TRAVELED BACK IN SPACE AS WELL AS TIME. WE'RE RIGHT BACK WERE WE STARTED.
YOU MEAN THAT AFTER ALL OF THAT... AFTER FINALLY GOING TO EARTH, AFTER REPAIRING A TIMELINE THAT WE NEVER KNEW WAS BROKEN BECAUSE WE HAD ALREADY REPAIRED IT, AFTER MAKING ANY NUMBER OF TEMPORAL PARADOXES, WE HAVE NOTHING TO SHOW FOR IT?
I WOULDN'T SAY THAT GOES FOR ALL OF US...

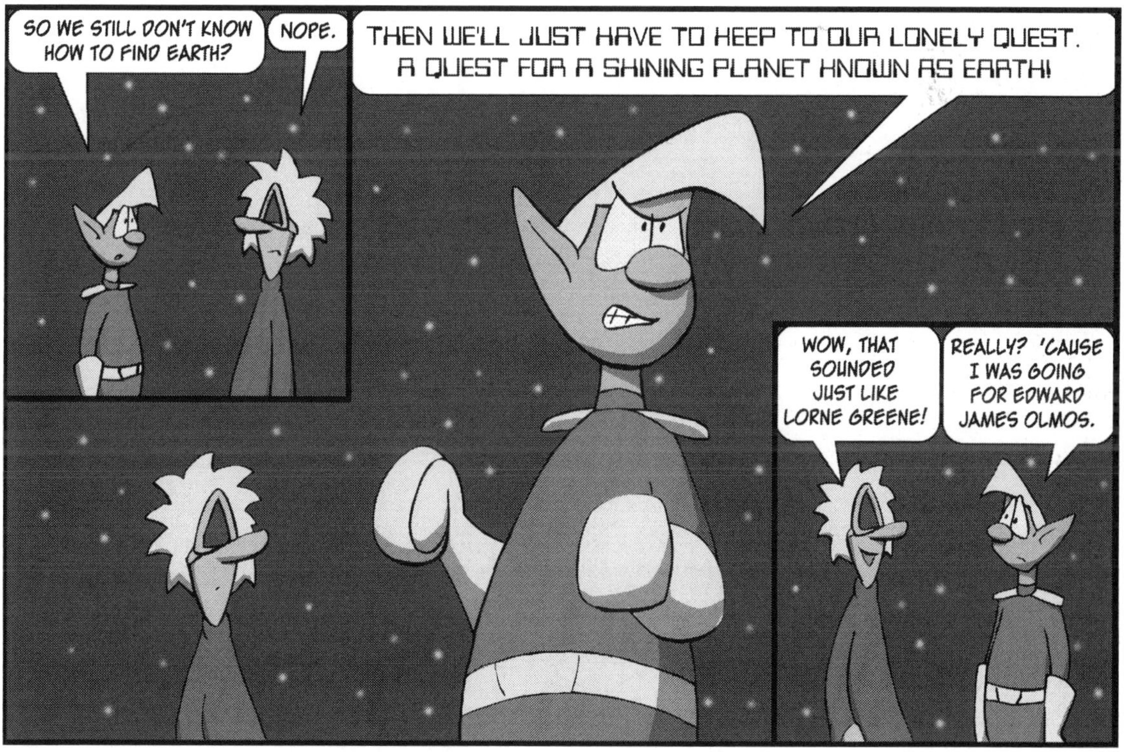
SO WE STILL DON'T KNOW HOW TO FIND EARTH?
NOPE.
THEN WE'LL JUST HAVE TO KEEP TO OUR LONELY QUEST. A QUEST FOR A SHINING PLANET KNOWN AS EARTH!
WOW, THAT SOUNDED JUST LIKE LORNE GREENE!
REALLY? 'CAUSE I WAS GOING FOR EDWARD JAMES OLMOS.

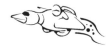

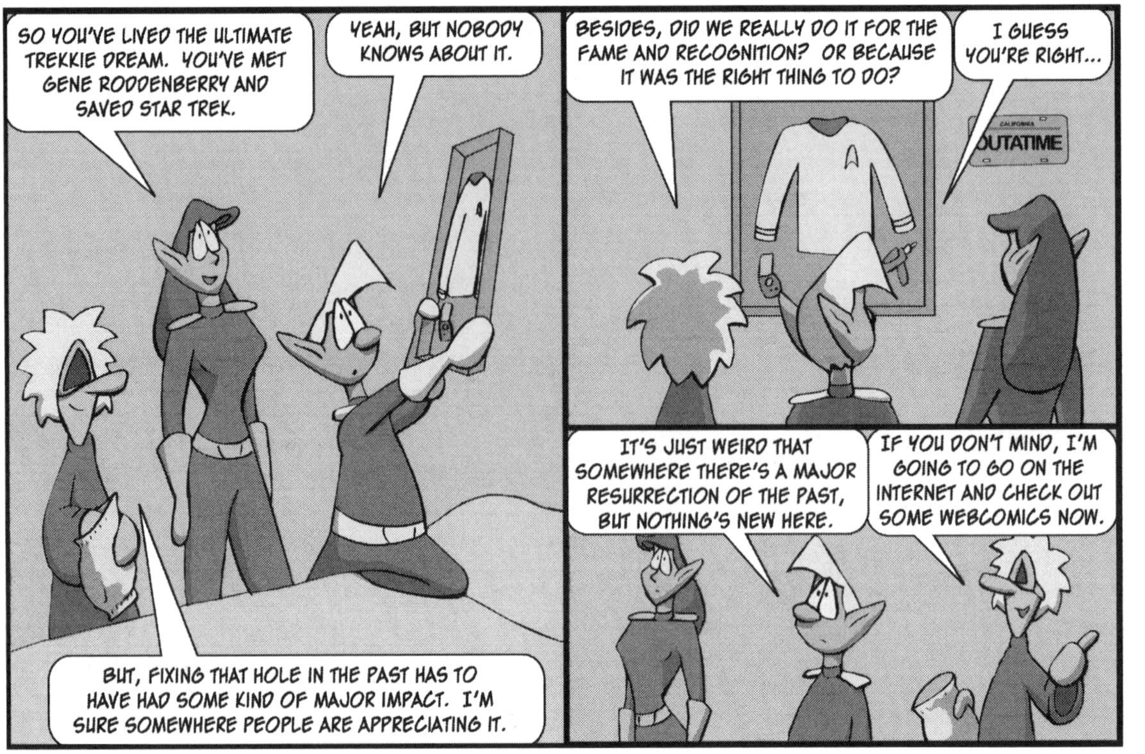
SO YOU'VE LIVED THE ULTIMATE TREKKIE DREAM. YOU'VE MET GENE RODDENBERRY AND SAVED STAR TREK.
YEAH, BUT NOBODY KNOWS ABOUT IT.
BUT, FIXING THAT HOLE IN THE PAST HAS TO HAVE HAD SOME KIND OF MAJOR IMPACT. I'M SURE SOMEWHERE PEOPLE ARE APPRECIATING IT.
BESIDES, DID WE REALLY DO IT FOR THE FAME AND RECOGNITION? OR BECAUSE IT WAS THE RIGHT THING TO DO?
I GUESS YOU'RE RIGHT...
OUTATIME
IT'S JUST WEIRD THAT SOMEWHERE THERE'S A MAJOR RESURRECTION OF THE PAST, BUT NOTHING'S NEW HERE.
IF YOU DON'T MIND, I'M GOING TO GO ON THE INTERNET AND CHECK OUT SOME WEBCOMICS NOW.

As a bonus, I included the Zortic strip that ran several months before the original **Melonpool/ Zortic Crossover** to clue in Mark's and my mutual readers (see page 55).

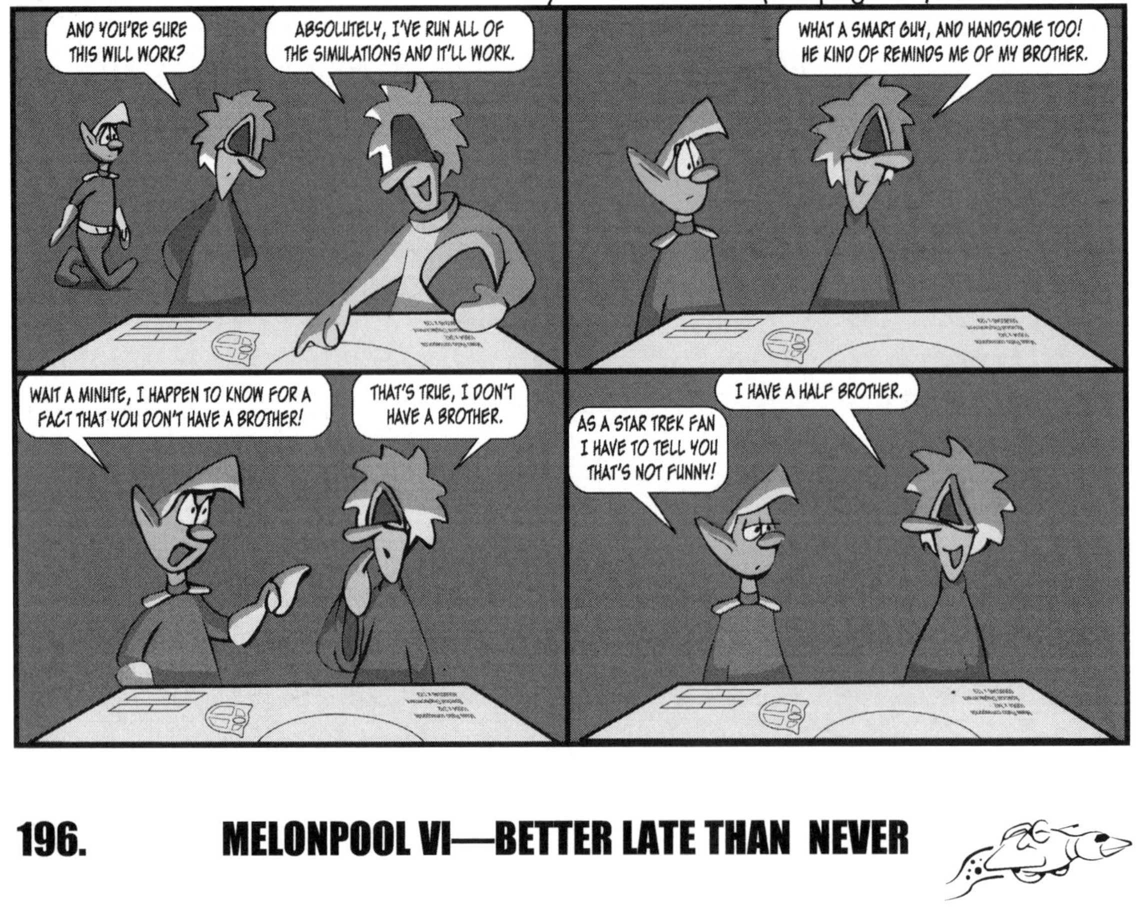
AND YOU'RE SURE THIS WILL WORK?
ABSOLUTELY, I'VE RUN ALL OF THE SIMULATIONS AND IT'LL WORK.
WHAT A SMART GUY, AND HANDSOME TOO! HE KIND OF REMINDS ME OF MY BROTHER.
WAIT A MINUTE, I HAPPEN TO KNOW FOR A FACT THAT YOU DON'T HAVE A BROTHER!
THAT'S TRUE, I DON'T HAVE A BROTHER.
I HAVE A HALF BROTHER.
AS A STAR TREK FAN I HAVE TO TELL YOU THAT'S NOT FUNNY!

MISCELLANEOUS MELONPOOL

Mark Mekkes wasn't the only one to keep Melonpool alive on the Internet. Yamcha Hibiki (AKA Robbie Allen) was so inspired by Teague Tyselling's re-imagining of the Melonpool characters (see TUM V, pages 57–59), that he took his own stab at it! After seeing his character studies, I asked if he'd do a guest week.

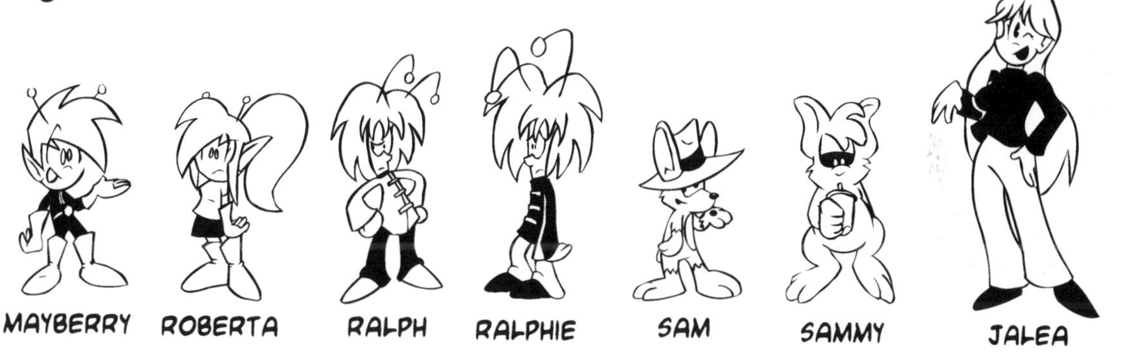
MAYBERRY
ROBERTA
RALPH
RALPHIE
SAM
SAMMY
JALEA

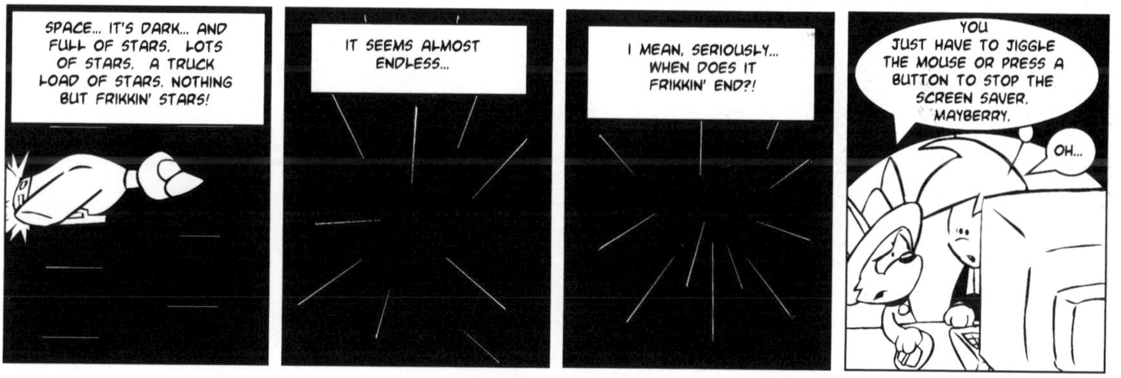
SPACE... IT'S DARK... AND FULL OF STARS. LOTS OF STARS. A TRUCK LOAD OF STARS. NOTHING BUT FRIKKIN' STARS!
IT SEEMS ALMOST ENDLESS...
I MEAN, SERIOUSLY... WHEN DOES IT FRIKKIN' END?!
YOU JUST HAVE TO JIGGLE THE MOUSE OR PRESS A BUTTON TO STOP THE SCREEN SAVER, MAYBERRY.
OH...

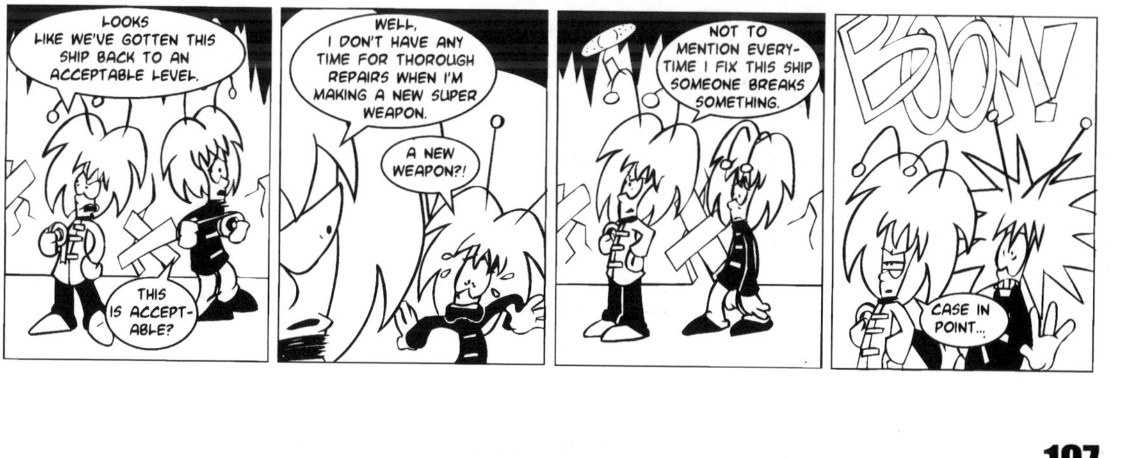
LOOKS LIKE WE'VE GOTTEN THIS SHIP BACK TO AN ACCEPTABLE LEVEL.
THIS IS ACCEPT-ABLE?
WELL, I DON'T HAVE ANY TIME FOR THOROUGH REPAIRS WHEN I'M MAKING A NEW SUPER WEAPON.
A NEW WEAPON?!
NOT TO MENTION EVERY-TIME I FIX THIS SHIP SOMEONE BREAKS SOMETHING.
BOOOM!
CASE IN POINT...

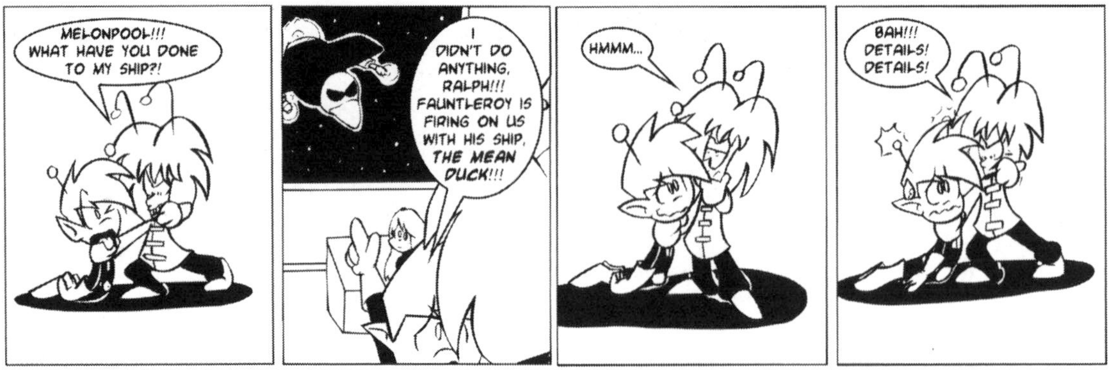
MELONPOOL!!! WHAT HAVE YOU DONE TO MY SHIP?!
I DIDN'T DO ANYTHING, RALPH!!! FAUNTLEROY IS FIRING ON US WITH HIS SHIP, THE MEAN DUCK!!!
HMMM...
BAH!!! DETAILS! DETAILS!

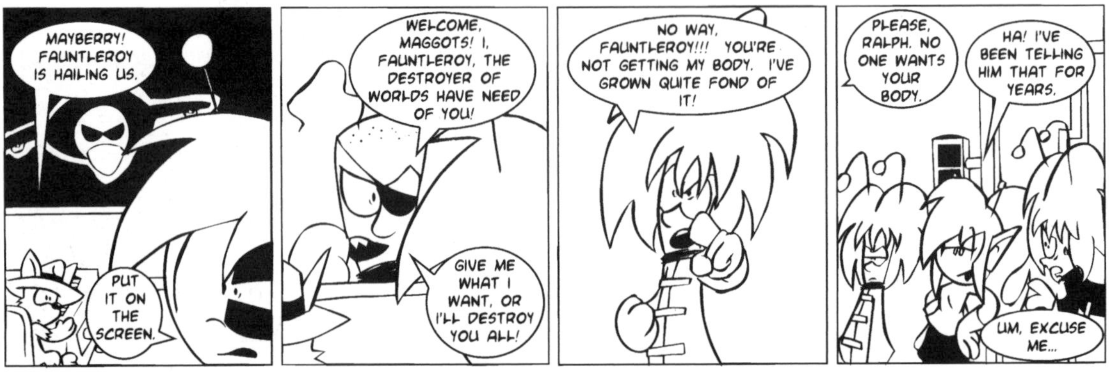
MAYBERRY! FAUNTLEROY IS HAILING US.
PUT IT ON THE SCREEN.
WELCOME, MAGGOTS! I, FAUNTLEROY, THE DESTROYER OF WORLDS HAVE NEED OF YOU!
GIVE ME WHAT I WANT, OR I'LL DESTROY YOU ALL!
NO WAY, FAUNTLEROY!!! YOU'RE NOT GETTING MY BODY. I'VE GROWN QUITE FOND OF IT!
PLEASE, RALPH. NO ONE WANTS YOUR BODY.
HA! I'VE BEEN TELLING HIM THAT FOR YEARS.
UM, EXCUSE ME...

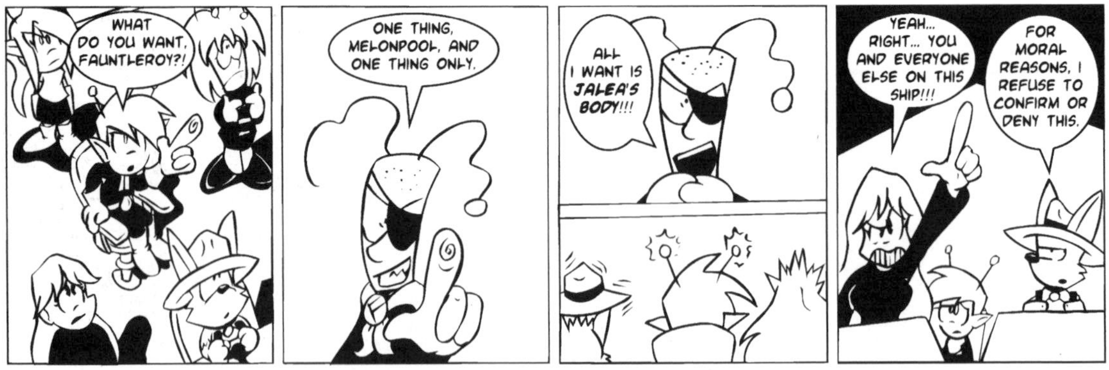
WHAT DO YOU WANT, FAUNTLEROY?!
ONE THING, MELONPOOL, AND ONE THING ONLY.
ALL I WANT IS JALEA'S BODY!!!
YEAH... RIGHT... YOU AND EVERYONE ELSE ON THIS SHIP!!!
FOR MORAL REASONS, I REFUSE TO CONFIRM OR DENY THIS.

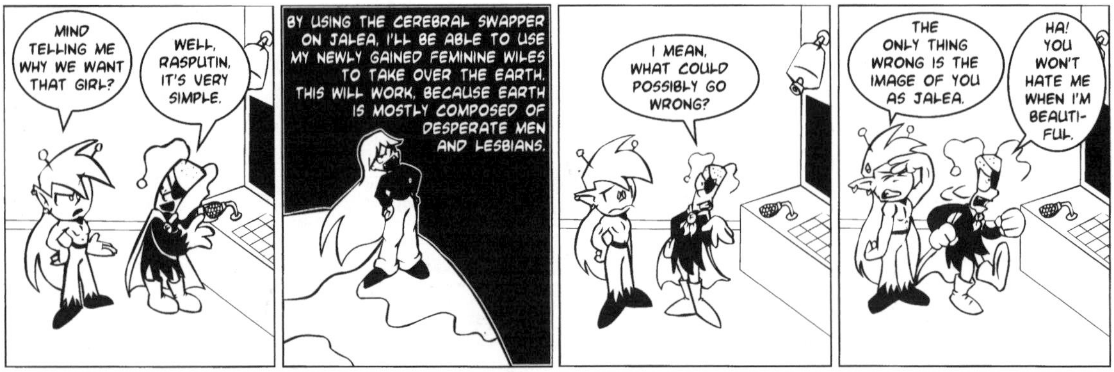
MIND TELLING ME WHY WE WANT THAT GIRL?
WELL, RASPUTIN, IT'S VERY SIMPLE.
BY USING THE CEREBRAL SWAPPER ON JALEA, I'LL BE ABLE TO USE MY NEWLY GAINED FEMININE WILES TO TAKE OVER THE EARTH. THIS WILL WORK, BECAUSE EARTH IS MOSTLY COMPOSED OF DESPERATE MEN AND LESBIANS.
I MEAN, WHAT COULD POSSIBLY GO WRONG?
THE ONLY THING WRONG IS THE IMAGE OF YOU AS JALEA.
HA! YOU WON'T HATE ME WHEN I'M BEAUTI-FUL.

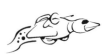

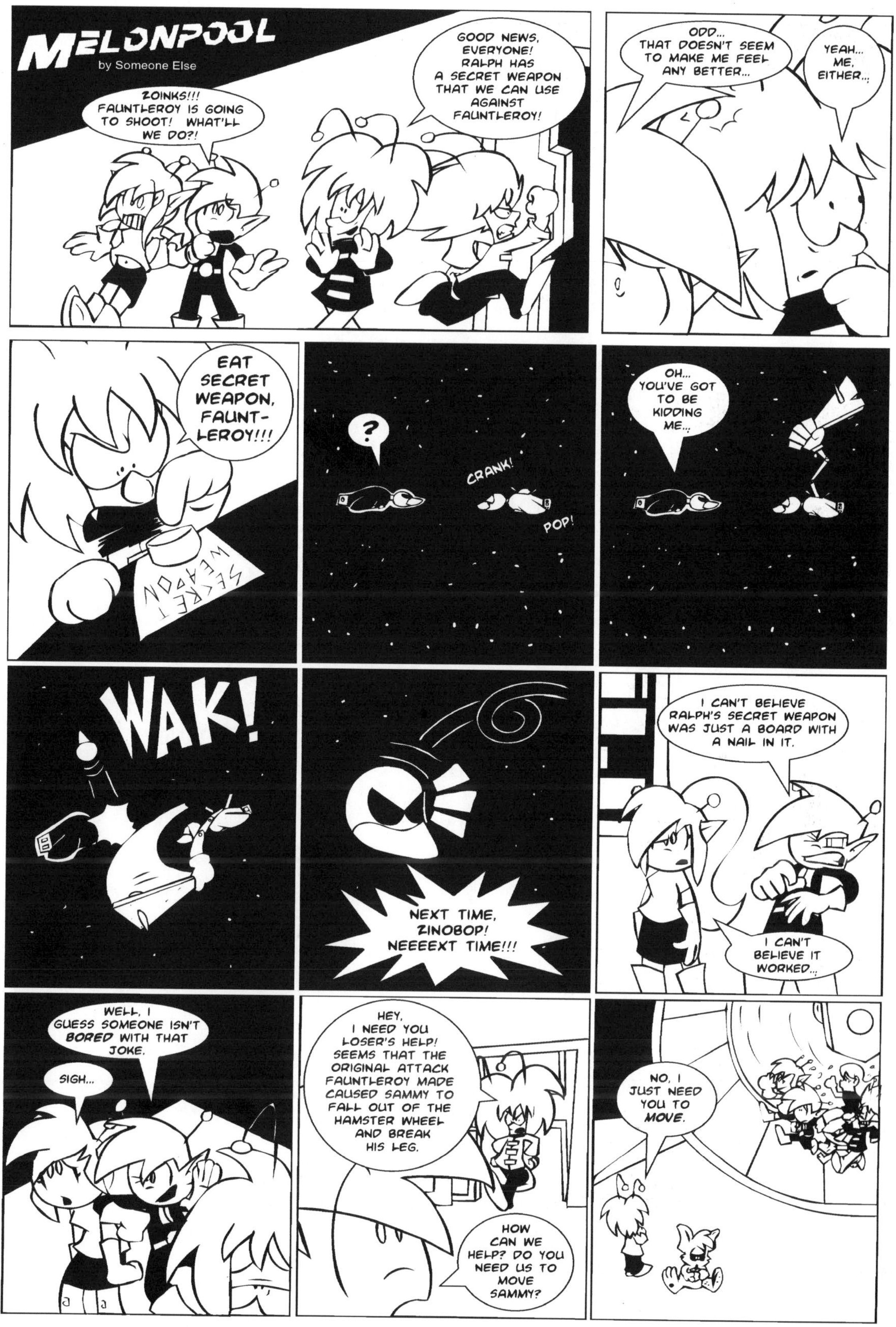
MELONPOOL
by Someone Else
ZOINKS!!! FAUNTLEROY IS GOING TO SHOOT! WHAT'LL WE DO?!
GOOD NEWS, EVERYONE! RALPH HAS A SECRET WEAPON THAT WE CAN USE AGAINST FAUNTLEROY!
ODD... THAT DOESN'T SEEM TO MAKE ME FEEL ANY BETTER...
YEAH... ME, EITHER...
EAT SECRET WEAPON, FAUNT-LEROY!!!
SECRET WEAPON
?
CRANK!
POP!
OH... YOU'VE GOT TO BE KIDDING ME...
WAK!
NEXT TIME, ZINOBOP! NEEEEXT TIME!!!
I CAN'T BELIEVE RALPH'S SECRET WEAPON WAS JUST A BOARD WITH A NAIL IN IT.
I CAN'T BELIEVE IT WORKED...
WELL, I GUESS SOMEONE ISN'T BORED WITH THAT JOKE.
SIGH...
HEY, I NEED YOU LOSER'S HELP! SEEMS THAT THE ORIGINAL ATTACK FAUNTLEROY MADE CAUSED SAMMY TO FALL OUT OF THE HAMSTER WHEEL AND BREAK HIS LEG.
HOW CAN WE HELP? DO YOU NEED US TO MOVE SAMMY?
NO, I JUST NEED YOU TO MOVE.

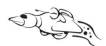

Dan Shive, of *El Goonish Shive*, was dabbling in hand lettering. I gave him a few tips and he, in turn, drew up three *Melonpool* comics to test out his new-found skills. Dan was also kind enough to allow me to use some of his characters as extras in a few of my strips (see page 89).

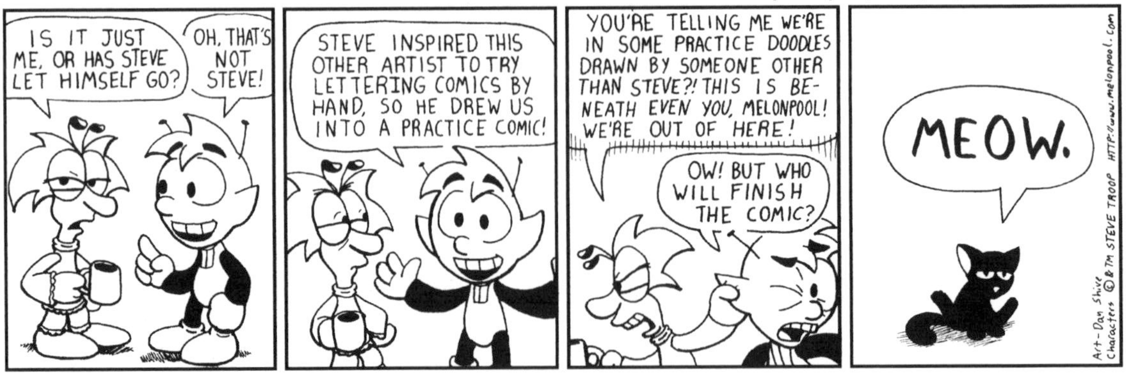
IS IT JUST ME, OR HAS STEVE LET HIMSELF GO?
OH, THAT'S NOT STEVE!
STEVE INSPIRED THIS OTHER ARTIST TO TRY LETTERING COMICS BY HAND, SO HE DREW US INTO A PRACTICE COMIC!
YOU'RE TELLING ME WE'RE IN SOME PRACTICE DOODLES DRAWN BY SOMEONE OTHER THAN STEVE?! THIS IS BENEATH EVEN YOU, MELONPOOL! WE'RE OUT OF HERE!
OW! BUT WHO WILL FINISH THE COMIC?
MEOW.
Art-Dan Shive Characters ©&TM STEVE TROOP HTTP://www.melonpool.com

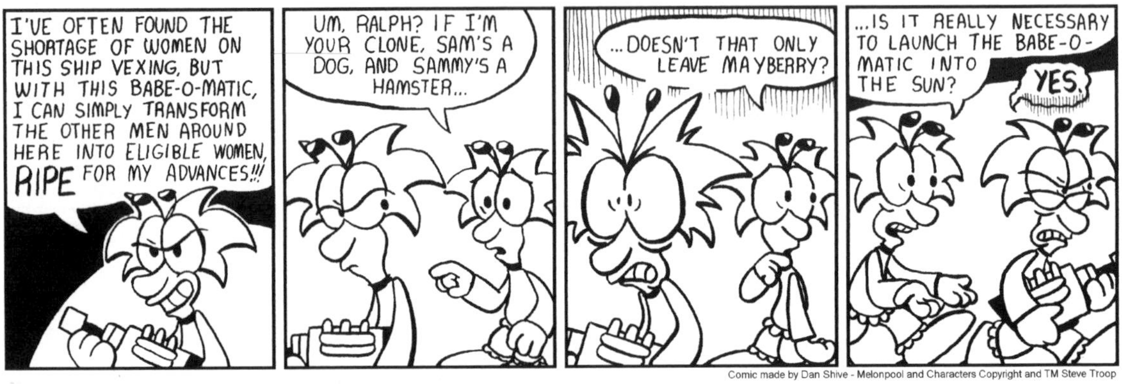
I'VE OFTEN FOUND THE SHORTAGE OF WOMEN ON THIS SHIP VEXING, BUT WITH THIS BABE-O-MATIC, I CAN SIMPLY TRANSFORM THE OTHER MEN AROUND HERE INTO ELIGIBLE WOMEN, RIPE FOR MY ADVANCES!!!
UM, RALPH? IF I'M YOUR CLONE, SAM'S A DOG, AND SAMMY'S A HAMSTER...
...DOESN'T THAT ONLY LEAVE MAYBERRY?
...IS IT REALLY NECESSARY TO LAUNCH THE BABE-O-MATIC INTO THE SUN?
YES.

Comic made by Dan Shive - Melonpool and Characters Copyright and TM Steve Troop

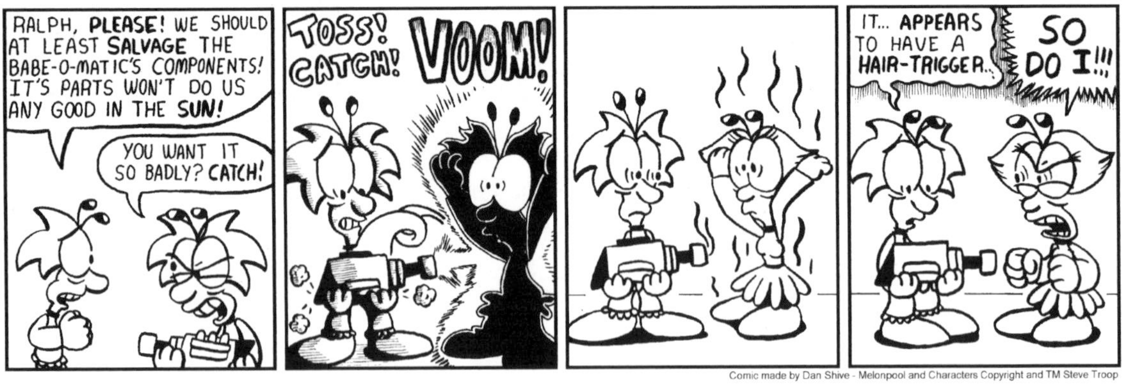
RALPH, PLEASE! WE SHOULD AT LEAST SALVAGE THE BABE-O-MATIC'S COMPONENTS! IT'S PARTS WON'T DO US ANY GOOD IN THE SUN!
YOU WANT IT SO BADLY? CATCH!
TOSS! CATCH!
VOOM!
IT... APPEARS TO HAVE A HAIR-TRIGGER...
SO DO I!!!

Comic made by Dan Shive - Melonpool and Characters Copyright and TM Steve Troop

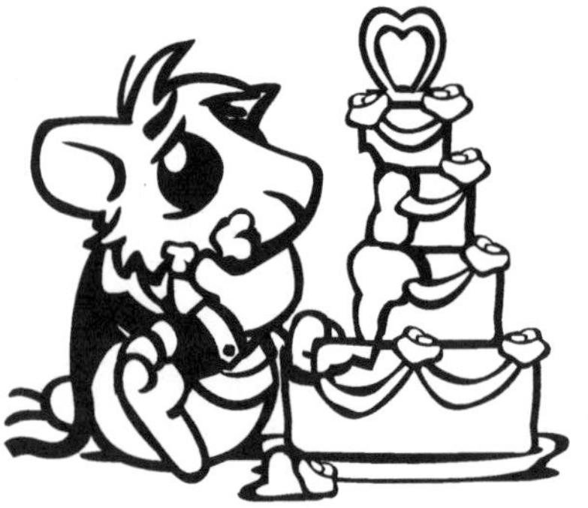

This final bit isn't a piece of fan art at all—but rather a piece of art I drew for Chris Gleason (puppeteer of Sammy the Hammy) and Linda Shaver (FortyTwo on the *Melonpool* forums) for their wedding.

The Gleasons actually met on my forums, so they asked me to design playing cards for their wedding reception. Unfortunately, I wasn't able to attend—I got an ear infection just before I was supposed to fly to Chicago for their wedding.

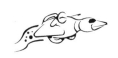

THE ADVENTURE CONTINUES...

Somehow, I knew I wasn't done with Melonpool. Even I realized that my "final" strip was a less-than-satisfactory ending for the series. More importantly, there were a few plotlines—such as Ralph's Cellular Degeneration (see pages 127–134) that I had never bothered to wrap up.

So, almost two years to the day after I abruptly ended Melonpool, I came back for one last storyline. But unlike all of my other hiatuses, I decided to pick up the story as if two years had passed in the Melonpool universe as well.

There were two major changes to this batch of strips. First, I decided that I was done drawing Sundays. I would instead try to keep a better balance with my non-Melonpool life by only updating four times a week. Second, these strips were created digitally using a WACOM tablet in Adobe Illustrator. Even the lettering was a digitized version of my own handwriting.

While this sped up the process a lot, ultimately, I stopped updating the strip as a daily at the conclusion of this storyline. Occasionally, I still update the strip in a Sunday format, but I've switched back to drawing the strips by hand with India ink and a brush. I found that it took longer to try to make the strips look hand-drawn using a computer than it did just to hand draw them.

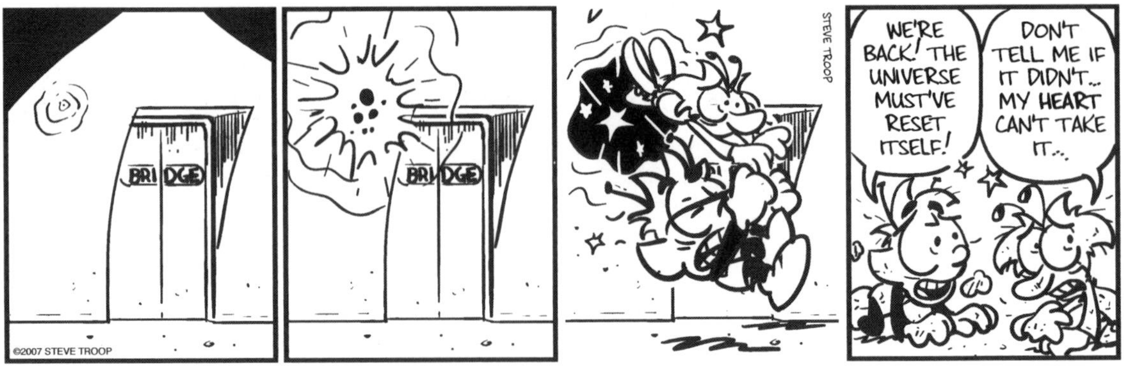
BRIDGE
BRIDGE
STEVE TROOP
WE'RE BACK! THE UNIVERSE MUST'VE RESET ITSELF!
DON'T TELL ME IF IT DIDN'T... MY HEART CAN'T TAKE IT...
©2007 STEVE TROOP

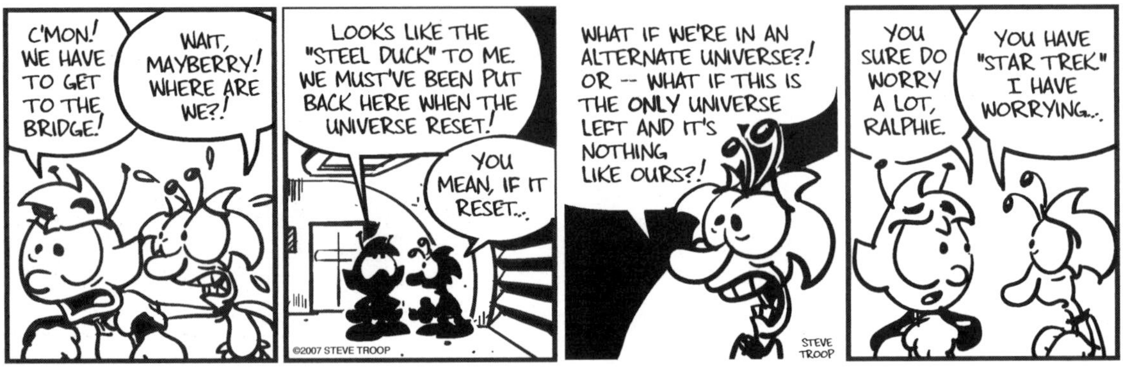
C'MON! WE HAVE TO GET TO THE BRIDGE!
WAIT, MAYBERRY! WHERE ARE WE?!
LOOKS LIKE THE "STEEL DUCK" TO ME. WE MUST'VE BEEN PUT BACK HERE WHEN THE UNIVERSE RESET!
YOU MEAN, IF IT RESET...
WHAT IF WE'RE IN AN ALTERNATE UNIVERSE?! OR -- WHAT IF THIS IS THE ONLY UNIVERSE LEFT AND IT'S NOTHING LIKE OURS?!
YOU SURE DO WORRY A LOT, RALPHIE.
YOU HAVE "STAR TREK." I HAVE WORRYING...
©2007 STEVE TROOP
STEVE TROOP

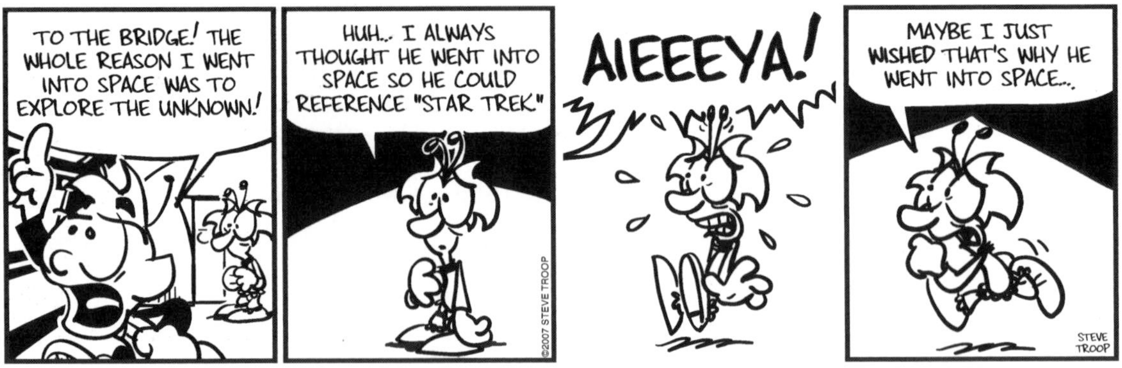
TO THE BRIDGE! THE WHOLE REASON I WENT INTO SPACE WAS TO EXPLORE THE UNKNOWN!
HUH... I ALWAYS THOUGHT HE WENT INTO SPACE SO HE COULD REFERENCE "STAR TREK."
AIEEEYA!
MAYBE I JUST WISHED THAT'S WHY HE WENT INTO SPACE...
©2007 STEVE TROOP
STEVE TROOP

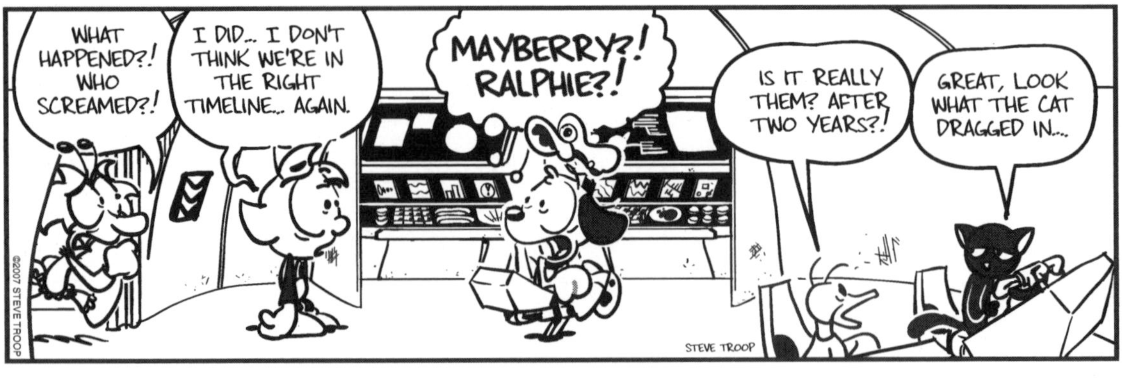
WHAT HAPPENED?! WHO SCREAMED?!
I DID... I DON'T THINK WE'RE IN THE RIGHT TIMELINE... AGAIN.
MAYBERRY?! RALPHIE?!
IS IT REALLY THEM? AFTER TWO YEARS?!
GREAT, LOOK WHAT THE CAT DRAGGED IN...
©2007 STEVE TROOP
STEVE TROOP

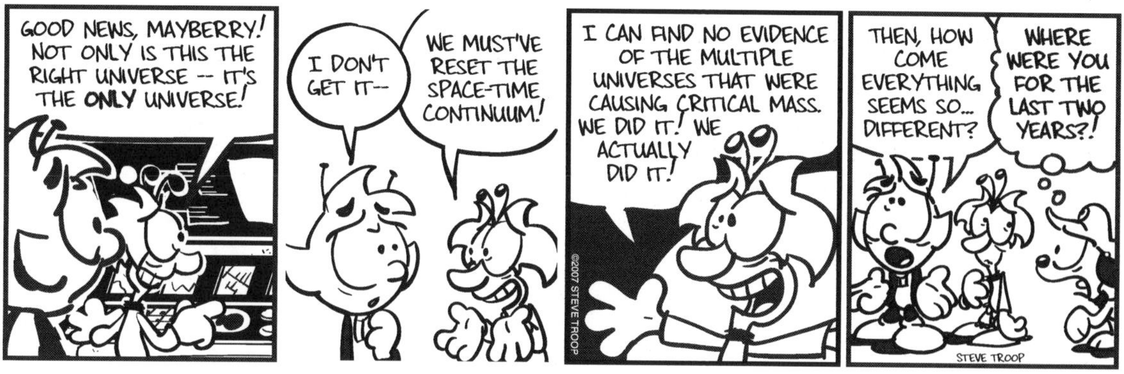
GOOD NEWS, MAYBERRY! NOT ONLY IS THIS THE RIGHT UNIVERSE -- IT'S THE **ONLY** UNIVERSE!
I DON'T GET IT--
WE MUST'VE RESET THE SPACE-TIME CONTINUUM!
I CAN FIND NO EVIDENCE OF THE MULTIPLE UNIVERSES THAT WERE CAUSING CRITICAL MASS. WE DID IT! WE ACTUALLY DID IT!
©2007 STEVE TROOP
THEN, HOW COME EVERYTHING SEEMS SO... DIFFERENT?
WHERE WERE YOU FOR THE LAST TWO YEARS?!
STEVE TROOP

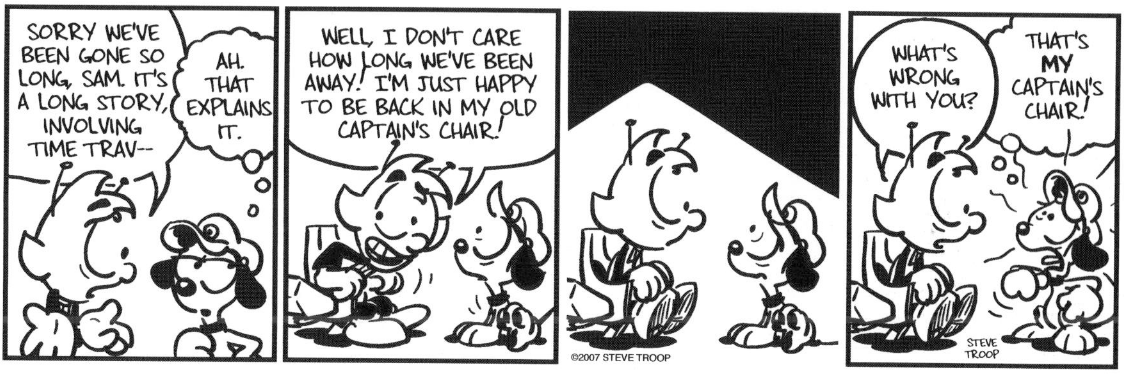
SORRY WE'VE BEEN GONE SO LONG, SAM. IT'S A LONG STORY, INVOLVING TIME TRAV--
AH. THAT EXPLAINS IT.
WELL, I DON'T CARE HOW LONG WE'VE BEEN AWAY! I'M JUST HAPPY TO BE BACK IN MY OLD CAPTAIN'S CHAIR!
©2007 STEVE TROOP
WHAT'S WRONG WITH YOU?
THAT'S **MY** CAPTAIN'S CHAIR!
STEVE TROOP

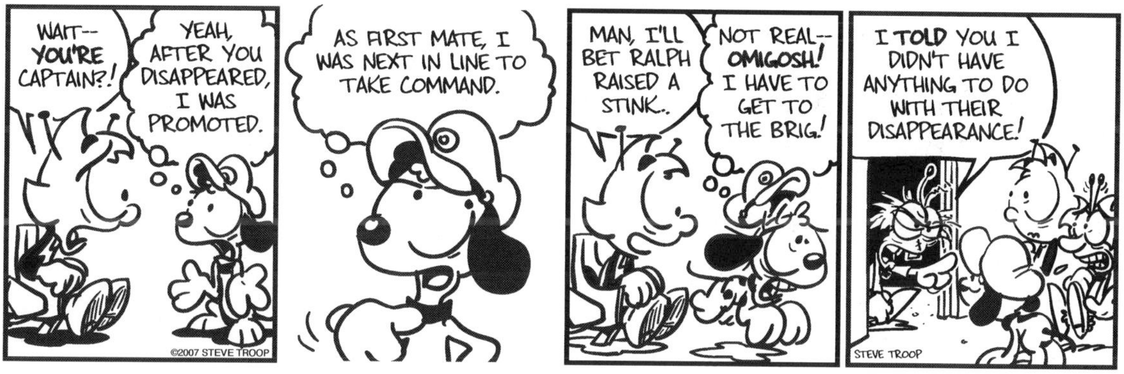
WAIT-- **YOU'RE** CAPTAIN?!
YEAH, AFTER YOU DISAPPEARED, I WAS PROMOTED.
©2007 STEVE TROOP
AS FIRST MATE, I WAS NEXT IN LINE TO TAKE COMMAND.
MAN, I'LL BET RALPH RAISED A STINK..
NOT REAL-- **OMIGOSH!** I HAVE TO GET TO THE BRIG!
I **TOLD** YOU I DIDN'T HAVE ANYTHING TO DO WITH THEIR DISAPPEARANCE!
STEVE TROOP

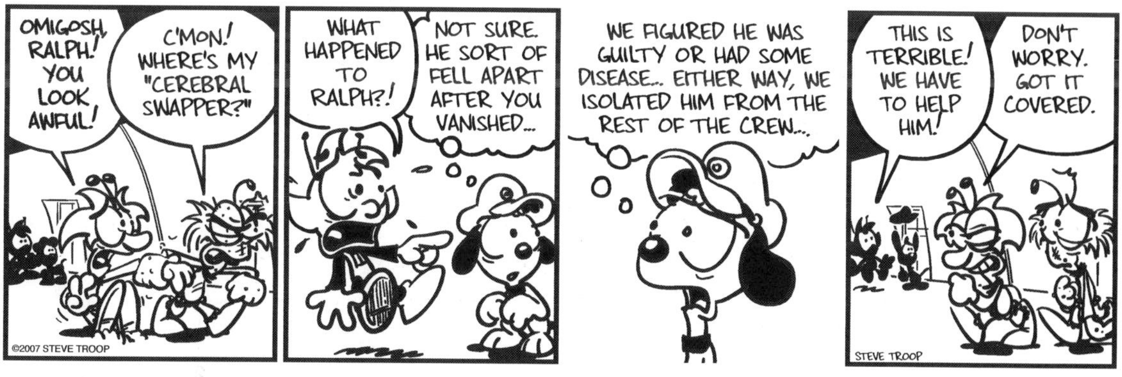
OMIGOSH, RALPH! YOU LOOK AWFUL!
C'MON! WHERE'S MY "CEREBRAL SWAPPER?"
©2007 STEVE TROOP
WHAT HAPPENED TO RALPH?!
NOT SURE. HE SORT OF FELL APART AFTER YOU VANISHED...
WE FIGURED HE WAS GUILTY OR HAD SOME DISEASE... EITHER WAY, WE ISOLATED HIM FROM THE REST OF THE CREW...
THIS IS TERRIBLE! WE HAVE TO HELP HIM!
DON'T WORRY. GOT IT COVERED.
STEVE TROOP

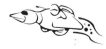

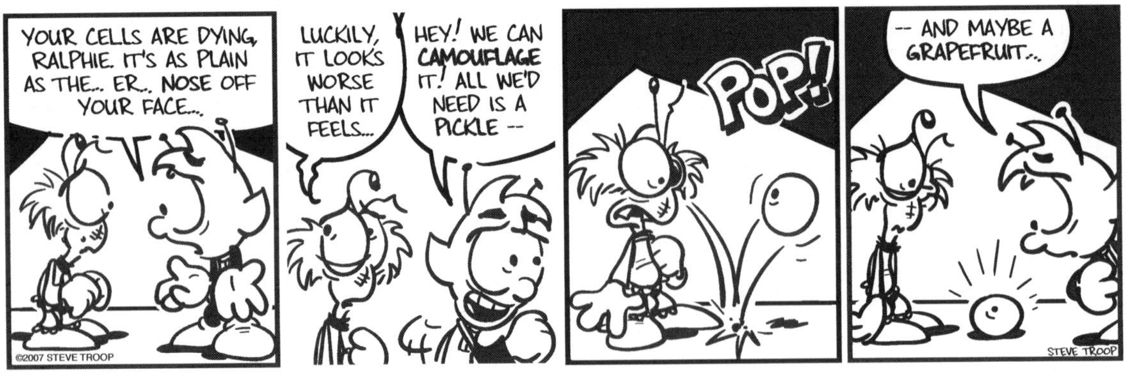
YOUR CELLS ARE DYING, RALPHIE. IT'S AS PLAIN AS THE... ER... NOSE OFF YOUR FACE...
©2007 STEVE TROOP
LUCKILY, IT LOOKS WORSE THAN IT FEELS...
HEY! WE CAN CAMOUFLAGE IT! ALL WE'D NEED IS A PICKLE --
POP!
-- AND MAYBE A GRAPEFRUIT...
STEVE TROOP

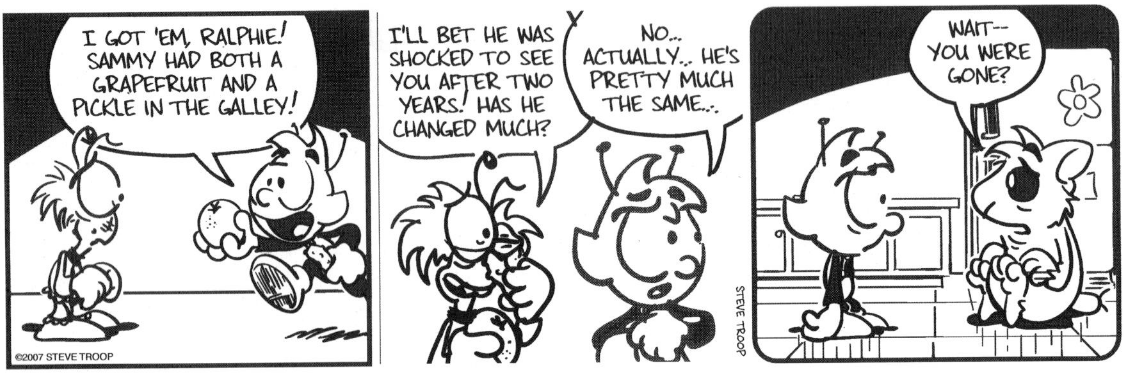
I GOT 'EM, RALPHIE! SAMMY HAD BOTH A GRAPEFRUIT AND A PICKLE IN THE GALLEY!
©2007 STEVE TROOP
I'LL BET HE WAS SHOCKED TO SEE YOU AFTER TWO YEARS! HAS HE CHANGED MUCH?
NO... ACTUALLY... HE'S PRETTY MUCH THE SAME...
STEVE TROOP
WAIT-- YOU WERE GONE?

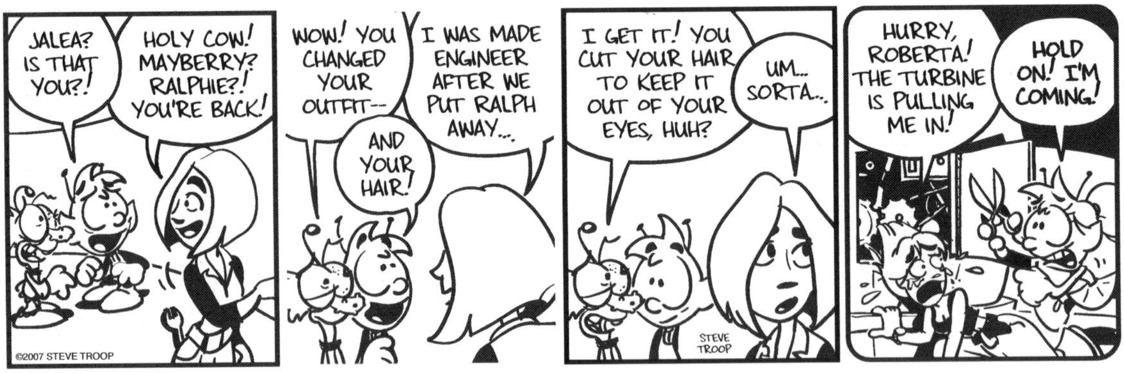
JALEA? IS THAT YOU?!
HOLY COW! MAYBERRY? RALPHIE?! YOU'RE BACK!
©2007 STEVE TROOP
WOW! YOU CHANGED YOUR OUTFIT--
AND YOUR HAIR!
I WAS MADE ENGINEER AFTER WE PUT RALPH AWAY...
I GET IT! YOU CUT YOUR HAIR TO KEEP IT OUT OF YOUR EYES, HUH?
UM... SORTA...
STEVE TROOP
HURRY, ROBERTA! THE TURBINE IS PULLING ME IN!
HOLD ON! I'M COMING!

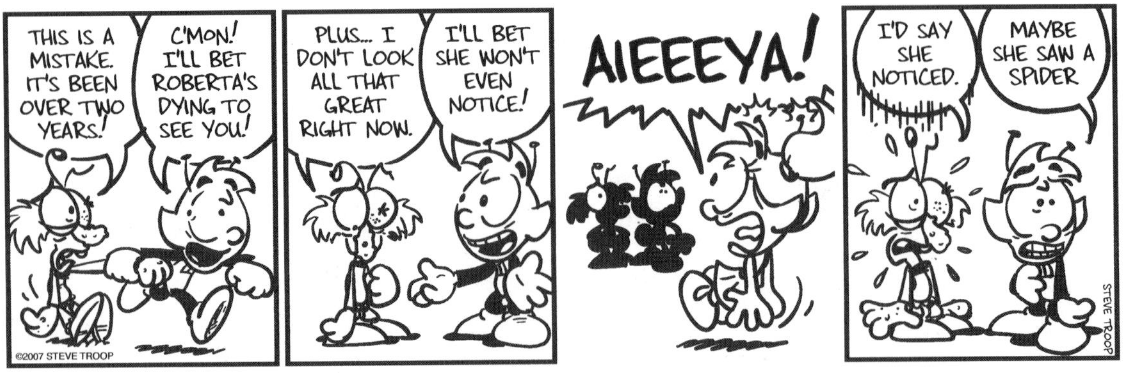
THIS IS A MISTAKE. IT'S BEEN OVER TWO YEARS!
C'MON! I'LL BET ROBERTA'S DYING TO SEE YOU!
©2007 STEVE TROOP
PLUS... I DON'T LOOK ALL THAT GREAT RIGHT NOW.
I'LL BET SHE WON'T EVEN NOTICE!
AIEEEYA!
I'D SAY SHE NOTICED.
MAYBE SHE SAW A SPIDER
STEVE TROOP

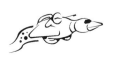

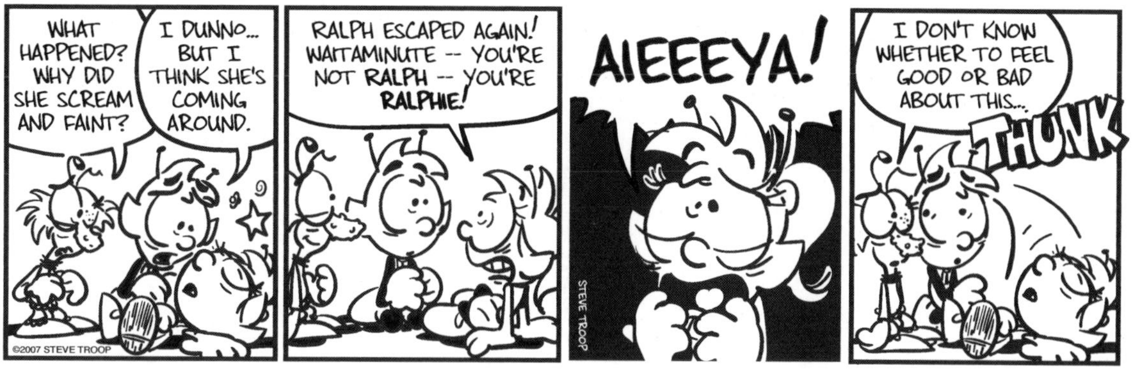
WHAT HAPPENED? WHY DID SHE SCREAM AND FAINT?
I DUNNO... BUT I THINK SHE'S COMING AROUND.
©2007 STEVE TROOP
RALPH ESCAPED AGAIN! WAITAMINUTE -- YOU'RE NOT **RALPH** -- YOU'RE **RALPHIE**!
AIEEEYA!
STEVE TROOP
I DON'T KNOW WHETHER TO FEEL GOOD OR BAD ABOUT THIS...
THUNK

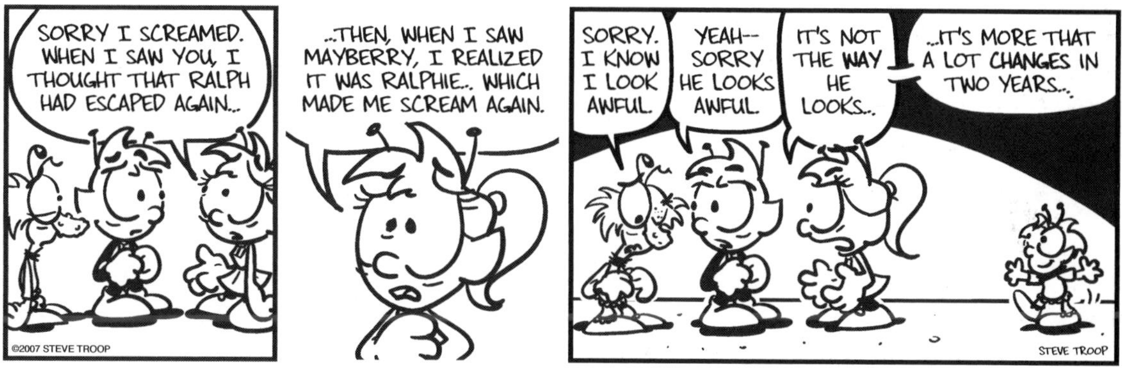
SORRY I SCREAMED. WHEN I SAW YOU, I THOUGHT THAT RALPH HAD ESCAPED AGAIN...
©2007 STEVE TROOP
...THEN, WHEN I SAW MAYBERRY, I REALIZED IT WAS RALPHIE... WHICH MADE ME SCREAM AGAIN.
SORRY. I KNOW I LOOK AWFUL.
YEAH-- SORRY HE LOOKS AWFUL.
IT'S NOT THE **WAY** HE LOOKS...
...IT'S MORE THAT A LOT **CHANGES** IN TWO YEARS...
STEVE TROOP

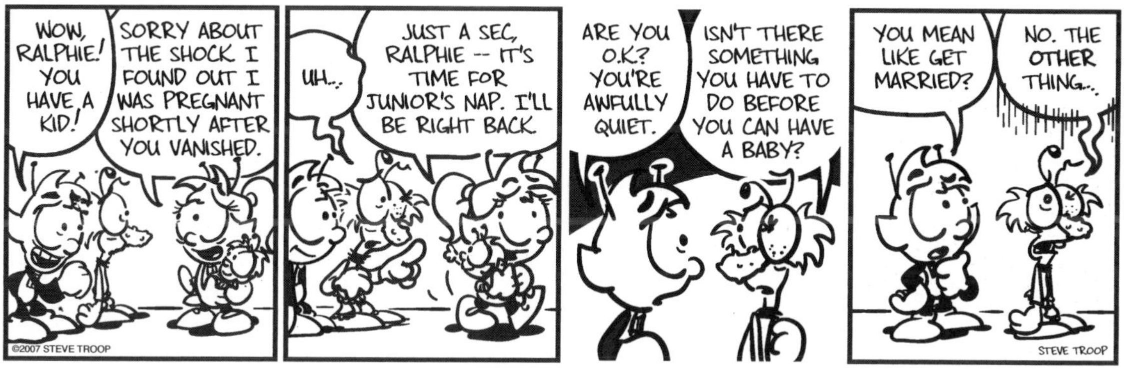
WOW, RALPHIE! YOU HAVE A KID!
SORRY ABOUT THE SHOCK. I FOUND OUT I WAS PREGNANT SHORTLY AFTER YOU VANISHED.
©2007 STEVE TROOP
UH...
JUST A SEC, RALPHIE -- IT'S TIME FOR JUNIOR'S NAP. I'LL BE RIGHT BACK.
ARE YOU O.K.? YOU'RE AWFULLY QUIET.
ISN'T THERE SOMETHING YOU HAVE TO DO BEFORE YOU CAN HAVE A BABY?
YOU MEAN LIKE GET MARRIED?
NO. THE **OTHER** THING...
STEVE TROOP

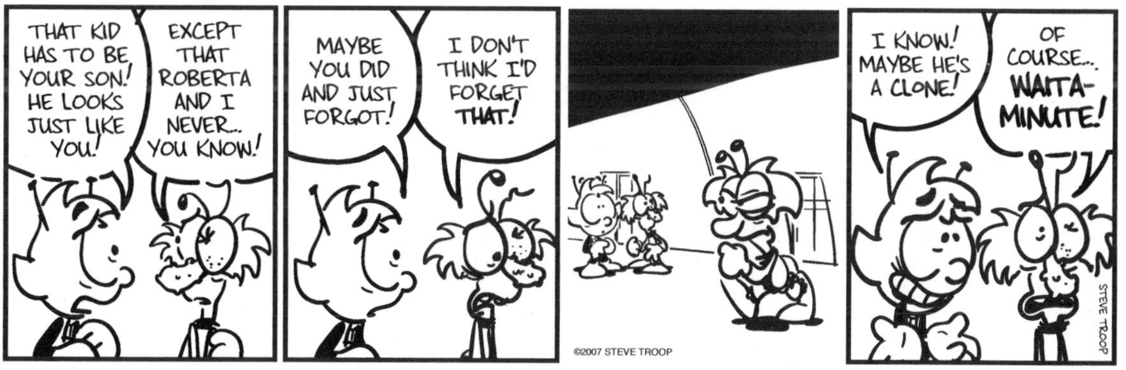
THAT KID HAS TO BE YOUR SON! HE LOOKS JUST LIKE YOU!
EXCEPT THAT ROBERTA AND I NEVER... YOU KNOW!
MAYBE YOU DID AND JUST FORGOT!
I DON'T THINK I'D FORGET **THAT**!
©2007 STEVE TROOP
I KNOW! MAYBE HE'S A CLONE!
OF COURSE... **WAITA-MINUTE!**
STEVE TROOP

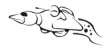

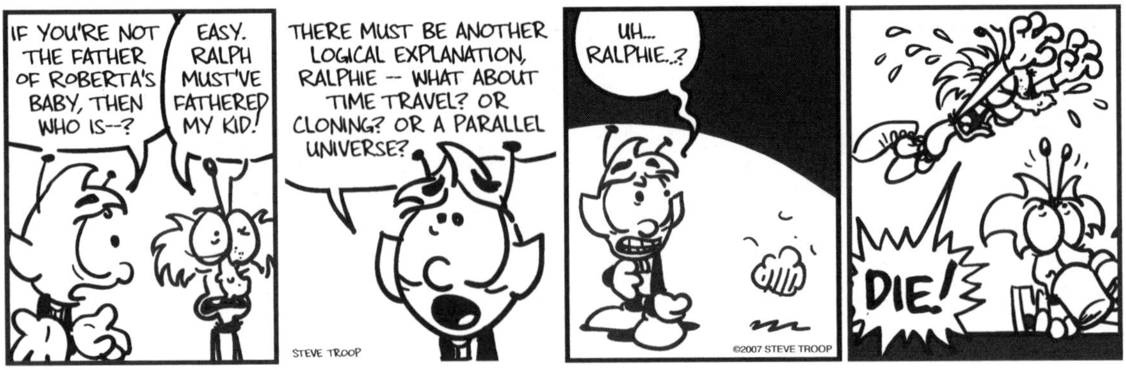
IF YOU'RE NOT THE FATHER OF ROBERTA'S BABY, THEN WHO IS--?
EASY. RALPH MUST'VE FATHERED MY KID!
THERE MUST BE ANOTHER LOGICAL EXPLANATION, RALPHIE -- WHAT ABOUT TIME TRAVEL? OR CLONING? OR A PARALLEL UNIVERSE?
STEVE TROOP
UH... RALPHIE...?
©2007 STEVE TROOP
DIE!

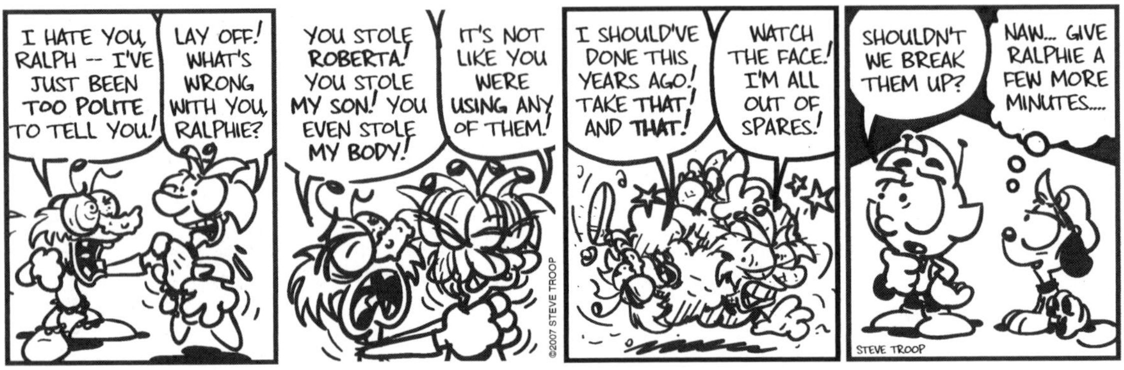
I HATE YOU, RALPH -- I'VE JUST BEEN TOO POLITE TO TELL YOU!
LAY OFF! WHAT'S WRONG WITH YOU, RALPHIE?
YOU STOLE ROBERTA! YOU STOLE MY SON! YOU EVEN STOLE MY BODY!
IT'S NOT LIKE YOU WERE USING ANY OF THEM!
©2007 STEVE TROOP
I SHOULD'VE DONE THIS YEARS AGO! TAKE THAT! AND THAT!
WATCH THE FACE! I'M ALL OUT OF SPARES!
SHOULDN'T WE BREAK THEM UP?
NAW... GIVE RALPHIE A FEW MORE MINUTES....
STEVE TROOP

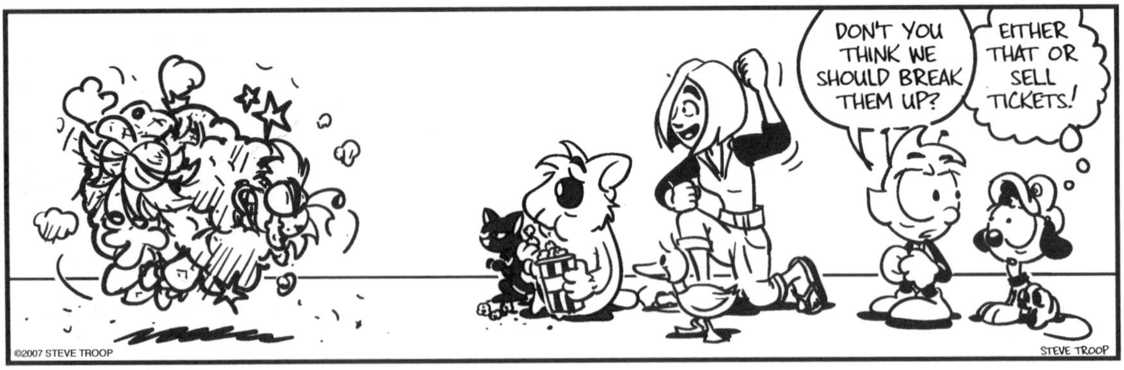
DON'T YOU THINK WE SHOULD BREAK THEM UP?
EITHER THAT OR SELL TICKETS!
©2007 STEVE TROOP
STEVE TROOP

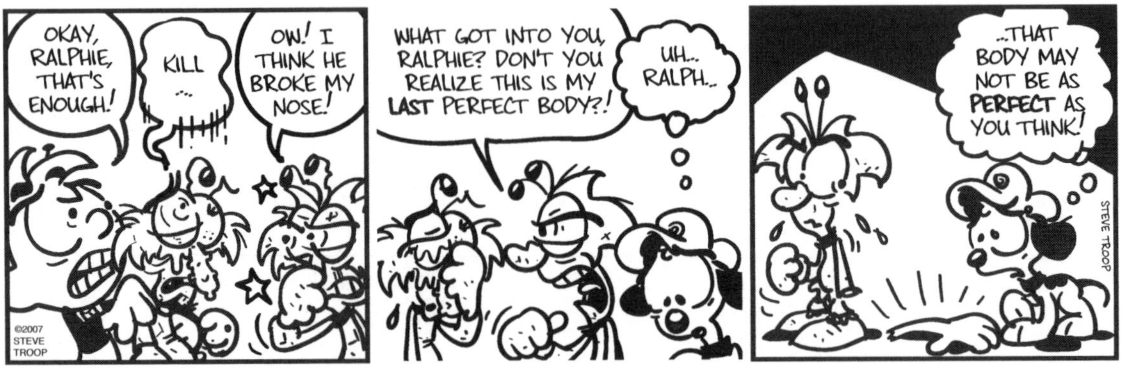
OKAY, RALPHIE, THAT'S ENOUGH!
KILL ...
OW! I THINK HE BROKE MY NOSE!
©2007 STEVE TROOP
WHAT GOT INTO YOU, RALPHIE? DON'T YOU REALIZE THIS IS MY LAST PERFECT BODY?!
UH... RALPH...
...THAT BODY MAY NOT BE AS PERFECT AS YOU THINK!
STEVE TROOP

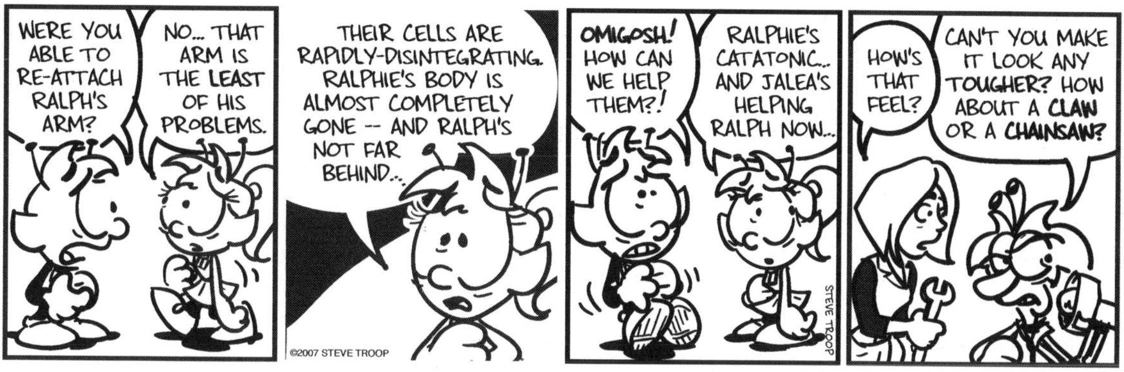
WERE YOU ABLE TO RE-ATTACH RALPH'S ARM?
NO... THAT ARM IS THE LEAST OF HIS PROBLEMS.
THEIR CELLS ARE RAPIDLY-DISINTEGRATING. RALPHIE'S BODY IS ALMOST COMPLETELY GONE -- AND RALPH'S NOT FAR BEHIND...
©2007 STEVE TROOP
OMIGOSH! HOW CAN WE HELP THEM?!
RALPHIE'S CATATONIC... AND JALEA'S HELPING RALPH NOW...
STEVE TROOP
HOW'S THAT FEEL?
CAN'T YOU MAKE IT LOOK ANY TOUGHER? HOW ABOUT A CLAW OR A CHAINSAW?

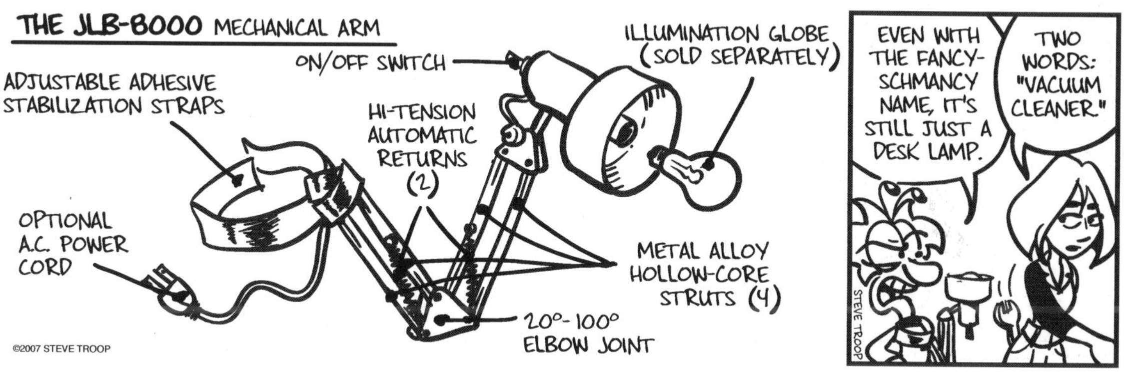
THE JLB-8000 MECHANICAL ARM
ADJUSTABLE ADHESIVE STABILIZATION STRAPS
ON/OFF SWITCH
ILLUMINATION GLOBE (SOLD SEPARATELY)
HI-TENSION AUTOMATIC RETURNS (2)
OPTIONAL A.C. POWER CORD
METAL ALLOY HOLLOW-CORE STRUTS (4)
20°-100° ELBOW JOINT
©2007 STEVE TROOP
EVEN WITH THE FANCY-SCHMANCY NAME, IT'S STILL JUST A DESK LAMP.
TWO WORDS: "VACUUM CLEANER."
STEVE TROOP

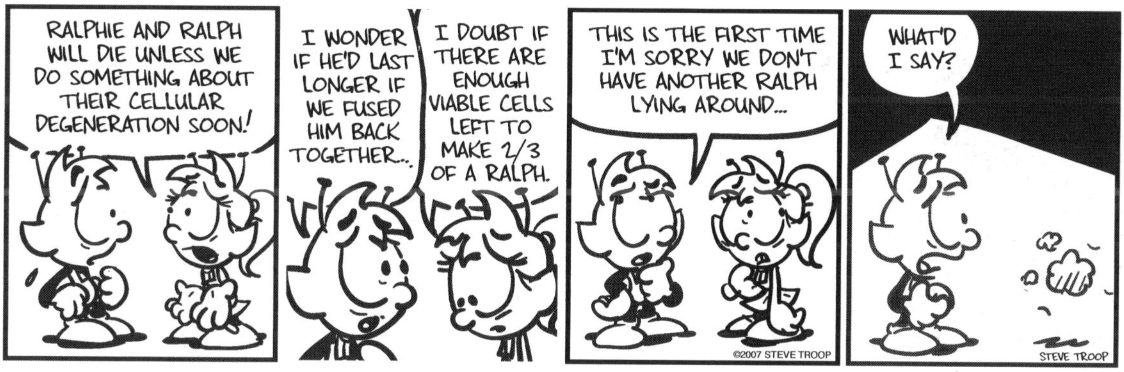
RALPHIE AND RALPH WILL DIE UNLESS WE DO SOMETHING ABOUT THEIR CELLULAR DEGENERATION SOON!
I WONDER IF HE'D LAST LONGER IF WE FUSED HIM BACK TOGETHER...
I DOUBT IF THERE ARE ENOUGH VIABLE CELLS LEFT TO MAKE 2/3 OF A RALPH.
THIS IS THE FIRST TIME I'M SORRY WE DON'T HAVE ANOTHER RALPH LYING AROUND...
©2007 STEVE TROOP
WHAT'D I SAY?
STEVE TROOP

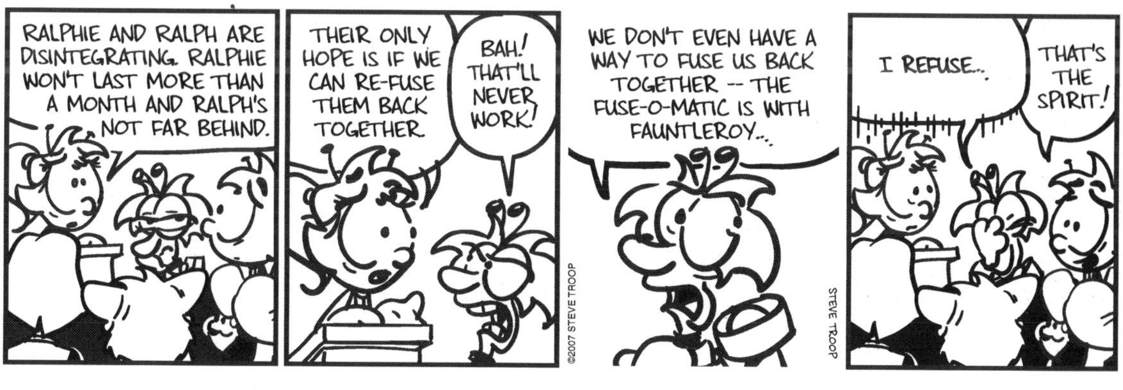
RALPHIE AND RALPH ARE DISINTEGRATING. RALPHIE WON'T LAST MORE THAN A MONTH AND RALPH'S NOT FAR BEHIND.
THEIR ONLY HOPE IS IF WE CAN RE-FUSE THEM BACK TOGETHER.
BAH! THAT'LL NEVER WORK!
©2007 STEVE TROOP
WE DON'T EVEN HAVE A WAY TO FUSE US BACK TOGETHER -- THE FUSE-O-MATIC IS WITH FAUNTLEROY...
STEVE TROOP
I REFUSE...
THAT'S THE SPIRIT!

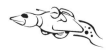

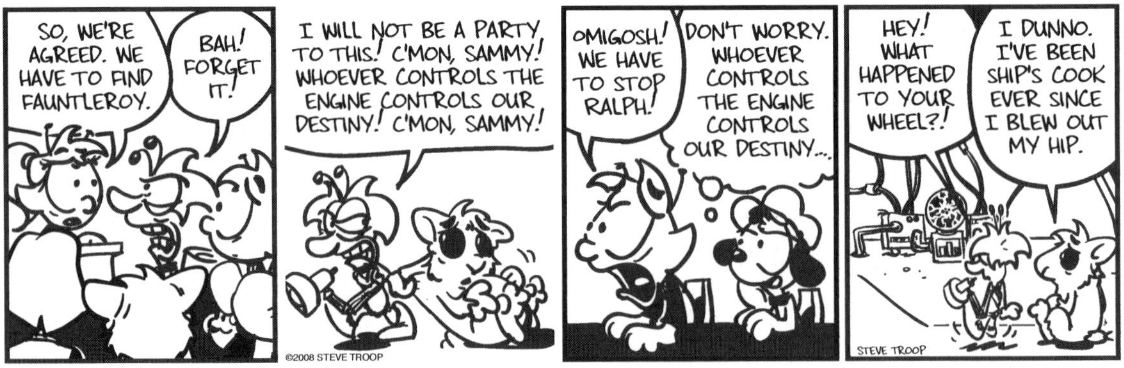
SO, WE'RE AGREED. WE HAVE TO FIND FAUNTLEROY.
BAH! FORGET IT!
I WILL NOT BE A PARTY TO THIS! C'MON, SAMMY! WHOEVER CONTROLS THE ENGINE CONTROLS OUR DESTINY! C'MON, SAMMY!
©2008 STEVE TROOP
OMIGOSH! WE HAVE TO STOP RALPH!
DON'T WORRY. WHOEVER CONTROLS THE ENGINE CONTROLS OUR DESTINY...
HEY! WHAT HAPPENED TO YOUR WHEEL?!
I DUNNO. I'VE BEEN SHIP'S COOK EVER SINCE I BLEW OUT MY HIP.
STEVE TROOP

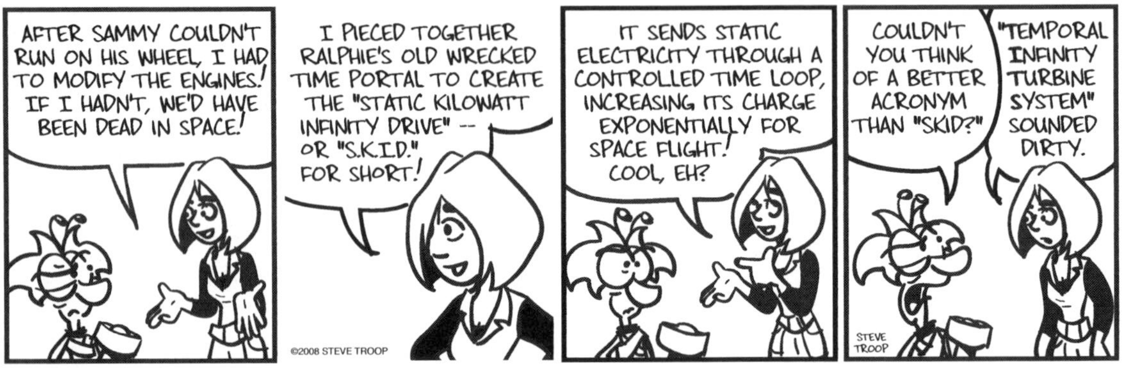
AFTER SAMMY COULDN'T RUN ON HIS WHEEL, I HAD TO MODIFY THE ENGINES! IF I HADN'T, WE'D HAVE BEEN DEAD IN SPACE!
I PIECED TOGETHER RALPHIE'S OLD WRECKED TIME PORTAL TO CREATE THE "STATIC KILOWATT INFINITY DRIVE" -- OR "S.K.I.D." FOR SHORT!
©2008 STEVE TROOP
IT SENDS STATIC ELECTRICITY THROUGH A CONTROLLED TIME LOOP, INCREASING ITS CHARGE EXPONENTIALLY FOR SPACE FLIGHT! COOL, EH?
COULDN'T YOU THINK OF A BETTER ACRONYM THAN "SKID?"
"TEMPORAL INFINITY TURBINE SYSTEM" SOUNDED DIRTY.
STEVE TROOP

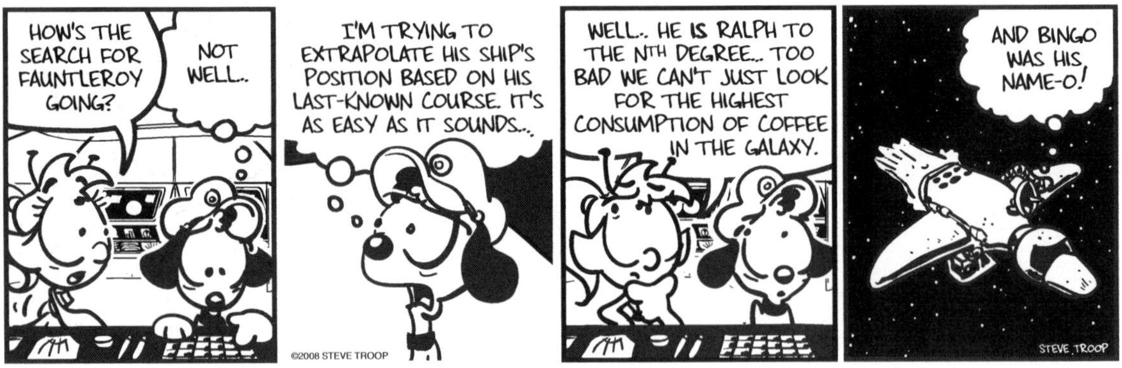
HOW'S THE SEARCH FOR FAUNTLEROY GOING?
NOT WELL..
I'M TRYING TO EXTRAPOLATE HIS SHIP'S POSITION BASED ON HIS LAST-KNOWN COURSE. IT'S AS EASY AS IT SOUNDS...
©2008 STEVE TROOP
WELL.. HE IS RALPH TO THE NTH DEGREE... TOO BAD WE CAN'T JUST LOOK FOR THE HIGHEST CONSUMPTION OF COFFEE IN THE GALAXY.
AND BINGO WAS HIS NAME-O!
STEVE TROOP

That was the last *Melonpool* strip I inked using my WACOM tablet in Adobe Illustrator. It was a fun experiment, but as the storyline progressed and become more and more ambitious, I was able to reuse less and less of the illustrations that I had created for earlier comics. It was fast becoming less of a chore to just go back to drawing the comics by hand.

What's more, the storyline was getting rather complicated, so I made the decision to tie up all of the loose ends in one last Sunday comic, drawn traditionally, paving the way for one-shot comics whenever I feel the need to draw something.

So far, I've felt this need over 30 times (and counting)!

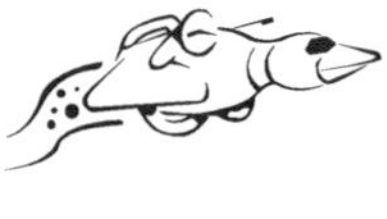

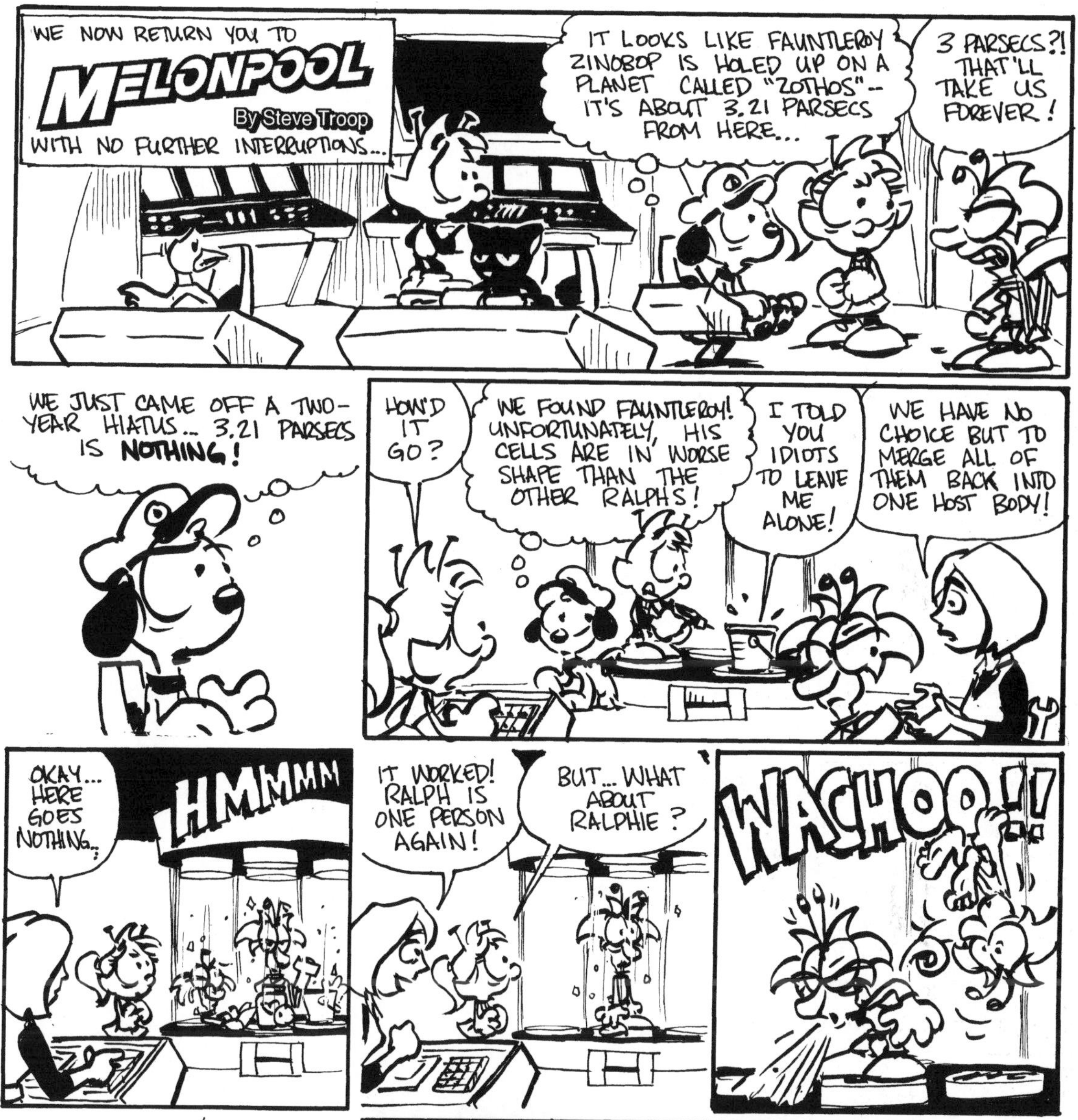
WE NOW RETURN YOU TO
MELONPOOL
By Steve Troop
WITH NO FURTHER INTERRUPTIONS...
IT LOOKS LIKE FAUNTLEROY ZINOBOP IS HOLED UP ON A PLANET CALLED "ZOTHOS"-- IT'S ABOUT 3.21 PARSECS FROM HERE...
3 PARSECS?! THAT'LL TAKE US FOREVER!
WE JUST CAME OFF A TWO-YEAR HIATUS... 3.21 PARSECS IS NOTHING!
HOW'D IT GO?
WE FOUND FAUNTLEROY! UNFORTUNATELY, HIS CELLS ARE IN WORSE SHAPE THAN THE OTHER RALPHS!
I TOLD YOU IDIOTS TO LEAVE ME ALONE!
WE HAVE NO CHOICE BUT TO MERGE ALL OF THEM BACK INTO ONE HOST BODY!
OKAY... HERE GOES NOTHING...
HMMMM
IT WORKED! RALPH IS ONE PERSON AGAIN!
BUT... WHAT ABOUT RALPHIE?
WACHOO!!
LET'S NEVER SPEAK OF THIS AGAIN...
I HAVE A BETTER IDEA!
THIS WAS YOUR IDEA?! RESETTING EVERYTHING WITH MORE TIME TRAVEL?!
IF WE RELIED ON LINEAR STORYTELLING, WE'D NEVER GET ANYTHING DONE!
STEVE TROOP

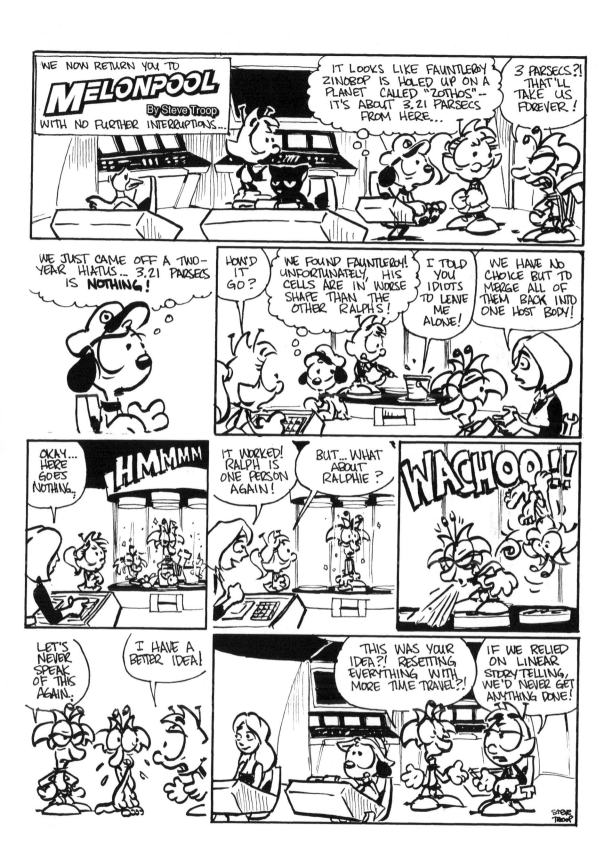

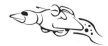

WHERE DO WE GO FROM HERE?

So, I hope you're not too sad, now that you've come to the official end of the Melonpool daily webcomic. It's been a lot of fun, and I hope, for the most part, it's been a satisfying journey.

And Melonpool isn't gone. I still update the site from time to time with Sunday installments. Eventually, I'll probably have enough for another collection. Or collections. You never really know.

Plus, there's the movie to look forward to. After almost 20 years, the same cast that helped make the original Melonpool Movie in 1994 has reassembled to make Melonpool—The Motion Picture. With filming slated to begin in February, 2013, there's plenty more Melonpool coming in the future.

Maybe even a comic adaptation of the movie!

Photos by Greg Skinner

THEN AND NOW:

Ralph (Erik Przytulski, standing), Sam (Roger Przytulski), Mayberry (me) and Sammy (Chris Gleason) on the Bridge set from the original *Melonpool Movie* (2004) and again in 2010 on the partially-completed bridge set for *Melonpool—The Motion Picture* (2014).